THE ART OF COMPROMISE
The Life and Work of Leonid Leonov

THE ART OF COMPROMISE

The Life and Work of Leonid Leonov

BORIS THOMSON

UNIVERSITY OF TORONTO PRESS
Toronto Buffalo London

© University of Toronto Press Incorporated 2001
Toronto Buffalo London
Printed in Canada

ISBN 0-8020-3537-X

Printed on acid-free paper

Canadian Cataloguing in Publication Data

Thomson, Boris
   The art of compromise : the life and work of Leonid Leonov

   Includes bibliographical references and index.
   ISBN 0-8020-3537-X

   1. Leonov, Leonid, 1899–1994. 2. Authors, Russian – 20th century –
Biography.   I. Title.

   PG3476.L5Z76 2001   891.73′4   C00-933010-0

University of Toronto Press acknowledges the financial assistance to its publishing program of the Canada Council for the Arts and the Ontario Arts Council.

This book has been published with the help of a grant from the Humanities and Social Sciences Federation of Canada, using funds provided by the Social Sciences and Humanities Research Council of Canada.

University of Toronto Press acknowledges the financial support for its publishing activities of the Government of Canada through the Book Publishing Industry Development Program (BPIDP).

To the memory of Leonard Woodd-Smith (1875–1960)

Contents

PREFACE ix

A NOTE ON TRANSLITERATION xiii

1 Early Years and Literary Debut 3
2 *The Badgers* 1924 32
3 *The Thief* 1927 52
4 Stories and Plays 1927–1928 78
5 *The Sot'* and *Locusts* 1930–1931 99
6 *Skutarevsky* 1932 125
7 *The Road to Ocean* 1935 149
8 Three Plays 1936–1940 173
9 The War Years 1941–1945 191
10 *An Ordinary Man* and *A Golden Coach* 1940–1946 203
11 *The Russian Forest* 1953 215
12 The Late Revisions 1955–1962 239
13 *The Pyramid* 1994 265
14 The Art of Compromise 285

APPENDIX *Zapis' na bereste* 295

ABBREVIATIONS 303

NOTES 305

BIBLIOGRAPHY 361

INDEX 401

Preface

For some thirty years after the publication of his first novel *The Badgers* (*Barsuki*) in 1924 Leonid Maksimovich Leonov (1899–1994) was one of the most widely admired of Soviet writers both in Russia and abroad. His reputation was largely based on what was felt to be something heterodox lurking beneath the surface of the ideological and materialistic pieties that his works seemingly proclaimed. His elaborate style was often flecked with an elusive irony and was further complicated by allusions to esoteric historical and cultural figures and events. An avoidance of explicit authorial evaluations and a certain ambiguity about the endings of his major works seemed to hint at moral or intellectual reservations. In particular, his affinity with Dostoevsky in the recognition of the power and persistence of human irrationality and wanton destructiveness suggested some misgivings about the official doctrine of the supremacy of the will and reason.

It was not easy, however, to substantiate these impressions. It was rumoured (correctly as it turned out) that Leonov was a practising Christian, but his treatment of the church and clergy seemed little different from that found in most Soviet literature of the time. His novels of the 1930s with their Communist heroes and paeans to Soviet industrial and agricultural achievements seemed to offer little encouragement to look deeper, and in general Soviet critics, except for the years 1936–40, remained respectful. His works were issued in large editions, he was the recipient of many Soviet literary awards, and he was even selected for membership of the Supreme Soviet. Readers began to ask whether his reputation was based on a mystification.

These suspicions gradually diminished public interest in Leonov and his works, until by the mid-1950s he was no longer felt to be a contemporary writer, but rather a survivor from another era. A new generation with different tastes had arisen, one which found his style and themes irrelevant; the public readings of the young poets Evtushenko and Voznesensky and the ballads of Okudzhava, Galich, and Vysotsky spoke more immediately to its interests and concerns; the gradual rediscovery of the great Russian writers of the Silver Age, whose works had been suppressed since the 1920s, mercilessly exposed the limitations of what had passed for literature for so long; and finally the appearance of openly dissident literature in 'Samizdat' made the occasional veiled expressions of dissent of earlier decades seem contemptibly cautious and indeed pointless. His novel *The Russian Forest* (*Russkiy les*, 1953), if read carefully, is one of the most damning indictments of the Stalin period, but it was soon overshadowed by the more outspoken products of the 'Thaw.' The early charges that Leonov was merely a stylistic virtuoso, whose hints at mysterious revelations, concealed behind a screen of complex and allusive stylistic play, were empty, began to reappear, and he was written off in both East and West. The very fact that he had been able to publish throughout the Stalin years now served to discredit him. By comparison with such writers as Akhmatova and Mandel'shtam he was seen as fatally compromised.

After having been one of the most widely read Soviet authors inside and outside Russia, Leonov is little read nowadays, and his former reputation has virtually evaporated. Reading lists for the period in graduate schools in North America seldom include any of his works, while inside Russia it is unusual to find anyone from the younger generation who has read even one of his books. This neglect seems to me unjustified.

The aim of this study is then to provide a general introduction to Leonov's oeuvre in its historical context, and to identify the nature and extent of his seventy-year-long debate with the Soviet version of Marxism, which he was eventually to outlive. His last novel, *The Pyramid* (*Piramida*), published a few weeks before his death, has helped to clarify many of the ambiguities surrounding his work and to demonstrate the consistency of his entire oeuvre. Here his beliefs are stated openly, and his judgments on the revolutionary period are unequivocal. But I do not think that he has jumped belatedly on to the anti-Stalinist bandwagon. That would be pretty anachronistic in this day and age. Rather he is concerned to show that the views he expresses here can be traced in his earlier works, going back to the 1920s and perhaps even further. In *The Pyramid* we find the clearest expression of what I take to be the major theme of his work, namely the claim of Communism to have replaced Christianity with a superior culture:

> After the abolition of Christianity will the new theory [Marxism] have strong enough wings to sustain mankind in its flight on even its previous insignificant level?[1]

If at first he treats the idea with scepticism, later, probably by the end of the 1940s, he came to reject it altogether.

My approach then is a chronological one. I shall trace the development of Leonov's thought over the years in the light of contemporary political and social developments and the events of his own life. His novels and plays are for the most part set firmly within contemporary reality, indeed to such an extent that they will soon require footnotes to clarify the allusions to contemporary debates and policies. But at the same time the specific problems and debates of his time are seen as local versions of timeless dilemmas about the human condition.

In this respect Leonov continues the traditions of the Russian writers of the nineteenth century. Like them he believes that the writer has a responsibility to the reader: to entertain him, certainly, but above all to teach him and make him think. He rejects relativism – the consequences of which were all too evident in his time – and believes in absolutes, that there is an ultimate truth, though it is unlikely to be attainable. He is interested in character and has created some memorable ones, but he does not aim at a polyphony of voices. There is a single, central, controlling vision in all his books, though this is not always clearly identifiable. Irony plays an increasingly important role in his work, and one of his most effective techniques is to play on the expectations of the Soviet reader, literary and political, in order to question if not subvert them.

Given the circumstances of his times Leonov's art is an art of compromise. It is the extent of this compromise that interests me. How far was he himself compromised in the process? It is not quite enough to say that the romantic ideal of the wholly uncompromising artist was always unrealizable, for the compromises that Leonov was compelled to make were sometimes unpardonable on an artistic level, even if understandable enough on a human one. He seems to have internalized the need for compromise and contrived to exploit it for artistic ends. He created a style which gave him extraordinary freedom within the straitjacket of socialist realism, and so when the pressures were gradually relaxed after the death of Stalin, just when his contemporaries, like Erenburg, were able to jump on to the new bandwagon, he found it difficult to adapt to the new situation. Above all, he was acutely conscious of the flawed nature of his work and expressed the hope that literary scholars of the future would write understandingly 'of our works, at which we ourselves look back... with mixed feelings of an obligation fulfilled, inescapability, and despair.'[2]

In this study of Leonov I have concentrated on his published work. I have not consulted his manuscripts; I am concerned with what he thought he could say, and what he was prepared to settle for when that proved impossible. This is not simply a case of self-censorship or faint-hearted acquiescence; rather, it served

Leonov as a sort of technical challenge which he came to relish. After all, according to Marx, 'freedom is the recognition of necessity,' and, as Leonov well knew, art works more effectively through indirection than through a frontal attack. I have, however, paid special attention to changes introduced between the first versions of his works in one or other of the 'fat' journals and the book-editions that usually followed within a few months. The latter often show traces of further screening by the censor.

A careful reading of these works often reveals a host of ambiguities and possible alternative readings. In *The Pyramid* Leonov makes his views and judgments unequivocal, but to my mind it is misleading to read them back into his earlier works; not because his views changed during the intervening years – I think that they did not change substantially – but because such a reading falsifies the experience of contemporary readers and their attempt to make sense of Leonov's works. I am concerned above all with what these readers can have expected and been expected to see in his works. In his works of the Soviet period he only rarely permits himself a flat contradiction of the official line; he prefers to raise the possibilities of other interpretations, but without giving them any authorial backing; his works ask questions and require readers to do the same.

I am ruefully aware that to try to convey the spirit of any writer in another language is rather like discussing a composer on the basis of the librettoes he sets – it leaves out the very reason why we became interested in him in the first place. This applies with particular force to Leonov, who is known in Russia less for his ideas than for his virtuosic use of language and syntax. As partial mitigation, in a few cases I provide the Russian text to illustrate some points that are lost in translation. Elsewhere my versions try to convey something of the spirit of the originals, in the hope of drawing readers to discover Leonov for themselves.

A Note on Transliteration

I have employed the following system of transliteration.

а	a	р	r
б	b	с	s
в	v	т	t
г	g	у	u
д	d	ф	f
е	e	х	kh
ж	zh	ц	ts
з	z	ч	ch
и	i	ш	sh
й	y	щ	shch
к	k	ъ	"
л	l	ы	y
м	m	ь	'
н	n	э	e
о	o	ю	yu
п	p	я	ya

Surnames, including pseudonyms, e.g., Gor'ky, are transliterated with a final '-y' rather than 'iy' or 'yy.'

THE ART OF COMPROMISE
The Life and Work of Leonid Leonov

chapter one

Early Years and Literary Debut

Like many other Soviet writers of his generation Leonid Maksimovich Leonov (1899–1994) came of an urban and petty bourgeois family.[1] His paternal grandfather, Leon, was of peasant origin (from the village of Polukhino in the Kaluga *guberniya*) and had moved to Moscow in 1882. There he took over a small shop in Zaryad'e, a district traditionally associated with the merchant class. The business was successful, and his son Maksim (1872–1929) was clearly expected to follow him into it. The boy was taken out of school at the age of ten, but he was a bookish child and managed to educate himself. After coming across some poems by Ivan Surikov he decided to become a poet and actually had a book of verse, *First Sounds* (*Pervye zvuki*), published in 1889 when he was seventeen. It must be said, however, that his poetry showed little originality,[2] and this side of his activity became less productive with the years. In the 1890s he became an energetic editor and publisher for the peasant poets of the period.

Maksim's family had no sympathy with his lack of commercial instincts or his interest in literature. Relations were no doubt further strained by his political activities. He was a prominent member of a workers' cooperative and was temporarily exiled to the northern city of Archangel in 1892. Nor was this the last of such experiences. In the brief period of liberalization that followed the 1905 revolution he opened a publishing house in Moscow called 'Iskra,' in partnership with his fellow poet Fedor Shkulev, where he published several works by Karl Liebknecht and Rosa Luxemburg. This venture led to a fresh arrest in 1908, which led to an eighteen-month jail term. On his release he was not allowed to remain in Moscow, and chose to return to Archangel where he remained until his death. After 1917 he worked for several Soviet institutions, the ROSTA news agency, and the newspaper *Trudovoy sever*; he headed various committees on cultural matters, and served as the manager of a newspaper office, before falling out of favour later in the 1920s.[3]

Maksim and his wife had separated even before his final arrest; Leonid, the oldest of the five children, seems to have taken his father's side. He never mentions his mother, Mariya Petrovna Petrova (1877–1968),[4] in his autobiographical writings and interviews, even though as a schoolboy he lived with her in Moscow and spent the shorter school holidays with her family in the village of Eskino.[5] For the summers he would visit his father in Archangel. These unsettled early years left their mark on his work. Childhood plays almost no role in the formation of his characters, and relations between parents and children are rarely discussed. His heroes and heroines look back at the past, if at all, with distaste; while their relations with their own children are cold and uncomprehending. This is particularly striking in view of Leonov's own happy marriage.

The Archangel that Maksim Leonov had moved to was a growing and comparatively prosperous city with a population of some 30,000. Maksim soon became one of the leaders of the local intelligentsia and founded a newspaper, *Severnoe utro*, which was characterized by liberal and populist sympathies. His own contributions to it consisted mainly of poems and a series of essays on the peasant poets of Russia from the time of Kol'tsov until that of his own contemporaries, Klyuev and Oreshin. It was in this paper that in 1915 his son made his literary debut.[6]

Leonid was educated at the well-known Third Gimnaziya[7] in Moscow, and here he displayed a wide range of talents from the start, particularly in music, literature, and the visual arts;[8] he edited the school magazine, and contributed poems, stories, and illustrations to it. He was particularly interested in the stage, and spent many evenings at the Moscow Arts Theatre. As a result he was entrusted by his father with the reviewing of plays produced in the theatres of Archangel.

He had begun writing verse at an early age, sometimes producing as many as six poems in a day. Naturally, these early efforts display the usual weaknesses of immaturity, but they show clear evidence of wide and intelligent reading. Maksim Leonov took a keen interest in his son's work. In one poem he blesses him on his artistic career and defines his mission as one of service and succour to the Russian peasantry.[9] It seems, however, from the surviving poetry that his son had different ambitions. Nekrasov, Surikov, and the flood of patriotic verse prompted by the war were indeed his first models, but not for long. In 1916 he came under the spell of the Russian Symbolists and, in particular, Blok and Bely. The social and national responsibilities of the poet give way to a concern with matters of language and technique. Even the turbulent events of 1917–18 seem to have made little impression on him. Only a handful of poems such as 'Flutter, flutter, you red flags of freedom!..' ('*Veytes', veytes', krasnye flagi svoboby!..*'),[10] written in response to the February Revolution, display any awareness of them, while the Bolshevik Revolution eight months later is not mentioned at all. In one of his last publications in Archangel he wrote, 'in choosing between life for art's sake and life for its own sake, the decision for almost all artists is clear and definite; there can be no two decisions! Art of course!'[11] In the years to come he was to discover that in twentieth-century Russia the choice was not so simple.

In May 1918 Leonov graduated from his school with a silver medal, and left for Archangel fully intending to return to Moscow in the autumn in order to study medicine at the university.[12] But he was apparently still nurturing literary ambitions: a book of his early poetry was being prepared for publication later in the year[13] and he had made arrangements to meet Bryusov on his return to Moscow in the autumn.[14] All these plans, however, came to nothing because of the outbreak of the the Civil War in August, which had the effect of confining him to Archangel. His early poems were never republished, the unpublished ones were burnt in 1920 (he later said that he wished he could have destroyed the published ones too) and his medical interests found expression only in his fiction.

The political situation that he discovered on his return to Archangel in May 1918 was extremely confused. In 1917 an Allied Expeditionary Force had been stationed in Murmansk, since the port, being ice-free, provided the best route for conveying war materials into Russia.[15] A substantial quantity of these materials had already been imported and transferred to Archangel when the Bolsheviks seized power, with the declared intention of pulling Russia out of the war with Germany. The Allied Powers therefore had two concerns in the north: first, to ensure that Russia remained in the war, and, second, to try to retain control of the materials that had been delivered. The situation was complicated by the fact that different regions in the area supported different factions. By February 1918 the Bolsheviks had managed to secure themselves in Archangel. Murmansk, however, was controlled by a moderate-socialist Soviet, which did not accept the Brest-Litovsk treaty of March 1918; it continued to consider itself at war with Germany and to provide assistance to the Allies. This stance put it at odds with both the central government in Moscow and the authorities in Archangel. The rising tensions culminated in the British decision to attack Archangel, and on 1 August, with the assistance of anti-Bolshevik elements within the city, the Allies captured it. The Bolshevik elements withdrew but continued to harass their opponents from the surrounding countryside.

A chaotic period ensued: the Allies were unable to coordinate their policies, while the local authorities were bitterly divided between monarchists and socialists. Within the city all parties succeeded in discrediting themselves with the local inhabitants who found themselves looking more and more to the Bolsheviks. With the signing of the Armistice in November 1918 the original raison d'être for the intervention in northern Russia disappeared, while the force had in any case been too small to influence events. It continued to remain there, however, until September 1919, when it finally withdrew, leaving its few Russian supporters to carry on by themselves.[16] The Bolshevik forces reentered Archangel on 19 February 1920 and took a terrible revenge on those who they thought had collaborated with the enemy.

Leonov was in Archangel for these events, but we know very little of what he was thinking or doing in these months. After June 1918 only a handful of poems and stories appear in the local press over his name. He was, however, apparently forced by the Whites to enter a cadet school for young officers (with the rank of *praporshchik*); on another occasion the captain of an English ship in the harbour offered to evacuate him and his father.[17] He declined, but the profound and lasting consequences of these two incidents for his life and work may be compared to Dostoevsky's involvement with the Petrashevtsy and near-execution in 1849. His enrolment in a school for officers and even the very thought of emigration were to become capital offences within a few years, so it is not surprising that for several decades he felt acutely vulnerable, and he was not able to tell his children about these events until the 1990s. Almost all his fellow cadets were to be later hunted down and executed, but Leonov was lucky enough to be shielded by a young woman commissar. In the circumstances his survival is almost miraculous; even more miraculous is the fact that a document confirming his enrolment in the school has apparently survived.[18]

Soon after the return of the Bolsheviks Leonov made his decision. In the summer of 1920 he became the editor of a Communist wall newspaper, *Krasnaya vest'* and, he volunteered for the Red Army; he was promptly drafted to the Fifteenth Infantry Division, serving in the south.

There are two works in which Leonov seems to refer to the Archangel period: one is the story *White Night* (*Belaya noch'*, 1928), which will be discussed later; the other is the poem *A Note on Birchbark* (*Zapis' na bereste*) that he wrote in May 1923, but published only in 1926.[19] The poem is Leonov's last published piece of original verse and has never been reissued. The complete text is provided in the index. It is a narrative poem of 256 lines (sixteen sections of sixteen lines each), written in a free *dol'nik* rhythm and unrhymed, quite different from his earlier verse. In it a certain Andrey tells how he and two of his friends decide to escape from an unnamed city to the north, as yet unaffected by the Revolution. When they arrive, however, they are immediately conscripted by the foreign interventionists. They soon desert and settle down to an idyllic existence in the forest. Before long, however, their ammunition runs out and

Andrey is sent off to the city to get some more. He returns with a young woman as well, Elena. At first she lives with Andrey but, in a scene strongly reminiscent of Pushkin's *The Gypsies* (*Tsygany*, 1824), he wakes up one night to find her gone. He goes out and finds her exchanging kisses with one of his friends. Andrey hands his rival a gun and tells him to leave, that if they meet again one of them will have to die. Soon afterwards they do meet and Andrey shoots the man dead. He then returns to the cabin to discover that Elena has departed with his other friend and that he is now completely alone. The poem ends at this point: we are not told what happens to the narrator.

Lev Fink, who first drew attention to this work, interprets it as a rejection of the arguments for remaining 'above the struggle' (a Soviet expression that does not appear in the poem).[20] This is true enough, but only up to a point. At the beginning of the poem Andrey says,

> Even the flowers of the fields
> Smelled dimly of gunpowder.[21]

These lines are not really about remaining 'above the struggle' – rather, they express a protest against all violence. Nature has been polluted and defiled by it ('the smell of gunpowder'); the 'red' of the Revolution is also the colour of the blood spilt in its name. The hero tries to find a refuge in 'silence' (*tishina*), a recurrent image in Leonov's early work of a haven from the violence and deceit of men:

> It [the forest] does not reject the newcomers,
> does not betray secrets or cries,
> does not mock,
> and remains silent.[22]

But this idyll is soon shattered.

> Once we met an elk;
> it did not run away, but listened.
> I never missed;
> that evening we had a fire.[23]

The innocent and trusting elk is shot by Andrey – natural enough perhaps, but the episode is still shocking. The refugees from the violence of the outside world have brought their own violence with them, and at the end of the poem Andrey shoots his unarmed rival in the back:

> How was it that my red eyes
> did not kill him at once? [...]
> Everything had become red to me; the vegetation, the birds,
> the cries of the owls, and the very murk of the swamps...
> Everything had become as red as the flags of revolution.[24]

The parallel between the 'red' of the Communist banners and that of blood is drawn once again, but now the violence that Andrey had sought to escape is inside and not outside him. At the end of the poem the silence of nature seems to be one of condemnation:

> That day the terrified birds
> cried no more above my roof.
> And that evening I cooked my meat
> and sat by my fire alone.[25]

Particularly revealing are the lines:

> Мне и теперь непонятно,
> чему улыбались дети,
> когда так бурно и страшно
> вскипала отцовская кровь.
>
> Знаю, что смысл обреченности
> в этом непониманьи.
> Но, может быть, это и лучше –
> не понимать до конца.[26]

['Even now I cannot understand what the children were smiling at, when their fathers' blood seethed so stormily and grimly. I know that in this lack of understanding lies the meaning of being doomed. But perhaps it's better that way, not to understand fully.']

The theme of the children's smiles achieved at the expense of the fathers' blood, the sacrifice of the present in the name of a hypothetically better future, recurs in different guises throughout Leonov's work. It is an old theme in Russian literature, whose origins go back at least to Pushkin's *Bronze Horseman* (*Mednyy vsadnik*, 1833). What is new here is the narrator's sense of guilt at his own scruples. The idea of 'not understanding' appears three times in these eight lines; 'even now,' when the time has moved to the present, outside the chronological frame of the poem, he still does 'not understand.' Still more significantly, he 'knows' that this 'not understanding' is tantamount to a death sentence (the Russian expression *smysl obrechennosti* is less vague than the literal English translation, 'the meaning of being doomed'). He continues with an unanswered question: 'But maybe it's better that way, not to understand fully?' But the listless intonation is no match for the preceding 'I know...,' and reads only as a half-hearted attempt at evasion. The emphasis on 'not understanding,' while apparently intended to divert responsibility from the hero, seems at the same time to acknowledge it.

Clearly, one must be careful about treating *A Note on Birchbark* as autobiographical, or identifying the 'I' of the poem with the author. But since Leonov himself was in this very place at this very time there are certainly some grounds for such an interpretation, though we need not take all the details literally. (For example, we know that unlike the narrator of the poem Leonov returned to the city – if he had ever left it – and that he volunteered for the Red Army.) On the other hand, if one rejects the autobiographical approach one is left with a very inconsequential piece of writing. I suspect, therefore, that this poem describes a course of action that Leonov was tempted to take, even if he later rejected it.

In Leonov's later novels and plays the years 1918–20 are time and again associated with the idea of a vain attempt to evade the Revolution – through study or pacifism or emigration, or perhaps even some form of collaboration with the Whites. This theme is almost always accompanied by the motif of a young woman whose love is betrayed. The symbolic function of this figure is difficult to identify. It may refer to the commissar who saved his life; alternatively, in the light of Leonov's later work it may be an image of Russia; thirdly, it may refer to the writer's own inner nature. But however one chooses to interpret it, the point is that it is the hero who is found wanting. Somewhere in these years Leonov incurred the sense of guilt and being 'doomed' that haunts much of his fiction. It is noticeable how often he is at pains to show that people with such tarnished pasts can become excellent Soviet citizens, in some ways even better than those whose records were clean, but for all that can never feel entirely secure. For all its silences *A Note on Birchbark* seems to me to contain a clue to many of Leonov's most fundamental motifs and themes. Even if one rejects the biographical approach it still remains a provoking and even prophetic work.

A Note on Birchbark is the first work in which Leonov's characteristic combination of daring and timidity appears. The typical features of this dance with danger are first of all the use of a narrator who is clearly distinct from the author. In this way the author can disguise himself even while exposing himself; the disguise is both transparent and deniable. The sense of danger emerges from the very vagueness of the narration. The reader is invited to read into it what it itself refuses to say. It is a game that the author cannot win, for his confession can damage no one but himself. Even if his bluff is not called this time, he will feel the same compulsion to try the act again and even more daringly, as we shall see in Leonov's later writings.

Leonov's military service was brief and comparatively uneventful, for he saw only one month of action in the Civil War, though he witnessed the storming of Perekop, the campaign that effectively ended it.[27] Most of the time he spent working as a proofreader and general assistant on the divisional newspaper *Byulleten'*. By October he had become editor-in-chief. In April 1921 he was transferred to the central newspaper of the Southern Army, *Krasnyy boets*, and a few weeks later to Moscow, where he became one of the three founders of another military organ, *Krasnyy voin*, the publication of the local garrison.[28] His contributions to these last two publications have survived and give some idea of his outlook during these years.

The poems and articles he wrote for them are almost all propagandist in nature and show the influence of Mayakovsky and Demyan Bedny. Many of them stress the need to be on guard against the machinations of the Entente and remind the demobilized soldier that though the Civil War may be over, the final victory over capitalism still has to be achieved. Besides warning and admonishing his readers Leonov also tries to make them aware of the achievements of the revolution, such as the expansion of libraries, hospitals, theatres, and schools. He points to the interest shown by serving men in attending lectures to show that education is accessible to all classes; he reads work submitted by soldiers and edits it for publication.

Some pointers to the future may, however, be noted. Leonov's preferred *noms de plume* in these years are Laptev and Lapot' (from a peasant's bast shoe), indicating that he instinctively identified not with the proletariat but with the peasantry. On the hundredth anniversary of Dostoevsky's birth he published a poem in his honour: 'If you had lived you would be with us... Yes, you are the brother of the working folk. The light that you lit has not been quenched. You did not know that the miracle would happen, but I know that you believed in us.'[29] The sentiments are banal enough, but the significant thing is that Leonov actually thought of honouring the writer in such a setting. It is ironic in view of later Soviet attacks on him for his excessive interest in Dostoevsky, that his first published utterance on the subject should have anticipated the lines along which Soviet critics were later to try to rehabilitate the great novelist.

Leonov's months in the Red Army could hardly fail to affect his style and outlook. His first efforts are still hampered by his previous habits of phraseology, and even later when he had acquired greater ease in the handling of colloquial speech and vulgarisms the rhythms are frequently unsteady and the rhymes forced; but in his prose, which gradually displaces the verse, he shows a steady development. He learns how to create character in a few lines of dialogue and the brevity of his sentences gradually becomes the result of compression and not just of short-windedness. Even so, it would be an exaggeration to claim that Leonov's schoolboy and Red Army writing contributed any more to his literary apprenticeship than the self-confidence that comes of familiarity with publication; in fact, his time in the Red Army is hardly reflected at all in his later writings; indeed those of his fictional characters who experience it are often enough condemned by the author. The two blank years in Archangel left much deeper traces.

Leonov thus entered the new age with an extraordinary range of experience. He had first-hand knowledge of life in Moscow, in a provincial city and in a Russian village. He had lived in Archangel under both the Allied intervention and the Bolsheviks. He had seen military action and something of the intellectual and artistic world. This vast stock of experience helps to account for the variety of backgrounds that he was to create in his later stories, novels, and plays.

Leonov was seconded from the Army to Moscow in May 1921. Although he was not officially demobilized until the summer of 1922, he was permitted to apply for a place at Moscow University, where preference was given to servicemen. At first, he was undecided whether to devote himself to art or literature (he seems have abandoned his earlier plan of studying medicine); but on applying to the philological faculty of the university he was rejected (he later claimed that he was failed for declaring his admiration for Dostoevsky),[30] and his artistic ambitions were thwarted when he was turned down by the Stroganov Academy, or, as it had been renamed, Vkhutemas, the acronym for the All-Union Artistic and Theatre Studios. As a result he was forced to look for work and lodging. He was unable to trace his mother's relatives in the city, but was taken on by an acquaintance of theirs, the locksmith A. Vasil'ev, for whom he worked in exchange for lodging. Before long he was offered a slightly larger space by the artist, V.D. Falileev, and this move was to set him on his literary career.

During these months Leonov worked intensively from nine until five in the office of *Krasnyy voin* and from five until eleven in Vasil'ev's workshop. Despite this he also found time in the smallhours to compose some stories. Occasionally he would read these to Falileev[31] and his friends, and before long the reputation of these readings had attracted some influential figures, in particular, the artist Il'ya Ostroukhov,[32] who was to become something of a mentor to Leonov in the next few years, Mikhail Gershenzon,[33] whose exchange of letters with Vyacheslav Ivanov, *Correspondence from Two Corners (Perepiska iz dvukh uglov*, 1920) is often alluded to in his work, and the publisher Mikhail Vasil'evich Sabashnikov (1871–1943).[34] Leonov became a close friend of the Sabashnikov family[35] and in 1923 he married their younger daughter Tat'yana (1903–1979).[36] Falileev's wife painted a portrait of Leonov at this time: in front of him there is an ikon, behind him a portrait of Dostoevsky.[37] Two of the most important elements in his life are thus recorded at the very beginning of his career.

Leonov considered his true literary debut to be the publication in early 1922 of his story *Buryga* (*Buryga*, 1922) in the almanac *Shipovnik*, an issue that also contained poems by Akhmatova, Pasternak, Khodasevich, and Sologub. This was followed by another ten stories all written in the same year, though some of them were not published at the time. These works are written in a variety of styles and display an extraordinarily rapid development in one who was still churning out propaganda for a Red Army newspaper. By the end of 1922 his name had become familiar to a small but select group of readers.

The literary world that Leonov now entered was a stimulating and challenging one. Many of the most influential writers of the previous generation were no longer part of the scene: Leonid Andreev, Blok, and Rozanov were dead, while others, such as Bely, Bunin, Gor'ky, Kuprin, Merezhkovsky, Remizov, and Aleksey Tolstoy had emigrated. The field was wide open for young writers. They might lack literary experience, but they found advice and guidance in a few representatives of the old cultural intelligentsia, such as Evgeniy Zamyatin, the mentor of the Serapion Brothers, and Maksim Gor'ky who from western Europe maintained close contact with the literary scene in Russia.[38] The variety and vigour of early Soviet literature owe an incalculable debt to these men; but, of course, their good advice and encouragement would have been wasted on lesser talents. The prospects for publication were also good. With the introduction of the New Economic Policy in May 1921 private enterprise was once more tolerated and this led to the re-appearance of independent publishers such as Mikhail Sabashnikov.

Broadly speaking, the artistic world of the twenties was divided into two groups: those who supported the Bolshevik Revolution wholeheartedly and considered that the writer's primary duty lay in unquestioning service to the Communist cause; and those who, while supporting the new regime in general, reserved the right to criticize errors, warn of dangers, and express doubts. This group was aptly called *poputchiki* (fellow-travellers) by Trotsky. Although the term was later to acquire connotations of political unreliability, in the early 1920s it did not carry any such stigma.

These two main camps were further subdivided into a multitude of smaller groups. On the Left they fell into two main streams: 'Proletkul't' (abbreviation for 'proletarian culture')[39] and the official Party organization, 'Oktyabr'' ('October,' after the month in which the Bolsheviks had brought off their revolution). The former and its later offshoot, 'Kuznitsa' ('The Smithy'), saw themselves as the cultural arm of the 'dictatorship of the proletariat,' the transitional period that, according to Lenin, would be necessary after the Revolution before true Communism could be attained. The 'Proletkul't' envisaged the creation of a new culture constructed round the values and aspirations of the proletariat, and, accordingly, they often denied the nonproletarian classes any role, or indeed any rights, in its creation.

It was to counter such ideological deviations that 'Oktyabr'' and its more militant wing 'Na postu' ('On Guard'; later 'On *Literary* Guard') were founded. These institutions were organs of the Party rather than of any particular class of society. Their aesthetic criteria were based on considerations of social utility and ideological correctness. These values came increasingly to mean the justification and glorification of the Party's policies and, on the critical side, the detection and suppression of counter-revolutionary propaganda and political heresy. These two groups, Proletkul't and Oktyabr', which might have seemed natural allies, were in fact bitterly hostile to one another and resentful of the toleration that the authorities at first extended to both impartially. In consequence, they were as occupied with squabbles among themselves as with attacking the common enemy, the *poputchiki*.

The *poputchiki* had no literary organizations comparable to those on the Left, though there were several subgroups within their ranks. They were loosely connected by their membership in the All-Russian Union of Writers, a literary club that offered little more than a meeting place. Where the 'Oktyabr'' group emphasized the ideological significance of the arts, the *poputchiki* tended to believe that artistic values were independent of ideological and political considerations. The 'Union' was open to writers of all sympathies; there was no common platform to which members were expected to subscribe and, accordingly, few internal polemics. Indeed, the atmosphere proved so attractive that many writers deserted their own more partisan associations for it.

The *poputchiki* usually published their work in *Krasnaya nov'* (*Red Virgin Soil*),[40] a monthly that had been established in 1921 under the editorship of Aleksandr Konstantinovich Voronsky (1884–1943). Although the journal was originally intended to reflect all the literary trends of the time, Voronsky's insistence on literary merit led to the *poputchiki* virtually monopolizing its pages. It was only natural, therefore, that the left-wing organizations should regard it with the greatest hostility. The *poputchiki*, however, received official blessing in the Party's decree of 2 March 1925[41] with its admission that the proletarian and Party writers lacked the gifts and skills possessed by their rivals; if they wanted to replace them they would have to learn from them first.

In the early days of Soviet power few Communists doubted that this would soon come about and that the superiority of socialism would be reflected in a flourishing new culture. As the decade continued, however, the Bolshevik leaders either lost this confidence or became impatient. The attacks on Voronsky and *Krasnaya nov'* were renewed and the Party gradually transferred its support and sympathies to 'Oktyabr'' and its allies. This campaign culminated in the disgrace and exile of Voronsky in 1927 and the decline of *Krasnaya nov'*. Its place was taken by a new journal, *Novyy mir* (*New World*), which had been founded in 1924. Similarly a forum for the *poputchiki*, it was regarded by the end of the 1920s as the leading cultural monthly of the Soviet Union, a position that it was to retain for several decades.

Despite his service in the Red Army and his prolonged spell as a propagandist Leonov did not join any of the committed left-wing groups. On the contrary, throughout the 1920s his name was invariably linked with the *poputchiki*. Even more surprisingly, none of his later novels or plays makes any reference to his military service or bears any signs of his experience in the Civil War. In this he affords a marked contrast with the majority of his contemporaries, for whom the crowded events and searing impressions of those years provided an inexhaustible stock of material. Indeed, he displays a scepticism about the Revolution and its myths that is more characteristic of older writers such as Zamyatin. It is this that no doubt accounts for the fact that none of his early stories was to be republished in the Soviet Union between 1928 and 1960.

The eleven stories that Leonov wrote in 1922 are astonishing for their variety of styles and settings. They range from the dark and portentous *The Ruin of Egorushka* (*Gibel' Egorushki*), set on an island in the Arctic Ocean, to the colourful and heroic *Tuatamur* (1922), which purports to be the autobiography of one of Jenghis Khan's generals; from the irrepressible wood demon Buryga (in the story of that name) to the introverted psychology of *The End of a Petty Man* (*Konets melkogo cheloveka*); from the imitation of Persian love poetry in *Khalil'* (*Khalil'*) to the marionettish movement of *Valya's Doll* (*Valina kukla*).

None of these stories is written in standard literary Russian, but the reader is always conscious of a sophisticated writer playing with forms and narrative styles and the expectations they arouse. In particular Leonov exploits the possibilities of the *skaz* technique, usually associated with Nikolay Leskov (1831–1895), whereby the story is narrated by a character within it, almost always in nonstandard and/or regional language. This narrative form had been undergoing something of a revival in the 1920s under the influence of Remizov and Zamyatin, partly as a reflection of the collapse of the old literary language, now associated with a discredited social class; partly as a consequence of the regional nature of many of the campaigns in the Civil War and the sense that no overall vision of the conflict could yet be written.

In Leskov's *skaz* the narrator is usually named and introduced by the author. In Leonov's works, however, the narrator is often not distinguished explicitly, though the use of nonstandard Russian vocabulary and syntax make his presence immediately evident to the reader. *The Ruin of Egorushka* opens with an imitation of a traditional *zachin* (an opening formula characteristic of folk tales):

Каб и впрямь был остров такой в дальнем море ледяном за полуночной чертой, Ньюньюг-остров, и каб был он в широту поболе семи четвертей, – быть бы уж беспременно поселку на острове, поселку Нель, верному кораблиному пристанищу под угревой случайной скалы. (1. 60)

[If there really were such an island beyond the midnight horizon in the remote and Arctic sea, N'yun'yug-island, and if in girth it were more than seven quarters across, then there would be a settlement Nel' on that island, a trusty haven for ships under the shelter of a chance cliff.]

Analogous devices can be found in the other stories: *Khalil'* and *Tuatamur* each purport to be narrated by their central heroes; they read like translations from the Persian and Mongol respectively; they are studded with foreign words running sometimes into whole sentences. Later editions were actually supplied with glossaries to assist the reader, but this rather misses the point, for the exotic and incomprehensible language is part of the story's effect.[42]

It may be observed, though, that Leonov's use of *skaz* is not so much *skaz* as a stylization of *skaz*. Thus *Buryga* begins:

In Spain there lived a Spanish count. And he had two sons, Rudolph and Vanya. Rudolph was ten, and Vanya even less. (1. 35)

The language clearly evokes expectations of *skaz*, with its nonstandard word order and naive intonations, but the incongruous names of the two brothers reveal an author who is self-consciously playing with the device. If Leskov was sometimes thought to have done no more than transcribed stories from illiterate peasants, such was his success in submerging his own personality in that of his fictional narrator, Leonov's control of the narrative is plain.

Critics have therefore tended to see in these stories only imitation or stylization. In the words of one critic, 'Leonov's own personality could not be discerned beneath the imitations.'[43] The name of Remizov has been mentioned in connection with such stories as *Buryga* and *Yakov Pigunok's Little Adventure* (*Sluchay s Yakovom Pigunkom*), while Andersen and Hoffmann are discernible in the group of stories, *The Knave of Diamonds* (*Bubnovyy valet*), *Valya's Doll*, and *The Wooden Queen* (*Derevyannaya koroleva*), which are concerned respectively with a playing card, a doll, and a chess piece. In a more general way the influence of Zamyatin and Bely can be detected in the deformations of the literary language, used for comic or distancing effects.

This view of Leonov as a brilliant stylist without very much to say has sometimes been extended to his later works as well.[44] But if in the early works his exploration of the possibilities of the *skaz* form is primarily an expression of linguistic exuberance, it later evolves into an ideal vehicle for the peculiar Leonov combination of self-exposure and elusiveness, as we have seen in *A Note on Birchbark*. Western critics who require Soviet authors to expose the evils of the system have accused him of literary 'coquettishness,' of hinting at more than he is prepared to deliver. But the point of Leonov's style is not so much that he never quite dares to say what critics would like him to say, but rather that he is trying not to blurt out what some inner urge keeps on the tip of his tongue.

For all their seeming remoteness from contemporary events the stories of 1922 adumbrate many of the themes and literary devices that were to preoccupy Leonov for the rest of his life. They fall into two main groups, those written in the first eight months of the year, and the final three, *The Breakthrough at Petushikha* (*Petushikhinskiy prolom*, November 1922), *The End of a Petty Man* (December 1922), and *Notes on Certain Episodes Made in the Town of Gogulev by Andrey Petrovich Kovyakin* (*Zapisi nekotorykh epizodov, sdelannye v gorode Goguleve Andreem Petrovichem Kovyakinym*, 1922–3), which all to a greater or lesser extent deal with the post-revolutionary period, written or begun at the end of the year. The story *Ham's Departure* (*Ukhod Khama*, July 1922) stands somewhat apart from both groups, though it has its own significance.

The early stories begin with a prelapsarian self-sufficient way of life, whether of children, or animals, or remote times and places, which is then corrupted or destroyed. The simple but idyllic existence of Egorushka and his wife is destroyed by the coming of the monk Agapiy; Tuatamur discovers that his position and fame are worthless when Ytmar' does not return his love, and again later when he is disgraced by Jenghis's successor. The timeless round of life in Petushikha is shattered by the 1914 war and its consequences.

The loss of Eden is not simply a personal disaster for these heroes; it is reflected on a cosmic plane in the alienation of man from the rest of the cosmos, an expulsion from Paradise, for which he is guiltless. In *The Ruin of Egorushka*, for example, man is at first completely in harmony with nature. The round of the seasons provides all the framework that he needs for his life:

> And so they live. Egorushka sails round his little bay in his broad-breasted boat, he lowers the sails, and his wife steers his course with a practised oar. The wind purrs its song to them like a kitten. The waves run in, hurrying to their destruction. A vast expanse for the eyes and a comfort for the soul. (1. 61)

In this pantheistic world there is no distinction between animate and inanimate; the wind purrs like a kitten, the fishing boat has a woman's breast. The waves run uncomplainingly to their destruction. But the story ends:

> The waves run in and fade away on the sand. The winds hum in the heights. It is open for the seagulls, spacious to the eye, but is it sweet to the spirit?.. (1. 83)

These lines suggest a new alienation between man and nature. The wind hums ominously overhead, the waves fade into the sand; and in the final sentence the vast northern expanses comfort only the seagulls not the humans. The archaic bardic style of the narrative conveys the melancholy of the narrator. The sense of loss runs through all these stories. In each one the narrator is clearly distinguished from Leonov himself, but the overall effect adds up to an authorial comment.

The myth of a lost Eden is, of course, a universal one, and it may bear many different meanings. Nonetheless it is tempting to see in the recurrent patterns of these stories a response to the events of the Revolution and Leonov's own role in them. We must also remember the lost two years in Leonov's own life between June 1918 and June 1920, and recognize that this loss of innocence and the impossibility of escaping the twentieth century is the central theme of *A Note on Birchbark*. For these stories are not simply an elegy for a lost Eden; they recognize that change is inevitable and that some of its aspects may seem in some eyes to be 'progress.' Buryga's human masters try to educate him; the monk Agapiy tries to bring religion to Egorushka and his wife.

In these stories the Revolution is present only by implication. The last three stories, however, *The Breakthrough at Petushikha*, *The End of a Petty Man*, and *The Notes of Kovyakin*, confront it explicitly. The author's evaluation seems to vary from story to story, and is not always clear-cut within each story, but one of Leonov's major themes begins to emerge from this kaleidoscope of settings and styles and voices, namely, the place of the Revolution in Russian history.

The Breakthrough at Petushikha purports to be an account of a north Russian village from the time of its foundation to the coming of the Bolsheviks. At first sight it seems to follow the same pattern as its predecessors; the life of the village fair displays the same sense of 'cosmic unity' as *Buryga* and *The Ruin of Egorushka*, though it is even more colourful:

Течет, кипя разнозвучным гулом ильинского дня бесшабашная ярь, расплясался с пономарем заедино достоенского колокола на колокольне развеселый, запьянцовский звон. А небо распростирается синей степью над головами, и по той степи летит, звеня серебряной подковой, свирепого Ильи гривастый конь... И небо все – как кибитка, быстронесомая тем конем, и пляшущий гик поповского трезвона, и ярманкино сердце как кибитка, которая не знает: обрыв, дорога или удерж где... (1. 178–9)

[The anarchic ferment runs on, seething with the multitudinous din of St Il'ya's day; the lusty drunken tolling of the Dostoynoe bell kicks up its heels with the bell-ringer in the belfry. And the sky spreads out like a blue steppe above their heads and through those steppes there flies the thick-maned horse of the ferocious Il'ya, tinkling its silver hooves. And the whole sky is like a wagon, swept away by that horse, and the kicking cacophony of the priest's bells and the heart of the fair are all like a wagon that no longer knows what lies ahead, a precipice, a road, or any curb...]

The universe celebrates alongside the peasants – indeed, the human celebrations are only a pale reflection of processes at work in the macrocosm.

This primordial unity disintegrates in 1917, with the abdication of the Tsar and the proclamation of official atheism:

And then one day there was a crack and a fracture. [...] It turned out that the Tsar was no longer Tsar and in his place yeputies [*sic*]; it was said that the priests and even God himself were no longer required, since it had turned out on inspection that there was no God, just an empty hole into nothingness in his place. (1. 190)

In the face of these rumours the priest Mel'khizedek 'felt that now, just when it was needed, there was no faith in him or hope or love of anything' (1. 19').

At the climax of the story the Communists open up the sacred relics of Pafnutiy, the founder of the monastery, and reveal them to be nothing but mouldering bones:

At once, Comrade Ustin, as though fearful of what he would find, bent down to the ear of Arsen Petrovich with a few brief and nervous words. But the latter simply looked back at him with his blue eyes, and glanced at the expressionless Mel'khizedek and at the whole crowd frozen in fear and curiosity.

'Pull yourself together, comrade. You should have thought of that before.' [...]

Underneath the lacy silver of the lid lay the heavy gold of the embroidery. Pale, but outwardly calm, Savos'yan's keen nostrils detected the faint, musty smell of decay. [...]

And there underneath the embroidery, stripped naked by the light of day and several hundred eyes fixed in passionate expectation, lay a handful of dark bare bones and Pafnutiy's shrunken skull on some pale and faded silk. There was a sense of greyness and the sponginess of the decomposing wood, and the touching sadness of an offended child. Then the horror of the truth, plain for all to see, struck. (1. 198–9)

The issues raised by this passage haunt Leonov for the rest of his life. The destruction of faith has left a void (*pustota*), an empty hole (*pustaya dyra*) or a pit (*yama*); the words 'bare' and 'naked' contrast with the richness of the vestments and the coffin.

The question that lies implicit in this scene, though it is not yet formulated explicitly, is whether Communism can provide a set of values and sustain a way of life as rich as the old one. In this story Leonov's verdict is unequivocal. It does not matter that the Church is corrupt, that its sacred relics are frauds, that its leaders are unimpressive or even cynical impostors. Culture is more than material relics; the mere fact of continuity and tradition gives these objects and churchmen their dignity and authority. Leonov's depictions of the decay of the Church, then, need not be seen as an attack on Christianity (though, admittedly, he does little to prevent them being read as such in the Soviet context). His affirmation of values (religious and cultural) is embodied in individuals not institutions.

The events of the story are observed from the side by two simple Russians, the old bee-keeper, Savos'yan, and his grandson, Alesha. They play no part in the action but represent the inarticulate masses who are the main victims of historic upheavals. Young Alesha buys a clay whistle in the form of St George (the patron saint of Russia) on his horse. The image of the horse, as in the passage describing the village fair, symbolizes the inchoate energies of the Russian spirit and the need for a leader to moderate its excesses. In Alesha's dream St George and his horse carry him off to a cave where he meets three devils guarding a leaden chest (recalling the silver coffin in which Pafnutiy lies), on whose 'cold floor lies Joy, bound and captive' (1. 186). After the desecration of Pafnutiy's relics Alesha returns to the cave in another dream:

The leaden chest still stood there, but the three devils were nowhere to be seen.

Alesha turned to look and saw – everything was bathed in red, and the red was shimmering and burning endlessly.

Alesha smiled: 'Any moment now and I will see the joy of men.' He lifted the lid and saw a dark, cold empty place, with no bottom to the sickening void. (I. 203)

For Leonov, as for Dostoevsky, a belief in God entails also a belief in devils. The abrogation of the one entails the disappearance of the other. Leonov emphasizes that it was the devils who had taken Joy captive, but their abolition has not liberated it. He was from the first suspicious of all promises of happiness, whether as a religious or as a socio-political goal. In the red light of the revolution these promises prove as empty as the coffin of Pafnutiy. In *A Note on Birchbark* the narrator had felt guilty at his lack of 'understanding'; now his perceptions are not so limited and inadequate, but 'plain for all to see.' As a result the implications of the story go far deeper. They are no longer merely pathetic but inexorably tragic.

The story ends with one final dream of Alesha's:

That night Alesha awoke and heard a humming sound. He opened his eyes and gazed into the heights above him. In the starless fearsome heights above he saw St George on his horse.

He was surrounded by vast crowds, many of the folk of Petushikha among them, and all of them gazed at the saint's blackened face, twisted in agony.

Then St George cried out:

'Lead them, Alesha Kharablev, lead them to the chest of lead. Let them see for themselves. Take them straight to it. Do you remember the way?'

Alesha answered like thunder: 'I know it.'

And he went ahead. And it seemed that mountains went with him.

Are you, are you, sweet Alesha, to become the unknown leader of the pack of wolves? (I. 210–11)

The story apparently ends on a note of pathetic hope, but for Leonov the ending remained something of a mystery. He told Natal'ya Groznova: 'The sentence sprang out of some movement of the unconscious, unexpectedly and inexplicably. But I will never change it.' Her comment 'These words from a story of 1922 retain even today the apprehension of some great secret, some inscrutable tragic fate'[45] rightly emphasizes their significance. This blend of realism and mysticism was perceived by the story's first critics,[46] and, though it can hardly be detected in most of Leonov's works of the Soviet period, it resurfaces in his last novel, *The Pyramid*, to which some words of the story might serve as epigraph: 'People call it famine, but we call it death, that fateful year of resurrection. Clearly our road to the bright heights is to be paved with corpses!' (I. 205).

The Breakthrough at Petushikha is the first of Leonov's works to deal with the Bolshevik Revolution, and to set it in a historical context. If the earlier stories had seen change as an irreparable rupture, here Leonov considers the revolution in the light of Russia's historical experience. The 230 years of Petushikha's existence coincide with the Petrine period of Russian history. The name of the young hero, Alesha, recalls both Aleksey Mikhailovich,[47] the father of Peter, and Peter's son, who was killed by him for his sympathy with the Old Church and his opposition to the reforms. If the Bolsheviks are seen as continuing Peter's work of Westernization, then the invocation to Alesha raises the possibility of returning to a still older tradition.

This theme is particularly associated with Boris Pil'nyak, who regarded the whole St Petersburg episode in Russian history as a mere aberration, and felt (at least in the early 1920s) that the Bolshevik Revolution had enabled Russia to shake off her artificial Westernization and return to her Asiatic heritage. Unlike Pil'nyak, however, Leonov sees the St Petersburg period, Peter the Great, and even the 'false Peters,' the impostors, who in turn father new dynasties, as no less of a Russian tradition. The village priest, Mel'khizedek, had once been known as Bald Mitrokha, a notorious drunkard and brawler, before his sudden conversion. Talagan's conversion from horse thief to revolutionary leader (Comrade Ustin)[48] is no different. It is then significant that Talagan himself tries to prevent the desecration of the relics, but is overruled by the Communist from the city, Arsen Petrov. The outcasts and rejects of Russian society can by a shift of the historical kaleidoscope turn out to be at the centre of events and better citizens than their former persecutors.

Closely related to the debate over the Russianness of the Revolution is the question of nature. Man is both part of nature and at odds with her. Nature is amoral and apparently anarchic, but she is vitally alive (as the many nature descriptions throughout Leonov's works attest), and she functions according to her own laws, however inscrutable these may be to the intellect. Her indiscriminate fertility and infinite variety are a constant reproach to the triviality and narrowness of human life. Man's attempts to introduce his own values of culture and morality into a world where they do not otherwise exist can therefore rarely succeed and may even backfire. In this respect Leonov rejects Marxism with its insistence on the will as a necessary accelerator on the intolerable slowness of the historical process. The infinitude of factors at work behind even the most trivial event makes nonsense of human attempts to systematize and regulate life. Thus it is not Bolshevik propaganda that prepares the peasants for the Revolution, but rather the spontaneous appearance of rumours, and these in turn are spread not so much by the soldiers deserting from the front as by the various demons of Russian folklore:

> Once again the rumours set off along the railroads, past the telegraph poles, on all fours through the ravines and gullies. Rumours started from the arm of an armless soldier, from a hitching post on a city pavement, from a rotting tree stump on an autumn night, a time of star showers and wild dreams. (1. 190)

Nature is thus deeply ambiguous: it may signify freedom and natural beauty, but it also stands for cruelty and irrationality. In Leonov's early work it is symbolized by the image of the 'wolf' (*volk*).[49] The villagers are compared to a pack of wolves: 'When one stumbles the others tear him to shreds' (1. 173). The human counterpart to the wolf, lawless, but no less natural and national, is the thief (*vor*; the Russian word is very similar to that for wolf). Thus in the story, *Yakov Pigunok's Little Adventure*, there are several comments on horse thieves, for example: 'A horse thief may drink, he may commit murder, and still not forget God. A horse thief is a Russian' (1. 128).[50] Indeed, it is even hinted that the Russian propensity for thieving may save the country from the excesses of Communism. Thus in *The Breakthrough at Petushikha* one of the peasants objects to the Bolsheviks' plan to communalize all private property: 'What do you mean, "all in common" when I dare say every man among us is a thief? No, this is not for us' (1. 192). The motif of the 'thief' plays an important part in Leonov's early work, and culminates in his first two novels, but does not quite disappear even then.

Thus the final pathetic appeal to Alesha raises a multitude of unanswerable questions. Savos'yan's bees have all died; human beings have reverted to the state of wolves. Even so Leonov still clings to some hope of a future redemption. In its blending of a passionate desire to believe and a scepticism bordering on despair *The Breakthrough at Petushikha* is Leonov's first masterpiece.

The End of a Petty Man (December 1922) provides a complete contrast to all the stories discussed so far.[51] The scene shifts from remote and exotic times and places to the apartment of an intellectual in a large city in the year 1920.[52] Despite this major difference the story is concerned with essentially the same themes of rupture and continuity, but Leonov here focuses specifically on the issue of culture, a concern that is to run through all his later fiction.

For many Communists the old culture seemed to have been so tainted by its origins in an unjust social and economic system that nothing in it was worth preserving. Such views, abetted by a campaign to remove non-Marxist writers such as Plato from public libraries, horrified many Russian intellectuals by their vandalism; the Communists in turn treated the intellectuals as potential counter-revolutionaries. *The End of a Petty Man* reflects both these attitudes. The Revolution is the death of existing culture, and there seems to be little reason to regret its passing, but there is as yet no prospect of a new one worthy of the name coming to take its place.

Fedor Andreich Likharev's magnum opus, a treatise on the climate of the Mesozoic age, has been interrupted by the Revolution. His work is not just a work of scholarship but an affirmation of cultural continuity, stretching back into the prehistoric past. The Revolution, however, intervenes and deprives Likharev of the material conditions he needs in order to complete his work. At the end of the story he goes mad and burns his manuscript.

The palaeontological imagery of the story recalls Zamyatin's *The Cave* (*Peshchera*, 1922). Both see Russian cities reverting under the strain of revolution and civil war to a condition of savagery, cavemen in Zamyatin's story, prehistoric monsters in Leonov's. In Zamyatin the conceit serves as an extended metaphor controlling the development of the entire story; the author himself does not use it to evaluate the revolution explicitly (though, of course, most readers do). In Leonov the image is primarily evaluative, and is used by both sides. Likharev ostentatiously prefers the prehistoric past to his own times in a parody of the Russian intellectual's supposed nostalgia for 'the good old days' before the Revolution; indeed, he 'had penetrated so deep into the unfathomable depths of palaeontology and other related sciences that you might say he had spent his whole life in an antediluvian somewhere, regarding the present as an insignificant reflection of those irrevocable days' (1. 215), and he is actually addressed as 'Mesosaur' and 'Mesosaurich.'

The story opens with Likharev running up to a man carrying a horse's head. In fact he is planning to offer to buy it, but his appearance is so terrifying that the man drops it and runs for his life. Likharev takes the head home, and with the help of some soda manages to turn it into a sort of soup. For all his high cultural pretensions Likharev turns out to be another Russian thief, but without the justification of Talagan. He himself rationalizes his actions as a consequence of the physical privations of the period, the lack of food, heating and shelter, but it becomes plain to the reader that his moral sense has been no less diminished. From an involuntary act of theft he degenerates into a state of utter selfishness, so that even the death of his sister, who has sacrificed everything to look after him, affects him only as a tiresome inconvenience. For Likharev the masses' sole raison d'être is to provide support for the cultural elite: ' "somebody has to feed me [...] I'm not a slacker, you know, I've worked all my life –

it's for them I've worked" – and he jerked a finger at the street feebly buzzing on the far side of the frosty glass. "Is it my fault that they wanted to set up all this topsy-turvydom?"' (1. 219).

The End of a Petty Man introduces the theme of the modern city into Leonov's work. Unlike other early Soviet writers he does not set town (bad) and country (good) against one another, but writes about both with sympathy. The countryside is associated with the past of Russia, with its cultural traditions; it is closer to the world of legend and the irrational. The city, on the other hand, is usually treated realistically; for all its occasional touches of Gogolian unreality, it tends to draw out Leonov's Dostoevskian allegiances, his interest in complex psychology and moral problems, and as his works become more city-based so they become more Dostoevskian.

The End of a Petty Man is the first of Leonov's works to be written under the influence of Dostoevsky. Indeed so strong is the identification that one tends to assume that the story takes place in St Petersburg rather than, as is more probable, in Moscow. This is reflected partly in the style, which recalls the seedy, sardonic intonations of *The Double* (*Dvoynik*, 1846). But *The End of a Petty Man* is more than a stylistic pastiche in that it also engages with the ideas of its sources. This is most obvious in the figure of the *fert*, who visits Likharev after he has stolen the horse's head. The word is never explained but it is obviously a contamination of Ivan Karamazov's devil (or *chert*), by the German word *Pferd* (horse),[53] betraying Likharev's feelings of guilt over his theft. The word thus loses its usual meaning of 'fop' or 'dandy' and comes to acquire the sense of a diabolical double who boldly expresses the repressed doubts of the hero, as if challenging him to act on them. At the end of the story he persuades Likharev that the only way to warm himself is by burning his life's work.

Leonov links this idea to an image in Dostoevsky's *Notes from the Underground* (*Zapiski iz podpol'ya*, 1864):

> Well, I for one would not be in the slightest surprised if suddenly, for no reason at all, amid all the general reasonableness of our future [Utopia], some fine gentleman with an ignoble, or rather, a retrograde and irreverent physiognomy, should not put his hands on his hips and say to us all: 'Well, gentlemen, shouldn't we just kick all this sweet reasonableness to smithereens once and for all for the sheer pleasure of sending all these logarithms to Hell and living once again according to our own stupid desires?'[54]

The 'gentleman with his hands on his hips' is standing in the posture called *fertom* in Russian (from the shape of the letter used in Cyrillic for the sound 'f').[55] In Dostoevsky the *fert*'s scepticism is directed at the Crystal Palace,

Chernyshevsky's image for the socialist Utopia. In *The End of a Petty Man* it is aimed at contemporary discussions of 'building socialism.'

Likharev's fellow intellectuals express incredulity at Russia's ever achieving such a goal with her backward and feckless population. Elkov asks:

> Do you really think it's possible to get anywhere with such people? Do you really think it's possible, my friend, to erect delicate buildings with dirty hands? Forgive me, but they will tear the whole delicate structure apart, brick by brick.[56] Why are you laughing? Mark my words, you'll see in another five years or so. If you were to give them all a good flogging, then, just possibly, and... No, even then, nothing would come of it. (1. 243)

Likharev is at first shocked, but on his way home he overhears a fragment of conversation: '... But Van'k, you've killed [him]!'[57] which seems to confirm all his prejudices about the Russian people. That night he is visited again by the *fert*, who spells out his fears and hopes:

> 'The petty man is taking an exam, his knees are shaking, his heart's in a flutter, and what if he should pass it?[58] Here's Elkov assuring us that they'll pull it apart, brick by brick, but what if Elkov is a fool and a liar? He wants its ruin, because that would be his justification. No, joking aside, they won't pull it apart. [...] There's Van'ka, you just heard him, knocked off a guy, but tomorrow that very same Van'ka will get out and lay bricks to create an elegant building to the amazement of the whole world and the terror of millions of Elkovs, damn their eyes. We'll lay our bricks and shed tears... We will flood the world with tears of repentance, my dear Fedor Andreich. That will be the day, a real epic!' And the fert, unable to restrain himself, began to shake all over with silent laughter. (1. 247–8)

Little by little the *fert* has passed from expressing Likharev's official optimistic sentiments to a grotesque parody of them (this is a technique that Leonov develops in his later works, most effectively in the figure of Gratsiansky in *The Russian Forest*). Likharev is shocked:

> 'You should stand up when you talk of such things, not pull faces.'
> 'Stand up? You and me stand up? Heaven preserve us! I just trotted out all this stuff to make you laugh,... to cheer you up. Do you believe that they really won't pull it apart. But they're not people, just bubbles, bubbles on the slime of ages, and a bad smell inside [...] And as for that Van'ka [...] pulling the brick out, who can blame him or throw the first stone? Why, between ourselves, you yourself,

you will pull it out yourself, without any evil intention, and use it as a paperweight to put on your desk.' (1. 248)

The focus has shifted from the inadequacy of the 'people' (Van'ka) to the inadequacy of the intelligentsia as the *fert* foretells that Likharev will eventually destroy the intellectual edifice that he has spent his life erecting.

The architectural imagery also recalls Pushkin's poem *The Bronze Horseman*, which contrasts the glorious city of St Petersburg with the monstrous cost in human suffering that its building had entailed. If for Pushkin, writing a hundred and thirty years after the event, the rights and wrongs were still agonizing, how much more so for those on the verge of comparable upheavals in the name of an as yet hypothetical Utopia? Thus there are two lines: the Pushkinian line of the historical injustice behind great events and the Dostoevskian sense of some ineradicable human impulse to destroy the good and the beautiful. In most of his early stories Leonov is closer to the Pushkinian view, but in *The End of a Petty Man* he raises the Dostoevskian questions for the first time, and it is these that will occupy him at the deepest level in his later works.

In earlier stories, particularly *Buryga* and *The Breakthrough at Petushikha*, we have seen the idea of the organic unity of the whole universe. Likharev is the first of Leonov's characters to express this as a philosophical idea: 'The world is so set up that everything is interwoven. Pull out a twig and the whole thing will fall apart.'[59] However anachronistic his work may be in revolutionary Russia, and despite his personal narrowness and pettiness, it has its own value. Is it possible to separate the achievements of human culture from the personal inadequacies of its representatives and the Mesozoic 'slime of ages' out of which they had sprung? The struggle with this problem is central in Leonov's work. One may not feel that any great catastrophe is likely to result from the loss of Likharev's manuscript; but in later works culture will prove to be an essential element in the unity of the cosmos.

The bleak conclusion to *The End of a Petty Man* will prove to be untypical of Leonov; in his later work he sees culture as indivisible and all-inclusive, and the trauma of revolutionary change is therefore as much a philosophical as a moral or emotional problem for him. Like many of his later works *The End of a Petty Man* contrives to end on a note that seems to be ideologically acceptable, but on closer reading seems to be profoundly ambivalent. Leonov himself remains a Russian *intelligent*, irreparably torn between two incompatible sets of values, justifiably distrustful of the old intelligentsia, while remaining sceptical as to the cultural pretensions of the new rulers and the masses they exalt. *The End of a Petty Man* contains a savage attack on the petty malice and snobbery of the Russian intelligentsia. But there is nothing to suggest that Leonov's view of the Russian people is any more optimistic. There are no ordinary Russian workers or peasants in the story (I am not suggesting that there should be such representative 'positive' elements, simply that Leonov does not think of providing any). The 'wolf' imagery ('wolves, sheer wolves';[60] 'wolf speaks to wolf, and the wolves do not understand'[61]) continues from *The Breakthrough at Petushikha*. Perhaps (to adapt Santayana) those who are wilfully ignorant of the Mesozoic age are compelled to relive it.

The last of these stories, *The Notes of Kovyakin...* is also written as a *skaz* and purports to be the memoirs of a provincial graphomaniac covering the last years of the nineteenth century and breaking off in 1920. So brilliantly is it executed that some critics are said to have taken it for a genuine work that had accidentally come into Leonov's possession.[62]

The backwardness of the town of Gogulev and its chronicler are suggested as much by the style as by the sentiments expressed. It gradually emerges, however, that the banal reflections of Kovyakin are essentially the same questions as those raised in the other stories. Historical change, whether in the form of modern science or the Bolshevik Revolution, has destroyed the old certainties. Just like Likharev, who feels 'there's no purpose left in life. It's been expropriated,[63] so too in 1918 Kovyakin is unbalanced by discovering the facts of evolution.

> Yes [...] from the apes, except that man came from the wolf [...] And the wolf from the worm or the flea [...] and the flea from damp [...] And dampness – from sheer boredom. It was boring, became damp; that's how it all started. (I. 339–40)[64]

As the date shows, modern science (at least since Darwin) is equated by Kovyakin with the Revolution.

Like Likharev he is appalled by bloodshed and the loss of life. 'Blood wasn't made to water the ground with' (1 325). Accordingly, he rejects all militarism:

> How can you teach a man to kill, your Excellency? Why that very same man could one day stab you too in the stomach. How easy it is once you've got into the way of it, yes, you can even enjoy it. Where will it all end? [...] Yes, in spite of everything, Kovyakin's afraid for mankind. He suffers, he even sheds tears. And don't laugh at Gogulev, your Excellency. Laughter is washed down with human tears, and tears are mopped up with human flesh. It's a vicious circle. I could give

up my life to stop bloodshed [...] any mistake can be corrected except bloodshed. You can't, begging your pardon, pour blood back into the veins. (1. 331–2)[65]

and indeed any involvement with historical events:

> Then I wept for the years when not a single important person visited Gogulev: no, not in spirit, not even in dreams. As I see it, the more important people there are the worse it is. They all insist on bloodshed. But it seems to me that a drop of human blood is worth more than anybody, however important, flesh, bones and all. It will be wonderful to live on earth when the last important person is dead: peaceful and undisturbed. (1. 341)

As a 'text' taken in isolation *The Notes of Kovyakin...* presents many difficulties of interpretation. The self-pity and parochialism of the narrator and his milieu seem to be as self-incriminating as the pretensions of Likharev and his circle in *The End of a Petty Man*. This might suggest that the backwardness and limited horizons of the citizens of Gogulev are not merely pathetic and comic but a threat to the evolution of Russian society into socialism. In the context of Leonov's other stories of 1922, however, *The Notes of Kovyakin...* can be seen as expressing the same concern at the violence of historical change,[66] the temptation to withdraw from the arena altogether, and the realization that such a hope was quite impossible. Kovyakin may seem contemptible, but the great men and their ambitious schemes for changing the face of the world are deeply distrusted by Leonov, and we should hesitate before interpreting the work as merely an attack on Russian provincialism. The horror of violence and bloodshed, whatever ideological justifications may be adduced for them, remained with Leonov for the rest of his life and is expressed most forcefully in his last book, *The Pyramid*. We have already noted these sentiments in the hero of *A Note on Birchbark*, with whom Kovyakin shares the name Andrey, and, like the hero of that poem, Kovyakin disappears at the end of the story.

The name Kovyakin itself seems to be a hybrid, composed of Kovalev, the protagonist of Gogol''s *The Nose* (*Nos*, 1836) and Golyadkin, the eponymous hero of Dostoevsky's *The Double*. Just as the meek and downtrodden clerk Golyadkin gives rise to his arrogant and aggressive alter ego, so Leonov conceived of the possibility of Kovyakin rebelling against the Revolution and the Soviet system; this idea eventually became the germ of his first novel *The Badgers* (1924). In later years he continued to return to the Kovyakin type and its metamorphoses under Soviet conditions.

One more story from these years, *Ham's Departure*,[67] turns out to have been no less prophetic; Leonov himself valued the work highly and drew my attention to it. The story relates the story of the Flood and the building of the Ark. Noah and his family brutally drive away all outsiders hoping to be saved with them. Ham is appalled by the cruelty that is the price of salvation, but his protests are overruled. Here we may see another version of the events related in *A Note on Birchbark*, for the Flood is a common image in these years for the Revolution, as in Mayakovsky's *Mystery-Bouffe* (*Misteriya-Buff*, 1918). The peace-loving hero is inevitably implicated in the crimes inseparable from salvation.

There is also a personal reason for Ham's disfavour:

Then Ham saw something monstrous to the reason. He raised his fist above his head and ran to his brothers, who were eating sheep cheese in the shade of a great tree. He called them and they came, and Ham leapt and pointed with his finger at the disgrace of his father, sleeping under a vine in the languor of love with Ham's wife, Kesil'. But his brothers covered their faces and did not see. (1. 142)

Ham sees what others refuse to see. He is cursed by his father and driven out, but he is not destroyed, and his story survives. For Leonov Ham is the archetypal artist (he is frequently depicted singing), and his burden of knowing and telling the truth that others do not want to know carries a prophetic charge into the later history of Soviet literature. The truth is unacceptable and it becomes a secret that he must keep to himself, even though he is its victim rather than its perpetrator. This link between the possession of guilty secrets, both personal and collective, that have to be concealed, and the need to keep the memory alive is the fate of the artist, at least in Soviet conditions. This aspect of the writer's calling was to be justified only too horrifyingly in the 1930s.

Leonov, however, is interested not so much in the abuse of totalitarian power as in the literary possibilities of this idea, and in his later works the focus shifts from *what* the hero knows, to the psychological consequences of his knowing it. In Leonov's writings of the '30s this motif reappears in the flirtation with forbidden and even unthinkable possibilities, in defiance of internal and external censors. Here too Leonov's activities in the years 1918–20 seem to lurk in the shadows behind the texts.

There is one more element in this story that anticipates Leonov's later works. This is the heretical Creation legend that Ham tells his family:

Hearken: this is my song of the beginning. In the beginning there was void and the world was without form. Silence covered everything. The Father said: 'Let there be earth and sun.' [...]. The earth conceived of the sun and bore an apple tree, a man, and a bee. Selah! The sun lay in the right hand of the Father, and in the left the earth. [...] The voids and the depths were filled with the waters of darkness, and the Father was reflected in them. Then the reflection that was in the water came silently. When he was close he seized the earth out of the hand of the Father and leapt into the depths and the voids. There he became the second Father of the earth. (1. 139)

This Manichean account of creation introduces a theme that is to become central in Leonov's oeuvre. The forces of creation produce their own shadow or reflection, secondary in order but indistinguishable from it. In this story the identities of the Father and his Shadow may seem clear enough, but in the conditions of everyday life, not least in Soviet Russia, it proved not so easy to distinguish one from the other.

The one constant in these stories is change, and Leonov emphasizes its traumatic effects in almost every one of them. It may be observed, however, that in most of the stories the break comes from outside, from forces that seem alien and unpredictable to those on the inside; the characters are passive victims of incomprehensible events. Only in *The End of a Petty Man* does the final break come from the actions of the hero, when Likharev burns his manuscript. In the city human agency is more effective and more characteristic.

The myth of a lost Eden is, of course, universal, and it can be taken in many ways – hostility to the twentieth century, to the Revolution, to urbanization, to industrialization, or simply as a lament for lost innocence. The fact remains that such a preoccupation is surprising in a young man who had only recently been serving enthusiastically in the Red Army.

The sense of continuity and cosmic unity that is later to play such an important part in Leonov's work is present in these early stories chiefly as a 'victim' of change, as can be seen most clearly in *The Breakthrough at Petushikha*. Even in these early works, however, there is a sense that continuity somehow exists on a deeper level than the disruption, though their relationship is as yet unclear. Only in *Tuatamur* is the hero destroyed unequivocally, and here the motivation may well be the fatalism generally attributed to Islamic literature. *Buryga* ends without the reader discovering whether the little wood demon succeeds in finding his way back to Russia; in *The Ruin of Egorushka* the hero and his wife lose their child, but they may still have other children, and the story ends, as does *The Breakthrough at Petushikha*, with a question mark. *Ham's Departure* ends not so much with any conclusion as with a new beginning as Ham and his family make a new life for themselves away from Noah. Few things are final. Loss, grief, and displacement are traumatic but not necessarily devastating experiences. They are part of the cycle of life. In Leonov's work one comes across many allusions to 'fate,' and, undeniably, there is in almost all his works a strong sense of man's vulnerability to external assaults; but, at the same time, people are seldom destroyed by them. It is their response to them that is of much greater significance.

These assaults take many forms: the clash between town and country; the conflict between morality and expediency; the survival of the past in a world of change. What gives these oppositions their force is not only Leonov's ability to see both sides of the argument, but also the fact that Leonov himself is divided. The conflicts may seem to come to some sort of a resolution in the closing pages of his books, but on a closer reading they almost all prove to be open-ended, either as camouflage for politically or ideologically unacceptable conclusions (as in some of his works of the 1930s), or simply for reasons of artistic balance. In *The End of a Petty Man* and *The Notes of Kovyakin...* this ambivalence may leave the reader confused, but in *The Breakthrough at Petushikha* it is handled with complete mastery. In the light of Leonov's later development this story stands out not only as the finest of his early works, but as one of the greatest in his entire oeuvre.

The stories discussed in this chapter were written in little over one year. Their appearance in print, however, was spread out over some four years. This time lag only makes the rapidity of Leonov's rise to fame all the more remarkable. In some cases, notably *Tuatamur* and *The Breakthrough at Petushikha*, it was assisted by public readings given by Leonov himself. The brilliance of the language, the importance of the questions raised, the ability to treat these problems in artistic form, and, above all, the individuality of the stories, such that any one of them can be identified by a single sentence taken at random, all attracted the attention of critics, whether among the 'fellow-travellers' or on the Left.[68] More than twenty articles appeared on *The Breakthrough at Petushikha* within a year of its publication.[69] Far from being a false start to his later career, as was once supposed, these stories contain the seeds of all his later themes and techniques. With the publication of his first novel, *The Badgers*, in 1924 Leonov finally achieved general recognition as a major writer.

chapter two

The Badgers 1924

The growing length and complexity of the stories of 1922–3 indicated that Leonov was moving away from shorter forms. Indeed, apart from five short stories written in 1927–8, he now virtually abandoned the genre in favour of the novel, the novella, and the full-length play.

He worked on his first novel, *The Badgers*,[1] from 1923 to 1924. The steady trend towards contemporary events, discernible in the preceding stories, is here carried a stage further. The action covers a period of thirteen years (1909–22), but the greater part of the book is set in the months between the summer of 1921 and the spring of 1922.[2] Although the material is hardly autobiographical, it does draw on personal experience, particularly in the first part, set in Zaryad'e, the merchants' quarter of old Moscow[3] where Leonov had spent much of his childhood. The events of the second and third parts are based on a peasant rising in the Yaroslavl' region, the area from which his father came and which he knew at first hand.

In the opening section Leonov introduces Egor Brykin, a barrow boy who has brought the peasant lads, Semen and his brother Pavel (aged thirteen and sixteen, respectively), to Moscow to find work with the grocer Bykhalov. The two boys react very differently: Pavel, self-reliant and uncommunicative, rebels against the inhumanity and monotony of life in Zaryad'e and runs away to work in a factory. Semen too is embittered, but instead of rebelling against the system he sets about trying to make his way within it; he courts Nastya, the daughter of a rich tradesman, but soon discovers that her father is unwilling to give her away to a mere shop assistant. The first part ends abruptly with the outbreak of war, Semen's conscription, and the first shots of the Revolution.

In the second part Semen and Brykin are seen returning after the Civil War to their native village of Vory. Brykin has deserted; Semen appears to have been demobilized. Soon afterwards the Bolsheviks enter the village to requisition the villagers' grain. Semen protests and has to take refuge in the woods. Here he becomes the leader of a gang composed of deserters, bandits, and other disgruntled peasants, who take the name of 'badgers' from the underground hideouts in which they live. Brykin has tried to kill his wife's lover, the commissar Polovinkin, but murdered another Communist by mistake, and so has also had to flee the village. Nastya from part 1 now reappears with her new lover, Mishka Zhibanda, and they too join the rebels. But the revolt is short-lived; the Badgers are torn by dissension and undermined by traitors, chief among them Brykin. Finally, Semen surrenders himself to the Communists led by the dreaded commissar Anton, who turns out to be none other than his brother Pavel. Nastya and Zhibanda escape. There is no chronological break between the second and third parts; the division simply marks the moment when the peasants flee to join the deserters already hiding in the woods, and the rebellion begins.

The germ of the novel lies in Leonov's wish to compose a sequel to *The Notes of Kovyakin...*,[4] tracing the adventures of the hero after his disappearance from Gogulev and his metamorphosis into the leader of an anti-Soviet rebellion. In the event few traces survive of this idea. Kovyakin has nothing in common with Semen, and it seems more likely that he evolved into the figure of Brykin, who plays an important structural role through his constant association with Semen. It is he who takes the two boys to Moscow at the beginning of the novel, and his return to Vory at the beginning of part 2 closely resembles that of Semen a few pages later. When he murders a Communist the deed is generally attributed to Semen, whose leadership is thereby confirmed, while his last return to Vory anticipates Semen's own last visit to his mother.

Brykin is a kind of Dostoevskian double of Semen, reflecting his actions and destiny in a distorting and less flattering mirror. But this line is never fully integrated into the overall design of the novel, and indeed the plot could be summarized without any mention of him. If the Kovyakin connection adds nothing to the finished work, the idea is still significant because the Golyadkin-like transformation of the meek and downtrodden 'little man' into a dangerous threat is to become a dominant concern of Leonov's later in the decade.[5]

Thus the novel changed direction in the course of composition, and in almost every respect – plot, characterization, structure, and style – the finished version contains traces of earlier plans only partly assimilated. Another design for the novel can be deduced from its original title, 'The Brothers,'[6] from which it would appear that at one stage Leonov intended to make the Semen-Pavel axis central. Thus the epigraph to the novel is taken from one of the traditional songs sung by blind beggars: 'Once upon a time there were two brothers; one mother gave them suck and divided her fortune between them; to the one riches, to the other beggary' (2. 5).[7]

The scheme of siblings fighting on different sides of the barricades is, of course, a common one in times of social upheaval,[8] but Leonov does not really follow it through. If the epigraph is intended to prepare the rivalry of Semen and Pavel it is misleading because the two go different ways and do not meet again until the end of the book. Meanwhile the narrative has dealt only with the story of Semen, who appears either in person or by name in all but ten of the novel's fifty-six chapters. The opposition between two closely related figures provides the basis for most of Leonov's later novels, though not necessarily in the form of a straightforward conflict. Rather the antagonist takes the form of an envious shadow, who cannot exist without the main figure. At a deeper level these opposing principles represent a split within the hero, and beyond that within the author himself. In this respect the relationship between Semen and Brykin is more indicative of Leonov's later development.

A more important myth than that of brotherhood is that of the 'orphan.' Semen and Pavel are effectively orphaned in that they are removed from their parents and their childhood environment. The motif is common in the literature of the '20s, not least because of the large number of homeless children roaming the streets of the major cities after the Civil War. They serve as a constant reminder of the injustice of the old world and of the suffering involved in breaking away from it. The image has, in addition, philosophical consequences, for Marxists assign the formative factors on human nature to the environment. In that case the creation of an ideal social system should remove undesirable bourgeois characteristics, such as crime, within a generation; if, on the other hand, genetics plays the decisive role, the prospects for creating a better society would be beyond the control of politicians and social engineers, at least in the near future. Orphans thus provide a kind of laboratory for determining the relative importance of environment and genetics.[9] In *The Badgers* Leonov holds the balance between them. The boys may be brothers, but they still develop in different ways until they end up on different sides. Semen is influenced by his life in the city, but he still reverts to his peasant origins when he joins the Badgers. The debate over the primacy of genetic or environmental factors is not prominent in Leonov's early work, but in his last two novels it is to form the basis of his criticism of Soviet Marxism.

The structure of the novel with its formal split between city (part 1) and countryside (parts 2 and 3) suggests yet another reading. At first the Zaryad'e section may seem no more than a lengthy introduction, but the opposition between town and country soon proves to be thematic, and in fact provides one of the few unifying elements in the structure. As a young man in Moscow,

Semen recalls how he had seen his father being publicly flogged by the Cossacks for his part in the peasant disturbances of 1905. Semen never forgets or forgives this experience: 'Who else but the city, stealing up like a thief in the night, bringing with it its laws and the knut, who else did Semen threaten with his puny boy's fist?' (2. 75).

The antagonism between city and countryside is endemic to all urban societies, and can be expressed in certain almost universal stereotypes, but it has acquired its own specifics in Russia. In the city the buildings are constructed out of the inanimate materials, stone and iron; in the country they are made of wood, a living substance in the minds of peasants. The city is noisy and aggressive; the countryside is quiet and submissive. If the countryside stands for a 'natural' way of life, the city is 'artificial' and associated with constant change and interference. It drains the life out of the village through taxation and military conscription.

The two represent different kinds of knowledge, the traditional wisdom of the peasantry handed down over the centuries, and the artificial, bookish learning of the city. Accordingly even such apparently progressive benefits as industrialization and education are regarded with suspicion just because they come from the city. In Russia this dichotomy has entered into the Slavophile-Westernizer debate: the countryside is seen as essentially 'Russian'; the cities by contrast are Westernized and rootless. Leonov who had lived in both the city and the countryside is able to sympathize with both sides, but in this novel he follows the usual stereotypes. Imagery taken from nature is invariably favourable: the young Nastya in Zaryad'e is compared to a cherry tree in blossom, Semen to a young foal. Conversely, the imagery of metal and stone is invariably pejorative: in Zaryad'e even the sun is compared to a five-kopeck coin.

The Communists were confronted by this complex of age-old prejudices in their turn. They were based in the cities and drew their strength from the urban proletariat, whereas the peasantry had for the most part supported the Social-Revolutionaries in the elections to the stillborn Constituent Assembly. The very word *Communist* was felt to be a Western rather than a Russian word, and therefore alien and suspect.[10] If at first the peasantry was disposed to welcome the Revolution as an opportunity to take control of the land, the forcible grain requisitions imposed in the first years after 1917 only caused the old antagonisms to flare up with renewed bitterness. In the early 1920s this hostility was the cause of much official concern, and the catchword *smychka* (union, fusion) was coined to express the relationship that should ideally exist between two mutually interdependent ways of life.

Leonov seems to pay at least lip service to this platitude. The peasant Chmelev, a self-taught but somewhat eccentric type, in what appears to be a 'key speech' – it used to be quoted with approval by Soviet critics – defends the need for mutual cooperation and understanding: 'We need you like an elder brother. And then, of course, you need to understand him, the peasant... if you don't, you might as well try to get bread out of a stone' (2. 162). The motif of the 'elder brother' might seem to relate this conflict to the polarity of Semen and Pavel, but the idea is not followed up or supported by the events of the novel. Chmelev's lessons are ignored by the Communists; the peasants regard him as an eccentric stargazer; and the Badgers murder him for his Communist sympathies. There is no particularly encouraging moral to be drawn from this figure. For the mass of the peasantry the city is identified with government, and its political complexion makes little difference.

For their part the Communists are shown as ignorant and dismissive of the culture of the peasantry. The commissar who comes to Vory to persuade the villagers of the rightness of the Bolshevik Revolution and the necessity for requisitioning their grain 'was not a bad man, but, to his misfortune, he did not know the village' (2.148). At first he gets a sympathetic hearing, but then throws it all away:

> The visitor spoke for a long time. Somewhere on the edge of the village Frol Popov was playing his evening melody on a home-made pipe, summoning the cattle home for the night. And the villagers of Vory were nodding their heads in agreement that it would be very much worse to hand themselves back into the power of the Svinulins [the previous landowners]... When suddenly the visitor – getting carried away and remembering his instructions from the regional centre to be firm and strict in his speeches so that the peasants didn't get any wrong ideas of some inopportune relaxation – suddenly began to abuse the damned deserters hiding out in the forests around Vory, and to threaten anyone who had any dealings with them with the full severity of the law.
>
> The meeting became agitated, the older peasants virtually to a man turned their backs on the speaker and Prokhor Stafeev, an old man with a long white beard, went up to him and said firmly and calmly:
>
> 'Look, jack, don't shout like that at the deserters. They are our sons. Do you think we're going to stop talking to our own children? If you've come to talk, talk, but don't try to threaten us.' (2. 147)

This tactlessness and failure to appreciate the realities of village life only confirm the villagers in their opposition.

The mutual incomprehension between city and country culminates in the third of the three stories told round the Badgers' campfire. It is prefaced by a discussion of the city's 'high-handed treatment of many matters, God among them.' The peasants agree on the whole that eventually nature will overcome even learning: 'A son cannot go against his mother' (2. 222). This sets the scene for 'The legend of the Fanatical Kalafat.'[11] Once upon a time in the Golden Age everyone and everything had performed their appointed tasks without any fuss; but one day the young prince Kalafat, who had been educated, decided to conduct a census of his country, cataloguing and docketing everything, animals, trees, and even the blades of grass. Finally, despite warnings from a wise old man, he built a great tower to reach the heavens from which to observe his achievements: 'And while we're about it, we'll brand the stars too' (2. 223). But the immense learning he has acquired has made him grow to a correspondingly immense size. When he climbs the tower his bulk simply thrusts the tower back into the ground, and after five years' climbing he finds that he is still only at ground level. Meanwhile, Nature has flung off all Kalafat's hated dockets and passports, 'All his jeometry had gone for nothing (*nasmarku*) [...] and so he achieved nothing at all' (2. 224).[12]

Few readers can have doubted that the story expresses the author's own convictions, though he avoids making this explicit: the story is a 'legend' (albeit one composed by Leonov himself), and it is attributed to a very minor character. But, as will be seen, the device of expressing sceptical, even heretical, views through apparently non-authoritative spokesmen is to become Leonov's favourite method of nudging his readers into considering the possibility of viewpoints other than those of the official ideology.

The story with its echoes of the Tower of Babel[13] reflects a universal distrust of 'big government,' but in this context it is clearly aimed at the atheistic and 'scientific' pretensions of Marxism.[14] The only indication in modern editions that Leonov originally identified Kalafat with the Bolshevik regime occurs in a remark of Polovinkin's; in a dream he calls out to some haymakers: 'Every blade of grass counts, every blade' (2. 99). But this happens long before the telling of the legend and so is easily missed. In early versions, however, the legend was explicitly connected with the traditional resentments of the countryside, now updated to the post-revolutionary period and in the present tense:

> We give you bread, blood, and an army. Have you forgotten that? *Then beat him, the fanatical Kalafat with staves and famine and the plagues* [...] Like ants we'll pull apart the stones from the tower. We can't just be forgotten – there are multitudes of us.[15]

The italicized words were omitted from the 1952 and all subsequent editions for obvious reasons. They are important, however, because the words echo Likharev's fears of the worker Van'ka, and the power of the ignorant and the deprived to destroy even the most 'exquisite buildings.' They thus provide a link between *The Badgers* and *The End of a Petty Man*. But there is an important difference. If in *The End of a Petty Man* the sentiment betrayed the intellectuals' distrust and fear of the urban proletariat, here it receives a more sympathetic presentation on the lips of peasants, where it is sanctioned by centuries of bitter experience. It reflects a clear scepticism about the superhuman aspiration to reach the stars that will reappear in many of Leonov's later works.

This impression is only strengthened by the minimal space devoted to Semen's brother, Pavel-Anton. For a figure who might be expected to be the central hero of a Soviet novel he plays very little part in the action, except to reappear at the end like a *deus ex machina*, or at least like Talagan in *The Breakthrough at Petushikha*. He appears in only seven chapters in part 1 and the last three of part 3. His character if not his ideology has been formed early in life:

From childhood Pavel's life had been painful and agonizing. He had seen much that was invisible to others, and so his childhood seemed a deliberate and stupid affront. When the accident with the cows happened and the villagers beat him [...] he kept silent, not stooping to cries or complaints, merely covering his head with his hands. His head was his most sensitive part, there he stored up his grievances [...] Pavel looked out at the world warily, and the world responded with silence. (2. 23)

His reliance on reason rather than emotion places him in a long tradition of literary revolutionaries, such as Rakhmetov and Pavel Vlasov, the heroes respectively, of Chernyshevsky's *What Is to Be Done? (Chto delat'?*, 1863) and Gor'ky's *Mother (Mat'*, 1907), later to become the models for all Soviet 'positive' heroes and their epitome, Pavel Korchagin in Nikolay Ostrovsky's *How the Steel Was Tempered (Kak zakalyalas' stal'*, 1934–6). Leonov's Pavel-Anton is distinguished by some of the features that characterize most Communist heroes of the period, for example, a 'leather jacket' and 'steel-blue eyes.'[16] Like them too he is austere to the point of asceticism and has little time to spare for the opposite sex.[17] He is taciturn with a somewhat sardonic turn of wit, and has a reputation as 'the commissar of death' (2. 285). Other Communists seem to be more frightened of him than the rebels are. It may be observed that this ideal is very different from the picture of the laughing confident revolutionary found in the novels and plays written before 1917. The state may have changed, but the roles of rulers and ruled have not.

Anton's isolation from the ordinary run of mankind is symbolized by a limp, the result of a brutal injury incurred in childhood.[18] It serves as a perpetual reminder of the injustice of the old world, but also as a sort of stigma, a mark of suffering that is the price of being a forerunner. This thinly disguised echo of Christian martyrdom for the sake of future generations soon becomes a regular feature of Soviet literature. In many of these works the forbidding exterior of the Communist hero is all that the reader is allowed to see, reinforcing the impression of difference from normal humanity. In Pavel-Anton, however, it is presented rather as a mask or shield protecting the hero's 'real' character. By the end of the 1920s the motif of the austere Communist with a sensitive heart beneath the surface was to become almost universal in Soviet literature. In *The Badgers*, however, the motif has not yet ossified into cliché. Pavel-Anton is allowed to reveal one touching moment of humanity, which is quite unprepared by anything that has come before. He and Semen are both supposed to come to their meeting in the forest unarmed and alone. Semen naturally disregards both these requests.

> 'Well, I left my horse there in the ravine,' [Semen] said airily, ashamed to admit that he had not come alone, breaking his brother's conditions.
> 'Me too...' and he shot a glance at Semen.
> They came to the edge of the ravine [...] and both looked at one another sheepishly. Pavel too had not come alone. (2. 306–7)

Pavel has brought a bodyguard with him and he too has come armed. One cannot imagine the hero of any other Soviet novel making such an anachronistically chivalrous deal with a rebel leader – nor, assuming the possibility, could one imagine him admitting that he had not kept his word, still less with the shy charm that is revealed here. In this scene the climactic confrontation modulates unexpectedly into a revelation of the mutual recognition of the two brothers; the age difference and the temperamental estrangement that had marked their relations in the first part of the book fall away, and the sense of mutual understanding and sympathy that comes from a shared family background is conveyed winningly.

For Leonov the events of these years, however cataclysmic, served only to confirm the cyclic nature of Russian history and the permanence of its national characteristics. Thus the very name of the village that provides the setting for rebellion, Vory (thieves), carries the same associations of Russianness as in the early stories. The Badgers not only come from this village, but are identified as 'wolves': 'Like wolves the Badgers spread throughout the whole region' (2. 271); and Mishka Zhibanda, when asked by a villager 'Are you the Badgers?,' replies, 'Yes, grandad, badgers we are, badgers... and wolves.' (2. 235).

As in *The Breakthrough at Petushikha* Leonov presents the revolution and even the city-village conflict in a longer perspective as mere side-effects of the age-old continuities of Russian history. In the chapter 'The History of Zinka's Meadow,' he offers an interpretation of the rebellion that is totally at odds with the Marxist version of events. For more than a hundred years Vory and the neighbouring village, Gusaki (geese), have been squabbling over a field.[19] Although the land belongs to the former it has never been used by them, because they have enough pasture land of their own, and the meadow is too far away, while Gusaki is surrounded by barren land except for this meadow which is conveniently close. The people of Vory, however, refuse to sell the meadow to their neighbours, or even to allow them to make any use of it. The dispute is abruptly settled after the Revolution, when the new government awards the meadow to Gusaki. Naturally the village then supports the Bolsheviks and Vory goes into the resistance. But even the people of Gusaki are not entirely happy with this solution: 'We've been quarrelling for a hundred years, and how many heads we've broken in that time... and you come along and slash! with a single stroke of the pen. I'm telling you, people won't like it' (2. 125), says one of the more responsible peasants of Gusaki.

The story of Zinka's meadow might seem to be merely a comic interlude, but its demonstration of the complex historical roots of the rebellion is confirmed elsewhere. For instance, many important episodes take place in a wood called Krivonosov Bor, whose name, we are told, commemorates one of the lieutenants of Pugachev, the eighteenth-century rebel. It is here that Leonov places the climactic meeting between Semen and Anton at the end of the novel.

Each brother tries to establish his superiority by appealing to nature but, ironically, both fail. Semen would seem to have the advantage as he has been living in the woods with the Badgers, but he fails to notice that Pavel has been sitting in the appointed place for some twenty minutes, a mistake which a true countryman could hardly make. Pavel tries to emphasize his origins by claiming to smell mushrooms though Semen tells him that it is still too early for them:

'Why do I keep smelling mushrooms?' Pavel seemed not to hear Semen as they walked together out of the forest. 'Yes, this is what I want to say,' he went on, 'Whatever happens you [plural] will come over to us – and not just because we're safeguarding the land for you. No, without us the village has no future, you'll see! You [sing.] are not condemned by me... but by life itself. And I can tell you straight – I will smash your [sing.] little band! We are building – how can I put it? – nature's own process and you are obstructing us... Look, here are the mushrooms. You said there weren't any.' (2. 306)

Even nature seems to have turned against Semen: if the Bolsheviks are 'building nature's own process,' then both Marx and the peasants should be satisfied with the Revolution.[20] But in the very next line all these facile assumptions are shattered. Semen takes one look at the so-called mushrooms: 'But they're toadstools.' Pavel's cocksureness about 'natural processes' is fatally undermined. If the city can so disorient a peasant that he can no longer distinguish between mushrooms and toadstools, then the gulf between city and village is even vaster than had been feared.[21]

Eventually Semen and Pavel emerge from the woods to find their men peacefully chatting among themselves. 'They were all smoking amicably, and there didn't seem to be any reason why they should have to come together, perhaps tomorrow, for the decisive struggle' (2. 306). Pavel's driver appears to be telling the Badgers about the quelling of some other disturbances, but this temporary advantage is offset by the fact that Semen's driver, true to the traditions of Vory, has surreptitiously removed his weapon. Thus the potential for conflict evaporates. Instead, what emerges is the sense of community between all peasants as the realities of village life reassert themselves over the opportunism of political alliances. The Bolshevik Polovinkin is abandoned by his peasants when the spring comes and they need to sow their crops; two pages later Semen is similarly reproached by his own men: 'We've won back our land, but there's no one to plough it' (2. 308). Pavel and Semen have both become alienated from their origins. They have more in common with one another than with the peasants that they nominally lead.[22]

Their debate continues down to the last page of the novel:

On the large porch there was a table, on the table a candle. Its flame never stirred; there was no wind. Anton was sitting on the steps dictating something to Afanasiy Chigunov, who had professed his willingness to work for Anton in the position of a temporary clerk – Afanas had been a clerk in the army earlier.

'Aha,' said Anton, without a flicker of surprise, 'So you've come? Well, so you see...'

'I've come to say that maybe you were right this morning, in the forest,' replied Semen just as calmly.

'You mean about the peasants?' Anton frowned and glanced sideways at his brother who was standing with head bowed.

Afanas did not look at Semen; he just chewed the handle of the pen he was writing with.

'What's that on your leg, is it blood?' asked Anton, leaning forward.

'Yes. I cut myself crossing the stream,' replied Semen apathetically.

> Anton said nothing and looked up at what Nastya and Misha were looking at also at that very moment – at the moon – a fresh sliver of birchwood, that had been swept behind the clouds by some mischievous prank of the wind. (2. 316)

Semen may seem to have capitulated to the higher arguments of the Bolsheviks; but the ending is curiously ambivalent. Leonov has given the 'correct' solution to the issue, and there is of course no doubt that the rebellion is a hopeless cause. The reader's sympathies, however, remain with Semen, the anti-Bolshevik rebel. He has been the focus of interest throughout the novel, by comparison with Pavel-Anton who has been absent for almost three hundred pages and is no more than a cipher. The contrast only adds to the sense that a 'natural' human movement has been crushed by impersonal forces.

The last words of the novel, however, turn away from the humans to the natural elements, the wind, the moon and the clouds high above them.[23] As in *The Breakthrough at Petushikha* Leonov suddenly switches the angle of vision from men and politics to a natural (the moon is like birchwood) or even cosmic standpoint, from which the concerns of the Kalafats of the world seem trivial. The words 'fresh' (*svezhuyu*), 'game' (*igroy*), 'mischievous prank' (*udal'stvom*), and the picture of a celestial game of hide-and-seek are suggestive of youth, even childlikeness, which make Semen, Pavel-Anton, and their entourages seem distinctly solemn. In the light of Leonov's later work this image of irrational joy in the here and now acquires even greater significance. Nature – in Leonov's work virtually synonymous with life – is the ultimate touchstone. It is nature that overthrows Kalafat. This conviction foreshadows Leonov's later defence of the Russian forest and his support for the Soviet environmentalist movement.

One of the most remarkable features of this ending is its general peaceableness. Apart from a slight scratch on his leg – a memento of his rite of passage across the river rather than of any more sanguinary encounter – there is no bloodshed, a conclusion that is as rare in Soviet fiction about such risings as it was in reality, though the eventual fate of Semen is easy to imagine. If *The Badgers* is hardly a pacifist work it does reveal some parallels with *A Note on Birchbark*. In both the flight to nature offers an alternative to the noise and violence of the city, and as in the poem so too in the novel there is no peace to be found. Violence follows the heroes from the cities; indeed it is already inside them.

Casual brutality and domestic violence are a feature of *The Badgers* from its opening pages. It is the peasants' anger against Pavel and Semen for letting the cows they are herding eat some poisonous reeds that triggers the plot. The boys are given a severe beating and have gone into hiding. It is to rescue them from this milieu that their father begs Brykin to take them to Moscow. This violence becomes murderous in the recurrent pitched battles between the two villages and in the mutual slaughter of the Civil War. Even the land surveyors who have come to investigate the rights and wrongs of Zinka's Meadow are chased away by the very villagers of Gusaki who have most to gain from their findings.

Naturally, the peasant uprising too is bloody and merciless. The villagers send out messengers to the nearby settlements to encourage them to join in:

> To an outsider their dark utterances about the sweep of the fields and the hush of the forests, about space and freedom, would have been incomprehensible, but they all had only one meaning: blood. (2. 191)

It is then significant that Semen and Pavel, though both have the reputation of being ruthless, are in fact shown as being remarkably pacific, particularly if one remembers the historical realities the novel purports to reflect. When the Communist Polovinkin brings the Badgers a message from Pavel-Anton, the rebels want to take him hostage, but Semen insists that he be given safe conduct. This act of clemency leads to the rejection of Semen as leader.

> 'He [Polovinkin] turned my whole house upside down and threw every vegetable out of my garden [...] and you let him go without getting anything out of him. There's no justice in you. You've deeply insulted me,' complains one of the peasants. (2. 308)

Semen himself is horrified by violence. When the rebels raid the village of Gusaki they are surprised by a group of pro-Communist peasants:

> Some of them had armed themselves with the first thing that came to hand when the alarm had been raised. One of them, running along at their side, was brandishing a bright scythe high above his head. A nimble old man with a long beard and in ragged underpants was out in front cracking a whip [...]
>
> It was this that attracted all Semen's attention – the whip with which the old man hoped to evade the clutching paws of the Badgers. Semen was overwhelmed with pity for this old man armed with a child's whip. Just at that moment a machine-gun rattled out over the peasants. (2. 236–7)

As Semen knows, it is Nastya who is firing: 'Don't shoot... I'll kill you, Nastya.' There was no answer other than the repeated rattle of the machine-gun. Semen would rather shoot his trigger-happy ally than his fellow-peasants who happen to be on the other side. A horror of violence runs through Leonov's works at least until 1941, and then re-emerges all the more strongly in the 1960s.

But Leonov's treatment of the issue is now more complex, as can be seen in his changing evaluation of 'silence' (*tishina*). In the early stories it had served as a symbol of peaceful, harmonious, natural life. Thus Kalafat is advised by a 'wise old man' to abandon his ambitions and live 'more modestly' (*v tikhosti*). In *A Note on Birchbark*, however, 'silence' stands not only for 'natural' values, but also signifies the hero's running away from the complexities and dangers of real life. It begins to acquire the associations of stagnation, a stubborn resistance to change. The silence of Zaryad'e at the beginning of chapter 3 is quite different from the silence of the countryside: it is a deadening, Philistine, deathly silence, and it is associated increasingly in Leonov's works of the next few years with the petty bourgeois mentality (or *meshchanstvo*).

The novel thus embodies and illustrates the changes taking place in Leonov during the process of composition. This can be seen above all in the changing narrative procedures. The book opens in a gaudy *style russe*, reminiscent of the description of the fair in *The Breakthrough at Petushikha*.

Прикатил на Казанскую парень молодой из Москвы к себе на село, именем – Егор Брыкин, званьем – торгаш. На Толкучем в Москве ларь у него, а в ларе всякие капризы, всякому степенству в украшенье либо в обиход: и кольца, и брошки, и чайные ложки, и ленты, и тесемки, и носовые платки... Купечествовал парень потихоньку, горланил из ларя в три медных горла, строил планы, деньгу копил, себя не щадя, и полным шагом к своей зенитной точке шел. Про него и знали на Толкучем: у Брыкина глаз косой, но меткий, много видят; у Брыкина прием цепкий, а тонкие губы хваткие, великими делами отметит себя Егорка на земле.[24]

[For the feast of Our Lady of Kazan' a young lad from Moscow – Egor Brykin by name, a barrow boy by trade – hied back to his village. In the Tolkuchiy Market in Moscow he has his own stall, and in his stall all sorts of trinkets for all manner of gentlefolk, for adornment or for everyday: rings and brooches and teaspoons and ribbons and bows and handkerchieves... The lad traded in a small way, bawling out of his stall fit for three brass throats, making his plans, accumulating his pennies, not pampering himself, but marching ahead to his zenith. In Tolkuchiy Market they all knew about him: Brykin might be cross-eyed, but he was sharp enough and saw everything; Brykin's grasp was tenacious and his thin lips hungry – Egor would distinguish himself by some great works on this earth.]

The inversions of standard word order – 'Prikatil... paren',' 'paren' molodoy'; the occasional use of rhythmical and rhyming prose – 'i kol'tsa i broshki i chaynyye lozhki'; the formation of sentences by the accumulation of short phrases without any subordinate clauses; the use of subliterary expressions such as 'gorlanil,' 'den'gu,' and the pretentious stylistic solecism 'k... zenitnoy tochke' are all indicators of *skaz* style. [25] They characterize the narrator as someone who is of the same class as Brykin, who understands his mentality and ambitions. The gaudy colour of these paragraphs is not, however, functional; it does not serve to characterize Brykin himself, who is a rather morose and insecure individual. It is a display of verbal and stylistic fireworks largely for its own sake, and this style is soon modified until it disappears altogether.

When Brykin returns to Moscow with the boys at the beginning of chapter 3, the atmosphere changes abruptly:

> Life here is stern and hard. The stone slits of the houses are like traps where all sorts of people, tribes and trades had been squeezed in, the inarticulate small change of people, lesser kin to the ants. The windows in the house are tiny, and hold on to their warmth tenaciously. Pigeons live in the overhangs, the sparrows dance around in swarms. The sounds and crackles of the city don't penetrate here; the people of Zaryad'e appreciate their silence (*tishina*). All is muffled and solemn as though beneath the waters of a great river. Only the familiar murmurings of the pigeons, only the tearful squeals of a barrel organ, only the sound of the evening bells. Silence and snow. Life here is like a slow wheel, but all its spokes are askew. (2. 17–18).

The *skaz* element has virtually disappeared and we are aware of an author speaking, not a narrator. The style and syntax are much closer to standard literary Russian. After the colour and vitality of the opening pages and the streetwise banter of Brykin's salesmanship we seem to be in the backstreets of Gor'ky's novels about Russian provincial life. There is a clear sense of moral and aesthetic condemnation. But it is not to be taken too seriously: the author is clearly enjoying himself; the colours and sounds may have changed, but the scene is no less vivid for that.

In part 1 each tableau serves to motivate or reveal a single aspect of Semen's character; the effect is of a series of isolated snapshots with the hero presented in one dimension at a time, with little sense of continuity or inevitability. The other characters exist only for their contribution to the development of Semen; they have little individuality of their own. In parts 2 and 3, on the other hand, a number of minor characters, Marfa-durochka, Polovinkin, and Yuda all act independently of Semen. They are not just influences, but autonomous individuals with whose wills and actions Semen has to come to terms. Their impact on Semen is not formative but constraining. The narrative is now more closely textured. For example, Semen's 'love' for Nastya is complicated by his identification of her with the hateful city, with her intrusion into his all-male world, and his jealousy of her relationship with Mishka Zhibanda. Thus it is Leonov's own developing skills as a novelist that account for many of the inconsistencies of the book.

The narrative tone too is much more consistent in the second and third parts. There is only a slight colouring of peasant vocabulary, idiom, and syntax, and the focus shifts from external physical description to internal, intellectual, and psychological analysis. The scene where Semen waits for his brother in the juniper grove illustrates the change of literary style and character analysis that looks forward to Leonov's later development:

А был май, полз копытень под ногами, купена цвела. Ее восковые зеленовато-белые цветы хрупко свисали с наклоненных стеблей, как крохотные ушки, настороженные слушать тишину утра, проникнутую острой лесной цвелью. «Еще не приехал, – сообразил Семен. – Можно будет подглядеть, один придет Павел или нет...» И тотчас же эхом отозвалось внутри, что затем и приехал не один, чтобы хоть чем-нибудь воспротивиться надвигающейся издалека жесткой воле брата. Боясь упустить приезд Павла, он ходил по лесу, вблизи самой опушки, делая как бы круги. Вдруг понял, что круги эти и есть признак его волненья. (2. 302)

[It was May, the wild ginger stirred underfoot, the Solomon's seal was in bloom. The waxy greenish-white flowers hung fragilely from the tilted stalks, like miniature ears, pricked up to catch the stillness of the morning, impregnated with the tart smell of vegetable decay. 'He hasn't come yet,' thought Semen, 'I'll be able to see whether he comes alone or not...' And at once like an echo from within he realized that the reason he had not come alone was the wish to make some kind of resistance to the unyielding will of his brother now approaching from afar. Afraid of missing Pavel's arrival he walked round the wood, close to the edge, going round as it were in circles. Suddenly he understood that these very circles were a sign of his nervousness.]

Here even the delicate 'greenish-white' colours are far removed from the gaudiness of the opening pages. The most striking difference, however, lies in the syntax and its psychological implications. The sentences are no longer accumulations of short phrases placed side by side as in the earlier passages, but complex units, encrusted with subordinate gerundial and participial clauses and embodying the interrelationship between the external world and inner psychological processes. The nature description is clearly a metaphor for Semen's inner state – indeed the last sentence of the quotation which confirms this is almost bathetic in its obviousness – but the point here is a new self-consciousness in Semen, as he observes himself thinking. Leonov is no longer using the external world to evoke corresponding internal reactions; the inner world now colours the apprehension of outer reality. It is a device which one might expect to find in *The End of a Petty Man*, but there the hero's thoughts are used to reveal the extent of his self-deception, not his self-knowledge.

For Leonov this technique also has the advantage of suggesting the interrelatedness of all phenomena (Likharev's: 'Pull out a twig and the whole thing will fall apart'), an idea that is to become the cornerstone of Leonov's later philosophy. The relationships that can be perceived and identified are only a minute fraction of the infinitude of factors ultimately involved. Dostoevsky's greatness as a novelist lay for Leonov in his ability to convey more of these interrelations than any other writer. It is this quality that Leonov is trying to emulate in the later pages of *The Badgers*.

The Dostoevskian strain creates particular tensions in Leonov's attitudes to morality. At times Semen is condemned on moral grounds for his egoism; but on other occasions – and increasingly towards the end of the book, where the Dostoevskian influence is most marked – he is presented as a man whose actions are not to be judged by conventional ethical standards, but rather as a unique individual answerable to no one but himself. Leonov's attempt to elevate personal authenticity over morality is resumed in his next novel, *The Thief (Vor)*. But the debate reappears in his later work and is never completely resolved.

One consequence of this interest in psychological and intellectual problems is that Leonov is from now onwards more comfortable with intellectual, even introverted characters: all his major heroes are a few years older than he himself at the time of writing about them. In his early stories he had depicted innocent, unreflecting types, whether Buryga or the large cast of *The Breakthrough at Petushikha*. They are portrayed from the outside because they are no different on the inside. In *The Badgers* the balance begins to shift. Uninhibited, spontaneous, extroverted characters like Mishka Zhibanda become increasingly strange to him and soon disappear altogether from his work. These changing sympathies naturally draw him back to city settings, where the complexities of modern life are most concentrated. There is thus a paradox in Leonov's work. The cult of the 'natural' does not extend to human beings.

The novel, then, is a transitional work in which the later chapters have little in common in style, atmosphere, or even philosophy with the earlier ones. In some respects, the use of *skaz* and the interpolation of short stories which could well stand independently (though they acquire added significance from their place in a larger design), it has more in common with the early stories than with his later novels. The prolonged temporal hiatus between the end of part 1 and the beginning of part 2 also marks the move from city to countryside with a corresponding shift in subject matter, style, and indeed characters. The split is underlined by the fact that the title of the novel refers exclusively to the later parts. There are in fact very few characters who play important roles in both halves of the novel. Semen and Brykin[26] are the chief ones; Pavel-Anton and Nastya may be important in terms of the plot, but they appear in only a few chapters.

Leonov's silence over the events of 1917–21 is as significant as any of the events that he does describe. We know next to nothing about Semen and Brykin in this period and absolutely nothing about Pavel-Anton. The omission is extraordinary in the design of a book to which these years are crucial and which was written in their immediate aftermath. It is extraordinary too by the conventions of Soviet literature, which naturally require that these years be treated as decisive in the formation of character and political loyalty. In the light of the missing years in Leonov's biography, however, the reasons may lie less in technical incompetence than in some inner psychological compulsion. An artist who had had no personal experience of this period might well have been tempted to invent some suitable incidents; but for Leonov, who had lived through two years in Archangel under the interventionists and the Bolsheviks and had witnessed the final campaigns of the Civil War, the difficulty is more likely to have lain in knowing too much rather than too little. As in *A Note on Birchbark*, also written in 1923, the year in which the novel was begun, Leonov finds himself unable either to write about these years or to resist drawing attention to the fact. As in the poem so in the novel the hero finds himself guilty 'without understanding' how or why, though in this respect the poem probes rather deeper. If in *The Badgers* the effect is merely disconcerting, in his later novels Leonov succeeds in preserving his silence while also placing these years at the centre of his design.

In view of Leonov's later mastery of the art of narrative continuity, it is perhaps surprising that his first novel should be so formally naive and artless – indeed his first story, *Buryga*, shows considerably more sophistication in the handling of flashbacks than this novel does. It is told in a straightforward, chronological way, with a few independent narratives inserted into the text, clearly set apart with separate titles. These stories can, as in the case of Semen's story 'About the year 1905' in part 1, be seen as flashbacks, but they are inserted as separate and detachable items: the interweaving of past and present that is such a feature of Leonov's mature novels is not in evidence here. This may reveal a desire to emulate the most influential writers of the day, Boris Pil'nyak and Vsevolod Ivanov, in whose work the device of jerky, disconnected narrative was deliberately exploited as a stylistic equivalent for the chaos of the times. But, apart from the former's *Naked Year*[27] this device generally proved more suitable for short stories than for full-length novels.

For all its formal flaws, however, *The Badgers* occupies a special place in Leonov's oeuvre. It is less homogeneous than the later novels, but it still has its own character; almost any sentence taken at random from its pages could be recognized and placed unhesitatingly. It is the last work of his to display a light touch in dealing with weighty issues. In spite of its depressing atmosphere, its materialism, inhumanity, and monotony, Zaryad'e with its sights and sounds, and particularly its smells, emerges as a lively and colourful place. The sexual adventures of the Communist Polovinkin are related humorously and without any of the disapproval, and even revulsion, that they will elicit in his later work. The passions of the Civil War in which Leonov himself had taken part only a few years earlier, are regarded with a sceptical and amused eye. It is peasant feuds rather than social class or ideological convictions that determine the choice between Reds and Whites. The wiles of the peasants in avoiding the confiscation of their grain are seen as comic rather than as counter-revolutionary. When the Badgers cut the telegraph wires they cannot think of anything better to do than string them into their balalaykas. Leonov's later heroes seldom laugh, and the author's own humour becomes increasingly sardonic and moralistic.

Leonov was still a young man at this time and, to judge at least from his writings, had no particular interest in political ideology and little idea that it might matter to a writer. In the mid-20s Marxist ideology had not yet begun to regulate the content and techniques for Soviet literature. Leonov had made his decision to commit himself to the Revolution in 1920, but this did not preclude him, or so he must have thought, from expressing reservations about some of its consequences. This may be seen in his cheerful indifference to Marxist interpretations of the Revolution (at least in the countryside). But a deeper scepticism can also be discerned. During the brothers' meeting in the wood, Pavel-Anton unexpectedly muses: 'generally speaking, there's more incomprehensible than there is comprehensible in people. A couple of days ago I suddenly thought: perhaps man is not meant to be?... if the prototype is no good – should it just be scrapped (*nasmarku ego*)? But no: with a few repairs we should get an excellent model!' (2. 305). Such a reflection is totally alien to the anthropocentrism of Marxism, and the Communist heroes naturally feel that a bit of social and political engineering should solve any problems. Leonov's question goes far deeper; his use of the word *nasmarku* relates Anton's remark to the legend of Kalafat; but whereas there it had referred to the failure of human attempts to surpass nature and challenge God, here it serves to discredit the very creation of mankind, whatever its origins, natural or divine. The idea that humanity has not justified its creation is an idea that runs through all his work. It is first expressed in the heretical Creation myth of *Ham's Departure*, and at the end of his life the idea of a Satanic hijacking of God's creation provides the germ of *The Pyramid*.

For the most part Soviet critics welcomed the novel. They were impressed by the way in which Leonov had combined his vivid and imaginative language with a more realistic approach than he had applied in any of the preceding stories. Several critics considered that his sympathies lay with the peasants rather than with the Communists;[28] others commented favourably on his objectivity in showing the faults of both sides and in not forcing the plot to meet the requirements of Marxist theory.[29] Gor'ky wrote the young author an enthusiastic letter in which he praised him for his fresh and unsentimental depiction of the peasantry.[30] There was only one unfavourable review and that was aimed at Leonov personally rather than at his work.[31] The author, a well-known Marxist academic critic of the time, considered that Leonov had been spoilt by excessive praise. Leonov, he wrote, had mistaken formalism for stylishness, photographic fidelity for realism, and ignored all the positive forces at work in the village; if village life really bore any resemblance to Leonov's picture of it then the whole Revolution had been in vain. These accusations anticipate the charges of 'formalism' and 'bourgeois objectivism' that were to be made of Leonov in the years to come.

In spite of this *The Badgers* was to remain one of Leonov's most favoured works in the Soviet period and it was reissued more often than any other of his novels. This continued approval seems rather surprising and it is apparently based on the fact that Pavel-Anton and the Bolsheviks triumph on the last page. But the picture of the Communists is not particularly flattering. Pavel himself is cold and impersonal, while Brozin, Polovinkin, and Grokhotov are memorable more for their human weaknesses than for their ideological conviction. Events are seen from the peasants' angle, whether they are submitting to the requisitioning of their grain or raiding pro-Bolshevik villages. Accordingly, the triumph of the forces of law and order is largely obscured by the defeat of the hero Semen.

Soon after the novel appeared a stage adaptation of it[32] was commissioned by the Third Studio of the Moscow Arts Theatre (better known today as the

Vakhtangov theatre). The dramatic version, however, is less satisfactory than the novel.[33] The episodic structure of the work is particularly ill-suited to the requirements of the theatre. Perhaps by focusing on the character of Brykin (as he had originally intended) Leonov might have succeeded better in unifying the play, but the theatre insisted that he make the revolt of the Badgers the centre of interest. Leonov rearranged his material with considerable ingenuity, and re-wrote much of the Zaryad'e material in order to condense it into a single act. Even so, there is no central plot to the play, while the large number of episodic characters and the inability to develop situations purposefully prevent it from achieving any real unity. Apart from an enthusiastic review by Lunacharsky,[34] who considered it an ideological improvement on the novel, the play was a failure; one critic even regarded it as positively harmful.[35] Both the production and the actors came in for criticism. The only unanimously agreed success was the acting of Boris Shchukin in the part of Pavel. In spite of this failure Leonov was later to collaborate in dramatizing two more of his novels, but with no more success.

chapter three

The Thief 1927

*Hamlet rebelled against the falsity
in which the royal court was stewing,
but if he were alive today
he would be a bandit and thief.*[1]
                Esenin, 'The Land of Scoundrels'

The Thief (*Vor*), the first of Leonov's novels to deal with contemporary life, was written between 1925 and 1927.[2] It is set in the period from the autumn of 1924 to the spring of 1926, and so ends after the time that Leonov began composition. The greater part of the action takes place in Moscow; but whereas in *The Badgers* the city scenes had been confined to Zaryad'e, the merchants' quarter, *The Thief* is set for the most part in Blagusha,[3] an area to the north-east of the centre and one traditionally associated with the underworld. Leonov had been introduced to the region by Esenin, who frequently visited it during the last months of his life.

    The novel is set firmly in its historical period, which not only provides a background to the action, but also dictates many of its problems. By 1921, after seven years of continuous warfare the economy was in ruins and there was widespread dissatisfaction, expressed in the form of peasant risings (such as the one depicted in *The Badgers*), industrial unrest, and above all the Kronstadt mutiny. The government met this crisis with the New Economic Policy (NEP), by which the prohibition of private enterprise, introduced in the years of War Communism (1918–21), was temporarily relaxed, at least for smaller businesses; the 'commanding heights' of the economy remained firmly under state control. (This phase of Soviet history lasted until 1928, when it was abruptly curtailed by the inauguration of the First Five-Year Plan.)

In retrospect the NEP has acquired an aura of glamour from the colour and vigour of its artistic and intellectual life, not least by comparison with the horrors of the decades that followed; but at the time it seemed a shameless surrender to the commercialism that the Revolution had once repudiated. As Pasternak later wrote, it was 'the most two-faced and false of all the periods of Soviet history.'[4] On the one hand it was a period of reconstruction and optimism: by 1928 the economy, both in industry and in agriculture, had regained the levels of 1913, the last year before the outbreak of war; culturally, too, the relaxation of controls encouraged the establishment of private presses and so stimulated the great upsurge of creativity that characterized the decade. On the other the emphasis on economic self-reliance led to the reappearance of glaring social inequalities. Many found themselves out of work, while others enriched themselves, sometimes honestly, but often enough through the black market, through embezzlement, or through the State-run lotteries. Not only orthodox Bolsheviks and veterans of the Civil War, but many ordinary citizens, were dismayed by this turn of events. As one of the characters in Leonov's novel observes: 'Perhaps you'll tell me that the train is still deep in the tunnel, hasn't yet burst out into the blue glimmer at the far end. But hasn't the tunnel gone on rather long? What if there's no way out of it?' (174).

It is this peculiar historical conjuncture that gives *The Thief* its unusual intensity and urgency. In the words of the novelist Firsov: 'All this is fantastic and can never be repeated. Only at the intersection of two epochs, at the moment of a gigantic reorganization are such agony and such bewilderment possible' (134). These words refer in particular to Dmitriy (Mitya) Vekshin, the 'thief' of the title.[5] A former commissar in the Red Army, he had been expelled from the Party for indiscipline and, in particular, for murdering the White officer who had killed his beloved horse. In spite of this disgrace he had continued to fight loyally until the end, only to run into the traditional problems of the demobilized serviceman, further exacerbated by the special conditions of the NEP period.[6] In protest he turns to crime and soon becomes one of the most brilliant and daring leaders of the underworld.

The Thief raises a vast number of issues and presents a wide range of characters and settings. The main action takes place in the criminal underworld, a milieu which permits Leonov to spice up his narrative with thieves' slang and a style of repartee that sometimes recalls Babel''s Odessa stories. Vekshin's sister, Tanya, is an acrobat in a circus, and this provides the opportunity for some more unusual and specialized vocabulary. A great deal of the action takes place in a communal apartment where Vekshin is living under the modest alias Korolev, but there is also a scene in the office of a highly placed Communist. Besides these there are glimpses of the Russian countryside where Vekshin spent his childhood and which he revisits at the beginning of part 3. Somewhat apart stands the tinsmith philosopher of Blagusha, Emel'yan Pchkhov, who observes and comments on the action but does not participate in it. On yet another level stands the novelist Firsov, who is also writing a novel about Vekshin.

The novel is divided into four parts which mark distinct stages in Vekshin's spiritual Odyssey. The first is in the nature of an exposition: his youth, his army career, and his criminal beginnings are framed between his release from prison in the opening pages, and his return to it in the final ones. He seems to be caught in a vicious circle. In the second part he is again released from prison and again continues his criminal activities, but this time he contrives to escape arrest. In the third part he begins to recognize the futility of crime and essays various new solutions: he returns to his native village in the hope of rediscovering his roots; he tries to find some release in love, whether for his sister, Tanya, or for his childhood sweetheart, Masha Dolomanova and, finally, even in Christianity, but all in vain. His demoralization culminates in a physical and spiritual collapse. He is finally forced to acknowledge the damage he has caused in the life of Masha and his closest friend San'ka Babkin, and to realize that this had led them to betray him. In a rather abrupt conclusion he sets off eastwards to work as a lumberjack, with the prospect of eventual rehabilitation through physical labour and education.[7]

The ending may seem rather surprising, since Vekshin's evolution seems to have been a steady decline (reflected in the progressive deterioration of his clothes). But Leonov is determined to show that Vekshin's energies are potentially fruitful. Firsov writes of him: 'Vekshin is eternal. He is the best that mankind can produce. He is the suffering that since times immemorial has accompanied all the great cataclysms. He will never be loved but what degradation would ensue if he ceased to exist' (513-14). At one point he is compared to 'a planet that has been torn from its orbit' (154), and each of the four parts of the novel ends with the word 'sun,' as a reminder of its irresistible but life-giving attraction. The 'sun' may represent Vekshin's ideal of the Revolution, as in his thoughts of the Civil War years: 'Oh, what a sun stood over Mitya in those days!' (478), or the constructive potential of Vekshin himself. In the last words of the novel the rising sun is compared to a 'unsaddled horse searching for a rider,' the symbolic animal whose death had begun his troubles.

Vekshin is not so much interested in the policies and reforms of the revolution as in the idea of revolution as a counter to the danger of stagnation and routine. Hence the NEP, which was viewed by the leadership as a breathing space, is even in principle, let alone its practice, deeply repugnant to him. But he cannot tolerate anyone else expressing these doubts. When the drunkard Tolya dares to confront him with his own fears: 'The revolution is dead,' he flies into a passion: 'I will never forgive you for those words [...] The revolution is first and foremost a flight, onwards and upwards, onwards and upwards' (408–9).[8] This endless cycle of aspiration is the touchstone by which he evaluates the various solutions open to him, and explains his indignation when his friends turn their backs on their romantic past: his former batman San'ka Babkin, once a partner in his military exploits, and later in his crimes too, decides to take a wife and go straight; his former dare-devil friend, the commissar Atashez, has become a government official.

Vekshin thus represents the romantic ideal of the Revolution, but he also illustrates the dangers inherent in a cause that claims to override all other obligations; his protest against the NEP leads him unintentionally into robbing his sister and later the office where Atashez is now working. In the 1982 version of the novel Leonov added some words that clarify the role of Vekshin:

> It was only for the sake of masking his intent, which was later to be justified only too tragically, that Firsov had set off for the shady underworld of the capital with his risky theme; he did not dare embody it in any loyal category. This is where one should look for the reason why Vekshin [...] with his aristocratic trade of a cracker of fireproof safes received in the aforementioned tale the appellation of thief, the most slippery and perhaps even offensive of all the criminal trades. (3. 506–7)

Firsov's (and Leonov's) caution springs from the identification of Vekshin with the revolution ('He is the best that mankind can produce.'). It is not necessary for him to be a thief[9] and his role in the novel could be played in its essentials by any of the 'loyal categories.' There are, however, certain parallels between Leonov's hero and the Bolsheviks. The grain requisitions (depicted in *The Badgers*), the removal of gold and other valuables from the churches (depicted in *The Breakthrough at Petushikha*) and, not least, the extortionate demands of the Soviet tax collectors,[10] could all be seen as robbery, however noble the cause in whose name they were executed.

Leonov is mainly concerned, however, with the sacrifice of the individual in the name of a hypothetical 'better future' and 'ultimate happiness':

> In those days they fought for a better life for man, but took little thought for the men themselves. A great love shared out equally among all gives no more warmth than a wax candle [...] Loving the whole world with the love of the plough cleaving the soft flesh of the earth, Vekshin bestowed love's tenderness only on [his horse]. (50)

San'ka Babkin remarks: 'The things that you and I did, guv. We wanted to win the ultimate happiness for the world, and look what a mess has come of it' (400). Vekshin is shocked when Tolya stamps on a cockroach:

> It's vermin and I am the king of creation [...] in the future era there must be no vermin, no speculators in human flesh, do you understand? Everything must flourish and shine [...] People will be passive, reliable [...] Vermin demonstrate the imperfection of life. Vermin are an insult to the new man... we must sterilize both the world and man. Yes, it's time at long last to replan the universe. It's absurd: the glory of collective reason... roses and tulips... and then suddenly a cockroach. (410)

But he still does not recognize that this is the consequence of his revolutionary idealism. Though it is largely obscured by the mass of ideas and incidents in the novel the realization that the extermination of vermin could lead to the sterilization of humanity is to become central not just to *The Thief,* but to all Leonov's work.

There are two crucial events in Vekshin's biography. The first is his killing of a White officer whom he had taken prisoner during the Civil War. The truth about this episode emerges only gradually, as for a long time Vekshin cannot admit the truth even to himself. The other is his betrayal of his childhood sweetheart, Masha Dolomanova. Soon after the outbreak of the Revolution she had not only helped him escape arrest, but had also offered to run away with him. He refused, and soon afterwards she was brutally raped and infected with syphilis.[11] In the first version of the novel Vekshin had already left town and so was unable to help her, but in later versions his absence is explained by his attending a meeting of the local Communist party, thus reinforcing the theme of placing the general and abstract above the individual human being.

Both these themes recall Dostoevsky. Vekshin's murder of the White officer recalls Raskol'nikov's killing of an old moneylender in *Crime and Punishment*, on the grounds that society will be better off without her; the betrayal of Masha evokes the history of Nastas'ya Filippovna in *The Idiot*.[12] These allusions are quite deliberate. In his reply to a questionnaire on the relevance of classical Russian writers to the conditions of the present day, Leonov declared unequivocally that Dostoevsky was the most appropriate model.[13] We have seen the beginnings of this influence in *The End of a Petty Man* and in the later chapters of *The Badgers*. In *The Thief* it is unmistakable. For Leonov Dostoevsky is of all writers the one who penetrated most deeply into the problems of the modern age. In particular he shared Dostoevsky's rejection of social and political remedies as a panacea, and this was to make him suspect to Soviet critics for many years to come.

The influence of Dostoevsky can be seen not only in Leonov's ideas, but also in his literary methods: the device of surrounding the hero with doubles who reflect different aspects of himself (for example,'with hatred and fear they recognized themselves in one another,' 408); the fondness for scenes culminating in a dramatic outrage (*skandal*); the belief that character is best revealed when subjected to superhuman strains and intolerable situations, and consequently the paradoxes of pride and humiliation (thus Mitya enters a low tavern only to order tea with lemon, and then responds very placidly to an insult). No less reminiscent of Dostoevsky are the unremitting intensity of the narrative (unlike *The Badgers The Thief* contains virtually no scenes of comic relief) and the fondness for allusive conversations whose meaning only becomes apparent later. Dmitriy Vekshin, the inarticulate, violent, but redeemable hero, resembles his namesake Dmitriy Karamazov; the old landowner Manyukin, now reduced to beggary, is a literary descendant of Marmeladov. Even such comparatively minor features as the association of patronymics from Fedor with sensuality, as in Mariya Fedorovna Dolomanova, contribute to the strongly Dostoevskian atmosphere of the novel.

The greatest single influence, however, is that of *Crime and Punishment*. Not only does the theme of the permissibility of murder in certain circumstances recall Dostoevsky's novel, but the whole design of *The Thief* is modelled on it. Like Raskol'nikov Vekshin takes to crime as a means of self-assertion; like him he is tormented by the contradiction between the logical justification for killing an enemy of society and the natural human revulsion against it.[14] Vekshin too discovers that in killing someone he has killed a part of himself, and just when he seems past redemption he instinctively intervenes to rescue a woman from rape. The final crisis is, as in *Crime and Punishment*, precipitated by a prolonged illness. Even the closing words of *The Thief* are a deliberate echo of the end of Dostoevsky's novel, not just in their promise of redemption through corporal punishment and hard labour, but in the author's hint at the possibility of a sequel:

> As for the rest – how Mitya fell among lumberjacks, how he was beaten at first and then welcomed [...] how he regained the name that he had lost: all this lies outside the scope of the present narrative. (540)

In particular it is the exaltation of suffering that relates the novel to the world of Dostoevsky.[15] 'You should judge a man not by his joys, but by his sufferings,' says Pchkhov (284). As Zina tells her over-persistent suitor, Chikilev:

> You'll never be put in prison, you'll never get drunk – you'll never even catch a cold. Vekshin – he's the last fearless and unhappy man left alive, and you aren't fit to follow in his footsteps.(190)

Firsov writes a story about a sailor who throws up his idyllic happiness with a fairy and returns to 'wander across this starving homeless earth,' because 'human happiness is pretty shameless [...] Happiness is always bourgeois. Happiness is when there's no further to go; when everything has been achieved' (395). If universal happiness is the goal of the Revolution then it is incompatible with the 'onwards and upwards' ideal of Vekshin. The Revolution as end and the Revolution as process are irreconcilable.

The introduction of a novelist, Fedor Fedorovich Firsov,[16] into the fictional world[17] may likewise be seen as a development of the narrator-figure glimpsed in Dostoevsky's *The Devils* and *The Brothers Karamazov*. As a character in the novel Firsov is one of the most actively engaged in the action: he falls in love with Man'ka Dolomanova, narrowly escapes arrest during a police raid, and is constantly begged by the other characters to write about them. But at the same time he stands to one side. He is the first character to appear as he enters Blagusha in search of local colour, and the very opening words introduce him as 'A citizen in a check *demisaison*.' The French word for the writer's light overcoat suggests that he is a foreigner in this milieu; the word *citizen* indicates that he is not a Party member, but also implies a certain irony at defining someone in terms of his civic role; on the other hand in its application to a writer it recalls Nekrasov's poem 'The Poet and the Citizen' (*Poet i grazhdanin*, 1856). His first impressions culminate in a flash of revelation:

> 'Before me the expanses of virgin land, sufficient for man to be born on, suffer his fill and die. Above me, in the expanses mirrored a thousand times in every direction rage the stars; down below – man: life. And without life how empty and meaningless all this would be! Filling the whole world with yourself and your sufferings you, man, create it anew...'
>
> [...] The first snowflake fell from the sky and danced in the air. Firsov caught it in his palm and gazed at it intently as it melted and acquired the timid likeness of a tear. Suddenly a blast of cold and darkness blew into Firsov's face; black as soot, some birds that had been hiding in the frozen market gardens suddenly took off noisily, proclaiming the onset of winter.
>
> And then Firsov saw as in reality... (8)[18]

The revelation encompasses both what the artist sees in the external world and the work of art that he will make of it. The dancing snowflake that turns into a tear, the onset of cold and darkness that leads to an uprush of bird-life (a traditional symbol for art) express Firsov's own sense of the unity and interconnectedness of the universe and the role of human consciousness in giving it meaning. To create means entering the darkness of winter, like nature herself, in order to emerge in the spring with new life. All Leonov's six novels of the Soviet period begin in the autumn and close in the spring.

Firsov often serves as a mouthpiece for ideas that for one reason or another Leonov does not wish to state in his own name. This technique has the advantage of forcing the reader to decide for himself how to take the ideas and who to attribute them to. Leonov does not stress those points on which he is in agreement with Firsov, partly because they seem obvious to him, and partly because they are supported by the author speaking in his own person elsewhere in the novel. Thus Leonov composes imaginary reviews of Firsov's novel and uses the opportunity to anticipate and answer the charges of ideological shortcomings that were later to be laid at his own door.[19]

At times he uses Firsov as a supplementary source of information. Thus we are given several accounts of the origins of Vekshin's psychological trauma. Firsov attributes it to the moment when he cut off the hand of the White officer who had killed his horse (51); on the next page San'ka Babkin tells him that Vekshin's downfall originated in a drunken binge in which he had rejected the internationalist aspirations of the Revolution and claimed that the revolution was 'a national one, it was Russian blood bubbling over before its unprecedented flowering,' and that it was for this heresy that he had been expelled from the Party (52). Immediately after this we are given yet another explanation, this time by Leonov himself, which blames it all on the NEP: Vekshin had been publicly humiliated by the wife of a profiteer, who thought that he was after her purse when he tried to open a door for her. Later on it will transpire that the horse never belonged to Vekshin anyway, but to the officer, and that he did not merely cut off the officer's hand, but actually killed him (467). The function of these conflicting stories is not to give the impression of progressing through false explanations to the true one; still less is it intended to suggest that there is no way of telling what the true reason is, or even if there is one. It is rather to create an impression of psychological complexity – the different explanations, or 'coordinates' in Leonov's word, accumulate to suggest the innumerable factors behind human behaviour. In such cases Firsov and Leonov supplement one another, and the reader is not expected to distinguish between them.

But at the same time Leonov keeps his distance from his fictional novelist; indeed he often uses him as an example of what a contemporary novelist should *not* be doing. The last line of the prologue might seem to be a modernist play with the conventions of fiction. It could then be translated: 'And then Firsov saw as though in reality,' and would express the ineluctable fictionality of even the most realistic forms of writing. But the words can also be interpreted...' as it was in reality,' and it is clear from the context that this is Leonov's real meaning. What follows is Leonov's novel, not Firsov's. Firsov may 'see' it, but it is Leonov who tells us what he sees, and he draws attention to Firsov's falsifications of this reality. Here Leonov follows in the tradition of the great

Russian writers of the nineteenth century, for whom the highest function of art is to interpret life. Thus when Firsov tries to treat the characters as his own creations, this is to be taken not as a reminder of the arbitrariness of the artistic process, but as Leonov's own ironic comment on the pretensions of his alter ego:

> Secretly glancing at Mitya, who was feeling in his pockets for some matches, Firsov fondly breathed in the February air, and thought: 'It is I who have created you the way that people will always know you. I dragged you out of your obscurity, you think with my thoughts, even the blood in your veins is mine. Everything, even this expensive coat which I will never have, this face that so alarms the world, and these birds, that seem to be rocking pensively in the frosty azure, this whole unrepeatable morning – all this comes from me, it is me!'
> Actually at this moment Mitya's face was unutterably sick and haggard. (139).

Leonov's ironic comment at the end of this passage makes it plain that Vekshin has a reality outside that of Firsov.

In trying to systematize and manipulate reality, 'the meaningless wisdom of life' (202), Firsov frequently makes a fool of himself: 'Life burst in and upset all Firsov's ingenious combinations' (202). The complexity of life defeats any attempt to understand it as even Firsov sometimes admits:

> 'Well, let's have a look!.. A sweet child sucking its mother's breast, with its angelic arm thrown out to one side. And what is it holding in its tiny hand? An unopened lily perhaps? No, a piece of tongue sausage [...] And what's that on the cupboard? A cooing dove perhaps? No, just a half-empty bottle.' He grimaced wearily. 'Life [...] can never resist putting a twist in things, and our misfortune lies in the fact that in planning our mighty works we always fail to take the human coefficient into account. That is the source of all our major embarrassments [...] Never be surprised by the coefficient. It contains all the sap and sanctity of life. Otherwise any ignorant knowall, having drained it to the dregs, would laugh at it... and put a bullet through his skull, because his brain would have outgrown any purpose in life! Whatever happens, live. A living person is the finest thing that nature has created!' (236–7)

The artist's supreme allegiance must be to life in all its complexity and disorder. A frequently recurring image is the 'puddle,' which contains the dirt of this world but also reflects the sky,[20] and the first part ends with the words: '... no matter how unpromising the day, there will always be room in it for a bit of dung and sunshine!...' (170). Vekshin watches a funeral procession go past, when the horse drawing the coffin suddenly stops to relieve itself: 'nobody was surprised by this: the horse was alive' (277). This side of Leonov relishes the messiness of life, its tangle of dung and sunshine, the dirty diapers of Firsov's baby, and the novel he is trying to write.

It leads to Leonov's lifelong polemic with the tendency already emerging in Soviet Russia to settle for an optimistic, sanitized version of reality. Censorship has begun to extend to the nightclub where Zina performs:

> On special instructions from above the programs of the cabarets were perceptibly cleaned up, and the check-costumed humorists were reminded of their obligation to sing only about useful matters. As for Zina she was simply sacked; she only sang about various human weaknesses, unrepresentative of the glorious opening of the new age. (300)

Firsov, too, in adapting his novel for the screen[21] shamelessly complies with the approved formulas of Soviet art:

> He crammed into it more than half the characters in his story, merely simplifying them to make them instantly intelligible [...] Manyukin goutily danced while Dolomanova enthralled them all out of class considerations. Don'ka she destroyed simply out of the lust typical of her class [...] 'What do you think of it?' asked Firsov. 'It's not a film, it's a bowl of cherries. Who of the Revolution's founders could have dreamed of such a triumph? Virtue on the left, vice on the right, all neatly lined up like soldiers in a barracks.' (373)

Leonov's fears about the oversimplification of culture and the attempt to make it a tool of political correctness were to be tragically realized in the following decades. Firsov himself well understands the dangers of depicting the contemporary scene:

> '... our time should be captured only in facts, without any commentaries...'
> Here Firsov shamelessly failed to complete his thought; he just drew a picture of a little house with bars across the windows. (391)

Leonov continued to reflect on these issues to his dying day, though for many years of course he had to frame his expression of them with some caution.

Behind all the characters and events of the novel stands the question of defining a socialist society and culture. The revolution of November 1917 had taken the form of a coup, a historical short cut, which had then been followed by a civil war and a thoroughgoing refashioning of society and its institutions in line with Marxist principles. The fact remained, however, that the Revolution had been achieved in a society that in Marxist terms was not yet ripe for it. More than half the population consisted of peasants with no experience of urban or industrial conditions. There would therefore inevitably be a transition period ('the dictatorship of the proletariat') before a fully classless society could emerge. At first this did not seem to present any cause for concern. If, as Marxists believe, consciousness is determined by the social and economic environment, then a socialist system should soon be able to transform human nature and produce a 'new man.' In the purely material sphere of technological advance culture can no doubt be appropriated easily enough. Thus Vekshin's former commissar, Atashez, boasts: 'We're beggars, counting our kopecks, yet we're flooding the country with electricity, we're building' (146). The problems arise over the artistic and spiritual culture of the past.

Some Marxist groups, notably the Proletkul't and LEF (Left Front of the Arts), asserted that insofar as the culture of the past had been created largely by classes inimical to socialism, it could have no place in the new revolutionary culture; others considered that it could play a useful role if only as a storehouse of artistic techniques that should be acquired by Soviet artists, though here too it seemed to follow that it could be discarded once these lessons had been learnt. On the other hand the *poputchiki*, Leonov among them, for the most part regarded the culture of the past as somehow essential to mankind, whatever the social and economic injustices of the societies that had created it. In his reply to a questionnaire on the place of the classics in a socialist society he replied with an unequivocal rejection of the Marxist approach: 'Classical literature is that which has given us the best and most memorable about man, his faith, his aspirations, his mistakes, his joys and his disillusionments. Classical literature is above all the literature of everyman, without attaching him to the passing accidents of time, place, nationality, etc. All these conditions are merely the material for creating the eternal image of man on this earth.'[22]

For Leonov the issue of culture is not merely a theoretical talking point, but a matter of passionate concern. He was the son of a self-taught poet, and he had been brought up in an atmosphere of reverence for Russian literature. When he was demobilized from the Army it was thanks to members of the Russian intelligentsia, Il'ya Ostroukhov, Dmitriy Falileev, and above all Mikhail Sabashnikov, that he had become a writer. The defence of Russian culture, and indeed of culture, *tout court*, became then something of a debt of honour with him. Throughout his life he read extraordinarily widely, not just in literature, but in history, philosophy, and the sciences. In his later years he would join such figures as Dmitriy Likhachev and Mikhail Alekseev in composing letters to the press on matters of cultural significance.

An episode from Vekshin's childhood raises the question in allegorical form. The region of Demyatino is visited by an itinerant photographer and bookseller who uses his trade as a cover for spreading revolutionary propaganda among the peasantry. He scratches his message deep into a venerable birch tree: 'Klochkarev Andrey. Down with violence!'

> From this fateful word cut into it, the old tree fell sick. [...] A horrifying arboreal sickness penetrated into the tree through this narrow window. The wound swelled up with a black cork-like growth; it cracked and spread, pulverizing and destroying the timber. In its struggle with death, the old tree vigorously shed its bark each spring, in the hope of shaking off this accursed brand. A storm put an end to the struggle. One morning the old lady crashed down along the whole meadow, lying there in the dust, and revealing to the skies her secrets turned inside out and the agony of her naked roots. [...] The old lady's collapse made a mess of the whole clearing; but the fateful word, overcome by death, fell off like a scab... Even in death the old lady did not concede victory; out of the broken root a tender, fragrant new growth sprang up in the spring. (69)

The revolutionary gospel is shown as a cancer, and the storm, a transparent image for the revolution, is shown as completing the work of destruction.[23] But the point of this symbolic episode is to be found just as much in the conclusion, in which new life appears irrepressibly out of the ruin of the old. The point is not the damage done by the Revolution, but rather the natural ability of the country to absorb this damage and transform it into other and no less healthy forms of growth. This new life owes nothing to the Revolution, and everything to the soil of the old tree out of which it springs. As in the legend of Kalafat the continuity of nature and culture triumphs over the unnatural designs of mankind.

Within the novel this principle is illustrated by the figure of the old landowner Manyukin, now penniless and unwanted, eking out a living by telling fantastic stories in taverns for a few kopecks. He is the only character in the novel who is given a family tree, traced back, significantly, to the time of Peter the Great. In his diary he writes:

> The generations differ one from another, struggle to the death, but they never realize that one cannot exist without the other. They never remember that it is on the stout shoulders of their elders that the young build their dizzying structures. And they in turn never foresee that they too will be hammered into the foundations by their appreciative but hard-headed successors. (178)

The words capture both the denial of continuity that the new man affects, and the fact of continuity overriding all temporary delusions. The diary, clearly a metaphor for the accumulated culture of the past, is addressed to Manyukin's son, Nikolasha, who seems to have served in the White Army, and is now presumably either dead or in emigration. He has apparently rejected his father and would be unlikely to read the manuscript even if it came into his hands. Have the links with the past been finally severed, or is there some prospect of continuity?

The only Nikolay in the novel is the peasant turned black marketeer, Zavarikhin. It emerges, however, during the course of the novel, that Vekshin himself is the illegitimate son of Manyukin, and there is a suggestion that the diary is in fact addressed to him. Later, on his visit to his native village, Vekshin meets his half-brother, Leontiy, who has also, it turns out, been fathered by Manyukin. Leontiy displays another face of the peasantry, the secretive, resentful, but nonetheless powerful force of inertia in Russia. Which of these, if any, is to be the heir to Manyukin's legacy?

In the 1920s it seemed to many Russians that the rising power of the peasantry constituted the main threat to the survival of the Revolution, a fear that was exploited at the end of the decade to justify the brutalities of forced collectivization. Firsov shares these misgivings:

> The earth gives birth to Mit'ka and Zavarikhin in one and the same hour, indifferent to their differences, dispassionate in her creative energy. The former is on the way down, the latter on the way up: where their paths intersect – catastrophe, collision, and hatred. The former will die a cruel and splendid death, the latter will triumph over death three times. Both are right, the former in his nobility and will-power, the latter in his strength. The two are harbingers of the newly awakened millions. (48)

Leonov too sees them in antithetical terms, for example, 'meat versus metal' (35). If he holds out the hope of Vekshin's eventual reintegration into Soviet society he is also resigned to the prospect of Zavarikhin's becoming the 'head of a firm' and his business 'world-famous' (14).[24] As the novel proceeds, however, Zavarikhin becomes a peripheral figure, and he appears only briefly in the later stages.

Vekshin embodies the cultural void created by the Revolution (the 'hole into nothingness' of *The Breakthrough at Petushikha*). Firsov claims that he is 'a block from which the ancestor of the new man of the future will be born' (378), but unfortunately Vekshin is hardly an adequate vehicle for such a weighty theme; the suggestion that he is a Hamlet figure (479) seems quite gratuitous.

Firsov, for all his admiration of his anarchic insatiability, realizes that the age requires other abilities: 'Mitya is a disaster, because he cannot be harnessed even to a windmill; no organization, no culture, no restraint – and the result – catastrophe' (378). Vekshin himself seems to be totally without culture in the normal sense of the word, so much so that it comes as a surprise when Firsov claims to have seen him in the theatre, and in the third row of the stalls at that (392).

As Leonov was to explain in an interview three years later: 'Mitya's desires were egoistic in the extreme, and once he had satisfied them, he had no idea what he should do next. This is what creates the narrowness of his outlook and his total lack of culture. As a child he had dreamed of chocolate and... sleeping in the Tsar's bed, and thanks to the Revolution all this had come about. But then what? It is just here that the drama of his inner emptiness, the drama of his cultural growth comes out.'[25]

Chocolate, a good horse, sleeping in the Tsar's bed – all these can be and have been achieved by the Revolution. But the suspicion that the old world possessed some secret that cannot be acquired so easily fills Vekshin with envy. In a comment on Firsov's novel Leonov remarks: 'In the interests of complicating the plot, the author had introduced some extremely ingenious developments. At one critical moment Masha was alleged to have said to [Vekshin]: "Yes, you killed, but not in anger, rather out of envy that you could not capture his last and most precious treasure, that has neither weight nor measure"' (420). And he continues:

> It was just this passage that incurred the wrath of the most prominent critic of the age: '[we must] study, not just in words but in deeds, with the energy and courage that our fathers and older brothers showed when they fought for the glory of socialism. By a veritable feat of heroism we must capture for ourselves that central citadel with its view of earth and heaven, where the banner of victorious labour must first of all be unfurled.' (The critic failed to note that if Firsov's story had inspired him to these words, then it was relevant enough to the times that the country was living through.)

Wasn't this just what the author had written at the end of his ill-fated fifth chapter that '... all this coincided with the happy moment when the Ministry of Enlightenment [Education and Culture] acquired an importance equal to that of the Ministry of the National Economy, when the universities, purged of idlers and other scum, were invaded by the young, and the older ones discovered, at long last, why it is that water boils, that rivers flow downhill, and the sky is blue'? By proclaiming the slogan of 'the acquisition of culture' Firsov ran the risk of oversimplifying the individual fate of his hero to that of a cartoon, but nobody understood or appreciated this. [Vekshin] was regarded as a counter-example of the revolutionary man. (420–1)

Vekshin's attempt to 'acquire' culture at a single blow[26] is not an isolated excess; it is true of the Revolution as a whole. What has been accumulated over the millennia cannot be disposed of or acquired so easily. The result is bound to be superficial and unsatisfactory. The sarcastic comments on the takeover of the universities by the Party in the second half of the '20s, with the expulsion of the old intelligentsia and the debasing of higher education to elementary levels ('the older ones discovered at long last why it is that water boils,' etc....) are attributed to Firsov, but Leonov shows in several places that he fully agrees with him, and his later novels continue the polemic. The attempt to make culture serve political ends, however apparently humane and admirable those ends might be, is to pervert its role and significance.

There may seem to be a contradiction in Leonov's ideas of culture. At times he treats it as timeless and indestructible: to attempt to deny it or abolish it is just absurd, for it will continue whether or not it is officially recognized. But at other times he sees it as under threat from the Communists. If the former is true then the enemies of culture would be engaged in a hopeless task, and Leonov might just as well sit back and let history look after itself. But this would hardly explain the passion with which Leonov has returned to this issue throughout his life. The answer is to be found in his idea of culture as the most nearly complete record of the experience of mankind, the evil as well as the good. It too is a 'puddle' that reflects the heavens in the prose of life. But this is not an easy tolerance. Leonov, like Dostoevsky, is fascinated and appalled by man's 'breadth,' his capacity for encompassing the ideals of both the Madonna and Sodom.[27] Later he will borrow the image of culture as 'original sin' from the *Correspondence beween Two Corners* of Vyacheslav Ivanov and Mikhail Gershenzon. Ham's shameful knowledge cannot be wished away, however painful it may be. There is no other way of knowing ourselves; ignorance leads not to liberation but to further enslavement, and it is the artist's mission to remind his readers of this truth.

Leonov holds out one possibility of an outlet for Vekshin's energies. When he leaves his brother's home in part 3 he comes across a new power station being constructed:

Suddenly he began to understand from his heart what previously he had tried to understand with his brain... 'This was where they were needed, those reins of electricity. We must direct the chaotic mass of mankind [...] into a single wise turbine and there purge the great reserve of human power of all its dross. On the far side of that turbine we will find the new man.' (345)

Accordingly, the end of the novel with its promise of Vekshin's redemption through hard work and education is better prepared than has generally been allowed by Leonov's critics. But, as in the early works, Leonov still has his doubts as to man's (Van'ka's) propensity for wanton destruction. Mitya's reflections on the power station take a pessimistic turn: 'And what if the new man should fail us?' (345), and later he returns to these thoughts:

> Mankind needs a shepherd [...] Don'ka has a song: 'Beyond the pass the sun is shining, but the way through the pass is terrifying!..'[28] Remarkable words, mark them well. Man has to be harnessed with an iron yoke and brought to the light. This summer I had a good look at the peasant: he too needs an all-loving father, but one wearing a policeman's uniform. [...] Without a shepherd they'll kill one another, choke in their own filth, lift their snouts to heaven and wail to God [...] The human race is worn out; the grain has been thrashed out of the sheaf. Let's burn the sheaf then and wait for another. (416–17)

This despairing view of human nature recalls Pavel-Anton's momentary loss of faith at the end of *The Badgers*. They expose the antinomies at the heart of Leonov's attitude to the Revolution. Like Dostoevsky he insists on the necessity for human freedom, however it may be misused, but like Dostoevsky he also recognizes the human inability to remain constant to any ideal, and the consequent temptation for tyranny to protect human nature from itself.

This aspect of human nature is reflected in Petr Gorbidonovich Chikilev,[29] as is shown by the fact that his name contains the same four consonants as the Russian word for 'man' (*chelovek*). A minor clerk under the old regime, he has shown himself able to adapt to post-revolutionary conditions without any difficulty:

> Chikilev was cunning – painstakingly he was whittling out a little niche for himself in the new life – in days gone by he had been recommended for the St Anne's medal, but he had never received it because of the revolution. (111)

He is a further development of the figures of Kovyakin and Brykin, but now he has been given a taste of power, like Golyadkin's double. Firsov sums him up as 'Akakiy Akakievich gone berserk' (392).[30] Chikilev is less affected by the events of the novel than any other of the protagonists:

> I am eternal, steadfast and unalterable – an army tunic, a peasant's overcoat, a jacket, a morning coat – they all fit me. I am as unalterable as God himself [...] Life is ours; we are laid at its very foundations. (535)

He is voted out of his position as chairman of the house committee, but he soon regains it, and even though he loses both wife and child he is not disheartened. (It may be noted that the moments of humiliation and suffering are the only occasions when Chikilev is shown with some humanity, but when he is restored to favour he returns to his former arrogance.)

Like so many of Dostoevsky's heroes Chikilev is characterized more by his ideas than by his actions. Where Vekshin stands for man's duty to search and aspire at whatever cost, Chikilev sees equality and homogeneity as the only basis for happiness, and, as tax collector, he has the power to cut exceptional individuals down to size:

> It's happiness we're working for, isn't it? But why has nobody ever thought of producing human beings to a single pattern, of having them all born the same size, height, weight, and all that? As soon as one of them begins to draw attention to himself (*zashebarshil*), then snip to his wings. And there'd be no unhappiness, but all of them in unison. Break one and it's no loss: dead – and you can forget it. (191)

If happiness is the goal then unhappiness becomes an expression of dissent, of social and political alienation: 'All the critics unanimously demanded an elevated rosy-cheekedness from Firsov, forgetting in their haste where real colour ends and makeup begins' (458). But, as Firsov had observed earlier, 'There are no rosy-cheeked people, no one is unscathed, we are all cripples' (90).[31]

Kovyakin's distrust of 'important persons' is now shown in a different light. In the name of establishing the earthly paradise individual freedom may seem a small price to pay. Thus Chikilev dreams of the day when it will become possible to read people's thoughts:

> In the future state which will come about in a thousand years there cannot be any secrets. Everyone must be able to visit anybody and observe his life at any moment of the day or night, perhaps even with a magnifying glass. Maybe you're harbouring the idea of destroying the whole of humanity? [...] You must keep an eye on mankind, never leave him unobserved. No secrets, out in the open, this way, citizen, into the square and tell us all frankly what you live by. Then everyone'll have to be honest whether they like it or not, and just put up with it. If

I, let's say, were the boss of the whole world, I would have a machine with an antenna, like at the post-office, put on everyone's head. Every morning the duty clerk would read and table a resolution... and in just the same way everyone would be able to look into the boss's head too. Thought – that is the source of all suffering. The one who abolishes thought will be commemorated forever by a grateful humanity. (253)[32]

This paean to equality betrays Chikilev's megalomaniac ambitions: 'If I [...] were boss of the whole world...'[33] Like Dostoevsky's Shigalev he starts from the premise of absolute equality[34] and progresses logically to the conclusion of absolute despotism, and in this guise he recalls Ivan Karamazov's Grand Inquisitor: 'Sin away; Chikilev will forgive you everything and even find you a justification' (535).

Like Shigalev too Chikilev understands the problems of inequality not just in terms of material conditions but also of intellectual and spiritual qualities. His real motivation, however, is envy, and so he desires not to raise people's potentialities but to reduce them to their lowest common factor. In Firsov's words, he does not ask 'Why have I got what they haven't got?' but 'Why have they got what I haven't?'[35] (503). At the time Leonov does not seem to have been aware that Chikilev's envy is hardly to be distinguished from that of Vekshin,[36] but when he came to revise the novel in 1959 this recognition becomes crucial to the re-evaluation of his hero.

It is natural to see reminiscences of Dostoevsky here, in view of his influence on so many other aspects of the novel, but, as far as the ideas go, an even closer source would of course be Zamyatin's *We* (*My*, 1920), with its sterile glass city (itself a reference to the Crystal Palace mocked in *Notes from the Underground*) and its portrayal of a state ideology of 'mathematically infallible happiness'[37] achieved at the price of freedom. Though never published officially in the USSR, *We* was undoubtedly known to most members of the intelligentsià in the 1920s. In Leonov's novels and plays there are so many echoes of Zamyatin's work that it would be implausible to explain them as merely coincidental.

Chikilev's ideas, however, originate not only in fiction. They may be seen as an grotesque version of the views expressed by some of the most influential thinkers in the Bolshevik hierarchy. In their remarkable book, *The ABC of Communism (Azbuka Kommunizma*, 1919) (also a source for Zamyatin's *We*), Bukharin and Preobrazhensky outlined a view of the Revolution and the future classless society in exclusively materialist and collectivist terms.

The reorganization of society and the plannning of all its activities on the basis of statistical information should, they believed, turn society into 'a well-oiled machine.'[38] The provision of kindergartens, communal dining halls and the reorientation of education at all levels should lead to 'a new world with new people and new customs' within a decade or so.³⁹ Above all, the authors did not hesitate to advocate the use of terror in the cause of hastening the arrival of their ideal society and the exclusion from all rights in it 'of those classes that are hostile to the proletariat and the peasantry [...] in order to end the exploitation of one human being by another.'⁴⁰

Bukharin himself denied that socialism inevitably involved any levelling down, but there is a strain of anti-intellectualism running through *The ABC*: 'Let us suppose, for instance, that the intelligentsia should have so narrowed the gap with the working class, that it has ceased to murmur against it, has come over wholeheartedly to the Soviet position in its work, and has merged with the proletariat.'⁴¹ The word I have translated as 'murmured' (*shebarshit'*) is rare in literary Russian, though common enough in everyday speech. It means to 'rustle' or 'scurry,' and is applied usually to vermin, rats, mice, cockroaches. Its use by Bukharin and Chikilev (where I translated it as 'draw attention to oneself') in a metaphorical sense is most unusual, and I have no doubt that Leonov's recourse to the same word is a deliberate allusion. Its implications for the intelligentsia are unmistakable, as one remembers the drunken Tolya stamping on a cockroach.

This point is confirmed by the parallel between Chikilev and the only two Communists in the novel. Chikilev asks, 'God? What does that mean? You can see Lenin lying in the mausoleum. I can go along and see for myself; but where's God?' (190); he rejects beauty: 'It ought to be forbidden *in the name of higher morality* – to prevent people being made unhappy' (189); and the soul: 'We'd be better off without it; it's driven enough people to the gallows' (202). These ideas are echoed by the Communist Matvey, who is enraged by the fact that his sister Zina should be in love with Vekshin, a thief:

> 'Love? [...] There you are, read all about it,' and he furiously turned over the pages, looking for the ones most likely to offend Zina's love. 'Got it? No mystery at all [...] just the mutual attraction of cells [...] When people have found out everything, weighed it, measured it, summed it up [...] when they can change everything then there'll be happiness. You'll be able to manufacture it like galoshes or light bulbs.' And he nodded up at the fixture in the ceiling where a feeble electric bulb struggled feebly against the twilight. 'We must study. Then happiness too will be painless.' (195)⁴²

The parallel between Chikilev's and Matvey's views is emphasized by setting them in adjacent chapters.⁴³ In the same way the commissar Atashez tells Vekshin: 'I know all about you. One only needs to know the chief cog in a man for all the rest to be plain.' Vekshin retorts: 'A man can make a machine that will produce sweets, but to produce a single berry, no, not in forty centuries. You can never understand man just by reasoning' (445).[44] Many of the Communists in Leonov's later works will display the same aggressive materialism, though its petty bourgeois roots will not be so explicit. The later course of Soviet history showed that the Chikilevs presented a greater threat to the Revolution than the Zavarikhins, and when Leonov came to rewrite the novel in the late 1950s Chikilev's role was significantly expanded.

So far *The Thief* seems to have been a novel of irreconcilable conflicts and antinomies. Somewhat apart and even above, stands the local odd-job man and herbal doctor, Emel'yan Pchkhov,[45] who, like Firsov, both participates in the action and stands outside it as observer and commentator. He is presented as a universal man in his experience and his skills: 'His reason, like his hands, was blessed with the inscrutable gift of being able to handle everything' (16), and in the past he has been both a soldier and a monk. Like Pavel-Anton in *The Badgers* he limps, but his limp is not a stigma, it is rather a reminder of the price of his freedom (he broke his leg when returning to the monastery after visiting one of the local girls). Where the other characters are concerned with change, progress, and the future, Pchkhov stands outside and detached:

> He loved his solitude, and when he was alone with his wood his ear fed sweetly on the silence. His chisel panted as it uncovered beauty, the curled slivers of wood, liberated by the plane, rustled, and the wood screamed as the saw divided it. Above him life seethed, men struggled and fell, old faiths perished, and new ones arose, but master Pchkhov in his semi-basement continued to affirm his absolute right to winkle out the laughing layers of wood, and to smile at the eternal rebellion of mankind. (120)

Pchkhov reflects the quietist side of Leonov (seen earlier in Savos'yan in *The Breakthrough at Petushkikha*). He represents an ideal of *tishina* far removed from the restless aspirations of Vekshin and the materialist culture of the Revolution. The scenes involving him almost all take place at night, intensifying the air of mystery around him. This prepares the revelation that he is a Christian, and at the end of part 3 he invites Vekshin to go to confession and take Communion. Vekshin's rejection of the offer provides one of the most moving scenes in the novel:

> 'You know your wisdom and I know mine. There are times when I revere you, Pchkhov. You are the only who is different from all the others, and no one can follow in your footsteps... But I know where you are leading me. Everybody

wants to comfort me and so trap me. Everything in the world is a trap and there is nowhere to escape and be free.' (451–2)

After this rejection 'Pchkhov's face collapsed, his arms dangled helplessly along his body; he had given everything he had and was now clearly broken,' and he plays little part in the rest of the action. When Leonov came to revise the novel thirty years later he moved this scene up to the very end, just before Vekshin's final departure for Siberia, where it acquires even greater force.

The scene is one of several which have led to the widespread assumption that Leonov was a practising Christian.[46] But the outcome of this scene is worth noting. The suspicion that Christianity with its promise of eternal bliss might be only another trap continued to trouble him to the end of his life: how is Christian 'bliss' to be distinguished from Communist 'happiness'? Leonov's Christianity is based on the acceptance of suffering, and the distrust of any man-made solutions to it.

Pchkhov displays the scepticism over progress that we have seen in 'The Legend of the Fanatical Kalafat.' He says to Firsov: 'you say that if you don't keep in step with progress, you'll be trampled underfoot, but I say, just wait and people will rebel: "that's enough of building a cage for ourselves"' (138). In a free adaptation of the biblical story he relates that when Adam and Eve were expelled from Eden the Devil offered to help them find their way back again. They foolishly agreed and ever since mankind has regarded Paradise as just around the corner, but whether on foot, or on wheels, or even in aeroplanes, man seems to have got no closer: 'And still the ancient Adam presses on, shrunken and smelly and decaying – nothing can allay his thirst' (138). The parable is of course wasted on Vekshin, who can only reiterate his 'Onwards and upwards, onwards and upwards, that's what's needed.' Pchkhov reminds him: 'When the angel of darkness fell at the beginning of time he too flew onwards and upwards... headfirst. No, my friend, there is no up or down there' (138). The collision between these two views of life is absolute. It is human nature to be dissatisfied and aspire, but wisdom lies in recognizing the value of life for itself, not as it might be.

Pchkhov recognizes that man is unlikely to be the final goal of history or evolution, but he accepts this without the despair of Pavel-Anton at the prospect of human inadequacy. At one point Firsov records some of his thoughts:

> ... and perhaps, the world doesn't exist for the sake of people, but for some birds or animals, as yet uncorrupted. (Uncorrupted by what? Thought perhaps?) Then in reply to my question what will happen when mankind has achieved everything that it could dream of (because to achieve your dream is degrading) he said:

'Lucifer and Beelzebub [...] are constantly struggling in the universe, and there has been no third for a long time. When one gets on top, then he immediately splits into two, and the two halves start fighting one another all over again. And so it is always.' 'To the end?' I asked him. 'No,' he replied, 'but until they learn.' (388–9)

The dialectic itself denies the possibility of any final state.[47] The dualism of *Ham's Departure* reappears here, but without the Manichean despair of that story. There the idea of dualism had implied an unbridgeable gulf between polar opposites. In *The Thief* it means rather the poles on an infinite continuum, within which everything is interrelated.

This is a lifelong conviction of Leonov's: 'Everything is interconnected by the force of an inextricable knot. If the leaves did not fly from the trees, then this biting wind could not blow – for what could it do alone in the empty field?' (8). This applies not only in space but also across time: 'We [...] are the direct heirs of the great achievements of the past, and we, in the person of our grandfathers, ploughed its mighty fields' (50).[48] If the ancestors are present in the works of their descendants, how can the descendants not be present in the achievements of the past? And so Vekshin, when invited to sit down by the psychiatrist, is suddenly appalled by the incalculable consequences of the decision that he must make:

I can sit on this one or that one [...] and if you imagine that all this is now past, then I have already sat on one of them [...] So, I must sit on the right one, the only one. I must not make a mistake. (422)[49]

It is man whose consciousness achieves this integration:

Before me the expanses of virgin land, sufficient for man to be born on, suffer his fill, and die. Above me, in the expanses mirrored a thousand times in every direction rage the stars; down below – man: life. And without life how empty and meaningless all this would be! Filling the whole world with yourself and your sufferings you, man, create it anew... (8)

By contrast, at the end of *The Badgers* Leonov had depicted the moon sailing high above the human actors, far removed from their concerns, as though life were merely an excrescence on the rest of Creation. These two views of man's purpose coexist uneasily in Leonov's work until despair finally overtakes him in *The Pyramid*.

In Leonov's work *The Thief* occupies a pivotal position. In some respects it shares with the early stories the sense of a lost Paradise, whether childhood or old Russia or the culture of the past, and a suspicion that none of the vaunted changes and innovations of the Revolution had been able to take their place. Yet at the same time it expresses the feelings held by many Russians at the time that the Revolution had not gone far enough, that the signs of continuity were perhaps merely evidence of stagnation. These conflicting attitudes can be seen in the varying associations given to the image of 'silence.' It is on the one hand an emblem of the ideal, of the forests of Petushikha and the island of Nyun'yug; in *The Thief* it is associated with the childhood idyll of Mitya and Masha; it is the state of serenity attained by Pchkhov. But 'silence' is also the lifeless, inhuman ideal of Chikilev and the Communist Matvey. Leonov was to revert again and again to the two faces of this image.

Certain weaknesses common to most of Leonov's work can be found here, chief among them his awkwardness in depicting female characters. The three women associated with Vekshin – Tanya, Masha, and Zina – represent different Russian literary stereotypes, the 'good,' the 'demonic,' and the simple 'loving' woman, respectively. They may also be regarded as different faces of Russia herself. None of them exists as an independent individual, but rather as an object of the needs of the various male characters.

The main problem, however, lies with the figure of Vekshin. Not only is it difficult to see him as an adequate vehicle for the transmission of culture, but the prospects of his redemption seem to be steadily diminished in the course of the novel. At the beginning he is recognized by the other denizens of the underworld as somehow more than a thief: 'You are only protesting, but it's our food and drink' (102). But by the end the word has lost all these glamorous and exculpatory implications, and he himself comes to recognize the reality behind his pretensions: 'Yes, sister, I am just a thief, who ought to be exterminated. I live from one robbery to the next' (415). His unscrupulous abuse of San'ka's devotion justifies the reproach: 'You mocked me and robbed me: you are a thief' (528), and in the closing pages Dolomanova says to Zinka: 'You see him as a puppy that's been run over, but he's just a thief' (534). The word has quite lost its earlier romantic and national associations; so too references to wolves are invariably negative.[50] In this light the prospects for Vekshin's eventual redemption would appear to be minimal. It seems that Leonov's desire to find a positive conclusion for his novel and his allegorical hero finally overrode the internal logic of Vekshin's character.

The Thief, like almost all Leonov's works, is remarkable for its sustained inventiveness in the areas of incident and imagery. If in his earlier work this imaginative power was primarily ornamental in its effects, it is now applied more to finding metaphors and symbols for the ideas at issue. For *The Thief* marks the beginning of Leonov's turn to making ideas rather than events or characters the foundation of his works. Elements of *skaz* can still be found in, for example, Manyukin's Münchhausen-like tales, and the eccentric speech patterns of such characters as Pugel', Tanya's trainer. But these features become less prominent in Leonov's later work, as the focus shifts to historical and philosophical questions such as the conflict between socialist ideology and Russian humanism.

The complexities of the novel have challenged critics ever since it first appeared. After the first two episodes had been published the left-wing critic Ermilov took the unusual step of welcoming enthusiastically a novel that had appeared from the rival camp of the *poputchiki*. He declared that Leonov was the first Soviet writer to try to show a 'living man' in all his complexity.[51] If Communism was a higher stage of development then human nature would inevitably become more complex and, at least in the early stages, this would lead to sharp inner tensions. The contradictions within Vekshin, even his criminality, could then be understood as expressions of his multifarious and still evolving character.[52] Ermilov was a notoriously ignorant critic, and his reading was based on only the first twenty-three chapters of part 1 of the novel so his views have usually been treated with disrespect.[53] It seems to me, however, that something like this is at the heart of Leonov's conception, and one may detect a similar process at work, but worked out rather more skilfully, in his later novel, *The Road to Ocean* (1933–5).

Apart from Ermilov, only Gor'ky, in a private letter to the author, praised the novel unequivocally,[54] singling out its characterization and its original construction for special admiration. Most Soviet critics were unsympathetic to it. Those on the Left found it symptomatic of the problems it depicted rather than offering any constructive solutions to them. On the liberal wing, two of the most respected critics, D. Gorbov and A. Lezhnev, who had praised Leonov's earlier work, found the book forced and pretentious, both in content and in style.[55] Apparently even Stalin found time to read it; a copy is said to exist with passages marked and even crossed out in his red pencil.[56] In the West the novel has been widely praised, largely because of its misfortunes in the Soviet Union, but no serious analysis of the book has yet appeared.

Yet for all this the novel marks a great advance on *The Badgers*. In its accumulation of a large number of short chapters *The Thief* at first sight resembles it structurally, but Leonov now demonstrates greater compositional skill in leading from one into another. The first signs of this have been noted in the third part of *The Badgers*, but the technique is applied consistently throughout *The Thief*. Groups of short chapters combine to form extended tableaus, culminating in dramatic climaxes; when switching the scene Leonov moves to a related series of events and so creates a sense of continuous development. This can be seen in the fact that though Vekshin is absent for long stretches of the novel his presence is constantly felt and his central position is never in doubt. Moreover Leonov now succeeds in unifying his style so that the narrative does not break down into a series of *skaz*-narrations, as sometimes happens in the earlier novel. The four parts of the novel form a logical progression and, if with certain reservations, an artistic whole.

In retrospect 1927 was the climax of early Soviet literature. Besides *The Thief*, the year also saw the publication of Olesha's *Envy* (*Zavist'*), Pasternak's *Lieutenant Shmidt* (*Leytenant Shmidt*), Fedin's *The Brothers* (*Brat'ya*), Sel'vinsky's *Fur Trade* (*Pushtorg*). This in itself says something about the climate of the period, a time of intense soul-searching on the part of Soviet intellectuals, as though time were fast running out. The attacks on the liberal literary monthlies, and particularly *Krasnaya nov'*, were already increasing in ferocity. In July 1927 Voronsky was dismissed as general editor of the journal; he remained on the editorial board for a few more months, but was finally dropped in December. In 1928 he was expelled from the Party and arrested. After this Leonov virtually ceased submitting his works to *Krasnaya nov'*, and began to publish instead in the other major poputchik organ *Novy mir*.[57]

It may be noted that the July issue of *Krasnaya nov'* (Voronsky's last) also contained the last episode of *The Thief*. In the journal edition the first part contained 125 pages, the second 90, the third 77, and the fourth 49.[58] These figures show that the fourth part was much the shortest, and suggest the possibility that it may have been a casualty of the political intrigues at *Krasnaya nov'* at this time. Vera Alexandrova has indeed stated that the publication of the novel in *Krasnaya nov'* was interfered with, and that Leonov had to change the course of the narrative accordingly.[59] Her interpretation, however, is based on a misreading of Ermilov's article, which was anyway based only on the first two instalments, and I would therefore discount it. It seems more likely to me that Leonov simply did not know how to end the novel, for it is the last two parts, and in particular the very last chapters, that were to be revised most extensively.

In all, some six editions of the novel came out, the last in 1936, the year of Gor'ky's death. After that it was never reissued in Russia, and for many years Soviet critics either passed it over in silence or regarded it as a youthful indiscretion. Thirty years later, however, Leonov returned to the novel, explaining that the original version had been shamelessly botched for the sake of a 'happy ending.'[60] In 1927 Leonov wanted to believe that the dangers latent in the ideology of the Revolution could yet be averted; Firsov may foresee a disastrous end for Vekshin, but, despite all the evidence, Leonov continued to hope. By 1959 he had lost this hope. For this reason a discussion of the revised version belongs to a later stage.

For all this the first version of *The Thief* occupies the central place in Leonov's oeuvre. He himself regarded it as his major work – 'everything comes from *The Thief*'[61] – and the ideas and problems raised in it were to occupy him for the rest of his life.

chapter four

Stories and Plays 1927–1928

Soon after the publication of the last instalment of *The Thief* in July 1927 Leonov and his wife went abroad to visit Gor'ky in Sorrento. The meeting led to a close friendship, which was to be of great importance to Leonov in the next few years. He shared his ideas for future works with the older writer, in particular his plans for the novel that eventually became *The Road to Ocean*, and gained his approval.[1] For his part Gor'ky was as impressed by Leonov as by his books, and he was later to recommend him to Stalin as one 'who has the right to speak on behalf of Russian literature.'[2] These words were to serve as protection for Leonov for many years.

Gor'ky took a keen interest in everything that was happening in Russia, and Leonov had hoped to tell him of some of the things that it would have been risky to put in a letter:

> I visited him in 1927 with the firm intention of speaking to him face to face, heart to heart, about several disturbing goings-on in Russian life. Such a conversation could, of course, have put a serious chill on our friendship, then at its peak. But he welcomed me so warmly, with such unfeigned sincerity [...] that all the time I was in Sorrento I literally couldn't find a minute for such a conversation. The sense of an unfulfilled obligation poisoned all my natural pleasure at entering the wider world for the first time, and in my next letter I did not fail to hint at my regrets.
>
> To be frank, I thought that he would find some way of showing an interest as to the nature of my hint, but in a single sentence, which you will easily find in our correspondence, he seemed to reject this debate, which, when all is said and done, did not commit him to anything, although immediately after his arrival in Moscow in 1928 [...] such a conversation almost got started, but never materialized, through no fault of ours.[3]

Gor'ky's unwillingness to hear negative information about developments in the Soviet Union was to be one of the factors that led to a cooling of their friendship.

The stories and plays that Leonov wrote in the next two years provide an insight into the processes that led to the apparently more conformist works that he was to compose in the next thirty years. As will be seen, this development cannot be explained entirely in terms of political pressures; it also reflects the outcome of some tendencies within Leonov himself. The works of this period explore the theme of *meshchanstvo*, which he had first raised in *The Notes of Kovyakin* and *The End of a Petty Man*, and which becomes prominent in *The Thief*. In this concern Leonov was not alone. If in the first half of the 1920s the characteristic subject of the *poputchiki* had been the 'breakthrough,' the destruction of the old by the new, in the second half they were more concerned with the dangers of stabilization. No longer do they lament the death of old Russia; instead they complain that there has been no revolution in the mentality of the population. Zamyatin in his speech on Fedor Sologub (1924) and Mayakovsky in such works as *About This* (*Pro eto*, 1923), had anticipated these developments; towards the end of the decade, however, this theme became much more prominent in the Soviet press, and it was formally launched in February 1929 by Gor'ky's article 'On *meshchanstvo*' (*O meshchanstve*).[4] In some cases, as Nadezhda Mandel'shtam has pointed out, the word simply became a code name for the campaign against the independent intelligentsia.[5]

Immediately after the publication of Gor'ky's article a questionnaire was circulated among Soviet writers, and Leonov joined the general chorus of denunciation: 'I consider *meshchanstvo* to be the most vicious danger still threatening us. The disease is deep-rooted; there is no easy cure. The patriarchal *meshchanin* is nothing beside his post-revolutionary descendant. His present-day successor has been tempered in the fires of the Revolution and is cunning, ingenious, and spiteful [...] He is enamoured of quietness (*tishina*), protected by the militiaman [...] Deprived himself of any creative spirit, he is terrified of the elemental upsurge of creative energy that has fired the whole country.'[6]

Although these words were written after the works to be discussed in this chapter they reflect their general tone. The type represented by Chikilev in *The Thief* seems to have triumphed over the revolution. The town of Untilovsk (in the play of that name) has 'slept right through this stormy and heroic epoch' (7. 20). So too Voshchansk in *A Provincial Story* (*Provintsial'naya istoriya* 1927)[7] is 'the lowest depths of that life which rages up there' (1. 429). It is 'a miserable place, and its inhabitants are halfwits. Not gardens and groves as they say in the geographies, but an inexplicable desert (*pustynya*)' (1. 393). It is not surprising then that its leading citizen is called Pustynnov. In the same way the name Chervakov in *Untilovsk* recalls the Russian word for a worm, *chervyak*.

The new valuation can be seen most clearly in the way Leonov handles the image of *tishina*. In the earlier stories, for example, *Buryga*, *The Breakthrough at Petushikha*, and *A Note on Birchbark*, its loss is invariably pathetic. But in *The Thief* a different attitude is already apparent. It is now the archetypal *meshchanin*, Chikilev, who defends *tishina*: 'Shouting, I can't stand any shouting in life' (*Vor*, 191), 'all noise in life is forbidden' (251). In the same spirit Chervakov reproaches his antagonist Buslov: 'You're a noisy man. You're always shattering the silence somehow,' and is told: 'That's what life is – a continual shattering of silence' (7. 12). In *The Taming of Badadoshkin* (*Usmirenie Badadoshkina*),[8] silence becomes an image for the concealment of crime: 'But our times are coming. Save your energy and your money. [...] But we must do it quietly, folks, quietly...' (7. 88). In *A Provincial Story* the progressive-minded Yakov comments, 'This silence of yours, it's so sticky. I can't stand it' (*Teatr*, I. 103); while his father's love of nature and contemplation has not stopped him betraying his friend Godlevsky to the Tsarist police.[9] In *White Night*[10] the silence of the town is an image of the White occupation and ultimately of death.

The most direct attack on *meshchanstvo* is to be found in *The Taming of Badadoshkin*, in which the characters are openly referred to as merchants and usurers.[11] The work is a savage farce, owing something to the comedies of Sukhovo-Kobylin and, to a lesser extent, Ostrovsky. The plot revolves round Badadoshkin's scheme for selling off aristocratic titles and estates under a hypothetically restored Tsarist regime. Although he meets with little opposition within the play, the absurdity of the scheme is never in doubt and, as in Leonov's later works, immorality is shown to be self-defeating. At the end of the play Badadoshkin's son Nikitay runs off with the money that has been contributed and takes his father's young wife as well. The final curtain line, Badadoshkin's curse on his son: 'Somewhere they'll strangle you too' (7. 138), recognizes the logical consequence of the cycle of greed and deceit.

In *The Thief* Leonov had revealed some sympathy for his NEP profiteer Zavarikhin; he reveals none at all in *The Taming of Badadoshkin*. The imagery of thieves and wolves that in earlier works had suggested an ambivalence about certain aspects of the Russian character and, by implication, the claims of the Revolution, is now almost always negative. Badadoshkin tries to justify thieving in terms that Vekshin could never have accepted: 'They're selling off happiness on the cheap, and you start worrying whether it's been stolen? [...] Good God, in Russia all our greatest undertakings have begun with a bit of jiggery-pokery. Russia's always been like that: she's gone with the one that grabs her' (7. 91). And the image of wolves reappears from the early stories when Badadoshkin realizes that he has been outwitted: 'What truth is there among wolves? Wolves only have teeth!' (7. 135). The play contains some amusing scenes, but it is one of Leonov's least interesting works. It occupies a place in his development, however, because it is the first work in which he uses 'things' (*veshchi*) as a metaphor for the bourgeois mentality. The stage directions introducing each of the three acts call for settings that emphasize the quantity and size of 'things.' Badadoshkin's dining room is 'piled with an abundance of things, bought for a song on the off chance. The mark of possessiveness lies deep on everything' (7. 84). Frequent references are made to these objects. The porter who has to carry the trunks remarks, 'You might say we were lugging people's misery around' (7. 125). The theme of material possessiveness, often grotesquely exaggerated as it is here, can of course be found in other Soviet works of this period as a means of characterization, but in Leonov's later work the image reappears often in unexpected contexts.

As this play shows, Leonov's boyhood love of the theatre reawakened in these years. But in fact only one of these plays, *The Taming of Badadoshkin*, seems to have been conceived entirely in terms of the stage. The others almost all originate in prose narratives: between 1925 and 1927 Leonov was working on the stage version of *The Badgers*; his first independent play, *Untilovsk*, was based on a novella that he had written in early 1925 before devoting himself to *The Thief*; *A Provincial Story* survives both as a novella and as a play. With one or two exceptions Leonov's thirteen plays are not as important as his novels and novellas, and the prose-narrative form would seem to be both a more congenial and a more suitable medium for his gifts. A comparison of the two versions of *A Provincial Story* will help to explain why this should be so.

The prose version of *Untilovsk*, the earliest of these works, was written in the winter of 1924–5 immediately after *The Badgers*, but was never published on the advice of the painter Ostroukhov, one of Leonov's early mentors. Leonov then decided to rewrite it as a play. The first draft was completed by December 1925 and the first act was published by itself in 1926.[12] However, although the Moscow Arts Theatre and its director, Stanislavsky, had from the first expressed an interest in the work, another five drafts (worked out in collaboration with P. A. Markov and L. M. Leonidov) were required before the theatre would accept the play for production. The play received its première on 17 February 1928, but was taken off after only twenty performances.

A remote town in the far north, Untilovsk has been inhabited mainly by exiled political dissidents, whether under the Tsars or under the Communists. It may be seen as a microcosm of Russia and the dominant image is 'snow,' with its suggestion of insulation against any change. But change, however distant, is inevitable. The name of the town is taken from the English word *until*,[13] with its promise of an eventual end to the waiting. Accordingly the play is set in late winter and ends with the words: 'Never mind, there never was a spring without snowstorms' (7. 80).[14]

The hero, Viktor Buslov, a former priest, had been defrocked and exiled to Untilovsk for saying a Requiem Mass over a student terrorist in 1905. But even though the Tsarist regime has fallen he still feels unable to leave. The desertion of his wife, Raisa, the provincial tedium of the town, and above all the influence of Chervakov, who has led him into alcoholism, have combined to sap his willpower. In his name and his immense physical bulk Buslov is clearly intended to recall the legendary folk hero Vasiliy Buslaev, who repudiates his drunkenness and returns in the nick of time to save his people from their enemies, but this prospect is left to a vague future after the play has ended. Buslov has abandoned his faith, but he has not found anything to replace it. In this respect he embodies Leonov's view of post-revolutionary Russia.

His antagonist Chervakov is a more interesting figure. Like Kovyakin he regards the coming of the new age with fear rather than hostility; but at the same time he is a force for negation who denies any possibility of change for the better:

Everything has passed, everything passes. Everything will pass. And nothing will be left. Every object has its hole, invisible, but waiting there just the same. An object is born, and at the same moment is born a hole, eager to swallow it up (7. 71)

Like Van'ka in *The End of a Petty Man*, he has no faith in the glorious buildings promised:

'But don't run down our region. Our soil is solid enough, and we are firmly rooted in life. And the silence... that green-eyed maiden... we respect it. [...] thousands of crazed Buslovs out there are piling up a tower, only to make it all the more terrifying when it comes crashing down and pelts us with bricks. But we can live in our hovels. We're fed up with these edifices of Babel.' (7. 44)

But Leonov himself has seen the 'hole into nothingness' (in *The Breakthrough at Petushikha*) and expressed his reservations about Kalafat's tower in *The Badgers*. In his works from now on he continues to voice such sentiments, merely attributing them to apparently 'negative' characters. Only in his last novel *The Pyramid* does he explicitly identify himself with them once again.

Battle is joined when Buslov's first wife, Raisa, returns to Untilovsk with her second husband who has been exiled by the Soviet government. The outcome is a Pyrrhic victory for the forces of light. All the male characters, except for Buslov, proceed to fall in love with Raisa, but she disappoints all their expectations and eventually leaves alone. Buslov does not follow her; he does not even leave Untilovsk. The task of redeeming him is left to the unlikely figure of the widow Vaska, the purveyor of home-distilled vodka to the local population. It is she who at the end of the play engineers the departure of Raisa and helps Buslov get rid of his piano, a memory of his supposedly happy years with Raisa, but actually the symbol of his surrender to idleness; she even apparently cures his drinking. Chervakov is driven out into a blizzard.

This optimistic conclusion is prepared in part by Buslov's profession, schoolmastering, in part by his enthusiasm for the achievements of the Komsomol who are occasionally heard singing offstage,[15] but above all by the promise of artistic talent in his pupil Vasyatka. There is thus some justification for his remaining. The issue remains in some doubt, however. Vasyatka and the Komsomol never appear on stage, and it is unclear whether Chervakov's jibe that Buslov has 'joined the Sovkids' (7. 75) has any truth in it. As a result the scenes of provincial stagnation are far more convincing and memorable.[16] The appeal to the cycle of the seasons to bring round a more hospitable and fruitful climate is in any case a flawed one, since the same cycle must inevitably bring back the winter with its snows.

A Provincial Story was originally conceived as a play, but Leonov apparently felt the need to develop his ideas in narrative form also, and for a time he was working on both versions simultaneously. In the event the novella version was finished first (before the end of 1927). The stage version was probably completed some time in 1928, though it was not published until 1935. The survival of two different forms of the work provides an opportunity to look at the differences between them and to relate these in turn to Leonov's own changing outlook.

The plot is concerned with Vasiliy Pustynnov and his two children, the 'prodigal son' Andrey and the 'dutiful son' Yakov.[17] Old Pustynnov is a pillar of local society, who is prone to uttering mawkish sentiments that parody Leonov's (or rather Firsov's) style:

> Does the world become any more beautiful if you add to it the possibility of God? Without Him the world is stronger, men are wiser, and more grandiose that plain on which man rages, pulls down false idols, falls with them only to rise again. Man torments himself; his brain outstrips his physical capacity. This is as it should be; anything that is not the fruit of suffering is unstable. Misery makes people shameless and happiness makes them trite. Only suffering irradiates. (*RP*, 398)[18]

These atheistic pieties lead to the revelation that Pustynnov had worked as an *agent provocateur* for the Tsarist Okhrana, and had actually betrayed his friend

Godlevsky to arrest and execution. When Andrey discovers this secret he is so demoralized that he embezzles state funds and becomes the leader of a gang of 'strekulists,' runaways like himself from Soviet justice. As with Ham[19] and Vekshin, a personal affront leads to disillusionment and thence to antisocial behaviour. Old Pustynnov understands Andrey's reactions – 'He is my reason and my conscience; if you only knew what whores they become once they have been violated' (*RP*, 395) – and he tries to raise the money to replace what Andrey has stolen, as much of course to protect himself as his son.

By comparison Yakov is a simpler character. In the novella he plays a comparatively minor role, but this is considerably expanded in the stage version, though without altering his character in any essentials. He is an architect, currently working on a hydro-electric project 'which he intended to present to his people at least as a blueprint. He passed through life uncompromisingly, and everything came to him easily and painlessly, because no expense of energy deterred him from the final great goal' (1. 395). Yakov's constructive purposes would be seen as unambiguously positive in the work of other Soviet writers, and even seem to be advocated by Leonov himself in the 'turbines' passage of *The Thief*; here, however, the words *easily* and *painlessly* suggest considerable irony. Yakov's insensitivity recalls that of the Communist Matvey in *The Thief*. The only occasion on which he displays any emotion is in the final scene, a rather unconvincing declaration of love for Liza Godlevskaya, and he has no sympathy for his brother's torments: 'If you must suffer, suffer decently, without disturbing the peace' (*Teatr*, I. 145).

Yakov knows nothing about his father's past and he greets him with the following rhapsody:

> Father, I honour in you a young man who can still be inspired by the noblest impulses of mankind. I bow down before your unquenchable fire. You are radiant; may I be the same. I hope that you will never be ashamed of me. (*Teatr*, I. 111)

Indeed he has to be protected as far as possible from knowing the unromantic truth:

> 'Does Yakov know? Don't tell him.' 'No, better not to. Yakov will live, he'll be an engineer. He's intelligent but naive. He thinks that they'll give him palaces and towers to create. No, they'll make him build barns and kennels.' (1. 432)

The Crystal Palaces of the Communist Utopia may turn out, as Dostoevsky had foreseen, to be fit only for domesticated animals, and the shock may effect in Yakov a disillusionment no less nihilistic than Andrey's. If he is to remain a positive, constructive personality his innocence must at all costs be protected from the dangers of Ham's crime of knowing too much.

The major difference between the novella and the play lies in the fact that the former is narrated by a certain Akhamazikov, for whom there is no place in the play (some of his remarks are shared out among the other characters). Akhamazikov is not just a passive chronicler of events, but an active participant in them. The psychological processes, the moral crises, the complicated intrigues of bluff and passion are refracted through the distorting prism of his limited horizons:

> In silence are we born and in silence we die, in truth like those prickly freaks that inhabit real deserts. Only the desire to justify myself in the eyes of the world has impelled me to this narration. My home is as empty as the pockets of that cad who stole my little girl from me; outside it is snowing. I am no longer afraid of anything, not God, not the police, not the wrath of progressive minds, not even the ironic laughter of Vasiliy Prokop'ich, whom only recently I revered to the point of self-neglect, even self-hatred. (1. 393)[20]

The narrator's voice may at first recall Kovyakin's; they are both 'little men,' easily unbalanced by unforeseen events, however trivial. But Akhamazikov is a cut above Kovyakin; he is not a graphomaniac, he is better educated, and his literary style is considerably more sophisticated. He represents the same resistance to change, however, and even after the truth about old Pustynnov has been revealed, he does not want to let it affect their friendship. The story ends with no prospect of change :

> The snow was early this year. Voshchansk was rejuvenated, the wounds all healed; our winter wilderness [*pustynya*] is quite enchanting. Nothing now disturbed our secluded friendship, whose burden I bore uncomplainingly. I never spoke to him about this Voshchanskian comedy, to laugh at which I now invite all progressive minds... (1. 438)

Akhamazikov's role as narrator allows for a certain amount of indeterminacy. With the excision of this figure in the dramatized version issues are naturally simplified and to some extent coarsened. Thus the reason for Sukovkin's decision to settle with the Pustynnovs remains unclear in the story; only from the play do we learn that he was the hangman who executed Godlevsky. The differences can be seen particularly in Leonov's changing evaluations of the brothers. In the stage version the role of Yakov is expanded, and he is given the programmatic last word in the play: 'Life is beginning anew in this house!...' (*Teatr*, I. 147), while Andrey's sufferings are no longer romanticized; rather they are mocked by being likened to those of Razderishin, an unsuccessful black marketeer.

Certain passages in the novella are reinterpreted in the play by being put into a different context or by being given to a different speaker. Thus in the novella old Pustynnov regards Andrey's sufferings as evidence of a higher and richer nature than Yakov's constructive but simplistic energies:

> All the same I'm proud of Yakov, Akhamazikov. I bless you, Yakov!.. And one day people, wise decent people, not like us, will walk over your building and say: 'Hats off – a man laboured here!..' But Andrey, my eldest, – in a thousand years who will say: 'Hats off – a man suffered here!..' [...] Posterity, I despise you! (1. 433)

In the stage version, however, the equivalent of this speech is given to Andrey himself:

> Let me tell you a secret: I am proud of Yakov! In a thousand years people, wise decent people, not like us, will walk over Yakov's building and say: 'Hats off – a man laboured here!..' But I too have sown my strength and tears in this earth, and who will say: 'Hats off – a man suffered here!' [...] Posterity, I despise you! (*Teatr*, I. 130)

Put into the mouth of a third party (even old Pustynnov) this judgment carries some authority; but on the lips of Andrey the suspicion immediately arises that it is prompted by guilt and envy rather than any objective assessment.

This reinterpretation is confirmed by a letter Leonov wrote to Gor'ky in December 1927:

> I am coming more and more (admittedly rather late in the day) to the idea that this is the time for work with a capital W. It's time to work, to make things, pyramids, bridges, anything that can absorb the accumulated energies of mankind. It's time that Russia stopped suffering and moaning and started living, breathing, and doing a decent job of work. And it's no accident that history has pushed on to the stage men who are tough, thick-skinned, men who have finally demolished our age-old stagnation (by which I mean the traditionally turbulent Russian soul) and banged a good solid pile into an as yet unknown, but evidently, to judge by the pile, impressive building. In the story that I have written this hasn't been properly worked out, but I mean to do so in the play.[21]

The 'traditionally turbulent Russian soul' is no longer evidence of a higher nature, but of 'stagnation' and the answer to metaphysical problems is now to be found in the self-fulfilment of physical labour. This idea had already appeared at the end of *The Thief*, in the tentative suggestion that Vekshin might find redemption in lumberjacking (though even there it was bracketed with education). Work now becomes a panacea for all personal and social difficulties. When Raisa tells Buslov: 'You should respect a man even for his torments,' he replies: "In that case we'd have no time for anything. This is the time for hard work [...] Cobbler, cobble your shoes; builder, build your towers; teacher, teach. When the river flows not a single molecule dare stop; otherwise it stagnates.' (7. 38). Or as Vaska puts it to Raisa: 'You silly woman! You should have kept an eye on him! You can't keep Viktor idle. People's energies decay in idleness, they rust like iron. And, what's worse, human energy decays with a nasty smell' (7. 65).

For Vekshin and Firsov suffering had been a means of intensifying life, the only answer to *meshchanstvo*, for 'happiness is always bourgeois' (*Vor*, 395). But with the transformation of the earlier meek and downtrodden individual into a virtual counter-revolutionary, the idea of suffering becomes synonymous with egoism and hypocrisy. Thus the adventurer in *The Taming of Badadoshkin* introduces himself: 'I am no fiend, I am simply the suffering Gramatsky' (7. 115). Firsov's most cherished views are now discredited by being given to old Pustynnov.

The apparent turn against the Dostoevskian values of suffering and meekness in favour of physical labour reflects Leonov's closeness to Gor'ky in these years. Gor'ky serves also as a model in technical matters. *The Taming of Badadoshkin* is influenced by Gor'ky's play *The Petty Bourgeois* (*Meshchane*, 1901); while certain characters from *The Barbarians* (*Varvary*, 1906) reappear in *Untilovsk* ; even the name Redozubov (Gor'ky) is remarkably similar to Redkozubov (Leonov);[22] similarly the game of draughts with which *Untilovsk* opens recalls the game of chess in Gor'ky's play *Cottagers* (*Dachniki*, 1904); the rather laboured symbolic significance is the same in both.

These similarities extend to the plots. In Gor'ky the heroes adopt the only expedient supposedly open to them in pre-revolutionary Russia and leave; Leonov's works, written after the revolution, naturally prefer to end with the expulsion of the villain. In the works discussed here, however, both patterns can be observed. Korotnev (the hero of *The Taming of Badadoshkin*) asserts his liberty and vitality by voluntarily leaving a stagnating society. Raisa leaves Untilovsk in the hope of drawing Buslov with her, but he remains behind to stay and fight; Chervakov, meanwhile, is expelled. In the novella version of *A Provincial Story* Sukovkin is driven out (though Akhamazikov and old Pustynnov remain), while Yakov and Liza leave to find success and victory in another life.

In the play, however, they choose to remain in Voshchansk to continue the fight, while old Pustynnov dies and Andrey is expelled. This oscillation reveals a less than total confidence in the eventual defeat of *meshchanstvo*.

Like Gor'ky's plays, Leonov's early plays lack any central theme, or at least the ability to bring it out. They are shamelessly episodic, a fault that is emphasized by Leonov's tendency to exaggerate irrelevancies until they become almost an end in themselves, as in the scene between Sukovkin and the house painter that opens the stage version of *A Provincial Story*. Some scenes are crudely naturalistic, while others are ponderously symbolic.

The names of many of the characters are often self-explanatory in an almost eighteenth-century vein, for example, Pustynnov, Sukovkin, Chervakov, Razderishin; others such as Badadoshkin, Redkozubov, Radofinikin, Akhamazikov are Gogolianly absurd, and prevent the reader from ever taking the character seriously. Most of the minor figures are characterized by catchphrases or speech defects. Leonov adds humorous descriptions to his list of dramatis personae. Thus Sukovkin is simply described as 'scum' and Nal'ka as 'just like that' (*Teatr*, I. 97). In general Leonov's plays are cruder in their methods and morals than his prose works.

Soviet critics were only too happy to see Leonov's attacks on *meshchanstvo* as evidence of his acceptance of the Party's view of art. But the sense of disgust extends to many other features of the contemporary scene. *Meshchanstvo* is not confined to the anti-Soviet camp. The clearest example of this can be seen in *The Taming of Badadoshkin*, where each act contains a stage direction mocking the banalities of Soviet radio programs, and the final curtain comes down on 'the revolting twanging of balalaykas from the radio' (7. 138). In *Untilovsk* Aleksandr Gugovich, the second husband of Raisa, the 'bespectacled intellectual' as he is called in the dramatis personae, is so insignificant ('But one cannot deny the uses of science. The whole world around us is incomprehensible. We want to understand it, and this is the origin of science,' 7. 40), that a government afraid of his opinions is as absurd as he is. Even the name of the executed revolutionary Godlevsky has strongly negative associations because of its phonetic resemblance to the root 'gad' (reptile) and its many derivatives.

In these works Leonov is far less optimistic than he had been in *The Thief* that some way out could be found. Besides the contempt that he feels for most of his characters he also displays a Tolstoyan revulsion against sexuality, especially in women. Each of these works contains conversations laced with vulgar innuendoes: between Anna Petrovna and her stepson in *The Taming of Badadoshkin*, between Nal'ka and the churchmen in *A Provincial Story*, and in the two Agniyas' constant search for husbands in *Untilovsk*. It appears also that an 'unbridled sex scene' was the cause of Leonov's suppressing the original short story version of *Untilovsk*.[23] This is rather surprising; sexuality was a common theme in Soviet literature of the 1920s, usually as an image of liberation. But the cheerful sensuality of Polovinkin in *The Badgers* never reappears in Leonov's work. His later heroes and heroines are seldom happy in marriage; they may feel affection, respect, or gratitude for their partners, but never passion. This is the more surprising in that Leonov's own marriage was a notably happy one.

Leonov seems to have planned an extended series of *Unusual Stories about Peasants* (*Neobyknovennye rasskazy o muzhikakh*, 1927–1928) but in the event only five were completed: a group of three stories (published in *Zvezda*) that fully justify the title, and two more that do so only tenuously.[24] These stories are all set in post-revolutionary Russia, though authority is exercised by the traditional village community, the *mir*, rather than any Soviet institution, and in their subject matter they could have taken place in a Russian village at almost any time in the preceding two hundred years (apart from such obvious signs of modernity as a radio, which are anyway presented as if they were fantastic). Thus the hero of *The Return of Kopylev* (*Vozvrashchenie Kopyleva*, 1927) tries to protect himself against the wrath of the peasants by appealing to his privileges as a holder of the Tsarist medal of St George.

The first of these stories is called *Dark Water* (*Temnaya voda*, 1927).[25] The title comes from an old Russian expression meaning blindness, but this meaning is not immediately obvious to modern Russians, who will tend to relate it to the folk expression 'living water' (*zhivaya voda*), by which the dead can be brought back to life. The epithet 'dark' introduces instead a sinister note, which in another writer would probably presage a death by drowning. Leonov prepares the introduction of this motif in the second and third paragraphs of the story through a common and similar-sounding expression, *temnaya beda* (a dark or obscure trouble). The peasant woman Mavra has been hideously disfigured by a growth that suddenly appeared on her cheek; her fiancé has left her and people in the village begin to fear her as a witch. As a result she has become embittered and solitary. Then her eyes begin to fail:

...темная нахлынула на Мавру беда.

Мавра не приметила ее прихода; потому и страшился мир Маврина сглаза, что остры и зорки были черные ее очи. Но однажды, когда еще таился снег в овражках, озябла Мавра, и взгрустнулось ей о платке. Она поискала и, увидя на лавке, протянула руку взять, но взъерошился платок и цапнул когтем старухин палец. Она устрашенно отдернула руку, еле признавая во враге своем сердитого соседского кота; она ударила кота скалкой, и кот убежал, но не растаяла в ней уже возникшая тревога: в хваленое ее зрение темная просочилась вода. Ночь она промаялась в испарине животного страха, а утром надела лучшую свою юбку и, подоткнув, чтоб не забрызгать грязью, торжественно, как на богомолье, отправилась в больницу за шесть весенних верст. (1. 347–8)

[... A dark misfortune swept over her.

Mavra didn't notice its approach; it was just because her black eyes were so sharp and piercing that the *mir* was afraid of her spells. But one day when the snow was still lurking in the gullies Mavra began to shiver, and felt the need for a scarf. She looked around and, seeing it on the bench, stretched out her hand, but the scarf suddenly bristled and scratched the old woman's finger with a claw. In a panic she pulled her hand away, hardly recognizing her neighbour's vicious cat. She hit it with a rolling pin and the cat ran away; but her alarm refused to subside; a dark water had begun to seep into her famed eyesight. All night she tossed and turned, sweating in an animal panic, and next morning she put on her best skirt and then, hitching it up so that it wouldn't get spattered with mud, set off on the four-mile walk to the hospital, as solemnly as though she were going to church.]

The process is presented from Mavra's viewpoint. Because of the various superstitions associated with cats the animal seems at first in some obscure way to have brought on her loss of sight. But the reader can see that if the once sharp-eyed Mavra can no longer distinguish a scarf from a cat then no black magic is needed. Stylistically, the passage reveals a new aspect of Leonov. There are now no traces of *skaz*, or nonstandard Russian. The narration is unmistakably, almost self-consciously literary. The verbal texture with its interrelations of sound and meaning comes close to poetry: the expression 'snow was lurking' (*sneg tailsya*) is very similar to the expression that might be expected here: 'the snow was melting' (*tayal*). This root appears a few lines down as *rastayala*, where it is related to her growing alarm and the darkening of her vision. In this way the coming of spring and the black melting snow are both related to the 'dark water' of her incipient blindness.

For Mavra this misfortune holds out also the possibility of regaining a place in the community: 'Her trouble was the only important event in her entire life – her trouble made her equal with other people and the *mir*; her grief was sweet...' (1. 350). But the local nurse can give her nothing to help; instead she advises Mavra to go to the nearest town for an operation. Deeply disappointed, Mavra returns home but then she hears about the fantastic possibilities of glasses. She goes back to the nurse, and, not finding anyone in, steals some money from a drawer: 'it seemed to her that now she had revenged herself on the *mir* for depriving her of her happiness' (1. 351). When she returns a third time intending to steal some more she is caught, for she is now so blind that she cannot see that the room is full of people; Mavra returns home in greater isolation than before.

Thus the motif of 'thieving' reappears in *Dark Water* (and indeed in several of the other stories in the group), but it is now freed of the explicit allegorical significance it had accumulated in the preceding stories and novels. It is presented as the action of an envious and disappointed woman, embittered at her 'loss of happiness,' not as an archetype of the contradictory Russian 'soul.'

Dark Water works powerfully on a straightforward level. It is only gradually that one comes to see its deeper and darker implications. The story of Mavra's rejection is set in early spring, the conventional image of rebirth; the dark water of the melting snow serves as an ironic parallel to her blindness, while her final humiliation takes place on a Sunday, in Russian the day of 'resurrection.' Much as Vekshin's hopes of acquiring culture take the form of cracking safes, Mavra's plan to regain her sight ends with her stealing money. But in place of Vekshin's Promethean ambitions Mavra's aspirations are pathetic and futile. The title of the story now recalls the Russian epithet for the peasantry, *temnyy narod*, the dark or ignorant people. The symbolic pretensions that overburden *The Thief* are here left implicit.

The other stories of the group in their different ways repay close analysis and rereading as generously as *Dark Water*. The eponymous hero of *The Return of Kopylev* had been responsible for cruelly subduing his village during the Civil War. Now, returning to his village in peacetime, he knows he will have to expiate his guilt. But he frustrates the *mir*'s death sentence by pretending to have died in his bed; eventually his ingenuity and endurance in sustaining the fiction win the peasants' admiration and he is reprieved. After being beaten within inches of his life he is pardoned and welcomed back into the society he has injured: 'You came back to us an orphan, and we've made a son of the outcast. And now you're more than a son to us' (1. 364).

A similar situation is developed rather differently in *Ivan's Misadventure*. The *mir* has gathered to punish a horse thief, the local blacksmith; but at the last moment it realizes that there is only one blacksmith and that the village cannot afford to lose him. Justice, however, must still be done; luckily the village boasts four carpenters, and the sentence is therefore executed on one of them, the deaf half wit Ivan: 'He was an orphan, he was a carpenter; he was wretched with no one to grieve for him; he was guilty because the *mir* required his guilt' (1. 371). Ivan submits without protest, but the very fact of his sacrifice is sufficient to reinstate him with the *mir*: 'We'll bury you like our own son' (1. 371).

The original group of three stories is particularly remarkable. They are all based on the conflict between the individual and the community, though this community is not contemporary Soviet society but the traditional village unit, the *mir*, whose customs and practices continue, quite unaffected by the Revolution. Whereas the *narodnik* writers had seized on the fact that the word *mir* can also mean 'world' and so implies that society at large should be based on the same principles, in Leonov the *mir* is a tightly knit closed community which cannot tolerate any difference, whether it takes the form of physical deformity or distinctiveness of character. The alien element must either be expelled or re-assimilated or rather re-affiliated (to retain the mother-son imagery of some of these stories).

The subordination of the individual to the needs of the community is the dominating theme of the other two stories later included in this group, *The Tramp* and *Revenge*, although the peasant angle is not essential to them. In the former the peasant Chadaev is thrown off balance by his wife's infidelity and as a result he fails to pay his taxes in time. To escape the consequences he becomes a tramp, thus putting himself even further outside the law.[26] In the story *Revenge* a young delinquent Nikitka suddenly realizes what power he possesses by being an outcast. 'Nikitka could be reconciled with people only by a catastrophe capable of evoking his pity' (1. 384). His act of revenge on society leads into just such a catastrophe and so prepares the way for his rehabilitation.[27] But in neither of these two stories does the *mir* play any part in prosecuting or punishing its erring children. In each case the hero's quarrel is with the state and with himself, not with the *mir*.

These five stories form a special group within Leonov's *oeuvre*, and point to a direction that his talent might have taken in a different socio-political situation. His interest in them is focused above all on human character. The stories *can* be read as attacks on the poverty, superstition, and injustice prevalent in a backward society, but they make no effort to strain towards such familiar conclusions, and in a different context they could even be seen as Slavophile works extolling the superior wisdom of the peasant way of life. But it is nonetheless tempting to look for wider implications. Just as the recurrent theme of the 'breakthrough' serves to unify the early stories and so suggest Leonov's own inner reservations about the speed and extent of the revolution, so these stories written at the end of the decade seem to express a concern that goes beyond the ostensible theme of the backwardness of the Russian village. Their recurring pattern of the individual being rejected, or accepted only at a exorbitant price, can be interpreted as a reflection of the increasing devaluation of the individual in Soviet society. In the next few years, with the campaigns against Zamyatin and Pil'nyak and the first show trials, these concerns were to prove all too justified. Chikilev's dreams seemed to be coming true. Before long Leonov himself would be feeling their effects.

The *Unusual Stories about Peasants* are among the most sustained and flawless works in Leonov's oeuvre. Uniquely compact among his prose writings, they suffer hardly at all from his besetting tendency to overwrite. Even the shortest of them develops unhurriedly. The recurrent images of his early period, 'thieving' (as in *Dark Water*) and 'silence,' now spring naturally out of the context (e.g., the carpenter Ivan is surrounded by silence because he is deaf) and acquire their own complex meanings from that context rather than from their use in other works of the period. The language and style are instantly recognizable as the work of Leonov, as are several of the mannerisms: the fondness for epithets formed from nouns (e.g., *Mavrin, starukhin*), the gift for creating unusual juxtapositions of words (e.g., *bespokoynyy dar*, 'the restless gift' – for the cock with which Mavra intends to pay the nurse), the inversion of normal word order, are features of all his works. In these stories Leonov achieves his ideal of a closely woven literary texture in which words and phrases acquire additional meanings from their interrelations with other words, and, finally, in the light of the whole. On another level they satisfy the ambition that Leonov had expressed in *The Thief*, that a work of art should convey something of the infinity of factors that gives any historical moment its individual flavour. All Leonov's major works aspire to achieve this, but few manage it with such success and none on so small a scale.

The remaining work of this period, *White Night*, stands somewhat apart. It opens thus:

Огромная розовая лужа стоит на въезде в Няндорск; она спит, потому что утро. В неверном, опрокинутом виде отразились в ней смешное, растрепистое облако и косматая придорожная ветла, – вот так же, розово и зыбко, явь отражается в снах. Белая ночь тает, ржавой позолотой расцвечивает тундру день... все еще длится прохладная тишина, насыщенная тонким комариным звоном. Но вот конь ступает в воду, проваливается в черную жижу колесо, и скрипит ось, мутится ил, и меркнет розовое очарованье лужи. (1. 439)

[A huge pink puddle stands at the entry to Nyandorsk; it sleeps because it is early morning. In distorted topsy-turvy fashion an absurd ragged cloud and a long-haired wayside willow are reflected in it; just so is reality reflected in dreams, pinkly and tenuously. The white night wanes as the new day tints the tundra with a rusty gold... a cool silence filled with the whine of mosquitoes still persists. But now a horse steps into the water, the wheel plunges into the black goo, the axle creaks, the mud rises from the bottom, and the pink magic of the puddle dulls.]

This passage sets the scene: the place name Nyandorsk evokes northern Russia (compare the name Nyandoma, a town about halfway between Vologda and

Archangel).[28] The events are utterly prosaic and even trivial, apparently devoid of any symbolic or allegorical potential. The words of the title, 'white night,' are introduced unobtrusively with as yet no hint as to their significance. One may, however, recognize some images from *The Thief*: the sleepy puddle, with its deceptively pretty reflections coexisting with the filth beneath, which is shattered by the intrusion of the horse, an image often used in the 1920s for the Revolution. The silence that is only deepened by the whining of mosquitoes is clearly not the idyllic silence of Petushikha or Nyun'yug, but as in *A Provincial Story* a presage of stagnation.

White Night is set not in contemporary Russia but in 1919 during the British intervention in the north. The story is an account of the last twenty-four hours in the life of Lieutenant Pal'chikov, commandant of a White garrison surrounded by the Reds. When the story begins, a British colonel has just been assassinated by a student, and Pal'chikov has been ordered to take reprisals on the civilian population. Though disenchanted, however, Pal'chikov is not brutalized and he refuses to carry out these massacres. He stands out among the White officers who are bestial and cynical, and the English interventionists who regard Russia as simply another Africa to be exploited. In consequence he is disliked by his own subordinates and he, for his part, is under no illusions as to their worthlessness.

Pal'chikov is another 'little man' – his name suggests the Russian for Tom Thumb (*mal'chik s pal'chik*) – who finds himself on the wrong side. He claims to be fighting for Russia and her people, but at the same time he sees that the Whites' 'defeat would harm the country less than their victory' (1. 460). In the same way he cannot understand how Egorov, the son of an artisan, can be fighting in the White Army: 'But you will be killed by your own side. What right have you to fight against the Bolsheviks?' (1. 459). He alone understands and accepts the fact that with the defeat of the Whites 'a new era in the life of the country would ensue in which there would be no place for them' (1. 460), and at the end of the story he commits suicide.

Such a sympathetic portrayal of a White officer is exceedingly rare in Soviet literature, and *White Night* contains one of the last examples.[29] But the story occupies an important place in Leonov's work not only for this reason. Pal'chikov may be decent enough as an individual, but, like Andrey in *A Note on Birchbark*, Leonov's only other work to deal with this period in his life, he is guilty and acutely conscious of it, even though 'not understanding' how or why. Leonov's attraction to this type surely springs from his own uncertainties in 1918–20 under the British intervention in Archangel, and it is to play an even greater role in his later work.

The story of Pal'chikov is framed inside an episode in the life of the peasant,

Kruchinkin, who has been supplying milk to the town. When, 'like a large stupid fish swimming into a net' (1. 439), he pays his regular visit to the town doctor he finds that the man is being interrogated by Pal'chikov, since it was his son who had killed the British officer. Kruchinkin too is arrested and put in the death cells as a hostage. At the end of the story, however, he is set free by Pal'chikov's last caprice and returns home to his village.

Kruchinkin himself is an utterly unremarkable character:

> You could see at once that he was a jolly, harmless fellow. True besides his peasant calling, Kruchinkin knew nothing at all [...] In his heart he even laughed at the pointless custom whereby people wasted good material on their mourning; an indifferent spectator of those grim years, he had seen clearly that widows' tears dry up, orphans grow up and learn to knock back their vodka, but you can't bring back a wasted piece of calico. (1. 440)

He is irresponsible in his attitude to politics and no less so in his private life; he has deliberately chosen to leave home on this particular day because his wife's baby is due; the need to buy a new teat provides him with a pretext. This unimpressive figure is explicitly allegorical:

> That same Russia, whose commandant [Pal'chikov] had hoped to be, was sitting in front of him, beseeching him with his beggarly, senseless eyes. (1. 452)

Amid the disintegration of the White Army he seems totally unaffected by the historic events going on around him. He comes from the village of Gory (mountains), a name that differs by only one letter from that of Vory (thieves) in *The Badgers*. This name is no less symbolic: it evokes a more dynamic kind of journey 'onwards and upwards.' The mountains are an image of time as much as they are an image of space, representing the better future that socialism should bring.[30] The associations of discomfort and endurance necessary before the goal can be achieved are an essential element in this image. In *The Thief* Don'ka's song runs: 'Beyond the pass there shines the sun, but the way beyond the pass is terrifying.' So too the snows of Untilovsk are cut off from warmer climes by the mountains. Redkozubov says, 'You're a learned man, Chervakov. Tell me, to get to warmer lands does one have to cross the mountains, the high mountains?' (I. 44–5). One way or another the mountains have to be crossed. In this context the name Gory would appear to suggest that the peasantry constitutes the chief mountain that the Revolution has to cross. The Revolution is no longer seen as an external destructive force invading traditional communities, but rather as a remote ideal to be attained only after much sacrifice and suffering.

Kruchinkin's role as a frame is paralleled within the story by the figure of Anis'ya, the innkeeper and procuress, who possesses 'no less power than Pal'chikov himself' (1. 463). Where Kruchinkin stands for the peasantry she stands for the class of *meshchanstvo*. Like Kruchinkin she is distinguished from the others by her vitality: 'she alone really *was* in this room; the others were merely present' (1. 466). For a brief moment in the fortune-telling scene Pal'chikov's destiny seems to be linked with hers, but the cards separate and Pal'chikov is called away. When he has committed suicide she still remains, as powerful as ever.

White Night continues the sardonic tone with which Leonov regards Russian life in the works of this period. As in *A Provincial Story* and *The Taming of Badadoshkin* this disgust frequently focuses on the subject of sex. Thus Pal'chikov is temporarily stirred out of his apathy:

'... I'm not wearing my corset,' [Katya] added quite unexpectedly.
'How naughty of you,' answered Pal'chikov with loathing. [...] And leaning over (and she at once moved closer to him) he whispered a few words, not so much vulgar as insulting. 'Suit you?' he asked her out loud. [...]
'Naughty, naughty man...' and she covered her face with her tankard, 'but charmingly, charmingly naughty.' (1. 463–4)

This sense of disgust extends often enough to life in general. Again this is true to some extent of other stories and plays that Leonov wrote during this period, but there this revulsion can partly be explained as an expression of dissatisfaction with the prolongation of the NEP period and the apparent consolidation of the *meshchanin*. But *White Night* is set in 1919, before the NEP period had begun, and Leonov's disgust is directed not just at the Whites but at human nature in general. Pal'chikov has to inspect 'the files of suspicious citizens, living and dead, containing the hidden filth of the town, a repellent mixture of fiction and truth, where the latter was worse than any libel' (1. 448). If these citizens are suspect to the Whites they are presumably potential supporters of the Communists, but they are hardly depicted as 'progressive' forces. Like Chikilev they adapt easily to political change: 'any one of them could serve as a model citizen under any regime: they were all men of property on a modest scale; they all went to church, but only because there were no theatres in the town; and they were unanimous in their support of any government so long as it didn't affect their pockets' (1. 470). Even the student who assassinates the British colonel is not actuated by any noble ideals but rather 'out of fear that Katya Gradusova would think him a coward' (1. 471), and, as the scenes in Anis'ya's inn reveal, Katya's opinion is hardly worth having one way or the other. This tone of contempt for human fallibility is naturally reduced in Leonov's later works, but it never quite disappears.

The story ends, however, with an epiphany. Like a 'large stupid fish, swimming out of a net' (1. 480), Kruchinkin returns home, apparently quite unaffected by the momentous events that he has witnessed. He drives through the same puddle,[31] which after a brief disturbance settles back into its torpor. But the birth of the child to which he had been so indifferent affects him quite unexpectedly:

> The house was filled with the crying of the new child and Kruchinkin, hearing it, at once pulled off his cap. Before looking in on his wife, or crossing himself before the ikon, or greeting the neighbour who was busy at the stove, he went on tiptoe to the cradle, suspended on strings by the window, as though to a mighty sovereign of life. [...] The baby's plump cheek attracted his gnarled and grubby finger irresistibly. But at this moment his brow furrowed, and the stubble on his cheek bristled: 'And I forgot to buy you a teat!' he exclaimed in vexation, and it almost seemed as though he considered no one but himself to blame for his unkept promise... (1. 480)

This brief glimpse of a new and less selfish side to Kruchinkin, even more than the traditional symbol of the birth of a baby, suggests that perhaps changes to the puddles and silence of Russia are on the way, and that they will be for the better. Perhaps too Kruchinkin's horse and cart will yet re-enact the magical transformation of Chichikov's *brichka* into a *troyka* at the end of *Dead Souls*. Thus this cycle of stories and plays, which had been almost unrelieved in its sense that stagnation was the natural fate of Russia, revolution or no revolution, ends on a note of tentative optimism.

The works discussed in this chapter form the crucial link between *The Thief* and *The Sot'*. Artistically, *White Night* and the *Unusual Stories about Peasants* remain unsurpassed in Leonov's oeuvre. They mark the transition from the *skaz*-oriented narratives of the 1920s to the deliberately literary style and omniscient narrators of his mature work. They may not aspire to the titanic all-inclusiveness of *The Thief*, but they are more successful because of it. The straining after philosophic significance that had overburdened that novel is now left implicit. Instead of hyperbolic language and passions we find a more compact and restrained style that does not advertise its profundity, but entices readers into discovering it for themselves. Some of the promise contained in these works was undoubtedly dissipated by the political pressures of the following years, but they represent an ideal which Leonov never quite renounced.

It may well be that in other circumstances Leonov's talent might have developed in a different direction from the one that it actually took, but the reorientation in his style and standpoint that took place at the end of the 1920s can also be seen as consistent with his own internal evolution. Like many Soviet intellectuals he was clearly repelled by the greed and inhumanity of the NEP period. It was only natural for him to welcome the inauguration of the First Five-Year Plan in 1928 and to see in it some prospect of change to the historic Russian failings of sloth and backwardness. But, while willing to accept the need for a revolutionary transformation of the moral and physical stagnation of Russia, Leonov had less confidence in the culture that would replace it. This was to become the underlying theme of all his subsequent novels and plays.

In spite of the deep seriousness of these works and the high level of their artistry there is no stage of Leonov's life that has been so little studied.[32] This is partly due to the fact that of these works only *Untilovsk* has received any wide recognition.[33] The other two plays have never been staged and indeed were not even republished between 1935 and 1960. As for the prose works, three of them, *Ivan's Misadventure*, *The Return of Kopylev*, and *A Provincial Story*, were not reissued between 1930 and 1980, and the others only in 1960. The explanation of this neglect in the Soviet Union lies in the rejection of any 'rosy-cheeked' optimism, for which Leonov was angrily criticized at a discussion of his work held on 31 January 1929.[34] But for the most part they were hardly noticed in the literary journals of the day. Lip service was paid to their literary merits, but their implications were ignored. This very neglect might have alerted Western critics to their significance, but they passed unnoticed outside the Soviet Union too.[35]

chapter five

The Sot' and *Locusts* 1930–1931

By the end of 1928 Stalin had succeeded in crushing his rivals to the Left and Right, and he proceeded to impose a series of policies that in many respects effected an even greater revolution in the social, economic, and political life of the country than the events of 1917 had done. The year 1929 was dubbed 'the year of the great breakthrough' and it was to shape the face of the Soviet Union for the next sixty years.

The relatively free market of the NEP period was now replaced by a centralized planning authority that controlled every aspect of the economy. In industry the system of Five-Year Plans laid the foundations for the future industrial and military power of the Soviet Union; in agriculture the peasant smallholders were forced into collective farms. The social and environmental costs of this revolution were, however, immense. A once prosperous agricultural sector was effectively ruined; the destruction of families by headlong industrialization and the mass arrests and executions of recalcitrant peasants created generations of cowed and embittered citizens. The exploitation of natural resources and the gross pollution of the environment took their toll on the health of the population, and led eventually to the economic crises of the 1980s and 1990s. These dangers were already apparent to thoughtful observers in 1928, though at the time they could say so only with extreme caution.

The literary world was not exempt from these changes, and the *poputchiki* now found themselves under attack not just for their aesthetic beliefs, but for alleged disloyalty and even treachery. Soon after being dismissed from the editorial board of *Krasnaya nov'* Voronsky was arrested on a charge of Trotskyism (he was later exiled), and at the end of the year three of the most prominent *poputchiki* were publicly criticized. Zamyatin, the secretary of the Leningrad branch of the Union of Writers was denounced for his novel *We*, which had been published in Prague in 1927; Pil'nyak, the secretary of the Moscow branch, came under attack for having sent the manuscript of his story *Mahogany* (*Krasnoe derevo*, 1929) abroad for publication before it had appeared in the Soviet Union;[1] Erenburg, whose sensational novel of life in Russia during the NEP, *The Grabber*, had been issued in two versions, one of them bowdlerized for consumption within the Soviet Union, was at first included in this group, but as he was in Paris at the time, he was safe, and the attacks on him were soon dropped.[2] The persecution of Pil'nyak and Zamyatin, however, continued. In the face of these pressures Pil'nyak capitulated with abject apologies,[3] but Zamyatin fought back energetically with a letter to the press (which was published),[4] and finally with a letter to Stalin himself.[5] Pil'nyak later perished in the Purges, but Zamyatin was allowed to leave Russia and settle in France, where he died in 1937.

The aim of these moves was to discredit the *poputchiki* and facilitate the centralization of the country's diverse literary groups under the control of the Party (parallel developments took place in the academic world and the other arts too). A proposal for just such an amalgamation had in fact been mooted earlier in the 1920s, but then it had been rejected by the more committed writers' groups for fear of ideological contamination. In the later 1920s, however, these began to form their own umbrella organization, the Russian Association of Proletarian Writers (RAPP). An energetic recruitment drive enabled them to increase their membership dramatically until they had become far and away the largest writers' organization, and by 1928 they were ready to advocate a merger.

In the summer of 1929 the leadership of the old Writers' Union – the association of the *poputchiki* – was disbanded, and a new organization, a temporary Union of *Soviet* Writers, instituted in its place. Leonov, as a writer comparatively untainted by his *poputchik* past, was selected as the president of the union. In the event his appointment proved to be only a token concession and he had little effective power. RAPP dominated the new union by sheer weight of numbers, and so was able to control its committees and dictate its policies. Some of the former groups tried to continue their independent existence within the larger body for a time, but relentless pressures from above led to their weakening and before long to their disappearance. At the time it seemed that the RAPP group had pulled off a coup within the literary world, and this enabled the Party to intervene in 1932 and pose as the liberator of literature from RAPP's 'sectarian' policies. But in fact, RAPP had done the Party's dirty work for it, and the Party's own policies proved not to differ in any significant way from those it claimed to be repudiating.

Despite the word 'proletarian' in their title, RAPP's program was in fact modelled on that of the 'Oktyabr'' group. According to Marxist theory the arts were a vehicle of propaganda for the ruling class. If in the nineteenth century the prevailing bourgeois ethos had dominated, then in the first stage of the socialist revolution there was nothing culpable about privileging the proletariat; indeed frank recognition of the fact was preferable to the hypocritical claims of independence and objectivity made by bourgeois apologists. The Soviet artist should then devote himself to the life and work of the proletariat and peasantry; if he knew nothing about them, then he ought to find out. As a result many writers, Leonov among them, were taken on visits to farms and factories. It should be recognized, though, that most were happy to participate in these excursions, at least in the early years of the First Five-Year Plan. They had been sickened by the forms taken by the NEP, and they felt a certain patriotic pride at the prospect of Russia becoming a major power and the role that they were called upon to play in the process. There was a desire too to impress foreign countries with the picture of a new Russia, committed to the creation of a society and culture on socialist lines. In this respect Soviet writers achieved considerable success, as foreign readers proved to be rather more sympathetic (or gullible) than those at home.

The definition of proletarian literature was not, however, to be left to the writers or even to the proletariat; this was appropriated by their self-appointed spokesman, the Communist Party, which proceeded to act on its 'mandate' ruthlessly. Engels had regarded 'realism' as the highest form of art, and with this doctrinal justification Soviet artists were expected to apply realistic methods. But 'reality' was not to be identified with an as yet imperfect present, but rather with an idealized future which should materialize soon enough to render any mention of current shortcomings quite irrelevant. From the very start, then, there was considerable pressure on the Soviet artist to produce a 'varnished' account of contemporary reality.

The artist was as much a servant of the state as any employee of a nationalized enterprise, and his job was to act as spokesman and apologist for his employers. Analogously, the critic received a supervisory role over the less than reliable artists:

> To work in a new way, to lead in a new way – this applies also to Marxist-Leninist criticism, an indispensable part of our literary development. [...] Sometimes people complain of the harsh and severe tone of our criticism, but this is not where its faults lie. Our criticism must be imbued with the spirit of the class struggle of the proletariat; only such criticism will be truly accurate, and an accurate class criticism cannot but be severe and harsh when the circumstances require it. [...] The strict evaluation of mistakes is one of Marxist criticism's means of helping the writer, who wishes to join the ranks of the allies of the proletariat, so that later,

provided he continues down this path, he can build the great art of socialism in the ranks of proletarian writers.[6]

This new status gave Soviet critics unprecedented powers, and many of them were no better than police informers. In such circumstances any open expression of dissent from official policy invited arrest and imprisonment, and, within a few years, could lead to death. Even the most cautious deviations from the line, however, seldom got through to the readers, who were as alarmed to find such ideas in print as most authors were frightened of expressing them.

In literary history the years of the First Five-Year Plan, 1928–32, are known as the RAPP period; after the variety of the 1920s the literature it produced is for the most part dishearteningly homogeneous. It is Party members who now occupy the leading roles in the works of all writers, even the former *poputchiki*. They serve as 'role-models,' they provide the initiative and pronounce judgment, and are themselves usually exempt from any but the most veiled criticism. This new hierarchy naturally involved the depreciation of the intelligentsia, who were suspected of giving only half-hearted support. It is therefore noteworthy that it is just at this period that Leonov turned to the sympathetic portrayal of intellectuals, and his later work returns again and again to their special situation in Soviet Russia.

A feature of the literature of the RAPP period was the re-canonization of the novel. In the 1920s the short story, the drama, the poem, had all been accepted as equally valid genres; the novel had been only one among many, and had actually been attacked by some Communists as the archetypal bourgeois form. But the novel can also be seen as the most universal form of literature in its accessibility and its ability to blur the distinctions between the descriptive and the normative, the prescriptive and the didactic. These qualities were well suited to the needs of Soviet propaganda, and from 1928 until the death of Stalin the novel was to become the dominant literary genre.

The Soviet novel in these years is remarkable for its adherence to the convention of the omniscient narrator. The 1920s had witnessed a wide variety of narrative styles with a predominance of first-person narrators and the use of *skaz*. Such narratives imply that the narrator carries no special authority, but is limited in his knowledge and understanding, is open to doubts and insecurities, is, in a word, not so different from the reader. The third-person omniscient narrator, on the other hand, speaks with the authority of one who not only knows the entire story, but even the unspoken thoughts and motivations of the characters. Here too Soviet theorists might claim to be returning to the traditions of the classical Russian novel, but where the omniscience of a Tolstoyan narrator was polemical, in refuting the pretensions to authority of unreflecting or interested parties, Soviet novelists were required to parrot the attitudes and judgments of their political leaders. The omniscient narrator dominates Soviet literature for the rest of the Stalin period. Leonov, whose early works had explored several varieties of *skaz*, had moved away from it in *Unusual Stories about Peasants* and *White Night*; he never returned to it except for episodic characters and for local colour. But he continued to investigate the possibilities of distinguishing between the narrator and the author within the third-person narrative, and there are several examples of this in *The Sot'*.

On his first appearance as chairman of the new Union of Soviet Writers Leonov introduced the organization with the words: '... the stumbling block that tripped up the leadership of the old Writers' Union was its notoriously apolitical and extremely vague ideological standpoint [...] The new leadership must first of all correct the mistakes of the old [...] for in our age any trifle, however insignificant, contains the germs of a large-scale political problem.'[7] Such sentiments were to become common enough before long in the Soviet Union, but, coming so soon after the works discussed above they are still surprising. It is true that in the 1920s Leonov was generally regarded as somewhat to the Left of his fellow-*poputchiki*,[8] but he was never remotely connected with RAPP, and indeed his harshest critics had belonged to that camp.[9] His response to Gor'ky's article 'On *meshchanstvo*' in 1929 had indicated some change in his stance, but even so, his espousal of explicitly ideological and political criteria in this speech smacks of compromise. The question is – how far was Leonov compromised?

In the context of the times Leonov's choices would have looked rather different from the way in which we see them today. Most writers believed that the suspension of artistic freedom was only temporary, and had no idea that these years were the first step in bringing literature under the total control of the Party. The difficulties encountered in the industrialization and collectivization campaigns and the risks of antagonizing large sections of the population may have persuaded Leonov and his colleagues that it was the duty of the Russian intellectual to support the progressive, even if ruthless, policies of the government, and they were of course ever mindful of the attacks on Voronsky, Zamyatin, and Pil'nyak.

In the later 1950s and early 1960s many writers were to claim that they had expressed covert dissent in their works of the Stalin period. Often these claims seem to be merely opportunistic self-exculpation in the more liberal climate of the post-Stalin 'Thaw.' But the issue is a serious one. How does one distinguish between works that take a stand, however unobtrusively, on certain values, and those that merely flirt with them? It is not enough to be merely ambiguous, to write words that can be interpreted one way today and another way tomorrow, according to the political weather. The Russian phrase *shish v karmane*, 'Cocking a snook in one's pocket,' wittily epitomizes such behaviour; it may be intended as a gesture, however circumspect, of defiance, but it is liable to be interpreted by the sceptical observer as mere self-gratification.

Those who evaluate a Soviet writer by the degree of his opposition to Communism will then often be disappointed in Leonov. He seldom comes out with a direct expression of opposition to the official line. He prefers to operate by quietly questioning the stereotyped Soviet versions of events, by suggesting alternative interpretations, and by challenging the reader to think for himself. In 1946 he said to Chukovsky about Leonid Grossman, whose play was under attack: 'Grossman is very inexperienced; he should have put his most cherished ideas in the mouth of some idiot, an obvious fool. If anybody had found fault he could say, "But that's only an idiot talking." '[10] This may be read as an account of Leonov's own practice. It may seem only a form of equivocation or 'mental reservation,' though in such times even St Augustine and Kant might have sympathized with his dilemma.

The official materialist and optimistic content of Soviet literature was for most of Leonov's writing career at odds with the sceptical and even tragic inclination of his own temperament, and many of his beliefs, as we now know from his last novel, *The Pyramid*, were in fact incompatible with Soviet Marxism, and could not be expressed directly or openly. But this is not necessarily a crippling restriction: history is full of instances where seeming limitations have in practice served to liberate an artist's imagination. Leonov, at least in his better works, can be seen as one of those for whom taboos and dangers have served as creative stimuli, both psychologically and artistically. By the same perverse logic, when those pressures were removed he no longer found it possible to respond as creatively as he had done in the past.

Today, with the general awareness of the existence and survival of such resolutely uncompromising writers as Anna Akhmatova, Nadezhda Mandel'shtam, and later Aleksandr Solzhenitsyn, Leonov's concessions to the realities of contemporary Soviet politics may seem rather shabby, and many readers came to regard him as little better than any other Soviet hack; others, mostly in the West, have argued that he remained true to his earlier ideals, though concealing and encoding them. The trouble with this argument is that it tends to identify political dissent as the chief aesthetic criterion for a Soviet writer, which is as absurd as its opposite. If one does not find Leonov interesting in his own right, then it really does not matter if any meanings are encoded or not.

By 1928 Leonov was no longer an up-and-coming writer, but already standing at the top of the tree. In the following year a four-volume edition of his works was issued (later supplemented by a fifth volume devoted to *The Sot'*).[11] A questionnaire circulated at the time reveals that he was the most widely read and appreciated contemporary author in the theatre world.[12] There is no reason to think that interest in his work was confined to this section of the artistic intelligentsia. His selection as chairman of the temporary Union of Soviet Writers in September 1929 may be seen as some recognition of this status.

At the same time this success involved a slight paradox, particularly in a self-consciously 'socialist' society. His reputation had been achieved on the basis of his depictions of the outcasts and underdogs of society. This incongruity was caricatured even at the time in a cartoon showing the now prosperous author surrounded by the disreputable heroes out of whose misfortunes he had enriched himself.[13] But with his administrative position in the Union of Soviet Writers this contradiction in his work virtually disappears. His new heroes are not underdogs but pillars of Soviet society; they are as emphatically 'in' as their predecessors had been 'out.' Leonov's romantic leanings still incline him to choose outstanding figures, but instead of a rebel or a criminal he now picks a scientist with a worldwide reputation or a prominent commissar. In the earlier novels Moscow had been represented by such marginal areas as Zaryad'e or Blagusha; from now onwards it appears as the capital of a major power and the seat of government. He renounces altogether the rebellious spirit of his early works; in one case, *Locusts (Sarancha,* 1930), it is shown to be a dead end, and in another, *Skutarevsky* (1932), to lead straight to sabotage and suicide.

In many respects *The Sot'*[14] is a typical Soviet novel of the First Five-Year Plan. It is concerned with the building of a paper mill on the banks of the Sot' (a fictional river in northern Russia)[15] and the obstacles encountered and eventually overcome there. Much of the material is based on personal experience, for Leonov had been taken to the paper mills of Syas'stroy and Balakhna in 1928, and some of the technical processes and industrial mishaps he witnessed there have found their way into the novel.[16] Apart from the commercial and industrial benefits the building of the mill becomes a metaphor for the construction of the new society, the establishment of a 'proletarian island in the great peasant ocean' (4. 52).[17] Finally, at the end of the novel it is the social reconstruction as well as the actual construction that is celebrated: 'the face of the Sot' was changing and the people too were changing.'[18]

Even the paper that the mill is intended to produce seems to be unimportant beside its social consequences: 'The idea that in producing paper the Sot' was contributing to culture was the weakest weapon in the debate; it was Potemkin's well-tried arguments about the proletarianization of the Sot' that finally carried the day' (4. 257). This belittlement of the actual uses of the paper, the deprecation of any suggestion that it might actually be used for cultural purposes indicates Leonov's continuing preoccupation with the fate of Russian culture under socialism. But it may be noted that the authorial voice does not necessarily sanction these views. It is the initiator of the project, Potemkin, who makes this point, and for him too it may be only a tactical concession.

The plot is simple enough. The novel opens in the spring of 1928 with the arrival of a group of engineers, headed by the Communist Ivan Uvad'ev, and their selection of a suitable site for the new mill. In spite of natural disasters and the opposition of *kulaks* and monks[19] the work is carried through satisfactorily, and when the novel ends a year later the factory is well on the way to completion. The saboteurs and ill-wishers have been routed; but it must be admitted that they never constituted a very serious threat: a shot is fired at Uvad'ev and a railway truck is derailed, but there is little else.

This minimizing of the element of conflict is a consequence of the RAPP view of art. The writer's task was to support government policy: where workers were struggling against almost insuperable difficulties it was necessary to persuade them that similar difficulties had been met and successfully overcome elsewhere; where *kulaks* were offering resistance it was obligatory to reaffirm that the Communists' victory was inevitable and all opposition doomed. The object of these works was above all propagandistic, and any suggestion of the possibility of failure could strike the censors as 'pessimistic.' 'Pessimism' was only a short step away from 'defeatism,' 'defeatism' from 'subversion,' and 'subversion' from outright 'treachery.' Faced with such a dangerously slippery slope, writers preferred to reduce the elements of conflict in their work, and most setbacks were assigned to the agency of nature, fires, floods, quicksands, inclement weather, or whatever. This tactic enabled the author to show the heroism of Soviet workers, while offering an easy way of resolving the crisis – what the elements had begun the elements could stop.

The novels of the First Five-Year Plan tend to subordinate the characters to the technical and political aspects of the project. The psychological complexity of the heroes of the 1920s gives place to a simpler and even cruder conception, which at times amounts to no more than an identification of political loyalties. Ivan Uvad'ev, the Communist who is in charge of the project, lives only for his work: 'he saw everything but the project in a grossly oversimplified light; even love was only a fuel which would treble his strength for tomorrow's journey' (4. 85). In his obstinacy and self-confidence he has something in common with Yakov Pustynnov in *A Provincial Story*. Yakov 'is right even when he's wrong, he's always right';[20] so too Uvad'ev declares: 'The truth – that's whatever I believe at a given moment' (4. 165). Leonov emphasizes Uvad'ev's toughness and militancy: he is 'a cart-horse of the Revolution' (4. 63), 'a human block fit to carry the foundations of a mighty house' (4. 65). In an echo of Chikilev he rejects beauty and the soul as immaterial by the side of food and work:

> Beauty – that's a strange sort of word [...] The soul – that's another one. I know what cotton is and bread and paper and soap. I've made them or eaten them or touched them [...] But I don't know what the soul is. What's it made of? Where can you buy it? (4. 42)

He calls himself 'a soldier: my job is to fight' (4. 175), and military imagery accompanies him throughout the novel:

> From the moment that Uvad'ev first stepped on to the shores of the Sot' a challenge was hurled at the river, and at the same time a challenge to the whole traditional way of life, in whose channel it had flowed. The very earth beneath his feet seemed to be hostile. (4. 44)

(It may be noted that Leonov here distinguishes between Uvad'ev, who is frankly hostile, and the river, which only 'seems' to be hostile.) When Burago invites him to listen to some Grieg he misunderstands this as the German word *krieg* . Leonov does not conceal the narrowness of Uvad'ev's life. Zheglov, the minister responsible for the paper mill, says to him: 'You are a machine [...], a machine fitted for independent existence. You consider nature herself to be contemptible [...] , but you are not living, you are only exercising your functions' (4. 248).

Despite this Leonov presents him with some sympathy:

> This beginning all over again, this question of the birth of the new man, for whom the world has only just been discovered, a man who has to find new names for everything, all this marks out *The Sot'* from my previous works [...] We carry on our shoulders the weight of centuries. We know the history of Syria, Babylon, and Egypt, the histories of vanished cultures and civilizations – we know too much. We can never quite liberate ourselves from it and this oppresses us. And so it is with affection that I write of a man like Uvad'ev, who knows nothing and accepts the world in a new way, in its materialistic essence.[21]

As the first representative of a new race Uvad'ev is naturally a lonely man. He is unable to get on with his men, but at the same time he desperately needs to be accepted by them: '... for a moment he longed to go in and sit on one of their bunks [...] to listen to the innermost thoughts of these workers from the fields and to drown his loneliness, even if only for half an hour' (4. 147). For their part the workers regard him with distrust and hostility. An inability to deal with the workers is in Soviet literature usually associated only with bourgeois engineers, but in Leonov's novels it adds to the note of dissatisfaction that so many of his heroes feel with themselves and their achievement.

Uvad'ev's marriage has been unfulfilling. In the literature of this period Communists are considered to be devoted to their public mission, and to have no time for such distractions as a private life. So Uvad'ev could never tell his wife about his revolutionary activities, and they have no children; one pregnancy ended in a miscarriage, the other in a stillbirth. He is ineffectually attracted to Suzanna, who eventually elects to marry a younger man, though no particularly deep feelings are suggested on either side. He makes an attempt to pick up a typist, but throws her out once she has taken her clothes off. In one strange aside we are told that he feels comfortable only with women from the now dispossessed classes.

This clumsiness in personal matters is characteristic of many Communist heroes in the literature of the period. Anything that smacks of human weakness sharpens Uvad'ev's suspicions. He resents

> Spring [...] that mush of feelings and emotions [...] in fact he had no love for anything that crumbled under the rough plane of his intellect, and if any springtime idyll had lodged in his memory, then he was ashamed of this murky page in his biography. (4. 8)

His contempt for the emotions does not save him from falling in love with Suzanna. These weaknesses are symbolized by his inability to give up smoking. Only in the closing pages does he finally overcome the temptation: he catches a sentry smoking on duty but unexpectedly restrains his anger at this breach of discipline:

> he inhaled the tickling smoke, visualized the smoking barrel of the cigarette aimed straight at him and threatening to make him forget everything. 'You're only poisoning yourself – chuck it! I gave up smoking long ago.' (4. 283)

This life of self-denial creates an aura of self-sacrifice and asceticism that has already been prefigured in the figure of Pavel-Anton in *The Badgers*. None of Leonov's Communist heroes has any children. In his work they have to content themselves with imaginary descendants, a silent comment on the ephemerality of the revolutionary project. Thus Uvad'ev's progeny is symbolized in the figure of an as yet unborn ten-year-old girl, Katya. He proudly sees himself as a 'machine manufacturing happiness, this awesome human happiness'[22] for her (4. 248–9), and so when a child is killed by a snapping wire during the flood he sees her death as an omen. Only when he discovers that the girl's name is Polya, 'her sister' (4. 175), can he relax. The comforting thought that his dream-child has been spared, while a real child has been killed, recalls Vekshin's preference for humanity in the abstract and his disregard for individual humans.

By comparison with other Soviet novels the technical intelligentsia are treated with some sympathy. Even the engineer Renne, 'a benighted intellectual, for whom the light went out when the Revolution began' (4. 69), is presented as not wholly negative. He works conscientiously on the project, despite the general hostility to him, but a technical miscalculation, for which he is not to blame, is interpreted as wilful sabotage on his part. He is mobbed by the workers and finally commits suicide. His daughter Suzanna is unmoved by his fate. This is normal in Soviet novels of the time – the younger generation is too occupied with the future to worry about the past – but it is difficult not to feel some pity for Renne.

The other older engineer, Burago, is one of the most attractive characters in the novel. By contrast with Uvad'ev he has firm roots in the past: he plays chess, appreciates music, and has many friends in the West. He is completely apolitical, but he works conscientiously, and is lucky enough to avoid the misfortune that befalls Renne. Though his training sometimes makes him sceptical of the grandiose ambitions of his Soviet masters, he is always ready to be convinced and to applaud their achievements. But although he can approve he cannot really accept the Party's leadership in technical matters: 'My job's building factories [...] and it doesn't worry me what you choose to call it. I'm yours to the end, but don't ask me to do more than I can' (4. 258). This type is to be explored further in Leonov's next novel, *Skutarevsky*.

The most intriguing figure in the novel is Vissarion Bulanin, the leader of the opposition, the first of the intellectual villains who are to play an increasingly important role in Leonov's work. We are told little of his past, except that he had fought in the White Army during the Civil War. Since then he has been hiding out in the local monastery, from where he lends his support to the kulaks and other disaffected elements in the community. The actual nature of these activities is not specified, though it is assumed by everyone and, presumably, by the Soviet reader, that they are 'anti-Soviet' and aimed at the destruction of the entire project. It is significant, however, that this side of Vissarion does not particularly interest Leonov, and there are only a few dark hints and token accusations to follow up this particular plot line.

Vissarion believes that all modern civilizations, capitalist and socialist alike, are in decline. This is because man has developed his intellect at the expense of the other elements of his nature. For the sake of the mind he has lost his 'soul';

he has come to rely on culture instead of nature, on memory and learning instead of instinct. Vissarion quotes Matvey's words in *The Thief*, 'Love is only the mutual attraction of cells,' as proof of this degeneration (4. 183): 'Man has poisoned himself with the lymph of his own learning; and so the soul is being driven out of the world with whips and scourges. The monster that gave birth to the Bible, the Koran, and the Iliad has become a worn-out nag' (4. 183).

The problem is how to rejuvenate the soul. Vissarion's solution is to go back to the beginning, 'Back to the thesis!' (4. 183), and start again. Accordingly he dreams of a new Attila, who will destroy a decadent and oppressive culture and prepare the way for a new and richer humanity. The Revolution had seemed at first to be doing just this, but it had stopped halfway and would now end in a restoration of the old idols:

> In the years of war and beggary this child was coming to birth in Russia, the perception of the truth was imminent. All the Livies, Thackerays, and Miltons of all countries were cheerfully rolled into cigarettes, and if any Rubenses fell into the maelstrom they were prized only for the calories contained in their antiquated canvasses. Men, clothed in wrath, raised their hands against museums and the Midas-like riches within them, those portraits of the world's foremost scoundrels, hypocritical saints, half-crazed conquerors, madonnas, card sharpers, tricksters, and idiots. These men valued their freedom above Pythagoras's theorem or the Cathedral of *Notre Dame*. They said: 'Let the dead rot in the ground and not tyrannize the living through their geniuses.' Man took his revenge on the beauty that he had created and which had made him a slave [...] – yes, the same old story, gunpowder followed by satiety. But [Attila] will return and bring back the soul that we have lost and teach us to appreciate the taste of bread, to love the tart smell of the campfire. (4. 188–9)

Vissarion's assault on the burden of culture weighing on the modern psyche recalls Gershenzon's complaints in *Correspondence from Two Corners*. Where Gershenzon had mused:

> What happiness it would be to dive into Lethe and wash away the memory of all religious and philosophical systems, of all knowledge, art, and poetry, and emerge on the shore again, naked like the first man, unencumbered and happy, and to stretch out one's bare arms freely to the skies, remembering only one thing from the past – how oppressive and stuffy it had been in those old garments, and how delightful it was without them.[23]

Vissarion declares:

> We must cauterize this poisoned legacy, because the dead... all these Homers and Shakespeares govern us more powerfully than any tyrants. We must destroy this elephantiasis of the brain, these noble cells, where the microbes of degeneracy have made their nests. [...] Humanity has no alternative but to forget its past and start again. (4. 186)

and he dreams that

> a new memory-free generation will be born. Only in songs sung round their gigantic campfires will they remember the stupid fish who was lucky enough once to leap out of the enchanted nets.[24] So be it: a song is like a tombstone: it helps one to forget... The boundaries between regions will dissolve. The whole planet will become man's home, the words love and sun will regain their primal meanings. (4. 188–9)

The role of Vissarion is the most problematic feature of the entire novel. At the time the name Attila would have reminded contemporaries inescapably of Zamyatin's play of the same name, which was being prepared for production in Leningrad, but had been suddenly withdrawn at the end of 1928;[25] attacks on the author continued throughout 1929. Vissarion's views can be read as a distorted version of those expressed in Zamyatin's play, and might then be taken as a sign of Leonov's desire to ingratiate himself with the RAPP leadership. He may have felt himself peculiarly vulnerable at this time, because his own early work had owed much to the example of Zamyatin, both in technique and content (as was frequently remarked in literary criticism of the time), and had been singled out by him for special praise.

By the autumn of 1929 *The Sot'* was far advanced (it was completed in November) and it is therefore inconceivable that Leonov's references to Attila could have been merely coincidental; the campaign against Zamyatin could not have passed unnoticed by anyone connected with the literary world, and Leonov was in fact present at a meeting at which his work was discussed.[26] It appears moreover that the Attila theme was a late addition to Leonov's original scheme. Vissarion's long tirade is contained in a single chapter which is not closely related to the rest of the book; there are just two other allusions to Attila in the rest of the text, in both of which he is associated with anti-Soviet movements,[27] and these could easily have been inserted at a later stage.

It may be noted too that Vissarion's views, and in particular, the slogan of the 'naked man' are directly related to those of Savva, the anarchist hero of Leonid Andreev's play of the same name (1906).[28] But Vissarion has never been an anarchist, he was an officer in the White Army. The only ex-anarchist in the novel is Suzanna, now a model Communist engineer, who takes the lead in denouncing him.[29] There is thus a certain incoherence in the development of this figure, which only adds to the impression of opportunism on Leonov's part, all the more distasteful in view of his debt to the older writer.

But Vissarion's tirade can be read in a different way. His denunciation of culture, the 'joyless wisdom of the world' (4, 133), is a mirror image of the rejection advocated by many Communists at the time. His views are only a more demagogic expression of the crude materialism of Uvad'ev. Just as Vissarion dreams of 'a new memory-free generation that will inherit the earth,' so Suzanna declares: 'the generation to which life belongs has broken its links with the past. It has grown up in a storm and will not be distracted by the fripperies of the past' (4. 187). Leonov remarks of Uvad'ev: 'every kind of forgetfulness came to him with enviable ease' (4. 89).[30]

At times Vissarion sounds like the Underground Man: 'Right in front of the gates of the promised city, full of the most magnificent social architecture, he was planning the last revolt' (4. 223). His views might seem to be not so much an expression of any particular social or political philosophy as part of the general twentieth-century revolt against the culture of the past, but they have a more specific target too:

> On this cooling planet man too is cooling down [...] everything is turning into crystal, everything is approaching its final equilibrium: no, not Clausius yet, just democracy and a new unheard-of man. [...] The world is in an unprecedented state of decline, based on hatred and vengeance, its laws are for swindlers, its technology for weaklings, its art for madmen... Civilization is the process, decadence its fruit... (4.182)

In this passage Vissarion bases his arguments on the Second Law of thermodynamics, first propounded by Clausius in 1865. According to this law it is the passage of heat from a warmer to a cooler body that creates energy, and so it follows that differences of temperature will diminish with time and eventually disappear, resulting in the loss of energy and 'heat death' of the universe. Berdyaev and others had transposed these ideas into social terms to argue that socialism's goal of abolishing inequality, the source of human energy, would lead only to the stagnation of the race; for if there are no differences then there cannot be any development: 'The world will perish from the inexorable and ineluctable drive towards physical equality. And isn't the drive to equality in the social world just the same entropy, the same destruction of the social cosmos and culture in the equitable distribution of heat energy, no longer transferable into cultural energy?'³¹ Here Vissarion joins Berdyaev and Leonov in rejecting the egalitarianism of Chikilev and Bukharin.³²

The occasional depictions of the proletariat are therefore worthy of comment. The workers are shown in a suitably positive light, and there is no hint at any justification for Likharev's fears that they might pull down the edifice they are constructing with such heroic self-sacrifice. On the other hand, Leonov seems to have no great interest in them and the general impression is of a faceless mass: 'They crept out of the trucks, grey in the half-light and all looking alike' (4. 96–7). In his drafts Leonov commented 'Tower of Babel' on this passage.³³ With its associations of Kalafat the phrase casts an ironic light on the scene. Even in Potemkin's dreams of the completed factory it is the swarm rather than the individual that dominates: 'Under electric light the peasants collectively eat their multicalorific dinner; with grateful glances at the portrait of the works they listen to canned music from the wireless' (4. 53).

There is a perceptible note of irony here; in the immediate context it is aimed primarily at Potemkin's dreamy nature, but the picture of a homogenized euphoria inevitably stirs memories of Bukharin's communal refectories and Chikilev's dreams of a standardized humanity. The one exception, Faddey Akishin, is an eccentric individualist who spends his spare time building latrines, not one of the occupations envisaged by Bukharin in his optimistic visions of the versatility of workers under Communism, but as essential to life as sunshine. As he explains to a somewhat bewildered Western visitor:

> the smell here must be dry, pitchy, and woody. In your city, I dare say, even the trees smell of stone – and there's no soul in stone. The soul can't live in stone. There's no support for it there. As far as I can see the soul's being driven out of the world nowadays and the brain's taking her place. (4. 102)

With allowances for Akishin's idiom, the sentiments could have been uttered by Vissarion.

Leonov's names are never lightly chosen, and the name Vissarion is both rare and striking. There is nothing in the life of the saint Bessarion that is of any relevance to Leonov's hero, nor does the example of the critic Vissarion Belinsky provide any clues.³⁴ I suggest that it alludes to the patronymic of Stalin, the architect of the Five-Year Plan and the new cultural policies. By December 1929 he had finally established his supremacy over the Communist Party. He was called 'Lenin's first pupil,' and his name was listed at the head of the members of the Politbureau, instead of in alphabetical order among the others, as had previously been the practice. It is from this date that the cult of

Stalin may be said to have begun. Bukharin charged that he had become the 'Jenghis Khan of the Party.'[35] Are the associations of the great Khan so different from those of Attila? Many years later, Leonov declared that in Vissarion he had foretold the ideology of Fascism.[36] By then he had come to regard Stalinism as its mirror image. This perception is already presaged in *The Sot'*.

On the face of it the Communist Stalin and the individualist Vissarion may seem to have nothing in common, but Leonov's reading of Shigalev's paradoxes of egalitarianism and tyranny had already led him to foresee the appearance of the Chikilev type. Just as in Dostoevsky's novel the ideas of Stepan Verkhovensky are debased and vulgarized by his son, Petr Stepanovich, so in *The Sot'* the sophistries of Vissarion Bulanin seem to lead to the tyranny of Iosif Vissarionovich Djugashvili. Leonov's recognition of this connection can be seen in one curious change made between the *Novyy mir* edition of the novel and the book version. Originally Leonov had described the political situation thus:

> The ship listed now to one side, now to the other, and each time the waves hurled themselves on the shaky vertical. The rudders broke, they were replaced by new ones, and the absence of so many reviled leaders was appalling. Now the success of the expedition to regions that older humanity had never visited depended entirely on the crew.[37]

The first of these sentences was retained in later editions but the continuation was changed:

> ... The rudders broke, they were replaced by new ones; the success of the expedition [...] now depended entirely on the wisdom of the captain and the endurance of the crew. (4. 235)

The proletarian crew has had to surrender its achievements to the omniscient captain. The 'reviled leaders' are not just absent but unmentionable. In these alterations the new cult of Stalin is reflected.

Bukharin had not flinched at the prospect of the physical liquidation of class enemies, and Tolya Mashlykin in *The Thief* had seen no difference between killing enemies of the Revolution and stamping on a cockroach. In *The Sot'* Vissarion fondly remembers a certain Bimbaev who had successfully used poison gas against the enemy:

> O, Bimbaev, you great provocateur, who showed me the power of science. His magnificent machines contained no cannons, only test tubes, condensers, and a

multitude of pipes [...] The wheels are turning, the machine is ready, but [Bimbaev] still hopes to quadruple the number of its functions. Perhaps he is teaching it to fly, or to smile, or to articulate the word Mummy. (4.185)

The idolization of science leads to ever-increasing barbarism. So too the scientific pretensions of Marxism lead to the negation of humanity. Here Vissarion gives voice to thoughts that Leonov could not possibly have expressed in his own name, and these ten pages can be read as the most sustained attack on the assumptions of Bukharin and Preobrazhensky's *ABC of Communism* to be found anywhere in his work before *The Pyramid*.

The use of the name Vissarion reveals a suicidal readiness to flirt with danger that runs through Leonov's work of the Stalin period. Alongside and even inside apparently orthodox Soviet passages we come across comments and suggestions that question the whole structure of Communism.[38] The very unthinkability of such ideas no doubt prevented the censors from perceiving what Leonov had written. Indeed, at times one feels that in letting such passages stand Leonov himself could hardly have been fully aware of what he was saying. On the other hand, he is one of the most self-conscious and self-critical of writers, constantly revising his works and invariably writing them out by hand; it is hardly conceivable that he should overlook a slip of the pen, still less an unthinking choice of a name. In *The Pyramid* he confirms that such passages were indeed deliberate.

The emphasis on science and control in Soviet Marxism has produced as its corollary a distrust of the 'natural,' whether in nature itself or in human beings. The classic formulation of this paradigm in Soviet literature is to be found in Furmanov's novel of the Civil War, *Chapaev* (1923), which deals with the Party's attempts to bring a brilliant, but ideologically innocent, partisan leader under its control. With the industrialization drive of the Five-Year Plans this attitude only hardens: nature, including human nature, becomes simply a resource to be exploited, and its inadequacies indicative of its counter-revolutionary spirit. This distrust is applied in particular to the traditional Russian idealization of the 'natural' life of the peasantry.[39] In *The Sot'* the violence of the natural elements seems to illustrate this thesis. When a flood threatens to destroy the entire project, it is compared to a peasant rising (*bunt*):

[The river] chose its moment infallibly for taking its revenge on man, who had presumed to set it to work. It refused to enter the pipes, it wanted to flow smoothly down its old spacious channel, to spawn its rich fish, and preserve its wise torpor. It seemed to acquiesce now, but Potemkin could hear it calling into space for support for its rebellion (*bunt*). A wild power hymned in our epic *byliny* was awakening; it was becoming threatening, imperious, and now the winds, those enraged bargees of the skies, had dragged up their waterlogged vessels, the winds were whispering, the birds circling, and in the river's violated womb thousands of new springs were coming to birth. (4. 164)

It is then noteworthy that whereas other novels of the First Five-Year-Plan bear such grandiose industrial names as *Hydrocentral*, *Energy*, *The Great Conveyor Belt*, Leonov names his after a small river, and it is only natural that the ambivalent image of silence should play an important part in the novel. One of the monks tells Uvad'ev: 'But justice comes from beauty, you know, and beauty is born of silence, and you are smashing it, the silence, with your picks' (4. 42). Silence too is the specious argument of *meshchanstvo*; the *kulaks* suggest that the factory will 'affect the peasants' health; and that a nature reserve should be established to preserve the forest and the people in their pristine wilderness, which would be a sure attraction for foreign tourists' (4. 244). But if these remarks are discredited by the ideology of the speakers the following dispassionate comment comes from the author: 'Here, where silence had once sweetly caressed the ear, the intermittent buzz of a locomotive was breaking in' (4. 124).

The Sot' is, paradoxically, the only one of Leonov's novels to open with a nature scene:

An elk was drinking water from a stream. The stream ran sweetly through the silence. It was gorged with happiness like a dream come true.[40] With its legs splayed the elk listened to its heart in some bewilderment. Drops of water fell from its moist timid lips, creating transparent circles on the water. Suddenly it started and vanished into the darkening forest, like a stone into a pond.

No doubt all the inhabitants of the entire forest knew about this secret path to the water. This was clear from the tracks leading to the stream. An old and gnarled man emerged from behind a tree. Besides the sky and last year's yellowed sedge, the water reflected also a dogskin cap and disproportionately long arms dangling from their sleeves. The old man flared his nostrils and listened to the deafening racket of life awakening... At this crowning hour of the dying day the forest was beginning to snort, bark, sing, each to its own amorous organ. First the chaffinches began to moan, and somewhere in a nearby marsh, a secluded spot for avian dalliance, a snipe responded with deepest sympathy. In the heights gilded by the setting sun an osprey lamented over its victims, now being born on the earth, a turtle-dove sobbed out its appeals to its crested mate, a bittern wailed... and a first tender star appeared over the swamp. The magic urges of the spring had now spread to the old man, he was ready any moment to jump up and roll in the grass like the impassioned birds, but a whiff of sulphur tickled his nostrils. He sneezed, frowned, and withdrew into the shadows. A withered juniper bush now stands by the stream, and not even the most turbulent spring will be able to awaken him.

The woods darkened, and the amorous choruses fell silent; only those carefree inhabitants of the forest, whom April had already begun to warm, lazily busied themselves on their hillock. In the face of unprecedented disaster they abandoned themselves to a vain agitation, some tried to block the entries with beams, others simply lay flat on their backs, impatient to fight and perish in battle. A crimson, jointed thundercloud had forced its way into their round world, and in vain they tried to drag it to their implacable judges for execution. And even though the man's hand was actuated by sheer high spirits, they calmed down only when the sinister warmth ceased to stream from above. Uvad'ev took his finger out of the anthill and sniffed it; it smelt of the tart sweat of ants. (4. 7–8)

This remarkable passage could only have been written by someone with a profound knowledge and love of nature, but it is also clearly a metaphor for the changes that the communists are bringing to the monastery, and ultimately to the whole way of life of the north. The destruction of primordial unity links this passage with Leonov's first stories; the startled elk is a descendant of the one killed by Andrey in *A Note on Birchbark*. The shedding of blood in the name of a future Paradise reinforces one of Leonov's major themes.

Naturally, the Communists see this scene rather differently:

forest, nothing but forest – standing there, withering away and rotting. And anything you care to think of inside it – mushrooms, bears, hermits, and goblins – everything except hard sense and strong will. (4. 50)

Here the features of the opening paragraphs, the wild animals (an elk rather than bears), the mushrooms, the goblins (the old wood demon in the second paragraph), the hermits (the monks with whom the engineers are soon to find lodging) are seen through very different spectacles. The 'hard sense and strong will' make their appearance in the third paragraph, with Uvad'ev's finger penetrating an anthill, and the desperate but hopeless resistance of the ants.[41]

The feminine gender of the Russian words for 'nature' and 'silence' extends also to a distrust of femininity in general. Love and particularly sexual desire are regarded as hostile and dangerous forces, which a Communist should resist. It is therefore significant that one aspect of the opening section is conspicuously omitted in the Communists' view of the forest, namely the intense feeling of eroticism attributed to nature here (and in other passages in the novel). It is spring, and the birds and animals are all ready to mate, but the human beings seem quite impervious to such feelings. It may be noted too that despite their evocation of pristine nature the opening paragraphs in fact contain a wide variety of sounds evoking the forest's spring awakening. On the other hand the novel ends in utter silence, with Uvad'ev alone amid the falling snow, dreaming of his future city, which is well-lit, but apparently soundless. The paradoxes of ends and means reappear: Is noise acceptable if it is required to build a noiseless Utopia? Is a Paradise without birdsong worth living in?

It is in this connection that one apparently peripheral character in the novel acquires her significance. This is Uvad'ev's mother, Varvara. She is not essential to the plot of the novel but she dominates every scene in which she appears by her disconcerting vitality. In view of Leonov's usual difficulties with depicting female characters his success in this case is all the more remarkable. An unashamed sensualist, she might seem to be a complete antithesis to Uvad'ev, but in fact the two are deeply attached to one another. Her irregular private life fully justifies the epithet *gullivaya baba* (a lusty wench), a term that is actually applied by Uvad'ev disapprovingly to the spring (4. 8).

The maternal relationship is particularly significant in a novel that is so concerned with the relationship between the natural and the man-made worlds; her name, Varvara, also acquires greater significance in view of the debate over culture and barbarism that lies behind much of the argument. At the end of the novel, with her life in Moscow having fallen apart (she has left the black marketeer to whom she was briefly married, and she has given up her job as a traffic policeman), she comes north to keep house for Uvad'ev, with the sneaking hope of marrying him off and so seeing a grandchild. However, her plans do not work out, and she finally returns to Moscow. Uvad'ev goes to see her off:

> Varvara's face was glowing: she was rejuvenated by her return to life. Neither of them encumbered the moment of parting with assurances about letters or with unnecessary pleas and pleadings; only at the last moment, when the motor was already running, did she suddenly stick her head out of the door:
>
> 'If you hear bad news – don't come. I don't like it. It's bad enough lying there, and then people start wailing...' And she fell back on her leather seat, and her son realized that she was referring to her death.
>
> It was thus, with her lips tight sealed, that she became fixed in Uvad'ev's memory. The metal gave a frozen screech, the railcar moved off, and Varvara did not even look out to embrace her last relative for the last time. Nor was there any need for her son to wave his handkerchief after her and call out the unavoidable

word of parting. The railcar had disappeared behind a clump of trees. Uvad'ev turned his back and went home. (4. 282–3)

In this bleak conclusion mother and son finally realize their incompatibility. She leaves the building site in a screeching metal vehicle that stands opposed to everything natural. She is 'returning to life' and 'her face is radiant.' As a comment on the emptiness of her son's life it is devastating.

Leonov was later to return to this type, but Varvara's subsequent incarnations in his work (e.g., Konstantsiya in *An Ordinary Man* [*Obyknovennyy chelovek*, 1940] and Tabun-Turkovskaya in *A Golden Coach* [*Zolotaya kareta*, 1946]) retain only her vulgarity and none of her vitality and warmth; they are never redeemed, but are invariably condemned and expelled with ignominy.

Although the general tone of the novel is triumphalist, occasional authorial asides point to a less rosy picture. Rumours of crop failures and setbacks to collectivization circulate. The building of the mill requires the eviction of peasants from their homes and their resettlement in new buildings, but they will still have to pay for the drilling of the new wells needed (4. 109). There are references to lay-offs, food shortages, and even the lack of funds to pay the workers (4. 208–9). The housing is cramped and insanitary (4. 44), but Uvad'ev is not sympathetic to complaints and recalls 'a tiresome health-inspector who came every day to insist that the workers' dormitories be enlarged, [...] and he reflected that even before starting work on the project they should lay a boardwalk which they had easily managed without until this month's break in the weather' (4. 194–5). Rumours spread about pollution of the air and water. One of the peasants complains: '"When they start building the stench will spread out to us." Apparently he had in mind the sulphuric acid, an inevitable and imperceptible byproduct of the production process. "The gas will spread and everything will be permeated by it, the rivers and the land. Our cows will eat the grass, but you won't want to drink their milk!"' (4. 180).

Leonov raises once again the question of *The Breakthrough at Petushkiha*, of whether Communism has anything better to put in the place of the culture it has destroyed. There is no sympathy in any of Leonov's works for the church as an institution, but it still stands for certain values. The young monk Gelasiy has come to despair of the monks' pettiness: 'Swindlers and idiots... they spend their time pulling out one another's hair; and the truth gets left to one side – and there's no beauty either. Do *you* possess the truth?' (4.20) Later one of the kulaks raises the same question: 'What sort of a temple will you erect in place of our monastery?' (4. 110).

In *The Sot'* Leonov does not commit himself unambiguously to a dissident account of Soviet industrialization – such a book could not have been published in the conditions of the time, nor would the author himself have survived.[42] Rather he nudges the reader into seeing the possibility of alternative interpretations, as in the treatment of nature, and even into thinking the unthinkable, as in the long section devoted to Vissarion. The fact that few if any readers understood the full implications of *The Sot'* does not prove that Leonov was excessively cautious; rather it was the readers who were unwilling to hear what they were being told. Ham's difficulties in that early story proved to be all too prophetic: the meanings were there for anyone prepared to follow up Leonov's words.

This perhaps accounts for the widespread sense that Leonov was somehow heterodox, though nobody (at least in print) was able to explain quite how or where. Each of his novels of the 1930s was initially welcomed as an advance on his previous work only to be soon disparaged and even attacked. Undoubtedly he owed much to the support of Gor'ky who praised his first three novels lavishly, and in 1931 introduced him to Stalin, a meeting that was to have important consequences later.[43] As will be seen, Leonov's relations with Gor'ky later cooled, but his real difficulties only began after Gor'ky's death.

Early in 1930 the Turkmenistan Ministry of Education invited a group of prominent Soviet writers to tour the republic and produce a book about Soviet achievements there.[44] Besides Leonov, Vsev. Ivanov, Lugovskoy, Pavlenko, Sannikov, and Tikhonov also took up the invitation, and altogether they spent some two months in Central Asia. They toured canals and industrial projects; they gave readings from their works, lectured on such subjects as 'Soviet woman' and 'atheism,' and founded literary organizations.

Of Leonov's various publications on this episode the most important is the novella *Locusts*.[45] The theme of the story he formulated thus: 'It was particularly difficult for us as writers not to succumb to the charms of this museum of exoticism. But in fact the struggle in Turkmenistan for a new culture, for a new way of life, is no less than a struggle with the famous exoticism of Central Asia, so attractive to the eyes and camera of a Western tourist, but so ruinous for the working population.'[46]

This idea is worked out in the figure of Petr Maronov. At the beginning of the story he is an inexperienced youth, completely under the spell of his dead brother's romantic outlook; fresh from three years in the Arctic[47] he is ready and eager to be overwhelmed by Central Asia. He feels guilty at having been born too late 'to take part in the sacred scrap with which his epoch had opened' (4. 288). By the end of the story, however, he has developed into a mature man, and has come to realize that the Five-Year Plan is no less romantic than the

Civil War had been. The transformation is effected when a plague of locusts hits Turkmenistan. Maronov is swept up in the crisis and forced to participate actively. At first a mere observer, he gradually becomes involved, until at the end of the story he is addressed as 'Comrade,' a sign that he has now joined the Party.

In *The Sot'* Burago's indifference to politics had not affected the quality of his work for the Communists; but in *Locusts* Maronov's maturity is seen entirely in terms of political awareness. At first he pooh-poohs the political approach to every problem, but he is reluctantly convinced at the height of the crisis that 'apart from the visible forces, people and the elements, there were invisible political forces at work around him [...] sometimes a mysterious hand would remove the coloured flags [...] sometimes the poison, intended for the locusts, would disappear, even if only in small quantities' (4. 323). As in *The Sot'*, the religious authorities – this time Islamic – are shown as actively cooperating with the *kulaks* against the Communists. The mullahs even try to prevent the people from killing the locusts on the grounds that 'They are God's guests and remember – a life for a life' (4. 312).

Parallel to the main theme runs the story of Maronov's relations with Ida Mazel', the wife of the local Party boss, and once his brother's mistress. In fact it had been mainly in the hope of an affair with her that he had made this trip to Central Asia. At their first meeting she behaves with dignity in the face of his schoolboyish innuendoes. She justifies her conduct: 'We try not to pronounce this word [love], not because we have been coarsened, but because the word itself is a weakness. And so if I feel like it I'll live with Akiamov or with Zudin or with you – without any qualms or internal pangs' (4. 298). But this frank apologia for free love, which had been a characteristic of the 1920s, was no longer fashionable, and Ida Mazel' is shown to be a degenerate. Leonov tries to prejudice the reader against her by calling her 'the woman' (4. 297), or by her surname.[48] The revulsion for casual sexual encounters (Pal'chikov and Katya in *White Night*, Uvad'ev and Zoya in *The Sot'*) reappears in this story too:

... And suddenly – not with his eyes, but through some ingenious turn of thought – he realized that she was naked, almost naked.
'Cover yourself,' he said brusquely.
'Don't come near me...'
'You were Yakov's wife, cover yourself!'
Possibly his words didn't penetrate her consciousness; in the last resort she was prepared to be the wife of all the brothers of Maronov who could be found.[49]

This episode was later substantially modified for the book version, no doubt in conformity with Soviet prudery, but it provides another meaning for the title of the story: in a later scene her husband points out a heap of locusts:

'... why are they sitting one on top of another?'
Maronov shivered, and despite his need for sleep, he laughed: 'You are an ideal husband [...] You can see and not understand. This is love, Mazel'.' (4. 328–9)

The later replacement of the original title 'Saranchuki,' denoting a multitude of individual locusts, by a single collective noun 'Sarancha'[50] unfortunately blurs this point, and reduces the significance of the episode.

The interest of *Locusts*, however, does not lie so much in the characters or situations as in Leonov's attempt to depict Maronov's development in stylistic terms. His romantic dreams are suggested in the opening description of an Eastern city in early spring with many non-Russian words such as *khudzhur* and *bakshi*, which would have been incomprehensible to most readers. But they are used strictly factually and with a minimum of exotic overtones. At the same time the reader is made aware of the dirt and poverty and the depressing reality; it is drizzling. The story begins: 'Maronov yawned' (4. 287) with boredom and disillusionment even before he has properly arrived in Central Asia.

By contrast, the pages devoted to fighting the locusts abound in hyperboles and superlatives: 'men at the limits of their endurance continued to dig trenches amid the shattering silence of the night' (4. 338); 'the sun as though in hysterics' (4. 331); and 'eyes that were catastrophically closing' (4. 329). So too in *The Sot'* Leonov had painted the heroism and endurance of the engineers in hyperbolic terms: 'this unprecedented struggle' (4. 277); 'the level of the quicksand was rising catastrophically' (4. 263). This rather artificial excitement was inspired by the desire to show that the period of the First Five-Year Plan was as rich in romantic potential as the Civil War.

In the final section of the story, however, Leonov abandons all obvious romanticism. It is drizzling again; it is autumn, and Maronov is waiting for the train that is to take him back to the Arctic. For all their apparent lifelessness and even disillusionment these few sentences bring the story to a triumphant close. Maronov has indeed been disillusioned, but in a positive sense. He is full of enthusiasm now to return to the north: 'It's better up there in Novaya Zemlya' (4. 338). The progress from spring to autumn is also unique in Leonov; all his other major works end in the spring or early summer. Not only does the autumn correspond to Maronov's new-found maturity, but it reflects the severer conception of romanticism that is the theme of the story.

Since the theme is worked out largely in stylistic terms it would seem that Leonov himself is closely involved in this work. In this farewell to the romanticism of his earlier works there is a certain note of reluctance or even nostalgia. He obviously relished the possibilities of Oriental description, just as he had done in *Tuatamur*, and in fact the first book version of 1932 was even more colourful, and required a glossary of 121 words, most of them of Asiatic origin. The text was revised and simplified for the edition of 1945.

Leonov himself was acutely aware of the artistic risks involved in writing these two works. For the first time he had ventured into a world in which the material setting and not simply the historical period was of prime importance. In *The Badgers* he had described the events of some three or four years previously, while *The Thief* was not begun until the fifth year of the NEP period. *The Sot'* and *Locusts*, on the other hand, were begun within a few months of the events on which they are based, and called for specialized knowledge. It was only natural, therefore, for him to feel that he might have confused the proportions and that his book would prove ephemeral: 'When Stendhal wrote he looked forward to an audience a hundred years away. We have only one year, or five at the most. This is what makes us afraid.'[51] Yet for all their concern with the new age and a new culture these works are not revolutionary or even proletarian; the masses play only a peripheral role. They are conventional novels and constitute no more than Soviet variants on traditional forms.

The narrative style, self-consciously literary, involved, and elaborate, has more in common with his later works than with *The Badgers* or *The Thief*. For the first time Leonov employs the device of indirect speech for revealing the thoughts behind the words, and even more significantly for dissociating himself from the sentiments expressed. This enables him to touch on such topics as the Zamyatin affair and the damage caused by rapid industrialization in apparently conventional Soviet terms, while refraining from giving them any authorial sanction. I think that this is not merely a form of 'mental reservation,' since Leonov's true beliefs are also present in the text, and can be shown to be consistent within it.

For the first time too there appear in Leonov's work the tiresome circumlocutions that often disfigure his later writing: on one occasion the population sets fire to the locusts and Leonov comments: 'the magnificent spectacle of these mobile fires had a discouraging effect on the general well-being of the locusts.'[52]

Initial reaction to both works was cautious. Gor'ky praised *The Sot'* warmly, and Soviet critics welcomed it as an indication of the new attitudes now prevailing among the former *poputchiki*. They considered it less striking than *The Thief*, but a step forward in Leonov's ideological evolution. The tone of criticism changed in the autumn of 1931. At a discussion of the novel by the Union of Soviet Writers Leonov was subjected to several attacks.[53] One critic declared that none of the factories that he had visited bore any resemblance to Leonov's paper mill; he complained that the author had failed to show his workers in the conditions of city life, and had shirked composing a final triumphant conclusion to his work; while two technical errors proved that he had failed to master his material. *Locusts*, on the other hand, passed almost unnoticed and Leonov himself disparaged the work in later years.[54] It is indeed one of his less interesting works. After Stalin's death, however, both books were frequently reissued and enjoyed unqualified official approval.

chapter six

Skutarevsky 1932

> '... *the universities, purged of idlers and other scum, were invaded by the young, the older ones discovered at long last why it is that water boils, that rivers flow downhill, and the sky is blue.*'
>
> The Thief

Leonov's fourth novel, *Skutarevsky*, continues many of the themes and concerns of *The Sot'*, but the setting now shifts from the proletariat and the construction of a factory in a remote province to high intellectual circles in Moscow and grandiose schemes for harnessing the nation's energy resources. The subject matter thus enables Leonov to reflect on the changes that had affected the intellectual life of the country in the recent past.

The success of the November Revolution had persuaded the Russian Communists that they had indeed mastered the science of history, and that they had therefore little to fear from the other sciences. Indeed it was science that would prove the instrument for creating Communism. Technology would create the basis for universal prosperity, while the rational organization of research would ensure a far sounder and broader coverage than the individualistic and commercialized methods of the bourgeois West. The furthering of science could only help to strengthen the socialist revolution, and scientists, whatever their social origins, were therefore to be valued.

This respect for science and its practitioners did not, however, succeed in turning the intellectuals into active supporters of the regime. By 1928 less than 6 per cent of all scientific workers were members of a trade union. The Academy of Sciences, the most distinguished scholarly institution in the country, still did not contain a single party cell.[1] This dearth of reliable technicians and scientists now seemed to threaten the whole program of industrialization.

As a result the Party had become increasingly impatient with the scientists' inclination towards research rather than application, their apparent political indifference, and above all the prestige and power that their intellectual independence attracted. Where so many were acting out of faith and enthusiasm their caution and objectivity seemed almost disloyal. Their way of life too seemed provocatively bourgeois and they were frequently suspected of, and sometimes even charged with, sabotage.

These resentments and suspicions found an outlet in the various show trials, such as the 'Shakhty' case of 1928 and the 'Prompartiya' affair of 1930. Leonov seems at first to have taken them at face value. He wrote to Gor'ky: 'We have a wreckers' trial going on here, and the impression is overwhelming... some of my friends are urging me to write something (like a novel) about it. [...] The significance of the trial is enormous, above all because it shows just what the hopes of our intellectuals are leading to. [...] These people organized the destruction of the work and efforts of millions...'[2] But it is possible that Leonov was here being cautious in case his letters were being intercepted, because in conversation he was rather more sceptical. On his second visit to Sorrento in 1931 he was one of those who heard Gor'ky read his new play on the subject *Somov and Others* (*Somov i drugie* 1931). Leonov failed to respond as enthusiastically as Gor'ky had hoped and when he was forced to explain himself, he said, 'I cannot understand how an engineer who has built a magnificent bridge can raise his hand against it. How can you destroy grace and beauty with your own hands? I cannot understand this [...] I don't know what to say. I cannot lie, I don't know how to. And if I did you would see it...'[3] This scepticism can be discerned between the lines of *Skutarevsky*, and it was one of the disagreements between the two men that led to their later estrangement.

Besides the show trials, which were intended, rather like the campaigns against Zamyatin and Pil'nyak, to 'encourage the others,' the pretensions of the intellectuals also came under scrutiny on purely doctrinal grounds. The theoretical issue which was used for this purpose was the question of the place of Marxism among the sciences. For some, the 'mechanists,' it was just one of the sciences, subject to the same processes of constant revision and refining as other scientific theories; for others, however, followers of Deborin, the senior Marxist scholar in Russia, Marxism had a special place, it was the 'science of the sciences,' on which all other studies were dependent. In the later 1920s this school of thought became dominant, providing a justification for subjecting the direction and energies of Soviet research to the requirements of the political leadership. In other words, Soviet science became the victim of the same evils of unplanned and changeable demands as bourgeois science was accused of. In the case of the sciences of genetics and quantum theory (to name only the most striking examples) these policies were to do serious and lasting damage to the Soviet economy.

In 1928 the Party began its campaign of 're-educating the intelligentsia' (*perestroyka intelligentsii*), and in the following years the Academy of Sciences was completely taken over. First, a new Charter was drawn up, enabling the party to nominate and appoint members; as a result more new members were admitted in 1929 than in all the years since 1917 put together. The admission of still more Party-backed candidates in the next two years left the old academicians without even a one-third representation with which to block unacceptable measures. These tactics were repeated throughout the academic pyramid. The various scientific societies were first infiltrated and then taken over from within. To ensure that the next generation would be totally loyal the universities were required to admit a thousand Communists into their graduate courses in engineering regardless of their qualifications. In the drive to maximize productivity, classes were examined and graduated in groups rather than on individual performance. During the First Five-Year Plan the student body trebled and the number of teachers doubled. The older scholars were treated with suspicion, threats, and in many cases open hostility.

In 1932, however, there was an abrupt change of line: Stalin and Molotov now began to advise Communist students to treat scholars with respect; the mere fact that an engineer or a scholar was middle-aged did not after all mean that he was necessarily a criminal or a saboteur. The excesses of student activists began to be deplored; the use of 'shock-brigade' tactics in the sciences was condemned. Academic excellence became once again the chief criterion.

Thus much the same policies were applied to the scholars as to the artists during the years of the First Five-Year Plan, and the relaxation of these pressures occurred at much the same time also. On 23 April 1932 the Central Committee announced its decision to abolish all existing literary organizations and to create a new Union of Soviet Writers, this time under the leadership of the Communist Party. The 'dogmatism' and 'narrow-mindedness' of the preceding four years were all blamed on the RAPP leadership, although they had in fact been the direct outcome of the Party's policy in promoting RAPP in the first place. Now, by disgracing RAPP, the Party was able to pose as the saviour of Soviet literature and to disguise the fact that a new despotism was being substituted for the old. At first, however, it seemed that the repudiation of RAPP indicated a change in official policy, and it ushered in a brief period of comparative liberty.

Sympathetic articles on the 'fellow-travellers' began to appear in the press; publishing houses too became more liberal in their choice of authors and subjects. The authors themselves were allowed to return to the sympathetic treatment of intellectuals and even to the techniques of psychological analysis. This period was, however, only short-lived, for by October 1932 the policies previously associated with the RAPP movement were being reimposed, and the pendulum began to swing once more against the independent Soviet writer.

Leonov's *Skutarevsky*[4] may be seen in the light of these developments. It is set in the winter and spring of 1930–1.[5] The sabotage trials of 1929 and 1930 and the installation of Communist activists in academic institutions form the immediate background of the novel. But whereas in *The Sot'* Leonov had been dealing with unfamiliar subject matter, in *Skutarevsky* he was turning to an issue and a milieu with which he could personally identify, namely the liberal intelligentsia.

Professor Skutarevsky is an eminent Russian physicist who had made his reputation long before the war, although, due to the low value placed on scientific work by the Tsarist regime, he had often found himself compelled to sell off practical applications of his research for commercial exploitation. He has an impeccable liberal record. As a young man he had attended Marxist seminars, but he had been forced to give them up because of pressure of work. After the February Revolution he had refused a post in the Provisional Government of Kerensky and remained politically independent even under the Bolsheviks. He is eventually summoned to meet Lenin and prepare schemes for the electrification of the entire country, to which he responds with a cautious 'Yes, but...' (5. 42). He appreciates the opportunities that he is given under the new government for continuing his work, but he sees no need to prove his gratitude and loyalty by joining the Party. In the philosophical debates of the time he would pass as a typical 'mechanist.'[6]

Skutarevsky's subject, the wireless transmission of energy, is ideally suited to the new criteria for Soviet science.[7] It involves both high theory and highly practical issues in a country whose reserves of fossil fuels are mostly remote from the industrial centres. His climactic experiment, however, is a failure[8] (here Leonov deliberately chose a problem that had not yet been resolved, and so was able to avoid the triumphal ending obligatory in Soviet novels),[9] and he tries to resign his position in anticipation of disgrace. Instead the Party only increases its support for his work.[10] The novel ends with a May-day meeting at which the lonely professor at last breaks out of his intellectual isolation. He has only to say the word 'Comrades' to be greeted by a wild ovation from the workers. His ideological conversion quite overshadows the failure of his experiment.

As many critics have pointed out there is a close connection between *Skutarevsky* and the early story, *The End of a Petty Man*. Both Skutarevsky and Likharev are prominent men of science, but where Likharev's subject – palaeontology – is at the furthest possible remove from the practical needs of the famine years, Skutarevsky's is of vital economic importance and has been sanctioned by Lenin himself. Likharev's bitterness at the interference of the Revolution with his life's work is a reasonable motive for his fear and resentment of the Communists; Skutarevsky's loyalty to the Party, on the other hand, is only increased by the technical assistance and demonstrations of confidence that he receives. Likharev becomes progressively more and more isolated from reality until he finally loses his reason. Skutarevsky, on the contrary, breaks out of his personal isolation into friendships, a love affair, and finally acceptance by the masses. The young proletarian, capable, in Likharev's opinion, of pulling down the building that he has just erected, becomes in *Skutarevsky* the ambitious young Communist, Cherimov. These comparisons show not only the parallels but also the fundamental differences between the two works, at least on a first reading.

Two years earlier in *The Sot'* Burago had urged: 'My job's building factories, and it doesn't worry me what you choose to call it. I'm yours to the end, but don't ask me to do more than I can. Socialism? – I couldn't say' (4. 258). This declaration of neutrality is of course deceptive. Burago is not really uncommitted; his loyalty to the cause and his confidence in the success of the project make him a Communist in all but Party membership card. In *Locusts*, however, and again in *Skutarevsky* even this limited kind of neutrality is rejected as inadequate. Accordingly, Skutarevsky's young Communist assistant, Cherimov, takes a hand in his re-education and finally persuades him that his non-political attitude is tantamount to treachery and even counter-revolution. The issue is a somewhat artificial one, since no reader of the book is likely to suspect Skutarevsky of treason, and this led some Soviet critics to complain that Leonov had not shown any change of heart on the part of the intelligentsia, but merely how a good and loyal scientist had become even better and more loyal.[11]

As a result the book possesses little narrative tension, and the obligatory plot line of skulduggery is perfunctory and unconvincing. The other members of Skutarevsky's family are openly anti-Communist; his brother-in-law, Petrygin, who occupies 'a high position from which the threads of control ran out over the entire sector of electrification' (5. 45), is also the leader of a gang of saboteurs, that is trying to recruit Skutarevsky's son, Arseniy. Like Vissarion, Petrygin is a follower of the 'pessimistic philosophy of Clausius' (5. 44); he too preaches a gospel of destruction, and the Napoleon of his dreams bears a strong resemblance to the mythical Attila awaited by Vissarion in *The Sot'*. But the saboteurs constitute no threat. They are melodramatic and frequently absurd figures. They are briskly rounded up at the end of the book, and Arseniy, who has come to recognize the true nature of their activities, commits suicide.

As in *The Taming of Badadoshkin* counter-revolution is virtually synonymous with *meshchanstvo*. Petrygin and his sister (Skutarevsky's wife) are the children of a tavern-keeper, whose way of life has been shattered by the proletarian revolution. They try to put the clock back by surrounding themselves with quantities of things (*veshchi*), bourgeois comforts, and status symbols, which soon threaten to squeeze Skutarevsky out of his own flat. It is no surprise when these valuables, supplied by the art dealer Shtruf, all turn out to be fakes; it is an obvious metaphor for the pretentious claims and illusory hopes of the counter-revolution.

Petrygin and his entourage serve as Dostoevskian doubles by voicing Skutarevsky's own mechanist beliefs and taking them to unacceptable conclusions:

> Only the practical sciences and technology are capable of changing the face of life; it all depends on the efficiency of the machines, not at all on the class struggle. The invention of the weaver's loom has benefited humanity more than any socialist program. (5. 34)

In Dostoevsky the function of this device is to suggest that the high-minded intellectual arguments of a Raskol'nikov lead logically to the cynical amoralism of a Svidrigaylov. The prospect of Skutarevsky following out his theories until they lead him into sabotage, however, is manifestly absurd. His old-fashioned morality may turn a blind eye to the anti-Soviet activities of some members of his family, but he himself, even after the failure of his experiment, is never seriously accused of sabotage. His difficulties and delays are caused by conflicting loyalties, not by a conflict of good and evil within himself. Accordingly the parallels drawn between Skutarevsky and the saboteurs are artificial and misleading.

They come closest to convincing the reader in the portrayal of Skutarevsky's relations with his son. If at first Arseniy is presented as a disgruntled teenager, the child of an unhappy marriage, in later chapters Leonov depicts his situation with surprising sympathy.[12] Arseniy has been given considerable responsibilities but not the authority to carry them out, and so he is easily made the scapegoat for any failures. As he says in answer to his father's criticisms of his work:

> You have learned the official terminology for these things a bit too fast. You make your accusations without knowing the conditions under which this occurred. But then people here are always ready to look for scapegoats instead of asking why it happened. I read your report, and you have been infected with the same suspiciousness. (5. 53)

Leonov himself admits that Russian slovenliness was often indistinguishable in its effects from organized sabotage (5. 205).

Beyond this, Arseny voices his father's own suppressed doubts. Some of Skutarevsky's friends and colleagues have been arrested and even executed and he has not tried to help or defend them. Arseny's accusations are aimed ostensibly at Skutarevsky's materialist theories, but the reader is more likely to see them as veiled accusations of cowardice, while the references to Oriental despots and the torturers of the Inquisition raise analogies with Stalinism that were already being expressed:[13]

> You said yourself that there's no need to grieve over the loss of each individual. Even in the old days you could forgive this world anything, wars, brothels, crusades, dreamers like the Jenghis Khans and Torquemadas... and not just out of weak-minded magnanimity or knock-kneed intellectualism, but because you see all this simply as electrochemical processes [...] Your morality's not based even on biology but on physics. (5. 54–5)

The shock of Arseny's suicide forces Skutarevsky to recognize the inadequacies of his electromagnetic theory: 'Politics then, must divide the world into quite different molecules from the ones that we chemists and physicists divide it into' (5. 248).

This dawning political awareness is, however, not the only reason for the collapse of Skutarevsky's materialist philosophy. One night he is driving at high speed when he knocks down a young girl, Zhenya, who is running away from some unspecified difficulties with the Komsomol. He takes her home, and before long he has fallen in love with her. This provides a more conventional refutation: 'Didn't this suggest that some new unheard-of quality had been acquired by that lifeless matter which he had known and subjected to measurements, condensation, and attenuation..?' (5. 250) Zhenya teases Skutarevsky about his eccentricities and even offers to give him lessons in Marxism. When he is in despair after the apparent failure of his experiment she actually offers herself to him – 'If you want to, then live with me' (5. 287) – even though she is in love with Cherimov. Skutarevsky is realistic enough to perceive the impossibility of any such arrangement. It must be admitted that, as far as the reader is concerned, Zhenya is as unreal as Uvad'ev's Katya.[14]

This sub-plot leads, however, to the most promising narrative development, Skutarevsky's attempt to find a new flat for himself and Zhenya, whom he intends to train as his secretary. Petrygin soon finds him one for 30,000 roubles, but since this is far beyond Skutarevsky's means, he reduces the price to 29,000 (perhaps remembering Judas) and then offers to lend him the money in the hope of blackmailing him into working against the Communists. This intrigue reaches its climax in the central chapter of the novel, describing a fox-hunt. At the crucial moment the red-headed Skutarevsky becomes aware of a strange affinity between himself and the prey; he instinctively fires wide and the fox escapes. In spite of this warning, however, Skutarevsky still accepts Petrygin's loan.

> It recalled the recent trap [set for the fox], but this time the fates willed otherwise. Changing direction the fox came straight on towards Petrygin, unhurried and unsuspecting. Petrygin had time to take careful aim. (5. 155–6)

This promise of dramatic complications to come is not borne out. The next day Skutarevsky visits Petrygin to complete the deal, but suddenly changes his mind. It is Cherimov who now finds him somewhere to live. With the hasty termination of this narrative line the novel loses any tension, and the remaining chapters do little more than tie up the numerous loose ends.

The following chapter is devoted to the story of Skutarevsky's artist brother, whose career is a close parallel to that of the physicist. Before the Revolution a successful painter with left-wing views, he has had all his pictures bought up by the capitalist Zhistarev. Zhistarev disapproves of Fedor's politics and decides to punish him by destroying his paintings. Fedor is at first broken by this and after the Revolution he is reduced to faking Old Masters for Shtruf to sell to would-be connoisseurs, such as Skutarevsky's wife. After meeting Cherimov and other Communists, however, he makes a new start and goes off to paint some industrial murals for a factory in the provinces.

The introduction of Fedor into the novel was an afterthought.[15] Apart from one long chapter placed at the exact centre of the novel and by far the longest in it, he appears only incidentally. Formally and indeed stylistically, this chapter recalls the Vissarion episode in *The Sot'*. The action of the novel is suspended while a character expounds his ideas at length and with great passion. The main difference is that the subject of Fedor's monologue is art.

In many Soviet novels of the period an artist is introduced on the coat-tails of a scientist, as a way of suggesting that art functions in much the same sort of way. This is true of *Skutarevsky*, but with a difference.[16] Fedor does not see political propaganda as compatible with art, and like his brother he is suspicious of the Party's demands for immediate practical applications:

> 'So you'd like me to paint a combine on this field? [...] But I'd be cheating you if I did. The picture would be out of date before the paint was dry. Then you will look at your yesterday and grumble about art lagging behind the times. I am

offering you a gold coin, a yardstick, a human feeling, and all you want is a state lottery ticket!.. Sorry, I can only do what I can.'

'Does that mean you don't believe that a new art will be born on the other side of the pass?' Sergey Andreich quite understood that he was abusing the uncomplaining respect of his brother. Ultimately what was for one the source of a million torments was for the other just a means of relaxation, which required only that this relaxation should be as cosy as a comfortable armchair.' (5. 174)

The image of the 'pass,' first found in Don'ka's cabaret ditty in *The Thief* and recurring throughout Leonov's work, stands for the eventual emergence into Communism after the mountainous hardships of the transitional period. Sergey's question shares the Communist assumption that under socialism art will be quite different from any of its manifestations under previous social systems.[17] Skutarevsky would not accept this in relation to his science, nor can Leonov accept it of art, as he proceeds to show.

For there is a fundamental contradiction in the Communists' demands of art. The artist is required to produce something that is both topical and inspirational and at the same time comfortable and soothing. The point had been raised by Mayakovsky in his poem '*Home!*' ('*Domoy!*' 1925): 'I do not want to be picked like a flower of the fields after a hard day at the office; I want the State planners to sweat as they debate my assignments for the year.'[18] But where Mayakovsky had seen the role of art in total service to the Revolution and its immediate needs, Leonov argues that the 'younger generation of painters who had replaced painting by the new ideology and boring rationalistic experiments'[19] had in fact created only a thoroughly conformist kind of art that had no independent value of its own.

Leonov illustrates this in his account of the exhibition of Fedor's first Soviet picture, *The Skiers*, which the painter himself considered to be a 'key to the new art' (5. 210).[20] Leonov says of it: 'After the glut of crude battle scenes in post-revolutionary painting, whose naïveté was equalled only by their up-to-dateness, this brilliant apotheosis of youth and constant forward movement was a pleasure to the eyes' (5. 268–9), and he comments on 'the alchemy of genius which makes the black of the girl's sweater seem almost pink' (5. 268). But Cherimov is unhappy because the artist has depicted a tear in the knee of one of the ski-suits. He declares that this is a libel on Soviet workmanship that will soon make the picture out of date, and he suggests to the artist that noon would have been a more suitable time than evening for such a subject. Fedor replies that technical considerations of light and shade made this necessary (5. 270).

Leonov then draws his own contrast of light and shade. Cherimov and Zhenya go out of the exhibition into the cold evening drizzle: 'The twilight was thickening. The air was like damp cotton wool' (5. 271), and through Cherimov's confused reactions Leonov suggests that art works on a different level from the rationalist and utilitarian criteria of Marxist theory:

> He didn't like the picture; it just wasn't about the heroic struggles of Russia today. But, strangely enough, he couldn't forget it, it excited him, and not only because of the remarkable effect it had had on opening his eyes to Zhenya for the second time that day. With an almost ascetic distaste he remembered the restrained eroticism of *The Skiers* [...] surprisingly the hidden message of the picture was no longer at odds with his feelings. (5. 272)

This 'hidden message' finally breaks down the barriers of shyness between the two:

> And suddenly it was as though their mutual unnatural apprehensiveness had evaporated, as though the temporary withdrawal of spring and the bitter bone-chilling twilight had ceased to exist. With their arms intertwined, they swayed slightly as they strode out along the pavement, humming to themselves a semi-martial song, that columns of marchers often sing. And they laughed as they crushed the thin lacy layers of ice on the freezing puddles. Obviously the sun can shine even in the twilight, since the springtime of human beings comes from within. (5. 273)

Art does influence life, but it does so indirectly, and not necessarily immediately or consciously. Even the literal-minded and practical Communist Cherimov dimly understands that twilight does not stop the sun shining; the alchemy of genius can make even black appear pink.

Leonov's handling of this theme is the boldest in all his works of the Stalin period. Here he states unequivocally that art is about absolutes, not the relativities of Marxist dogma, and, even more important, that it is vital to the health of a society:

> At the risk of a banality that had been so often compromised [Fedor] emphasized the absolute value of certain imperishable words: spring, winter, love and death, joy and jealousy, those pebbles on the shore of the unexplored ocean of the universe, out of which the artist composes his intricate designs. Finally in a veritable fit of artistic aggression he threatened those who should ignore all *this* with spiritual scurvy. The very images were alien to Cherimov, a practical man and a believer in logical thinking, and the more vigorously he nodded the more he disagreed. (5. 270–1)

The story of Zhistarev's monopolizing Fedor's work may seem far-fetched to a non-Soviet reader, but it takes only a moment's reflection to realize that this very state of affairs existed in even more total form in the Soviet Union during the RAPP period, and was by no means a dead letter even after April 1932. Fedor's fate is sealed by an influential critic, one of those envious hacks

> who is kicked out of art only after many years of *slanderous* and destructive activity [...] Permanently nursing some unaccountable grudge, he found consolation in casting a paralysing fear over all true inspiration; it was probably he who had worked over Shunin just before his death, he who had *driven Evlashevsky into the grave, and chased Vasiliy Zerkal'nikov into emigration*, broken Berman, and if the rest had survived, then it was through no fault of his. Here he was again, and the opening phrase of his article, later to become a classic, was already maturing within him: 'Does the proletariat need art like this? No, it does not...'[21]

The bitterness of these lines springs from Leonov's own treatment by Soviet critics, and it confirms Leonov's suspicions that envy and the meanest form of egalitarianism are the inevitable consequences of Communist theory; the italicized words were cut or moderated in later editions (see 5. 269), but their force survives.

After the exhibition Fedor leaves to begin work on his murals, the project that will confirm his rebirth as a Soviet artist:

> ... in the contract it says: noon, a building site, barricades, a procession, spring, that is, all those epic words with which a new class begins its history. But inside myself I see only a mass of intersecting lines, of which some ascend far beyond the confines of my sketches, others struggle in the frenzy of their final agony, while yet others descend making way for the new ones that are destined to carve out the great expanses ahead... (5. 302)

The Communist who has commissioned Fedor assures him that 29,000 workers will see his work each day. This odd number recalls the 29,000 roubles that Petrygin was offering to lend Skutarevsky for his new flat, where it carried the taint of Judas's betrayal.[22] It is hardly coincidental, then, that Leonov's novel contains just twenty-nine chapters. He was constantly aware of the dangers of compromise, and the Skutarevsky brothers' plight was all too similar to his own. It was easier to escape Petrygin than the Communists, and in the scene of the fox-hunt we read that red flags are used to confine the animal within a certain area 'because red is the colour of cunning' (5. 148).[23]

Although the takeover of the sciences is one of the main concerns of the book, the young Communist Cherimov receives much less attention than is usual in Soviet novels. His thirtieth birthday occurs early in the novel, making him only a year or so younger than Leonov, but it is the aging Skutarevsky who is more understandable and appealing to the author. Almost all Leonov's heroes are older than their creator, and this gives his works a conservative cast, confirming his general scepticism about the benefits of change.

Many years later in a comment to Kovalev about *The Thief* Leonov remarked, '... the critics forgot that Vekshins were bound to appear in the future and make themselves known, for example, Cherimov in *Skutarevsky*.'[24] Unfortunately this conversation is not dated, but since Kovalev first made contact with Leonov in 1948, it probably dates from the later 1950s when he was working on the revised version of *The Thief*. If in the 1927 edition Leonov was still prepared to look for some way of redeeming Vekshin as a vehicle for the transmission of culture, in the new one he changed his mind. If we are to take his remark at face value, then it would appear that Leonov was already having second thoughts about Vekshin at the beginning of the 1930s.

Like Vekshin, Uvad'ev and Cherimov embody the Revolution's attempt to acquire culture. Vekshin had tried to seize it by a stroke of his sword; Uvad'ev is completely without culture; Cherimov intends to take it over by administrative coup. He contemplates Skutarevsky patronizingly:

> Cherimov's long-held beliefs were being confirmed: the old morality based on a servile and dishonest pity for mankind, the whole complex of antiquated and wrong-headed conceptions of love, kinship, and social relationships, were preventing Skutarevsky from following his own correct line in this matter. At times it was difficult for the old man, like a quadriped trying to walk on two legs... (5. 207)

The author's irony, audible in these lines, contrasts the opportunistic relativism of Communist thinking with the eternal human values of love and friendship. Both intellectually and morally Cherimov represents Leonov's fears for the future of culture.

Cherimov is nominally Skutarevsky's assistant, but it is clear that his appointment is a political one. In the occasional aside Leonov indicates his mindless iteration of party clichés: 'Cherimov felt himself defenceless without the pompous hackneyed words that are used to spice the tedium of ordinary meetings.'[25] He was responsible for removing the previous assistant, who was alleged to have been a prosecutor under the Tsarist regime (5. 64), and before long he is behaving like a prosecutor himself (5. 69). His 'I' often sounds like a 'we' (5. 205). Skutarevsky is naturally apprehensive about Cherimov's political connections and the extent of his commitment to science:

> On closer acquaintance it was easy to discern in the new deputy director a lurking obstinacy in the pursuit of certain aims, publicly concealed under a mask of total subordination to the scientific – and indeed not only the scientific – regulations of the director. Several rumours had already reached the ears of [Skutarevsky], and he was secretly afraid that someone even more intransigent could yet be sent. For that reason he was in no hurry to initiate Cherimov into his own work. (5. 88–9)

Towards the end, however, Cherimov has effectively taken control of the institute. Skutarevsky tries to resist some of his proposals:

> The institute was not designed for the purposes of metallurgy. Or do you have a directive?... When applied to science this word acquired a generally abusive sense on [Skutarevsky's] lips.
> 'It was designed to further socialist construction and defence,' Cherimov reminded him of the harshest and most pertinent clause in the charter.
> 'You are a monster. Right. So I'm on my own...,' muttered Skutarevsky, standing up and colouring. 'I've always been on my own. Everything is upside down. Cabbies are reviewing the sciences, scientists are producing electric kettles, yes.' (5. 237)

At first Skutarevsky sees Cherimov as a scientific threat, as the Faraday to his Davy, but this is hardly on the cards. Cherimov's scientific talents are confined to finding technological applications for his master's work and taking the public credit for it. Leonov comments sardonically:

> ... the discovery flowed entirely from Skutarevsky's own work on high frequencies [...]
> It was the general press rather than scientific circles that made all the fuss; the newspapers published a brief but exemplary biography of the young scientist, graced, admittedly, not by a listing of his scientific achievements, but rather of his official appointments.
> ... A fierce opponent of any kind of *Prometheanism* – and this word was aimed straight at Skutarevsky – [Cherimov] continued to assert that any invention should be credited to the entire research team and not just to its guiding spirit; considering the cumulative nature of technical culture he had no objection to sharing his triumph with all those who had earlier devoted their lives to the field.

And if there was something that amused him, it was not so much his sudden *Soviet* fame, as the *open* way in which it can be done. Lying in bed that morning he looked through the paper and smiled ironically at the headline, 'Our Future Academicians...' (5. 260–1)[26]

The image of Prometheus derives originally from the parallel between Skutarevsky's work on energy transmission and the theft of fire.[27] 'Prometheanism,' however, carries quite different associations for Leonov. It is the accusation made by the envious nonenities that batten on genius, and says more about them ('vultures') than their victims. Cherimov's attempts to discredit Skutarevsky relate him to the critics who hound Fedor, and the Chikilevs who distrust any individuality. No doubt Leonov was also thinking of his own experiences at their hands, and in his later work the reproach of 'Prometheanism' recurs in several significant contexts.

In one revealing scene Cherimov visits his old friend Fedor Butylkin in the hope of rediscovering his proletarian roots. This chapter is placed strategically, immediately after his visit to Arseniy and his bitter recognition that they have nothing in common. Leonov seems to imply that the same has happened in this relationship too. Cherimov proceeds to eat all his hosts' food, and his only gift for them is a copy of his one publication, translated into French (which he had originally intended for Arseniy); even his name on the cover is unrecognizable to Butylkin. At the end of the evening he returns home slightly tipsy and Leonov ironically comments on his painstaking progress: 'They were magnificent and impressive, the footsteps of a man who was on his way' (5. 88). The wider implications are hardly accidental.

The irony, often indeed sarcasm, with which Cherimov's character and behaviour are related, reflects Leonov's alarm at the subordination of culture to political ends. The rumours that circulate about Skutarevsky's imminent disgrace after the failure of his experiment show that Cherimov is not unusual, but rather typical of the intellectual climate of the age:

[Apparently] some gangs of half-educated youths had got together [...] to discredit Skutarevsky in the eyes of the higher administration. [...] That's how it is now. They've invented a proletarian physics, and are using it to criticize Newton. Last week they gave Galileo a worse going-over than the Vatican ever did. [...] Thus they explained the failure of the experiment as a treacherous plot, poured pitch over Zhenya, and even found two renegades within the institute who were prepared to swear under oath to the unprecedented squeeze on self-criticism by the director, depravity on a truly Roman scale, and on top of everything a reactionary mechanist deviation. Obscure rumours were already circulating in the institute to the effect that a letter of denunciation had been sent to the papers and that Skutarevsky would be relieved of his post once it had been published. The motivation behind all this, however, was not to show that a discredited Skutarevsky was not fit to head a scientific army, but rather to enable him to concentrate entirely on his scientific work... Skutarevsky felt a hot flush of revulsion. (5. 293)

This in turn is only a local reflection of the oppressive atmosphere of the first years of Stalinism. There are several pointed references to the 'conditions of the times' (5. 140, 218). Some indication of what these might be is given by the frequent references to malicious denunciations,[28] telephone tapping (5. 216), the following of citizens by police agents and worse: 'The news of his arrest was completely unexpected, but for some reason nobody was surprised by it' (5. 237).[29] In fact many of the changes and cuts made to the *Novyy mir* text before the novel was released in book form were designed to moderate these expressions of anger and bitterness. The following anecdote about an amateur who had written in to volunteer a site in Siberia for Skutarevsky's experiment was, not surprisingly, curtailed before being reprinted:

> They tried to trace the local antiquarian, they mailed letters, and according to the latest information it transpired that he was a mechanic, a former exile, who had long ago settled here, fifty-eight years old, married, all his taxes paid up, not convicted of any compromising family relationships, never involved in trade, a member of the union ... *As soon as it received the enquiry the local administration took the precaution of immediately sealing off his little meteorological station and putting the man himself under lock and key until his case could be heard. In fact he spent only two months inside, and to general delight actually put on some weight...*[30]

The narrator of *Skutarevsky* is often ironic and likes to pretend to a naive failure to understand the significance of what he is reporting: 'Admittedly, just a week before a certain harmless, even rather amusing episode had occurred in the institute, but one would have had to be insanely suspicious to draw any conclusions from it' (5. 183). The episode in question is the disappearance of one of Skutarevsky's notebooks from his office. The notebook does reappear, and so the episode is indeed 'harmless'; but the suggestion that one of the would-be saboteurs is the culprit makes the 'insanely suspicious' seem normal enough in Soviet conditions. Thus Leonov contrives to comment on the spy-mania of the period, while leaving it open as to whether or not there was any justification for it.

This sardonic attitude may be taken as a reflection of Skutarevsky's own hypersensitivity, but its prevalence throughout the book suggests that the author also shares these feelings. There is a whole series of running jokes about the fecklessness of Russian citizens and workers, and the shoddiness of Soviet products, cigarette-ends in the bread (5. 10, 116), nettles in the tobacco (5. 107), jam made out of seaweed and bones (5. 11), shellac in the wine (5. 54). The names of some of the episodic characters, Podushkin (pillow), Butylkin (button), Shirinkin (trouser-fly), suggest a Gogolian derision at human ordinariness. This tone is particularly marked in the *Novyy mir* version of the novel. When Shtruf offers to help Skutarevsky out of his family problems by finding him an apartment, the scientist tells him to 'chuck these *bordello* games, *but strangely he still did not dare raise his hand against this repulsive piece of meat stuffed with vodka and sperm.*'[31] The italicized words were omitted from the book version of the novel (see 5. 135).

As this last quotation suggests, Skutarevsky shares the disgust with sexuality that has been seen in Pal'chikov, Uvad'ev, and Maronov.[32] In this case there is some motivation in the memory of his seduction by Anna Petrygina and the disastrous marriage that it led to, but it also puts him on his guard against Zhenya. When she suggests that she might work as his personal secretary, he treats it as a sexual invitation: 'I have hardly any personal affairs' (5. 132). At the end of the novel, after the failure of his experiment, she offers herself to him, in the hope of restoring his self-confidence. The scene is introduced thus:

> Life that had given him mobility was like this: a cat stealthily crossing the moonlit field outside his window; it was thinner than its own shadow. At the dark edge of the park it made a sudden jump and then an agonizing wail pierced the silence. It was answered by another; her tousled lover was about the size of an Arctic fox. The two shadows approached and Skutarevsky turned away. At that very moment Zhenya came in; carefully, with her whole body she closed the door behind her. (5. 286)

As the first clause shows the scene is presented through the perception of Skutarevsky,[33] and the emphasis on 'her whole body,' has the effect of reinforcing this sense of physical revulsion. Rather strangely, beside these specific instances of sexuality, Leonov's work also contains such passages as the beginning of *The Sot'*, with its highly erotic depiction of the awakening of nature in spring, and the true significance of Fedor Skutarevsky's picture lies in its artistic representation of eroticism. There is a difference, evidently, between the ideal and the reality in Leonov's conception of sexual attraction, a gulf that he will try to bridge in his next novel.

Leonov's favourite technique for creating irony, however, is his use of indirect speech. Throughout his work there is a tendency to avoid direct authorial intervention in the narrative. In his early stories he uses the *skaz* type of narrator; in *The Sot'* he had dissociated the author from many of the views expressed by his Communist heroes; in *Skutarevsky* he discovers the possibilities of reported speech filtered through another consciousness and uses it to slide almost imperceptibly between the voices of the author and his characters:

> In particular Ivan Petrovich, who could not fail to notice the exaggerated interest in him shown by Cherimov, began to visit him. Affecting an intense intellectual confusion, which Cherimov could not refuse to help him with, he, who was certainly no chatterbox, expatiated unstoppably about his colleagues, about Skutarevsky, with whom he had finally broken, and about his work. Cherimov absorbed all this information with an air of polite interest and indebtedness; there was so much that he did not understand in this unfamiliar milieu. Ivan Petrovich would be thoughtful, often he would argue passionately for the need for the ideological re-education of the engineering community, and at times he would betray a tendency to raise alarming questions:
>
> 'Tell me, Nikolay Semenovich, do you still believe in the world revolution? And you don't feel burnt out?' and his dark and sticky gaze would envelop Cherimov.
>
> He liked to attach a significant almost Shakespearean tone to his tricksy question, which he calculated could not fail to flatter this ignorant upstart from the working classes; actually, Ivan Petrovich did not entrust his views even to his wife. (5. 123–4)

In his early *skaz* stories Leonov seemed to enter the skin of the speaker and to allow another individuality to emerge, but here the narration is monophonic and leaves no room for the emergence of a truly other voice. The passage begins as authorial and authoritative narration. 'Affecting an intellectual confusion' is the author's comment, but the expression 'he, who was certainly no chatterbox' is clearly Gerodov's opinion of himself; it is immediately contradicted by the author – 'expatiated unstoppably' (*vovse ne boltun, bez umolku...*). The narrative voice may seem to be continually shifting between author and character but Leonov retains firm control of the narrative, much as we do when retailing anecdotes about our friends or colleagues. We mimic their voices, their catchphrases, but even while pretending to let them 'speak,' we impose our interpretation on their words and the impression they hope to create. Leonov often underlines this effect by a blatant stylistic discord, such as the intrusion of vulgarisms into literary speech, or the pretentious insertion of Western words into a predominantly Slavic vocabulary, for example, *obyknovennyy, obyvatel'skiy konversas'on* (an ordinary trivial *causerie*, 5. 185).

The device is well suited to exposing the hypocrisy and self-deception of the villains Petrygin and Gerodov, and the depiction of strained friendships such as that between Petrygin and Skutarevsky. It is more problematic when applied to naive and innocent characters like Zhenya:

> When her provincial imagination conceived its first imprecise pictures of the future she saw a happy smartly dressed crowd in the huge and brilliant squares where the electric streetcars moved soundlessly beneath the steel constructions and scaffolding, among the lush and gleaming greenery and the statues, which would any moment now clear their throats and start a thunderous evening of reminiscences, in the light of the illuminated banners, glorifying the stern and unsmiling names and the decision of the latest congress of Soviets at the end of the Second Five-Year Plan. (5.130)

Here too the narration blends authorial and reported speech; the use of the colloquial expression *togo glyadi* (any moment now) clearly signals an attempt to convey Zhenya's thoughts and way of expressing herself. The author thus dissociates himself from the political pieties of the final phrases, which recall Potemkin's dreams of the workers' refectories. Their naïveté reflects also the limitations of Soviet education, a recurrent theme in Leonov's work.

Like *The Thief*, *Skutarevsky* is held together by the central figure, his character, and the ideas associated with him. Skutarevsky too is surrounded by 'doubles' representing different possibilities of development. The use of these 'doubles' is reinforced by a complex system of leitmotivs. These are not simply devices for individualizing and characterizing the various personages as they had been in *The Sot'*, but play an important structural role in tracing the development of Skutarevsky and his relationships to the other characters. One of the most important of these images is the 'mountain.' This first appears as a symbol of Skutarevsky's solitude, his single-mindedness, his exalted intellect, but it also suggests his refusal to commit himself and his wilful self-isolation. He shares this image with the bathhouse attendant Matvey Cherimov, uncle of the young Communist hero. He too has refused to commit himself to the Communist cause, even though he fully appreciates both the iniquities of the Tsarist regime and the achievements of the Communist party, but he is swept into the new age when he is elected local representative at a rather farcical election. Skutarevsky later meets the transformed Matvey and this moment plays a large part in his own eventual conversion, which Leonov compares to the sensation of descending a steep mountain (5. 304). On the other hand the young Party careerist Cherimov is explicitly aiming higher: 'even after scaling this lofty mountain he suffered as yet from no shortness of breath' (5. 73). This new, ambivalent assessment of the image is to be developed in Leonov's later works.

The image of the mountain is gradually displaced by the image of the tree. This first appears in the scene of Skutarevsky's delirium at the beginning of the novel. Skutarevsky is tormented by the prospect of old age, of a new generation completing his work and regarding his achievements as mere stepping stones. The image is given a deeper meaning by setting the novel over a time span extending from an autumnal September[34] to a triumphant close in spring, on May day. Skutarevsky himself is the tree: the old leaves, his outmoded loyalty to his family and his remaining traces of bourgeois ideology, must fall before the new ones can grow. For Skutarevsky this is an agonizing process. Only his love for Zhenya gives him faith to endure:

> ... he hid away this timid seed even deeper in himself, as though to increase the chances of its growing one day into a new tree, heavy with birdsong and leafy branches; the soil of Skutarevsky was still fertile. (5. 198)

Leonov opposes the mountain and the tree with the 'wind,' an image usually associated with youth and rejuvenation. This image too has a double aspect. The concept of the 'wind of electrons' (5. 212) forms the basis of Skutarevsky's materialist philosophy. At the same time he is pursued by a different wind, the wind of new ideas and attitudes which he is unwilling or unable to accept.

> bewildered, half-thought-out ideas, cast-off ambitions floundering in it, sounds, people, things, and finally the uttermost secrets that people encode and hide away even from themselves. (5. 12)

This wind is personified in the figure of Zhenya, and here Leonov's often ironic presentation of the girl suggests the simplifications and sacrifices required of Skutarevsky.

Skutarevsky's only hobby is playing the bassoon. Less obviously literary than the other images, it too serves to characterize him and mark the stages of his development. From the start Leonov stresses the eccentric character of the instrument and is ironic at the expense of Skutarevsky's amateur technique; but at the same time the bassoon represents one of the few lifelines leading out of his isolation. He plays duets, even if only with the saboteur Gerodov, and confides in his instrument as if it were a diary. Leonov describes these soliloquies as 'something like a brawl or even fighting with a phantom. No doubt this was the melody of his fate' (5. 23).

In the early part of the book the bassoon is associated with Skutarevsky's attitude to his family and the beginning of his rebellion against the conventional morality with which they protect themselves.

> And now it was born and took the form of a little homunculus... it was a mixture of a child's fairy stories and an old man's fears, merciless as murderers. It bore the likeness of Skutarevsky himself, but ludicrously diminished... Now *it* came out of his room... and moved with fists clenched in the direction of [his wife's] room, ready to smash it. (5. 109)

When he falls in love with Zhenya the bassoon sings of this rite of spring. Finally Skutarevsky returns to his bassoon for the last time after the failure of his experiment. It proves to have been only a stage in his development, which he has now outgrown: 'The valves gobbled at the air brokenly and feebly as though the angry little homunculus who had inhabited this magic pipe was dead' (5. 292).

Leonov's creative heroes are frequently accompanied by images of flying. Vekshin's defiance of the NEP is paralleled by his sister's acrobatic turn, the *shtrabat*. The brilliant Potemkin flies out of the Sot' to his death. Skutarevsky even drives his car as though it were an aeroplane; at the wheel he reflects: 'Flight – that's man's natural state; everything else is just a blasphemous lowering of the norm. Flight – that's the only way to die' (5. 96). The idea of flight is closely connected with the idea of danger, which stresses both the defiance and the heroism involved. For the Vekshins flight is tragic; for Skutarevsky it merely enhances the value of his work. He tells Khanshin, one of his assistants: 'You're a pedant; you're afraid of risks. But the Bolsheviks too took a risk in 1917' (5. 235). Skutarevsky's flights, however, are well insured, and a safety net is waiting for him as it never was for the Vekshins.

As in *The Sot'* and *Locusts* Leonov is searching for a style to convey the ethos of the First Five-Year Plan. Skutarevsky's son Arseniy is guilty, like Maronov, of looking back to the heroic feats of the Civil War, but Cherimov argues that the present is no less heroic: 'We make our own romanticism' (5. 75). Leonov seems to share this enthusiasm: in an article, which is closely related to *Skutarevsky*, he relates some of the extraordinary feats of Soviet workers under appalling conditions and concludes that only romanticism could do justice to such a reality: 'Romanticism is the hormone that raises the artist's craft to the level of true art. All art, if it is not to degenerate into petty naturalism must be romantic.'[35]

Accordingly the narrative is geared to a high pitch of intensity. At times it relapses into the novelettish excesses of *Locusts*: 'Time was catastrophically short' (5. 249),[36] but on the whole it now proceeds more logically from the character and interests of the central hero. Thus the vocabulary with its fondness for such words as 'matter' and 'substance,' 'atoms,' and 'molecules' leads the reader to perceive events and problems through Skutarevsky's eyes. In a revealing aside the narrator remarks that Skutarevsky's son was closer to him 'in his material substance' (*po veshchestvu*), where one would expect the word 'essence' (*po sushchestvu*) (5. 215). Even Arseniy's death is described in these terms:

> His substance was cooling and fading; it was undergoing a metamorphosis; it no longer appealed to itself; it wanted to enter the fields, the spaces, to dissolve in acids and winds, so that it could break out once again, whether as a tree, a cloud, or a simple little daisy, it didn't matter what. The complex salts were breaking up, the magnetic fields failing, the cell losing its electric charge. (5. 246)

Accordingly the novel is written in a style very similar to Skutarevsky's own. Events are not narrated by him in the first person, but, as it were, over his shoulder. Hence the extreme subjectivity of such observations as 'There was a tiresome autumn drizzle, or perhaps there wasn't.'[37] Even if Skutarevsky himself is not present at a certain scene the reader still sees events through his eyes and comes to his conclusions.

The narrative technique of the novel, its use of concrete images for conveying abstract ideas, and the interweavings of the various elements of the plot, relates Skutarevsky's materialist philosophy to Leonov's own conviction of the interconnectedness of all phenomena. The system of interlocking leitmotivs such as the 'mountain,' the 'tree,' and the 'bassoon,' thus plays an important structural role; indeed there is hardly a sentence in the entire novel which does not connect with one in another chapter. These images are used with extraordinary fluidity, and enable the narrative to move between different temporal and spatial levels with an ease that can be compared to the symphonic interludes in Wagnerian music-drama.

The most elaborate demonstration of this technique is chapter 18.[38] It opens with Cherimov's decision to visit Skutarevsky. He arrives when the professor is out negotiating with Petrygin and starts talking to Zhenya. Mme Skutarevsky meanwhile is eavesdropping on them and a lengthy digression now traces her recent history, her discovery that her collection of antiques is worthless, and her hostility to Zhenya. This in turn leads Leonov to clarify the relationship between Skutarevsky and the girl, and so return to the present of Cherimov and Zhenya. Soon afterwards Skutarevsky arrives home, and Leonov embarks on a description of his meeting with Petrygin only to drop it in order to introduce a new idea, Skutarevsky's fear that his wife might commit suicide. Finally he relates how Skutarevsky turned down Petrygin's offer and returned home. Most of the transitions in this chapter take place in mid-paragraph, thus further illustrating the fluidity of the narrative, but in spite of the seeming complexity of these methods the novel is surprisingly easy to follow.[39] Leonov never loses control of his digressions, and their place in the formal design is always clear. *Skutarevsky* is the most brilliant example of his formal mastery; the later novels are simpler and looser in their construction.

Like all Leonov's novels, *Skutarevsky* has its own individual sound; almost every one of its sentences, taken out of context, can be identified without difficulty.[40] It is characterized by a certain edgy nervous quality, partly created by the constant cinematic shifting from one setting to another, partly by a recurrent sardonic, irritable kind of humour that is integral to the book's main theme. For in many ways *Skutarevsky* is a bold challenge to the Party's attempt to muzzle and manipulate intellectuals for political ends. The conflict between the dogmas of ideology and the truths of science and art is eternal. Galileos are as suspect to the Kremlin as they had been to the Vatican.

The novel is memorable primarily for its many striking details, the contemptuous asides, the chapter on Fedor, and the brilliance of the language and the construction. But as a whole it is less satisfactory. This is most evident in the episode of the fox-hunt, a superb and gripping passage in its own right, which is then followed by a hasty retreat from the dangerous implications that the scene has threatened to raise. The surface conformism of Skutarevsky's 're-education' sits uneasily on top of these less orthodox themes. He reaches his predetermined end but his final conversion is hardly the logical outcome of the preceding events. The profound shocks, the treachery of his family, the failure of his experiment, the collapse of his mechanistic philosophy, and the loss of Zhenya do not in themselves suffice to explain why Skutarevsky becomes a Communist. Leonov's very success in creating the character makes such a transformation inconceivable.

The novel belongs very much to its time. Its sympathetic depiction of some members of the older intelligentsia reflects the repudiation of RAPP's anti-intellectualism in the month before the first instalment was published in *Novyy mir*. The attacks in the press that greeted the completed novel herald the restoration of RAPP attitudes and policies, albeit under another name and with the backing of the Party, in the autumn of the same year. Soon after the novel appeared a leading scientist declared that Leonov had completely misunderstood the problems of the intelligentsia.[41] Two months later a discussion of the novel was launched in the press. Two critics attacked the novel bitterly and uncritically;[42] a third attempted a rather weak defence of Leonov on both literary and political grounds.⁴³ Feelings were apparently running high, since two further discussions were called to establish the 'correct' attitude to the novel.

At the first,⁴⁴ the speakers seem to have divided into two factions. The former 'Serapion brother' and formalist, Shklovsky, and the party hacks, Kirpotin and Ermilov, found themselves allied in attacking the book, though from different standpoints. Leonov's supporters seem to have come from neither of the extreme wings and to have been more moderate in their claims. They were more outspoken at the second meeting, however; one of them asked why Leonov's novels should be singled out for special attack when their superiority to the mass of Soviet fiction was clearly marked,⁴⁵ and Leonov's detractors correspondingly moderated their tone. The editorial comment called for further opinions but apparently none were forthcoming; none at least were printed.

In view of the critics' strictures on the novel it is interesting to note that in another discussion held by workers and engineers the novel, apart from the patronizing suggestion that Leonov should make a thorough study of the works of Marx, Engels, and Lenin, was warmly received. Leonov himself was present and thanked the speakers for their 'serious, profound, and friendly' criticism. He admitted to certain 'mistakes and obscurities and promised that his next novel would be a better one.⁴⁶ After these partial justifications articles continued to appear throughout 1933 but without any particular intensity in approval or denunciation. The discussions were temporarily renewed by the appearance of a dramatized version⁴⁷ of the novel on the stage of the Malyy Theatre.

Leonov claimed that *Skutarevsky* had originally been conceived in dramatic form, but that he had reshaped it as a novel once he had seen the possibilities of Skutarevsky's painter brother, Fedor.⁴⁸ Serious work on the play, therefore, was only begun after the completion of the novel. The material was substantially rearranged; certain minor characters were introduced and others combined or omitted, but the basic situations and speeches are obviously the same. The fact that the play ends in a blaze of light with the success of Skutarevsky's experiment is simply a concession to the need for a spectacular finale and does not represent any ideological reinterpretation of the subject.

The most serious deprivation is the loss of Leonov's narrative. In the novel this carries the majority of the images and the main development. Some of the narrative was slightly rewritten in the form of stage directions, but the spectator in the theatre can hardly be aware of this. The character of Skutarevsky himself, as might be expected, suffers particularly severely, and his importance as the structural centre disappears. As with the dramatized version of *The Badgers* the psychological interest of the novel has been largely replaced by a social and political approach. Rybnikov, who created the role of Skutarevsky at the first production, won almost universal praise for his interpretation, but it is plain that his interpretation was based on the text of the novel, not of the play. The play was performed frequently in the 1930s and has been revived since the war with considerable success. Most Soviet critics, in fact, preferred it to the original novel.[49]

chapter seven

The Road to Ocean 1935

'Are you, are you, sweet Alesha. to become the unknown leader of the pack of wolves?'

The Breakthrough at Petushikha

The earliest ideas for *The Road to Ocean*[1] can be traced back to 1927, when Leonov shared his plans for the novel with Gor'ky in Sorrento. He did not begin work on the novel, however, until 1933, and it was completed only in 1935. In its subject matter it is loosely related to its predecessors, *The Sot'* and *Skutarevsky*, and in some respects it is even more topical than they were.

The action of the novel takes place between the autumn of 1933 and the spring of 1934, and the immediate context is the major purge of the Party that began in January 1933 and reduced the membership from over three and a half million to under two million in less than a year. Other contemporary issues such as the criminalization of abortions, the recent decision to appoint commissars on the railways, the role of the national minorities in the Soviet Union, and the current criticisms of Meyerkhol'd's innovations in the theatre are all worked into the design. The assassination of Kirov on 1 December 1934 and the ensuing purge fall outside the time frame of the novel, but for the reader of 1935 they too were inevitably part of the background.

The literary context is also important. *The Road to Ocean* is the first of Leonov's novels to be written after the proclamation of socialist realism as the method of Soviet literature. Although this doctrine was formally announced only in August 1934 at the Congress of Soviet Writers, discussions about it had been going on for at least two years. Many of the formulations were vague (e.g., the 'depiction of society in its revolutionary development,' 'socialist in content, national in form') and served less as specific guidelines than as slogans that could be used to approve or condemn works and their authors as the political climate might require. Rather more consequential was the demand for the portrayal of a 'positive hero,' meaning by this primarily an ideal Communist. The notion revived a dream of several critics and novelists of the nineteenth century,[2] and perhaps this made it more acceptable to the writers, artists, and composers of Soviet Russia in the 1930s.

The problem with the 'positive hero' is the expectation that he should counter the traditionally passive, self-analytical hero of the central works of the Russian literary tradition and offer a more active, constructive model. The art of literature is almost by definition better suited to the former, and this is one reason why the 'positive' heroes of Russian nineteenth-century literature, like Shtol'ts in Ivan Goncharov's *Oblomov* (1859) and Rakhmetov in Chernyshevsky's *What Is to Be Done?* (*Chto delat'?*, 1863), seem so unappealing. The same reservations apply even more strongly to the positive heroes of Soviet fiction, for the paramount Communist virtue of devotion to the Party involves, even in the most sanitized treatments, acts of disturbing inhumanity.

Leonov's solution to these difficulties is to show his hero, Aleksey Nikitich Kurilov, a newly appointed commissar for the railways, struck down by a fatal illness. His party activities, however unsavoury, can be assigned to the past and not examined too closely, while the novel concentrates on his attempts to come to terms with dying and death. At the beginning of the novel he has just arrived to investigate a series of accidents on the Volgo-Revizan' railway.[3] His initial suspicions of sabotage are reinforced by chance encounters with the one-time White officer Gleb Protoklitov and the now impoverished former factory director Omelichev, but his illness prevents him pursuing them in person, and at the end of the novel he dies after an apparently successful operation. The search for the saboteurs is left to the younger generation; the repairs to the railway line are left to the imagination. Thus the initial narrative impulse gradually fades into the background.

Marxism sees man in economic terms. Men and women who do not work are either exploiters or parasites. But what of those who are incapacitated or dying? For these universal experiences Christianity offers some answers, but what sense can Communism make of them? Uvad'ev had had little use for the dying Potemkin, once the driving force behind the project on the Sot', but now reduced to a 'thing' (a word all the more offensive for Leonov's regular use of it as a symbol of the bourgeoisie): 'If only people were made of rubber, eh? Break something, and off you go to a machine [...] and in half an hour a new man comes trotting out in his running shorts, eh?' (4. 231).[4] Skutarevsky had simply dismissed the thought of death by declaring that 'real life begins when you haven't got time to die' (5. 281), but Kurilov's predicament exposes the emptiness of this boast. In a culture where work is the only criterion for judging the value of a life, his forced inactivity seems to nullify the whole of his long and loyal service to the Party.[5] Communism is clear enough about what it requires from its subjects; it is much vaguer on what it can give them. Does it do nothing but fit a man to work for the cause? In *The Road to Ocean* Leonov once more raises the question, already broached in *The Breakthrough at Petushikha* and *The Sot'*, of how far Communism can take the place of religion.

Coincidentally, *The Road to Ocean* was written at the same time as Nikolay Ostrovsky's *How the Steel Was Tempered* (*Kak zakalyalas' stal'*, 1934–6), whose hero Pavel Korchagin was also struck down by illness and death. The novel is told in a straightforward linear manner, with special attention being focused on Korchagin's activities as a Party member (like Kurilov he has spent most of his active life on the railways); his final illness and death occupy only a few pages. Although the name of the hero has been changed and the narrative is written in the third person, the book is in fact autobiographical. For non-Communist readers the infallibility of the hero creates a somewhat priggish impression, while the explicit approval of actions that would be impossible to justify except by the demands of Party discipline is likely to alienate all but committed readers. For all that it should be recognized that *How the Steel Was Tempered* is the perfect socialist-realist novel. Although the hero may seem impossibly idealized the patently autobiographical element is guarantee of his reality, thus bridging the apparently incompatible requirements of the genre. *How the Steel Was Tempered* was not only studied in schools; it became a genuinely popular book and acquired the status of a quasi-religious text; even in the Khrushchev period it was possible to meet Communists who claimed to have modelled themselves on the hero. Thus *How the Steel Was Tempered* met Marx's demands for philosophy in that it did not merely 'contemplate the world but helped to change it.'

Despite the surface similarities, however, the two books offer fundamentally different answers. Leonov was later to write: 'The critics reproached me for not having shown Kurilov at work. I replied: "The railway is going badly, but a leading Bolshevik appears and all goes well again. That's the usual solution to the problem. I wanted to take a man with a vast inner world, tear him out of his usual setting and leave him quite alone. It's much harder for a man to bear with himself in solitude [...] That's when you see what a man is really worth." '[6] In the opening scenes Kurilov is shown as an efficient and even ruthless administrator in the tradition of Uvad'ev and Cherimov. The incompetent officials at the crash site are disconcerted to discover that 'this man with the shoulders of a stevedore and the brow of a Socrates had sent one man for trial, and on his own authority had put three others inside for stretches of varying lengths. In the past he had been a soldier in grey, one whom the age had taught to be pitiless' (6. 8).[7]

Like other Communist literary heroes Kurilov has had no time for any private life. His relationship with his wife had been 'a strictly honourable and sober friendship' (6. 30) and totally subordinated to his work. He does not spend any time with her as she lies dying or even attend her funeral. He 'had always had far too much respect for her ever to be happy with her' (6. 365), and they had had no children. Indeed in the opening pages he is shown as actively disliking children, and he is frequently annoyed by the presence of a courting couple who invariably take up their position outside his window wherever he happens to be. As the novel unfolds, however, he becomes more tolerant, even of children, and eventually he actually falls in love; in the epilogue, when his friends and disciples visit Ocean without him, their last impression is of a couple embracing.

Where Korchagin uses every minute of his last remaining days to advise and admonish younger Communists, Leonov makes little attempt to show his hero at work; instead Kurilov is thrown back on himself. At first he tries to reassure himself with thoughts of an anonymous immortality through the continuing lives of his friends, but ultimately it is neither his work nor his influence but his inner world, his vision of Ocean, that justifies him.

The image of Ocean can be interpreted on several planes. In the first place it is connected with Kurilov's childhood fascination with the sea and his dreams of becoming a sailor. At the same time it recalls Russia's historical struggles to find an outlet to warm waters: the eventual destination of the Volgo-Revizan' railway is Ocean, a Utopian city of the future, to be built on the site of the present Shang-hai. Kurilov and the narrator pay imaginary visits to this city, 'three and a half-thousand kilometres away, a mere ten-minute walk' (6. 110). It is thus natural to equate Ocean with the 'ocean of Communism into which the rivers of history will flow,' and accordingly the victorious general in the final triumph of Communism over capitalism is named Yang-Tse, the river on which Shang-hai stands. But to Kurilov Ocean is not simply the world-state of the future, but the condition of each member of that state. He himself traverses the road to Ocean, and serves as that road for others. He is compared to a 'lofty bridge over a mighty river, whose estuary reached out into the ocean. Yes, he was like a bridge, and people crossed over him into the future...' (6. 369). Each of his three collapses is juxtaposed with a chapter devoted to Ocean. Like Job he has been stripped of everything, his health, his work, and his presumed purpose in life, but he never betrays his faith: 'it was not with yesterday's but tomorrow's eyes that he looked at people' (6. 16).[8]

The image of Ocean carries the main philosophical burden of the novel. It represents an idea that is fundamental to Leonov and which can be traced back to *The Brothers Karamazov*: 'for everything is like the ocean; everything is connected and in a state of flux; if you touch it in one place it will have its effect on the other side of the world.'[9] In the infinite chain of interactions that can be observed in the movements of the sea Leonov sees a parallel to the seamless web of the universe. Marina, as she struggles to compile Kurilov's biography, observes: 'Truly one would have to recreate the whole world in order to isolate the existence of a single grain of sand' (6. 271).[10] This belief had been foreshadowed in Vekshin's dilemma over which chair he should sit on; it forms the foundation of Skutarevsky's materialist philosophy; in *The Road to Ocean* and in Leonov's subsequent works it becomes part of the philosophical underpinnings. In Ocean this property of matter is commercially exploited in 'amazing complex combines where everything was manufactured out of everything, for the substance of all matter is one and the same and everything can be found everywhere' (6. 371).

The interdependence of all phenomena is exemplified not only in space but in time, and its symbol is the photograph:

> It was a large photograph taken on the terrace of the house in Borshchnya on the day of the opening of the railway. On the back the date and the names of those in the party had been recorded. This particular document had suffered more than all the others: some spoilt child had embellished it to suit his own tastes [...] Peresypkin spent a long time sponging off this artless commentary [...] all these people were now dead and buried [...] Those times too were dead, but yet the moment had been preserved, sealed on silver bromide paper [...] the champagne that had intoxicated their brains had since then served as a cloud and a puddle and a wet snowball in the hands of a child; it had ascended into the heavens for the sole purpose of sparkling in one of the arcs of a rainbow; it had poured out of the eyes of a woman in pain or the bladder of some animal; it had made its way into the murky depths of the earth, pulverizing the rocks in its path, to re-emerge unrecognizable in a sun-filled bunch of grapes. And so through thousands of channels inaccessible to the intellect, it would finally flow into the shimmering ever wakeful Ocean. Matter passed dynamically through all these ghosts, who spread out their arms vainly trying to catch and arrest it. (6. 180–1)[11]

The structure of the novel also embodies this idea. The very first paragraph of the novel begins: 'Talking to a friend does not bring back one's youth' (6. 7). The 'friend' proves to be a railway carriage which Kurilov had used during the Civil War and which he now re-encounters as the base for his investigation. It may not bring back his youth, but it is material proof of the power of the past over the present. The paragraph ends with the ominous words: 'The circle was closing,' again relating the past and the future.

On the narrative level it is illustrated by excursions into the past, a peasant rebellion in the nineteenth century, and the future, the last battles before the attainment of Communism, and finally a visit to Ocean. But the past, for all its injustice and misery, cannot be ignored; it not only contains the seeds of the future, but continues to exist within it. Leonov illustrated this idea by the following diagram:

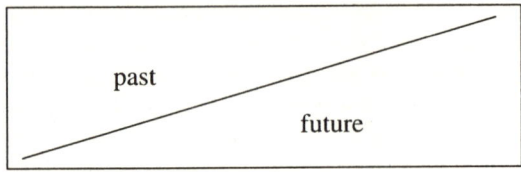

where the diagonal line represents the present. At the beginning the past is dominant, but as time passes so it diminishes, though without ever disappearing completely. Other events, which seemed important at the time, diminish, almost, but not quite, into nothingness in the light of the future. Thus, for example, the historian Peresypkin, looking for traces of Pokhvisnev in Ocean wants only to gaze 'into his faded eyes; perhaps at the very bottom there might be some reflection there of the incident on the river Psna' (6. 511). Formally the idea is illustrated by the copious use of footnotes in the chapters devoted to the past and the future: 'If our descendants are commentaries on us, then we are commentaries on our descendants.'[12]

The past is like a compost heap, constantly absorbing new amounts of material, breaking them down, and recombining them to create new forms of life. It is this conviction that underlies Leonov's scepticism about Communism and all other ideologies. He rejects any teleological view of history;[13] it is not working towards any predetermined end. Leonov observes of a blazing fire: 'Like everything in the world it was not a thing but a process' (6. 294). This constant flux means that no one view of events or people can hope to do justice to them. This is not because there is no such thing in Leonov's view as objective truth, rather that it is so complex as to be unattainable; but the photograph, however mutilated it may be, can still provide some information.

One way of conveying this complexity is through a variety of viewpoints and, although the greater part of the novel is narrated by an impersonal, apparently omniscient narrator, there are several figures in it who are actively engaged in writing histories of one kind or another. Marina Sabel'nikova is writing a biography of Kurilov, Aleksey Peresypkin is writing a history of the origins of the Volgo-Revizan' railway, the main narrator listens to the monologue of the historian Volchikhin. All these narrators discover that historiography is not so simple. Volchikhin's tale of the rise and fall of the Omelichev merchant dynasty contained elements of 'the heroic folk tale (*bylina*), of a criminal record and an economic investigation' (6. 228). So too Peresypkin's history covers not just the technicalities of railway engineering, but a peasant rising, a financial scandal, and an absurd love affair.

The most important of these secondary narrators, however, is the 'I,' who appears unexpectedly after some twelve chapters of traditional third-person narration: 'Winking at me to show I should wait for him, Kurilov...' (6. 109). This belated introduction of an narratorial 'I'[14] suggests that he is only another fictional character under the control of the overall narrator rather like Firsov in *The Thief*. He is a writer[15] and a personal friend of Kurilov, but he is presented as a simple, even naive observer who is perpetually being rebuked by his hero for his romanticizing tendencies. He is modest about his own qualities in the presence of the dominating Communist hero: 'all that is best in these sessions belongs to [Kurilov]; mine are only the imprecisions, the trinkets of imagery and the omissions inevitable in any paraphrase' (6. 111). He seems to accept Kurilov's opinions as infallible and binding. Thus in the text he observes (in parentheses): '(The constructor of our age is made out of the dreamer and the art of living has always been compounded out of the ability to look ahead),' but adds in a footnote: ' "Wrong, scribbler", Kurilov corrected me. "The constructor realizes not a dream but a cast-iron inevitability." I willingly agreed with him' (6. 110–1). As they argue over the likely causes for the future world revolution 'we agreed that it was the final goal that was all-important and not the preliminary variations' (6. 115), in direct contradiction of Leonov's own preference for process over goals and his distrust of 'cast-iron inevitabilities.'

The 'I''s modesty is thus ironic and Kurilov's certainties are unobtrusively contradicted:

> But, just as in creating his gods the savage endowed them with human characteristics, so we were unable to create a race of people distinct from our contemporaries. There too were to be found in due proportion the lazy, the envious, and the stupid. (I must make an exception here: Kurilov categorically denied the existence of dust, or flies, or accidents, or even that normal quantity of minor irritants that is inevitable in any human community.) (6. 118–19)

Kurilov, like Leonov's earlier Communists, Matvey and Chikilev in *The Thief*, Uvad'ev and Cherimov in the following novels, dreams of an oversimplified and sterilized Utopia. For Leonov, though, the sheer messiness of life is a guarantee of vitality, and the characteristic images of *The Thief* (the 'puddle' and 'dirt') that embody this theme reappear in *The Road to Ocean*.

On one of their trips to Ocean Kurilov and 'I' find themselves swept up by a giant vacuum cleaner; they are pinned to the wall and become an object of mockery to the inhabitants, and particularly the children. 'I' assumes that he is to blame, but in fact it is Kurilov's pipe (as his name suggests he is an inveterate smoker) that offends the sensibilities of the citizens. The whole episode is, of course, a product of 'I''s imagination, but such fantasy is quite unacceptable to the Communist:

> Kurilov categorically denied this incident. Apparently, he intended to turn the flying youngsters into well-brought-up, decently educated little goody-goodies.
>
> 'But you are trying to make a Christian Paradise out of our Ocean,' I cried, spitting out the muck that was flying into our faces. 'You want to populate it with cherubims and passionless statues. But let them have their fights, their sufferings, their separations... that's what life is.'
>
> '*You are slandering the children of the future, writer!*... And another thing, why are you always looking for dirt?'
>
> 'Well, if only because it indicates the presence of a living man. Man passes over the earth and leaves behind him his dirt, large and small, the ashes of his combustion.' And there was much else that I told him on this occasion. (6.119–20)[16]

The reference to Firsov's living man paradoxically redeems Kurilov. For all his horror of dirt, the visible evidence of human combustion, he blithely relights his pipe, impervious to the implications of the action that had got him into trouble in the first place.

For Leonov the novel, like the symphony for Mahler, must include the world. He prided himself on the immense range of his reading in the sciences, philosophy, religion, and cosmology. For his novels of the '30s he mastered the technical aspects of each new subject, the construction of a cellulose factory, the theoretical discussions of advanced physics, the administration of a railway, and the workings of a locomotive. Only a few years later (in his war story *The Taking of Velikoshumsk*) he was to impress army commanders with his detailed knowledge of the functioning and tactical possibilities of a tank. Only the artist, and specifically the novelist, is able to synthesize or, in Leonov's word, 'logarithmize' this mass of material. The successful author, and here Leonov's ideal is Dostoevsky, is the one who contrives to indicate the greatest number of 'coordinates' that plot a life. Above all the artist should not sanitize reality.

'Life,' in the words of *The Thief*, 'was wiser than all Firsov's ingenious combinations.' The good and the bad, the positive and the negative, the admirable and the deplorable, are inextricably intertwined.

The Communists, Uvad'ev and Cherimov, may 'forget with enviable ease,' but memory is the key to our humanity and any understanding of the past or the present is impossible unless this is recognized and accepted. The narrator, contemplating the horrors of the last wars before the attainment of communism, remarks ironically: 'No one could say whether there was more grandeur or more baseness in this inhuman tragedy. (What a good thing that the healthiest quality of the memory is to forget.)' (6. 112).

It is a hard lesson for Leonov's Communists to learn. Marina finds that Kurilov's account of his childhood and early years is hopelessly at odds with the myth-making requirements of Soviet propaganda.

> They would have sent her packing if she had noted down literally what he dictated to her. She needed something heroic, some concrete act of heroism or self-sacrifice. Like all her generation she romanticized the past, and the greater the gap between the old world and the new so the less the masters of old Russia were portrayed as people. (6. 122)

Kurilov cannot understand Peresypkin's determination to show the past from as many angles as possible:

> the Soviet system had so radically transformed all relationships, legal, financial, and the rest, that there was really no point in resurrecting the barbaric enactments of the nineteenth century. He even went so far as to say something to the effect that the history of the railway should be first and foremost the history of the revolutionary movement on it. (6. 177)

Even so, he recognizes that his protégé 'has devised a way of settling accounts with Russian history in artistic form. Determined to encourage by every means possible the development of the arts on railway themes, he facilitated Peresypkin's access to the railway archives' (6. 178). Kurilov's intentions may be good, but his view of art is very limited.[17]

Here Leonov restates Fedor Skutarevsky's rejection of 'that simplistic role-playing which was peddled under the guise of art for the masses' (6. 83). An (unidentified) play is condemned as a banal stereotype: 'The storyline had been deliberately simplified to the point of being a formula, and the spectators treated it as a fairy story, easily remembered and not requiring any thought from them. The content was easy to guess from the title [...] The fate of the cobbler was likewise obvious because plays with alternative solutions to their problems rarely made it on to the stage' (6. 193–4).

It is just such an alternative solution that Leonov offers in *The Road to Ocean*. It would seem from the early pages that Gleb Protoklitov was originally intended to play only a minor role in the novel, but in the second part of the book, as Kurilov's role diminishes, he comes to the fore. Before the Revolution Gleb's family had belonged to the upper bourgeoisie; his father was a judge who had once sentenced Kurilov to exile. Gleb himself was studying to be a railway engineer, but in 1918 he had been forcibly mobilized into the White Army where he had been engaged unsuccessfully in the pursuit of Kurilov. There are thus both general and personal reasons for the tension between the two men.

Since the Revolution Gleb has tried to rebuild his life; he has invented a blameless but fictitious past for himself, and he has worked hard for some ten years in railway administration. He has been so successful in this that when the novel opens he has been a member of the Party for some six years. But he is haunted by having lied in his *anketa*, the questionnaire that Soviet citizens were constantly required to answer.[18] Besides providing information about their own lives they were expected to indicate the social status of their parents and other family members, the existence of any relatives or friends in emigration, and any connections to officers of the White Army or ministers of the church.[19] Gleb is thus highly vulnerable: 'The accidents of his past were not enough to liquidate him physically but enough to make him stumble over them for the rest of his life' (6. 53).[20] Nor is he a popular figure; his arrogant manner and demanding standards have antagonized the workers. In an important sub-plot he opposes the Komsomol's insistence on making the unqualified Sayfulla an engine driver.[21] His misgivings are justified by events, but the Komsomol only regards him with greater suspicion as a result.

There is nothing, however, to suggest that Gleb's service on the railways has been disloyal.[22] Even his unsympathetic brother Il'ya, who has become a prominent Moscow surgeon, acknowledges him as 'a persevering man, uncomplainingly earning the right to live and have his mistakes forgotten' (6. 473). With the launching of a new purge, Gleb is at first tempted to reveal more about his past and throw himself on the mercy of the Party on the strength of his many years of unblemished work. The reappearance of Kurilov in his life makes this a much more risky course of action, and his situation becomes even worse when a long-forgotten fellow officer from the White Army unexpectedly resurfaces. Evgeniy Kormilitsyn begins with a letter asking for money, and before long he comes to live with Protoklitov. Gleb is forced to take him in and even find him a job. But when Kormilitsyn starts drinking and spreading insinuations about Gleb's past he tries and fails to murder him. Both men naturally turn to Moscow. Gleb appeals to his brother, who has been chosen to operate on Kurilov, and tells him that this is the man with whom Il'ya's ex-wife is now living; moreover, as the sons of a Tsarist judge they are both in danger should Kurilov live.

Kormilitsyn too flees to Moscow, in the hope of denouncing Gleb, but it is too late, for Kurilov is already in hospital. Instead he is referred to the surgeon, though he does not discover his name until later. Il'ya quickly grasps the situation; he feels no sympathy for Kormilitsyn, 'this failure who was no less guilty than the one [i. e., Gleb] whose head he had brought to Kurilov; his days too were numbered' (6. 472). But his attitude to his brother is also modified by this development: 'His friendly feeling for Gleb was breaking down into various fragments of pity and dubious sympathy, in which a certain censure was beginning to crystallize' (6. 473–4). Il'ya's first thought is to withdraw from the operation and he goes to the telephone to find another surgeon. 'Halfway there he turned back, but not at all because it was late, and the colleague who could have taken his place was already in bed' (6. 475). At first the operation seems to have been successful, but two days later Kurilov suddenly dies after a haemorrhage. Immediately afterwards Il'ya travels to Cheremshansk where he reveals Gleb's attempt to have Kurilov murdered, and smashes his false autobiography.

For a Soviet reader in 1935 (and indeed for the next twenty years) the issues would seem clear enough: Gleb is an unrepentant White officer whose aim in working on the railways is to attain a position of power and authority from which he can conduct his sabotage more effectively. Il'ya, by contrast, is a loyal though apolitical intellectual who unmasks his brother as soon as he understands his nefarious designs.[23] But Leonov has also provided enough evidence to suggest a different apportionment of blame and criminality, as more recent accounts of the novel have begun to admit.[24] Gleb's brother Il'ya is thoroughly bourgeois in his mentality and habits; indeed his collecting mania links him to the hoarder-saboteurs of *Skutarevsky*. And yet in spite of the death of Kurilov under his knife he is instantly redeemed; although he has kept quiet about Gleb for fifteen years his belated denunciation is accepted unquestioningly as evidence of a change of heart. It would seem more likely that by eliminating Kurilov and denouncing Gleb Il'ya is simply killing two birds with one stone. In this way Leonov presents a plot that can be read in two diametrically opposed ways.[25] The fact that Soviet readers would immediately assume the guilt of Gleb is itself a comment on the spirit of the times.

Gleb's character and his attempt to murder Kormilitsyn are unattractive, but less so than the characters and actions of his accusers, Kormilitsyn, Il'ya, and the embittered worker Gashin, whose chief allegation against Gleb is that he reads books on railway matters written in foreign languages. In fact his predicament is described with such intensity that one may suspect Leonov's personal identification with his fate:

> Of course it was mere chance that Gleb had once come home to his *father* for the *holidays* and the *town had been cut off by the Whites*, so that the student from the railway institute *found himself being mobilized in the name of restoring law and order*, so trampled by the Bolsheviks. [...] *The peaceful town suddenly found itself no longer deep in the rear but in the front line of the most dangerous of campaigns* [my italics]. It had become the capital of the Western Urals, and every inhabitant was to become familiar with the horrors of the Russian counter-revolution and later with the mechanisms of guerrilla warfare and the grim logic of the people's wrath. (6. 53)

If we transpose this passage from the western Urals to Archangel, the parallels with Leonov himself become obvious. He too had returned from school to his father in 1918, only to be cut off by the Civil War, while the medicine that he had hoped to study is given to Gleb's brother, Il'ya. The remote city of Archangel had then been in the front line, and during the White occupation Leonov had briefly attended a training school for young officers. His *anketa* was as incriminating as Gleb's. Leonov might seem to have redeemed himself by his service in the Red Army, but in the rising paranoia of Stalin's Russia this past remained a terrible liability and if any evidence of it had ever come to light he would have been arrested and executed. This compulsion to return to the crucial years and events in his own life just on the eve of the Great Purge explains Leonov's involvement in Gleb's fate. It also reveals something of the psychological processes underlying his fiction.

It is then significant that Gleb Protoklitov and Kurilov are in many respects doubles of one another. One might even say that they represent two versions of the same biography. Both have spent most of their lives working on the railways, and both are destroyed at the end of the novel. Kurilov's past is irreproachable, Gleb's on the other hand is a source of perpetual menace. Leonov even draws attention to their relationship. Gleb feels tied inextricably to the figure of Kurilov: 'He is like a great planet and I his insignificant satellite. For fifteen years I have been revolving round him and still I cannot break away' (6. 454). And so the news of 'Kurilov's death brought Gleb no joy. He experienced a feeling, inexplicable at first sight, not only of freedom but also of loneliness' (6. 498). The relationship between them is a parallel to the two lives that Leonov himself lived, his public face as a successful Soviet writer and his secret past in White-occupied Archangel.

In Soviet literature of the 1930s the portrayal of the opposition had always presented the author with a problem. How was it possible to provide a genuine and engrossing conflict while ensuring that the triumph of the Communist cause was never in doubt? Leonov's discovery of the type of the 'doomed hero' provides a brilliant solution to this problem.[26] He could not be accused of 'pessimism' since the inevitability of Gleb's eventual downfall prevents him from ever presenting any real threat. At the same time his predicament offers a psychological situation that Leonov was to continue to explore in later works. His life with its network of lies and concealment has become a mere shadow of life. Yet his deceptions are the direct consequence of Soviet policy towards 'class enemies' so that the situation is self-perpetuating and admits of no solution. His flight is not of his own choosing and in these circumstances his courage and individuality give him a tragic stature.

In *The Road to Ocean* Leonov intended to write a Soviet tragedy. Leonov has said several times: 'Every new hero must make his first appearance through tragedy.'[27] In Soviet aesthetics tragedy is a theoretical possibility, but in practice it falls foul of the propagandist demands of socialist realism, the assurance of a triumphal ending, and the victory of progressive forces. It is admissible only as 'optimistic tragedy' (the title of a play by Vsevolod Vishnevsky), in which the losses, though regrettable, are outweighed by the gains, as in a successful queen sacrifice in chess. In this respect Soviet artists are continuing, however simplistically, in the footsteps of such nineteenth-century masterpieces as Goethe's *Faust*, the music-dramas of Wagner, and Dostoevsky's *Crime and Punishment*. Kurilov's death too is an 'optimistic tragedy'; it may snuff out a life, but it enables him to discover how to live and to pass this on to the men and women around him.

This attempt to draw some consolation from tragedy seriously diminishes the central role that Leonov wants to give it:

> Here [in Ocean] man had attained his natural state; he was free to enjoy the fruit of his hands and brain without any exploitation by anyone. But although everything was theirs, work, bread, and even fate itself, we frequently came across people with careworn faces. We realized that they too could be sad and experience tragedies, but ones more worthy of man's lofty calling. (6. 371)

Careworn faces are hardly evidence of tragedy, while the idea of tragedies 'more worthy of man's lofty calling' seems to miss the point that the tragic hero is more often than not destroyed by forces that are *unworthy*. Would Kurilov's death be more tragic if it had been brought about by a heroic act of self-sacrifice?[28] If Leonov is bolder than most Soviet writers in treating the possibility of tragedy, he still hesitates before its starker implications.

In Leonov's view tragedy is a consequence of the limitless aspirations of human nature, and in his work it is generally associated with the idea of flight, as for example in the Vekshins in *The Thief*. In the defiance of gravity, the most inescapable of the natural forces, human aspirations find their highest fulfilment, both literally and symbolically. Potemkin the visionary who had conceived the project on the Sot', flies out to his death, Skutarevsky exults at the wheel of his car: 'Flight – that's the only way to die' (5. 96);[29] in *The Road to Ocean* Klavdiya, Kurilov's Old Bolshevik sister, embodies 'an unbending will to fly' (6. 480). The city of Ocean is 'the capital of men who fly naturally and effortlessly' (6. 118). The space flight that is the main subject of the third of the excursions into Ocean, is itself only an extension of Kurilov's own flights of imagination, though its tragic outcome (two of the three stratonauts die and the third is blinded), however painful at the time, is only a temporary setback.[30] It is then significant that the same image is extended to Gleb Protoklitov. Kurilov recognizes that he 'would make a good airman' (6. 45). If there is a tragedy in the classical sense in *The Road to Ocean* it is Gleb's, trapped as he is in a situation that is not of his making, but for which he has to pay the penalty.

The awareness of tragedy is the obverse of Leonov's distrust of happiness; dissatisfaction and suffering, even to the point of self-destruction, are far more creative and beneficent.[31] The idea that he found in Bukharin and Mayakovsky, and attributes to his Communists, Matvey and Chikilev, that happiness can be manufactured and planned, is utterly unacceptable to him. Since *The Thief* the theme of happiness had largely disappeared from Leonov's work. Skutarevsky had had no time to think about it and Uvad'ev seems to have regarded it as immoral. In *The Road to Ocean* it returns – Kurilov is a 'seeker of man's happiness' (6. 457) – and it is never far away in Leonov's later work. Many of the figures in the novel offer their definitions of happiness. The young Communist Shamin dismisses it in Uvad'ev-like terms:

> That word always annoys me. It has no social significance at all. Some people find it in their daily bread and butter, others in collecting antiques. If happiness is just the product of many factors which we will soon have learned how to mass-produce, then obviously everybody will be happy. (6. 299)

He goes on to describe happiness in terms of choosing clothes to match one's complexion, but, of course, 'the happiness of each individual must be consonant with the happiness of all the others' (6. 300).

Kurilov with his ascetic temperament feels that happiness is suspect unless it has been earned. He reminds Liza of her ambition to act the role of Mary Stuart:

> 'You told me once that your right to joy was to be found in this role. Fair enough: under socialism each man will be able to prove his right to joy by his activity.'

[*Liza*]. 'His right to joy or his right to bread?'

[*Kurilov*]. 'Don't confuse the issue. Even today all work entitles a man to bread, but only creativity to joy; and tomorrow all work will be creative.' (6. 284)[32]

But a happiness that has been 'earned,' as though it were some kind of service pension, that has become 'an entitlement,' is only another 'mechanical happiness,' and bears the same relationship to the real thing as a mechanical nightingale.

The rare moments of spontaneous unearned happiness are therefore worth examining. One of them is given to the Tatar Sayfulla, who celebrates his selection by the Komsomol to drive a new locomotive with a wild dance in the snow: 'Clouds, like snowdrifts, moved portentously overhead. This was happiness' (6. 335–6). The next day he crashes the new train. One might take this as punishment for his *hubris* in claiming an unearned happiness; but Leonov's point is that happiness is the more precious for its transience and vulnerability. This can be seen in the recurring motif of the courting couple that Kurilov finds so irritating. From the start the couple is associated with a tree, and at their first appearance Leonov explicitly invokes the story of Adam and Eve:

> A thick branch above them could be taken for the serpent of the biblical legend. Their whispers merged with the rustling of the foliage, and the couple in turn became a leaf, driven through the world by an irresistible force [...] At this point it would have been fun to put one's fingers in one's mouth and whistle, as the good Lord did on a certain occasion. That famous expulsion would then have been repeated, the enchantment of the garden would have faded, though the lovers would not be the losers so much as Kurilov. His curiosity was stirred for something that he himself had never experienced. (6. 29–30)

It is then significant that the lovers and the tree appear once more on the last page of the book in Ocean, only to disappear as they become aware of the presence of the omniscient and omnipotent narrator. Once more the enchantment fades, for the moment of happiness is also the moment of original sin. Every garden of Eden is only a prelude to expulsion. No happiness can be final, and the novel ends with the narrator and his companion setting out once more 'down the road that is obligatory for all who leave home in bad weather' (6. 512). The tree of life, once plucked, becomes the the tree of death, and Kurilov himself is regularly associated with a dying or wounded tree. Talk of rights and earnings is irrelevant here. The legacy of original sin, frequently invoked in Leonov's work, is no less powerful than the Communist promise of Utopia, but here Christianity displays a deeper understanding than Communism.

The case against the goal of human perfectibility is given, as so often in Leonov's works, to his least attractive characters. They may be morally discredited, but they can still talk sense. Thus Kormilitsyn observes to Gleb Protoklitov:

> 'Well, the people of the new world will still be the children of the old world, and just take a look inside yourself. Is everything there quite clear to you? [...] Well – who is going to supervise *them*?'
> 'And why should they need supervising? There will be no power then.'
> 'Who will tell them about good and evil – or where to go?'
> 'Who told primitive man?'
> 'But he didn't have the same kind of economy.'
> 'He didn't have the same culture either.'

So far Gleb has managed to parrot the Party line, but at this point a note of irony creeps in:

> 'The new man will create iron slaves in his own image and likeness. He will become a god. He will be the soul of huge mechanisms that produce food, clothes, and entertainment to order. These articulated metallic ignoramuses will work, sing songs, dance on holidays like Salome, even reproduce themselves.'

But Kormilitsyn is not interested in the wonders of technology, but in the nature of man:

> 'I'm talking about the man in whose hands all the threads of complete knowledge will come together. Don't take offence, but what if he turns out to be another Protoklitov, like you, proud, secretive, a mystery for everybody?'
> [...] 'Such a one will be powerless to do any harm. And anyway he will be perfect.'
> 'Can you remember a single god in history who had no faults? and anyway, why *harm*? He will do what is *right* according to his lights... In a word I don't believe you, Gleb. The revolution has killed its enemies and exalted its friends; but how many of both types still remain unrecognized?' (6. 328–9)

This remarkable passage contains the most explicit statement of Leonov's rejection of the goals of Communism. The fallibility of man, especially when entrusted with supreme power, and the inhuman ambitions of materialism recall Vissarion's 'machines able to articulate the word *Mummy*,' but are now set in an explicitly Soviet context.

This scepticism about the practical consequences of grand theories is further suggested by a pattern of frustrated expectations that runs through the novel. Literary and semantic associations often enough prove to lead nowhere. Thus old Pokhvisnev constantly boasts of his friendship with Bakunin, but this luminary eventually proves to have been an unknown schoolteacher, Sergey Petrovich, not the famous anarchist, Mikhail Aleksandrovich. There may be more point to the use of the name of Tyutchev for a friend of Kurilov's who is an important figure in theatre administration and could be be an indirect reminder that his nineteenth-century namesake was a government censor.[33] It is curious too that Marina Sabel'nikova, whose first name would seem to prepare her for an honoured place in Ocean, and who is the most interesting and sympathetic female figure in the novel, is repeatedly let down by Kurilov. Instead he takes up with an immature second-rate actress, Liza, whose absurd ambition to play the role of Mary Stuart in Schiller's play is shown up by the unsuitability of her name. During Kurilov's last days in hospital Marina comes to visit him every day; Liza, in whose arms he suffered his final attack, is in Moscow, but she is more concerned with the possibility of making a career for herself on the stage, and remembers to ask after him only four days after he has died. It is perhaps less surprising then that Marina's son, Zyamka, takes his name from the biblical outcast Ishmael.

This pattern of frustrated expectations and disappointments is particularly concentrated in two short stories inserted into the text. In the chapter 'Borshchnya'[34] the gardener tells Liza how, on returning from captivity after the war, he had decided to test his wife's fidelity. Without identifying himself he had seduced her only to discover that she had in fact been faithful to him; the encounter is completely joyless and brings only a sense of guilt to both of them: 'You are not my husband, you are my sin' (6. 296). He leaves the next morning and never returns. Later in hospital Kurilov tells Marina's son a fairy tale. A political adventurer discovers that according to the traditions of a certain country the coming of a white elephant will bring in an age of plenty. Accordingly he buys a suitable elephant from a travelling circus and sets off. But the elephant is alarmed by the noise of the crowds that have come to meet it. It runs amok and has to be destroyed. Luckily some ingenious machinery soon repairs the 'god' and all live happily ever after.

The bitterness of these two stories is complementary. In both cases the expectations of the faithful are mocked: the faithful wife is seduced and raped by her long-awaited husband; the 'god' is only recognized when it is dead and has to be animated by clockwork. Although the stories seem completely detached from the main lines of the novel, they are linked to it by their imagery.[35] The fact that it is a gardener who tells the first story relates it to the Garden of

Eden imagery that accompanies Kurilov's dreams of Ocean; Stalin too was often referred to as a 'gardener.' The second story is anticipated in the section on the religions of the world, where Leonov draws the reader's attention to the cult of 'elephants with a sacred mantra on their brows (and it is fascinating to trace what this image crystallized into in Kurilov's mind in the course of the next few months)' (6. 40). Both stories are variants on the motif of 'the usurper,' which runs through Russian history and literature, and is of course particularly charged in the conditions of post-1917 Russia.[36] The detail that the 'god' has come by rail, the visible symbol of the road to Ocean, conclusively undermines the ostensible theme of the novel. The tale has something in common with the legend of Kalafat and the stories of Pchkhov. Leonov is expressing his scepticism in all universal panaceas, whether of religion or politics. On another level they raise one of his oldest themes, the rejection of the idea that the end can justify the means. On the contrary, as these stories show, the means end up by perverting and betraying the goal to which they are meant to lead.

This pattern of great expectations and unfulfilled promise naturally prepares the subject of 'fathers and sons.' Leonov has always been more comfortable with depicting older figures; younger ones are either, like Zhenya in *Skutarevsky*, utterly unconvincing, or, like Cherimov, deeply unsympathetic to the author. In *The Road to Ocean* Leonov tries to redress the balance, and in his next works younger men and women play a more prominent role. But he still has little feel for them and they lack the complex pasts with their ambiguities and compromises that he easily creates for his older heroes. Lacking this background, can they ever understand or live up to the achievements of their elders?

At Kurilov's birthday party Kutenko, one of his closest friends, asks if their successors

> will know of the cloacas and graveyards that they have been rescued from by the generation now growing old. Do they know what efforts it had taken to smash these breaches in the centuries...? (6. 103)

These doubts are answered directly, but superficially, when the narrator later comments on the conversations of the young railwaymen:

> We should have brought Kutenko here to listen to their talk and to see how the rough drafts of the older generation were being put into effect. True, this new world looked rougher and solider, but then any craftsman's hands always are coarser than the miraculous power of the imagination. (6. 331)

This answer sounds conventional enough for a Soviet writer and is typically dishonest. As Leonov well knew, and as he was soon to experience in person, Soviet life had its own 'cloacas and graveyards.' His question should be read in a more general sense: won't the children of a hypothetical Utopia be crippled by their ignorance of suffering and injustice? This is not just a lack of historical knowledge; it is a psychological and cultural lacuna, closing off one of the dimensions of what it means to be human.

The new Soviet policies promoting the young and inexperienced to positions of responsibility had been illustrated in the figure of the unscrupulous Cherimov. In *The Road to Ocean* the young engineer Sayfulla is entrusted with driving a new locomotive on its maiden trip at the insistence of the Komsomol and against the advice of Gleb Protoklitov. These aspects of the younger generation, its ignorance, its naïveté, and its eagerness to sideline its elders are to become recurrent features of Leonov's later depictions of the younger generation. Ironically, it was the desire to encourage proletarian talent that had led to Gleb's rapid rise after the revolution:

His solid knowledge was accepted all the more enthusiastically as a consequence of natural talent, since it confirmed the widespread belief of the time that the culture of a generation could be acquired in the shortest of intervals. (6. 55)

The discussion of this point between Gleb and Il'ya Protoklitov was later cut in toto:

'Exciting times are coming, *and we are still not ready. The fools, they want to run trains on mere enthusiasm, when normally they require coal and and a well-trained population to run them decently. Enthusiasm is an expensive and volatile fuel. I would keep it only in hermetically sealed vessels. It can still come in useful...*'

Il'ya reflected: 'And what do you propose instead?'

'*In a word, I'm talking of culture. Material comfort without culture is essentially bourgeois, and a jemmy is no help here.*' [...]

[...] '*But you can't create a culture to order. You can't make it like galoshes and tractors. Remember how America developed its craftsmen, first-class whatever their profession, superb aviators, murderers, slave-dealers, great scientists...*'

'*That takes time, Il'ya. It takes time for that imponderable but all-powerful something that is transmitted from generation to generation by some mysterious process.*'

'*Yes, but you must admit that your Communist party has managed to shift our huge multinational monolith, and the kinetic energy released is quite incalculable. It's a great honour to have been part of it from the very beginning.*'

> *Gleb laughed naturally, but mirthlessly: 'If you think like that, you should be consistent and apply to join [the Party].'*[37]

This passage goes to the heart of Leonov's dissent from Soviet cultural policy. Ideological enthusiasm is not enough for building a culture. It cannot be acquired overnight (the reference to a jemmy recalls the attempts of the thief Vekshin to do just this), or manufactured like galoshes. It is an 'imponderable but all-powerful something that is transmitted from generation to generation by some mysterious process.' As so often Leonov gives his most cherished ideas to a man persecuted for his past. It is just such a past, complex and flawed, that is Leonov's conception of culture.

Ostensibly Leonov is attempting in *The Road to Ocean* to demonstrate the superiority of communism as a moral and intellectual system, but one may also detect a Christian ethos just below the surface. This may be seen in the virtues of forgiveness and tolerance that Kurilov advocates. Old Protoklitov had warned his sons in 1918:

> '... don't let those you have injured get away alive. Our generation didn't understand this. I've been going through old papers...' and with a gesture of passionate hatred he plunged his hand into a heap of archives waiting to be destroyed. 'So many of them have passed through my hands, and it's bitter to find out at the end of your life that you were just like the others, the same old humanist, truth-seeking, Russian shit.' (6. 54)

Leonov quietly deprecates this spirit of vengefulness which was being whipped up once again in the mid-1930s. So in the course of the novel Kurilov is transformed from an aggressive Communist searching for class enemies into a more tolerant figure. Before the Revolution his sister Frosya had married Omelichev, a factory owner, and even though brother and sister had naturally drifted apart because of Kurilov's Communist convictions, Omelichev had still taken in Kurilov during the Civil War and hidden him from the Whites. After the Revolution the Omelichevs became *lishentsy*, stripped of all their possessions and rights as members of the former 'exploiting classes.' Now when his sister comes looking for temporary shelter Kurilov willingly takes her in despite the disapproval of his older sister Klavdiya, a hard-line Bolshevik:

> '... the Revolution has not abolished the rights of a father, and, another thing, these people did something for me.'
> Yes, she had heard something, but what's so great about not being a swine? Then in a conciliatory tone, as though she wanted to reawaken an instinct by

which she had been guided all her life, she began to speak about being cautious [...] Now that everything has been taken from them they are embittered [...] Even a straw can be dangerous in the hands of a cornered enemy. You must be careful: sometimes even the dead can rise to shoot you in the back. I beg you at the very least not to keep important documents at home. It's not cowardice, just vigilance [...]'

He found it difficult to answer: 'I would help him get back on his feet, if he wanted to change himself.'

'It's too late, Alesha, for him to get back in the cradle.' (6. 254)

The subject of the *lishentsy* was effectively taboo in the Soviet Union of the time; their rights were restored only under the Constitution of 1936, and perhaps Leonov had been emboldened by rumours of this change to raise the topic. Even after their enfranchisement, however, the *lishentsy* continued to suffer various forms of discrimination, and their position continued to trouble Leonov for the rest of his life. As Frosya says: 'The grandfathers have sinned, but why do the grandchildren have to pay for it?' (6. 202). Just as the Old Testament morality of 'The fathers have eaten sour grapes and the children's teeth are set on edge' was superseded by Christ's injunction to forgive, so Leonov questions the morality of Soviet vindictiveness. It is then significant that the section on Kurilov's dreams of Ocean is followed immediately by another devoted to the history of religions, which ends with the words: 'suddenly Kurilov imagined that one day pages about himself would find their way into this book [the history of religions]' (6. 40).[38]

Formally, *The Road to Ocean* marks a break in Leonov's work. From *The Badgers* to *Skutarevsky* the importance and number of the images, the significance of the chapters, and the subordination of the parts to the whole had been steadily growing. It is difficult, indeed, to see how Leonov could have developed his technical mastery beyond the point reached in *Skutarevsky*. With *The Road to Ocean* Leonov reverses this trend and returns to the mosaic technique of *The Badgers*. As in the earlier novel the short chapters are all given titles, sometimes significant, sometimes playfully irrelevant, and they are often only tenuously connected with the main themes. Many chapters are virtually self-contained and could almost be printed separately, as for example the elaborately footnoted chapters devoted to the past and future.[39]

This weakening of the structural aspect has enabled Leonov to throw greater weight on to the narration and the characterization. *The Road to Ocean* is the best written of all his novels. The pseudoromantic hyperboles that disfigure its two predecessors now disappear, except possibly in the passages devoted to the past and the future. The opening paragraph implies a rich subtext of information and associations that are only gradually unfolded over the next 500 pages and ends with a baleful prophecy: 'The circle was closing' (6. 7); its ominous intonation casts a spell over the rest of the novel and encourages the reader to look for darker undertones.

In none of Leonov's novels are there so many memorable and sharply drawn figures. He allows them to speak directly rather then filtering their words and motives through his own narrative and commentary. This reduces the sense of authorial control and manipulation that is often oppressive in *Skutarevsky*, and enables the author to demonstrate his mastery of dialogue. Particularly effective are the scenes between characters who are tied together by family or a common past, but whose relations are strained, the more so because of their deep knowledge of one another.[40] A foretaste can be found in the relationship between Skutarevsky and his brother-in-law Petrygin; in *The Road to Ocean* the encounters of the two Protoklitov brothers and the dialogues between Gleb and Kormilitsyn display Leonov's skill in bringing out the unspoken thoughts of his characters, a technique that will prove invaluable when he starts to write for the stage. In the next eleven years he was to produce some seven plays.

As a result, the analysis of motives and thoughts also takes up much less room than in the preceding novels. Instead Leonov concentrates more on event and action, though these also have their psychological implications. Kurilov is clearly and consistently characterized in his ideologically irrelevant holiday with Liza; but Leonov's attempts to show him as a man of the future serve only to blur the image. The greater depth in characterization is achieved above all by a new use of leitmotivs. Less pliable than those of *Skutarevsky* they are used more sparingly and serve as ornamental labels: for example, Kurilov's pipe, the Protoklitov teeth, Pokhvisnev's Latin tags, and various catchphrases for some of the minor characters. On the other hand, the two central images contained in the title dominate the whole work. It is true that the idea of the road to emotional and spiritual maturity appears in other works by Leonov, but *The Road to Ocean* is remarkable for the multiplicity and variety of the roads traversed in the figures of Liza, Marina, Sayfulla, and of course Kurilov himself.

The Road to Ocean was not at first understood or appreciated in the Soviet Union, although its first instalment attracted favourable critical attention and a discussion was organized by the editorial board of *Novyy mir*,[41] at which the style and the depiction of Kurilov were unanimously welcomed as evidence of Leonov's complete ideological rehabilitation. The completed novel, however, gave rise to considerable perplexity. Throughout the first half of 1936 critics reproached Leonov for not having shown Kurilov in action. They were disconcerted by the death of the hero, especially when they compared him to Pavel

Korchagin, the hero of *How the Steel Was Tempered*. They felt that Kurilov had failed to rise above his sufferings and had been become a passive, almost a sacrificial figure. One critic was ready to admit that in purely literary merit *The Road to Ocean* might be superior, but warned his readers against over-valuing these virtues.[42]

On 5 May 1936 another discussion was held by the Union of Soviet Writers to review the completed novel. Although none of the speakers was as critical as at the previous meeting the lack of enthusiasm was widespread. The outcome was no more than an expression of tepid approval for the book.[43] Leonov himself spoke briefly to the effect that he could accept some of the criticisms made, but by no means all.[44] In the following months the tone of the critics was somewhat moderated, but the earlier enthusiasm was never recaptured. Whereas five editions of the novel appeared during the early months of 1936, the next came out only in 1950. Since the death of Stalin, however, the book has regained official favour, and Soviet critics have treated it with growing respect.

Even outside the Soviet Union *The Road to Ocean* has not yet been properly appreciated, except for some interesting observations by Rufus Mathewson.[45] Some Western critics have dismissed it as continuing the decline evident in *Skutarevsky*;[46] others seem to have misunderstood it altogether.[47] Yet *The Road to Ocean* has many claims to be considered Leonov's greatest novel. It certainly suffers from serious weaknesses. The chapters devoted to the distant past and future may be important for the philosophical scheme of the novel, but they do not earn their place. Leonov's difficulties in controlling his large cast is tacitly admitted by his need for an epilogue to tie up the various threads; it is the only time he resorts to this device in his works.

These faults, however, should not obscure the qualities of the book. The characterization is the richest, most varied, and the most realistic to be found in Leonov's novels. Even the female figures, usually so artificial in his works, are convincing portraits. The style is less hyperbolic than in the preceding novels, and all the more eloquent for it. Such scenes as the opening train crash, the dialogues of the two Protoklitov brothers, the idyll at Borshchnya, reach a consistently high level. Moreover the theme of the book, the re-examination of accepted values in the face of illness and death, is of universal appeal, though it acquires particular significance when seen against the background of Communism as a faith. It is also Leonov's fullest statement since *The Thief*, of his concept of culture as a seamless web linking past and future. It includes not only 'the best that has been thought' but also the worst that has been done; without it our understanding of ourselves is fatally limited. For all its faults *The Road to Ocean* is probably the most relevant and ambitious novel to have been published in Stalin's Russia. It sums up Leonov's novels of the '30s and establishes a pattern for his later works.

Leonov's works since *The Thief* had invariably aroused controversy. Although he was generally recognized as one of the major Soviet writers (if not *the* major writer) of the time, he was regarded with some wariness as a former *poputchik*.[48] Each new novel that he produced in the 1930s was initially welcomed by Soviet critics as an ideological advance on its predecessor, only to be later disparaged.

In his three novels of the 1930s Leonov tried to remain faithful to his earlier beliefs while outwardly conforming with the demands of the State. On the surface the story lines and value judgments are orthodox enough, but Leonov employs a variety of devices to indicate that events and characters can be read in a less conformist way. The most obvious is the expression of heterodox ideas by characters who seem to be suspect or even criminal, such as Vissarion and Arseniy Skutarevsky. Other methods include the juxtaposition of passages on apparently unrelated topics, which yet cast an ironic light on one another. Leonov consistently returns to the same concerns that occupied him at the beginning of his career. For example, Kurilov's first name relates him to the young Alesha Kharablev in *The Breakthrough at Petushikha*, and the mysterious question posed at the end of that story: 'Are you, are you, sweet Alesha, to become the unknown leader of the pack of wolves?' hovers even more enigmatically over *The Road to Ocean*. The Communist claim to solve all problems of morality and aesthetics by purely rationalistic methods, and the justification of injustices as the only means of attaining a future happiness, which had concerned him at the beginning of his career, will be re-examined again and again in the years to come. Certainly Leonov made his compromises, but taken overall, even on their own terms, without the benefit of hindsight, these works do show that art can coexist with compromise. The following years were to test Leonov's integrity even more severely.

chapter eight

Three Plays 1936–1940[1]

Leonov's reputation stood at its peak during the years 1929–36. Throughout this period he enjoyed large sales and widespread respect not only at home but also abroad, where his works were quickly translated.[2] In Russia seven editions of *The Sot'* were published between 1931 and 1935, seven of *Skutarevsky* between 1932 and 1935, and five of *The Road to Ocean* in 1936 alone. Even the two earlier novels were frequently reissued (*The Badgers* in five new editions and *The Thief* in three). None of them, however, was to be published again until after the war. One of them, *Skutarevsky*, only after Stalin's death, while another, *The Thief*, was never to be reissued in Russia in its original form. After having been one of the most widely read and frequently published of Soviet writers Leonov in these years fell into comparative obscurity.

This virtual suppression of his works was not necessarily the reflection of a decline in his popularity. Perhaps, indeed, his very success was a factor in his fall. Other prominent figures in the arts, for example, Shostakovich and Meyerhold, were disgraced in the first months of 1936, and one of the purposes seems to have been not so much to destroy them, as to 'cut them down to size,' to remind them that it was the Party that was the sole judge in artistic matters. After a period of sustained vilification they were given a chance to return to favour. (Meyerhold was almost alone in rejecting this offer and was promptly executed.) Leonov's difficulties were less sensational than theirs, but the experience left deep traces in his later work.

In those years personal rivalries and antipathies were also often exploited in the discrediting of prominent figures. In November 1933 the following letter appeared in the press.

An open letter to Vl. Lidin and L. Leonov.

Permit me to remind you of the following fact. On 5 November a writers' brigade, including yourselves, was due to leave for Yaroslavl'. The proletariat of Yaroslavl', which has followed Soviet literature with the greatest attention and sensitivity was awaiting the arrival of the writers from Moscow for the holiday celebrations [i. e., the anniversary of the Revolution]. At the very last moment before the train's departure you categorically refused to travel, though you were standing on the platform beside the coach with your luggage.

'Why?'

'Because the coach is "hard,"' you replied. 'And we were promised a "soft" one.'

No persuasion had any effect.

The train left without you.

I must point out that although the coach was a 'hard' one, it was well-fitted, clean and equipped with bedding. But this is unimportant – it is only a few hours' journey to Yaroslavl'.

I think that even if it had been a cattle-truck and the journey had required a whole day, you would still have been bound to travel.

The writers were being awaited by the proletariat of Yaroslavl', the Party organization and the general public.

These matters, dear comrades, are not to be treated lightly. It should not be forgotten that we are not merely writers but Soviet writers.

I am ashamed of your treatment of the workers of Yaroslavl'.

Explain your behaviour.

Valentin Kataev[3]

The answer of Lidin and Leonov puts a rather different complexion on these 'facts':

In his open letter Valentin Kataev demagogically accuses us of refusing to travel in a 'hard' coach to Yaroslavl' at the invitation of the Yaroslavl' workers.

It is true that we accepted an invitation from the secretary of the committee of the Union of Soviet Writers to visit Yaroslavl' for the October celebrations. There was no talk of any public appearances. The trip was suggested as a form of recreation. The membership of the writers' brigade, agreed by us, was as follows: Vs. Ivanov, Nikulin, Hidas, and ourselves. None of these other three proved to be at the station. The appearance of Kataev at the station was a complete surprise. It is silly and unworthy to suppose that an unsuitable coach could have been the reason for our refusal to travel. If we have disappointed the expectations of the people of Yaroslavl' then we willingly undertake to make amends, with, of course, the comrades who failed to appear.

The fact that Kataev's open letter was addressed to the two of us can only be explained by his complete ignorance of the membership of our brigade.

Vl. Lidin, L. Leonov[4]

This letter might seem to have refuted all Kataev's charges, but an editorial note added:

The editorial board is glad to note that comrades Lidin and Leonov admit their error and that they are ready to make amends.

It made no reference to the countercharges contained in the letter, thus contriving to give the impression that the two writers had been in the wrong throughout. The campaign against Lidin was to reach its climax a few years later with the attack on his novel *Son* (*Syn*, 1936). In Leonov's case it was to be prolonged over several years, coming to a head in 1939–40 over the plays that he wrote after *The Road to Ocean*, and flaring up sporadically at least until the mid-1950s.

In view of the deteriorating political atmosphere inside Russia it is perhaps surprising that Leonov had survived unscathed for so long. The reason is almost certainly his endorsement by Maksim Gor'ky. As we have seen, Leonov, like many other Soviet writers had corresponded with him and had twice visited him in Sorrento; Kataev had in fact been his travelling companion on one occasion. Gor'ky for his part had from the first taken a keen interest in Leonov's achievements and potential. He had frequently singled him out as the most promising of the younger Soviet novelists and had introduced him to Stalin with a strong recommendation.

It may seem surprising then that Gor'ky, who had welcomed *The Sot'* and *The Locusts* so enthusiastically, should have said nothing at all on the subject of *Skutarevsky* and *The Road to Ocean*. Some of the attacks on the former were so hostile that Leonov was quite shaken; but when Gor'ky was told of this by Vsevolod Ivanov early in 1933 he seems to have done nothing about it.[5] As for *The Road to Ocean* Gor'ky had in fact drafted a letter which was never actually mailed,[6] though his secretary read it to Leonov over the telephone.[7] The contents are startling: Gor'ky can find hardly a good word to say for the book, whose ideas and design he had approved only a few years earlier. Some of his complaints are justifiable, but many of them are merely quibbles or based on crude misreadings. The tone, moreover, is marked by an unmistakable personal animosity. When I asked Leonov about this[8] he told me that in 1935 one of his remarks had been misrepresented to Gor'ky by a fellow writer.[9]

The rift between the two men seems, however, to have been rather more complex than this might suggest. As far back as 1931 Leonov had found himself unable to join in the chorus of praise when Gor'ky read his new play *Somov and Others* to his guests.[10] Gor'ky was apparently deeply wounded by this, though Leonov's words contain not so much a literary judgment, as scepticism about the recent show trials. By this time Gor'ky had thrown off all his earlier reservations and had become an uncritical admirer of Stalin, so it may well be that he was offended by this expression of dissent. A few days later he took Leonov to task for the *Unusual Stories about Peasants*,[11] a criticism that he had not made at the time of their publication. Later in Moscow he was upset when Leonov was unwilling to show him the just completed manuscript of *Skutarevsky*: 'The manuscript was full of crossings-out, I couldn't present myself to him absolutely naked [...] So I said, "I can't. But as soon as the book comes out I'll send you a copy."'[12]

Gor'ky's death in June 1936 prevented him from clarifying the misunderstandings, but his endorsement was still to prove invaluable. Stalin, a poet *manqué*, had a reverence for art and was ever hopeful that some great writer would immortalize him for posterity.[13] Sporadic prods, however, served to remind the favoured few of their responsibilities. In the next few years the attacks on Leonov became more intense and more openly political. A fair amount can be reconstructed from the periodicals of the time, and no doubt there is much that was not recorded in the press. But the general drift of events and their consequences for Leonov are clear enough, for they find their way into the design of his works, where they serve to reanimate and reinforce the theme of guilt associated with his whereabouts and activities in 1918–20. The theme of persecution, which had already appeared in *Skutarevsky* and *The Road to Ocean*, now becomes a recurrent feature of Leonov's works. At first the persecuted figure is an enemy (this is a standard plot in Soviet plays of the late 1930s), but the emphasis gradually shifts, until the persecuted figure more often than not turns out to be the real hero, while the persecutors prove to be the villains. In this respect the Protoklitov brothers in *The Road to Ocean* establish a pattern that runs through Leonov's later work.

His novels of the 1930s had been remarkable for their scope. Their heroes are men who occupy important positions at the hub of affairs. They may be working in distant provinces but they are constantly in touch with the capital; they make frequent trips to ministries and are even vouchsafed interviews with the leaders. In the following works, and particularly the plays of 1936–40, Leonov chooses humbler figures in middle rather than senior management (people from the lower strata of Soviet life play only episodic roles in his work after the 1920s). Often enough these heroes have never been to Moscow in their lives. They live in the provinces; their work, on the land, in industry, or in local administration is important but never exciting or ostentatious. This growing interest in humble 'ordinary' men (to borrow the title of one of Leonov's later plays) would seem to reflect the author's own sense that he was slipping from the centre of the literary scene.

In another respect too, the works that Leonov wrote after 1936 may be said to mark a new stage in his development. If in his earliest stories (up to *The Badgers*) the basic pattern had been one of an established community destroyed by the irruption of external forces, the novels, plays, and stories that he wrote between 1925 and 1936 were clearly outward oriented. They looked to new horizons and prophesied new possibilities for human nature. From 1936 onwards, however, the pattern reverts to that of his earliest works and his sympathies switch to the community that is under threat from intruders. Up to *The Road to Ocean* his heroes had been associated with change and progress, but from now on they stand for consolidation and conservation.

This shift is symptomatic of what was happening in Soviet political life at the time, and it is reflected in the literature of these years. The works of the 1920s and early 1930s had revealed an openness to the outside world. European techniques are adopted, admired, and surpassed in the novels devoted to the First Five-Year Plan. Western technicians too make frequent appearances; but by the middle of the decade they are regarded with distrust and discarded as soon as their expertise has been exploited. The tendency gradually developed into an acute xenophobia, which assumed all foreigners to be spies or saboteurs. This trend can be discerned in the war episodes of *The Road to Ocean*, and it becomes blatant in Leonov's next works, a group of three plays, *The Orchards of Polovchansk* (*Polovchanskie sady*, 1938),[14] *Wolf* (*Volk*, 1938),[15] and *The Snowstorm* (*Metel'*, 1939).[16]

These plays follow on from Leonov's novels of the 1930s in their depiction of contemporary Soviet life and their more or less guarded hints at the discrepancies between official propaganda and the reality. The Stalin constitution of 1936 had proclaimed the triumph of socialism in the Soviet Union, and had backed this up by relaxing many of the measures (deprivation of education, voting rights, etc.) aimed at members and descendants of the former 'exploiting classes,' the bourgeoisie, the Church. In practice this made little difference to the lives of the *lishentsy*, for the climate of distrust that had accumulated over the previous fifteen years could not be easily dissipated. As the case of Protoklitov and the episode with the Omelichev family in *The Road to Ocean* show, Leonov found it easy to sympathize with these unfortunates, and this motif reappears in these plays. There is probably a personal reason for this. Leonov's father-in-law, one of the Sabashnikov tea-merchants, had founded a respected publishing house. Although he continued to work loyally under the Soviet regime he was subjected to various indignities as a member of the former 'exploiting classes' throughout the 1930s.

Each of these plays is set 'in the provinces and in our own times' (*M*, 2) and is constructed round a Soviet family whose security is threatened by the appearance of an intruder. This intruder is mysteriously involved in the past history of the family, and is invariably connected with emigration and/or foreigners. Each of the plays ends triumphantly with the expulsion of the intruder and the restoration of harmony. A further detail common to all three plays is that each was the subject of heated debate and none of them was successful on the stage.

In *The Orchards of Polovchansk* (set in the early autumn of 1937) Adriyan Makkaveev is the director of a model collective farm. Some eighteen years earlier his wife, Aleksandra Ivanovna, had had a brief affair with a soldier in the Red Army, Matvey Pylyaev, and had given birth to a son by him. Pylyaev was captured and is assumed to have been executed, so that his reappearance is traumatic for the family and gives old Makkaveev a heart attack.[17] It later transpires that he had managed to save his life only by agreeing to work for the Germans.[18] This sub-plot was a later addition demanded by Glavlit, the censoring authority, while the play was already in rehearsal:

> Pylyaev was not originally a saboteur. I had in mind a Mozart and Salieri situation. Here is a man who has created everything [Makkaveev], and here is another [Pylyaev] who has created nothing and leaves empty-handed. But I was obliged to give the play a political point. I did, and so he turned into a saboteur.[19]

The politicization of Pylyaev is curiously inconsequential. No explanation is given for his mysterious return to Polovchansk: it is suggested at one point that he has come to blackmail Makkaveev's wife, but since their affair is by now common knowledge this threat carries little dramatic potential. At the same time he appears to be waiting for some foreign contact to arrive, but nothing comes of this idea either. Pylyaev is in fact irrelevant to the structure of the play, and the author himself found it possible to summarize the action without even mentioning his name.[20]

If in *The Orchards of Polovchansk* the villain Pylyaev is alone in his invasion of the Makkaveev family, in *Wolf* the intruders on the Roshchins are fourfold: they include the elderly Magdalinin and three members of the Sandukov family, the former priest, Lavrentiy, and his two grown children, Luka (the 'wolf' of the title) and Kseniya. These figures are more than ghosts from the past; they are closely interwoven with the present-day life of the Soviet family. Kseniya is

Roshchin's wife and Magdalinin his trusted adviser. Here again foreign espionage and sabotage are implied. Magdalinin lapses into a German accent in moments of stress, and he is able to blackmail Luka into working for him. In this play, however, the distinction between 'good' and 'bad' characters is less clear, and Leonov contrives (as in *The Road to Ocean*) to intimate an alternative reading of the plot.

The same basic situation can be discerned in *The Snowstorm*. At the centre stands a similar family with a guilty secret: Katerina Syrovarova's first husband, Porfiriy, had been a junior officer in the White army and had fled the country in 1919.[21] He had continued to write to his family, but Katerina had burnt his letters without reading them and claims in her *ankety* that he is now dead. She had later married his brother Stepan, a factory director, and so gained some security for herself and Zoya, her daughter by Porfiriy. Stepan, however, has been embezzling funds from his factory and depositing them in his brother's Paris bank account in readiness for his own planned defection. Meanwhile Porfiriy has become disillusioned by life in the West; he volunteered for the Republican army in the Spanish Civil War, and lost an eye at the battle of Guadalajara. In this way he is presumed to have earned the right to return to Russia, so that on this occasion it is the apparent outsider, the émigré and former White officer, who is justified and welcomed back into the family, while the seemingly respectable Stepan is exposed as an ideological intruder and finally expelled.[22] The moral that a good émigré is better than a bad Communist in unique in Soviet literature of the Stalin period. At the end of the play Porfiriy goes off to work on a collective farm.[23]

Like Pylyaev and Magdalinin, Stepan Syrovarov has connections in the West, but unlike them he is not a spy; his only wish is to get out of the Soviet Union and enjoy the wealth that he has smuggled abroad. His wife says of him at the end: 'I thought that he was an enemy but he is only a thief' (*M*, 72).[24] He lives an apparently simple and unostentatious life, but this is a deception, deliberately intended to create the impression that 'here lives a man who values his crust of happiness' (*M*, 20). Leonov does not suggest that he is an untypical figure of his time, or even that the cause of his rottenness lies in the pre-revolutionary past. On the contrary Stepan is a product of the Soviet system and it is his astute manipulation of Soviet jargon and manners that has enabled him to survive and conceal his true nature for so long.[25]

There are many similarities between these three plays. The orchards of Polovchansk reappear in the other two works as the collective farms on which Roshchin and ultimately Porfiriy Syrovarov work. The intruders are compared to worms and moths, parasitic on this Soviet Eden.[26] Even the character types and their roles are strikingly similar. The negative figures are all associated with images of decay and death. This is suggested by Pylyaev's very name, which he himself pronounces Pylaev,[27] as though it were derived from *pyl* (vigour), whereas according to Leonov's orthography it is formed from *pyl'* (dust). To emphasize this point he is called 'a dusty man' (7. 171), and he characterizes himself with the words: 'I like it when there are moths' (7. 162). His first mysterious entry out of the silence of the night is echoed by his final disappearance into nothingness (7. 217). He is associated with images of cold, a symbol that will accompany all Leonov's later villains; the action of the first two acts takes place in a heat wave, but he never takes off his overcoat. The same images recur in *Wolf*: Elena says to Luka, who claims to have been working in north-eastern Siberia: 'Look at the moth in your jacket! Where has it all come from in the cold?' (7. 277).

As in his preceding works Leonov is torn between the desire to show that evil leads inevitably to its own punishment and the need to display the efficiency of the Soviet security forces. Pylyaev and the Sandukovs betray themselves by their obsessive guilt and fall into simple traps laid for them by mere children. They destroy themselves before the police have a chance to catch up with them. In *The Snowstorm* Porfiriy has closed his Paris bank account so that Stepan will find himself penniless when he arrives in the West. But since the NKVD officer has 'known all about him from the first' (*M*, 78) he will probably never find this out.

Leonov's novels of the 1930s reveal little sympathy for the post-revolutionary generation. Katya and Zhenya in *The Sot'* and *Skutarevsky* function as symbols rather than as individuals; in *The Road to Ocean* he made a more sustained effort, but the younger figures still remain peripheral to the main interest. In these plays Leonov returns to the search. His young heroes and heroines are usually required to prove that they are worthy descendants of their legendary predecessors, capable of performing some heroic feat or *podvig*,[28] a demonstratively brave or self-sacrificing action, habitually associated in Leonov's later works with the figure of a young woman and frequently with the idea of flying. Thus Masha Makkaveeva is a parachutist and Nastya Roshchina a devotee of gliding. There is the same image of flight, the same element of risk as in Tanya Vekshina's leap from the trapeze, but these are no longer sought for their own sake; rather they are undertaken in the name of the community, like the flight of the cosmonauts in *The Road to Ocean*. Where the Vekshins had been testing their potentialities to their furthest limits, these new heroes are simply undergoing initiation ceremonies, which they invariably complete successfully. They 'come of age,' and as a reward they are allowed to utter the final words in their respective plays.

This optimism, however, is only superficial, covering a much deeper scepticism. For Leonov does not subscribe to the standard Soviet cult of youth. He seldom shows the younger generation as possessing any inner moral or cultural life. This omission is not accidental; on the contrary, this cultural vacuum is to become one of his most serious charges against the Soviet regime. Several of these younger figures are afflicted with a psychological trauma that is to become a feature of Leonov's later work. Isayka Makkaveev, Pylyaev's bastard son, and Elena, Roshchin's mistress, are both acutely conscious that they are not full members of the family and are oppressed by a sense of guilt. Isayka regards his crippled legs as symbolic proof of his bastardy: 'Do you think I'm a Makkaveev? Are the Makkaveevs like this?' (7. 149). Similarly Elena says to Roshchin: 'We're like thieves, you and I – who am I in this house?' (7. 231). Each of them, however, plays a decisive part in unmasking the intruders and is assured of total reintegration.[29] In later works Leonov was to combine these two types, the flying heroine and the outsider-*lishenka*, into a single figure (for example, Polya in *The Russian Forest*); in fact this seems to have been his original plan in *The Orchards of Polovchansk*, for in the first draft of the play it is Masha and not Isayka who is the child of Pylyaev.[30]

In *The Snowstorm* the whole family is said to be 'sick' because of the émigré Porfiriy. His daughter Zoya finds it unbearable that she has to conceal this knowledge to protect herself and her family:

> I can't lie any longer. So many times, so many times now... thanks to lies I entered the Institute, got a scholarship, and won the friendship of my schoolmates. But all this is just stealing. (*She begins to cry*). I am ashamed to be so young and so worthless already. (*M*, 5)

When her mother reminds her that by being honest she may frighten off her fiancé she replies: 'I won't steal a husband as well as everything else. Sooner or later he will tell me that I am a thief' (*M*, 5). All her mother can say is: 'Get used to life' (*M*, 7). At the climax of the second act Zoya reveals her secret to the assembled New Year's party, and most of her friends promptly abandon her. Her fiancé, Serezha, coldly remarks: 'Where you find one lie you soon find another. I did not know of these circumstances. I will give you my answer tomorrow. You will have to wait' (*M*, 36).

Leonov describes Serezha thus:

> He loves Zoya just because she has appreciated his qualities of charm, talent, and strength, qualities which he really does possess. He will go far in life, because he will never do anything silly. In ten years' time he will be a merciless man. (*M*, 2)

Like Stepan Serezha is a product of his environment; he too has found in the Party a cover, both psychological and political, for his ambitions. His 'mercilessness' in pursuit of them presages a future even grimmer than the present of the 1930s. The sickness of the Syrovarovs is then to be blamed not on the Porfiriys but on the Stepans and Serezhas of Russian life.

Thus the three plays represent three variations on the same group of themes. Their crude treatment in *The Gardens of Polovchansk* is complicated but essentially unaltered in *Wolf*. The Soviet family is there shown as less homogeneous; the head of the house is vacillating where Makkaveev had been dictatorial; the intruders are more numerous and more plausible; but the basic situation remains the same. In *The Snowstorm* this situation is turned inside out. The apparent intruder proves to be a long-lost 'prodigal son,' while the real enemies prove to be the representatives of the Party and the Komsomol.

One may ask how the same author can have given such different accounts of the same time and place, and it is then worth taking a second look at the two earlier plays to see if they contain any hint of what becomes explicit in *The Snowstorm*. Leonov himself said in his speech at the first performance of *Wolf*: 'In some plays the author – and then the theatre – reveal everything to the audience from the opening scenes. It is at once made plain which character is positive and which negative, who is going to unmask whom, and what is going to happen at the end. There are other plays whose authors seem to say to the audience: "We will show you a piece of life, people as they really are; sit quietly in your seats, watch while the characters of men and the meaning of their actions are unfolded before you step by step; and judge for yourselves which of them is positive and which negative." This is the task I set myself when working on *Wolf*.'[31] These are not empty words, as Leonov had shown in *The Road to Ocean*, where the opening pages deliberately put the reader on the wrong scent.

Luka is the central figure of the play. Indeed in many ways Leonov's original title, 'The Flight (*Begstvo*) of Sandukov'[32] is more appropriate than *Wolf*. Its significance lies in the motifs of running[33] that accompany Luka from his first entry (7. 228) to his final disappearance (7. 269). Leonov here plays on the preconceptions of Soviet audiences, much as he had done with Gleb Protoklitov in *The Road to Ocean*.[34] Luka had left town on the day before he was due to marry Elena, and he has since been in Chukotka on unspecified work, though not for as long as he claims.

But his unexplained absence in the north is a traditional euphemism in Russian literature for administrative exile, and the play makes good sense if we take him as an escaped prisoner, or perhaps as a man on the run from arrest. Seen in this light his words to Elena: 'Are you unwilling to forgive me for leaving you then, before the wedding. Believe me, I couldn't do anything else. I had no right. We would have been prevented' (7. 273) take on a different meaning. His intense fear of all dogs and his 'flight' at the end of the play, when he fears that 'they' have come for him (actually 'they' turn out to be a group of schoolchildren), are all too understandable, and do not have to be an admission of anti-Soviet activities. He is given less opportunity to explain himself than Gleb Protoklitov, but his situation seems to be much the same.[35] As he says, 'Everyone is trying to catch ghosts. Even up there, in Chukotka' (7. 277).

This interpretation also does something to explain the actions of the other members of the Sandukov family. Lavrentiy, a former priest, now dependent on the charity of his children, is an embarrassment to the whole family. It may seem shocking that Kseniya will admit him only at the back door, but in the conditions of the time, as audiences would have known well enough, even this took some courage. More puzzling is Lavrentiy's attitude to Luka: 'If Lukashka comes chase him out *(with sudden fury)*. Stick a gun against his chest... He wants to escape into the depths, to save his soul, the son of a bitch. He can run as fast as he wants, but they'll break his paws' (7. 252). But this too may be seen as Lavrentiy's fear for his own position and the security of his other children.

Luka's sister, Kseniya, can also be seen in a different light. Throughout the first three acts she is consistently shown as an unsympathetic character (largely through her acquisitiveness and her bourgeois tastes in furnishings), but she is given a chance to defend herself in the closing pages. Her bitterness is explained plausibly enough by her husband's treatment of her (he is keeping a mistress in the same house); she has failed to bear any children, and her hopes of making a career on the stage have just been shattered. In these troubles she gets little sympathy from her husband's family. Her expulsion at the end of the play thus seems not so different from the fate awaiting Gleb Protoklitov.[36]

Behind the three members of the Sandukov family stands the sinister figure of Magdalinin, Roshchin's legal adviser. Magdalinin is one of Leonov's recurrent middle-aged philosopher types, in the line of Chikilev, Chervakov, and Petrygin, servants of the old regime who have adapted to the new one. He is a spirit of negation with nothing to offer but doubt and distrust: 'Victory begins with the first fearless smile... Let nobody smile even when he is alone. Kill the smile' (7. 287, 288). Unlike the Sandukovs he is not at first seen as an intruder; on the contrary he has made himself a trusted and influential Party member. He successfully persuades Roshchin that Ostaev and Tsiryul'nikov, both good Communists, are really enemies of the State.

In the light of these possibilities, we may take a second look at the first of these three plays. *The Gardens of Polovchansk* is, on the face of it, Leonov's most shamelessly Soviet work. The associations of the central hero's names,

Hadrian and Maccabaeus, his apple orchard and his seven children, deliberately evoke the most grandiose associations. The characterization is crude in the extreme: at one point Makkaveev calls on his sons to utter suitable sentiments to celebrate the family reunion. The three present, respectively a lawyer, a surgeon, and a boxer, respond as follows: 'It is good to live knowing that people need you. It is good to go into battle, father, and to feel one's neighbour at one's elbow'; 'My country is beautiful, but I will transfuse myself into her, and she will become yet more beautiful'; 'In the old days they said "An eye for an eye, a tooth for a tooth." But I say "two eyes for an eye, and a jaw for a tooth"' (7.178,179).[37] The humour is ponderous; the ethos of the play with its pervasive reminders of military exercises is chauvinistic to the point of parody (though it must be admitted that the jingoism of all Soviet plays of this period reads like a parody.) Seen in isolation, *The Orchards of Polovchansk* is hardly to be distinguished from the mass of Soviet plays of this period. The only moment in which the play breathes the same atmosphere as the other two occurs in a brief snatch of dialogue:

> *Aleksandra Ivanovna.* They took Pylyaev then to a place from which no one returned alive. You remember Grisha Odintsov and Il'ya Garpovenko. They knew who they were taking. And I was terrified that a man who was dead would come in.
> *Yuriy.* Well the dead can't walk. They sleep in a well sealed container.
> *Aleksandra Ivanovna.* O how many dead men are walking among us. That's what makes it difficult at times for the living. (7. 175)

The reference clearly goes beyond Pylyaev and might seem to be a justification of the paranoia about spies; but in the light of *Wolf* and *The Snowstorm* these 'dead men' could equally well be those who, like Magdalinin and Stepan Syrovarov, had successfully penetrated the Party. This does nothing to alter the fact that *The Gardens of Polovchansk* remains an embarrassingly bad play. It is perhaps significant that it was the Arts Theatre version that Leonov chose to publish in 1938 and afterwards (something that he did not do with *Untilovsk*, similarly rewritten by the theatre). Could it be intended as a parody of the 'banal stereotypes' mocked in *The Road to Ocean*?

Such a reading is supported by the recurrence of certain motifs common to all the plays. All of them treat the family as a metaphor for the Russian state:[38] 'I too am the people and Soviet power,' says Makkaveev of himself; 'I want your children to live well and honourably in the spacious home of my fatherland,' says the young hero of *Wolf.* Just as 'the boughs bend under the wind when Makkaveev walks in his garden' (7. 153) so Lizaveta says of herself, 'Not a single mirror can hold me; I go down to the lake when I want to look at myself' (*M*, 30), while of Aunt Marfa Porfiriy says, 'when you're abroad and remember her, it's as though you were back in the fatherland again' (*M*, 64).

But there also more ominous aspects to these figures. While Makkaveev is aggressively proud of the achievements of his five sons by his first marriage, his proneness to self-pity suggests a lack of self-assurance beneath the bluster. This is particularly evident in his relations with his two favourite children, Vasiliy[39] and Masha. He talks of Vasiliy to the virtual exclusion of his other sons, and insists on laying a place for him at table even when he knows he is not coming. (Vasiliy has been drowned on a dangerous mission to the Arctic.)[40] He is also a demanding and possessive father to his only daughter, Masha, an agronomist, who has taken up parachuting. In the first act he calls after her threateningly: 'You will fly away from me as your brothers have done' (7. 158), and he tries to prevent her friend Otshel'nikov, also an officer in the Army, from entering the house.

Roshchin, the head of the family in *Wolf*, is a similar character. He too regards his daughter's fiancé with disapproval. In this case the hostility is motivated by an anonymous denunciation rather than by jealousy; but there are personal reasons too: 'There's not much of the bridegroom about him; he's a bit dry, isn't he?' (7. 266). Nor is Roshchin's private life above reproach. Himself married to Kseniya Sandukova, he has been living with Elena for some time, though she is engaged to Luka. Unlike Makkaveev Roshchin is entirely to blame for his entanglement with the Sandukovs; his lack of vigilance has enabled the spy Magdalinin to deceive him with the utmost ease. The culture of unquestioning submission to the decisions of one's superiors has created the climate for such abuses. As Ostaev cautiously observes to Roshchin: 'In the history of science doubt has sometimes been a more progressive factor than absolute faith' (7. 291).

If one is to follow the logic of the family-state analogy then the heavy-handed and possessive father-figures of these plays point to Stalin. One hesitates to draw this conclusion, especially in view of the unequivocal condemnation of Stepan Syrovarov. A writer who had conceived such a parallel would surely conceal it a lot more cryptically than Leonov has done here. On the other hand the creator of Vissarion in *The Sot'* and the author of references to Jenghis Khan and Torquemada in *Skutarevsky* had raised such unthinkable suggestions before, and can hardly have been unaware of the implications of his words.[41]

The arrogance of Makkaveev and Roshchin leads them into distrust and acts of violence against their colleagues and dependants. In the case of Stepan Syrovarov it leads to blatant corruption. Makkaveev is responsible for the atmosphere in his home, but in the other two plays the climate of fear and suspicion comes from outside. Anonymous denunciations and frame-ups are used to discredit decent citizens and enrich cynics and criminals. Stepan's comment on the twenty years of Soviet power as 'a great university of distrust' (*M*, 56) is borne out by the events and atmosphere of these plays.

Stepan's conscience, 'the putrid sweat of waiting every night' (*M*, 40), is, of course, understandably troubled. When the play opens he is under investigation, but his actual crimes are almost irrelevant, and he is able to postpone the day of reckoning by sending a compromising anonymous letter to the son of a Party member, which, as he expects, is opened in the mail and leads to the young man's arrest and the subsequent suicide of his mother. When Porfiriy appears in the street outside the Syrovarovs's apartment he is at first assumed to be a secret policeman.

Even the younger and more innocent characters experience the same fears. Zoya is tormented with guilt at having a father in emigration and so needing to conceal the truth in her *ankety*. Her mother tells her that if she fills in her forms truthfully then 'Stepan's trip abroad will fall through [...] you yourself will end up without a diploma, and nobody will even dare nod to you through the window' (*M*, 6). Another character remarks, 'It's said they can listen through the light bulbs now' (*M*, 10). These undercurrents, discernible to a lesser extent in the other two plays, serve as a reminder of the atmosphere of the times. By a terrible irony it was in these years when Soviet society had been almost atomized by spy mania, mass terror, and the apparatus of denunciations, arrests, torture, exile, and executions that Soviet writers were expected to write ever more enthusiastically about the unity of Soviet families and the solidarity of the Soviet people. The Communist Matvey's prophecy in *The Thief* that happiness would soon be manufactured like light bulbs has come horrifyingly true. As Stepan sourly observes, 'The well-being of a home is to be measured by the quantity of women's tears shed in it...' (*M*, 7).[42]

Perhaps this is the explanation for the prevalence of scenes of physical violence. Magdalinin flogs Luka Sandukov, Stepan Syrovarov drives his wife round the floor on her knees. Nor is this behaviour confined to the villains. Anatoliy Makkaveev and Otshel'nikov conduct a boxing match, Unus tweaks Pylyaev's nose; old Marfa slaps Stepan Syrovarov's face, and there are various scuffles on and off stage. These rather clumsy devices are specially surprising in view of Leonov's preference elsewhere for psychological tension rather than violent action. The predominantly visual nature of drama tends to give these scenes a disproportionate impact. Leonov's later plays do not make any use of such devices.

The three plays are further linked by the motif of 'ghosts from the past.' While this theme undoubtedly reflects the atmosphere of the period of the Great

Purges, when saboteurs and foreign agents were suspected everywhere, it also corresponds to a recurrent obsession in Leonov's own work. The crucial events (eighteen years ago in *The Gardens of Polovchansk*, twenty in *Wolf* and *The Snowstorm*) take us back each time to the missing years in Leonov's life between 1918 and 1920; the same themes of emigration, service in the White or foreign armies, and a betrayal in love recur in all of them. As in *The Road to Ocean* the witch-hunts of the age triggered the writer's guilty secret in an almost suicidal gesture of self-revealment.

It may be noted that Makkaveev and Pylyaev, Roshchin and the Sandukovs, and the two Syrovarov brothers form pairs of antagonistic doubles. In each case the wife, Aleksandra Ivanovna in *The Gardens of Polovchansk*, Kseniya in *Wolf*, Katerina in *The Snowstorm*, is the link between the two camps. Pylyaev appears when Makkaveev is absent or sick, and has fathered one of the Makkaveev children; Roshchin has married into the Sandukov family; Stepan Syrovarov has married his brother's wife after his emigration. This use of doubles reflects, I think, Leonov's own sense of an alternative biography, or rather biographies. He too had a foot in both camps, his life too could have gone either way. The pattern of a pair, one of whom has a 'clean' biography and the other a guilty secret, recurs in several of Leonov's later works, and gives them a tension quite different from that between, say, Semen and Pavel/Anton in *The Badgers*. It is largely for this reason that the heroes with guilty secrets, such as Gleb Protoklitov, are often more sympathetic than their apparently blameless counterparts.

Some of these discordant subtexts may have been suspected by audiences at the time. For the first performances of *The Gardens of Polovchansk* and *Wolf*, after being initially well received,[43] brought down on the author a torrent of abuse, innuendo, and political threats unlike anything he had experienced before.[44] The two plays had their first performances on the same day, 6 May 1939, and Leonov himself was inclined to attribute these attacks to professional envy of his success. There was certainly a personal note to the attacks, but the thrust was even more political. Nonetheless the two theatres that had produced the plays, the Moscow Arts and the Malyy, at first stood by Leonov.[45]

In an attempt to clarify the situation the dramatists' section of the Union of Soviet Writers called a meeting to discuss both Leonov's plays and the criticism to which they had been subjected. The wording of the notice was as follows:

The Section of Dramatists considers that the attitude shown by several newspapers (*Sovetskoe iskusstvo, Moskovskiy bol'shevik, Komsomol'skaya pravda*) does not represent a fair appraisal of the work of Leonov as a dramatist. The discussion is to establish the correct attitude of dramatic and theatrical opinion to

188　The Life and Work of Leonid Leonov

Leonov's latest plays and their realization by the Malyy and Moscow Arts theatres.[46]

At the meeting Leonov himself said only a few words: 'The harshness of the criticism has not convinced me. Critics are free to treat my works how they choose, but the author has the right to expect a higher level of criticism than that on which the discussion has so far been conducted.'[47] The meeting, however, failed to vindicate Leonov. He was not helped either by an unpleasant scene after the discussion when Sudakov, the producer of *Wolf*, demonstratively refused to shake hands with Tal'nikov, the critic from *Sovetskoe iskusstvo*.[48]

Finally, even the idea of holding such a discussion came under fire in the official summing-up of the meeting: 'The organizers of the discussion were not justified in circulating, in the name of the Dramatists' Section, an agenda in which they expressed a definite point of view on a work of art, until the section as a whole had come to an opinion. This is doubly reprehensible since the organization, in issuing invitations to a discussion which should have reflected various points of view, tried to predetermine the tendency of the speeches, and so, indirectly, to influence the composition of the participants in the debate.'[49]

In spite of this apparent turn against Leonov and his plays, a leading article in *Teatr* at this time came out boldly in their defence.[50] It contains some interesting revelations of the campaign that had been conducted behind the scenes. But this unexpected support could do no more than postpone the final showdown.

After the first round of attacks Leonov had concluded that he would soon be arrested, and his wife went to Peredelkino in the hope of finding advice or even support from Fadeev, the Secretary of the Writers' Union, with whom Leonov was on friendly terms. However he refused to admit her, and spoke to her through the window, leaving her standing in the rain. (This episode was later used in *The Russian Forest*, where Fadeev's role was given to the Party careerist Cheredilov.) The next day, however, a long and laudatory article appeared in the government newspaper *Izvestiya*, and Fadeev promptly telephoned to congratulate him.[51]

Meanwhile Leonov's fate remained in limbo. Without having been officially disgraced he still remained something of a pariah. Some indication of the change in his fortunes can be seen from the drastic reduction in his appearances in print. Since 1927 he had contributed at least six articles a year to various newspapers and magazines; in 1939 ten had already appeared by August. Apart from *The Snowstorm*,[52] only a handful of unimportant articles were to appear in print between then and March 1941. His position had been fatally weakened, and when the attacks were renewed no one was prepared to come to his defence.

Ironically enough the initial reception of *The Snowstorm* had been wholly favourable. The play had proved a success in the provinces[53] and was in rehearsal for production at the Malyy Theatre.[54] In August 1940 it was actually shortlisted for a Stalin Prize, but only a few weeks later two articles appeared simultaneously under the same title, 'A Slanderous Play,'[55] making the same accusation, namely, that the image of the snowstorm was intended to represent the 'chaos' of Soviet reality, and that only the villains had been shown as possessing any character or intelligence; but Leonov's real crime was to have contemplated the possibility of redemption for a White officer. One of the articles ended with the ominous words: 'The work is dead, the images false. Such a playwright must inevitably become the channel for influences both foreign and hostile to us.' Other critics and the Committee for Artistic Affairs also came in for criticism for their misplaced enthusiasm over the play.

On the following day Leonov attended a discussion of the play at the Union of Soviet Writers. I have not been able to find any accounts of this meeting, but it must have been unfavourable, since several more articles appeared in the next two months reiterating the same charges.[56] The work was eventually banned by the Council of People's Commissars as a 'maliciously libellous and counter-revolutionary play,'[57] and it appeared that Leonov's arrest was imminent. At the end of 1940 he was dropped from the editorial board of *Novyy mir*, where he had served since 1932. He was never to return to it.

While Leonov believed that Stalin had been impressed by Gor'ky's praise of him, and had even intervened several times to protect him, he was fully aware of the dictator's capriciousness.[58] He had been told that Stalin had been through the entire text of *The Thief* with a red pencil, and he was in no doubt where the order to ban *The Snowstorm* came from: 'I had a difficult time after Stalin gave the order to kill *The Snowstorm*. I knew that the order came from Stalin himself. I thought they would come to arrest me, and I lay awake expecting it night after night.'[59]

> ... for two weeks my wife and I could not sleep, waiting for the knock on the door. Suddenly there was a telephone call from the theatre: 'Furtseva [the people's commissar for culture] is on her way, and we would like to perform the play for her with the author present.' In the second interval the management and I met Furtseva and her entourage. She addressed herself to me as the author: 'Most interesting, most interesting; now you should try to write something more up to date.'[60]

But this cynical gesture of reprieve did not extend to the play itself, and for more than twenty years it was not mentioned again in the Soviet press. None of Leonov's works was suppressed so completely. The play was reissued only in

1963 in a substantially revised version. This will be discussed in its place with the other revisions of the '50s and '60s.[61]

As works of art these plays occupy only a modest place in Leonov's total oeuvre, but the stage in his development that they mark is of considerable importance. Many of the situations and images of these plays and the dangers which they had occasioned were to exercise a compulsive, almost obsessive power over the author in his ensuing works.

chapter nine

The War Years 1941–1945

The nightmare of the Great Purges seemed to be winding down when the German invasion of 22 June 1941 brought new sufferings to the people of Russia, the appalling loss of life in the early campaigns, the acute food shortages that followed the devastation and loss of the Ukraine, and the physical hardships of evacuation. Even so the mass of the population regarded this new ordeal almost with relief. After the pall of fear and suspicion of the preceding years it was a comfort to rediscover mutual trust and unity in the common cause of repelling the invader. In literature the artificial themes of sabotage and espionage gave place to studies of actual war conditions and the image of a clearly defined enemy, though, as will be seen, the experience of the preceding years was not always easy to forget.

For Leonov the war provided an opportunity to rehabilitate himself. Three short articles of his appeared in the first few weeks after the invasion, though not in the most important periodicals, or in any particularly prominent position within them. As the *Wehrmacht* approached Moscow his wife and daughters were evacuated to Chistopol',[1] and he himself joined them at the end of November.[2] During the war years he made several trips to the front, which provided material for patriotic despatches, and once his rehabilitation was completed with the award of a Stalin Prize he became a regular contributor to *Pravda*.

Leonov's wartime articles, like those of other Soviet writers, at first appeal primarily to Russian patriotism and national pride, but by 1944, with victory now assured they begin to emphasize the role of the Communist Party. The names of Lenin and Stalin are dragged into a speech supposedly commemorating Chekhov; the enemy ceases to be just Nazi Germany and becomes the 'old world.' The concept explicitly embraces even Russia's nominal allies in the West, who are now accused of unleashing Hitler against an innocent Soviet

Union. The age of the 'cold war' was dawning even before the 'hot' one had ended.

During these years Leonov wrote two plays, *Invasion (Nashestvie)*[3] and *Lenushka*,[4] and a novella, *The Taking of Velikoshumsk (Vzyatie Velikoshumska)*.[5] The situation that underlies all these works, the expulsion of an invader-intruder, is closely related to that of the preceding plays, and each work ends with the defeat of the Germans either prophesied or achieved. In *Invasion* the family of Dr Talanov find themselves occupied by the Germans in the winter of 1941–2. Among the intruders are such relics of the pre-revolutionary past as Fayunin, now collaborating with the enemy, and the Talanovs' only son, Fedor, who has just returned unexpectedly from three years in prison. Since his return coincides with the German invasion he is naturally, under Soviet conditions, regarded with distrust. At the end, however, he is redeemed by his *podvig*, when he takes upon himself the name of Kolesnikov, the leader of a group of partisans. Fedor is hanged, but his self-sacrifice enables the real Kolesnikov to escape. The play ends with the landing of Russian paratroops and the news that the Germans have just suffered a reverse outside Moscow.

Originally Fedor was conceived as an innocent victim of the Purges, but this was not acceptable to the censors,[6] and so Leonov provided another explanation for his imprisonment, the attempted murder of his mistress (for which his release after only three years seems more plausible).[7] In the revised version of 1964, completed after the XXII Party Congress and the second round of de-Stalinization, Leonov returned to his original conception.[8] This makes much better sense of Fedor's intense bitterness and the wariness with which he is regarded by the other characters.

It is surprising how few changes Leonov needed to make in order to clarify this point, and several phrases acquire new meanings in the changed context. Thus when Dr Talanov advises his son: 'Your sickness is curable... And the prescription has already been written. It is – to be fair to people' Fedor explodes:

> Fair? and the people you have cured over the past thirty years, have they been fair to you? You were the first, long before the big names, to perform operations on the heart. It was you who got the polyclinic started, on your own hard-earned money. You have become a feature of the town, a piece of public property like the fire engine... and now the Nibelungs are moving east, destroying everything. People are fleeing, taking what they can with them... but why have they forgotten you? (7. 471)

In the first version the remark characterizes only the speaker; in the second it serves to evoke the atmosphere of the times and, in particular, Dr Talanov's difficulties with the Party.

Like Leonov's previous intruders Fedor is associated with images of cold and death. These suggest his loneliness and alienation, as he cannot forget or forgive his unjust imprisonment, even in the face of his people's sufferings. Only when he sees Aniska, a young Russian girl who has been raped and tortured by the Germans, can he overcome his bitterness and perform a *podvig*: he murders a German officer and takes the name of Kolesnikov. In the last act when all around him are freezing he alone feels warm, and at his interrogation he can claim of himself: 'I am a Russian. I am defending my country' (7. 511). His physical return is thus transformed into a psychological return, so that in all versions up to the 1983 edition the play ends with his mother's ecstatic cry: 'He has returned, he is mine, he is ours.'[9] In this way the play's refrain, 'The Russians always return,' acquires a new meaning. Like Porfiriy Syrovarov in *The Snowstorm* Fedor is a social outcast whose return at first inspires only fear and suspicion until he manages to justify himself.

The figure of the collaborator, the former merchant Fayunin, recalls Pylyaev from *The Orchards of Polovchansk*. He had left Russia twenty-five years ago, in 1917 – it is implied that he had been a Tsarist police agent – and has now returned as town governor under the Nazis. He is characterized in the dramatis personae as 'returned from the dead' (7. 461); and he even introduces himself as 'Lazarus' (7. 477). He first appears mysteriously out of the darkness, when the power is cut (7. 477). He likes to hint at his similarity to Fedor and his criminal past; he reminds Talanov: 'Perhaps our sons slept in the same bunks at public expense' (7. 482–3). He recommends Fedor to the Germans – 'You will have heard of the son of Mr Talanov as a fighter against Soviet power' (7. 485). But he has little confidence in his German masters and he is convinced that the Russians will eventually triumph: 'Russia, my friend, is the sort of pie that the more you eat the more remains' (7. 500). Accordingly he does not betray Fedor or Kolesnikov to the Germans even when it is in his power to do so, in the naive hope that this service will be taken into account when at last the Russians do return. There is no suggestion that it will.

Leonov for some time contemplated a sequel to *Invasion*, to be called 'Retribution,'[10] in which one of the minor characters of *Invasion*, the boy Prokofiy Statnov, was to have played an important part. Nothing came of this project, but some scenes and ideas originally intended for *Invasion* later found their way into the play *Lenushka*.

The main action concerns a group of villagers whose homes have been requisitioned by the Germans. They have joined the partisans but they have become aware that there is a traitor among them, and the plot is built on finding out who this is. He proves to be Stepan Drakin, a former *kulak*, and it is his brother Biryuk who plays the major role in unmasking him. The conflict of the two Drakin brothers bears a close resemblance to the situation of the brothers Syrovarov in *The Snowstorm*. In each case the villain is called Stepan. Much as the unmentionable émigré Porfiriy proves superior to his Soviet brother, so in *Lenushka* the apparently respectable Stepan Drakin is eventually shown up by his brother, the social outcast, Biryuk (the word means 'lone wolf').[11] The wolf image thus temporarily regains the potentially positive associations that it had had in Leonov's early works; the 'thief,' however, is now beyond redemption.

But this denouement is poorly prepared and so feels merely arbitrary. At the beginning of the play Stepan's patriotic gesture of offering to share all his possessions with the villagers and his hostility to Biryuk and another peasant seems to identify the good guys and bad guys conclusively. Biryuk and Potapych are outsiders in the village community, and even their supposedly admirable actions would be open to doubt elsewhere in Leonov's work. Thus of Potapych's heroic death we hear only from Biryuk, while Biryuk's *podvig* consists in bringing in the head of a German officer; but since none of the other Russians (except the now dead Potapych) has ever seen this German, this is not conclusive proof of his loyalty. Biryuk is regularly denigrated, not only by Stepan but even by the stage directions: 'People expect some evil from this man of the woods' (7. 535), while the small boy Don'ka asks, 'Is it true that Satan lives in his cap?' (7. 535). In fact were it not for Stepan's improbable admission of his hatred for the Soviet regime there would be few grounds for believing in his guilt.

To some extent this confusion can be justified as a sign of how the breakdown of trust and confidence over the preceding years continued to poison relations even during the war. Pokhlebkin, the incompetent, garrulous, and self-centred president of the village council, tells Travina, another Party member, that he cannot be sure even of her: 'Documents can always be stolen off a corpse' (7. 558). On the other hand, although Stepan has been a *kulak* he has no difficulty in finding credulous ears for his slanders on three loyal Soviet citizens. Indeed some Soviet critics have considered Biryuk to be no better than his brother, but redeemed by the death of Potapych, as Fedor Talanov was by the sight of Aniska in *Invasion*.[12] It would seem, however, from certain hints in Act 1 that Leonov intended to contrast the two brothers from the very beginning. For example, Biryuk warns the villagers against accepting Stepan's seemingly generous offer, and he is shown in a favourable light in the scene where he meets his long-lost friend Turkin. Leonov often makes use of reunion scenes to indicate his characters' moral steadfastness or degradation.

Lenushka's fiancé, Il'ya Drakin, is perhaps the most interesting character in the play. He too is descended from a prototype in *The Snowstorm*, the young Communist Serezha. But there is an important difference between them. Like Serezha Il'ya is shown at first as a selfish individualist, but unlike him he finds the strength to overcome the *kulak* instincts he has inherited from his father, and proves capable of a *podvig*: he risks his life to capture a German doctor in the hope of saving the man who has supplanted him in Lenushka's affections.

The heroine, Lenushka, is a seventeen-year-old girl who has volunteered for the partisans. Strictly speaking she is only tangentially related to the main action, and serves more as a symbolic figure representing the spirit of Russia. In the course of the play she develops and matures, though this is signalled more in the stage directions than by anything she actually says or does. At the end of Act 2 her father is amazed by her 'new and commanding intonation' (7. 563), and in the final scene Leonov comments, 'How unlike she is to herself as she was at the beginning of this tale!' (7. 591). Like Masha Makkaveeva and Nastya Roshchina in the earlier plays she achieves maturity, and finally sums up the play with the curse that she pronounces on the Germans.

Although the two plays are set in different milieux, *Invasion* among the intelligentsia of a provincial town, *Lenushka* among a group of peasants, with all the differences of speech-idiom that this implies, the two plays are related to one another much as *The Orchards of Polovchansk* and *Wolf* had been. The clear distinction between friends and enemies in the former play is blurred in the second, but where in *Wolf* Leonov suggests a possible alternative reading of the characters and events, in *Lenushka* there is no such suggestion. The two war plays are further linked by the image of 'medicine,' which here means the experience of suffering that reunites the alienated hero with his people. They are also similar in construction. At the end of the second act the figure of a mutilated Russian, Aniska in *Invasion,* Temnikov in *Lenushka*, is introduced as a silent reminder of the human cost of the war, while in the third a younger character is strengthened in his resolve by the assurance that Stalin is watching him personally. In both plays the dramatic action is essentially complete by the end of the third act, and the fourth is limited to tying up loose ends and underlining the message.

The same basic elements, the war, the Soviet family, and the concept of the *podvig* provide the framework for Leonov's only piece of war fiction, *The Taking of Velikoshumsk*. The family here, however, is not founded on blood relationships but on national and supranational affinities. Thus several of the characters, both central and episodic, bear the same surname, Litovchenko; a variant of this name, Litovtsev, also appears (8. 45). The name embraces the whole Soviet population: 'At this point all these people belonged to the one family of the Litovchenkos, passing drivers, the general, [...] stern-faced peasants from Vologda, the Tatar Aleksey, [...] and even the gods peering out of their paper flower-bed' (8. 26). This sense of kinship between the different strata of the population is reinforced by the unanimity of the different nationalities within the Soviet Union. Thus the Ukrainian name of Litovchenko in itself includes the meaning Lithuanian; in the same way the four protagonists of the story come from widely separated parts of the country, Ukraine, the Kuban', the Altay, and Siberia, and yet other nationalities appear episodically.

Unlike the plays which reflect the desperate situation of the first two years, the novella depicts the turn of the tide. The action covers four days over the winter solstice (20–23 December 1943) when the Russian advance was temporarily halted to regroup and secure communications, and the Germans launched a powerful counter-attack. The strategic significance of the action is thus underlined not only with reference to the Ukrainian front but to the whole course of the war. The story itself is devoted to a daring raid carried out by a lone tank, No. 203, behind the German lines, and the eventual destruction of the tank and half its crew.[13] The raid, however, plays an important part in securing the Russian advance and the liberation of the town of Velikoshumsk. Thus the story deals with a temporary setback in a generally triumphant progress, and this was recognized not only by the work's first readers but the author himself as he composed the story. This naturally affects his attitude to events.

As in the two plays the *podvig* bears both an individual and a public character. For one of the heroes, Dybok, the *podvig* in No. 203 is a necessary step on his road to fame; for the young Litovchenko it represents initiation into maturity. At the beginning of the story, as an inexperienced driver he lets his tank slide off a ramp, thus delaying the movements of the whole division; by the end of the story he has become an expert.

But it is the idea of the *podvig* as patriotic sacrifice that is predominant in all these works, and the word regains something of its original religious associations – that to lose one's life in a worthy cause is the surest way of finding it:

> a hero performing his duty fears nothing in this world except oblivion. But even oblivion is not frightening when the *podvig* exceeds the bounds of duty. Then the hero enters the very heart and brain of his people; his example inspires thousands, and with them he changes the course of the river of history like a great cliff, becomes a part of the national character; such was the *podvig* of No. 203. (8. 116–17)

As with Fedor Talanov the *podvig* becomes an affirmation of the unity of the individual and the community. Such a *podvig* is the exclusive prerogative of the Soviet people, the final proof of the superiority of Soviet man. General Litovchenko declares:

It is not enough to give a detailed account of material improvements or to enumerate paragraphs from a program not yet fully achieved [...] We have decided to help history and shorten time [...] We hold the fate of progress like a fledgling in our roughened palms. We have discovered that no one holds it as dear as we do. [Our] devotion to the idea is measured by our readiness for endurance and sacrifice [...] the ordinary poor mortal imagines that he lives on the very edge of time; pain blinkers his gaze into the future. But my soldiers [...] gaze ahead and almost hold in their hands the newspapers of the twenty-first century [...] that is where the Soviet soldier finds his immortality. (8. 48–9)

This sense that the future is already discernible in the present recalls *The Road to Ocean* and in one passage, 'Great rivers never hurry. They flow into the ocean' (8. 90), Leonov explicitly refers back to the novel. Ocean had been rendered accessible by the October Revolution, and now nothing stands in the way of its attainment but the Germans:

We who flung open our prison doors with our own hands and burst upon the expanses of Ocean – we fear nothing. What of Fascism? We will pass through it as through the smoke of the last campfire left by savages. (8. 50)

And in another passage these same expanses are the 'parents of wings' (8. 49). Thus the image of wings once more underlines the kinship between the two works and unites the ideas of the *podvig* and the future.

Accordingly the Russians are linked throughout with images of life. Even their shells are not destructive but life-giving. Dybok cries as he fires on a German tank: 'Drink up our Russian *kvas*. It's the elixir of life; take your fill of it' (8. 82). Nature herself is on the side of the Russians against the invaders: 'Every stone tore at [the German] entrails, every bush fired a shot after them' (8. 73). Even the sun, 'that cold brazen luminary, was conspiring to ruin Germany' (8. 110). In their identification with Nature and the forces of life the Russians are enabled to overcome the physical limitations of ordinary humanity so that even death, 'like a mongrel scrounged at the feet of these immortals' (8. 77).

The Germans by contrast are shown as subhuman. In *Invasion* they are seen first as grotesque phantoms, silhouetted through smoked glass; when they come on stage they are described in the stage directions as animals. In *The Taking of Velikoshumsk* they are shown as monsters, revealing the true face of German culture:

high-quality German death, tested in government laboratories, liquid, solid, and gaseous, death that travelled round our land in gas chambers [...] here was everything that over the centuries had been concealed in the vaults of German universities – whips for our peasants, nails for crucifying children for target-practice, unslaked lime and metal gloves for torturing prisoners, black paste for sealing the nostrils of children at the breast... (8. 111–12)[14]

They frequently display their barbarism by talking in German, and when they do speak Russian their cruel maltreatment of the language indicates their soullessness and brutality. In *Lenushka* not just the German language but even its script becomes the object of loathing. The Germans are frequently shown as cowards; even their courage is only suicidal and gains no admiration from the Russians. Long after they have destroyed No. 203 they continue to bombard it: 'Only an animal fear that the tank might yet come to life again [...] could explain this frenzied and ignoble shelling' (8. 116).

But although the victory of the Russians is assured Leonov does not pretend that it can be achieved cheaply. An essential element in all these works is the hideous and irreparable suffering involved: the rape of Aniska in *Invasion*, the figure of the dying Temnikov in *Lenushka*, and the stage directions with their reminders in the form of explosions and burning villages. In *The Taking of Velikoshumsk* the scene with the demented woman screaming, 'War, where are my children?' acts as 'a spur to the furious energy of the crew' (8. 109). Such scenes are intended to mobilize not only the fictional characters but also readers and audiences. Thus in *Lenushka* one of the homeless peasants driven out by the Germans reminds his blinded leader: 'Filipp Dem'yanych, your countrymen are sitting here in front of you, they are waiting to hear the truth. Tell them how you defended your country with your breast,' and the villagers stand, 'their faces severe and solemn as if they had been born anew' (7. 541). The exhibition of suffering on the stage and the use of speeches addressed as much to the audience as to stage characters link these works to the propaganda articles that Leonov wrote during the war.

Leonov himself said that he was inspired 'by the suffering that Hitler had brought to children. The Nazis' mass burials in Kerch' still haunt me. *Invasion* was built out of this.'[15] Thus where the Germans callously murder defenceless children the Russians see them as the supreme issue at stake, an embodiment of the people's hopes for the future: 'Is there anything we wouldn't do for them, for children, for the children of the world? We'd make bridges of our bodies to save them from wetting their shoes in blood. I'd drink all the filth of the world at a single draught to spare them even a drop' (8. 93). At its simplest this is an appeal to sentiment, 'all the children of the world cry in the same language' (10. 109), but at the same time it recalls Dostoevsky's sense that of all sufferings those of small children are the most hideous.

All three works introduce some references to religion, particularly ikons, but the references are generally negative. Fayunin ostentatiously crosses himself; while in *Lenushka*, with its setting among the peasantry, religion is generally shown as an aspect of an archaic way of life. The heroine persuades her father to pray to an ikon in the hope of saving Temnikov's life. When Temnikov dies, Lenushka dismisses God as an 'old black stone' (7. 591).

The war years mark the beginning of Leonov's rehabilitation. He made certain concessions to the requirements of the time in both his journalism and his plays with numerous adulatory references to Stalin, 'the sage of Gori.'[16] Most of these were removed after the denunciation of Stalin at the XX Party Congress in 1956, but some were retained as true to the spirit of the war years. Similarly, he refrained from describing *Invasion* as a tragedy, preferring the noncommittal 'play in four acts' (7. 459).

At the same time these plays show Leonov's attraction to danger. For the basic plot, the return and redemption of a prodigal, is essentially the same as that of *The Snowstorm*, the play that had almost destroyed him. Indeed, in writing these works he was in an analogous position to his heroes, Fedor Talanov and Biryuk, and the target of similar distrust. Unlike most of his previous works which had been printed in pride of place at the front of the journals in which they appeared, *Invasion* was tucked away inconspicuously in the middle. Theatres too were in no hurry to stage the play.[17] Tairov to whom the play had originally been offered never put it on, and the first performance was given only in an amateur production in Chistopol' with Leonov himself directing. Leonov's still shaky position can be seen from a telegram purporting to come from the Kazan' repertory committee: 'What is the justification for putting on this play?'[18] which reached Chistopol' on the night of the first performance. It was only after it was awarded a Stalin Prize in March 1943[19] that the play began to be accepted.

Since then it has enjoyed an uninterrupted triumph. In the Soviet Union it was the most frequently performed of his plays and probably the best known of all his works. One Soviet critic went so far as to claim that it was among the masterpieces of world literature.[20] A film version was produced in 1944, and some critics regarded it as an improvement on the play.[21] As an opera, however, it was less successful.[22]

Leonov was apparently encouraged by the success of *Invasion*, for he boldly called his next play *Lenushka*, a 'folk tragedy' (7. 529), though with rather less justification than in the case of *Invasion*. Unlike its predecessor, however, this play has never enjoyed favour in the Soviet Union. It had to wait three years for its Moscow premiere, and it was then greeted by a scurrilous attack in the press.[23] The main charges against the play were its 'fatalism' and 'pessimism'; by the latter was meant not simply the grisly picture of the German occupation, but also the admission that some Russians had collaborated with the Nazis. The play was accused of being false and malicious, and, more sinisterly, a return to the style of Leonov's pre-war plays, an allusion to *The Snowstorm*. The use of language was compared to Zoshchenko's, another serious accusation after the attacks on Zoshchenko and Akhmatova made by Zhdanov in August 1946, only two months earlier. The article also contained a personal attack on Leonov for his alleged vanity. Konstantin Simonov made a half-hearted attempt to defend the play;[24] but he was careful to dissociate himself from *The Snowstorm* and Zoshchenko.

The same embarrassment over *Lenushka* has been felt by Russian critics up to the present day. It is still one of the least discussed of Leonov's major works, but this neglect is undeserved. It is, admittedly, a less straightforward play than *Invasion*, and a less successful one. But this should not disguise the fact that it is a much more complex and ambitious work. The preceding plays had followed the conventional dramatic structure of a central hero, surrounded by lesser figures necessary for the sake of the narrative or the construction. In *Lenushka* several characters are studied in depth, and there are at least four who perform a *podvig* of greater or lesser significance. Biryuk and Potapych display heroism of the type of the earlier submariners and parachutists. For the boys Don'ka and Il'ya Drakin, the *podvig* is rather more than a display of heroism; it is also a sign of their coming of age, both physically and morally. Il'ya, in particular, not only risks his life, but does so for the sake of Lenushka's lover, thus equating the *podvig* with self-sacrifice, a characteristic feature of Leonov's later works. Leonov may not combine and develop these themes with quite the mastery displayed in his two best plays, *An Ordinary Man* and *A Golden Coach;* but *Lenushka* is an essential step on the way.

The Taking of Velikoshumsk was received on its first appearance with guarded praise, but it remained in favour throughout the Soviet period. At the same time it has received much less critical attention than Leonov's other major works, justifiably, for the story does not possess the individuality of the novels, in which almost every sentence taken out of context can be identified; indeed in certain passages, such as the relationship between the veteran Sobol'kov and the inexperienced Litovchenko, one is reminded of Fadeev's *The Rout* (*Razgrom*, 1927). This is partly due of course to the limitations of most war writing, which easily descends into the clichés of melodrama and propaganda.

More damagingly, the style has been infected by some of the mannerisms of Leonov's wartime journalism. The aphoristic simplifications and the stereotypical strong silent men have not worn well:

> ... each one completed his personal affairs without any trace of nerves, they became for a moment sterner, as though on the eve of some distant journey, and

[young Litovchenko] understood that it was just here that people understood life most profoundly and did not mention the name of its mighty antagonist even in their thoughts. (8. 67)

Or again:

And something had happened with Dybok: he placed his hand on Sobol'kov's knee, squeezed it in a vice-like grip, and words that at other times could not have been extracted from Dybok even under torture burst from his lips:

'Hey, Lieutenant...' and something shook in his voice, 'they're good people who live on my land, *my* people. I would lay down my life for them seven times in a row. Then I'd rest a bit... and lay down another one.' (8. 90)

Some critics have seen in the tale a Soviet version of 'Taras Bul'ba,' an impression that is reinforced by Leonov's deliberate introduction of Gogol' and his works into the narrative, but the epic tone is occasionally deflated by such embarrassing miscalculations as 'It had turned dark again; the moon had been removed until next time, *so that it shouldn't wear out* (8. 93; the words italicized were later added to the *Novyy mir* version).

The story further irritates by its claim that the people and events in it are not only absolutely unparalleled, but at the same time utterly typical of the Soviet war effort. Thus the exploits of tank No. 203 did not at once 'reach the ears of the whole country only because it was lost in a dozen similar ones' (8. 109). But this is belied by the general hyperbolic tone of the story and a succession of remarkable, not to say incredible, coincidences. On one occasion No. 203 and its crew are saved from certain annihilation by a hare crossing the field and distracting the attention of the German gunners; on another by the rising sun blinding the Nazis; on a third occasion the Russians succeed in firing a shell down the barrel of a German tank: 'Such good fortune is not bestowed on even the most illustrious aces. This was not just accuracy, but a coincidence bordering on the inconceivable' (8. 80).

All three works are tragic in intention, but the tragedy is still 'optimistic.' The deaths of the heroes and heroines do not endanger but rather secure the eventual triumph. A more serious limitation is the emphasis on hatred and revenge as responses to the German atrocities. German casualties evoke in Leonov only contempt; and often enough even their existence is ignored, as in the scene in which No. 203 successfully blows up a bridge when it is crowded with soldiers.

Nationalism has always been a feature of Leonov's outlook, and official propaganda in the first years of the war appealed deliberately to Russian patriotism rather than to Soviet or Communist ideals, but here it becomes unpleasantly chauvinistic. 'A foreigner wouldn't understand a thing in this mystery or the source of the strange and haunting magic of Russian song, because the secret does not lie in the notes or in the words either' (8. 59). The West is denounced in *Lenushka* for its failure to support Russia in the war. Thus when Biryuk brings in the head of a German officer Pokhlebkin is shocked: 'All Europe is watching us, and you, you're a man of the night, of the deep forest, that's what you are. We are fighting savages, and then you...' Biryuk replies, 'Why do you try to frighten me with Europe. When we were struggling with these bandits hand to hand, where was your Europe then? They buried Turkin in a well, they pulled up Ustya's skirts, and hanged her... and your Europe was drinking coffee, I supppose?' (7. 577). The emergence of such sentiments during the wartime alliance was an ominous presage of the Cold War soon to unfold.

Admittedly, the glorification of the heroism and nobility of one's own soldiers and citizens and the deliberate cultivation of hatred and contempt for the enemy are features of war literature anywhere. But a comparison of these works with the sensitive and indirect treatment of the equally bitter Civil War in Leonov's early stories, a war in which Leonov himself had been even more actively engaged, and the pacifist sympathies of his works of the '20s and '30s, points to a narrowing of the author's vision. It is true that his works of the war years were not intended for aesthetic contemplation; they were designed to mobilize and direct public opinion. But many works of art, dictated by specific events, have acquired a universal significance that was never foreseen by the author. Leonov's work of 1941–5 is unlikely to be remembered in this way.

chapter ten

An Ordinary Man and *A Golden Coach* 1940–1946

The plays *An Ordinary Man* (*Obyknovennyy chelovek*)[1] and *A Golden Coach* (*Zolotaya kareta*)[2] are the finest of Leonov's dramatic works, and reveal such skill in dramatic construction that it is surprising that he wrote no more plays after them. Perhaps the difficulties in getting them produced played a part in Leonov's subsequent loss of interest in the form. *An Ordinary Man* had to wait four years for its first performance; *A Golden Coach* was accepted for performance by the Malyy Theatre in 1946, but was soon afterwards banned by Zhdanov,[3] and has still not been performed in its original version. In 1955, when the Moscow Arts Theatre expressed an interest in performing it, Leonov subjected the play to far-reaching revisions, and it is this version that is generally known. It will be discussed in its place with the other late revisions.

An Ordinary Man is described by Leonov as a 'comedy in four acts,' and it reveals a much sunnier kind of humour than any of his works since *The Badgers*. This is the more remarkable since it was written in the difficult period in Leonov's life that followed the banning of *The Snowstorm* and was completed in February 1941.[4] No trace of these events can be detected in the play, however, and it seems likely that Leonov found some relief from his situation in composing it. Even more surprising is the fact that it was published while Leonov's reputation was still under a cloud. The fact that the play was not performed or even noticed at the time is natural enough in the desperate conditions of the first years of the war.

Unlike Leonov's previous plays *An Ordinary Man* is not easily summarized. The parallels linking it to its predecessors are deceptive. Like them it concerns a Soviet family: Ladygin, a prominent operatic bass,[5] his wife, and their nephew, Aleksey, a young and brilliant biologist. With them is staying a young divorcée, Kira, to whom Aleksey has for some time been on the point of proposing. Konstantsiya, Kira's mother, and Svekolkin (an old friend of Ladygin's from the days of the Civil War) and his daughter Annushka play the part of intruders. These last two help to bring about Aleksey's marriage to Kira, although by this time Annushka has herself fallen in love with him. Konstantsiya, on the other hand, has her own ideas of a successful marriage for Kira and tries to draw her away from Aleksey to the older, wealthier (and married) Ladygin instead. All three intruders leave the Ladygin household at the end of the play. Konstantsiya is virtually expelled and is taken away by the Svekolkins, who are invited to come again; but we are given to understand that they will not do so. They have successfully completed their mission.

The play is unique in Leonov's oeuvre in that it deals with the comfortable and leisurely life of the Soviet cultural elite. The first act is set in a luxurious apartment in Moscow, and the last three in an isolated and spacious *dacha*. The setting and the storyline give the play the appearance of a 'drawing-room comedy.' But the final marriage proposal is not a prelude to 'living happily ever after.' Aleksey, we are to believe, loves Kira sincerely enough, but his work in the lab will always take precedence over his private life. Kira is more calculating; she is torn between the rival attractions of an established figure in the artistic world and an up-and-coming young scientist. Leonov clearly gives his preference to the scientist (probably because the vanities of the artistic elite were better known to him). At the end of the play, however, the two are still on formal '*vy*' terms, suggesting that their marriage will not so much unite them as accommodate their different interests.

The guiding spirit behind the play is Pavel Svekolkin,[6] the 'ordinary person' of the title. He stands apart from the others and serves at times as a mouthpiece for the author. He is a figure of unchallenged authority; he foresees all the moves in the game and advises the various characters accordingly. It is he who engineers the engagement of Aleksey to Kira, and he is an influential member of the committee that awards an important prize to Aleksey. In fact he is a People's Commissar and a prominent scientist, but because he is a 'small man of humble appearance' (7. 296) Ladygin takes him for a bank clerk, and so asks him to pretend to be something grander; Svekolkin cheerfully assumes his real identity and acts the part with such success that Ladygin comments: 'An extraordinary man' (7. 299). Even when Svekolkin's name is publicized in connection with the prize committee, Ladygin cannot imagine that it might be the same person.

This aspect of the play recalls Chekhov's short story, *The Grasshopper* (*Poprygun'ya*, 1892). Just as Ol'ga Ivanovna's passion for 'extraordinary people' had led her to neglect and even betray her apparently ordinary, but in fact outstanding, husband, so in *An Ordinary Man* the modestly ordinary Svekolkin proves to be exceptional, while connoisseurs of the extraordinary turn out to be merely vulgar. The moral is underlined by the toast to 'heroic ordinariness' (7. 346) which closes the third act.

The cult of the 'extraordinary' is caricatured in the figure of Konstantsiya. She has arranged one disastrous marriage for her daughter Kira, and is now on the lookout for another. Leonov mocks her absurd language and clothes, but she is more than a figure of fun. Like many of the characters of Gogol' she is a figure of evil under a mask of silliness and vulgarity. Ladygin is in danger of falling into the same trap. He has been corrupted by success and his desire for 'things,' the material evidence of it. His apartment looks like 'an antique shop with a multitude of objects wrapped up in gauze covers and yellowing newspapers' (7. 275),[7] while he flatters himself that 'All this has been given me by my people' (7. 289). Leonov, however, does not oversimplify his failings and he is treated with some indulgence; Ladygin says of himself: 'When I was a child they were always chasing me out; it was always, No, no, no. I had to wait too long for it to be Yes, yes, yes' (7. 289). Even so, the signs of his later egoism were visible some twenty years ago when he had first known Svekolkin. Just as he had then failed to notice the girl that his friend later married, so he is now unconcerned by the news of her death.

The visible symbol of Ladygin's materialism is his latest acquisition, a large picture. He cannot remember what it represents, only the price that it fetched before the Revolution. When finally it is taken out of its wrappings and hung, it crashes on to the settee where he had been sitting only a few minutes earlier. The moral is plain: 'things' can threaten one's very life. Ladygin decides to get rid of the picture, but even then it resists to the last: 'A lifeless thing, but it seems to have grown roots,' comments the maid Parasha (7. 359).

The other main focus of interest is Svekolkin's daughter, Annushka, the most attractive of Leonov's young heroines. Like her predecessors in Leonov's novels and plays of the '30s she is an incarnation of honour and innocence; but unlike them she has no great ambitions and suffers from no burden of guilt; instead she is blessed with an irrepressible sense of humour. Her moment of decision occurs when she falls in love with Aleksey and is tempted to take advantage of his temporary disenchantment with Kira. At this point Svekolkin says to her:

> Suppose you found happiness lying in the road. Large and smart, but belonging to someone else. Would you take it home with you to bury at your own front door, or even try it on yourself? (7. 342)

She rises to the challenge and is rewarded, like her predecessors in Leonov's plays, by being allowed to utter the final condemnation of Konstanstsiya:

You wicked, evil woman, you're the wickedest woman in the world!.. Look at her face, blackened with age and experience... Give us a chance to live, you black people. Get out. (7. 337)

Thus summarized the figure of Annushka sounds intolerably priggish, but Leonov presents her youthful innocence and impulsiveness persuasively. Certain aspects of her role, however, suggest possible dangers. These will become clearer from a comparison with *A Golden Coach*.

The atmosphere and problems of this play seem at first to be utterly different from those of *An Ordinary Man*. As will be seen, however, the two plays are closely related. *A Golden Coach* is set in a small unnamed provincial town[8] immediately after the end of the war.[9] Some twenty-seven years earlier[10] a young schoolmaster, Nikolay Karev, had proposed to Masha Poroshina; but her parents had forbidden him to see her again until he could provide a golden coach for his bride, and she had not had the courage to elope with the man she loved. Karev left the district to work in the Pamir mountains and eventually became an outstanding geologist. In the meantime Masha too has risen in the world. As Mar'ya Sergeevna she has for several years been unchallenged as the mayor of the town (in fact the original title, 'The Mayoress,' placed her at the centre of the drama).[11] She is married to a factory director, Chirkhanov, and has a daughter, Mar'ka.

When the play opens Karev has just returned for the first time in all these years; he is on his way to the Pamirs once again, this time prospecting for oil. He is a widower now, with a grown son, Yakov, only just demobilized from the army. The older people discover that they are still drawn to one another, and they begin to think of a marriage between their children. But the situation is no longer the same: the girl Mar'ka loves and is loved by the soldier Timosha, who has been blinded in the war; so that it is Timosha who is now in the position of the former schoolmaster, while it is Karev and his son who now flaunt their 'golden coach.' The tension and denouement of the play are built round these two alternatives with their various symmetries and asymmetries. Will Mar'ka follow Yakov to the Pamirs or stay behind with Timosha, despite his lack of prospects? Will the children make up for their parents' broken happiness? – which in these circumstances would be to repeat their mistake – or will they defy their parents' wishes and so avoid their errors? This is the most elegant plot in all Leonov's work and it secures a balance of interest and sympathy between the various protagonists. The fairy-tale associations of the title add to the complications and are recalled in such details as a pair of slippers, intended for Mar'ka, and the presence of a benevolent magician. But Mar'ka is no Cinderella, while Timosha would be insulted to be seen in such a role.

In the first version of *A Golden Coach* Mar'ka elects to marry Yakov Karev. Leonov in his commentary on the play admits that she is making a mistake, and suggests that she does so only because she cannot marry Timosha for some years yet. He adds that she will be happy with Yakov, but will still occasionally regret her decision.[12] Accordingly the play ends on a subdued note; the children have repeated their parents' mistake.

This minor-key ending is in keeping with the generally austere tonality of the play's setting and subject matter. Timosha is blind, his commanding officer Berezkin has returned home shell-shocked to discover that he has lost his wife and daughter in an air raid; the travelling conjuror Rakhuma has lost his entire family at Babiy Yar. The town has been devastated; there is a sense of exhaustion rather than elation at the victory over the Germans and a recognition that the war had produced cowards as well as heroes. The ruined church visible in the background (according to the stage directions) that had appeared in Leonov's three wartime works and will be found again in *The Russian Forest*,[13] is a reminder not only of the destruction wrought by the Nazis, but also of the Communists' assault on religion in the 1920s and 1930s. As one of the characters in *A Golden Coach* remarks, 'If you want to destroy a people you start with its sacred places' *(ZK, 5)*. Not altogether surprisingly the play was found unsuitable for production and it was suppressed soon after its appearance in print.

The negative features are concentrated in the figure of Mar'ya Sergeevna's husband, Chirkhanov, a factory director, an army officer, and, though it is not explicit, a Party member. His importance to the design is indicated by his position at the head of the dramatis personae: he is constantly being referred to; his entry appears at times to be imminent; he is heard scurrying in the corridors, but he himself never materializes. Emptiness, death, and nonexistence are recurring symbols for evil throughout Leonov's work. Untilovsk is 'one large hole'; Osip Shtruf in *Skutarevsky* is introduced punningly as Mr Trup (corpse); in the war plays the foreign agents and the Nazis are 'shadows' or 'returned from the dead.' Chirkhanov is the culmination of this line. As with Gogol''s Chichikov and Khlestakov, what is horrifying about him is not so much what he does as the fact that he exists at all. Such figures are blasphemous incarnations of void and nothingness. Like Gogol''s archetypes too Chirkhanov is successful in everything; he has a powerful position, he is an irresistible womanizer, he has had a good war. True, the matches that his factory produces are notoriously non-inflammable, his love affairs have wrecked his marriage, and his war record is one of utter cowardice. Despite this he continues to present a smug and triumphant face to the world.

His former commanding officer, Colonel Berezkin, 'the conscience of the war,' has returned home with the intention of revealing Chirkhanov's war record and so disgracing him in the eyes of his family. But before he can do this he learns that his own family has been wiped out in an air raid. In his works of the war years Leonov would have used this to intensify Berezkin's desire for revenge; here the opposite happens. Berezkin discovers that Mar'ya Sergeevna has no illusions about her husband and as he realizes that his revelations will hurt Mar'ka far more than her father, he gives up his plan. It is this gesture of renouncing revenge that helps to create the unusual atmosphere of the play.

Eventually Chirkhanov's sordid affairs and the endless ramifications of his cowardice and falsity drive him from the town. There is no need for Leonov to invoke the NKVD, as he had done in *The Snowstorm*: 'Now every rustle behind the door will make him think of the coming of a judge; his own shadow on the wall at evening – of the shadow of an avenger. And even when we have forgotten him the wind of war will still hound him like a leaf in autumn' (*ZK*, 56). Just as Katerina tells Zoya that Stepan Syrovarov's crime is not that he is 'an enemy, but that he is a thief' (*M*, 92), so too Mar'ya Sergeevna answers her daughter's question: 'What has he stolen?' 'Life' (*ZK*, 59).

Despite this bleak picture of the times *A Golden Coach* can be seen as the most soberly affirmative of all Leonov's works. It tells of human failures, but it tells too of human responses to these failures. Thus Karev and his son, Mar'ya Sergeevna and her Mar'ka, all make their mistakes and have to cope with the consequences for the rest of their lives. But the past does not take the form of a guilty secret, like, for example, Aleksandra Ivanovna's bastard son in *The Orchards of Polovchansk*; it is a stimulus to further endeavour. It is thanks to their mistakes that Karev and Mar'ya Sergeevna have now achieved positions that they could never have dreamed of. Although they cannot repair these painful mistakes, cannot even avoid imposing them on their children, their lives are the richer for them. Karev says to Mar'ya Sergeevna: 'I owe everything to you' (*ZK*, 48). This too is to be projected on to the younger generation. Timosha, happily married to Mar'ka, would have been content to play the accordion in cinemas and at local parties. Unhappiness spurs his ambition as it had done Karev's; and beyond this Leonov holds out the hope of redeeming the sufferings of the preceding years.

Accordingly, it is the image of aspiration, the Pamir mountains, rather than the image of success, the 'golden coach,' that dominates the play; the former phrase occurs some thirteen times in the text, the latter only three times. It was the mountains that had set Karev on the road to success and he is now returning there with his son and daughter-in-law to be. Timosha's hopes of becoming an astronomer are a symbolic equivalent of the Karevs' dreams of the Pamirs.[14] His blindness may have thwarted this ambition as well as his hopes of marrying Mar'ka, but he resolves to continue his studies.

Timosha's renunciation of Mar'ka, like Annushka's of Aleksey, is a new version of the *podvig*. In the plays of the late '30s and the war years, the young characters perform their heroic feats as a demonstration that they have come of age, that they are worthy of their parents. The *podvig* involves physical danger, perhaps even death. In *A Golden Coach*, however, as in *An Ordinary Man*, it is an act not of affirmation but of renunciation. Asceticism has replaced the romantic gesture.[15]

Leonov's early works, particularly *Buryga* and *The Badgers*, had been abundant in good humour and joie de vivre. but by the time of *The Thief* 'happiness is always *bourgeois*,' and suffering is much to be preferred. This ethos persists throughout the first part of the '30s, where Uvad'ev and Skutarevsky would have had no time to be happy even if their private lives had been less wretched. The idea is re-examined in *The Road to Ocean*, and from now onwards it becomes one of Leonov's main concerns.

Konstantsiya and Ladygin, even Kira and Vera Artem'evna scheme to ensure happiness for themselves and their protégés, but they are invariably thwarted. Many of the characters in *An Ordinary Man* are in fact characterized – and judged – by their definitions of happiness: Konstantsiya's 'To live and not to have to do a single thing' (7. 335), Ladygin's 'You need to break life like a honeycomb and eat it out of your hands' (7. 288), Aleksey's 'the awareness that you have helped humanity rise by even a single step' (7. 360).

There are two quite different kinds of happiness in Leonov's work, and he is attracted now to one side, now to the other. One, like Aleksey's, is set in the future and has to be earned by hard work and sacrifice. It is the goal of Communism, and as Leonov later reminds us, of Christianity too. Such a state of permanent happiness, however, even if it could be achieved, is hardly compatible with human nature, and is generally treated by Leonov with considerable scepticism. The other is spontaneous and quite ummotivated, here and now in the present tense, the joy of the elk at the beginning of *The Sot'*. It is unpredictable and transient: in *The Road to Ocean* Sayfulla's wild dance in the snow ('This was happiness') is followed by his wrecking of a train.

An Ordinary Man and *A Golden Coach* both prefer the former; present happiness is defined in terms that make it almost morally reprehensible. Of the Chirkhanov family, and this includes Mar'ya Sergeevna and Mar'ka, it is said: 'They have everything you could ask, everything except want and unhappiness' (*ZK*, 13). And at the end of the play, when Mar'ka yields to her mother's persuasion and follows Yakov to the Pamirs, she feels 'ashamed of her happiness... as if she had committed the gravest crime of her life' (*ZK*, 60). Karev cannot resist asking Mar'ya Sergeevna: 'Are you happy with your husband?' (*ZK*, 47), and so reducing her to tears. His ancient grudge may be satisfied but if that is happiness she wants none of it. At best happiness can be seen as the reward for a hard but blameless life, symbolized in the image of 'black bread,' with its idealized associations of the life of the Russian peasant. In *An Ordinary Man* Kira reproaches her mother: 'If it hadn't been for you, I'd be a chemist in some factory – eating my black bread and making friends with people whom I now envy' (7. 343). In *A Golden Coach* Berezkin defines happiness as not 'chandeliers and golden coaches... but to come home and your daughter waving out of the window and your wife cutting the black bread of happiness... and a plain wooden table' (*ZK*, 57–8). But even this minimum happiness is now unattainable for him after the loss of his family.

At times this cult of austerity runs the risk of cutting out happiness altogether. In *The Road to Ocean* and the war plays suffering had been acceptable only when overcome and transformed into positive action. In *An Ordinary Man* and *A Golden Coach* the sacrifices of Annushka and Timosha become almost an end in themselves. This may seem to recall the cult of suffering that had characterized *The Thief* and Leonov's other works of the later NEP period. But Vekshin had welcomed suffering as a means of intensifying experience. To the characters of Leonov's new works it is rather a test of one's worth. To have passed it once as Ladygin and Karev have done is no guarantee of continuing salvation. On the other hand a single failure carries the threat of becoming a Konstantsiya or a Chirkhanov.

The evolution of the idea of happiness can be further traced in Leonov's recurrent image of the road through the mountains to the plains and the sea beyond, first formulated in Don'ka's song in *The Thief*: 'Beyond the pass the sun is shining, but the way through the pass is terrifying!..' (*Vor*, 416–17). But the idea of a seaside holiday as a reward for a life devoted to study or administration, still less as the eventual destination of the historical process, can hardly satisfy the later Leonov.[16] When Mar'ka tries to comfort her mother: 'Never fear, the darkest tunnel is already behind us. Only the last defile remains. Even now, if you climb a rock you can see the sea and the shore' (*ZK*, 45), her words express only her ignorance of the difficulties and complexities of her mother's life. A still more revealing clue can be found in the mixed metaphor of the toast to Aleksey Ladygin after he has won his prize: 'Drive our broad red sail on to the eternal heights of human happiness' (7. 444). Earlier in Leonov the mountains had been the last obstacle before attaining a sunny seashore on the far side. Now the seaside is just a temporary respite before resuming the ascent. This may be acceptable on an individual level, as in Vekshin's 'upwards and onwards, upwards and onwards'; it is less attractive as a program for universal application.

In the preceding plays the *podvig* had been an act of personal initiative; now, however, it is performed under pressure from an older man. Annushka needs the guidance of Svekolkin to ensure that she make the right decision; Timosha, already reconciled to losing Mar'ka, is still hoping to find a reason for staying near her, but his arguments are all rejected by Berezkin:

> *Berezkin.* ... and when you finally attain your Pamir we will visit them one evening in a golden coach. We will go in and see a table, and a woman, whom you will recognize at once, even before she turns round, will be cutting the black bread of happiness. She will ask, 'Who are you?' and we will reply, 'We are war! We have come to wish you good night. Are you well fed? We made it possible. Are you happy? We gave it to you. Every part of ourselves we have given to you. There is no one richer than us in the whole world!'
> *Timosha.* Your words make me feel cold and happy, colonel... as though I were looking at the world from the top of a high mountain.
> *Berezkin.* We'll stay a little longer and then [...] hurry for the night train. Make up your mind, but you must do it now. Now.
> *Timosha.* Yes... but let me just say goodbye to them, colonel.
> *Berezkin.* Have some shame, soldier. You can write to your father afterwards [...]
> *Timosha.* Yes... I'll just take my accordion with me.
> *Berezkin* (*kicking the accordion under the sofa*). No. We take nothing from here. When you set out for the stars you must travel light. (*ZK*, 57)

Berezkin's demands recall those Christ made of his disciples: 'Verily, I say unto you, There is no man that hath left house, or wife, or brethren, or parents, or children for the kingdom of God's sake, Who shall not receive manifold more in this time, and in the time to come eternal life' (Luke 18. 29–30). Christianity and Communism may agree in rejecting present happiness for the sake of a better future, but Leonov seems at times to distrust even the prospect of happiness.

The intervention by Svekolkin and Berezkin in the lives of Annushka and Timosha might seem to diminish the significance of their *podvigi*. Paradoxically, however, it emphasizes the pain and hardship involved in the act of renunciation, as though the characters could not be trusted to make the right decision without such guidance. If this provides less of a moral example, it is more humanly affecting. On the authorial level, however, these interventions are more problematic. In *The Road to Ocean* and the following works Leonov insists on the dangers of spoon-feeding children (and indeed the population as a whole) with politically correct sentiments, on the grounds that our mistakes are more instructive than any teacher. Thus Svekolkin tells Annushka: 'You must be strict with yourself if you don't want other people to do it for you' (7. 290), but evidently the young cannot yet be trusted to be strict enough. Berezkin's speeches to Timosha alternate between addressing him as 'you,' which leaves him his freedom to choose, and 'we,' which implies orders that he cannot refuse. In this light Svekolkin and Berezkin, as the instruments of the author's designs, appear rather less benign. Much as he advocates leaving his characters their freedom Leonov can hardly ever bring himself to let them have it.

The exception is Mar'ka. Of her own accord Mar'ka has decided to refuse the Karevs' offer, or at least to postpone her decision. It is her mother who reads her mind and persuades her to go. Mar'ya Sergeevna may believe that she does not want her daughter to throw away the opportunity that she herself had not dared to take; in reality she is repeating her parents' mistake in looking for a good marriage for her daughter. As this play shows, however, such mistakes have ultimately enriched the lives of both herself and Karev, and there is no reason why they should not do so for Timosha and Mar'ka in their turn.

It is then deeply revealing that nine years later Leonov rewrote the play with a new ending in which Mar'ka makes the right decision, and elects to stay with her mother and Timosha. Evidently Leonov felt that Mar'ka had not been 'strict enough with herself,' and needed some help. The consequences of this authorial intervention for the balance of the play will be discussed in chapter 12.

On the face of it *An Ordinary Man* is a comedy set in a *dacha*, and *A Golden Coach* a predominantly serious play set in the aftermath of the war, but there are many similarities between them. This can be seen most clearly in the pairs of parallel character types – Svekolkin and Berezkin, Ladygin and Karev, Annushka and Mar'ka, Konstantsiya and Tabun-Turkovskaya – which play analogous roles in the two works. Mar'ya Sergeevna too can be seen as a development of the rather faceless Vera Artem'evna Ladygina.

Above all they are related through their common moral standpoint. Surprisingly this element is less obtrusive in *A Golden Coach* than it is in *An Ordinary Person*. Annushka's whole life and character seem to depend on her decision; she is faced with the alternatives of Svekolkin or Konstantsiya. In *A Golden Coach* life is more forgiving. Mar'ka indeed makes the wrong decision like her mother before her; but it is her mother's destiny that awaits her, not the gross vulgarity of Tabun-Turkovskaya; and this is not such a disaster. In this play Leonov recognizes that the mistakes of the past cannot be undone, but far more important than this is the response of people to the consequences of their mistakes. Karev and Mar'ya Sergeevna rise to this challenge, and there is no reason to doubt that their children will. The two tendencies of Leonov's work, the insistence on moral 'purity' and the recognition that life is necessarily impure, here coexist in a balance that can only be achieved in a work of art.

In this continuing debate within Leonov one may discern a parallel process to the one described in Dostoevsky's *Dream of a Ridiculous Man* (*Son smeshnogo cheloveka*, 1877), in which the hero is transported into an Edenic world, innocent of the Fall. His very appearance there, however, contaminates it with sin and corruption, and yet he and his new fellow-citizens perversely believe that this fallen world is somehow preferable to their earlier innocence. So too one side of Leonov dreams of a world of purity, but the artist in him knows that dust and dirt are essential for the breadth and variety of life.[17] Two irreconcilable ideals war within him, and the struggle continues throughout his later works.

In *A Golden Coach* Leonov succeeds as nowhere else in conveying the complexity of people's motives. The play is rich in subtexts which illuminate the characters, often unexpectedly. Thus when the Chirkhanovs offer Timosha a magnificent accordion, he at first thinks that it is Mar'ya Sergeevna who is trying to bribe him to renounce her daughter (actually it comes from Chirkhanov who is trying to buy his silence). This sidelight on Mar'ya Sergeevna is extended by the parallels between herself and Tabun-Turkovskaya, an even more monstrous figure than Konstantsiya in *An Ordinary Man*, who is also trying to engineer a marriage for her adopted daughter (as it happens, to Chirkhanov). Here Mar'ya Sergeevna's own hopes for Mar'ka are reflected as in a distorting mirror, but are not totally unrecognizable. Even the most virtuous figures in the play are not beyond reproach, but Leonov succeeds in persuading us that their virtues are inseparable from their vices. *A Golden Coach* conveys, as no other of his plays, the mistakes made for the best of reasons by decent people and the mixed emotions of retrieving at least a second-best from a seemingly lost situation. Nowhere else in his works is he so successful in showing the necessity for life's impurities.

So far as I know, *A Golden Coach* has never been publicly performed in its original version. Even *An Ordinary Man* was at first misunderstood by Soviet critics.[18] The first two notices clearly misinterpreted Leonov's intentions and failed to appreciate the counterpoint of the various themes. Since then, however, the play has received general acclaim and has been turned into a successful film.[19] Surprisingly enough, the play has not yet been translated into English, though its merits should have made it particularly attractive to Western readers and theatre-goers. Few Russian plays since 1917 are so universal in theme and require so little knowledge of contemporary Russia for their appreciation. Even the word 'Soviet' appears only once in the play, and then on the lips of Ladygin.

Perhaps the most surprising aspect of these two works after the crudities of the earlier plays is the complexity of their subject matter and the technical mastery with which Leonov handles his material. The contrapuntal ideal of dispensing with a single 'central' hero, to which he had aspired in *Wolf* and *Lenushka* is here successfully achieved. In *An Ordinary Man* the cast is small, at least by Leonov's standards. But of the eight speaking parts, seven are full-scale characters, who are not only essential to the structure but are each associated with a theme of their own. It is the interplay and sum of these themes that gives the play its unique texture. The only character who can be called minor is the maid Parasha, but, as in the traditional drawing-room comedy, she is nonetheless essential to its construction. She and Svekolkin are the only ones who fully understand all that is happening, and the ironic wit of her comments on the changing situations does much to disguise the essentially didactic nature of the play. *A Golden Coach* has a rather larger cast and is less tightly constructed, but the numerous sub-plots and individual dramas are handled even more skilfully. The various parallels and symmetries are less obtrusive, so that the situations seem more natural and the characters freer, even to the point of making the 'wrong' decisions. The 1946 version is one of Leonov's most profound and moving works. One must hope that it will one day be reprinted and staged. Without it any picture of Leonov's work will be seriously deficient.

These two plays reveal a side to Leonov's talent that does not emerge anywhere else in his work. The plots are cleverly designed to form an integral part of the content, and the climaxes of the drama coincide naturally with the climaxes of the argument. The most notable contrast with the preceding plays lies in the moderation of Leonov's language and imagery, which hardly ever exceeds the possibilities of normal conversation, while the imagery (the unwanted picture, Aleksey's monkey) flows naturally out of the everyday circumstances of the action. The symbolic and ethical ramifications extend, as in all Leonov's work, far beyond the surface of the text, but the surface is less obtrusively portentous. The aims and achievements of these two plays mark the summit of Leonov's work for the stage. At the same time they have their own distinct character, and are as individual in their styles as each of the novels.

chapter eleven

The Russian Forest 1953

Leonov's standing had improved during the war years largely as a result of the success of *Invasion* and his many patriotic articles, and in 1945 he was selected as *Pravda*'s correspondent at the Dresden and Nurenberg war trials. Such honours brought with them certain obligations, and Leonov came under increasing pressure to write panegyrics to Stalin; to this end he was subjected to two hours of 'massage' from Polikarpov, the official who had organized the campaign against *The Snowstorm* six years earlier. A single quotation from the resulting article, 'A Word on the First Deputy' ('Slovo o pervom deputate,' 1946)[1] should suffice to give the general flavour of the piece: 'Here my people and my conscience command me to say a word about Comrade Stalin, the first deputy of our land. I am not a sea, not even a smiling northern lake to reflect the merest fraction of the grandeur of the luminary that can now be seen from every corner of the universe. I am only a drop in the great river of our national life, that has been touched by the sharp and vivifying ray of a star.'[2]

Leonov was duly rewarded: at the beginning of February he was elected to the Supreme Soviet and a week later he was awarded the Order of Lenin. Such marks of approval, however, effectively turned their beneficiaries into hostages, for a fall from favour involved disgrace not only for the individual concerned but also for his family. As Stepan Syrovarov observes in *The Snowstorm*: 'On the heights that you and I have attained, the shift of even a grain of sand can start an avalanche.'[3]

Leonov was indeed living close to an avalanche. The Zhdanov decree of August 1946 with its notorious denunciations of Akhmatova and Zoshchenko put an end to any hopes of greater liberty that the war years might have encouraged. It inaugurated a new spell of Party dictatorship in the arts, in some ways even more repressive than that of the later '30s. For Leonov the year saw the sudden suppression of *The Golden Coach* and a flurry of attacks on

Lenushka; a new selected edition of his works projected for 1947 came to nothing;[4] and for the first time in his life, a fallow period ensued.[5] It was not until 1953 that he produced a new work of fiction, *The Russian Forest*.[6]

He was not, however, disgraced. He continued to publish articles on approved subjects, Soviet anniversaries, the Cold War, and later the Soviet peace offensive, and of course eulogies of Stalin. Perhaps the most shaming of these articles is the one, commissioned for Stalin's seventieth birthday, in which Leonov foresees a time when the day will be celebrated worldwide as the 'Day of Gratitude.'[7] Critics who regard Leonov as irreparably compromised by these and similar effusions should, however, remember that defiance would have destroyed not only him but also his family; one returns to the recurrent dilemma of his work – how far can one sacrifice others in the name of one's own ideals? I suspect that as early as the 1930s Leonov had come to feel that he should not be held responsible for his journalistic publications; indeed he later claimed that several articles had been attributed to him without his consent, or even knowledge.[8]

His publicistic writings have received plenty of favourable attention in Soviet critical and academic publications, if anything rather more than his novels and plays. After all, the Marxist conception of art is of class ideology dressed up with some aesthetic frills, so straightforward propaganda is felt to be morally preferable and more suitable for adult audiences. For the creative writer, however, it involves certain dangers, especially when indulged in over several years. Most of Leonov's pre-war novels and plays (with the possible exception of *The Orchards of Polovchansk*) require some intellectual or imaginative effort on the part of the reader or spectator; alternative interpretations of events and characters are suggested through such figures as Arseniy Skutarevsky, Gleb Protoklitov, and Luka Sandukov. Effective propaganda, however, demands a clear message: the standpoint of the author must be unmistakable; issues are reduced to black and white. But for a writer of Leonov's type such crudities are incompatible with the discriminations and ambiguities that distinguish his best work; the irony that glints through his writings of the 1930s is replaced in the war years by a heavy sarcasm. Unfortunately, the coarsening of judgment and style, understandable enough in journalistic work, inflicted serious damage not just on his wartime works, but also on those still to be written, notably *The Russian Forest*.[9] In the long term it discredited him with the reading public and prevented him from ever regaining the respect that he had enjoyed before the war.

Like most propaganda Leonov's journalism is dated and almost unreadable now. We can hardly doubt his patriotism or his horror at the German invasion and the atrocities that followed. But his repeated assertions of Russia's democratic traditions and reverence for culture, his mockery of Hitler's 'cult of personality,' and his condemnation of German art and science for preparing the rise of Nazism are likely to alienate anyone who knows the Soviet Union's own history in the years preceding and following the war. He had lived through the Molotov-Ribbentrop Pact; he had personally experienced political persecution, he had seen his own books banned; he knew of countless Russian churches that had been blown up, or desecrated, or even turned into archive depositories for the secret police; he had himself contributed to the cult of Stalin. In other circumstances one might well suspect some irony, but can that really be the case here?

The issue is epitomized by Leonov's use in 1942 of a quotation from Blok's poem 'The Scythians,' foretelling a day '... when the savage Hun will rummage through the pockets of corpses, burn cities, drive his herds into the churches and cook the meat of his white brothers.'[10] Leonov treats these lines as though they referred to the present-day Nazis, but in fact the poet was thinking of the Asiatic tribes whom he regarded as the ancestors of the modern Russians. Blok is making the point that Russia had protected Western Europe from the Tatar onslaught at the cost of delaying her own development for centuries; but now she had her own revolutionary culture and was under no obligation to protect a decrepit West. The poem contains a threat to stand aside and let these elements destroy Western culture, unless it is prepared to accept the Asiatic, Scythian culture embodied in the Bolshevik Revolution. As propaganda, then, these lines would be more useful to the Nazis than to the Russians. To conceal his misreading Leonov omitted the first two words of the quatrain: 'We shall not stir when...'

This falsification of one of the most famous of all Russian poems raises some tricky questions. If we were dealing with a 'literary' text we would unhesitatingly recognize the reference as ironic and interpret it accordingly. But in the desperate days of 1942 when Russia was crying out for Western aid it is inconceivable that Leonov could have intended any such ambiguity, even subconsciously. How then can we be sure that we have found irony elsewhere and not been misled by our own desire to find it? Who is to say that in other cases the author may not have innocently (either through ignorance or laziness) laid himself open to the possibility of similar misunderstanding? Inevitably one is thrown back on one's own intuition in such cases, but the temptation to find irony where none was intended is always a danger in reading Soviet literature, and especially in the reading of Leonov. These questions are germane to our reading of *The Russian Forest*, a work that is heavily coloured by the atmosphere of the Cold War and specifically the Korean War. Thus the villain Gratsiansky's supporters wear 'Western' clothes and the Nazi agent who contacts him proves to be an Australian.

The problem is further complicated by the fact that after the XX Party

Congress of 1956 (the first official admission of the crimes of the Stalin era) Leonov removed all references to Stalin from *The Russian Forest*,[11] and most of them from reissues of his other works. If he had retained them they would have served as witnesses of the times in which they had been penned; whether or not they had been intended ironically in the first place they would certainly have been read as such in the changed climate of the 'Thaw.' To remove them some three years after Stalin's death in conformity with Khrushchev's new political agenda gets the worst of both worlds.[12] It looks opportunistic and it gives the lie to the lofty claims of Russian democratic values that are trumpeted interminably in the articles and *The Russian Forest*. Acquiescence in the new canons of political correctness, even with reservations, only perpetuates the same old habits of compromise.

These years, however, also saw the birth of Leonov's interest in the environment, and in particular in the management of Russia's forests, which was to become the main concern of his later years and was to involve him in several controversies. His first article on this subject, 'Let's think about our green spaces,'[13] which appeared in 1945, seems to have made little impression, but his next one, 'In defence of our friend,'[14] drew a wide response. He received thousands of letters containing information on the continuing indiscriminate and wasteful felling and he helped to found several societies for the protection of Russia's natural resources. In the next few years he travelled widely throughout the Soviet Union, collecting further material. He had as yet no thought of writing a novel on the subject, although his friends in forestry had apparently suggested it to him.[15] In 1950, however, the idea suddenly fused with a project that had long been in his mind, the relationship between an aging intellectual and his adopted son.[16]

Little now remains of Leonov's original scheme. The aging intellectual split into two figures, both involved in Russian forestry policy: one, Vikhrov, represents Leonov's position, the other, Gratsiansky, an opportunism not so different from that of the Soviet government. The former is eventually vindicated while the latter is discredited and apparently commits suicide. The theme of scientific rivalry recalls the antagonism between Skutarevsky and Petrygin,[17] but the conflict is now more intense because the rivals are working in the same field, and the rightness of one means inevitably the wrongness of the other. Moreover, since the debate is conducted over one of the most important of Russia's natural resources the issue is also one of patriotism. Vikhrov is reluctant to burn wood even in his own fireplace, while Gratsiansky's policy of wholesale felling suggests that 'he simply had no love for the forest or probably even his own country' (9.260).

The younger generation is now represented by two figures, Vikhrov's daughter, Polya, who has been living with his estranged wife Lena, and Serezha, his adopted son. Both children are ashamed of their origins: Serezha is the son of a *kulak* (who had been Vikhrov's childhood friend), while Polya is naturally prejudiced against her father; after reading Gratsiansky's attacks on him she has come to believe not only that he is an enemy of the state, but that she herself is tainted by the relationship. She never asks her mother about him and makes no attempt to find out his side of the argument. By the end of the book these misunderstandings are all cleared up and Polya and Serezha duly perform their *podvigi*. Serezha's father also redeems himself by enabling Polya to escape from her German captors at the cost of his own life; while Polya's mother, who had been adopted by a landowner before the Revolution and was later victimized as a *lishenka*, establishes her right to be reintegrated into Russian society.

The theme of the two generations is reflected in the structure. The novel opens in June 1941, on the eve of the German invasion. Polya has arrived in Moscow with the intention of entering the university and confronting her father. Chapters recounting her adventures in the first weeks of the war alternate with others devoted to the biography of Vikhrov from his childhood up to the same period. The first part of the book culminates in her attending her father's introductory lecture at the university and realizing that she has misjudged him. The second part follows a similar pattern, alternating events from 1941–2 and Gratsiansky's activities in 1910–12, so accounting for his behaviour in the Soviet period. The novel's centre of gravity, however, is to be found not in the wartime events, but in the older characters and the ramifications of their conflict.

It was most unusual for a Soviet writer to express concerns about the environment during the Stalin period. In the drive to build socialism in one country as quickly as possible such considerations were interpreted as obstruction, and even tantamount to sabotage. Consequently Leonov's hints at environmental damage in *The Sot'* had been expressed very cautiously and are really only perceptible to those who are looking for them. Nonetheless the theme of nature and particularly the forest has run right through his work ever since his first story, *Buryga*. One of the most striking anticipations of *The Russian Forest* may be found in the closing pages of *The Thief*, when Vekshin returns to the forest, 'his second homeland' (*Vor*, 540). In the train he overhears a conversation: 'They're felling the forests and the peasant worries that there will be less soil for the trees' roots. And when the last stump has rotted away the whole earth will soon shrink to the size of a nut' (*Vor*, 538).[18] In *The Russian Forest* Kalina remarks, 'and when you have felled the Russian forests down to the last tree, then, my friends, you will have to look abroad for your bread' (9. 92). Implicit in this concern is Leonov's natural tendency to identify nature with a cultural touchstone: 'The erosion of the soil leads inevitably to an erosion of the spirit, egoism and fear, the philosophy of overpopulation, barrenness of thought, and ultimately to the loss of faith in mankind's destiny' (9. 300–01).

In Russian culture concern for the forest has generally been confined to the intelligentsia. The popular epithet for it in Russian folklore, as Sinyavsky has pointed out, is not Leonov's 'green,' but 'dark' (*temnyy*). Klyuchevsky has tried to account for this attitude of hostility and fear: 'Despite all its benefits the forest was always a burden for the Russian people [...] the heavy work of felling and firing required to clear space for agriculture was exhausting and frustrating. This may explain the hostile or even irresponsible attitude of the Russian to the forest; he has never loved his forest. An unaccountable timidity would overwhelm him when he stepped into its twilit shade.'[19] So too Leonov's Vikhrov is at first shocked by the peasants' indifference to the forest, but he comes to understand that it is deeply rooted in Russian history.

Ever since the first primitive clearings for settlements and agriculture the destruction of Russia's forests has steadily accelerated through the mass fellings required for Peter the Great's shipbuilding program and the railway construction of the nineteenth century. The Revolution with its Marxist emphasis on the centrality of economics promised a more rational and orderly policy, and in 1918 at the Ninth Party Congress, a decree had been passed to safeguard the forests.[20] These good intentions were never fulfilled. In the 1930s the program of industrialization had been met largely at the forests' expense,[21] while the policies that Leonov and Vikhrov advocate were denounced as unpatriotic. Indeed several of the historical figures on whom Vikhrov was modelled had been disgraced and exiled.[22] Departments of forestry in universities and institutes were closed down.[23]

Leonov is careful, therefore, not to criticize this policy explicitly, for: 'it would have been disastrous for us today, under the onslaught of Fascism, if our people had not taken the direct road through the mountain passes in good time [...] We were poor but we bought foreign experience and machinery for the full cash price... and they took it all, those most Christian gentlemen of the West, the bread and butter of our children, the treasures of our museums, the forests that protected our water supplies – hoping to repair their own tottering economies on the heroism of Soviet workers. In our haste we felled everything, taking no account of age, species, or quality' (9. 304).

Instead the destruction of Russia's forests is blamed on wicked rulers, capitalists, and the foreign exploiters of Russia, though occasional comments such as 'even today ' (9. 291, 294) and the admission that statistics had been falsified (9. 306) provide a discreet counterbalance to these assertions. The short-term economic advantages of exploiting the forests had had serious long-term consequences for the environment as a whole, for the climate, for agriculture, and so for the economy. In the *Znamya* edition of the novel Leonov had written: 'For some time now the disruption of the water table has affected the well-being of Russians. Crop-failures assailed the country every ten years – 1891 – 1901 – 1911...'[24] The reader will naturally continue the series into 1921 and 1931, with their devastating man-made famines, aggravated not so much by forestry policies as by political calculation. In 1955 the second sentence was replaced by the less explicit: 'Crop failures assailed the country every decade beginning in the '90s...' (9. 296).

The fate of the Russian forest thus serves as an allegory for the history of the Russian people. The two are often bracketed by Leonov, but even when he does not do so the parallel is implicit, as, for example, in Vikhrov's lecture, from which the last three quotations have been taken. One is frequently reminded of the Russian proverb 'When a forest is felled the chips fly,' which was often used to justify the wastage of human life in the name of building socialism in the 1930s. The lumber exported to finance the industrialization campaign was mostly produced in Stalin's labour camps, as Leonov's readers in the 1950s would have been well aware. In the novel the liquidation of the *kulaks*, the victimization of the *lishentsy*, the denunciations and arrests of innocent citizens run parallel to the wholesale felling of the forests.

No less important in the image system of the book are the rivers, which nourish and drain the forests, and are endangered by their destruction. Without the river 'children cannot be born, nor bread nor song – a single draught of it sufficed our ancestors for exploits that have gained a thousand years of glory' (9. 74). Accordingly the source of the river, which Vikhrov discovers as a child, is the sanctuary of the nation.

> There were no ramparts or feudal walls close by, but the whole domain of the state, its endless fields, [...] its libraries and mighty industries, its forests, and the mountains on its frontiers served as a stout and trusty bulwark for this spring. And so the reason that the nation builds its impregnable fortresses of the spirit, keeps its frowning armies on the borders, and places its dearest children in ceaseless vigil, is to ensure that no one's foul footstep should penetrate here and sully, violate this clear stream. Ivan was not aware of all this at the time, but never again did he feel himself so insignificant as he did that evening in the presence of this seemingly defenceless spring, never again did he experience this radiant spontaneous sense of jubilation.
>
> When it had subsided the boys knelt down and drank the water; they took a breath and drank again – for the rest of their lives, for there was nothing else to take away. (9. 74)[25]

The moment is one of spiritual revelation – the boys kneel: Vikhrov's whole life follows from the experience. The Russian expression *zhivaya voda* (living water, or the water of life), which appears several times in the text, is thus integrated with the central images of the novel.[26] It is this river of life that carries Polya in and out of her various adventures: 'And now the current swept the blade of grass away,' serves as her catchphrase.

This spring is the source of life: if it should be blocked 'then it will blow up the whole world' (9. 74), and in the most dramatic scene in the novel this is just what Gratsiansky tries to do. For a moment the stream is checked, but then 'a clear vein of water bursts through the murk.' Vikhrov reacts with a violence that he shows nowhere else; he throws himself at Gratsiansky: 'I'll kill you' (9. 263).[27] The episode is a parallel to the German invasion of Russia, and so prepares the eventual disclosure that Gratsiansky is a foreign agent. At the very end of the novel Vikhrov returns to the spring to give an account of his life and work.

Vikhrov shares many features with his creator; their occupations, forestry and art, are both concerned with the future rather than the present day. Even their biographies are strikingly similar. Indeed some aspects of the book make better sense when read in a literary rather than a scientific context. Vikhrov's rise to fame in the 1920s culminates in his second book: 'Perhaps there were no original discoveries in this book, but from start to finish it was shot through with an urgent sense of concern for the future, hardly out of place in a Soviet scientist; before this very few people had spoken out so frankly about the forest' (9. 398–9).

Very similar words *mutatis mutandis* could have been written about Leonov's own second book, *The Thief*. Vikhrov's 'trial' in 1936 and the ensuing 'compulsory holiday' (9. 452) recall the attacks on Leonov after *The Road to Ocean*, and their culmination in the *Snowstorm* affair. Little is said of the next five years in Vikhrov's life, but in the first days of the war he is unexpectedly singled out for an important award. So too Leonov's period of disgrace was abruptly terminated by his return to favour with *Invasion*, and the award of a Stalin Prize. In the elaborate detail with which Leonov recounts Gratsiansky's attacks on Vikhrov there is a distinct personal note, as though he is thinking of the attacks on himself and other leading figures in Russian cultural life, and of the timidity of his colleagues: 'senior foresters kept their peace to avoid coming under the scrutiny of a microscopic review, but some of them would admit, in confidence, that Gratsiansky's abusive masterpieces, some of them only a page long, did not make any contribution to serious science' (9. 51).

Vikhrov is apparently apolitical, but in fact he is as loyal to the Bolsheviks as Burago and Skutarevsky had been in Leonov's novels of the 1930s, and he joins the Party on the outbreak of war. As a young man he had been arrested and exiled for his connections with a revolutionary group. He had spent the time in tramping the length and breadth of Russia and gaining a first-hand knowledge of her forests. It was this experience that brought him to the realization that 'salvation for the forests of Russia must be sought not in the voluntary self-restraint of the landowners but in a national revolution' (9. 152). Indeed, he sees his work in forestry as a model of 'socialist continuity' (9. 57). Yet, in spite of his loyalty to the Party he receives little support in return. Unlike Skutarevsky he is not favoured with personal interviews with Lenin or Stalin, nor encouraged to demand money and facilities for his work. Of his two closest associates in the Party, one, Kraynov, admits even after Vikhrov has been vindicated, that he is partially in agreement with those who consider his views to be alarmist (9. 647); while the other, his favourite pupil Os'minov, he actually suspects (wrongly) of having run off with his wife.

Vikhrov's antagonist is potentially the most interesting of Leonov's villains. In the years before the First World War Aleksandr Gratsiansky had flirted with the revolutionary movement and had conceived the idea of 'mimetism,' a scheme for penetrating the Okhrana (the Tsarist secret police) and then carrying its methods to absurd lengths, so as to 'blow it up from within' (9. 169, 450). The police chief, Chandvetsky, however, applies some mimetism of his own by affecting to share his political views, and finally traps him into becoming a police informer.[28] The outbreak of the Revolution thus threatens Gratsiansky with exposure, and so he undertakes a thesis on revolutionary movements in Russia before 1914, which will enable him to work in the archives and destroy any incriminating evidence. Adjusting his mimetism to the changed situation, he reinvents himself as a Marxist theoretician, and even manages to enter the Communist Party, continuing to mimic an ideology which he does not share. His carefully cultivated appearance gives him 'the model exterior of a stubborn fighter for something supremely noble' (9. 111). With such phrases as 'our brilliant reality' (9. 108), 'our proletarian truth' (9. 475), 'our sensitive, responsive, and progressive youth' (9. 692), he shows himself a master of Soviet 'political correctness.' Eventually, however, his past catches up with him, when he is approached by a mysterious visitor from Australia, apparently an emissary from Chandvetsky. It would seem that he has come to blackmail Gratsiansky, but Soviet readers of the time (the Korean War) would probably have interpreted the episode as evidence of Gratsiansky's working for the Western powers.

In some ways the introduction of mimetism is only a red herring, for the concept implies pretending to believe in one set of ideas in order to further a totally different one that is genuinely held. But Gratsiansky has no such beliefs.

He is actuated at first by a juvenile ambition and later by self-preservation. Like other figures of evil in Leonov, for example, Chirkhanov, he is a blank, an incarnation of nothingness, and he is accompanied by symbols of negation and death. On one occasion he introduces himself with the words: *'De nihilo nihil'* (9. 254). His own work contributes nothing to the science of forestry. His character and beliefs are just as empty as his life: he is 'a liquid which takes the form of any vessel it is poured into' (9. 345).[29] This fluidity is brilliantly conveyed in the name Gratsiansky,[30] which seems to acquire ever-changing associations as the revelations of his past emerge: at first it evokes an old-world graciousness; later we hear it as devious and ingratiating, and finally as gratingly expressive of his envy and malevolence.

In terms of Leonov's own work Gratsiansky is a descendant of Chikilev, or perhaps even Chikilev himself, after twenty-five years of Soviet power. In 1929 Leonov had defined the *meshchanin* as one who was 'deprived of any creative spirit and terrified of the elemental upsurge of creative energy that has fired the whole country.' In *The Russian Forest* Chandvetsky warns the young Gratsiansky:

> As you decline so your blood will turn sour with unfruitfulness and envy of your neighbour, his health, his talents, his digestion, and even the torments of his spirit... No doubt, in failing to make yourself a Prometheus, you will contrive to turn yourself into a vulture feeding on one; with the years you will come to love this intense, almost creative delight in devouring his liver, drowning his voice, blackening his character in the hope of resembling him even in the colour of your face. (9. 499)

Envy is the characteristic of the new revolutionary generation, cut off from historical tradition. Its creativity is spurious, a mere masquerade. So too Cherimov had boasted of his opposition to Skutarevsky's 'Prometheanism.' Gratsiansky's envy is even more poisonous, and it ramifies in many more directions. Leonov's success in characterizing a familiar type of Soviet operator has led to the coining of the word '*gratsianshchina,*' which is universally understood, even by those who have not read the book.

Gratsiansky does not try to refute Vikhrov on scientific grounds, but through a mixture of misrepresentation and personal insinuation: 'out of consideration for the intelligence of the general reader, and indeed secrecy, Professor Gratsiansky did not as a general rule adduce any figures or constructive suggestions [...] he displayed a comprehensive erudition (except, unfortunately in matters concerning forestry), a withering sarcasm, and in recent years a magnanimous refusal to specify the true sources of Vikhrov's misconceptions' (9. 51). During the purges he publicly accuses Vikhrov of 'contemplative objectivism and bourgeois economism, the malignant traces of uncommitted eclecticism, and mechanistic empiricism, and an incorrigible tendency towards idealistic nihilism and pseudoscientific vulgarism' (9. 401), charges that might seem parodistic if they had not been all too common in those times.[31] In some respects Gratsiansky recalls the charlatan Lysenko, who wrought such havoc in Soviet agriculture; in others Leonov seems to be thinking of a Soviet literary critic.[32] He is not just a hanger-on of the system; he is typical of it.

Soviet critics, ignoring the historical realities of the times, reproached Leonov for Vikhrov's apparent passivity in the face of Gratsiansky's attacks, but this is essential to the scheme of the novel. Vikhrov is bewildered by Gratsiansky's hostility and sincerely believes that it is purely due to an intellectual misunderstanding. Accordingly he makes little attempt to justify himself even to his own family. His life and work are sufficient justification. And, of course, any attempt to resist Gratsiansky would have been suicidal, or, as Leonov put it: 'his fate would have been wretched. He would not have survived to the end of the novel.'[33]

Paradoxically, however, Gratsiansky still needs Vikhrov as the vulture needs Prometheus, because without him he would be nothing. And so on several occasions he intervenes on his behalf, notably in 1936, when Vikhrov's destruction seems inevitable: 'It was to his advantage to support Vikhrov's reputation as one of the most controversial, perhaps, but nonetheless significant figures of contemporary forestry... The destruction of his opponent would involve annihilation for him too' (9. 401). He accompanies Vikhrov like a shadow. The two men even join the Party on the same day. This parasitism often leads to confusion.[34] Polya is completely deceived: she imagines that it is Gratsiansky who is actuated by love of the forest and her father who is the traitor. This inversion is only corrected when she visits Gratsiansky and discovers that the bourgeois comforts she had once attributed to Vikhrov are in fact Gratsiansky's natural element.

Gratsiansky is the first of Leonov's villains to have committed his crime before the Revolution,[35] and the critic Mark Shcheglov accused Leonov of following the convention by which all wrongdoing in the Soviet period was ascribed to survivals from the bourgeois past or to foreign enemies.[36] In fact Leonov's point is rather different. Under pre-revolutionary conditions Gratsiansky would have been simply a small-time informer. It is the Soviet system that has given power and apparent immunity to the most contemptible products of the old regime.[37] Far from rejecting such creatures it has encouraged and promoted them.

In the figures of Gratsiansky and Cheredilov Leonov is indicting the corruption and demagoguery of a substantial element within the Communist *nomenklatura*. Max Hayward even suggested that Gratsiansky's concern to destroy the archives relating to his work in the Okhrana was a hint at the rumour that Stalin himself had worked for both sides, and similarly destroyed the evidence.[38] One can extend these parallels further: like Stalin Gratsiansky studied for a time at a religious seminary, while his style of polemic, that is, distorting his opponent's position in order to insinuate some counterrevolutionary motivation, was a speciality of Stalin's.

In his early revolutionary posturings Gratsiansky often affects a Leninist lack of scruple in the pursuit of power. Thus he amplifies his theory of mimetism with the comment that 'great ends justify a few sacrifices, even human ones' (9. 169);[39] by which he means planting double agents in the Okhrana, who might have to betray the occasional revolutionary in order to protect their own cover. The only alternative, he goes on, is to sit back and wait for 'it to come about peacefully [...] any sacred cause is only strengthened by the blood of a few martyrs' (9. 169).[40] Vikhrov is of course horrified by this 'diabolical scheme' which he condemns as the ultimate in 'moral corruption' (9. 169). Vekshin had at least been sincere in believing that the Revolution's commitment to man in general justified its indifference to individual hardships. Gratsiansky's words are simply radical chic.

Later, Chandvetsky comments on Gratsiansky's 'somewhat young-Turkish project for an immediate seizure of power [...] I cannot approve your plan, as the future leader of Russia, to appoint ministers only from among the members of your organization. First of all, you simply won't have enough people to staff the government you envisage... and second, how do you propose to deal with the other parties which, just like yourselves, are also eager to bring the benefits of revolution to humanity?' (9. 492–3). Chandvetsky's prophecy anticipates both the way the Bolshevik Revolution was to be carried out in 1917 and the problems it encountered. Later still, in 1929–30, the year of the 'Great Breakthrough' of industrialization and collectivization, Gratsiansky acquires 'cold eyes, a calculating pragmatism, and a grasp like death' (9. 152). Significantly, even after Gratsiansky's suicide Vikhrov 'can't help wondering whether he has not left his hat and stick behind him in the hope of twiddling our naiver brethren round his little finger once again' (9. 716).[41] The death of Stalin did not necessarily mean the death of Stalinism.

The full implications of such passages emerge only at the end of the novel, when Polya visits Gratsiansky and sees 'a face with cold eyes of extreme ruthlessness: just like those of the airman who circled overhead during the raids on Moscow, and the soldier who shot old Paramonych in an open field instead of her, and then led her by the hand to the German dugout in Shikhanov Yam' (9. 693).

Gratsiansky, the champion of Communist orthodoxy, is indistinguishable from the Nazi enemy.[42] This has led Richard Peace to argue that Leonov is raising the question: 'Who are the fascists?'[43] Phrased in this way the question oversimplifies the issue. Leonov is not saying that the Communists are worse than the Nazis, but rather that many Communists are almost as bad. He makes no distinction between Nazis and ordinary Germans (or indeed people in the West generally). On the other hand the Russian people are idealized and there are even a few decent Communists to be found. This is consistent with Leonov's general standpoint. He is not writing from a Western liberal-democratic position. He has never been strongly attracted to Western culture, which, like Dostoevsky, he identifies with the misguided pursuit of progress. His objection to Communism is that it is pursuing the same illusory goal, and so falling into the same materialist traps.

Hence he sees no inconsistency in denouncing the West for its failure to come to the aid of Russia in the spring of 1942:

> Now that the first breach had been made in the enemy's battle morale, the opening of a second front could have significantly hastened the rout of Nazism and saved millions of soldiers' lives. The sacred, or so one might have thought, obligations of our allies were not fulfilled in that year [1942] nor in the following three purely out of long-term considerations. In this delay the people of Moscow recognized with some bitterness the truth of the Latin proverb, in which the third party waits for the vultures before coming to the scene of battle. [...] The entire burden of the duel fell on the shoulders of the Soviet people, and since one never forgets the behaviour of one's friends in time of battle, the Vikhrovs remembered for all time how for three years on end they and their neighbours had speculated on the forms a second front might take... every morning they had scanned the papers for news of the landing of the Anglo-Saxon armies on the mainland, only for their faith in soldierly friendship to be frustrated nine hundred times... and when on the nine hundred and first morning, the Germans launched their offensive in the Ardennes, the Muscovites could not refrain from smiling as they read the Allied telegrams appealing for help. (9. 681–2)

As Alexander Gerschenkron pointed out, the Allies appear to have come under attack in the centre of Europe even before they have landed.[44] This might perhaps be ironic, but I doubt it. The remarks stand outside the time frame of the rest of the novel and so cannot be attributed to any of the characters. They are authorial and their sarcasm relates them to the style of Leonov's propagandist writings.

Many of Gratsiansky's insinuations are aimed at Vikhrov's family connections. His wife Lena had been abandoned as a baby and brought up in a landowner's family, where she was constantly humiliated as a foundling. After the Revolution she was further victimized as a member of the former 'exploiting classes' and is not even allowed to complete her medical training.[45] Serezha, his adopted son, is subject to the same insinuations as the son of a *kulak*. Polya herself is so overwhelmed by Gratsiansky's attacks on her father that she is ashamed to bear the same name, and tries to disguise it by shifting the stress from the last to the first syllable. As so often in Russian and Soviet history, wives and children are made to suffer materially and psychologically for the supposed crimes of their relatives.[46]

Lena lives with a sense of 'unforgiven guilt' (9. 234), Polya with a fear that she might be 'expelled [...] from my people, from my country' (9. 118). Each has to win back the citizenship of which she feels deprived, Lena 'the right to breathe the air of her fatherland, as though anybody could take it away from her' (9. 365), and Polya 'the right to look her country squarely in the eye' (9. 396). Like Fedor Talanov they are associated with images of cold and illness, for which the medicine is a *podvig*, Lena's in her years of work as a nurse in a small village, Polya's in her heroic mission behind the German lines. The successful completion of the *podvig* gives Leonov's heroines the 'moral right' (9. 691) to execute judgment on the villain; accordingly Polya throws a bottle of ink in Gratsiansky's face (9. 694). But even when she has won the Party's confidence and is summoned for an interview to assess her suitability for a mission behind the German lines, she at first thinks that it may be connected with her father.[47]

The obsession with guilt and 'moral right' that characterizes these figures brings Leonov back to the cluster of ideas that had preoccupied him in *An Ordinary Man* and *A Golden Coach*. The antithesis between purity and happiness characteristic of the two plays is continued in *The Russian Forest*, but the two concepts are now supplemented by a third one, 'honour,' which provides a phonetic link between them: *chistota* – *chest'* – *schast'e*.[48] Their interrelationship becomes plain when Polya has completed the first part of her mission: 'Now Polya could eat her honourable (*chestnyy*) Soviet bread with a pure (*chistoy*) conscience [...] she could experience that blissful, dreamless exhaustion that is the essential seasoning to happiness (*schast'e*)' (9.542). The purity and the honour are clear enough, but the happiness lies outside conscious experience.

The word *chistyy* has a range of meanings extending from clean to innocent (as in a clear conscience) to pure,[49] and in Leonov's work it is associated primarily with the figure of a virginal heroine, Annushka, Mar'ka, and now Polya. Her Russian control preparing her for her mission seems indeed to be more worried by the thought of her being raped than of her being killed:

> You see, Polya, out there in the old world, there are many kinds of gentlemen who just adore pretty little Russian girls. You can be sure that all of us, every single one of us on this earth, will be watching over your every step, but there will be nobody to stand up for you there, so it's better not to put on any lipstick... no, better not. (9. 556)

The supposition that lipstick or the lack of it might make all the difference reveals a touching innocence in the would-be worldly wise NKVD officer.

But unlike virginity, purity in Leonov is not a quality that is innate and then lost; on the contrary Lena, Polya, and Serezha feel that they never had it and that they must earn it. It is located not in the past but in the future. Thus Polya explains her motives for volunteering for the front:

> I think of it like this... well, what do people aspire to? some people say – to happiness; but that's not right in my opinion. You should aspire to purity. Happiness is the chief reward, a sort of makeweight to purity. And what is purity? That there should be no war [...] no need to lock doors at night [...] and that everybody should work, because a man without work is worse than a beast. (9. 454–5)

Accordingly, it is only after her *podvig* that Polya is recognized as a 'pure being' (9. 687); she has no regrets about the war 'provided that our children can enter a pure house.' Her aunt Tais'ya takes this to mean that Polya is pregnant, and Leonov remarks: 'Polya in her purity was taken aback by the old woman's suspicions and explained herself in a clear and pure voice' (9. 690), as though he too would prefer her to remain 'pure.'

Vikhrov also shares this scale of values:

> it was his sincere conviction that the Revolution was not just a struggle for a fairer distribution of the good things in life, but first and foremost for human purity [...] and if progress consists in the multiplication of the instruments of well-being simultaneously with an increase in moral responsibilities (for only a perfect man is capable of attaining perfect happiness), then each man would have to have a perfect biography too, one that he would not be ashamed to tell out loud in front of his children [...] Hence it became plain just how much mankind was in need of a vast purification by storm and tempest. (9. 58–9)[50]

Later he and Kraynov drink a toast to a 'better life on a pure earth for their children and descendants' (9. 345). Perhaps even to think about happiness in an impure world is immoral. Thus when Lena, after leaving Vikhrov, falls in love with a young Communist she decides to stop seeing him in order to 'punish herself for the momentary temptation to take the easy short cut to the happiness she had never known' (9. 370). When he is seriously wounded during the collectivization campaign she nurses him back to life, but makes no claims on him: 'Her later daily experience helped her to understand that the joy of giving oneself to people is infinitely greater than the pleasure of taking from them, and that everybody in the world, without any exception, falls into one or other of these two categories' (9. 383).

That final judgment is not Lena's, but Leonov's (she comes to understand what he already knows), and it betrays his recurrent tendency to divide humanity into two classes, the damned and the saved. On this view happiness becomes less and less a reward and more and more a temptation, to which only the guilty succumb. By the side of Vikhrov's childhood moment of spontaneous 'radiant jubilation' at the spring happiness does not seem so important anyway.

The second image associated with purity is of cold mountain air, 'glaciered heights' (9. 316), in the words of Polya's fiancé, Rodion. There appears to be some attempt to soften the chilly atmosphere of the expression in the portmanteau word *ognevetrevys'* (fire-wind-height) that Rodion favours, but somehow that does not inspire much warmth either. For Vikhrov the Revolution is an 'invigorating, icy blast of air' (9. 240), and at the very end of the novel, with victory over the Germans now assured, he overhears a 'voice, pure as snow, like a stream from the foothills of Communism' (9. 697).[51] There is no longer any thought of a sandy beach and a warm sea beyond the mountain pass to reward the loyal Communist for his perseverance. Communism itself is the mountain.

And yet at the same time Leonov recognizes the inhumanity of 'purity' as an ideal, and one is reminded of Dostoevsky's *Dream of a Ridiculous Man*, in which the evil and sufferings of this world are still somehow preferable to the innocence and tranquillity of Eden. The associations of virginity and mountain heights suggest not only moral perfectionism but also sterility and barrenness. Polya's friend, Varya Chernetsova, the great advocate of 'purity, perhaps the chief among human freedoms' (9. 315), who dreams of a 'pure world, sterilized against evil' (9. 194), sleeps in a tiny child's bed of 'sterile purity' (9. 13).[52] Her surname with its monastic connotations betrays the same tendency. The concept of sterility appears in a grimmer context, when the Nazi officer Kittel's dream of 'simply sterilizing the entire expanse East of the Vistula' (9. 580) proves to be a euphemism for mass extermination.

But the main agent of sterilization in this novel is Communism itself. The police chief Chandvetsky warns Vikhrov against his revolutionary sympathies: 'You want to sterilize life, Mr Vikhrov... but absolutely pure elements exist only in scientists' test tubes, and frequently come at a price that make them impracticable for general use' (9. 347), and he warns the now irrevocably compromised Gratsiansky that he can never go back to his revolutionary friends: 'Only an absolutely pure man, that is, one with a hopelessly sterile centre, can stand up in such a wind. Well, just think about it: suppose they were suddenly to see through you... and on the very eve of that longed-for day were suddenly to read those thoughts that scurry furtively through your head. Doesn't that scare you just a little?' (9. 476–7). These comments are given of course to a discredited and untrustworthy character, but Leonov has since the time of *The Sot'* entrusted his boldest ideas to the enemy.

If purity is defined in terms of the future then the past is clearly impure, and the present is contaminated by any dealings with the 'old world.' Thus Lena, Polya, and Serezha are all ashamed of their origins and make no attempt to find out anything about their parents. The rejection of all the products of discredited social systems would seem to follow from Marx's historical materialism, but, rather inconsistently, he made an exception for the arts.[53] Leonov uses this loophole to expose the inadequacies of Communism as an ideology, and some of the most deeply-felt pages in his works are devoted to this theme.

The Soviet attitude to the culture of the past has always been ambivalent. While feeling obliged to counter the accusations of vandalism levelled at them since 1917 with campaigns for mass literacy and unprecedented subsidization of theatre and publishing, the Communist authorities have always been suspicious of art's potential for impurity and subversion. From the very first they have been concerned to ensure that Soviet readers would draw the politically correct lessons from works of art, or at least, in Leonov's words, 'to weaken the harm contained within them' (9. 384). In the same spirit one of the critics of *The Road to Ocean* had argued that though Leonov's novel might be artistically superior to *How the Steel Was Tempered*, that only increased its potential for harm.

The consequences of such assumptions are seen in Vikhrov's attempts to apply them to the education of his wife and adopted son. He reads to them and takes them to art galleries and concerts, taking care to prepare them for the experience by little lectures. Thus he takes Lena to a Bach organ recital, where he 'whispers into her ear some information about the composer and the programmatic content of the work to be performed, without which, he sincerely believed, no cultured person could hope to enjoy art. As always he had prepared himself in advance, and read up in the requisite literature; briefly enumerating the basic facts of Bach's biography, he paid particular attention to his Dresden contest with the organist Marchand' (9. 340).[54] Lena repeatedly asks him to stop talking, but in vain, and by the end of the evening she has, not surprisingly, resolved to leave him.

Vikhrov's methods prove equally unproductive when he applies them to Serezha:[55]

> The entire wisdom of the world was presented to Serezha in predigested form, – he had never had to struggle to find out the truth for himself. [...] Vikhrov had forgotten that it was the very hardships and the sheer protractedness of his search for a philosophy, the constant collisions with alien ideas that had helped the truth to mature in his own brain. The older generation, which had personally experienced the misfortunes of social disorder, was trying to inoculate its successors against the humiliations of poverty and to insure it against all possible diseases of the spirit. (9. 384)

The climax comes when Vikhrov takes Serezha to the Pushkin museum and sits him down in front of a copy of the Venus of Milo, 'created, as Vikhrov explains, by the people's poetic reverence for the productive energies of the earth,' but Serezha comments: 'So what, it's pretty expressive in the sense of, hm... the prolongation of the species. But all the same in view of the fact that it arose in a different age and latitude, I would prefer to see it clothed more effectively' (9. 388). This irreverence, however, is only a mask for Serezha's embarrassment at the sight of nudity. He 'lowers his eyes, as though to avoid temptation' and continues in a vein of criticism that in some circles still passes for Marxist:

> So what are the leading ideas of the age that so captivate you in this chunk of rock? Remember, no work of art exists outside its social environment – so tell me, can this piece assist me in understanding that remote epoch? The sculptor lived in the thick of the most appallingly cruel events, and yet did not notice the barbarism of ancient slavery, or the horrors of the Peloponnesian war, or the bloodthirsty campaigns of Alexander. In general, that word *beauty* is a pretty murky one. All too often it has served as a cover for injustice and criminality. Ruins are always attractive at sunset, but beware of the ancient reptiles that lurk in their crannies. (9. 389)

He goes on to say that the tragedy of Romeo and Juliet could easily have been averted if the human race had ever got round to analysing the problems and functions of what is called love. When Vikhrov reminds him that in that case a great tragedy would never have been written, Serezha retorts by quoting *The Road to Ocean* at him: 'our age will create new tragedies but ones more worthy of the human estate' (9. 388).[56] Vikhrov feels ill-equipped for such a debate, and he eventually concedes: 'Possibly you have got a point there; but I can't deny that I shall be sorry if you are right. Usually people come to doubt the good things of life only when they've drained them to the last drop' (9. 389).

At this point a stranger intervenes. After overwhelming Serezha with his erudition he proceeds to support Vikhrov with a well-worn quotation from Lenin: 'we can build Communism only with the aid of the forces and techniques that we have inherited from the old world' (9. 391). In fact the quotation is irrelevant because the discussion has not been concerned with the value of previous cultures as stepping stones for succeeding generations, but rather with the plain fact that cultures and their works are felt to retain their immediacy long after the collapse of the civilizations that produced them. Having provided Vikhrov and himself with this authority, however, Leonov can now go on to reassert the importance of the continuity of the cultural tradition. Morshchikhin reminds Serezha that Heine and Gleb Uspensky[57] had also sat in front of the same work of art: 'They considered themselves the legitimate heirs of all the best that had been produced by the titanic endeavours of their predecessors [...] How then can you give all this away, this well-loved home to the cave-men of our times – and the cavemen were probably more merciful than our present-day monopolists' (9. 391).[58]

To some extent Leonov is here refuting an attitude of which he himself had once been guilty. In 1927 he had offended Gor'ky by his unceremonious dismissal of the frescoes of Pompeii,[59] but he later came to the conclusion that the sublime and the vulgar coexist inseparably, however difficult this might be for ideologists (of whatever stripe) to accept. It is indeed quite unacceptable for most of Leonov's Communists: Uvad'ev in *The River Sot'* rejected the past out of hand; in *The Russian Forest* Serezha, remembering 'the lamentable fate of Lot's wife, would never allow the young to look back at the old world or to overload themselves with its seductive antiques' (9. 385). Chikilev's views have become official.

As such they are expressed by Gratsiansky in words that for all their qualifications and seeming concessions insist that the social role of art is paramount, and that artistic values are secondary and even suspect. The artist has no particular individual merit; his work belongs to the collective which is free to introduce corrections and modifications as it sees fit:

> Don't misunderstand me [...] I too quite agree that [...] the fabric of literature cannot take too much didacticism... but all the same literature is an aspect of the thought of society, which we can't just sell off to private individuals, *however inspired...* And if this may lower the formal value of their works, so what? Let them be a little bit worse, so long as they are more grandiose and universally accessible. [...] And I foresee the exalted pattern of our own literature of the

> future, from which the individual handwriting of the author will have been wholly expunged, when literature will have become the province of all and sundry, mutually engaged in correcting *and supplementing* one another; when *the various inequalities of labour will have been smoothed away and* the compositor at the linotype will introduce his own *creative* corrections into the works of his *brilliant* contemporaries. Oh, please don't take my suggestion as an attack on the direction of our *beautiful*, progressive, joyous, shadowless, *and, so to say, sterile* literature. After all, it is only because of its innate scepticism that my own generation earlier rejected the alcohol-free lives of the saints. (9. 472–3)[60]

The slippery irony of this passage works on several levels. Gratsiansky's elaborate charade of alternating denials and assertions barely conceals the fact that for him all this is a matter of contemptuous indifference. The immediate context of his remarks is the theory of 'conflictlessness' that bedevilled Soviet literature in the late 1940s. It was argued then that since Soviet society had attained a stage at which no social conflicts remained there was no reason why literature should attempt to depict any; to suggest otherwise was to deny the achievements of the Communist Party. Although the theory had long been discredited by the time Leonov completed *The Russian Forest* it represented for him the epitome of Soviet political correctness in its blandness and sterility.

The most interesting vindication of culture in all its ambivalence comes, however, from Vikhrov himself, though in view of the banality of his lectures to Lena and Serezha he makes an implausible mouthpiece. In conversation with Polya he relates the myth of the Gorgon and of how, after Perseus had killed it, 'there emerged from its blood poetry and a storm cloud, which in hot climates is associated with fertility. As you see, not such a bad reward for victory. But even Perseus turned away as he raised his scimitar over the Gorgon, though he had prudently equipped himself with a magic mirror' (9. 455–6).

The Gorgon's hair consists of snakes, no doubt the same ones that lurk in the crannies of ancient ruins. The poetry and fertility that emerge are the foundation of our culture. Perseus himself cannot bear to look at the sight, for fear of being turned to stone. But as we shall see in the revised version of *The Thief*, the artist is the one who insists on looking in spite of the dangers. In *The Russian Forest* Morshchikhin and Polya have to gaze into the icy, petrifying eyes of Gratsiansky if they are to master him.

The special role of art resides in its ability to encompass the whole of human experience. This idea is rooted in Leonov's conviction of the interconnectedness of all phenomena in space and time. The forest, like the ocean in Leonov's previous novel, serves as a natural image for the belief that 'prolonged treatment of any point of any of nature's organisms cannot but produce a reaction even at the furthest possible remove' (9. 172). On the last page of the novel Leonov draws the reader's attention to 'the setting sun reflected in a puddle' (9. 716), an image that has run through his work ever since *The Thief*.

In this universal interdependence good and evil are inextricably interlinked. In *The Russian Forest* the idea is reinforced by several references to Darwin's *Diary of the Voyage of H.M.S. Beagle*, the expedition which led to the theory of evolution. The final words of *The Origin of Species*, the book in which Darwin formulated these ideas, are: 'We must, however, acknowledge, as it seems to me, that man with all his noble qualities [...] still bears in his bodily frame the indelible stamp of his lowly origins.' Ironically, this book is Varya Chernetsova's bedside reading, but she does not see how it contradicts her ideals of purity.[61] So too the Nazi officer Kittel bears the name of one of Bach's pupils, without whom some of Bach's greatest organ music would not have been preserved, including perhaps some of the works that Vikhrov and his wife heard on that fateful evening.[62]

In Darwinism too Leonov finds an argument against the social and intellectual levelling, gloatingly foretold by Shigalev in *The Devils*, and enviously parroted by Chikilev. At the very beginning of *The Russian Forest* Leonov remarks ironically on 'the fashion of the time that aimed to equalize all citizens, so that none should feel hard done by' (9. 11). The irony is inverted when the police chief Chandvetsky reminds Vikhrov of the 'biological inequality of individuals and, consequently, the immutability of the time-honoured principles of human coexistence, and of the abyss into which Russia was being drawn by the overexcitable (and hence in particular need of strict paternal supervision) younger generation...' (9. 347). The principles of evolution and genetics conclusively refute the ideals of socialist egalitarianism.

At one point Leonov compares the relationship of Vikhrov and Gratsiansky to a 'strange double star' (9. 400), and it is tempting to see the two as another pair like Kurilov and Gleb Protoklitov, who had similarly been compared to a 'planet and its satellite.' But unlike Gleb, Gratsiansky is not a man who is trying to atone for a wrong decision taken many years ago; on the contrary his political orthodoxy is merely camouflage for a nature that remains essentially unchanged. Leonov treats him with sarcasm throughout – this is particularly obtrusive on rereading – and is constantly intervening to 'correct' or 'modify' his versions of events.

Nevertheless, like Gleb, Gratsiansky dominates every page on which he appears, and his real double is not the nominal hero of the novel, but his creator, Leonid Leonov. For what could better characterize Leonov's literary methods throughout the Stalin years than the word *mimetism*?[63] The slippery ironies and circumlocutions that characterize Gratsiansky are features of Leonov's style too. When we read Gratsiansky's double-edged presentation of Soviet orthodoxy we are at the same time reading Leonov's refutation of it. Both men owe their survival to their manipulation of official stereotypes. In drawing this parallel Leonov fully recognizes the ambiguities of his own position. Art is necessarily impure since it springs ultimately from our accumulated experiences. In the revised *Thief* Leonov is to compare our cultural heritage to original sin. The idea is not just a provocative speculation but is rooted in Leonov's own experience, going back to the events of 1918–20. He knew that his compromises had compromised himself and his art. Hence no doubt his fascination with the tangle of good and evil. Is his art then irreparably compromised, or can one make an art of compromise?

This view of the relationship between good and evil recalls the comparison with light and shadow made in Bulgakov's *Master and Margarita*; but where Bulgakov regards human greed and cowardice with Rabelaisian laughter, for Leonov, as for Dostoevsky, the problem is tragic. Evil is evil, and cannot be excused or condoned, and yet a world without evil would be worse than the world we have. We may also hear in this debate Leonov's continuing reflections on Zamyatin's *We*. The sterility of the glass structures of the Single State and its sexual regulations, the uniformity of its citizens, the fear of the green world[64] of nature beyond the wall, and the attempt to deny the role of genetics in the human make-up: all these are features of Zamyatin's sterilized city-state that find their reflection in *The Russian Forest*. They are not, of course, intended to reflect the realities of life in the contemporary Soviet Union literally. Rather they represent the logical conclusion of the aspirations of its ideologists.

The novel's combination of scientific debate and veiled historical comment made it an object of passionate debate from the time of its appearance. In January 1954, a mere month after the final instalment had appeared, a meeting was held in Moscow under the auspices of the Academy of Sciences, at which it was subjected to harsh criticism from Professor P.V. Vasil'ev of the Leningrad Institute of Forestry; further condemnations followed in the next few months, culminating in a demand that the novel should not be republished until it had been fundamentally revised.[65] The tide began to turn in May at a meeting of the Prose Section of the Union of Soviet Writers. Although the first speakers, among them Professor Vasil'ev and Leonov's fellow writer S. Zlobin,[66] were united in their attacks, Leonov was vindicated when Professor Anuchin produced statistics of developments since the publication of the novel to show that Leonov's predictions were substantially correct. Other professionals joined in and succeeded in reversing the course of the meeting. Vasil'ev was so shaken by this turn of events that by the end he was begging not to be identified with Gratsiansky.[67] The controversies continued, however, and only ended in 1957, when the novel was honoured with the first Lenin Prize, a new award intended to replace the discredited Stalin Prizes of the old dictator, and so was placed beyond any further attacks.

The Russian Forest was immediately hailed by Soviet critics as the author's masterpiece. In the twelve years after it first appeared more than a million copies were published.[68] It was adapted for the stage and the radio; Leonov and others gave public readings from it. No other of his works ever enjoyed such official acclaim. A mass of critical literature, innumerable reviews, two book-length studies, and dozens of dissertations and articles have been devoted to various aspects of the novel.

It is undeniable that *The Russian Forest* draws together many of Leonov's lifelong concerns, his deep love and understanding of nature, and his elaboration of the interdependence of the ecosystem into a metaphysical philosophy; his justification of the Russian intelligentsia, long vilified under Stalin, and his abiding fear that the younger generation may have been morally and culturally stunted by the decades of Stalinism. In its theme, its implications, and the profundity of its reach, it could have been the greatest novel of the Soviet period. The book remains essential reading, but few Russians have read it to the end except for those who admire Leonov already.

For it must be confessed that the novel is damaged by a certain self-indulgence in the style. It is expertly written, but it is the expertise of a practised raconteur. Gratsiansky and indeed most of the major characters in the book are seldom allowed to speak for themselves. Leonov reports in his own voice the vital pieces of information that Gratsiansky had 'forgotten' or 'confused'; 'All this was related in a shortened and somewhat expurgated version' (9. 500), but we are not allowed to see Gratsiansky's own narrative; instead we get the author's sarcastic account of his Pushkin speech, which we already know was never delivered. This fondness for repeating and embellishing the words of his characters sometimes leads to a confusion of their individualities in a single style, which is scarcely to be distinguished from that of Leonov himself.[69] Thus in chapter 2 Lena is told of Vikhrov's early life by his sister Tais'ya, but the author soon takes over the narrative from her. The role of controlling intelligence assigned to Svekolkin and Berezkin in the plays is now adopted by Leonov himself.

Another reason for the uneven quality of the novel lies in Leonov's lack of sympathy with the younger generation. They are shown as naive and superficial, and often provoke his irony. Not only Vikhrov and Gratsiansky, but a host of incidental characters from the early years of the century are described with greater vividness and understanding than Polya and Serezha and their contemporaries. This is expecially marked in the closing scene of the novel, in which the relationship of Elena Ivanovna and Vikhrov is of far more interest than that of the younger figures, who are supposed to have been covering themselves with glory in the war.

This aspect of the novel was particularly damaging, for when *The Russian Forest* was published in 1953 a new generation was already looking for a new kind of literature with a vocabulary and syntax closer to its own. Leonov's elaborate manner seemed dated and needlessly cautious, at least by comparison with the more outspoken criticisms voiced by Erenburg in his novel *The Thaw* (*Ottepel'*, 1953), which was to give its name to the new period. The young poets and 'bards,' Evtushenko and Okudzhava, seemed more relevant in both content and style than anything Leonov could offer. This gulf was only to widen in the following decades. In fact, as we have seen, Leonov's novel goes further in its denunciation of the Soviet system than anything officially published in the country until the emergence of Gorbachev, but to understand this requires an ability and a willingness to put together pieces of information and authorial observations scattered over many hundreds of pages.

In the last resort, however, the allegorical and symbolic elements of Leonov's novel and their political and ideological implications are only secondary. The literal meaning of the novel is the most urgent of all. The continuing destruction of the world's forests threatens mankind and indeed life on earth with a greater catastrophe than any conceived by Stalin or Hitler. The forty years that followed the publication of *The Russian Forest* offered Leonov no reasons for optimism, and his next and last novel, *The Pyramid,* is frankly apocalyptic in its vision of the approaching crisis.

chapter twelve

The Late Revisions 1955–1962

The years after the death of Stalin witnessed a gradual liberalization in the cultural climate of the Soviet Union. Authors who had been disgraced or executed were rehabilitated; works that had been suppressed were reissued; writers who had been almost forgotten began to find their way back into print. For all artists it was a period of greater freedom of expression, even if dangerously ill-defined. It may seem surprising then that after producing *The Russian Forest* with its comprehensive indictment of Soviet Communism, Leonov was to contribute nothing further to the literature of the 'Thaw,' unless we count the unimportant film scenario, *The Flight of Mr McKinley* (*Begstvo mistera Makkinli* 1961).[1] Instead, over the next ten years he devoted himself primarily to revising several of his earlier works.

This development began in 1955 when the Moscow Arts Theatre expressed an interest in staging *A Golden Coach*.[2] As usual Leonov decided to look over the work first, and soon found himself embarked on a substantial reworking of it.[3] This experience led him on to a series of other revisions, *The Thief*,[4] *The End of a Petty Man*,[5] and *The Snowstorm*[6] (works that had lain in obscurity if not disgrace for some twenty or thirty years); and in 1963 he finally released a novella, *Evgenia Ivanovna*,[7] originally composed in 1938 but simply unpublishable at that time. Other works, such as *Invasion*,[8] where he restored the original explanation for Fedor's imprisonment, were also reviewed in these years.

In the years of tight ideological control Leonov had developed a style which enabled him to express indirectly even the most heretical views; but when these controls were relaxed these evasions were no longer required, and I suspect that he was unsure as to how he should write under the changed conditions of the 'Thaw.' As we now know he had already begun work on his last novel, *The Pyramid*, but this was not to appear until the mid-1990s, and the rethinking of earlier works may have seemed a way of keeping his hand in during the meantime. So it is significant that the two most fundamental revisions, *A Golden Coach* and *The Thief*, were in fact the first. The later ones, *The End of a Petty Man* and *The Snowstorm*, are of less interest and will be treated here only briefly.

The rewriting of books had of course been a feature of Soviet literature under Stalin, but in the 1950s many writers took the opportunity of returning to earlier versions (though seldom the original version) of works they had been required to rewrite. Leonov similarly returns to works that had incurred displeasure on political or ideological grounds, but the accent is not placed primarily on these aspects, except in the case of *Invasion*. Rather he was concerned to reinterpret characters and situations that he had devised many years earlier.

This chapter will be devoted mainly to an examination of the differences of accent and the shifts in interpretation in the revised versions rather than those of style (a vast subject in itself). For the remarkable feature of Leonov's late revisions is that they have all gone far beyond the practice of mere stylistic repolishing. In each case he has left the structure virtually unaltered, but the changes have been designed to clarify the issues and indicate the author's position more unambiguously. There are thus gains and losses. The author's intentions are clearer, but the moralizing element also becomes more insistent. If in the case of *The End of a Petty Man* and *The Snowstorm* the new version serves to clarify the thrust of the originals, in the case of *The Thief* and *A Golden Coach* Leonov ends up with a dénouement diametrically opposed to that of the original work.

The 1955 version of *The Golden Coach* is the most fundamental and intriguing of the late revisions. While retaining the basic plot and structure of the original, Leonov has introduced changes at every level, from the names (for example, Chirkhanov now becomes Shchelkanov) to the general direction and overall ethos of the play. At the end of the new version Mar'ka rejects the chance of leaving for Pamir and chooses to stay behind with her mother and Timosha.[9]

Leonov said that he rewrote the play 'in order to be fair to Mar'ka.'[10] In other words he wanted to make it easier for her to resist the temptation of the 'golden coach.' If in the first version of the play Berezkin had intervened to help Timosha make the right decision, in the revised version the author himself intervenes to ensure that Mar'ka does. But in doing so he has shifted the delicate balance between freedom and morality that is so moving in the original. This lowers the purely dramatic tension of the work and emphasizes its moral dimension. By making the right decision easier Leonov has also made it less admirable. This new approach casts its shadow back over the entire play.

This is because being 'fair to Mar'ka' has involved him in considerable unfairness to most of the other characters, and above all to the two Karevs. This is done in various ways. First their plain and commonplace surname, Karev, is expanded into the more imposing form, Kareev,[11] and the father's patronymic, Mikhaylovich, is changed to Stepanovich, a name that Leonov reserves for his most dislikable characters (see Stepan Drakin and Stepan Syrovarov); he is distant to his boyhood friend Nepryakhin and finally earns his reproof: 'If by chance you should meet my old friend Mikolashka Kareev in Pamir, please give him my regards.'[12] Whereas in the 1946 version the purpose of his visit was to prospect for oil, in 1955 he is said to be on his way to a health resort before going on to Pamir (in other words he has now reversed the priorities of the seashore and the mountains). In the first version he had hoped to see his former girlfriend on the way, but now his main motive is revenge, to flaunt his 'golden coach.'

In the 1946 version he had asked Mar'ya Sergeevna if she was happy. The question could be interpreted in many ways, from the sympathetic interest of a former friend to the unpleasant bragging of a man who is confident he has done better. But when she bursts into tears he had responded – inadequately perhaps, but still decently: 'I owe everything to you.' In the new version his question reveals only a desire to parade his success:

Then, if it's not a secret, Mar'ya Sergeevna, allow me to ask you a question. Are you happy now? (*This is the culmination of Kareev's triumph, his consciousness of his previous insignificance and his present grandeur. The old wound which had fuelled him for twenty-six years of persistent and well-rewarded scientific labour is far stronger than his intelligence. He can see the rapid succession of complex feelings in Mar'ya Sergeevna's face, and it takes real cruelty to keep his eyes fixed on her at this moment.*) If you find it difficult, you don't have to answer my tactless question... though it's the only reason, as you observed, that I came down from Pamir. (VII. 565)

Mar'ya Sergeevna is now, however, quite unflustered and replies that she has found happiness in working for her people: 'It is pleasant to know that the workers in our town love me – yes, I think so, they love me. And you, I see, have found your happiness.' Kareev can reply only in terms of the books he has published, the reputation he has achieved, the awards he has gained, his foreign trips, and in particular a delicious pear that he enjoyed on the Champs Elysées in 1936 (VII. 568).[13]

Worst of all is the fact that he has managed to secure military exemption for his son: 'There are many wars, but I have only one son' (VII. 569). Some of this denigration inevitably rubs off on the boy, who is now renamed Yuliy, an ominously classy name by comparison with the unpretentious Yakov of the original. The amiable but undistinguished young captain of 1946 now becomes a rather uneasy 'lawyer with a geological slant' (VII. 570) and he is called a 'blockhead' (*lobotryas*, VII. 549) by one character; like Serezha in *The Snowstorm* he seems to regard Mar'ka as his property (VII. 565),[14] and even his sincerity is 'unexpected' (VII. 576).

This tendency towards moral devaluation extends even to the figure of Mar'ya Sergeevna. Like Kareev, though less disastrously, she too is guilty of having preferred a golden coach to Pamir. Whereas in the 1946 version it was Chirkhanov who had presented Timosha with the accordion in order to buy his silence, in 1955 it is Mar'ya Sergeevna who does so in the hope that he will make no claim on her daughter,[15] and at the very end of the play she makes one final bid to persuade Mar'ka to postpone her decision (VII. 587). In the earlier version human mistakes could still be redeemed if not repaired, but in the revision they are judged much more sternly.

In 1946 Leonov had presented a wide range of characters, none of whom was entirely black (with the exception of Chirkhanov and his mistress, who in any case never appear on stage). Instead there was a wide range of more or less fallible human beings. In the new version all the characters are steered into one or other of the two categories of givers and takers into which Lena Vikhrova had divided humanity. As a result the dilemmas of the first version now cease to exist. Mar'ka may have made the wrong choice then, but her situation was potentially far richer in its moral implications. Now the scales are heavily weighted: young Kareev has nothing to offer but his wealth and prospects, Timosha no drawbacks except for his poverty and blindness. Mar'ka makes the right choice because ultimately she has no other.

The same process can be observed in the imagery of the play. In the earlier version the golden coach had been an image of temptation, but the corollary of achievement was an important element in its complex meaning. The dominating image had been Pamir; the elder Karev and Mar'ya Sergeevna had all achieved it in their different ways, while their children aspire to it. In the 1955 version the golden coach becomes an image of corruption, pure and simple, while even Pamir is debased. Kareev is not ennobled by his achievements, and the rumours that he had died on Pamir now hint that, spiritually, perhaps he did, while his son fails even to recognize Pamir when he lands there. In other words the new version really is about the 'golden coach.'

Soviet critics found the revised play more optimistic than the original,[16] but this is hardly justified except on the most superficial level. In 1946 Leonov had tried to find some affirmation to set against the hardships of Russian history:

'We have passed the darkest tunnel now – only the last defile remains. Look, you can see the sea and the shore.' (*ZK*, 43). In the new version this remark is omitted, and the mountain climb continues for its own sake. When Mar'ya Sergeevna shows Kareev her plans for rebuilding the town he politely asks, 'And how soon do you expect to realize these ambitious dreams?' Her answer is extraordinary (not least in the context of a planned economy): 'In the circumstances, that's not really important' (VII. 567). If other Soviet writers have generally ignored the means in their pursuit of the all-justifying goal of Communism, Leonov seems to have fallen into the opposite trap of losing sight of the goal in his preoccupation with the means.

Thus the 1955 revision of *A Golden Coach* proved to be self-defeating. A happy ending is achieved but only at the cost of debasing several of the characters and virtually depriving Mar'ka of any freedom of choice. The generosity of the original version which had accepted the interdependence of human strengths and weaknesses has here narrowed into a joyless and puritanical severity. This is chiefly due to a shift in the balance between conflicting tendencies in Leonov's artistic make-up. On the one hand he has always been an idealist, interested in perfectionism. At the same time he is a realist, well aware of human frailties and inconsistencies. In his finest works, such as the first version of *A Golden Coach*, the tension between these two elements contributes largely to the profundity and complexity of the whole. But in the 1950s the dissatisfaction of the idealist with the weaknesses of ordinary men and women comes to the fore. This leads to a contradiction that sours the nobility of his moral conceptions. Leonov's characters all aspire to happiness and success. But in achieving it they lose their moral purity, like Kareev and Mar'ya Sergeevna. Therefore his heroes are shown only at the moment of achieving success or recognition, like Mar'ka or Vikhrov. After attaining the summit there is nowhere to go but downhill.

This development is paralleled by a significant shift in Leonov's imagery. Like Karev, Kalafat in *The Badgers* had gone off into the mountains to prepare himself for building his tower. Timosha, Leonov's preferred hero, is an astronomer. Where the image of the mountains presupposes a finite end to one's aspirations and is therefore suspect, the stars are unattainable. If in the 1946 version of *The Golden Coach*, there appeared to be little difference between these two ideals, in the 1955 revision it is crucial.

But even this solution did not satisfy the author, and in 1964 he brought out yet another version of the play in which he returned to the denouement of 1946,[17] with Mar'ka electing to follow Yuliy to the Pamirs. Again Leonov was actuated by a desire to help Mar'ka: 'an eighteen-year-old girl whom two real heroes sentence to a difficult life of service, even sacrifice, with a blind man, in expectation of the day when he will win worldwide fame. And this is done by Berezkin, that knight *sans peur et sans reproche*, a philosopher! Impossible! And what of Timosha, how can he not understand what he is dooming their love to?'[18]

Leonov's recognition of the practical human consequences of the 1955 version does not wholly remove the sense that Mar'ka still 'ought' to have chosen Timosha. The older Kareev is now less snobbish towards Nepryakhin, and his 'cruel' enjoyment of his moment of triumph is dropped altogether, but he still boasts of having procured his son's exemption from military service. Yuliy himself retains his impatience and possessiveness towards Mar'ka. The two are even less worthy of her than they had been in 1946, and there is now no balancing prospect of aspiration and success to offset the regrets for her mistake. Mar'ka, for her part, tries to persuade herself that she only wants to get a glimpse of Pamir, that she has not yet finally decided, that she will return in three years to marry Timosha, but her self-deception is exposed in her last words, uttered 'through tears and triumphantly': 'Goodbye, Mummy, and tell Timosha, for God's sake, that it's not my fault at all' (7. 666).

Leonov regains something of the pathos of the original version: Mar'ka is left to make her decision on her own (though Timosha still needs Berezkin's support), but her life with Yuliy looks even less promising than her prospects with Timosha. If in 1946 she was faced with a choice between two futures, equally attractive in their different ways, in 1964 they seem almost equally unattractive. The desire to help Mar'ka has only pushed her into making the wrong choice yet again.

Complex works of art are delicately balanced, and any attempt to improve them runs the risk of destroying this balance. Tovey tells the story of the musician Klindworth who re-orchestrated Chopin's F minor piano concerto in an attempt to correct what he perceived as the inadequacies of the original; having done so he discovered that he then had to rewrite the piano part too to restore the balance between them. Much the same thing happened to *A Golden Coach* in its successive rewritings.

In the case of *The Thief* too the initial stimulus came from outside. After the success of *The Russian Forest*, Leonov had been invited to reissue the novel, largely because of the wide demand from readers. At first he thought he could revise it in two or three weeks, but in the event it took him two and a half years of concentrated labour (1956–9), a longer period than it had taken him to write the novel in the first place: 'This work was perhaps the most difficult in the forty years of my life in literature. There were only a few pages left till the end. Suddenly I understood that in this new version I had "killed" my hero, Mitya Vekshin, stone dead.'[19] Even after completing the revision he continued to return to it, and new editions with substantial changes and additions appeared in 1970[20] and 1991.[21]

In its revised form the novel's original four parts have been reduced to three, the third of them corresponding to a rearrangement of the last two parts of the 1927 version. The first part of the novel has been changed the least. It has become longer, as the texture has been thickened with new epithets and modifiers in the style of all Leonov's prose since *The Taking of Velikoshumsk*, but it is not significantly different. Starting with the ninth chapter of part 2, however, Leonov starts elaborating the original text with new incidents, new motivations, and new commentary. The second part which in 1927 was rather shorter than the first part is now substantially longer, and is in fact the largest of the three. The new third part follows the original third part as far as chapter 15 (chapter 13 in the new edition); a new chapter is then inserted that has no equivalent in the earlier version. The remaining nine chapters of the new version then rearrange material from the original third and fourth parts to concentrate on the complicated plot involving Vekshin, Don'ka, and San'ka Babkin. Pchkhov's attempt to persuade Vekshin to find a Christian solution to his problems is now given even greater prominence as it is moved from the end of the third part to the very end of the novel, where it takes place on the eve of Vekshin's departure for Siberia. The epilogue dealing with the aftermath of Firsov's novel is a more sophisticated version of the reviews originally contained in chapters 1 and 2 of part 4 of the original. Whereas the original third and fourth parts together were longer than either the first or the second part, the new third part is almost exactly as long as the new first part, and substantially shorter than the second.

The basic plot line of the novel remains virtually unchanged, but the tonality and the conclusions are now very different. Leonov stressed the fact that the new version was not just of historical interest: 'Of course, the novel has become angrier [...] and in some ways better targeted. I myself consider that it is very timely and necessary just now (between ourselves!) As I put it in one interview: "the novel is written with today's hand and in today's ink."'[22]

The key to the new version lies in the reinterpretation of the significance of the old tree, poisoned by the revolutionary slogan scratched into its bark; in the original the tree had managed to recover and give birth to new forms of life. In the new version this optimistic sequel is removed and replaced by the ominous words:

Just as the old [tree] never managed to cleanse its wound with pure white bark, so too Mitya's heart was never able to shake off the disturbing speeches that the wandering photographer had incised on his young heart. (3. 69)

Whereas in the 1927 version Leonov had pardoned Vekshin as the embodiment of the spirit of the Revolution, however unjustified this might seem,[23] the 1959 version sees no possibility of redemption. Vekshin is stripped of his romantic aura and doubts are cast even on his heroic exploits during the Civil War. The contrast between the 'sun' of his aspirations and the depths of the underworld is reinforced by a new image: from the first he is a 'fallen' man, and the word and its derivatives recur some thirty times, with increasing frequency as the book nears its end. Whereas in the first version the state of Vekshin's clothes and his raccoon-skin overcoat had steadily deteriorated, in the new version his overcoat becomes even more luxurious. His descent into the underworld had been seen as a spiritual odyssey; in the revised version it is simply a study in accelerating moral decay. In 1927 the frequent references to illness and fever had served as Dostoevskian metaphors for Vekshin's psychological state; they now carry instead the implication of moral sickness. In the following decades Leonov continued to reflect on Vekshin's fate. A new edition of 1982 amplified a few passages, and in 1990 he composed a new 'Epilogue' in which Vekshin ultimately disappears in one of Stalin's labour camps. Paradoxically, this new ending does something to redeem Vekshin as a representative of the once noble ideals of the Revolution, their rapid perversion, and their final brutal destruction.

For all that, Leonov's condemnation is now absolute, and might seem to reflect the same process as the revision of *A Golden Coach*. But there is an important difference. In the play Leonov was concerned above all with personal morality; in the novel Mitya's failings now carry much wider implications because of his identification with the Revolution. As Leonov says, Vekshin is 'a fragment, not of the fortress that had been destroyed, but of the hammer that had pulverized it, which in its turn must be affected by the force of the blow' (3. 513). In 1927 Firsov had declared: 'In those days they fought for a better life for man, but took little thought for the men themselves. A great love shared out equally among all gives no more warmth than a wax candle' (*Vor*, 50). But there the remark had been left hanging. In the new version it is closely tied to Mitya's betrayal of Masha Dolomanova. In the earlier edition he had been far away and so unable to save her from being raped by Agey. In the new one, however, he was in town and had arranged to meet her that very evening only to fail her because he was delayed by a political meeting. Her ironic acceptance, 'Of course now even I can see that this was just a trifle, a special case, as they say nowadays... so really there isn't anything for me to forgive Mitya. But then again, why on earth should I forgive something that was so personal, so precious?' (3. 474), makes explicit the collision between two sets of values. Elsewhere she says of him:

I can even allow that he really does love – no, not people, but – mankind, and a pretty impersonal one at that, because it is infinitely distant, agreeably silent, and blurred in the vista of the centuries – and all the more lovable for that; but these are two very different things, perhaps even mutually exclusive. (3. 472)

This willingness to sacrifice the living for the unborn had worried Leonov in 1927, and again in *The Sot'* in Urad'ev's indifference to the death of Polya. It now becomes his main charge against Communism, and is to be further elaborated in *The Pyramid*. Here it leads directly into the central event of the novel, Vekshin's murder of the White officer.[24] Firsov comments in his notebook:

> The Biblical commandment 'Thou shalt not kill' refers to individual not social behaviour. [...] In the Middle Ages the value of an individual life was inversely proportional to the grandeur of the idea, state, or epoch, even though these had been devised by man himself. 'The more there is of something the cheaper it becomes,' as Pchkhov said once about apples. So what does true humanism consist of? the affirmation of the sanctity of each unique existence, or in the overcoming of this ancient taboo, that is becoming more and more archaic with the march of progress?
>
> I am always amazed by the quantity of broken bricks on our largest building sites. (3. 490)

Raskol'nikov's question is posed once again, and Leonov's answer is the same as Dostoevsky's: human life cannot be reduced to purely material considerations.

The apparently unrelated comment on bricks takes us back to *The End of a Petty Man*, but now it is not the cultureless Van'kas, but the builders themselves who value the individual bricks so cheaply. Thus the connection with the cultural theme is made much clearer. Vekshin's murder of the White officer is an assault on the culture of the past: 'I cut him down, then I bent over him, but it still shone, his eye, it wouldn't go out.' (3. 491).[25] In 1927 Vekshin had been a vehicle, even if unawares, for the transmission of culture across the revolutionary divide. Now he is identified with the forces of destruction and the envy of culture once attributed to Chikilev:

> The two principles of envy. A. Why haven't I got what you have? B. why have you got what I haven't? [...] And hence three solutions to the problem of acquiring the treasure. 1. Putting out the glint in the enemy's eye, so that there should be no

difference between our eyes. 2. Removing the conditions under which it can appear in anyone's eye. 3. Acquiring it oneself [...]
Which will Vekshin choose? (3. 493–4)[26]

Whereas in 1927 Vekshin had been contrasted with Chikilev, the bureaucrat and *meshchanin* who had infiltrated the Party, now the two are working towards the same end. Chikilev is the true face of Vekshin's revolutionary aspirations.

The democratic drive for equality: 'why haven't I got what you have?' has given way to the envious downward levelling of: 'why have you got what I haven't?' Thus Firsov explains '... the unusually unsociable character of Chikilev by his quite extraordinary and utterly involuntary lack of any talent and hence his justifiable indignation at the rest of humanity which, despite the equality it had won and now proclaimed, still continued to endow its favourites with qualities that were dubious and even potentially harmful (3. 116).

Chikilev's hostility is aimed particularly at Firsov 'in reprisal for his previous misdemeanours, in the hope of causing not only harm to the writer's health, but also [of winning] the gratitude of several interested literary personages for his vigilance' (3. 437). He plans his revenge to start

> immediately after the publication of Firsov's novel; a clear advantage of waiting till then would be to enable him to support his denunciation with a list of the most flagrant instances of heterodoxy, political slander, sexual licence – to be going on with – and, who knows, something else nasty might turn up too. And it wouldn't be a bad idea to collect a hundred or so readers' signatures, preferably illegible, from among his colleagues at work or even in his place of residence, though of course it would be still more impressive if they were to come from the region as a whole or even from the entire Central Black Earth district, which should dispose of this repulsive scribbler in a bed of lime in no time. And so, shuddering, almost fainting with hatred, Chikilev took up his watch in the gateway of serious literature, where a motley crowd of Firsov's good friends were already assembling with their ink-wells at the ready.' (3. 325–6)

Soon after the publication of his novel Firsov does indeed experience 'physically the displeasure of the powers he has offended' (3. 324). In such passages Leonov is no doubt thinking of himself, but there is hardly a Soviet writer who would not have felt the same at one time or another.

Chikilev has learnt from Gratsiansky how to dress up his resentments in the jargon of the times, and boasts that he is

> boundlessly devoted to the interests of the immediate future. [...] Every genius is

an extremely antisocial phenomenon, which threatens the moral humiliation of the great mass of workers, and if, just between ourselves, I was director of the whole world I would find some practical and administrative application for it! Even so I frequently wake up in a cold sweat at the thought: 'and what if you, Chikilev, are in fact the highest form of genius, only as yet unknown?' [...] If we could only get things properly organized I would not let any events happen in history, just one long avenue of progress! [...] I have a secret screwdriver[27] [...] and what is this screwdriver? I can honestly tell you it is the aspiration to the highest well-being, that everything around me should be better, rounder you might say, more attractive.[28] And such is my nature that no sooner have I established order at home than I will proceed to the streets in our vicinity and so on to the end of the universe, where there is still quite a bit of chaos around. (3. 363)

The ideals of the Communist Revolution, the creation of a new man and a new society based on equality and universal happiness are not just mistaken but murderous. In 1927 Vekshin had rejected happiness as the negation of his 'upwards and onwards' aspirations; now in Firsov's film scenario he figures as an 'inventor of a machine for automatic happiness,' in the spirit of Leonov's Communists. Happiness, as in Zamyatin's *We*, has become compulsory, and the consequences are to be found in the words of Tolya Mashlykin, the last and most degraded of Vekshin's doubles:

You wait, I'll still come in useful for polishing people off in tomorrow's universal cataclysm! [...] useful for you know what – for the happiness of humanity [...] just get me a seven-year warrant to do anything I like and no questions asked, and I'll serve you up the happiness of humanity on a plate, all nice and warm [...] and I'll wipe all the scum and their hangers-on clean off the face of the earth... so that one can sit down on the ground that's been cleared and rest. (3. 518–20)[29]

In 1927, at the height of the NEP, Leonov had thought that Zavarikhin, the peasant turned businessman, was the real threat to the Revolution and Chikilev merely a grotesque excrescence. Thirty years later Zavarikhin, whose drive to world fame had once seemed unstoppable, is said to have perished like the other NEP-men of the time in Stalin's labour camps. It is the Chikilevs and Gratsianskys who have triumphed. Shigalev's prophecies have been fulfilled.

As Leonov re-evaluates the central figures of his novel, it is natural that Firsov too should come in for re-examination. In 1927 Firsov's novel about Vekshin, 'The Misadventures of Mitya Smurov,' had been clearly distinguished from Leonov's *Thief*. The new Firsov is the author of a book that is very like the

1927 *Thief*. In 1927 it was Firsov who had killed off Vekshin, and Leonov who had held out hopes for his reintegration into society; now their roles are reversed. Leonov quotes the ending of the earlier version and comments: 'all this is a matter for the conscience of the omniscient Firsov' (3. 589).[30] Many of the young Leonov's effusions are now transferred to Firsov, and, as before, he takes pleasure in pointing out the falsifications, inconsistencies, and implausibilities of Firsov's work (3. 226). Thus at the end of the new chapter 18, part 2, which is closely modelled on the corresponding chapter in the 1927 version, Leonov unexpectedly adds: 'Well, the whole of this chapter, deliberately invented by Firsov to justify his hero, in reality never took place' (3. 354).

In many important respects, however, Firsov still stands for Leonov. The novel opens with the same moment of inspiration: 'And then Firsov saw as if in reality...' (3. 10); and it ends with the first presentiments of another: 'new profiles, situations, and speeches, vague as yet, were just beginning to crystallize out of the murk of disturbing premonitions' (3. 600). Firsov's novel also includes another Firsov, whose novel in turn does the same thing, and so on ad infinitum. Fortunately, we are not given extracts from this endless recession of fictional narrators, but Leonov comments, or rather confirms, that the device 'enabled [Firsov] to reproduce with mirror-like fidelity the most complex even taboo situations, and to shift the responsibility for the delicate nature of his subject matter as also for his own literary shortcomings on to the shadowy host of accomplices that he headed' (3. 102). Obviously these words are equally true of the author of *The Thief*, who has been applying this very technique throughout his novels.

Leonov now attributes to Firsov his own earlier determination to make Vekshin the vehicle for the transmission of culture across the revolutionary divide. In a passage that elucidates the aims of the original novel in the language of the later one Firsov tells Vekshin:

> In the scheme of my book, though outside its pages, people are destined soon to attain the culmination of happiness with all its concomitant benefits... according to the needs, taste, and imagination, naturally, of each individual. [...] with the special advantage for you that your cerebellum [...] will be utterly sterilized against all those griefs, doubts, and despairs that are so destructive of our optimism. When the day comes for humanity to quit the slums of modern life for its new domicile in the Promised Land everybody will stream there unanimously [...] On the day before armed commandants will finally dekulakize the old world, leaving it only the worthless lumber of the past, rocks worn away by tears and rains, memorials to pointless battles and insights, the temples of discredited deities. Not an hour will pass, however, on the journey to your destination before

your iron organism will be affected by a strange nostalgia... it won't touch anyone else, but it will seem to tie your very legs. And with every step you will be gripped ever more fatally by the compulsion to cast a farewell glance back at the grey wilderness, trodden from end to end by your ancestors. [...] But ever since the days of Lot's ill-fated wife it has been forbidden to look back at the conflagration just escaped, so as to carry no infection into the new world... and indeed nobody would dream of doing so; salvation will consist precisely in not looking back... But in my scheme you will look back – not out of a foolhardy defiance of the interdiction but out of some strange and seductive intuition... which is really why I was attracted to you, Dmitriy Vekshin, to my misfortune. But then I have never tried to deal with those who do not look back.

[...] At your back you will see an utterly deserted wilderness as though nothing at all had ever happened there, no life, no love, no tears. Only, propped against a headless tree, with the last apologetic sunset behind it, there will gaze into your eyes what was once the soul of yesterday. Not even the most practical or dictatorial scrutiny will find in it anything of any value worth nationalizing – except, possibly, for the naggingly knowing glint in the sorcerer's darkening eye. Nobody will pay any attention to such a trifle, but you will notice it unfailingly. And at that instant you will be fired with the realization that this insignificant something, this spark, hardly even a dot [...] is perhaps the most priceless treasure of existence, because it is the distillation of everything that is behind us, the entire experience of human history. In one way you will be drawn to this mysterious flickering, young man, as though it contained the supreme sweetness of damnation, and yet you will also be scared because all the fearlessness of youth is founded on its magnificent ignorance. And while you are working out a smart way of obtaining it, the soul of yesterday will stretch its glint out to you of its own accord [...] 'Take my treasure, Mitya, valuable if only because it can never be taken away or quenched or executed [...]' It would be better for your health if you didn't, but that's why I chose you, Dmitriy Vekshin, because you don't care one little bit about your health. Any sensible person would think twice, but you will just grab it like a drunkard and swallow it in a single draught. But this draught contains neither sweets nor alcohol, not even a merciful death, but the entire memory of the human race. In it are dissolved such trifles, by modern standards, as the dust of ruined temples, the cry of a traveller [...] It includes also the apparently unimportant griefs and sorrows of our ancestors, their fruitless hopes, their untimely doubts, and the disillusionments of heroes. (3.126–9)[31]

Since the beginning of history thinkers and reformers have dreamed of a Utopia that would be free of the burden of sin and injustice that we have inherited from the past. But alongside this urge there has also existed an awareness, inarticulate perhaps and shared only by the occasional 'ridiculous man,' of the value of the past, of Sodom and pre-revolutionary Zaryad'e, for all their horrors. This heritage is not a luxury, still less a recreation. It is an almost insupportable nightmare, a Medusa, such that perhaps 'salvation will consist in never looking back – but in that case will there be any need to save anything?' (3. 147).[32]

The irony is that in Leonov's scheme Vekshin and the Revolution have finally proved unworthy of this mission. None of the putative addressees of Manyukin's testament, Mitya, Leontiy, Zavarikhin, is likely to read it, still less to take it to heart. The only one to take him seriously is Firsov. This perception was latent in the first version, it emerges clearly only in the second. If that version had ended with the story of Vekshin, the new one ends with the figure of Firsov. Like his heroes Leonov too time and again looks back not only to the years 1918–20 but also to the politically incorrect culture of the past. The act is fraught with danger, but without it Leonov would have been a lesser artist.

It is indeed this idea that provokes the most extensive criticisms of Firsov's novel, which in turn recall the hypocritically solicitous insinuations of Gratsiansky:

> ... we are alarmed by Firsov's occasional tendency to dwell on the darker sides of human existence, on the pseudotragic themes of disillusionments, unrealized dreams, and intellectual catastrophes, a dangerous excess of attention to the discredited visions of the past, his very curiosity about human suffering, as though it and the memory of it, and not the all-embracing dream, united the experience of the world, as though suffering allied to reason could provide creative insatiability to our eternal search [...] As a result of this incomplete thinking the author indulges in such profound revelations (pardon the expression!) as 'Every great truth begins as a heresy' or the 'appearance of a new hero in art is only possible through tragedy,' [...] Firsov gaily marches into our tomorrow heels first with his face firmly turned to our yesterday and the notorious glint in the eye, with which he zealously attempts to corrupt his ward Smurov. And it is not so much the family tombs left behind, or the age-old cinders of our grandparents' campfires that attract his moistened gaze [...] no, he cannot bear to part with the comfortable but antiquated wilderness that we have abandoned forever for a settled and universally secure life, free of all industrial crises.' (3. 593)

In quoting from his own writings Leonov is speaking of himself. His reaffirmation of the place of the past in our present and future and his attempts to suggest a tragic dimension to life in a time of forced optimism have run through his entire creative life. This central theme in his work sprang originally out of the debates of the 1920s over the nature of a socialist culture and its relationship to the cultures of previous societies. In the 1950s, however, Leonov goes far beyond his original aim of justifying the achievements of the past to a sceptical present. Culture is not just a list of the triumphs of the human spirit; rather it is a record of the whole of the past, its triumphs and its failures, its joys and its sorrows, its glories and its horrors. It is a curse as much as a blessing, but it is what distinguishes humans from the animals:

> It is not only we who create our habits and our wealth... and in this sense the Christian myth of original sin doesn't seem to me such utter nonsense. The past treads on our heels inexorably; it is harder to escape from it than to fly off the face of the earth or to break out of the power of the matter that we are made of. Only pretty and tasty fish and various colourful butterflies are exempt from the agonizing sense of the past, and it is better, far better, that mankind should never attain that ideal state. (3. 127–8).[33]

It is a force that is beyond our power to control, and our dreams of progress are ultimately frustrated by the undertow of the past.

The memory's ability to condense the complexity of experience into an image means that it can be transmitted through the generations like a seed or a node in the chain of DNA, capable of expanding and unfolding and absorbing new experience on the way. This knowledge, properly understood, is like D.503's hairy hands in *We*, shameful, indeed almost unbearable, and it is this that art insists on recalling to us. The artist, like Ham in Leonov's early story, is possessed of a knowledge that is not welcome. It is natural, then, that well-intentioned reformers should try to spare us its full realization, like Dostoevsky's Grand Inquisitor, who was moved to simplify the demands made on the Christian by taking the responsibility on to his own shoulders. So too in Leonov the State tries to minimize the harm latent in culture by inoculating readers against the dangers lurking in its crannies. But the suppression of the past is a denial of our humanity and, far from ameliorating life, has actually unleashed the horrors of the twentieth century. The pursuit of purity has led not just to sterility but to forced sterilization.

From a technical point of view the revised version of *The Thief* gains from the accumulated experience of several decades. Whereas the earlier version had frequently failed to integrate its mass of events and characters, the new version is more successful in charting the multiple cross-currents of moods, motives, and influences, and relating them to the main themes of the book. The narrative lines of Vekshin and Masha Dolomanova, Vekshin and San'ka, and Tanya and Zavarikhin, are filled out and made clearer and more credible. Meanwhile the intellectual scope of the novel has been deepened and extended to embrace Leonov's mature philosophy, already immanent in the original.

On the other hand the new work lacks the vitality and contradictoriness of the first version. In revising the novel Leonov has seriously weakened the temporal specificity of the original. The narrative has become smoother, but the jerky, aphoristic, impressionistic movement of the 1927 version was better suited to the milieu and the psychological states depicted. With the passing of the NEP period the urgency that had once informed the work has diminished. Zavarikhin has lost the vitality which in the earlier edition had made him an object of fear and detestation but also of admiration. Vekshin's former Robin Hood posture is now reduced to an unfavourable comparison of his words with his actions. Even Tanya's stature is diminished as Leonov devotes more space to describing her training, 'the mechanics of this unusually impressive turn' (3. 260), than to her actual performances. 'It was simply the number of difficulties overcome that created the value of her show' (3. 563). She herself claims: 'We're not heroes; we just work terribly hard' (3. 67). In 1927 the dangers of her *shtrabat*, the constant challenge to the void beneath her, had made her an image of the artist. Now she has become one of the professionals of her particular guild.

But any attempt to promote one version of *The Thief* over the other would be a mistake. They are both very much of their periods, pre-Stalin and post-Stalin. One's understanding of the revision requires a knowledge of the original. As Leonov said: '*The Thief* is my main work.'[34] Any serious edition of his oeuvre will have to include both versions.

The revisions to *The End of a Petty Man* and *The Snowstorm* are less fundamental. In the former Leonov returns to an early work, which had seemed to be an attack on the pre-revolutionary intelligentsia for their hostility to the new age. Such a work might seem something of an anomaly in Leonov's oeuvre generally, and particularly in view of his concern with the non-Party intellectuals and his insistence on the need for knowing the past. However, Leonov has not so much revised the story as tightened it up, in particular by pruning the later sections. Likharev himself becomes even more unattractive. Earlier he had assumed that he 'who had devoted himself to science naturally had the right to be a bit unfair occasionally.'[35] Now he tries in vain to justify his egoism by the need '... to take care of himself for the sake of his future achievements... and at this point it occurred to him – but what would happen if the whole of Russia from shore to shore was to turn into just such a dead lump of fossilized heart, and then who would read all his learned rubbish?' (1. 248). His scientific pretensions are now mocked by the discovery that 'thinking is the most economical form of combustion, that the brain, even in making its mightiest decisions requires incomparably less energy than, say, the hand in scratching one's side' (1. 253). When he finally burns his manuscript he discovers that 'cultural treasures yield a very second-rate kind of warmth' (1. 254).

Nonetheless Likharev represents a culture under threat both from the Underground Man within and the proletarian Van'ka without, and Leonov has seen little in the intervening forty years to reduce these concerns. He has always been sceptical about the teleological claims of Marxism, though such heretical thoughts are usually attributed in his works to 'negative' characters such as Vissarion, Petrygin, and Gratsiansky. In the same spirit Likharev and his fellow-intellectuals refuse 'to look for any plan in this seething mass of matter, shifts of population, volcanic eruptions, hordes of locusts, worldwide atrocities' (1. 230). Their despair at human nature goes even deeper than it had done in the original story; perhaps it is 'the beasts who are the normal wheel in the chariot of nature – while mankind is a wheel that has come off its axle and now gallops through the ditches alongside the high road, in defiance of all logic' (1. 230). Similar apocalyptic sentiments are expressed by Leonov himself in his last novel, *The Pyramid*, work on which was already far advanced by this time.

One may ask why Leonov should have chosen to revise this work, if he was to make no fundamental reinterpretation of it. I would suggest that he wanted to draw attention to a work that had been almost forgotten and to show that his campaign on behalf of the Russian intelligentsia had been consistent throughout his life. Such a reading may hardly seem to be supported by the story taken in isolation and is based, admittedly, on the evidence of his other writings of the 1950s and 1960s. Leonov's works, however, do not exist in isolation from one another. They return to certain themes again and again and even quote from one another. The return to earlier works is part of the same process.

The first version of *The Snowstorm* was one of Leonov's least successful works, not only politically but artistically too, and this in itself suggests a reason for wanting to improve it. In a letter to Kovalev he said that he wanted to reconstruct it in the form in which it was originally conceived.[36] In the process, however, he could not resist the temptation to make the work rather bolder than it had been in 1940.

As a result the characters have become more explicitly and unidimensionally evaluated. Thus Stepan Syrovarov, who in the 1940 edition had been a successful 'factory director' (*M*, 2) is now downgraded to 'a director of something or other' in the 1963 edition (*P'esy*, 100).[37] In the 1940 version he had been an unpleasant figure, but with some justification for his hatred of life in the Soviet Union, 'the putrid sweat of waiting every night' (*M*, 40). In the new version he is actuated entirely by greed: he is not so keen to escape from Russia as he is to lay his hands on the money he has banked in the West, and his aspirations rise no higher than the Paris nightclubs. His paper on 'socialist morality' with its insistence on unanimity now recalls Chikilev rather more explicitly, and is quoted with apparent approval by the 'good' Communist Potashov: 'It's very true, as you say, many people nowadays, especially at public meetings, have learnt to speak in unison. But if only one could listen to what they say to their wives on stormy nights when there is no one to overhear...' (*P'esy*, 128). As so often Leonov's use of reported speech leaves it unclear who is uttering a particular sentiment, the character ostensibly being quoted, the character adding his own comments on these sentiments, or the author himself.

The political implications of the play have also been revised, though they still retain considerable bite. In line with official propaganda since the XX Party Congress Leonov tends to identify all illegality with the 'cult of personality,' 'Assyrian megalomania' (*P'esy*, 152),[38] and the little Stalins it engendered. Thus, like many apologists of the 1930s and 1940s, Stepan justifies the Terror by appealing to the precedents of Ivan the Terrible and Peter the Great, who had transformed Russia into a great power even if at a horrifying human cost. The more unpleasant features of the Stalin regime are now associated with the villains in the self-contradictory pretence that in any case it was only the guilty who had anything to fear. Thus Val'ka's words 'and they say that they can listen in through light bulbs now' (*P'esy*, 110) are in the revised version attributed to Stepan Syrovarov. Similarly the complicated story of Karyakina's arrest is now shown to have been entirely the handiwork of Stepan and Lopotukhin, not as an everyday occurrence of the time.

Even so, enough evidence remains to indicate that Stalin's paranoia had fallen on fruitful ground. The panic that overcomes the Syrovarov household at the news of Porfiriy's return, the cowardice and malicious curiosity of the friends and neighbours, the ingenuity shown by Party members in denouncing and compromising one another, provide a cheerless picture of Soviet life. The old matriarch Marfa says to Potashov, her comrade-in-arms in the Civil War: 'Let's drink... not to the quiet and the cunning ones, but to the decent and proud, as you and I used to be once, long ago. (*Potashov silently cleans out his pipe.*) All right I was only joking' (*P'esy*, 134). When Zoya is deserted by her friends, one of them still has the courage to ask: 'Who are we? builders of the world, or rats in a ship?' (*P'esy*, 132)

The most striking change to the original play is the scene between the two brothers at the end of Act 2 when Porfiriy first enters. Stepan delivers a long monologue of self-justification, claiming that he had helped Porfiriy escape from Russia and had then saved his wife and daughter from becoming *lishentsy*, though his feelings of fear, guilt, and shame are clearly conveyed. Porfiriy meanwhile remains completely silent (in fact he utters only one word in the entire text of the revised play, 'Guadalajara'). The device deliberately recalls the encounter between Christ and the Grand Inquisitor in *The Brothers Karamazov*. Porfiriy, of course, is hardly a Christ-figure, but his sufferings in emigration and the hardships awaiting him[39] in the Far North relate him to the innumerable Russian saints whose sanctity seems to be only enhanced by the enormity of the sins that they have to expiate.

The new version of *The Snowstorm* is still not among Leonov's masterpieces. Its resurrection at this stage in his career seems more like a personal attempt to lay the ghosts of his own past than to realize the unfulfilled potential of an unsatisfactory work.[40] The characterization of Stepan has been reworked, but the other characters remain symbols or stereotypes.

The origins of *Evgenia Ivanovna* go back to 1928, when Leonov and his wife visited Titsian and Nina Tabidze in Tbilisi. He began work on the story in 1934 after a trip with the Tabidzes to the Alazan' valley, where much of the action of the story was to take place.[41] As it now stands, however, the story is dated 1938-1963; this does not necessarily indicate continuous composition – the other revised works are similarly dated by the years of original composition and later revision. Leonov has said that he would return to the story every few years, so that several versions exist altogether, though only one has been published. Philosophically and stylistically the story in its present form belongs to the period of the late revisions.

Leonov's decision not to publish the story in 1938 is said to have been dictated by the risky nature of the subject matter (though this would seem to be considerably less provocative than that of *The Snowstorm*, which he was to write in the following year). After the Civil War Evgenia Ivanovna and her husband Stratonov, an officer in the White army, had fled abroad. In Istanbul after some months of abject poverty Stratonov had abandoned her; she assumes that he is dead, but in fact he has returned to Russia. Evgenia Ivanovna then makes her way to Paris, where she meets an English archaeologist, Pickering, who takes her on as his secretary and eventually marries her.[42] After a tour of Asia Minor the couple decide to return to England via the Soviet Union, so that Evgenia Ivanovna can visit her birthplace. On the way they travel through Georgia, where they meet Stratonov, now working as an Intourist guide, and the main part of the story is devoted to the few days they spend in that country, culminating in Evgenia Ivanovna's sudden decision to cut the trip short and return to England. The story ends with the information that Evgenia Ivanovna died the following year after giving birth to a child.

The story is simple enough in outline, but in its ramifications it is the most complex of all Leonov's works. At first sight it may seem to stand aside from its predecessors, for it is the only one of his major works to be set outside Russia, and the main characters are either émigrés or foreigners. But the theme of emigration and of former Whites has run through much of Leonov's work ever since the time of *The Road to Ocean*, the novel he was writing when he began work on what was eventually to become *Evgenia Ivanovna*, and can be traced back still further to the events of his own life in the years 1918–20.

The germ of the story lies in the figure that later became Stratonov. His betrayal of Evgenia Ivanovna and his ignominious return from emigration have destroyed his self-respect. His rootlessness is revealed in his lack of any firm beliefs: as a student he had espoused superficially democratic ideas only to end up in the White Army; as an Intourist guide he leaps to the defence, now of Alexander III, now of the emerging Soviet state. His life has been ordained by events and decisions which he is powerless to change or rectify and in the conditions of Soviet Russia he is a marked man, as he is well aware. He has to pay an even steeper price than Porfiriy Syrovarov for his return: 'he could only have obtained his job after an exhaustive screening, probably involving a public recantation in a crowded auditorium, and possibly under even harsher conditions excluding any repetition of this blunder' (8. 182). Unlike Porfiriy, Stratonov has no hope of eventual redemption. 'His life was empty and hopeless, without a woman to love him, and soured by continual fear' (8. 160). Less sympathetic than Gleb Protoklitov he nonetheless acquires something of the same tragic aura.

By comparison Pickering is less vividly imagined. With his gift for self-deprecation he fits a certain kind of English stereotype. In many respects he recalls Ivan Vikhrov, the decent and scholarly, but boring and unloved husband. His lectures to his wife on archaeology and aesthetics may not be as absurd as Vikhrov's, but both wives are left equally out of their depth. His relationship with Stratonov is one of Leonov's best depictions of the barbed relationship between two men who are forced to dissemble their mutual antagonism, though Stratonov's insinuations and provocations do occasionally stir Pickering to rage.

Of the three main characters, however, Evgenia Ivanovna is the most fully developed. In some respects, such as the trauma of feeling rejected by her country, she recalls Elena Ivanovna Vikhrova. She cannot believe her good fortune in meeting Pickering, and, like other Leonov heroines, she 'is appalled at the multiplication of joy in her life' (8. 138). Both women are grateful to their academic husbands for their rescue, but they are unable to love them.[43] Evgenia Ivanovna continues to be haunted by dreams of Stratonov long after he has deserted her, and when they meet again Leonov skilfully suggests the physical attraction she still feels for him contending with her contempt for his behaviour.

But where Leonov's other heroines overcome their traumas and earn an honourable place in Soviet life Evgenia Ivanovna marries a foreigner, settles in the West, and is fatally cut off from Russia. This is the true cause of her death:

> British doctors explained the death of [Evgenia Ivanovna] by post-natal complications; their diagnosis would have been more accurate if, besides the history of their patient's disease, they had had at their disposal the few scraps of information to be found in this story. In view of the fact that the English are never separated from their country, since they possess the wonderful faculty of carrying it with them to their new domicile, they apparently hardly ever suffer from homesickness in the Russian understanding of the term. (8. 195)

Evgenia Ivanovna can no more escape from her native country than she can from Stratonov; she carries around with her a newspaper photograph of her native town and her mother's house. As she tells Pickering: 'I am made out of this land' (8. 152).

There is thus a parallel between Evgenia Ivanovna's relations with Stratonov and those with Russia. Stratonov reminds her that 'we Russians suffer from ailments that can never be forgotten or healed' (8, 185). Similarly there is a parallel between the ways in which they treat her 'unfaithfulness.' She tries in vain to explain herself to Pickering: 'When a leaf is torn from a tree its life is finished. It may still sport at liberty, fly around the neighbourhood, even rise to undreamed-of heights, but it will still perish before its companions on the branch...' Pickering reasons with her: 'But surely this thought should release you from all ties [...] to the tree which has had no regrets in letting you go, rejecting you. It is unnatural to love what repays you with hatred...' Evgenia Ivanovna shrugs her shoulders: 'I see that it is easier for people of great intelligence to put down roots in alien soil than for us little ones.' She is under no illusions, however, as to the political realities of the time; her dreams of Russia 'are fortunately no reason for political persecution in Europe,' while in Russia she would inevitably 'become either a brick or a target.'

This mystique of the Russian soil is of course not peculiar to Leonov. It can be found in several pre-revolutionary writers too. What is unusual is Leonov's introduction of moral criteria into this irrational and even mystical concept. Evgenia Ivanovna's illness and death are not simply a consequence of her homesickness, but a judgment on her. She suffers her first attack of the mysterious illness that is to kill her on the eve of receiving her British passport. It is in the hope of laying these ghosts that she returns to Russia 'to ask permission to go, to be spared these nightly visitations and to be set free' (8. 152).

Her prayer is granted.

... all this no longer belonged to her. Evgenia Ivanovna realized this not with the longed-for feeling of relief, but with a sense of guilty, nagging unease, and irreparable loss. For now she was totally liberated from the sorrows of her former homeland, from its present hardships and those that awaited all these people in the future, from the sometimes superhuman burdens and ordeals of the age that had given them birth [...] They were so close that you could stretch out your hand and touch them, but already separated from Evgenia Ivanovna by cosmic mileages; and when from her infinite remoteness she smiled at them almost timidly, they smiled back at her kindly, but without any warmth – because to say goodbye to the foreign girl in the good old traditional way would have been impolite now, and even uncalled-for [...] Mrs Pickering felt herself unusually comfortable, almost to the point of weightlessness, even though with an aching sense of falling in her heart, a sense that in fact is bound to accompany any change of homeland. (8. 194–5)

Evgenia Ivanovna has become Mrs Pickering; she starts speaking of England as home; and in the title her name is given in the Latin not the Cyrillic script. It is almost as if her crime is worse than Stratonov's. The reader is not even told whether her child survived.

The rivalry between Stratonov and Pickering may be read as an allegory of the struggle between East and West for the soul of Russia, in which the prize is inevitably destroyed. It may then not be mere coincidence that the heroine's name and patronymic are a feminine version of Zamyatin's Evgeniy Ivanovich, one of the main themes of whose work had been the clash between East and West. His name has cropped up at many of the turning-points of Leonov's career. He had died in emigration in 1937, the year before Leonov completed the first version of his story.

Even so, it is strange that a tale of the Russian inability to live outside Russia should be set in Georgia. Of course the colonial mentality naturally inclines Russians to regard all parts of the former empire as naturally and inalienably parts of Russia, though Leonov's friendship with Titsian and Nina Tabidze, whom he came to know in 1928, would surely have disabused him of such a notion. In that case the fact that Evgenia Ivanovna gets no closer to home than the Caucasus becomes a metaphor for her inability to recover her Russianness.

But there are deeper reasons for Leonov's choice. The history and geography of Georgia, its role since times immemorial as a crossroads for the trade routes from South to North and East to West make it attractive not just to the archaeologist, Pickering, but also to Leonov, the believer in universal interconnectedness and interdependence. The natural fertility of the country, its rich literary, musical, and architectural culture, and its long history of invasion and oppression, make it the ideal setting for Leonov's views. And, of course, Stalin himself was a Georgian.

The main part of the story takes place at a fair in the Alazan' valley, renowned for its wines and for its spectacular natural beauty. The area was owned by the Chavchavadze family, one of the great aristocratic clans of the Caucasus, which also produced one of the area's greatest poets. The name is known to most Russians because the poet-diplomat Griboedov married Nina Chavchavadze in 1828 shortly before his murder in Teheran. Later in the century a group of Chechens under Shamil' kidnapped two of the Chavchavadze princesses and demanded such a high ransom for them that the family was ruined and their estate fell into decay. Subsequently the house was taken over by Alexander III as a summer residence, and later still by the Soviet rulers of Georgia. These historical associations are referred to in the story and are part of its complex meaning.

The most dramatic scene in the story occurs when Stratonov takes the Pickerings to the arbour where Griboedov was reputed to have proposed to his bride. As he explains:

'... unfortunately, tempted by the isolation of the spot, not all visitors have evinced the sensitivity due to this romantic grotto of love.'
With the air of a reluctant witness the guide stood back and the guests froze on the threshold with prolonged and unanimous exclamations of anger and shock. The floor of the summer house had been befouled, uniformly, down to the last centimeter, even to the corners [...] A network of questionable drawings and inscriptions in two languages covered the walls that still remembered the childish prattle of Nina Chavchavadze. (8. 167)

The scene operates on many levels. Stratonov has deliberately brought the newly-weds to this place as part of his revenge. But he is also pointing to the ruin of his own life:

when Russia's allies abandoned her in her trouble, I was forced to go abroad temporarily, until I decided to return home and offer my fatherland the service of which I was capable – even including the draining of marshes. To do this I had to go against my better self, betray my dreams, and even commit a vile crime, the memory of which haunts me even today... (8. 166)

It is as an example of what happened to such a dream, his love for Evgenia Ivanovna, that he has taken the Pickerings to the arbour. Thus the scene reveals the degradation not only of Stratonov, but also of post-revolutionary Russia. The desecration of a once revered culture reappears in *The Pyramid* as an indictment of Soviet egalitarianism and its envy of every kind of elitism. But beyond all this it is set against the background of the rise and fall of dynasties and civilizations that is the main concern of the archaeologist Pickering.[44]

Thus the choice of an archaeologist is essential to Leonov's scheme. Some forty years earlier, at about the time of the events described in this novella, Leonov had depicted the palaeontologist Likharev, and his revised version of the story was published only a few months before the first publication of *Evgenia Ivanovna*. The connection therefore is more than coincidental. Stratonov recalls these arguments when he snidely observes to Evgenia Ivanovna:

> [Pickering's] science of shards and fragments of a long dead world can surely wait. At a time when the smoking ruins of the homes of the living are crying out for revenge, and when the bloody sweat of war and revolution has barely dried, Russia can hardly take an interest in the publications of your husband.' (8. 181)[45]

On the contrary: Pickering's archaeology, the 'spade of history' (8. 137), is tangible and visible evidence of the principle of universal interconnectedness:

> [Pickering] reflected aloud on the gigantic concentrations of indefatigable human plasma that over the centuries had repeatedly risen out of the earth for the sole purpose, if the truth be told, of colliding face to face with hordes of other tribes, hacking at one another with their swords, all in the name of the demons who in those times governed the world, only to disintegrate uncomplainingly in the eternally blowing wind. Since then, Pickering concluded, the mass of dust and ash had been tormenting itself in the search for its former combinations, a girl's lock of hair, the throat of a songbird, a petal of saffron. (8. 142)

The past contains everything. This conservation is utterly unselective: the good and the evil are preserved uncritically, inextricably entangled – the images of the puddle, of dirt and weeds that have run through Leonov's work since *The Thief*, serve as constant reminders of these interconnections. Thus, at the beginning of the story Evgenia Ivanovna decides to drown herself and goes out for one last meal. But when she comes to pay the bill she drops her last coin and it runs away into 'a puddle full of cigarette-ends' (8. 131). Her pathetic attempts to find it lead to her meeting Pickering and beginning a new life. One of the last things that she sees as she leaves the valley of Alazan' is the 'wayside weeds' (8. 195). 'As far as the eye could see everywhere people were active, sweeping, working, painting, uncovering the beauty of life from beneath the layers of dirt and deliberate malice – without which it would not survive' (8. 135–6).

But the coexistence of good and evil does not exempt human beings from moral choices. The Georgians tell Pickering in their farewell toast: 'dig up your past [...] so that it will help the future to become more honest and beautiful' (8. 195), and it brings Leonov himself back to the paradoxes of the Russian Revolution. Undertaken in the name of human betterment it had led instead to monstrous evil and suffering. Stratonov speaks of 'Russia's historic mission, essentially the same old journey to the stars, but unlike previous, indirect approaches through the heavens, Russia intends to take the shortest route, through the mountains and straight ahead. I recognize that this will involve some casualties, but inspiration has implanted in the people of such epochs a cataleptic ability to endure, and a prolonged insensitivity to suffering' (8. 181).

The wording inevitably reminds the reader of Pchkhov's parable of Adam who tries every form of transport only to find himself no closer to the Promised Land, a passage that Leonov had left unchanged in the new *Thief*. The climbing of mountains is no substitute for the journey to the stars. Pchkhov's scepticism is now given to Pickering: '[he] cheerfully agreed with his new friends that to go on living in the old way was becoming more and more dangerous with such an inflammable civilization, and that progress should be subordinated to the issues of social humanism, which would ensure that the grandeur of any idea should be assessed by the benefits that it had brought to a population and not by the number of sufferings that had been inflicted in its name' (8. 191).

Any attempt by ideologists to discern a pattern or meaning in history is misguided and even dangerous, as the experience of Russia has shown; but the past must be studied because it is inextricably part of our present, though whether we can apply its lessons is another matter. It is understandable that few should want to look back at it, but that is the role of the historian, the archaeologist and above all the artist, unprotected by Perseus's magic mirror.

The scientist Pickering is thus a metaphor for the artist, and on several occasions he directly expresses Leonov's views on the role of art. Just as an archaeologist is able to recreate a vanished way of life from a few surviving artefacts, 'the miraculous gift of reconstructing the past out of veritable trifles' (8. 183), so the artist discovers the defining elements of our culture in the everyday trivia of existence. Observing a procession of blind men stumbling and falling exactly as in the Elder Breughel's famous picture, Pickering remarks, in the most explicit statement of Leonov's own views on the subject to be found anywhere in his works:

> ... [the function of art] consists not in the reflection of life in the narrow mirror of a limited technique, nor in imitation which is inevitably paler than the original [...] the aim of art [...] consists in understanding the logic of an event through the study of its muscular system, in the search for the shortest possible formula of its conception and birth, and consequently in the revelation of the original idea... (8. 177)[46]

In this respect, of course, the archaeologist is the very opposite of the artist. If the artist aspires to compress the maximum of information into the minimum of space, the archaeologist tries to reconstruct this wealth from the few surviving clues. The point is made when Evgenia Ivanovna comically confuses several myths: '... the drowning of Pharaoh and his chariots, as she now remembered, for having whipped the sea as a punishment for some stupid fish that had dared to swallow the imperial ring.' After a long silence Pickering tactfully replies, 'Well, Jenny, you have certainly discovered a most efficient and imaginative mnemonic system for... retaining historical information in concentrated form. But we archaeologists spend a lot of time and trouble in disentangling this method of contamination often practised by time and nature – I mean the excessive compression of such treasures, with the aim, I suppose, of fitting as much as possible into the space available' (8. 137).

Quite apart from the interest of the story and the ideas it contains, *Evgenia Ivanovna* grips the reader by its intensity and demands to be read at a single sitting. It is unusual among Leonov's later works, which are mainly concerned with ethical and intellectual problems, for the physicality of its descriptive passages, and particularly the fair, with its jostling crowds, the smell of meat cooking in the open air, the excitement of the wine, which recalls the early Leonov of *The Breakthrough at Petushikha* and *The Badgers*. The work stands apart in Leonov's oeuvre for another reason too. Evgenia Ivanovna is even more the victim of circumstances than Gleb Protoklitov or Porfiriy Syrovarov; she is completely blameless, though she is still punished. The 'impurities' that destroy her are those of history and life.

Leonov said in connection with *Evgenia Ivanovna*: 'since the most important parts of a work of art are those that in some fateful way have passed through the essence of its creator, it would be permissible to construct a second, shadow spiritual biography on their basis' (8. 312), and I think that the secret of the work is that Leonov himself is involved in all three of the main characters. These are three potential lives that he might have lived, and indeed did live, with the constant danger of their coming to light. He himself had come close to fighting in the White armies in a junior rank; he too had considered the possibility of emigration, and he too, I believe, had at about this time abandoned a woman who loved him; while in Pickering we may see the artist that Leonov might have become under different circumstances. Despite the injustices and insecurity of life in Stalin's Russia, Leonov, like Akhmatova, in the poem, 'Menya kak reku, / Surovaya epokha povernula...' ('The harsh epoch has redirected me like a river,' 1944), would not ask for any other. Originally conceived during the nightmare of 1938, when his position had already begun to crumble, *Evgenia Ivanovna* is Leonov's greatest achievement.

chapter thirteen

The Pyramid 1994

In spite of the success of *The Russian Forest*, the award of a Lenin prize, and semi-official recognition as the senior Soviet writer, Leonov remained under some suspicion throughout the 1960s and 1970s. His activities on behalf of forestry and other ecological causes had made him enemies in high places and in 1968 his refusal to sign the Writers' Union letter in support of the invasion of Czechoslovakia incurred further displeasure. This took the form of various petty humiliations. He was persuaded, against his better judgment, to let his name go forward for nomination to the Academy of Sciences, only for it to be rejected.[1] Celebrations for his seventieth and seventy-fifth birthdays, which he tried to avoid, were low-key and seemed to him to be more of a snub than an honour. On discovering that his apartment had been raided and the manuscript of *The Pyramid* read,[2] he came to suspect that all his correspondence was being intercepted by the KGB.[3] These experiences, although less intimidating than his ordeals of the 1930s and 1940s, contributed to a certain feeling of persecution, which is marked in many of the interviews that he gave in the last decades of his life, and partly accounts for the pessimism that pervades his last novel.[4]

Leonov later traced his first ideas for *The Pyramid*[5] back to 1922, but they began to take shape only at the beginning of the Second World War. The work was to obsess him for the second half of his life, and he regarded it as his major work: 'My new novel is the biggest and most important thing I have done.'[6] On several occasions he seems to have felt close to completing it.[7] Thus at the end of the 1959 edition of *The Thief* Firsov is asked about his new literary 'mistress.' 'Just to get away Firsov blurted out, "A priest's daughter."'[8] (3. 600). According to Natal'ya Leonova a version was completed in the 1960s, and it was probably this that was announced for publication in 1964 as a novella,[9] but it too was soon discarded.[10] In the '70s and '80s occasional cryptic hints to interviewers and two or three excerpts from the work appeared, but in the event the novel was never completed.

Leonov generally found it difficult to let his work go for publication and relied on his wife's judgment in such matters. Tat'yana Mikhaylovna, however, died in 1978 and this made it even harder for him to take the decision. In these years too his own iron constitution was at last beginning to weaken, and in the 1990s he lost his sight. But he continued to work on the book: his daughters helped him as amanuenses; they would read the text to him and offer advice on alternative versions. By this time, however, his material had become unmanageable. In the end it was a message from the Bulgarian clairvoyant, Vanga, that persuaded him to release the work for publication in 1994, incomplete though it was. It was published later that year,[11] just a few weeks before he died, more than eighty years after his first appearance in print in an Archangel newspaper.

The difficulties of completing the novel are almost entirely due to its encyclopedic and ever-expanding ambitions. As Ovcharenko writes: '*The Pyramid* was conceived as a work that would summarize the current cycle of human history. Summarize not only in regard to the life work of the senior Russian writer, but also the entire corpus of Russian, and, to some extent, of world literature' (*P.* I, 3). Certainly it is steeped in the classics of Russian literature, and, in particular, the works of Dostoevsky, who is mentioned by name on two or three occasions. Three works of the Soviet period, Zamyatin's *We*, Klyuev's long poem *A Time of Fire* (*Pogorel'shchina*, 1928–9), and Platonov's novel, *The Foundation-Pit* (*Kotlovan*, 1929–30), all suppressed during the Stalin years, are alluded to more or less explicitly in many passages. Still more important are the echoes of Leonov's own earlier works, in particular *The Breakthrough at Petushikha*, *The Thief*, and *The Sot'*, with an attempt to amplify and clarify their misunderstood or inadequately appreciated meanings. Thus the novel is a summation of a certain strain in Russian literature, and in particular of Leonov's own work. To call it a summation of world literature, however, is excessive.

On the face of it *The Pyramid* departs from the realistic manner of Leonov's preceding novels. It features an angel, various magical or fantastic episodes, and excursions into the remote future, rather in the spirit of H. G. Wells's *Time Machine*. But in Leonov's view these other levels are no less real than the specific time and place in which the novel is set, namely Moscow in the months between the peak of the Great Purges and the Nazi invasion, roughly from the autumn of 1939 to that of 1940. Almost every scene takes place against a background of terror, denunciations, eavesdropping, sudden disappearances, religious persecution, brutal interrogations, and death or exile. The knowledge of later events, notably the removal of Stalin's body from the mausoleum and the eventual collapse of Communism, also plays a role in the book. But such anachronisms are not merely self-indulgence in the futile wisdom of hindsight; rather they point to the patterns of recurrence in Russian and indeed world history that Leonov had first intuited in *The Breakthrough at Petushikha*.

The novel is primarily concerned, at least on a narrative level, with events inside Russia; the action takes place almost entirely in Moscow and its immediate environs with the exception of one or two fantastic excursions outside. It opens with the introduction of the author himself, complete with name and patronymic, still in fear for his life after the devastating attacks on *The Snowstorm*: 'In the late autumn of the last year before the war I was visited by one of those reverses, common enough in my profession, based on charges which on this occasion promised the worst possible consequences. In my letter to the Leader I explained the premiere of the disgraced play by the fact that the theatre had trusted too much to the literary reputation of the author, and asked that I alone should answer for it. For a week we slept without taking off our clothes, awaiting the nocturnal knock on the door' (*P.* I. 7). On an impulse he decides to visit a church on the outskirts of Moscow, apparently somewhere quite close to the Sparrow (or Lenin) Hills. Here he gradually becomes acquainted with the family of the Loskutovs, Father Matvey, a former priest, his wife, and their three children,[12] now living in utter poverty as *lishentsy*. Their dilapidated shack and the local church are threatened with demolition to make way for an 'International Stadium of Friendship.'[13]

It is the fate of this family that provides the main narrative line of the novel. The oldest and favourite son, Vadim, has rejected his family and become a militant Communist; his naive idealism, however, has incurred the suspicion of the authorities and some time before the novel begins he has been arrested and exiled to Siberia (it later transpires that he has been killed there). The younger son, Egor, has taken his parents' side against Vadim, and angrily rejects his brother's politics and materialist philosophy. But his very intemperateness has alienated his parents, and the author too treats him with some coolness. It is the third child, Dunya, who inadvertently triggers the action. One evening she meets an angel emerging from a door painted on a pillar in the local church. Dymkov, as he is called (he has no first name or, of course, patronymic), is as insubstantial as his name (a little mist or smoke) suggests; indeed most of Dunya's family and friends, and even the narrator at times, treat him as a mere figment of her imagination or a neurotic response to the events of the time. But he is real enough; he casts a shadow and even hard-headed Party members have no doubts about his reality.

In many respects Dymkov recalls Dostoevsky's Prince Myshkin;[14] he is childlike with a schoolboyish sense of humour and he is sexually impotent; it is even suggested that he is epileptic (*P*, I. 560). Like Myshkin too, through his naïveté and good intentions he succeeds only in exacerbating the problems he tries to resolve. But if he is not a Christ figure, Dymkov is still an angel and capable of performing miracles. It is this gift that is the object of the scheming of the novel's villains, who hope to acquire it for their own ends – for the most part, material possessions or power. He is adopted by a circus entrepreneur, Dyurso, another *lishenets*, who hopes to restore his fortunes by exploiting the angel's talents for his shows. Dyurso's daughter, Yuliya, becomes interested in Dymkov's potential for furthering her own career as an actress; she even dreams of becoming the mother of a new Messiah, though the book hints that any child is more likely to be an AntiChrist. Her friend the film director Evgeniy Sorokin, begins to dream of making a sensational film around her and the angel, which will win him international fame and perhaps even her love. Eventually Dymkov's growing reputation brings him into contact with senior members of the Party, who, after initial distrust, become intrigued by his potential; finally Stalin himself summons him to the Kremlin and invites him to become his partner in ruling the country.

Unfortunately, however, Dymkov's prolonged stay on earth, while rendering him more human – he begins to blush, and to experience the first signs of sexual arousal – has weakened his miraculous powers. An important engagement in front of a senior minister ends in fiasco (and the disgrace of the commissar who arranged it). Dymkov himself loses his confidence, and realizes that he will not be able to satisfy Stalin. He runs away rather than risk a second meeting with him, and by one last superhuman effort manages to transport himself out of this world. At which point the novel ends.

This fantastic plot is the surface for a story of cosmological scope. According to the Apocryphal Book of Enoch, which provides the basis for the novel,[15] it was God's decision to create man in His[16] own image and to subordinate the angels to this new creature that had provoked their rebellion: 'How couldst Thou subject the creatures of fire to the creatures of clay?' (*P*, I. 131).[17] The rebels set out to prove that man is unworthy of this favouritism, and God has been reduced to increasingly desperate measures to justify His creature, culminating in the sacrifice of His son.

The history of the following two thousand years seems to show that the rebel angels were right. In Leonov's words, 'Man was given the chance of becoming a god but has attained only to the level of an ape.'[18] The gifts of reason and freedom, the fruits of the Tree of Knowledge, have been grossly misused for ideological and political ends: the despoliation of the natural environment, the perversion of science for military purposes, and the uncontrolled rise in the world's population have finally exhausted God's patience with the human race and it can be left to destroy itself. With the removal of this impediment the rebel angels can be welcomed back and the celestial unity restored.

Not surprisingly then, an atmosphere of apocalyptic foreboding hangs over much of the novel. Reminders of Sodom and Gomorrah and references to the fate of Krakatoa (*P.* I. 414) and other such catastrophes recur frequently throughout the text. The author compares himself to St John on Patmos, and declares that his decision to publish his still incomplete book was 'dictated by the imminence of the most dangerous of all the calamities, confessional, ethnic, social, that mankind has ever experienced, and which are now terminal for the creatures of the world as a whole [...] the territorial conflicts among yesterday's good neighbours can easily boil over into an accelerating process in which people, crazed by their own infernal numbers, will sweep themselves away into nonexistence with their atomic broomstick in a frenzy of self-destruction – only a miracle can postpone the final agony for another century or two' (*P.* I. 6).

In retrospect one can see that these premonitions were present in Leonov's earliest stories, with their recurring pattern of a catastrophic irruption of alien and destructive forces. The recognition that mankind must sooner or later come to an end, either through the processes of evolution or the inexorable tendency towards entropy, whether physical or social, surfaces periodically in his works of the '30s. But more and more often these natural processes are reinforced by human activity. In the journal version of *Skutarevsky* Leonov had depicted a Soviet industrial town as another Herculaneum (this passage was omitted from the book version):

> From here it was easier to see that the town was dying. Like a beggar in a ragged cloak it sprawled there to one side of the main highways and the new capitals. It was as if it were already undressing; first the roofs were slipping off, spring shoots of fertile and lively greenery were already clambering on to the headless huts. Soot, smoke, and a blinding cement dust were settling on its tatters; the very wind overhead was saturated with a metallic grinding; it seemed as though a new race was coming in storm and tempest to settle this dreary land of exile and punishment. And then, with a leap of consciousness, Skutarevsky remembered Herculaneum; no doubt it too had dozed much like this on the eve of its destruction, and the same swarthy clouds had drifted overhead, their purple silhouettes reflected as disturbing and painful images in the memory.[19]

This passage is authorial, hence no doubt its suppression. More often, however, Leonov attributes such views to his 'negative' characters, such as Pokhvisnev in *The Road to Ocean*, with his dream of the moon crashing into the earth,[20] and Gratsiansky:

I fear that as our industrial capacity grows, and with it the complexities of international relations, such [peaceful interludes] will diminish further and further until humanity comes to its knees... or is transubstantiated into a gaseous nebula of purely local significance [...] Professors of astronomy in some neighbouring galaxy will say of our planet: 'Here lived some rather incautious and impulsive gods.' (9. 109)

Soviet critics have usually taken such views to indicate the moral and intellectual bankruptcy of the speakers. Thus, when Cheredilov asks: 'What is the point of life?' Vikhrov answers: 'When one has been given the sun, it seems ungrateful to ask what it's for' (9. 268–9). But the question is in fact Leonov's, and even Vikhrov is occasionally prone to doubts that recall comrade Anton's moment of despair at the fickleness of human nature:

... one day man took a look at himself under a new sun, and once again saw himself, not just naked, but also in blood, up to his elbows, and not just the blood of animals, but his own blood, his brother's. Everything was permeated with it, even his songs and books, the bricks of his temples, the treasures of his art galleries... And then every kind of illness, the erosion of the soil, the exhaustion of the forests, the shortage of food, the growth and elaboration of human desires, the entry of new awakening races into the civilized world... And all this in the face of the stubborn resistance of nature, that has intensified as we have penetrated into the microworlds where she hides her deepest mysteries and secrets. Here even a healthy mind can hardly cope, and yet it is undermined by the spirochetes of social greed, which convert the brain into a watery feeding ground for microbes of the basest passions. In other words it is time for humanity either to jump into a mass grave or to look for some new path... indeed sometimes one feels guilty in the face of the animals that we eat.[21] (9. 517)

Recurrent symbols of human unworthiness are the vandalized and unrepaired churches that have figured in all Leonov's works since *Invasion*. There it was possible to blame the Nazis, but the pre-war setting of other late works precludes such a reading. In *Evgenia Ivanovna* the desecration of the Chavchadzes' summer house had shown that this cynicism was endemic in post-revolutionary Russia and threatened not only religion but all cultural values. These scenes culminate in *The Pyramid* with the demolition of an old Russian church, 'a pearl of northern architecture' (*P*. I. 288):

The church was of pre-Petrine construction, consecrated to the All-Merciful Saviour. Made of white stone, and even on the brink of destruction still shining with the severe beauty of Russian antiquity, the church seemed to be dressed in a funereal cotton cloak to its feet [...] On the immense blue star-studded cupola a gilded cross still gleamed [...] but now after an unsuccessful attempt to knock it down, it tilted at a drunken angle, like [a criminal] after the ritual mug of vodka before execution... (*P*. I. 284)

The space behind the altar has been turned into a latrine for workers and officials:

None of the authorities had thought fit to cover up the abomination of desecration with a barrow or two of sand In his not infrequent later reflections on the fate of modern civilization Father Matvey assigned it to that pre-terminal phase of old age, when the sense of hopelessness, as he conjectured, gives way to a liturgical perception, in which one can turn one's back on yesterday's sanctuaries in the name of a sinless joy. (*P*. I. 286)

The apparently innocuous phrase 'a sinless joy' acquires terrible implications from its context, for it is the justification of those who desecrate 'yesterday's sanctuaries.' As such it is a symptom of the 'pre-terminal phase' of humanity itself.

The purpose of Dymkov's visit to the earth is to discover whether the world is indeed in a pre-terminal state: 'even if it had no concrete aims in mind it could serve as a sort of probe like those that are launched for the study of all sorts of unknown objects, which is, of course, a hundred times more sensible than the old way of unthinkingly hurling down on to the earth emergency brigades of prophets with Sodomic fires in their rucksacks' (*P*. II. 664). The mission, however, provides the rebel angels with the opportunity of finally discrediting God's creation, and their earthly representative, Professor Shatanitsky[22] is (as can be seen from his name) the diabolical originator of the various schemes designed to humiliate Dymkov and make it impossible for him to return to his angelic home (*P*. II. 621).[23] At times Shatanitsky seems to be an alias for Stalin, though some of his machinations are unknown to the dictator (*P*. II. 590–1); at others a sinister academic within the Soviet establishment, rather like Gratsiansky in *The Russian Forest*:

a perfectly ordinary creature of that history-making breed, who by means of flattery, manipulativeness, and socially acceptable *ankety* had attained the heights of the *nomenklatura*. His universal erudition in the most controversial aspects of cognition on the interface of the warring philosophies had given him in the eyes of the crowd the aura of a Coryphaeus of the progressive sciences,[24] while his implacable scepticism concerning the ideological and, particularly, the ethical delusions of the past [...] had created among his listeners the impression that the speaker had himself long been engaged in the affairs of humanity under the control of some even higher and mightier power, who ever since the appearance of mankind had been in serious disagreement with its Creator. (*P.* I. 27)

Soviet conditions are well suited to his schemes, and like Gratsiansky he finds Soviet jargon and Marxist ideology ideal for his purposes.[25]

This combination of worldly and supernatural power[26] marks him as the long-predicted AntiChrist, whose cosmic enthronement, according to certain signs, had already begun in some parts of the globe [...] in recent times the aforementioned gentleman had gone over exclusively to purely educational activities. (*P.* I. 587)

Accordingly he is identified with the militant materialism of the Soviet state, which, as Dostoevsky foresaw, is simply an inverted form of the religion it claims to reject:

... official atheism, in its endeavour to eradicate the Almighty by means of murdering his priests and desecrating his altars, had never once dared take a swing at his adversary, because the omnipotent leaders of the established regime saw in him an ally, a veteran with a record of revolutionary service a hundred times longer than the combined subversive experience of all the propagandists of compulsory happiness. (*P*. I. 19–20)

In Shatanitsky Leonov finds the ultimate source of the two interrelated aspects of the Russian Revolution that he had been questioning since the 1920s: the 'golden dream' (*zolotoy son*)[27] of universal happiness, and absolute equality. These issues are now amplified at great length and through a variety of spokesmen, culminating in Stalin's monologue to Dymkov at the end of the novel. In many respects this apologia recalls the Legend of the Grand Inquisitor in Dostoevsky's *The Brothers Karamazov*. Like his predecessor the Communist leader sees his task as the creation of a Paradise on earth. For Leonov, as for Dostoevsky, the consequence is dehumanization, the reduction of mankind to household pets or farmyard animals, but the process inevitably involves monstrous and widespread suffering. Universal happiness is unattainable so long as inequality persists, and therefore Utopia requires a ruthless levelling out of all differences between individuals. The sufferings incurred, we are to believe, will be more than repaid by the results, but we may well wonder, like Ivan Karamazov, if any Utopia is worth such a price.

These passages, however, add little to Leonov's earlier treatments of these ideas and indeed share much of the same imagery.[28] In *The Thief* (1927) they had been voiced by the tax collector Chikilev; in *The Pyramid* they are given to another tax collector, Gavrilov. The ambiguous image of the mountains, as an image of aspiration and simultaneously of a lifeless sterility also reappears throughout the novel. Stalin himself quotes *The Thief*: 'As a certain hack wrote almost seventy years ago: "Beyond the pass the sun shines, but the way through the pass is terrifying."'[29]

The pursuit of equality can be justified as a social and philosophical ideal, but Leonov suggests that it is peculiar to Russia. In a passage reminiscent of Vikhrov's lecture in *The Russian Forest*, but now in much more pessimistic vein, he traces its source to the facts of Russian history and geography and their paradoxical consequences: passivity alternating with anarchic outbursts, a sense of inferiority to Europe coupled to a messianic faith in Russia's destiny (*P.* II.129):[30]

> the Russians, all too sensitive to another's grief, and ready at the first puff of smoke to rush to help a neighbour with a bucket of water [...] now dreamed above and beyond all this of creating a common future for all on the basis of material equality, and for that matter intellectual equality too, to ensure that there would be no more bloody internecine conflicts, so that all should take their fair share of everything – right down to famine, cold, and homeless beggary. We were caught on the lure of universal beggary... I fear that God will soon punish us by granting our wishes... just look at how horrifyingly eager we are to scrape out and extinguish God's greatest gift, our reason, from our own brains (*P.* I. 56–7).[31]

The main motive, however, is an envious protest against 'biological inequality which is so offensive to the masses' (*P.* II. 594), Chikilev's 'Why do they have what I don't have?,' the 'primitive thirst for revenge and equality,' characteristic of the Russian village (4. 106), or the mean-minded levelling of 'If one person has toothache, then everyone else should be in agony too' (*P.* I. 309). It lies behind the malice of the communal apartment system, where citizens are encouraged to spy on and denounce one another (in *The Pyramid* one character spends half his pension on postage for his innumerable denunciations, *P.* I. 460). In such an atmosphere everything that is individual or exceptional becomes suspect: 'Talent was regarded by the lower orders as a socially immoral phenomenon, explicable only by the connivance of God, while in the eyes of science too it is seen as some pathological deviation from the norm, like a pearl, which is frequently accompanied by a series of unhealthy symptoms, while being counterbalanced at the other extreme by every kind of deformity.

Talent, concentrated in the concept of genius, has become an anarchic threat to the system of a planned state' (*P.* II. 595).

Leonov's argument against the fetishization of equality and happiness had always been that they are unnatural. Pchkhov had pointed out that if trees differ from one another, why should human beings expect or wish for uniformity? This argument is implicit in the very imagery of *The Russian Forest*, and it is further supported by the novel's allusions to Darwinism: the concepts of natural selection and the survival of the fittest are incompatible with egalitarianism.

The discovery of genetics at the beginning of the century further undermined the Marxist belief that human differences were largely the result of unequal social environments and could therefore be redressed in a classless society. It is not surprising then that the science was banned under Stalin,[32] or that opportunists and charlatans like Lysenko, who claimed to have proved that characteristics artificially acquired in the course of a single generation could be transmitted genetically, were honoured and rewarded, despite the manifest failure of their policies. In Zamyatin's *We*, composed at the very beginning of the Soviet regime, the legacy of the past, emerging in D. 503's hairy hands, had conveyed this warning. The facts of genetics stood stubbornly in the way of all attempts to create the new man, a classless Utopia, or universal happiness.

But in the last years of the Soviet regime a new threat had appeared in the technology of genetic engineering. The genetic code, specifying the individuality of each creature, had begun to reveal its secrets, raising the possibility of eradicating disease, physical defects, or socially undesirable characteristics, and so creating the ideal individual and the perfect society. At the climax of *The Pyramid* this is just what Stalin invites Dymkov to do:

> From the nocturnal confession of the leader Dymkov had understood only the external aspects of the mission entrusted to him – that he should thrust his arm into the dark entrails of humanity (since *his* arm was too short) and loosen a certain screw[33] that had been overtightened, before the thread should be ruined. The transformation consisted of a bloodless and painless stabilization of the intellectual potential of mankind at a level of biblical childishness, that is to say in a state of permanent and unclouded bliss. In general, no great problem, especially as further evolution was by no means ruled out within the parameters of strict genetic filters, to ensure the high quality of human reproduction – without the more gifted individuals outstripping their maternal average, that is to say, a harmonious social equilibrium, excluding the possibility of social storms in the future. (*P.* II. 637–8)

Even without fully understanding what he is being asked to do, Dymkov 'could not shake off the vile feeling that he was being commanded to blow up something vaster and holier than any temple' (*P.* II. 624).

The operation is an echo of the surgical procedure performed on D. 503 at the end of *We*. The ability to engineer genes will finally free mankind from the incubus of the past: D. 503's descendants will not have to worry about the possibility of hairy hands. The past and its legacy of original sin, culture, and memory will no longer torment the citizens of the new age. They can concentrate entirely on the future paradise. They will be spared the misgivings of those who know the fate of such endeavours in the past, and so they will not experience despair at setbacks along the way or any disillusionment when they eventually arrive at their destination.

Leonov realizes, however, that the objection to the goals of equality and universal happiness can also be lodged against the Christian Heaven. If the comparison between the two religion-ideologies is usually intended to make Communism more acceptable to Western liberals Leonov turns it against Christianity. What is the point of God's having created life in all its variety if the aim is to standardize it? If suffering is the source of man's noblest qualities, what is to be gained by removing it? Is the purpose of the Creation only to produce clones of the Creator, or are there certain qualities of humanity that are inaccessible to Him? God has created man with the freedom to choose sin: how can He then punish him for yielding to it? In that case, Father Matvey suggests, perhaps the original sin was not man's but God's? (*P.* I. 44–5).

Like Job,[34] who is invoked several times in the book, Leonov's mankind, just because of its mortality and its ability to suffer, possesses a vitality and a dimension that is unknown to God. Dymkov is sexless; he leaves no dirt or dust in his room (*P.* II. 535). But this is not possible for human beings. Their lives are as messy as the puddle outside Dymkov's earthly home. It is for this reason that the goal of purity is unattainable, though the search is natural and indeed essential to our humanity. Christianity may be inadequate, but the pretensions of Communism are infinitely more so.

In one scene Father Matvey comes home in a state of exaltation after seeing some chickens being sold in the market, and the crowds smiling at their antics.

> 'If it wasn't the sheer quantity of the chickens that made them so happy what was it?' he reflected, and came to the conclusion that it wasn't a matter of beauty or even of a full stomach, but that people's best impulses, their religions, and Utopias are all nourished by this wondrous spring, the mystery of matter infused by God. And since even Christianity had become less and less able to govern life,

where the dead weight of existence is partly lightened by the immortal soul's capacity for flight, then how poor Communism must suffer once the wings of faith had been cut! (*P.* I. 272)[35]

This moment of revelation cannot obscure the fact that the chickens will soon be slaughtered and eaten by the very people who are now happy enough just to look at them and who will perish in their turn. This does not prevent the chickens or the humans from enjoying the miracle of life for a few moments. The spectacle of matter infused by spirit transcends temporality and reveals truths that can be recognized, if not fully understood.

The idea of a permanent happiness is quite different. It precludes change; only unhappiness permits variety (to adapt *Anna Karenina*). If happiness is the paramount goal then the diversity of human experience must be reduced and eventually removed altogether; for as long as there is difference there is room for comparison and so for dissatisfaction. But this is to deny an essential element in human nature; happiness is not the product of some chemical or social formula, like galoshes or light bulbs; it does not lie in a hypothetical future, but in the here and now, the passing moment. Only when man realizes this simple truth is he likely to find happiness. Such a capacity is uniquely human and inaccessible to the immortals. At the very end of the book, as Dymkov prepares to leave, Dunya stops to pick a flower:

> an unremarkable grass, little better than a weed, but for Dunya there was no plant more precious in the world... and the same magic, hidden from the rest of the world, lurked within it [...] 'Look, Dymkov, how pretty it is! We call it pussy-toes...' Dunya was on her knees, smoothing the pale-pink dryish petals with the tips of her fingers, and suddenly with a tender pride for a world that was in spite of everything, in spite of everything, good, she asked Dymkov, standing behind her back, whether out there in the abyss of uncompleted time they had even one such tiny trifle, and also without a scent, so that after a hundred thousand years one would still want to return for the chance of touching it just once. (*P.* II. 675–6)

Leonov found it difficult to find a title that would embrace the full range of his concerns in the novel. To judge from an interview of June 1994, in which he refrained from actually naming the book, he was still undecided only a few days before the book was published.[36] The title eventually chosen comes from a poem written by the Communist Vadim Loskutov, in which he compares the great engineering achievements of the Stalin period and the colossal waste of human life and energy involved to the building of the pyramid[37] of Cheops. He naively hopes by this analogy to alert the dictator to the dangers of incurring the hatred of posterity (Cheops's pyramid was eventually pillaged and the body thrown out of its mausoleum, as was to happen to Stalin's corpse in 1962): 'The author's intention was that the awesome addressee should read the poem and see himself in the mirror of art (which is the only purpose of a writer's communication with the reader), should be shamed by the incriminating similarity of the facts, alarmed by the prophecy in the story, and, deeply moved by the courage of such a warning, should embrace him in eternal friendship' (*P*. II. 155). The poem is to prove the cause of Vadim's downfall. It is overheard, he is denounced, and arrested together with the professor of Egyptology to whom he had recited it.

Many years earlier Leonov himself had anticipated Vadim's poem. In *The Sot'* the name of the Egyptian Pharaoh had been one of the sobriquets applied to the Communist planner Potemkin, 'hinting no doubt at Cheops's unfortunate fate'[38] (4. 92). The association of the pyramids with Stalinism is implied too in *Evgenia Ivanovna* by the progression of Pickering's scientific interests from Egypt to Assyria, and finally to the Soviet Union.[39] Vikhrov had also raised this analogy in *The Russian Forest*, where his conventional pieties are treated with some irony: ' "... some factories of ours seem to me more immortal than the pyramids. They were the graves of human aspirations, but ours are the sacred cradle of joy itself. And so it is a pleasure for me to look into the faces of you engineers of happiness and defenders of life." Suddenly Vikhrov looked round shamefacedly at his bored audience...' (9. 517).

The pyramid, which might seem so antithetical to the idea of levelling, is at first identified with Western social structures: 'The other system, hostile to us, and correspondingly adopted by the West, was pictured by Vadim in the form of a class-pyramid, with an absolute ruler at the summit of a solid plutocratic elite; below them the remaining more or less captive classes, from senior bureaucrats to slaves, a voiceless rabble, oppressed by the weight above' (*P*. II. 57). But the hierarchy of Communist Russia turns out to be no less pyramidical in its structure: 'A repeat performance two days later was unexpectedly attended by the semipresident (with his wife and family) of something quite unpronounceable, virtually the right hand of a prominent comrade, who exercised curatorial capacities in an economic sector of almost prime importance, and as such had the right of reporting directly to the assistant to the secretary of the personal bureau of a shadowy colleague from the immediate entourage of a certain supreme figure, supreme not only in our hemisphere, but also as regards all previous ages, meridians and continents' (*P*. I. 253).

As Shigalev had discovered: 'Starting with the premise of absolute equality I arrive at the conclusion of absolute despotism.' In *The Sot'* Leonov's use of the name Vissarion had suggested that the extremes of individualism and social levelling were really two faces of the same coin. In *The Pyramid* this suggestion becomes explicit.

The pyramid is, among other things, an embodiment of the Hegelian triads which led to the Marxist dialectic, and is thus a monument to the epistemological theory on which the Soviet system is built. Against it Leonov sets the concept of the miracle, apparently, the epitome of the irrational, or at least of a rationality that lies beyond our understanding. Dymkov's supernatural powers are often expended on such pranks as decorating the faces of the men at a Kremlin banquet with identical Stalin moustaches, but they still raise serious difficulties for materialism, especially the Communist version, and for some time the authorities are unsure whether to treat Dymkov's shows as 'ideologically criminal' provocations (*P*. I. 642) or as harmless amusements. But if miracles exist then it is obviously desirable for the State to gain control over them, and so his performances are introduced by pseudoscientific lectures, much in the spirit of those Soviet prefaces 'designed to reduce the harm contained in books' that are mocked in *The Russian Forest*.[40] Needless to say the crowds perfectly 'understand the necessity of this clownish packaging as a safe way of concealing a miracle from being banned by the censorship' (*P*. I. 261).

But miracles are not freakish violations of the natural order. On the contrary, they are common enough. It is simply that they possess 'a self-protective ability to conceal themselves in an everyday wrapping, which helps to explain why they are noticed only comparatively rarely' (*P*. I. 678). But people's need for them is just as strong as their requirements for such basic goods as bread (*P*. I. 516). The miracle is manifested above all in art, and Leonov ridicules the Formalist idea that art is merely the sum of its devices.[41] It is a peculiarly human kind of creation, one that is inaccessible to God, whose

> misfortune lies in the fact that the concept of miracle requires the simultaneity of conception and execution, in other words the moment of imagination coincides with the act of creation, omitting all the intervening stages. The gods do not burn themselves out through work; for all their bliss they cannot know the pains of selection and doubt, nor the pride of overcoming them, nor the joy of completing a work, nor the blissful Sabbath exhaustion that flatterers have invented for them, and so, no creative satisfaction from their works. [...] From this you can see how lonely they are, how unhappy and indeed impotent for all their omnipotence. [...] The gods are benevolent but bodiless, in other words they are immune to feelings and sin, pure and naive like children. On the one hand they cannot understand how their azure dreamings could have created something so dirty and nasty; on the other they daren't condemn it because this same grubby impure substrate is the source of mysterious and intoxicating flowers, which cannot grow in the

sterile tranquillity of their eternal habitation. [...] They have had time enough, but there is nothing in heaven comparable to our fertile black earth, because they have nothing there that is capable of decaying. (*P.* II. 465–6)

It is through art that humanity discovers its godlike potential. Leonov likes to compare the genesis of a work of art to the concentration of matter on the eve of the Big Bang, or to a seed which contains the entire future development of a living organism in an apparently lifeless piece of matter. As Pickering says to Evgenia Ivanovna: '... once upon a time the universe itself was only an idea, a first stroke in a rough draft, and so could have been expressed on a scrap of paper no larger than the palm of a hand. The formula may seem cumbrous today, but as man matures so it will contract to the dimensions of a line of poetry, a hieroglyph, and eventually to the magic sign with which the the act of creation had once begun. The task of the artist is to pack an event into the space of a seed, so that once cast into a living soul, it may blossom out into the miracle that had originally captivated him' (8. 177). Where the original Creation had contained the future in embryo, human creativity, which comes in the middle or, as Leonov suggests, at the end of time, is primarily oriented to the past, 'the distillation of everything that lies behind us, the entire experience of human history' (3. 126–9).

Art then is similar to genetics in that it is made out of the accumulated past. Not for nothing does Leonov follow Gershenzon in likening it to original sin. For the fruit of the Tree of Knowledge has enabled man to create not only the marvels of his culture, his arts and sciences, but also their baleful corollaries, war, pollution, and overpopulation, so that man has become a threat not only to himself, but also to the whole planet. Our genes, our arts, our entire culture are all compromised by the impurity of our inheritance. But we would still be the poorer without them. Leonov's later novels, *The Russian Forest*, the revised *Thief* and *The Pyramid* all devote substantial space to the role of art. In fact the latter two novels end with the figure of the narrator alone.

In *The Pyramid* the representative artist is the film director Evgeny Sorokin, whose success is built on his willingness to gratify his political masters: 'Considered a leading figure in the cinema [he] conscientiously carried out all his official commissions within the limits of his flexible and universally versatile intelligence with the result that art never became for him the act of self-immolation that gives birth to masterpieces' (*P.* I. 110). He happily churns out socialist-realist films and is lavishly rewarded for them, but he has nothing but contempt for '... the socialist realism that is in fashion today, that is, historical projections for an hour, a week, or at most a year ahead. And if Disraeli said that there are lies, damned lies, and statistics (on which our doctrine is founded), then what would he have said about socialist realism, which is projected for at most a year or two ahead, if he hoped to escape a firing squad?' (*P.* II. 206).

One may well see in Sorokin a self-portrait of Leonov for their views on art are almost identical, and both men, as they are well aware, are compromised by their dealings with the regime. Nonetheless, the work of even these flawed and compromised artists challenges the egalitarian and utilitarian pieties of socialist orthodoxy, possessing a power, the 'glint in the eye,' that is not subject to rationalistic or sociological explanation. It is the work of the individual and successful only insofar as it is individual (see Gratsiansky's sneers at 'the handwriting of the individual' in *The Russian Forest*) and therefore resistant to any kind of levelling. It cannot be tied to narrow topical issues, because its roots lie in the remote past and it foretells the future more accurately than any political theory. This is why it outlives the economic and religious systems that supposedly give it birth.

Apart from explicit discussions Leonov also illustrates the workings of art through the form and structures of his works. In *The Pyramid* the alleged source of the author's information about events, whether terrestrial or extraterrestrial, is the young student Nikanor Shamin, Dunya's fiancé and eventual husband.[42] On the one hand he is of course a creature of the author, saying to him: 'I know only what you have managed to put into me, in recruiting me for your team' (*P*, I. 32). But at the same time he is the Virgil to Leonov's Dante (*P.* II. 360), explaining the cosmic order to him. Nikanor in turn has two sources, the saintly Dunya who tells him of her travels through the painted door into the remote future, and the sinister Shatanitsky, with whom he has managed to ingratiate himself by offering to write a book about him. Shatanitsky has agreed, apparently reasoning that 'the dim-witted student would, in the spirit of the modern age, justify his unsavoury activities, and so the young man's clumsy scribblings might become an important testimony to the inevitability of Evil in the history of the world' (*P*. I. 29). This might seem to compromise Nikanor's credibility as a source, but for Leonov art is inescapably a double game. Just as Gratsiansky's mimetism is a mirror of Leonov's own, so the author of *The Pyramid* has to cohabit with Dunya and Shatanitsky.

Leonov's consciousness of the unbridgeable gulf between the godlike potential of man and his utter unworthiness of this gift inevitably recalls Dostoevsky:

> ... even a man with a noble soul and a lofty intellect can begin with the ideal of the Madonna and end with the ideal of Sodom. Even worse, he can contain the ideal of Sodom without denying the ideal of the Madonna [...] Man is too broad, too broad, I would have narrowed him [...] What the intellect sees as shameful can be

pure beauty to the heart. Is beauty to be found in Sodom? Believe me, for most people, it is. It is horrifying that beauty is not only terrible but also mysterious. Here the devil and God wrestle with one another, and the field of battle is the human heart.[43]

Like Dmitriy Karamazov Leonov feels that human nature is too broad, and it is in the artist that this contradiction is seen most intensely. Despite all the sins of Sodom and Gomorrah Lot can still plead with God to spare them for the sake of a few righteous souls, and even after their destruction his wife defies all prohibitions for the sake of looking back at them one last time. For some inscrutable reason the past, for all its abominations retains a charm that outweighs the immaculate perfection of any Paradise. All Leonov's sympathies lie with those 'ridiculous men' who 'look back' like Dmitriy Vekshin and Firsov.

The past at which Leonov and his heroes look back is invariably associated with the fires that consumed Sodom, and so special significance attaches to the word *pogorel'shchina* (a place that has been destroyed by fire) and its cognate *pogorel'tsy* (people who have lost their homes through fire). The word provided the title for Nikolay Klyuev's long poem of the same name (probably written 1928–9), in which the Soviet assault on religion and the old way of life is seen as a parallel to the persecution of the old Russian Church at the end of the seventeenth century. Many of the Old Believers had committed mass suicide by taking refuge in their churches and then setting fire to them rather than compromise their faith. Thus the word comes to bear associations of martyrdom. Klyuev's poem was never published in Russia during the Soviet period, but Klyuev did give readings of it to small circles of friends and sympathizers. I think it likely that Leonov, through his friendship with Esenin, who was closely associated with Klyuev, would have known the poet and his work. This gives added point to his use of the word in *The Sot'*, *The Russian Forest*, and *The Pyramid*.

If the usual sense of *pogorel'shchina* is the destruction of the innocent (as in Klyuev's poem) in Leonov its associations also include Sodom and Gomorrah. Like Lot's wife, Firsov's Vekshin and Evgenia Ivanovna, the artist is ready to risk his life rather than turn his back on the past. Accordingly Leonov's last novel ends with the destruction of the Loskutovs' shack and their church, and its last words are:

Before leaving I felt I had to look back. [...] all one could hear was the crackling of giant bonfires. Columns of sparks spiralled up into the darkening sky as new armfuls of useless wood were tossed into the flames. It was beautiful to watch them soaring and dying out, falling back as ashes on to the trampled snow and the open spaces beyond the rubble of the demolished church, and on my own cupped hand, the hand of one whose home has been burnt out... (*P.* II. 684)

The author, witness to the horror and beauty of the conflagration, has himself become a *pogorelets*. Can there be a more fitting image for the artist in twentieth-century Russia?

The background of Christian myth, the relationship of Good and Evil, and the appearance of diabolic figures in Moscow in the time of the Purges naturally recall Bulgakov's *The Master and Margarita*, which was written in the 1930s, though it was not published until 1966. As in Bulgakov nothing could be more fantastic than the daily reality of Soviet life. The parallels extend also to the details: Sorokin's idea of making a film about Dymkov and the rebel angels recalls Bezdomny's novel about Christ. The treatment of the years of terror in largely farcical terms and jokes about hardened materialists being confronted with miraculous events are common to both books; the depiction of persecuted victims of the purges, and the ambiguous roles of officially approved artists are further parallels.

Leonov of course knew of the existence of Bulgakov's work, but it appears that he deliberately avoided reading it, so as to avoid any possible influence.[44] This may seem strange for such a widely read writer, who elsewhere showed little anxiety over such dangers; but for all the similarities, Leonov's novel does show a rather different approach. This is most marked in the treatment of the diabolical figures, who are dedicated to the frustration of the divine plan, whereas Bulgakov's Woland is ultimately an agent for good, however unwitting.

The Pyramid is a much bleaker work than *The Master and Margarita*. Leonov's earlier scepticism about the 'golden dream' of a Paradise on earth has now turned to despair, and the apocalyptic forebodings of the book are echoed in many of his utterances in his last years. The novel itself, however, ends on a fairly muted note. None of the major narrative lines has come to much of a conclusion; the catastrophes constantly promised throughout the book do not materialize: 'Only at the denouement, from the bird's eye view at the very end of the story, will the mechanism of the truly Satanic trap become visible, which only through pure accident failed to work at the crucial moment' (*P.* II. 277–8). Shatanitsky's plot seems to have led nowhere, and Dymkov manages to return, almost unscathed, to the intergalactic spaces from which he had appeared.

On the other hand nothing has been improved by Dymkov's sojourn on Earth; the imminent war with Nazi Germany is not averted, and the nightmare of Stalinism continues unabated. The final disappearance of Dymkov is paralleled by Dunya's loss of her mystical gifts, and she settles down as the dutiful wife of a professor at Moscow University. The catastrophe is still inevitable; the last attempts at averting it have failed, but it has been postponed to an indefinite future. Such an ending is really inevitable for any apocalyptic subject. As in Bely's *Petersburg*, history – and the assumption that someone will read the book – prevent the author from fulfilling his eschatological predictions. The side effect of such an ending is to suggest the possibility, despite everything, of a reprieve, rather as at the end of Thomas Mann's *Doktor Faustus*; but this seems irreconcilable with Leonov's views expressed elsewhere in these years.

The Pyramid is a vast novel, which is hardly to be summarized in a single chapter, and I can easily imagine another account of it that would not use a single one of the episodes or quotations I have discussed. But the overall interpretation would be much the same. This indicates the main weakness of the book. For all its many striking, even brilliant, passages, it remains a tract. Its characters are spokesmen for ideas rather than embodiments of them and the author's sympathies are unmistakable. In Dostoevsky one can see the attraction of the Grand Inquisitor's proposal: even while knowing we ought to reject it, most of us would happily accept it if given half a chance. In *The Pyramid* Stalin's offer to Dymkov is clearly diabolical. As a result the tension between alternative readings that had galvanized parts of Leonov's earlier novels has largely disappeared.

The novel is of course unfinished, not in the sense of being incomplete, rather that it is overloaded with material and requires drastic editing and pruning. Many of its weaknesses, the repetitions, the inconsistencies, the loose ends spring from this fact. For here Leonov wanted to break away from the techniques of indirection and irony he had evolved over the years and to speak openly and exhaustively. But the constraints of censorship had also had their benefits: they had challenged his ingenuity and helped to shape his works. Directness of speech, however, never came easily to Leonov, and in *The Pyramid* the heavy sarcasm (directed specially, but not exclusively, at Stalin and his accomplices) is clumsy when one recalls the elusive irony that had glinted through his earlier work.

It may be objected that the very gravity of Leonov's message cannot afford the luxury of aesthetic balance. But the author chose to present his warnings in artistic form, and, as the novel argues, art is the ideal way for treating the great questions of existence. The passion behind the book is indubitable, but unfortunately good intentions can be as counterproductive in art as in life. The decades of work on the novel have blunted its urgency while its style and repetitions are likely to alienate even readers already disposed to respond to its message.

Nonetheless *The Pyramid* for all its faults is essential reading for all admirers of Leonov. It can serve as a summary of his lifelong concerns and above all his rejection of the philosophical and ethical implications of Marxist materialism (and indeed all scientism) that have brought mankind to the brink of self-destruction. In place of the single-minded pursuit of purity he affirms the miracle of life and the 'glorious misery' that is mankind. The interaction of spirit with matter is necessarily impure, and all creation, whether divine or human, inescapably compromised; but it is still miraculous and infinitely to be preferred to the sterilities of intellectual and moral Puritanism.

chapter fourteen

The Art of Compromise

> *It proved to be absolutely impossible to get by without a kiss, the toll with which [...] the boy helped out his family in the big house, because resistance would of course have led to a mass of petty humiliations, only deepening their poverty. In the final analysis there was nothing so shameful in the aforementioned act of homage to a genius, a Croesus, a patriarch, even a benefactor, though the fact remains that apart from what he earned by his own hard labour he never received a single penny [...] for that kiss.*
>
> (*P.* I. 652)

Leonid Leonov lived an exceptionally long life; more than eighty years passed between his first publication in an Archangel newspaper and the release of his last novel. He lived in a century that witnessed revolutionary changes in almost every aspect of life, artistic and scientific, social and political. He spent his formative years under Tsarism, while almost his entire creative life was passed under the Soviet system, whose ignominious collapse he yet lived to see. Despite these upheavals his works are remarkably consistent in their concerns and values. They abound in cross-references to one another, they quote from one another, and the same set of images serves to unite them. The sceptical legend of Kalafat and the myth of the artist in *Ham's Departure*, both originating from before the Revolution, foreshadow the main concerns of his maturity. The image of the journey through the mountains to the Promised Land, first raised in *The Thief*, recurs in his later novels and plays with ever-deepening implications.

Fundamental to Leonov's outlook is his conviction of the reality of the spiritual dimension. In his work this is clearly illustrated in his lifelong preoccupation with the continuity of culture. But it may be noted that his favoured imagery for this theme is usually taken from the Bible, for example, the stories of Lot's wife, Noah and Ham, and the concept of original sin. This leads me to suspect that culture serves him as an analogue for the concept of religion, which was taboo during the Soviet period. His defence of culture thus implies a rejection of official atheism. The ruined and desecrated churches of his later work can and probably should be seen in both ways.

All his life Leonov was a practising and apparently orthodox Christian. He was married in church and attended religious services regularly. It would be difficult, however, to infer this from his works. Nowhere does he idealize the church; Father Mel'khizedek in *The Breakthrough at Petushikha* and the monks in *The Sot'* are depicted as unflatteringly as any Soviet commissar could have wished; Father Lavrentiy in *Wolf* is shameless in demanding protection for himself at the expense of his children. Where Leonov does make use of the scriptures, as in *Ham's Departure*, his treatment is usually heretical. In *The Pyramid* he draws parallels between Christianity and Communism, in that both promise eventual equality and unclouded bliss in some remote future, while perpetrating monstrous abuses in the present.

Nevertheless Christianity for all its inadequacies still answers to the side of human nature that instinctively recognizes moral and aesthetic values. Leonov therefore challenges the Communists' claim to have replaced it with a superior creed based on rationalism and utilitarianism. In *The Pyramid* Father Matvey asks,

> After the abolition of Christianity will the new theory [Marxism] have strong enough wings to sustain mankind in its flight on even its previous insignificant level? (*P.* II. 33)

In his works of the immediate post-revolutionary period his misgivings are plain enough, for example in the 'black hole' of *The Breakthrough at Petushikha* and the 'legend of Kalafat,' incorporated into *The Badgers*. But in the years from *The Thief* to *The Road to Ocean* he seems to have been prepared to consider the posssibility that socialism too might evolve such 'wings.' Later – on my reading, some time in the late 1940s, that is, between the first version of *A Golden Coach* and *The Russian Forest*[1] – he came to reject the Revolution and all its claims of moral and cultural superiority. His portrayal of the careerist Gratsiansky as a typical product of the Soviet system, and, as such, indistinguishable from the Nazis, his demolition of the pretensions of Dmitriy Vekshin in the revised *Thief*, and the sustained attack on the Revolution's basic presuppositions in *The Pyramid*, indicate how far his views had hardened. And shortly before his death he told Natal'ya Groznova that he was thinking of rewriting the scene between Semen and Pavel-Anton at the end of *The Badgers*:

'Semen himself comes to Pavel in the wood, wearing only a shirt, barefoot in the frost, and quite prepared to be shot. He says: "Why don't you come and get us? Mother is in the church, just waiting to die." Pavel silently begins to walk out of the wood down the hill and away from his brother. And here is the really subtle touch (Leonov's emphasis. N.G.). Pavel *turns his back* to Semen; he lays himself wide open to death; he wants to receive his punishment at the hands of Semen, punishment for what he has done. But...' And here the writer planned to give new life to the myth of Cain, who was doomed to an agonizing immortality for his fratricide. [...] According to Orthodox belief a murdered man becomes a sacrifice and is absolved of all the sins he has committed on earth. The author of *The Badgers* took the decision not to pardon the bloody sins of his hero. Semen was not to fire a shot into his brother's back and so release his soul from sin. No. Pavel was to receive Cain's eternal punishment.[2]

The Revolution is now equated with the archetypal sin.

In this predilection for seeing events in their mythical and symbolic dimensions Leonov, even though he was born and spent most of his life in Moscow, stands closer to the St Petersburg tradition in Russian literature, and, in particular, the work of Dostoevsky. The affinities between them can be traced on many levels. Both compose novels of ideas; their leading characters are associated with distinct, often irreconcilable, philosophies. Both regard rationalism and materialism as inadequate and dehumanizing solutions to man's spiritual needs. In both the unity of Creation is threatened by the duality of human nature.

In *The End of a Petty Man* Likharev had asserted: 'The universe is so set up that everything is interwoven. Pull out a single twig and the whole thing will fall apart,' and the idea dictates not just the content but also the structure of Leonov's works. The natural world is the symbol of this ideal unity, and any attempt to improve, redirect, or exploit it is misdirected, if not actually dangerous. The trees, fields, and stars that throw off Kalafat's labels and dockets, the groves from which Buryga is kidnapped, and the forests to whose service Vikhrov humbly devotes himself, are far wiser than man's clumsy and limited intervention, however well intentioned. The revolutionary slogan scratched into the old tree in *The Thief* almost kills it. The fate of the Russian forest is a visible reminder of man's arrogance and ignorance.

Man's peculiar position lies in the fact that he is both part of nature, and yet through consciousness and intellect is able to stand outside it. In his early work Leonov saw this duality as the key to the meaning of creation: 'Before me the open spaces of virgin land, sufficient for man to be born on, suffer his fill, and die. Above me, in the expanses mirrored a thousand times in every direction rage the stars; down below – man: life. And without life how empty and meaningless all this would be! Filling the whole world with yourself and your sufferings you, man, create it afresh...' (*Vor*, 1927, 8). Man stands as a bridge between the Creator and His creation. But at the same time he is caught between two worlds, and his being is therefore irreparably divided. In *Ham's Departure* the hero sings of how God's creation had been kidnapped and subverted by His shadowy reflection or double. The cosmogony underlying *The Pyramid* (taken from the Apocryphal Book of Enoch) essentially repeats the same idea: man is the battleground for irreconcilable forces.

This is the source of Leonov's distrust of those who would stress one aspect of human nature at the expense of the others. Two types recur in his fiction, which in their essentials can be traced back to *The Breakthrough at Petushikha* and *The Thief*. If Talagan and Vekshin and such later heroes as Uvad'ev and Skutarevsky represent the human need for aspiration, 'onwards and upwards,' the imposition of the will on a recalcitrant nature, the pacific Alesha Kharablev and the sceptical Pchkhov know that all striving is illusory: Adam and Eve will never make their way back to Eden for all their cars and airplanes.

The Communists belong to the former group: they are dedicated to the belief that mankind is capable of solving its problems. Leonov recognizes that such ambitions are valid and even admirable, but they take no account of man's potential for irrationality and destructiveness. For this reason he casts doubt on the ability of reform and still less revolution, to effect any real change, let alone improvement in the human condition. Open expression of such scepticism was of course unacceptable in the Stalin years, and so he could voice his reservations only through his so-called negative characters (e.g., Vissarion, Petrygin, Gratsiansky) or through the implications of the narrative (as in *The Road to Ocean*; it is only when he is dying that Kurilov comes to understand that life is to be valued for iself in the here and now, not for what one might be able to make of it in some hypothetical future). But in *The Badgers* the archetypal Communist Comrade Anton momentarily wonders whether the whole revolutionary project is not misguided: 'Just two days ago it suddenly occurred to me: perhaps it would be better if man didn't exist?... If the model isn't satisfactory, then just scrap it?' only to answer his own doubts: 'But no – with a bit of tinkering we could have an excellent model' (2. 205). Vekshin and Uvad'ev also imagine that a little bit of engineering can sort out the various inadequacies and weaknesses of mankind; but human nature cannot be changed to order and will inevitably reassert itself. As Leonov had foreseen in the character of Chikilev the good intentions of the first revolutionaries had prepared the way for the vicious intolerance of the Stalin years. On reading Solzhenitsyn's *Gulag*, he remarked: 'There's the postscript to *Das Kapital* for you.'[3]

The attempt to improve life is in fact the force that most threatens it:

> Here [Father Matvey] proceeded from the church tradition of the so-called last days with the enthronement of the thousand-faced AntiChrist. Also foretold was the gradual, logically irrefutable, and almost imperceptible readiness of humanity to shift its spiritual allegiance in exchange for the seductive gifts of science, technology, and comfort. Particularly sensitive observers like Father Matvey were perturbed by the strange resemblance of certain features of the modern age to the identifying marks of that awful antechamber, to wit, the universal decline in religious faith, the murderous wars, the multiplying of false prophets, the premature castration of souls [...] alongside the blindness of conceited intellects, the ever-growing energies devoted to self-destruction, and much else – right down to the alarming similarity of the new ruler in the form of, say, Armillius. to some of the leading figures of the age. (*P*. I. 410)[4]

Leonov's warnings are directed in the first place at Soviet Marxism; but Western societies are no less vulnerable to his criticisms, for they are equally committed to a narrowly materialistic conception of progress, and their methods are not so different.

Above all, like Dostoevsky, Leonov rejects happiness as a goal whether for the individual or for society, on the grounds that it can only be achieved by abolishing all individuality. Differences among people are as natural and desirable as those among trees, but Marxists regard them as the prime cause of unhappiness and have therefore tried to remove them from society. Beginning with material disparities the principle has spread to intellectual and spiritual qualities too. Envy, once an evil to be eradicated, has become instead a tool for pursuing the cause of egalitarianism – in the interests of a new elite. Dostoevsky's cynical Shigalev had first proposed these measures, fully aware that they would lead only to greater inequality and unhappiness, but in the twentieth century they were to be advocated in all seriousness by Bukharin and Preobrazhensky in their *ABC of Communism*.

In particular, the entire culture of the past came to seem culpable just because of its acceptance of inequality and suffering. Such views were indeed often voiced in the early years of the revolution. For Mayakovsky it was one of the masks of the counter-revolution:

> If you catch a White Guard you put him up against the wall.
> But haven't you forgotten Raphael? and what about Rastrelli?
> And why isn't Pushkin under attack
> and the other White Guards of our classics?[5]

These objections were based not just on the irrelevance of past cultures, but on their dangers, as though they contained a contagion that could infect and corrupt the citizens of a supposedly happier and healthier age; they should therefore be abolished along with the libraries and museums that house them. Even the culture-loving Gor'ky comes close to this view: towards the end of his autobiographical *Childhood* (*Detstvo*, 1913) he wrote:

> Remembering these leaden abominations of our savage Russian life I sometimes ask myself: is it worth talking about these things? Then with renewed assurance I answer myself: yes, it is worth it, because this truth is a vile and stubborn truth which is still not dead. It is a truth that one has to know to its deepest roots so that one can eradicate it from the memory of mankind, from the soul, from our entire life, so base and shameful.[6]

The past must be faced but only so that we can eradicate it more effectively. In practice the Communist leaders did not go to these extremes, but they felt fully entitled to decide what works were worth preserving, editing them, if necessary, in ways 'specifically designed to weaken the harm contained in them' (9. 304).

It is natural for well-intentioned reformers to wish to spare their children the nightmares of the past, but Leonov cannot accept such a remedy. The past and its record in our culture, impure though it may be, contains a fuller picture of human nature than is dreamt of by political economists. In place of a rationalized and sterile ideal it reveals the complex human potential for change and development. Zamyatin understood this when in his novel *We* he had lodged the opposition to the Single State in the Ancient House, with its relics of past culture, the poetry of Pushkin, and the music of Scriabin. So too for Leonov Lot's wife's backward look at the flames of Sodom is the primal act of disobedience that establishes our humanity.

Both Zamyatin and Leonov use genetics as an analogy for culture; D.503's hairy hands are a constant reminder of the past, latent in the present. The roots of our culture similarly lie inextricably entangled in the prehistoric, even prehuman, past. Nothing that we do can be immaculate; even humanity's highest achievements in the arts and sciences are vulnerable to perversion. In his wartime propaganda articles Leonov had pointed to the links between classical German culture in philosophy, science, and art, and the atrocities of the Nazi period;[7] Agey and Vekshin in *The Thief* had been tormented by the technologization of war. But the creative ambitions of science are even more obscene than its destructive powers:

> O Bimbaev, you great provocateur, who showed me the power of science! His magnificent machines contained not cannons, only test tubes, condensers, and a

multitude of pipes, propellers, and revolving discs... here chemistry is wedded to physics and mechanics [...] The wheels are turning, the machine is ready, but [Bimbaev] still hopes to quadruple the number of its functions. Perhaps he is teaching it to fly or to smile, or to articulate the word *Mummy*.' (4. 185)

This process culminates in *The Pyramid* with the prospect of genetic manipulation as a solution to the problematic inheritance of our genes.

But genetic engineering is not the answer. Human duality is not just a matter of a faulty gene or two; it is essential to our humanity. In this rejection of a technological fix Leonov echoes Dostoevsky's *Dream of a Ridiculous Man*, in which the author is torn between his yearning for a new golden age and his recognition that human life with all its squalor is still somehow priceless, and that something would be lost if humanity were really to achieve its goal. Human fallibility is better than a sterile purity. The horse that relieves itself in *The Thief* proves that it is 'alive.' The dung-heap is as essential to life as sunshine, and the abominations perpetrated in *Evgenia Ivanovna* and *The Pyramid* are as inalienably human as the values they desecrate. Like Ham, the artist has no magic mirror to veil the horrors that he has witnessed and at which he must continually look back.

Such a conception, however, does not spring from an Olympian detachment from the real world. On the contrary it is a difficult and unstable position, as can be seen from many of Leonov's works and, above all, the multiple rewritings of *A Golden Coach*, a play that is largely concerned with just this issue. Ivan Karamazov had rejected any 'harmony' that might be built on the sufferings of a child, but it seems to me that he was looking for not a harmony but a unison. Leonov sees that dissonance is essential for the realization of harmony, but also that its resolution can never be more than temporary. The enigmatic chord at the start of *Tristan und Isolde* is finally resolved only hours later in the last bars of the opera, in one of the most satisfying conclusions to any work of art; but it cannot undo any of the tragic events that have gone before, or bring the dead back to life. Nor did it deter Wagner from embarking on new works. Just because of its limitations art comes closer to an adequate representation of reality than any of the more idealistic physical or social sciences. Art then may be seen both as a form of religion and as a metaphor for it in Soviet conditions.

But art is still only ancillary to life, and it is in the areas where they overlap most conspicuously that the keys to Leonov's work and his chequered reputation may be found. The fact remains that for many readers, in Russia and in the West, he is irreparably compromised as much by having survived the Stalin years as by anything that he actually wrote or did. Living in an exceptionally barbaric age, the outcome, as Dostoevsky had foretold, of the combination of fantastic advances in science and a Utopian ideology, Leonov yet found himself required to idealize it according to the propagandist demands of the Party. In the face of these pressures many Soviet artists fell silent (if they had not already been silenced) or simply conformed. Leonov saw his duty in continuing to write, but this involved trying to steer a course between moral capitulation and the obligation to protect his dependents. One may feel that he sometimes compromised himself by excessive caution, but no one who has not experienced the pressures under which he and his colleagues lived and worked has the right to condemn him for his periodic misjudgments and failures of nerve. The appalling dilemmas created by these conditions in fact dictate the main concerns of his work.

Throughout the 1930s he continued to intimate a sceptical and even critical attitude, not only to what was being done but also to the ideology in whose name it was being done. The full extent of his dissent, however, was certainly not suspected at the time except perhaps by a very small number of readers. But if the implications of his work were not perceived at the time, one may ask what he achieved, whether his caution was not self-defeating. I think that the explanation lies partly in the fact that in any work of art the element of dissent constitutes only a small part of a larger whole and that anyway under such conditions most readers are unwilling to pursue subversive subtexts, as though mere awareness of them was tantamount to complicity in them.

For all his numerous honours and awards Leonov was never quite accepted as a 'Soviet' writer. Lip service was paid to his stylistic virtuosity and to the intellectual complexity of his work (though without examining it too closely), but there was a recurring resentment that he had not placed his talents more unequivocally at the service of the Party. Although his situation eased somewhat after the death of Stalin, he still remained suspect, as can be seen from the savage attacks on *The Russian Forest* when it first appeared, and the periodic harassments and indignities which he endured during the Brezhnev years. The celebrations of his various jubilees were somewhat strained occasions with official spokesmen confining themselves to generalities that had been used before and could be applied equally validly to many other Soviet writers. Only in 1989, when Gorbachev visited him to congratulate him on his ninetieth birthday, did he receive conspicuous and unequivocal recognition. Ironically, the honour brought him little satisfaction for he despised Gorbachev, and still more Eltsin, as opportunists who had destroyed not only the Soviet Union but also Russia in their greed for power.

The times he lived in and the conflicting demands made of him mean inevitably that Leonov is an uneven writer. He is best known as a novelist, but none of his novels is free from faults though they are all worth reading and each has its own distinct character. But any artist has the right to be judged by his best works, and these would have to include *The Breakthrough at Petushikha*, the first version of *A Golden Coach*, *Evgenia Ivanovna*, and some of the stories of the late 1920s which are still too little known. The rediscovery of these works should lead to a re-evaluation of his oeuvre as a whole. I do not believe that Leonov's genius was broken by the Stalin years, as many critics have averred; on the contrary it was shaped by them, stylistically and philosophically. But although the plots and character types of most of his stories and plays are firmly tied to their time and place his importance is not confined to the Stalin years or even to the Russia of the twentieth century. His warnings against the deification of the intellect, the cult of progress and the despoliation of nature, the idolization of happiness, the indifference to the past and the tendency of democratic ideals to degenerate into a mean-spirited egalitarianism, carry a universal message in the tradition of classical Russian literature.

In his speech on the fiftieth anniversary of the death of Lev Tolstoy Leonov said,

> As I see it, every great artist, quite apart from his main theme, inscribed by him upon the intellectual agenda of his age, is inevitably the vessel of a personal problem, sometimes irreproachably concealed, a complex spiritual knot, which he gradually unravels throughout the course of his entire creative career. (10. 423)[8]

When writers make such remarks about other writers one may suppose that they are thinking also of themselves, and it is therefore tempting to try to identify these themes in Leonov's own work.

The 'main theme,' as I take it, is the network of issues raised by Communism's attempt to replace Christianity with a new culture. The 'personal problem' is less easy to identify, especially if it has been 'irreproachably concealed.' But isn't the author contradicting himself by drawing attention to it in this way, and isn't the choice of adverb surprising? What is this 'reproach' that seems to be acknowledged, even as is it is being disowned, rather like the 'not understanding' in *A Note on Birchbark*? I believe that Leonov is thinking here of the years 1918–20 in Archangel, when he had been tempted by emigration and had almost taken up arms against the Bolsheviks, a past that could have destroyed him at any time in the next forty years, and was so unmentionable that he could tell his daughters of it only two or three years before his death, some thirty years after the Tolstoy speech.

Once one is aware of the significance of these years, one sees allusions to them right across Leonov's *oeuvre*, and no doubt further research will reveal even more. In all his works that touch on this period, from *A Note on Birchbark* down to *A Golden Coach* and *Evgenia Ivanovna*, it is associated not just with the temptation to evade or even oppose the Revolution, but also with the motif of having failed a woman. Among the many possible symbolic interpretations I would suggest a guilty sense that somewhere along the road, like Gleb Protoklitov, and not necessarily willingly, he had taken a wrong turning. Although his activities in 1918–20 seem to have remained unknown to the Soviet authorities he was still regarded with some distrust as a former *poputchik* and the author of *The Thief*. This continuing awareness of his vulnerability led him to make some damaging compromises in the Stalin years. Thus the two main concerns of his work, the guilty memory and the identification of culture with original sin, are seen to be different aspects of the same experience. Leonov was compromised in more senses than one.

But this is true of us all. Human nature is irreparably compromised. As a lifelong carver of wooden imps and goblins Leonov would have appreciated Kant's conclusion that 'out of the crooked timber of humanity no straight thing can be made.' Short of genetic engineering there is no way that it can be purged of the legacy of the past, and perhaps our horror at the very thought reflects our awareness of the mixed blessings we have inherited.

It is only fitting that such reflections should come from a writer who made his compromises and was often enough compromised by them, but who also showed that art can and sometimes must be made out of compromise.

Appendix: *'Zapis' na bereste'*

1.
Вот я запишу про счастье,
которое казалось близким,
но улетело птицей,
и больше счастья нет.

И я записал, как умею,
слова о недавней встрече
размером случайным и шатким
на белой простой бересте.

История моя все та же,
о какую разбивают сердце
поэты и глухонемые,
мудрые и глупцы.

Она кратка, моя повесть
с начала и до крайней точки,
за которой умер пришелец
и родился лесной человек.

2.
Когда листаешь страницы,
спокойный и равнодушный,
кажется дымным и чадным
любой из вчерашних дней.

В те дни и весенние ветры
жалили подобно змеям,
порохом пахли глухо
даже полевые цветы.

Мне и теперь непонятно,
чему улыбались дети,
когда так бурно и страшно
вскипала отцовская кровь.

Знаю, что смысл обреченности
в этом непониманьи.
Но, может быть, это и лучше –
не понимать до конца?

3.
Сергей – мой старый приятель,
с которым учились вместе,
а Павел – поэт немножко,
мечтатель и полусвятой.

Из города, где ежечасно
свирепей становилось время,
на север, еще не красный,
мы сговорились бежать.

А тут еще весна случилась,
мутная, горькая, сырая,
у меня отняли друга,
а у Павла – отца.

А зачем, кому они нужны,
истине или человеку –
под суровым, обожженным небом
красные, небыстрые ручьи?

4.
Когда же мы пришли на север,
нас послали на фронт, а на
    фронте
думали спасать Россию
штыками чужих солдат.

И мы бежали оттуда
в бескрайнюю, мертвую тундру,
болотами шли до Тоймы,
а в Тойме свернули в лес.

Мы несли с собою винтовки,
топоры, котелки и пули.
Не про нас ли в какой-то книжке
уже придуман рассказ?

А когда миновала неделя,
я сказал своим на ночлеге:
«Здесь, по моему, гораздо лучше, –
и тише и умней».

5.
Если люди тебя обманут,
и тебе средь них не будет места,
приходи бездорожною ночью
в эту глухую дебрь.

Она не прогоняет приходящих,
Не выдает ни тайны, ни крика,
не насмехается,
молчит.

Тогда – это было под утро –
кричал коростель в канаве,
а в небе как будто розы
горстями рассыпал май.

Мы шли и молчали, а Павел
вдруг сказал и засмеялся тихо:
«Весна, и любовь, и розы...
глядите, глухарь на току».

6.
На веселой, зеленой поляне,
в глубинах темного бора,
поставили мы наш домик,
простой и в четыре окна.

Тогда зацветали рябины,
брусника таилась в топях,
а на опушках белела
земляника прозрачным цветком.

Вверху были солнце и птицы,
и не было нам тесно с ними.
Хватало и неба и леса,
не то, что с людьми в городах.

Мы встретили однажды лося:
Он не бежал а слушал.
Я промаху не дал ни разу:
вечером был костер.

7.
Целыми днями блуждал я,
разыскивая пищу.
Зоркими, как у птицы, стали
серые мои глаза.

Сергей оставался по дому,
а Павел уходил с зарею
к голубой полутьме перелесков
рвать фиалки, которые цвели.

Сергей – это наша Марфа,
которая заботилась о многом.
А Павел – это Мария,
избравшая лучшую часть.

Я же познакомился с каждой
неприметной даже лощинкой
и узнал, что ночью ветер гуще,
а перепел кричит к дождю.

8.
И когда выходили патроны,
мы бросили вольный жребий,
кому отправляться завтра же
в недолгий, но неясный путь.

А о том, что разрывалось этим
наше милое, лесное братство,
и о том, что солнце шло на убыль,
не подумал тогда никто.

В зеленых высях кукушка
крикнула и улетела.
Плыли сумерки. Над самым ухом
жалобно звенел комар.

«Нет патронов – не будет мяса.
А без мяса – плохое дело».
Так решили мы на совете,
и жребий пал на меня.

9.
Как случилось – рассказывать
   долго,
а чужому и непонятно,
что принес я не порох, не пули,
а женщину с собой привел.

Я встретил ее случайно,
она казалась несчастной,
звали ее Еленой,
я полюбил ее.

И сказал ей: «В лесу, за тундрой,
глушь и лоси, комары и болота.
Мы недавно там живем. Трое.
Остальные – Павел и Сергей.

Если я тебе не противен,
имя Андрей не противно,
то пойдем туда со мною вместе».
Она ответила – да.

10.
Елена была красива.
Сергей себя за ус подергал,
а безусый Павел смутился
и мигом умчался в бор.

Она подружилась со всеми,
пела песни и варила мясо,
а ночью была моей женою.
Потом недели прошли.

Однажды я проснулся в полночь,
и не было со мной Елены.
Я надел сапоги и вышел,
сонный, хмурый, злой.

Белый пар стелился по бору.
Я шел, а душа кричала.
Молчали березы и ели,
они умеют молчать.

11.
Обнявшись, она сидела с Павлом,
и Павел целовал ее руки,
и, кажется, стихи о встречах
с поцелуями мешали они.

Летние ночи прозрачны,
а слова Елены были тихи,
а небо было розово и тонко.
Я спрятался и молчал.

«Ты единственный и любимый.
Ну, какой ты поэт? Ты глупый,
как тихая ряска на болоте.
И в глазах твоих – печаль.

И Андрей – он тоже прекрасный,
но такой молчаливый, умный.
С ним всегда и скучно и страшно,
а тебя я люблю, люблю...»

12.
Дальше я не слушал. Я увидел,
что подобно поздней бруснике
горели губы Елены.
Мох был не стоптан, а смят.

Тогда я не стал таиться.
Я пошел и принес винтовки,
положил одну перед Павлом
и сказал ему так:

«В какой-то из двух Америк
есть обычай славной охоты.
Если двое поспорят насмерть,
то уходят в леса и поля...

И оттуда, зоркие, как волки,
приближаясь лукавыми путями,
сходятся подстерегая
меткой пулей своего врага».

13.
Я и Павел, – мы решили так же,
речи были коротки и скупы.
Волк, когда выходит на добычу
также дышит ровно и легко.

Я пересчитал свои патроны,
поровну их разделил, сказавши:
«Целься лучше, Павел». Тут Елена,
испугавшись, убежала в дом.

Он молчал и улыбался, Павел.
Нагибаясь и беря винтовку,
он ответил мне, но я не слушал:
«Если ты убьешь меня, – прости».

Он пошел на юг, а я на север.
Там, где бор переходил неспешно
в дикую, колючую щетину,
я присел на мох и закурил.

14.
Целый день я шел, остерегаясь,
чутким ухом карауля шорох;
держать на прицел винтовку
не уставала рука.

К вечеру засинела опушка.
Я увидел на поляне Павла,
и была, как ковер та поляна
вышита желтыми цветами.

На траве валялась винтовка,
и сам он стоял возле,
так спокойно, как стоит дерево,
вишня, например, – в цвету.

А я ему целил в спину,
в кожаную потертую куртку.
Как его сразу не убили,
красные мои глаза?

15.
Боровые ветры, что ломают,
как солому вековые сосны,
не разгонят даже на мгновенье,
темных чар твоих, любовный чад.

Всю ту ночь я пробродил по бору.
Все мне было красным:
    зелень, птицы,
крики сов и самый мрак
    болотный...
Все мне было красным, как
    кумач.

А когда я пришел обратно,
дом был пуст, дверь была
    настежь.
На столе белела записка:
«Мы уходим к людям. Сергей».

Пели птицы, вставало утро,
но уже багровые розы
отцветающего июля
осыпались на облака.

16.
Я – высокий, сухой и сильный –
перед этим домом запустелым
скакал, в клубок сжимался,
делал прыжки, кричал.

Потому что припомнил Павла,
как лежит он на желтой поляне
и разорванные паутинки лета
протянулись по его лицу.

Значит, Сергей был ближе,
значит, он стал милее,
чем убитый мечтатель Павел
или убийца Андрей...

В этот день распуганные птицы
не кричали над моею крышей,
А вечером варил я мясо
и сидел у костра один

A NOTE ON BIRCHBARK

1. And so I will write about happiness, which had seemed so close, but has flown away like a bird, and now there is no more happiness. And I wrote down, as best I could, some words about a recent encounter in a random and shaky meter on plain white birchbark. My story is the same old one for which poets and deaf mutes, wise men and idiots alike break their hearts. From start to finish it is short enough, my story, for which one man died and a man of the forests was born.

2. When, calm and detached, you turn the pages, each one of those yesterdays seems smoky and acrid. In those days the spring winds stung like snakes, even the flowers of the field smelled dimly of gunpowder. Even now I cannot understand what the children were smiling at when their fathers' blood seethed so stormily and grimly. I know that in this lack of understanding lies the meaning of being doomed. But perhaps it's better that way, not to understand fully.

3. Sergey is an old friend, we were at school together; and Pavel – a bit of a poet, a dreamer, and almost a saint. From the city where with every hour the times were becoming more barbarous we decided to flee to the North. And then too it was springtime, tart, confusing, and raw. I lost a friend, and Pavel his father. Do people or the truth need these slow red rivers under the harsh scorched sky?

4. When we got to the North we were sent to the front, where they hoped to save Russia with the bayonets of foreign soldiers. And we fled from there into the endless barren tundra. We made our way to Toyma through the marshes and in Toyma we turned into the forest. We took with us our rifles, axes, billycans, and bullets. Hasn't someone already made up a poem about us in some book? And when a week had passed I said to my friends in our bivouac: 'I think it's much better here, quieter and wiser.'

5. If people betray you, and you no longer have a place among them, then one pathless night come into this remote covert. It does not reject the newcomer, does not betray secrets or cries, does not mock, but remains silent. There towards morning, the corncrake would call from the ditch and the sky like roses scattered in handfuls by the spring. We moved in silence until Pavel suddenly spoke and laughed quietly: 'Spring and love and roses. Look, the mating dance of the woodgrouse.'

6. In a green and smiling clearing, in the depths of the dark pine forest we built our house, plain with four windows. The rowanberry was in flower; the cowberry was hiding in the swamp, and to the side white strawberries with their translucent flowers. Above us the sun and the birds, and their presence was not oppressive: there were sky and forest enough, not like people in the cities. One day we met an elk; it did not run away, it was listening. I never missed; that evening we made a fire.

7. Whole days on end I would roam, hunting for food. My grey eyes became as sharp as a bird's. Sergey would stay at home, while Pavel went off at dawn to pick the blossoming violets in the half-light of the copse. Sergey was our Martha, occupied with many things, and Pavel our Mary, who had chosen the better part. I became familiar with even the humblest hollows; I learned that at night the wind is dense, and the quail's call means rain.

8. And when our bullets were running low we threw lots to decide who should leave the next day on the short but hazardous trip. None of us ever

thought that our forest brotherhood would be shattered by this, or that our sun had passed its zenith. In the green treetops the cuckoo called and flew off. A mosquito whined piteously over our ears. 'Without bullets there is no meat, and without meat things will go badly.' So we decided in our council and the lot fell on me.

9. It is too long to tell, and anyway an outsider would never understand how it was that I brought back with me not gunpowder or bullets, but a woman. I met her by chance. She seemed unhappy. Her name was Elena, and I fell in love with her. I said to her: 'Far away in the forest, on the far side of the tundra there is nothing but elks, mosquitoes, and swamps. We haven't been there long. There are three of us. The others are Pavel and Sergey. If you don't find me repulsive or my name, Andrey, then let us go there together.' She replied: 'Yes.'

10. Elena was beautiful. Sergey twitched at his moustache, and the beardless Pavel was abashed and ran off into the trees. She made friends with all of us, she sang songs, she cooked our meat, and at night she was my wife. Weeks passed. One midnight I woke up. Elena was not beside me. I put on my boots and went out, sleepy, frowning, angry. A white mist was spreading through the forest. And as I walked my soul was screaming. The birches and firs kept silence. They know how to keep silence.

11. She and Pavel were sitting embracing. Pavel was kissing her hands; they seemed to be mingling poems about their meetings with their kisses. Summer nights are transparent and Elena's words were quiet and fragile. I hid and said nothing. 'You are the only one I love. Well, what kind of a poet are you? You are silly like the duckweed of the marsh and your eyes are sad. Andrey is handsome too, but he is so silent, so wise. Being with him is boring and frightening, but you I love, I love.'

12. I listened no further. I saw that Elena's lips were burning like cowberries in the autumn. The moss was not trampled, just crushed. Then I hid no longer. I went up to them with the rifles, placed one of them in front of Pavel and this is what I said: 'In one of the two Americas the hunters have a grand custom. If two men quarrel to the death they go into the forests and fields... And from there, keen-eyed as wolves, each spies on his enemy, with his bullet ever ready.'

13. Pavel and I agreed to do the same. Our words were brief and spare.

When a wolf goes after its prey its breath is even and light, as ours was. I counted up the bullets and divided them equally: 'Take good aim, Pavel!' Elena was frightened at this and ran into the house. Pavel smiled and said nothing. Bending down to pick up the rifle, he replied, but I was not listening: 'If you kill me forgive me.' He went to the South, I to the North. Where the forest slowly turns into wild, sharp bristles I sat down on the moss and lit a cigarette.

14. The whole day I was on my guard, listening keenly to every rustle; my hand never wearied of holding my gun at the ready. At evening the edge of the forest began to darken. I saw Pavel in a clearing; it was covered with yellow flowers like an embroidered carpet. His gun was lying on the grass and he stood beside it as calmly as, say, a cherry tree in blossom. I took aim at his back. How was it that my red eyes did not kill him at once?

15. The forest winds that can snap the age-old pines as though they were straw will never for a moment dispel the dark enchantment of love. All that night I wandered through the forest. Everything had become red to me – the vegetation, the birds, the cries of the owls, and the very muteness of the swamps. Everything had become as red as the flags of revolution. And when I returned the house was empty, the door open, and a note on the table: 'We are going back to mankind. Sergey.' The birds sang, the morning was dawning, but the red roses of the dying July were already dropping on to the clouds.

16. I, so tall, so reserved and strong, threw myself at the empty house, curled up into a ball, leapt, and screamed. Because I remembered Pavel lying in the yellow clearing and the ragged cobwebs of the summer stretched over his face. So, then, Sergey was closer to her, dearer than the dead dreamer Pavel and the murderer Andrey. That day the terrified birds cried no more above my head. And that evening I cooked my meal and sat by my fire alone.

Abbreviations

Chit i pis.	*Chitatel' i pisatel'*
DMZ	*Dekada moskovskikh zrelishch*
Izv.	*Izvestiya*
KazPr	*Kazakhstanskaya Pravda*
KomPr	*Komsomol'skaya pravda*
KN	*Krasnaya nov'*
KrGaz (vech)	*Krasnaya gazeta (vecherniy vypusk)*
KrVoin	*Krasnyy voin*
K i zh	*Kul'tura i zhizn'*
L.	Leningrad
LenPr	*Leningradskaya pravda*
LesProm	*Lesnaya promyshlennost'*
LitGaz	*Literaturnaya gazeta*
Lit i Isk	*Literatura i iskusstvo*
Lit i Zh	*Literatura i zhizn'*
LitLen	*Literaturnyy Leningrad*
LitOb	*Literaturnoe obozrenie*
LitR	*Literaturnaya Rossiya*
LitTat	*Literaturnyy Tatarstan*
M.	Moscow
M	*Metel'* (Moscow, 1940)
MosBol	*Moskovskiy bol'shevik*
MosKom	*Moskovskiy komsomolets*
MosPr	*Moskovskaya pravda*
NLP	*Na literaturnom postu*
NM	*Novyy mir*
Og	*Ogonek*

Okt	*Oktyabr'*
Pr	*Pravda*
RabGaz	*Rabochaya gazeta*
RP	*Rannyaya proza* (Moscow, 1986)
RabM	*Rabochaya Moskva*
RusLit	*Russkaya literatura*
SevD	*Severnyy den'*
SevU	*Severnoe utro*
SEEJ	*Slavic and East European Journal*
SovIsk	*Sovetskoe iskusstvo*
Sovkul't	*Sovetskaya kul'tura*
SovR	*Sovetskaya Rossiya*
SovT	*Sovetskiy teatr*
T	*Teatr*
Tzh	*Teatral'naya zhizn'*
30 dney	*Tridtsat' dney*
TLS	*Times Literary Supplement*
UchGaz	*Uchitel'skaya gazeta*
VechM	*Vechernyaya Moskva*
VopLit	*Voprosy literatury*
ZarV	*Zarya vostoka*
Zn	*Znamya*
ZK	*Zolotaya Kareta* (Moscow, 1946)
Zv	*Zvezda*

Notes

PREFACE

1 Leonid Leonov, *Piramida* (M., 1994), vol. 2, p. 33.
2 Quoted from Oleg Mikhaylov, *Mirozdanie po Leonidu Leonovu: lichnost' i tvorchestvo: ocherki* (M., 1987), p. 123.

CHAPTER 1   Early Years and Literary Debut

1 The main sources for Leonov's early years are the introduction that he wrote for the 1954 edition of *The Road to Ocean* (*Doroga na Okean*, 1935), and an interview that he gave to E. Starikova in 1959. Both are reprinted in *Sovetskie pisateli: Avtobiografii* (M., 1959), vol. 1, pp. 660–6. See also *Leonid Leonov v vospominaniyakh, dnevnikakh, interv'yu*, ed. Viktor Petelin (M., 1999), pp. 5–22.
2 For a discussion of Maksim Leonov's poetry see V.A. Kovalev, *Tvorchestvo Leonida Leonova: k kharakteristike tvorcheskoi individual'nosti pisatelia* (M.-L., 1962), pp. 8–19, and V.A. Kovalev, 'Poet-surikovets M. L. Leonov' (*RusLit*, 1957), no. 1, pp. 257–9. A selection of Maksim Leonov's poetry can be found in *I. Z. Surikov i poety-surikovtsy* (M.-L., 1966), pp. 374–80.
3 S.P. Mel'gunov is mistaken in asserting that Maksim Leonov was executed by the Bolsheviks in 1920 (see *Krasnyy terror v Rossii 1918–1923*, Berlin, 1924, p. 96), though it is clear that he had some difficulties with the regime in the 1920s. He was arrested twice, the second time resulting in a lengthy prison sentence, which seriously weakened his health. In the later 1920s he worked as a salesman in a toyshop (*I. Z. Surikov i poety-surikovtsy*, p. 374). For more on Maksim Leonov's later life see *Leonid Leonov v vospominaniyakh...*, pp. 169–71, 540.
4 A striking illustration of this can be found in *The Russian Forest*, where Vikhrov reflects:

> I lost my mother when I was young... I don't remember if I ever managed to say a kind word to her. A peasant's mother is his closest contact with nature, and possibly this is why I still feel her mournful scrutinizing gaze, as though I was leaving home for ever. You can never escape from her any more than from the sky. This is why Russians feel the need of constant contact with their country; this is why Russians feel so lost when they are abroad.

(Leonid Leonov, *Sobranie sochineniy*, 10 vols. M., 1981–4, vol. 9, p. 284. In future all quotations will be taken from this edition unless otherwise specified, and will be indicated in the text by volume and page numbers.)

For a time it is not clear whose 'gaze' Vikhrov is aware of, since the antecedent of 'her' is ambiguous. At first it appears to refer to the mother, but gradually it emerges that Leonov is speaking of his country, or rather of nature. The Russian sense of motherland is well known, but it is difficult to think of another Russian writer for whom it would supplant even his own mother.

A portrait of Mariya Petrova in her youth can be found in F. Kh. Vlasov, *Poeziya zhizni* (M., 1961), opp., p. 48.

5 In the Soviet period Leonov made arrangements for her housing in Moscow.
6 This is generally agreed to be a poem, 'Vecherom,' published on 4 July 1915. In 1913, however, Maksim Leonov had published excerpts from his son's letters, describing the strikes and disturbances in Moscow (*see SevU*, 25 and 26 Sept. 1913). Technically these were Leonov's first publications, but they were hardly intended as such (see V.A. Kovalev, *Leonid Leonov: Seminariy*, M.-L., 1982, p. 11).
7 One of his teachers at this school, Nikolay Platonovich Kul'kov, is commemorated in the story *The Taking of Velikoshumsk* (1944).
8 In later life Leonov retained these talents. He possessed a fine singing voice, he was an excellent photographer, and he became a skilled carver in wood. His children inherited some of these artistic gifts. The older daughter, Elena Leonidovna (1929–1999), was a painter, and the younger, Natal'ya Leonidovna, is an architect and poet.
9 M. Leonov, 'Zavet synu' (*SevU*, 4 Sept. 1915). The poem is quoted in Z. Boguslavskaya, *Leonid Leonov* (M., 1962), p. 4.
10 *SevU*, 15 March 1917.
11 *SevD*, 9 June 1918, 'Otgoloski zhizni.' *Severnoe utro* changed its name to *Severnyy den'* in April 1918.
12 L. Fink, *Dramaturgiya Leonida Leonova* (M., 1962), pp. 17–18.
13 *SevD*, 1 May 1918. The book was said to be coming out in the next few days with an introduction by Anatoliy Dobrokhotov.
14 Mikhaylov, *Mirozdanie po Leonovu...*, p. 21. Natal'ya Leonova told me that she had heard nothing of her father's attempt to contact Bryusov, but she knew that he

had visited Khodasevich with a selection of his poems. Khodasevich told him to come back later, but Leonov never did. He had a similar experience with the artist Favorsky in 1921 after demobilization.
15 The following account of the Allied intervention in the Archangel region is based on George Kennan, *Russia and the West under Lenin and Stalin* (New York, 1961), pp. 65–90.
16 Their leader, General E. Miller, escaped but was later kidnapped in Paris and taken back to the Soviet Union, where he was executed.
17 *Leonid Leonov v vospominaniyakh...*, p. 16.
18 Ibid., p. 169.
19 'Zapis' na bereste. Poema Leonida Leonova,' *30 dney*, 1926, no. 1, pp. 45–50. The poem is dedicated to 'M.V.S-u,' presumably his father-in-law, Mikhail Sabashnikov. The dating of the poem's composition is taken from V.A. Kovalev, *Leonid Leonov: Seminariy* (1982), p. 14. The complete text of the poem is printed in the appendix.
20 See L. Fink, *Dramaturgiya Leonida Leonova*, pp. 18–21.
21 *30 dney*, 1926, no. 1, p. 45.
22 Ibid., p. 46.
23 Ibid., p. 47.
24 Ibid., p. 50.
25 Ibid.
26 Ibid., pp. 45–6.
27 For some of Leonov's reminiscences of this period see *Leonid Leonov v vospominaniyakh...*, pp. 54–61.
28 For a detailed study of Leonov's work on Red Army newspapers see V.A. Kovalev, 'Leonid Leonov – sotrudnik krasnoarmeyskhikh gazet,' *Voprosy sovetskoy literatury*, vol. 1 (M.-L., 1962), pp. 329–41, and S. Ya. Yakovlev, 'Pervye shagi (k nachalu publitsicheskoy deyatel'nosti Leonova)' in *Tvorchestvo Leonida Leonova: Issledovaniya i soobshcheniya*, ed. V.A. Kovalev (L., 1969), pp. 395–430.
29 'Tebe, nashemu,' *KrVoin*, 12 Oct. 1921.
30 See S. Romov, 'Vstrecha s Leonidom Leonovym,' *LitGaz*, 24 Sept. 1930. For clarification see *Leonid Leonov v vospominaniyakh...*, p. 27.
31 Leonov's first published story, *Buryga*, is dedicated to Falileev.
32 The story *Petushikhinskiy prolom* is dedicated to Ostroukhov.
33 Mikhaylov, *Mirozdanie...*, p. 39.
34 The story *Gibel' Egorushki* is dedicated to Sabashnikov.
35 For an account of the Sabashnikov family and in particular of their publishing house see *Zapiski Mikhaila Sabashnikova*, ed. A.L. Panina and T.G. Pereslegina (Moscow, 1995).
36 Leonov and his wife were married in church, a brave and provocative gesture at

the time. See Leonov's remark to Blinov 'How does a man feel who has not sanctified his marriage in church?' (*O Leonove*, e.d V. Chivilikhin, Moscow, 1979, p. 42).

37 See *Tvorchestvo Leonida Leonova* (1969), p. 416.
38 For a selection of Gor'ky's correspondence with Soviet writers in these years see *Gor'ky i sovetskie pisateli. Neizdannaya perepiska, Literaturnoe nasledstvo*, vol. 70 (M.-L., 1963).
39 The origins of Proletkul't go back to 1910, when Lunacharsky, Gor'ky, and Bogdanov conceived the idea of opening a school for the education of Russian proletarians on the isle of Capri. The project came to nothing at the time, largely because of Lenin's implacable opposition to it. It was revived, however, in 1917 under the Provisional government, when Lunacharsky became commissar for education and culture.
40 For a detailed study of the history and profile of this journal see Robert A. Maguire, *Red Virgin Soil* (Princeton, 1968).
41 See 'O politike partii v oblasti khudozhestvennoy literatury,' *Pr*, 1 July 1925. This statement was drawn up by Bukharin, probably with the assistance of Trotsky.
42 In the first edition of *Tuatamur* even the chapters were headed by numerals in Arabic script.
43 N. Smirnov, 'Leonid Leonov,' *Izv*, 18 Aug. 1924. But see A.K. Voronsky, 'Literaturnye siluety,' *KN*, 1924, no. 3, for a deeper analysis of Leonov's early stories.
44 In the West this view has been expressed by Helen Muchnic in her essay on Leonov in *From Gorky to Pasternak* (London, 1963).
45 N.A. Groznova, 'Leonid Leonov – grani leonovskoy metafiziki,' in *Nauchno delo akademika Milosava Babovicha* (Podgoritsa, 1996), p. 21.
46 See, for example, V. L'vov-Rogachevsky, *Revolyutsiya i russkaya literatura* (M., 1923), vol. 2, p. 82.
47 Aleksey Mikhailovich's traditional epithet is 'Tishayshiy' (the Quiet One), again recalling the importance of silence in early Leonov.
48 The name is derived from the Latin name Justinus, and so is as ironic as Bald Mitrokha's adoption of the name of the first high priest of Israel.
49 Leonov's use of the image of the 'wolf' is not unusual in early Soviet literature. It is used with very much the same connotations by Pil'nyak, notably in his novel *Machines and Wolves (Mashiny i volki*, 1924), and by Esenin (see, for example, his poem, 'Mir tainstvennyy, mir moy drevniy...,' 1922).
50 The classic statement of this idea may be found in an early story of Leskov, which contains a legend of how the various nations receive their traditional occupations from God: the English are associated with commerce, the French with military prowess, but the Russians distinguish themselves by thieving, and receive God's

blessing for it: 'Go out and steal all your life long.' See M. Stebnitsky [pseud. of N.S. Leskov], 'V tarantase' (In the Carriage), *Severnaya pchela*, 1862, no. 119. Similar comments on the thieving propensities of the Russian people can be found in other Leskov stories, e.g., *The Spendthrift* (*Rastochitel'*, 1863), *Shameless* (*Besstydnik*, 1877), *Choice Grain* (*Otbornoe zerno*, 1884), and *The Life of a Peasant Woman* (*Zhitie odnoy baby*, 1863).

Similar sentiments can be found in Pil'nyak: 'You won't win yourself a stone palace by honest work – if you're not caught you're no thief; an object in Russia has only two purposes, one is its nominal function, the other to be stolen...' in *Machines and Wolves* (*Sobranie sochineniy* (M.-L., 1930), p. 20.

The anecdote of Vertinsky's return to Russia from emigration further illustrates the prevalence of this myth. At the border he looked around at the Russian landscape which he had not seen for some twenty years and commented: 'Somehow I don't recognize my country.' He then knelt down to kiss the earth. When he rose he looked round once again and saw that his luggage had been stolen while he was on his knees. 'Now I recognize my country,' he remarked.

51 The story was first published in *KN* (1924), no. 4. In 1959 it was substantially revised, with the latter sections completely rewritten.
52 *The End of a Petty Man* is generally taken to be the first of Leonov's works devoted to the intelligentsia. But there is an earlier story, 'Professor Ivan Platonych,' which I have not seen. For a discussion of this story see V.P. Krylov, 'Vremya, geroy, ideal khudozhnika' in *Tvorchestvo Leonida Leonova* (1969), pp. 18–21.
53 This was first pointed out by Nathan Rosen in his unpublished PhD dissertation, 'The Fiction of Leonid Leonov' (Columbia University, 1961), p. 29.
54 F.M. Dostoevsky, *Polnoe sobranie sochineniy*, 30 vols. (L. 1972–87), vol. 5, p. 113. Henceforth this edition will be abbreviated to *PSS*, followed by volume and page number.
55 This gesture is explicitly identified in another part of *Notes from the Underground*: 'Two times two equals four is all the same quite insufferable. Two times two blocks your path, looks like a *fert* with his hands on his hips and spitting...' (*PSS*, vol. 5, p. 119). Leonov's *fert* prefers to sit on the bed with his legs crossed, like Ivan Karamazov's devil.
56 The motif of 'bricks' also has its origin in *Notes from the Underground*, cf. 'And so long as I live and have desires, may my arm wither up if I ever consent to bring a single brick (*kirpichik*) to this building' (Dostoevsky, *PSS*, vol. 5, p. 120). The word is quite common in Soviet literature of the '20s and can usually be traced back to this source. Thus the citizen-numbers of Zamyatin's *We* (*My*, 1920) are called 'bricks' (*My*, New York, 1952, p. 128); see also Pil'nyak's story *At the Door* (*Pri dveryakh*, 1919). It is used quite unironically, however, in Nikolay Ostrovsky's *How the Steel Was Tempered* (*Kak zakalyalas' stal'*, 1934–6).

57 Leonid Leonov, *Sobranie sochineniy*, 5 vols. (Khar'kov, M.-L., 1928–30), vol. I, p. 253. This episode was omitted in the 1959 revision.
58 Cf. Gor'ky's words of 1919: 'The Russian worker-socialist has attracted the attention of the whole world. He is as it were sitting an exam in political maturity in full view of the world, and he is showing himself publicly to be the creator of new forms of life...' in 'Sovetskaya Rossiya i narody mira,' *Sobranie sochineniy v tridtsati tomakh* (M., 1949–55), vol. 24, p. 195. Henceforth this edition will be referred to as *SS*.
59 Leonov, *Sobranie sochineniy* (1928–30), vol. I, p. 233.
60 Ibid., p. 228.
61 Ibid., p. 247.
62 See A. Pridorogin, 'Leonid Leonov,' *Knigonosha* (1925), no. 31–2. Kovalev notes that Leonov had indeed seen such a work, *Stikhotvoreniya kuptsa-samouchki M.A. Polikarpova, s ego avtobiografiey* (St Petersburg, 1908). See his *Romany Leonida Leonova* (M.-L., 1954), p. 19.
63 Leonov, *Sobranie sochineniy* (1928–30), vol. I, p. 249.
64 Similar interpretations of Darwinism can be found in other Soviet works of the period, e. g., Pil'nyak's *The Snowstorm* (*Metel'*, 1921), in which the origin of life is traced back to '*ozorstvo*' (irreverent brashness, cheek). See Peter Alberg Jensen, *Nature as Code: The Achievement of Boris Pil'njak 1915–1924* (Copenhagen, 1979), p. 61. Leonov's interest in Darwin reappears in *The Russian Forest* and *The Pyramid*.
65 Compare: '[The International] is eaten with gunpowder [...] and spiced with the best blood' in Isaak Babel''s story *Gedali* (I. Babel', *Izbrannoe*, M., 1968, p. 52).
66 Compare the dedication of 'Khalil'': 'Let me present you with fourteen *kasydas* about Khalil', of whom no memory has remained in men's hearts, because he did not shed another's blood and did not crush other people's hearts with his vain dreams and did not build unneeded cities.' The story was dedicated to Leonov's future wife, Tat'yana Sabashnikova.
67 Kovalev says that this story originated in a long poem 'Earth' (*Zemlya*) written in 1916 (see his *Tvorchestvo Leonida Leonova*, 1962, p. 24). According to Mikhaylov (*Mirozdanie po Leonovu...*, pp. 39–40) Leonov turned to Gershenzon for Jewish interpretations of the Flood.
68 Among many tributes one should single out Zamyatin's praise in 1923. See 'Novaya russkaya proza,' *Russkoe iskusstvo*, 1923, no. 2/3, pp. 57–67.
69 Boguslavskaya, *Leonid Leonov*, p. 17.

CHAPTER 2 *The Badgers* 1924

1 First published in a slightly shortened version in *KN*, 1924, nos. 6 and 7–8. The

KN edition omits from part 3 the three inserted stories in chapters 4, 5, and 6, and chapter 13, 'Egor Brykin loses the thread of his life.' The *KN* text was substantially revised for the first complete edition, which came out in book form in the following year. The first part, in particular, was drastically shortened though without any significant change to the overall sense; the second part has been left largely unaltered; the third part again shows several differences, mostly of a stylistic character, but some of them do serve to reinterpret events and motivations. The cuts and changes involved are aimed mainly at curbing the stylistic and narrative exuberance of the young author; in some cases details that might be thought mildly risqué, such as Katya's seduction of Semen, were modified. Leonov continued to make revisions to the novel in later years, some of them clearly under the pressure of the censorship.

2 There is some confusion over the dating. Most critics set the last two sections in 1920–1. This agrees with the historical conditions of the period. The few chronological indications in the novel, however (the Great War breaks out just five years after the beginning of the novel, and the later action begins just twelve years after the beginning), would make 1921–2 the only consistent dating for the latter part of the book. Of Soviet critics only A.K. Simonova sets the revolt of the Badgers in these years. See her article 'Barsuki,' *Nauchnye trudy*, Erevanskiy gosudarstvennyy universitet, vol. 66, vyp. 6, ch. 1 (Erevan, 1958).

3 In 1958 the Moscow City Council planned to pull down the Zaryad'e area, but was prevented from doing so by a protest of 71 Soviet artists, among them Leonov. See *New York Times*, 6 April 1958, p. 26. It was, however, eventually demolished to make way for the hotel Rossiya.

4 E. Starikova in Leonid Leonov, *Sobranie sochineniy*, 9 vols. (M., 1962), vol. 2, p. 359.

5 When in 1925 Leonov was invited by the Vakhtangov Theatre to adapt his novel for the stage his first thought was to return to his original plan and construct the play round Brykin. In the event he was overruled (see L. Leonov, 'Ot romana k p'ese,' *SovT*, 1927, no. 5, p. 70), but the very possibility of such a thought shows that he still saw the figure of Brykin as central to his conception. By now, as will be seen, the type of Brykin had acquired a different significance.

6 Kovalev, *Tvorchestvo Leonida Leonova* (1962), p. 42.

7 The idea is taken up again when the two brothers meet for the last time in Zaryad'e and listen to a barrel organ 'playing something melancholy and discordant such as blind beggars sing at a fair' (2. 64). This is the only reference to the song in the novel. In the stage version, however, Leonov directed that it should be sung sporadically throughout the performance.

8 See, for example, Pil'nyak's *Machines and Wolves*, Erenburg's *The Grabber* (*Rvach*, 1925), and Fedin's *The Brothers* (*Brat'ya*, 1928), some of the many works on this theme composed in the decade.

9 See Hongor Oulanoff, *The Prose Fiction of Veniamin A. Kaverin* (Cambridge, Mass., 1976), pp. 82–3.
10 On the other hand, when the Communists were identified as 'Bolsheviks' the Slavic origin of the word was more likely to attract peasant sympathy. Hence the slogan attested by many writers, among them Pil'nyak in *The Naked Year* (*Golyy god*, 1922): 'We are against the Communists but for the Bolsheviks.'
11 The story is said to be based on a poem, since lost, that Leonov wrote in 1916. See Kovalev, *Leonid Leonov: Seminariy* (1982), p. 12. This chapter was omitted from the *KN* edition, but references to the story elsewhere in the novel were retained.
12 It is interesting to note that Kalafat is called *duraley* (fool). This unusual word is also used by Esenin in his poem 'Sorokoust'(1920) for the foal that tries to race against the locomotive. In Leonov the word is applied to the rationalistic twentieth-century mentality that vainly tries to outwit nature, and so acquires just the opposite sense.
13 Groznova has shown that in Dostoevsky, the myth of the Tower of Babel is associated with the ambition of reaching Heaven by purely materialistic means, so obviating any need for religion. (See her *Tvorchestvo Leonova i traditsii russkoy klassicheskoy literatury: ocherki*, M., 1982, pp. 173–81.)
14 Czeslaw Andruszko identifies Kalafat with Peter the Great. (See his book *Romany Leonida Leonova 20–kh godov*, Poznan', 1985, p. 46). This is not wrong; as in *The Breakthrough at Petushikha*, Peter the Great is seen as the ideological ancestor of the Revolution, but his agency here is only indirect. The direct target of the legend is the city, which is identified with the Communists.
15 *Barsuki* (M., 1950), pp. 256–7. Compare *Barsuki* (M., 1952), pp. 263–4, and all subsequent editions.
16 See, for example, the early works of Pil'nyak, Nikitin, Fedin, and Vsevolod Ivanov.
17 This has led one critic to speculate on his tendencies towards homosexuality. See Dale Plank, 'Unconscious Motifs in Leonid Leonov's *The Badgers*,' *SEEJ*, vol. 16, no. 1 (spring, 1972), pp. 19–35.
18 It is then significant that both Semen and Brykin re-enter the novel in part 2 limping. Brykin is simply malingering, but Semen's injury is real enough, like his bleeding leg at the end of the novel. It leaves open the possibility of seeing Semen too as a martyr.
19 For a similar episode used in a similar way see Boris Pil'nyak's story, 'Times and Dates' (*Chisla i sroki*, 1921, in *Sobranie sochineniy*, 1930, vol. 8, p. 183). Compare also the origins of the feud between Il'ichevsky and Barsukov (Badger) in Kuzmin's story, 'Raid on the Barsukovs' ('Nabeg na Barsukovykh'): 'The origins of this dispute had been long forgotten; they went back at least to the grandfathers and probably consisted in the unfair division of some piece of land, the mowing

of a neighbour's meadow [...] trifles to our mind, that had become blood-feuds,' M. Kuzmin, *Proza*, vol. 4 (Berkeley, 1985), p. 299. In Esenin's play *The Land of Scoundrels* (*Strana negodyaev* 1922–3) one of the rebels is called Barsuk.

20 This is one way of looking at the Marxist theory of history, as a natural evolutionary process. Before the end of the 1920s, however, the emphasis in the Soviet Union had shifted to stressing the role of human will and intellect in shaping and accelerating the slow and even reactionary processes of nature.

21 For an extended discussion of this scene see Groznova, *Tvorchestvo Leonida Leonova i traditsii* ... pp. 158–91.

22 At the end of the novel one of the peasants says to Semen: 'You don't understand the peasant heart' (2. 338).

23 The reader has no doubt that as the game continues the moon will emerge from behind the clouds. Only Semen does not lift his head to look at it. The suggestion of a moon-Zhibanda parallel introduces the motif of the 'elusive bandit' who defies all efforts of the authorities to catch him. For examples in early Soviet literature see Esenin's *Land of Scoundrels* and Sel'vinsky's *Ulyalaev Rebellion* (*Ulyalaevshchina*, 1924). For obvious reasons this motif disappears from Soviet literature before the end of the decade.

24 *KN*, 1924, no. 6, p. 3. The quotation has been taken from the *KN* edition. The slight differences from the eventual book version give some idea of the stylistic revision to which Leonov subjected the first part of the novel.

25 One may also note the ironic wit with which Leonov follows up the word 'potikhon'ku' (in a quiet way) with its apparent antonym 'gorlanil' (bawled).

26 In part 2 of the novel Brykin's name appears in 10 of the 15 chapters, Semen's in only 8. It is part 1 that places Semen so much in the centre of events that one naturally focuses on him in later sections.

27 Pil'nyak's novel is itself composed out a number of short stories, some of which had been published independently, some of them even before 1917.

28 See for example, G. Lelevich, 'Barsuki,' *SovIsk*, 1925, no. 2, and G. Kolesnikova, '*Barsuki*. Roman Leonida Leonova,' *Okt*, 1925, no. 9–10.

29 A. Voronsky, 'Literaturnye zametki,' *Prozhektor*, 1925, no. 5, and V. Lunin, 'Barsuki,' *Knigonosha*, 1925, no. 29.

30 M. Gor'ky, letter of 8 Sept. 1925, *SS*, vol. 29, pp. 441–2.

31 P.S. Kogan, 'O leonovshchine,' *KrGaz (vech)*, 1 July 1925.

32 The play was first performed in the Vakhtangov Theatre on 22 Sept. 1927 in a production by B.A. Zakhava. The text of the play was first published in Leonid Leonov, *P'esy* (M., 1935). This text is very different from the one that was actually used by the Vakhtangov Theatre and still survives in the archives there. The play was subjected to a further stylistic revision before being republished in *Teatr*, the two-volume collection of Leonov's plays published in 1961.

33 But see Fink, *Dramaturgiya...*, pp. 74–8 for an interesting defence of the play.

34 A. Lunacharsky, 'Barsuki,' *KrGaz (vech)*, 14 Oct. 1927.
35 V. Golubov, 'Barsuki,' *Zhizn' iskusstva*, 1929, no. 13.

CHAPTER 3 *The Thief* 1927

1 Sergey Esenin, *Sobranie sochineniy*, 5 vols. (M., 1961–2), vol. 4, p. 205. Vekshin is addressed as 'Hamlet' in the novel *Vor* (M.-L., 1928), p. 479. All subsequent page references to this edition of the novel will be included in the text.
2 The novel was first published in *KN*, 1927, nos. 1–7. The version accepted by the editors was ready by 18 October 1926; but Leonov continued to work on the text, and the definitive version was ready only on 22 March 1927, by which time two instalments had already appeared. It came out in book form later in the same year. There are many differences between these two versions, particularly in the first 23 chapters of part 1, i.e., those contained in the first two issues of *KN*. In 1959 Leonov released the novel in a new and drastically revised version. This was in turn further modified in new editions of 1982 and 1990. These will be examined in chapter 12.
3 As prophesied in the text this name was changed shortly after the book came out; in 1928 the region was renamed Stalinskaya. It is known today as Baumanskaya.
4 Boris Pasternak, *Doktor Zhivago* (Milan, 1957), p. 477.
5 The name Vekshin comes from *veksha*, a northern name for a squirrel. Since the verb 'metat'sya' is frequently used of him, the choice of name is perhaps intended to evoke the idiom, 'metat'sya kak belka v kolese' – to run like a squirrel in a wheel, an image of ceaseless but fruitless activity. The root *vek-* also suggests that he embodies the problems of the age.
6 Compare Aleksey Tolstoy's stories 'Azure Cities' (*Golubye goroda*, 1925) and 'The Viper' (*Gadyuka*, 1928) for other studies of this type.
7 It is usually assumed that Vekshin has gone to Siberia, but in fact he gets off the train after little more than a day. This would not be enough to get him to Siberia. In the 1959 version he travels for 'several' days.
8 The Russian for this expression, '*vpered i vverkh*,' echoes Gor'ky's prose-poem 'Man' (*Chelovek*, 1903), with its refrain of 'onwards and higher' (*vpered! – i – vyshe!*). Leonov's use of this motif has been studied by Helen Muchnic in her chapter on him in *From Gorky to Pasternak*.
9 The image plays an important structural role in the novel. Almost all the characters are associated in one way or another with the motif of 'stealing.' Even the novelist Firsov calls himself a thief, 'only my thefts are never noticed' (117). Cognates of words associated with stealing, such as *vorovski* and *kraduchis'* (stealthily) occur frequently.
10 Mayakovsky's poem, 'Conversation with the Tax-Inspector about Poetry'

('Razgovor s fininspektorom' o poezii, 1926), is a well-known complaint on this theme. For Leonov's own problems with the tax collector Filimonov see Kovalev, *Etyudy o Leonide Leonove* (M., 1978), p. 260, and Mikhaylov, *Mirozdanie po Leonovu...*, pp. 71–2.

11 This is not explicit in any of the versions of the novel. Leonov makes the point in his interview with Inna Rostovtseva, 'Negativ, proyavlennyy vechnost'yu,' *LitGaz*, 1 June 1994.
12 Vera Alexandrova has mentioned Grushen'ka in *The Brothers Karamazov* in this connection. Another influence is Blok: Masha's name in the underworld is Man'ka-V'yuga (Mary the Blizzard), an allusion to the erotic associations of the snowstorm in Blok's poetry, notably in the cycle 'The Snow Mask' (*Snezhnaya maska*, 1907), and its revolutionary connotations in *The Twelve* (*Dvenadtsat'*, 1918).
13 See 'Nashi pisateli o klassikakh,' *NLP*, 1927, no. 5–6, p. 57. Leonov first read Dostoevsky when he was 13, and he gave a paper on his work to a school seminar in 1917. See Groznova, *Tvorchestvo Leonida Leonova i traditsii...*, p. 37.
14 His double Aggey declares that he lost his sense of right and wrong when his commanding officer praised him for killing an enemy soldier: 'But, I said, I've killed a man, your Excellency' [...] I spent three days inside for those words, and really I'd enjoyed it. It's easy work, and you get medals for it' (128).
15 This subject was first discussed in E. Polyakova, 'Dostoevsky v otrazhenii sovremennikov,' *Literatura i Marksizm*, 1929, no. 6.
16 Even his initials, F. F. F. (the letter 'f' or 'fert'), which are to a Russian eye grotesque, make it difficult to take him entirely seriously. This is not, however, intended to suggest that the doubling of the two novelists implies any diabolical relationship between them.
17 A parallel to this device can be found in André Gide's novel *Les Faux-Monnayeurs* (1925); the novel was translated into Russian by A. Frankovsky and published by the 'Academia' press in Leningrad in 1926. Leonov told me that he had never heard of the novel, but this is perhaps to be explained by forgetfulness, since the similarity had been pointed out by critics in the 1920s. It is noteworthy too that the subject of Gide's novelist, 'the struggle between what reality offers him and what he himself desires to make of it' (*The Coiners*, trans. Dorothy Bussy, London, 1950, p. 207), is one of the chief problems worked out by Leonov in the person of Firsov.
18 The last sentence of this passage was added only in the first book-publication of the novel.
19 This device is also found in Sel'vinsky's novel in verse, *Fur-trade* (*Pushtorg*, 1927).
20 Compare '... un roman est un miroir qui se promène sur une grande route. Tantôt

il reflète à vos yeux l'azur des cieux, tantôt la fange des bourbiers de la route. Et l'homme qui porte le miroir dans sa hotte sera par vous accusé d'être immoral. Son miroir montre la fange, et vous accusez le miroir!' Stendhal, *Le Rouge et le noir*, part 2, chap. 19. Leonov's admiration for Stendhal is confirmed in an interview with Kovalev (see *Tvorchestvo Leonida Leonova...*, 1962, p. 142).

21 This should not be taken as an attack on film as such. Leonov regularly refers to Firsov as *sochinitel'*, a word which for all its disparaging connotations was adopted by Dziga Vertov as a self-description. The most intelligent review of Firsov's novel singles out its cinematic qualities (459).

22 *NLP*, 1927, 5/6, p. 57.

23 In the *KN* version the sickness of the tree is attributed also to the depredations of a passing peasant and a monk hoping to tap it for syrup. The omission of these two culprits from the book version leaves the responsibility entirely on the agitator.

The image of the tree and revolutionary propaganda had been anticipated by Khlebnikov: 'On the blue bark of a marsh-birch I scratched the names of ships taken from a chronicle [...] Which is stronger: the simple-hearted birch or the fury of a sea of iron?' V. V. Khlebnikov, 'Vlom vselennoy' (c. 1921), *Sobranie sochineniy*, 5 vols. (1928–33), vol. 3, p. 94.

24 At the end of the novel, when Vekshin is travelling eastwards to begin a new life, he dreams that Zavarikhin is travelling in the same train. The point of this allusion is obscure. Some critics have taken it as a prophecy that Zavarikhin himself would end up in Siberia. But in the dream Zavarikhin is free: he is playing his accordion and swinging his legs, and, of course, Vekshin himself is travelling voluntarily. I take it rather as an allusion to the parallelism between the two characters. Zavarikhin also has the potential to begin a new and totally unforeseen way of life. In view of his fate in the 1959 revision of the novel – when he *is* sent to Siberia – some critics have been tempted to read this back into the earlier edition.

25 Sergey Romov, 'Vstrecha s Leonidom Leonovym,' *LitGaz*, 24 Sept. 1930. Leonov is commenting on a passage in *The Thief* (see p. 281).

26 In connection with Leonov's interest in the 'acquisition of culture,' Kovalev has some valuable observations to make on the concept of the 'primitive' or 'elemental' mentality current in Soviet psychology of the 1920s. Some of these ideas are undoubtedly relevant to the figure of Vekshin. See Kovalev, *Tvorchestvo Leonida Leonova...* (1962), pp. 237–43.

27 See Dostoevsky, *PSS*, vol. 14, p. 100.

28 This motif of the pass through the mountains (or, sometimes, tunnel) becomes still more important in Leonov's later work. It probably originates in Serafimovich's novel *The Iron Flood* (*Zheleznyy potok*, 1922).

29 The exotic patronymic is another Dostoevskian fingerprint in *The Thief*; often it is more suggestive than the first name or family names.
30 Compare the self-portrait of the petty clerk Okonnyy, who dreams of being the Napoleonic leader of a counter-revolution against Soviet power: 'Like a dead fly in a jar I sleepwalked in a commercial bank, counting up other people's roubles. Akakiy Akakievich? Makarushka Devushkin [the hero of Dostoevsky's first story, *Poor Folk*? in Il'ya Sel'vinsky, *Komandarm – 2* (M., 1928), p. 22.
31 See also the sarcastic reference to 'the official campaign for the rosy-cheeked' (468).
32 Compare Shigalev's ideas in Dostoevsky's *The Devils*:
> Each member of society keeps an eye on every other, and is required to report on him. Each belongs to all, and all to each. All are slaves and equal in their slavery [...] the main thing is equality. The first thing is to lower the quality of education, science and talent. A higher level of science and talent is accessible only to those with higher abilities, but we don't need these higher abilities. They have always grabbed power and turned into despots. Higher abilities cannot but be despotic, and have always brought more harm than benefits. They are to be exiled or executed. Cicero will have his tongue cut out, Copernicus his eyes gouged out, Shakespeare stoned to death: that's Shigalev for you. Slaves must be equal: without despotism there has never been any freedom or equality... (Dostoevsky, *PSS*, vol. 10, p. 322)

The similarities between Shigalev and Chikilev have been pointed out by many critics, among them Gleb Struve (in *Twenty-five Years of Soviet Russian Literature 1918–1943*, London, 1946, p. 48). Names on the pattern of Ch–v are given to many of Leonov's more sinister characters: Chervakov, Chirkhanov, Cheredilov. Cherimov in *Skutarevsky* also belongs in this family.
33 So too Shigalev had suggested
> dividing mankind into two unequal parts. Ten per cent will receive personal freedom and unlimited rights over the other ninety per cent, who will have to surrender their individuality and turn into something like a herd; through total obedience and after a series of transformations they will achieve a primal innocence, similar to that of the Garden of Eden, though, admittedly, they will have to work. (Dostoevsky, *PSS*, vol. 10, p. 312)
34 The Russian word for this concept is usually the neutral *ravenstvo*, but other words are *uravnenie* and *uravnilovka*. The former suggests some kind of mathematical process of evening out the differences between people; the latter (which occurs only twice in the novel) carries strongly negative connotations, and is generally denounced in Soviet writings, at least since the end of the 1920s as a petty-bourgeois heresy, no better than its near anagram *nivelirovka* or 'levelling.'
35 Apparently this aphorism was contributed by Leonov's wife (*Leonid Leonov v*

vospominaniyakh..., p. 454). It had, however, been anticipated by Nietzsche: 'This revolting feeling is the summit of envy, which argues: because there is *something* I cannot have, the whole world shall have *nothing*! The whole world shall *be* nothing!' (See Aphorism, no. 304, *Daybreak*, trans. R. J. Hollingdale, Cambridge, 1982, pp. 304–5.)

36 Many years later, in conversation with Kovalev, Leonov remarked: 'I failed to make Vekshin's main aspiration clear, his envy of those who possess culture (an envy quite different from the envy of Chikilev, who would like to reduce all cultured people to his own level), and his turn towards culture.' See Kovalev, *Tvorchestvo Leonida Leonova...* (1962), pp. 236–7.

The mention of envy naturally recalls Yuriy Olesha's novel of that name. But there is an important difference. In Olesha it is the intellectual Kavalerov who is envious of the new world. In Leonov it is the new rulers who are envious of the culture of the past.

37 E. Zamyatin, *My* (New York, 1952), p. 6. For further examples see the idea of standardizing all noses (ibid., pp.10–11), the idea of the Benefactor as a 'Tamerlane of happiness' (ibid., p. 73), and the 'rubbery, round and ruddy cheeks, the foreheads, unshadowed by the madness of thought.' (ibid.)

38 N.I. Bukharin and E. Preobrazhensky, *Azbuka kommunizma.* (n.p., 1921), p.49.

39 Ibid., p.50

40 Ibid., p. 115–6.

41 Ibid., p. 116.

42 Some of these words have since acquired additional meanings that can hardly have been foreseen at the time of writing. Lighting fixtures came to be used for concealing bugging devices, and 'goloshes' became Soviet slang for condoms.

43 This was pointed out early on by Kirpotin in his book *Romany Leonida Leonova* (M.-L., 1932), pp. 34–7. No later Soviet critic was prepared to make the point.

44 Compare the Communists Zhmakov and Bormotov in Platonov's story 'Gorod Gradov' (1926). Bormotov, like Chikilev, also lives in apartment no. 46.

45 Henry Elbaum in his unpublished PhD dissertation says that the figure of Pchkhov was based on the locksmith Vasil'ev, with whom Leonov lodged when he returned to Moscow in 1921. His name is really Pukhov, but in painting his shop sign he confuses the letters for 'u' ('у' in Cyrillic) and 'ch' ('ч'). The similarity between his name and that of the eighteenth-century peasant rebel Emel'yan Pugachev can hardly be accidental, but I do not know what to make of it.

46 This was not confirmed until the Gorbachev years. Probably the first published statement of Leonov's Christianity is to be found in Ronald Hingley, 'Leonid Leonov,' *Soviet Survey*, no. 25, 1958, pp. 69–74.

47 Compare in *We* the recognition that there can be no final revolution any more than there can be a final number (*My*, p. 149).

48 Compare Nietzsche: 'And are not all things bound fast together in such a way that this moment draws after it all future things?' in *Thus Spoke Zarathustra*, trans. R.J. Hollingdale (Harmondsworth, 1961), p. 179.
49 This philosophy had been foreshadowed in *The End of a Petty Man*: 'You have to put up with it; the world's so designed that if you pull out a single splinter the whole will collapse.' It is therefore significant that just before these words Likharev has himself sat in the 'wrong' chair:

'Sit down,' repeated Elkov, and himself sat down in a chair that had once been covered in plush, piercing his patient with a keen and agitated look.

'What are you staring at me like that for?' asked Fedor Andreich in some curiosity; he sat down in the other chair and immediately fell to the floor with the chair.

'Oh, you're a one, you've sat in the wrong chair; this one's leg has fallen off in the damp. Try this one, there's no danger in sitting on this one...' (Leonov, *Sobranie sochineniy*, 1929, vol. I, p. 227)
50 The word is associated with Agey (86) and Chikilev (112).
51 V. Ermilov, 'Problema zhivogo cheloveka v sovremennoy literature: *Vor* Leonova,' *NLP*, 1927, no. 5/6. As another critic pointed out, few literary schools have advocated the ideal of a 'dead man.' See A. Lezhnev, *Literaturnye budni* (M., 1929), p. 31.
52 Compare Dostoevsky: 'All the convicts stink like pigs and say they can't help behaving like swine, "the new man", or so they say,' *PSS*, vol. 28, bk. 1, p. 170.
53 For a detailed rebuttal of Ermilov see A. Lezhnev, *Razgovor v serdtsakh* (M., 1930), pp. 146–53.
54 See Gor'ky, *SS*, vol. 30, p. 91.
55 A sentence from *The Thief*, 'Do you know how many bullets have rusted away in pining for Mit'ka's forehead?' (*Vor*, p. 46), is quoted in Veniamin Kaverin's *Scandalist, or Evenings on Vasil'evskiy Island* (*Skandalist, ili vechera na Vasil'evskom ostrove*, 1928) as an example of the excesses of contemporary fiction. See V.A. Kaverin, *Sobranie sochineniy*, 6 vols. (M., 1963), vol. 1, p. 357.
56 See Mikhaylov, *Mirozdanie po Leonovu...*, p. 95.
57 Leonov's only publications in *KN* after 1927 were two very short stories, 'The Tramp' (*Brodyaga*) and 'Revenge'(*Mest'*) in nos. 5 and 6 respectively of 1928, and the novella *Locusts* (*Saranchuki*) in nos. 9 and 10 of 1930. Nadezhda Mandel'shtam claims that after the dismissal of Voronsky many of the *poputchiki* boycotted *KN* (see her *Vospominaniya*, New York, 1970, p. 118); but it could also be argued that some writers were actuated by self-interest.
58 In the book publication, parts 1 and 2 are virtually the same length. The disproportion between them in the *KN* version is explained by the fact that the first 23 chapters of part 1, contained in the first two instalments, were drastically cut by

Leonov before republication in book form. In February Leonov was still working on the novel and so had no time to revise the early chapters. From the March instalment onwards, however, the text is very much as it appeared in the book publication.
59 Vera Alexandrova, *A History of Soviet Literature*, trans. Mirra Ginsburg (New York, 1963), pp. 181–2.
60 Inna Rostovtseva, 'Negativ, proyavlennyy vechnost'yu,' *LitGaz*, 1 June 1994.
61 Ibid.

CHAPTER 4   Stories and Plays 1927–1928

1 Boguslavskaya, *Leonid Leonov*, p. 234.
2 Leonov told this to many people over the years, among them Harrison E. Salisbury. See his *The Soviet Union: The Fifty Years* (New York, 1967), pp. 130–1.
3 *Iz tvorcheskogo naslediya russkikh pisateley XX veka*, ed. N.A. Groznova (St Petersburg, 1995), p. 462.
4 *NLP*, 1929, no. 4/5.
5 Nadezhda Mandel'shtam, *Vospominaniya*, pp. 345–6.
6 See Leonid Leonov, 'O meshchanstve,' *NLP*, 1929, no. 6, p. 27.
7 This work exists in two forms. As a novella it was first published in *NM*, 1928, no. 1. This text has been reprinted virtually unaltered in the 1986 edition of Leonov's shorter prose, *Rannyaya proza*. References to this edition will be indicated in the text by *RP*, followed by page number. As a play it was first published in Leonid Leonov *P'esy* (M., 1935). So far as I know, it has never been performed. References to this version will be taken from the two-volume *Teatr: Dramaticheskie proizvedeniya, stat'i, rechi* (M., 1960) and indicated in the text by *Teatr*, 1 and page number.
8 First published in *KN*, 1929, no. 3. So far as I know, the play has not been performed.
9 For similar uses of the image of *tishina* in the literature of this period, see Andrey Platonov's story, *An Inhabitant of the State* (*Gosudarstvennyy zhitel'*, 1925), Tikhonov's poems, 'Silence' (*Tishina*, 1925) and 'The President's Night' (*Noch' prezidenta*, 1926), and the poetry of Mayakovsky, passim.
10 First published in *NM*, 1928, no. 12.
11 Such language is not, however, confined to this work. In *A Provincial Story* Razderishin is described in the dramatis personae as 'a young merchant of our time' (*Teatr*, 1. 97). The same type reappears in *Untilovsk* in the figure of Redkozubov.
12 *KN*, 1926, no. 8. The complete play was first published in *NM*, 1928, no. 5. The differences from the 1926 version are stylistic rather than thematic. Four different

drafts of the Arts Theatre version exist in the archives of the theatre, none of them apparently the same as the text that was published (G.N. Shcheglova, *Zhanrevo-stilevoe svoeobrazie dramaturgii Leonida Leonova*, M., 1984, p. 57). In 1947 Leonov undertook a revision of the work for a projected edition of his collected works, but after revising one and a half acts he abandoned the idea.

13 See Kovalev, *Tvorchestvo Leonida Leonova...* (1962), p.117–18. Hence the name of the town should be pronounced with the stress on the second syllable. Other associations are with 'reptile' and the French 'inutile' (ibid.).
14 The symbol is, of course, a cliché, but it may be noted that A. E. W. Hutchinson's once best-selling novel *If Winter Comes* was translated into Russian and published in 1924.
15 This device was later borrowed by Gor'ky in his play *Egor Bulychev and Others* (*Egor Bulychev i drugie*, 1932).
16 In the performance at the Moscow Arts Theatre these weaknesses were apparently accentuated by an outstanding performance by Moskvin as Chervakov. Ershov, who took the part of Buslov, was completely eclipsed according to all the critics and indeed Leonov himself. See N. Abalkin, *Sistema Stanislavskogo i sovetskiy teatr* (M., 1954), p. 240.
17 These characterizations are taken from the dramatis personae of the play (see *Teatr*, 1. 97).
18 Compare Firsov's words at the beginning of *The Thief*: 'Before me the open spaces of virgin land, sufficient for man to be born on, suffer his fill and die. Above me, in the expanses mirrored a thousand times in every direction rage the stars; down below – man: life. And without life how empty and meaningless all this would be! Filling the whole world with yourself and your sufferings you, man, create it afresh...'
19 Old Pustynnov explicitly compares himself to Noah at one point (1. 404).
20 Leonov himself began collecting cactuses, those 'prickly freaks' in the 1920s, and his fascination with them lasted for the rest of his life.
21 *Literaturnoe nasledstvo*, no. 70 (AN SSSR, M.-L., 1963), p. 252.
22 For a more detailed examination of this question see A. K. Simonova, 'Pervaya drama L. Leonova, *Untilovsk, Nauchnye trudy* (Erevanskiy gosudarstvennyy universitet), vol. 57, vyp. 4, ch. 2 (Erevan, 1956).
23 See Boguslavskaya, *Leonid Leonov*, p. 136.
24 *Dark Water* (*Temnaya voda*), *The Return of Kopylev* (*Vozvrashchenie Kopyleva*), *Ivan's Misadventure* (*Priklyuchenie s Ivanom*) all published in *Zv*, 1928, no. 1; *The Tramp* (*Brodyaga*) and *Revenge* (*Mest'*) were published in *KN*, nos. 5 and 6 respectively.
25 According to Pil'nyak the name Mosk-va (Moscow) means 'dark waters.' See his story 'Sankt-Piter-Burkh' (1921) in *Sobranie sochineniy*, vol. 8, p. 71. I don't

think that this etymological *trouvaille* plays any role in Leonov's story, but it would certainly not be out of character for him to use it in such a way.
26 N.P. Malakhov has some interesting suggestions on Leonov's choice of name, and suggests that he is here polemicizing with the views of Petr Chaadaev. See *Leonid Leonov: Tvorcheskaya individual'nost' i literaturnyy protsess*, ed. V.A. Kovalev and N.A. Groznova (L., 1987), pp. 199–200.
27 'Revenge' as a form of hostility to culture is associated with the 'primitive mentality' in the work of Soviet psychologists of the 1920s. See V.A. Kovalev, *Tvorchestvo Leonida Leonova.* (1962), pp. 237–43.
28 The region of Nyandy was later to become a Soviet labour camp.
29 Other notable examples are Vs. Ivanov's novella *Armoured Car 14–69* (*Bronepoezd 14–69*, 1922) and Bulgakov's novel *The White Guard* (*Belaya gvardiya*, 1924).
30 Future time is often associated with the image of mountains in the poetry of Mayakovsky.
31 The puddle now recalls the one in Gogol''s 'Story of how Ivan Ivanovich and Ivan Nikiforovich Quarrelled' (*Povest' o tom, kak possorilsya Ivan Ivanovich s Ivanom Nikiforovichem*, 1834). Leonov's story then may suggest that the Revolution is no more than a replay of their absurd and interminable feud, like the squabble over Zinka's meadow in *The Badgers*.
32 A.K. Simonova, a scholar of the University of Erevan, is an exception to this generalization. Her contributions to the *Nauchnye trudy* of that university in 1956, 1958, and 1960 deal almost exclusively with this period of Leonov's work and are of great interest.
33 The play was revived on the Soviet stage in the 1970s.
34 A detailed account, somewhat hostile to Leonov, of the meeting is given in 'Po literaturnym vecheram,' *NLP*, 1929, no. 4–5, p. 126. A rather more neutral account may be found in A. Kut, 'Doklad I.M. Nusinova,' *VechM*, 1 Feb. 1929.
35 A translation of *Ivan's Misadventure* may be found in J. Cournos, *Short Stories out of Soviet Russia* (London, 1929).

CHAPTER 5   *The Sot'* and *Locusts* 1930–1931

1 In fact this was standard practice at the time. Communist Russia had refused to sign the Berne convention on copyright, and so Soviet writers had to arrange for publication in the West to protect their rights. After the Pil'nyak case no Soviet writer could send his work abroad for publication without official permission.
2 For a fuller account of this campaign see Alex M. Shane, *The Life and Works of Evgenij Zamjatin* (Berkeley and Los Angeles, 1968), pp. 55–81.

3 He rewrote *Mahogany* in a form more acceptable to the authorities. It was published under the title *The Volga Falls into the Caspian Sea* (*Volga vpadaet v Kaspiyskoe more*, 1930).
4 See *LitGaz*, 7 Oct. 1929.
5 See E. Zamyatin, *Litsa* (New York, 1955), pp. 277–82.
6 Kirpotin, *Romany Leonida Leonova*, pp. 3, 5.
7 Leonid Leonov, 'Kak reorganizovat' Soyuz Pisateley,' *LitGaz*, 30 Sept. 1929.
8 See, for example, V. Polonsky, 'Oktyabr' i khudozhestvennaya literatura,' *NLP*, 1926, no. 3, pp. 24–5, and *Izv*, 7 Nov. 1928.
9 In 1928 Leonov was invited by S. Kanatchikov, a senior Bolshevik and the RAPP representative on the Federation of Soviet Writers, to deliver the keynote speech on the occasion of the 30th anniversary celebrations of the Moscow Arts Theatre. The proposal was disputed by the Secretary of RAPP, V. Stavsky, who offered his own candidate, V. Kirshon, a member of RAPP. When Leonov heard of this he immediately withdrew. (For more details see Mikhaylov, Mirozdanie po Leonovu..., p. 92.)
10 K. Chukovsky, *Dnevnik 1930–1969* (M., 1994), p. 175.
11 Leonid Leonov, *Sobranie sochineniy* (1928–30).
12 See 'Anketa sredi deyateley teatra,' *NLP*, 1928, no. 3, p. 38.
13 See 'Provintsial'naya idilliya,' *NLP*, 1928, no. 6, p. 88.
14 Leonov wrote the novel between December 1928 and November 1929. It was first published in *NM*, 1930, nos. 1–5, and came out in book form in the following year. There are some differences between the two versions. Few of them are of a political nature, though a reference to the 'fall of Trotsky,' used primarily for dating the narrative, was omitted (see *NM*, 1930, no. 1, p. 66). Leonov also wrote a libretto (so far unpublished) for the Leningrad Academic Theatre of Opera and Ballet. In *LitGaz*, 12 May 1932, it was announced that the composer M. Starokadomsky was setting it to music. Nothing seems to have come of this project.
15 There is a river of this name in the Yaroslavl' district, where Leonov was living in 1926, while working on *The Thief*. The action of *The Sot'*, however, clearly takes place very much further north. On the evidence of the place names, many of which have a strong Finnno-Ugrian component, it appears to be set in south-central Karelia. The nearest large city mentioned in the novel is Vyatka.
16 The writers' brigade that visited Balakhna was later criticized in the Soviet press for the shoddy works that it produced (see Lazar' Fleishman, *Pasternak v tridtsatye gody*, Jerusalem, 1984, p. 77). Syas'stroy is about 120 km. east of Leningrad; Balakhna about 40 km. north-west of Nizhniy-Novgorod.
17 Even the name of the project, Sot'stroy, punningly suggests 'sots-stroy,' or the 'building of socialism.'
18 *NM*, 1930, no. 5, p. 36. In all editions after 1945 these words were made more

emphatic by a shift of the final verb into the perfective: 'the face of the Sot' was changing, and the people too *had* changed' (4. 284).
19 These scenes are apparently based on Leonov's visit to a monastery in northern Russia in 1926.
20 Leonid Leonov, *Teatr*, vol. 1, p. 146.
21 S. Romov, 'Vstrecha s Leonidom Leonovym,' *LitGaz*, 24 Sept. 1930. In *The Sot'* similar words are given to the non-Party engineer Burago: 'A new Adam is coming to distribute names to creatures that existed long before him [...] I am an old man: I can remember the French Revolution, and the death of Icarus and the Tower of Babel' (4. 258). In this passage the historical events are significantly all examples of overweening ambition and catastrophic failure. Once again the idea of Revolution is linked with the Tower of Babel and so with the legend of Kalafat. By contrast, in the newspaper interview the historical precedents are not so much failures as 'vanished cultures and civilizations.'

The sentiment recalls the words of Gershenzon to Vyacheslav Ivanov in *Correspondence from Two Corners*: 'The cultural heritage weighs on the individual with a pressure of 60 atmospheres and more' (see Vyacheslav Ivanov *Sobranie sochineniy*, Brussels, 1971–, vol. 3, p. 390).
22 These lines recall Mayakovsky's poem 'Domoy!' ('Home!,' 1926): 'I feel myself to be a Soviet factory, manufacturing happiness' (Vladimir Mayakovsky, *Polnoe sobranie sochineniy*, vol. 7, p. 94). Henceforth this edition will be abbreviated as *PSS*. It is perhaps not coincidental that this chapter of *The Sot'* appeared in the April issue of *NM*, the month in which Mayakovsky committed suicide.
23 Vyach. Ivanov, *Sobranie sochineniy*, vol. 3, p. 385.
24 The image of the 'stupid fish' refers back to the peasant Kruchinkin in *White Night*, and casts a new light on his role as the embodiment of the spirit of Russia, stubbornly impervious to the pressures of the new age.
25 Zamyatin continued to work on this theme in emigration, but as a novel, 'The Scourge of God' (*Bich Bozhiy*), not a play. It remained unfinished at his death in 1937.
26 See 'Leningradskie pisateli solidarizirovalis' s moskovskimi; soprotivlenie reaktsionnykh elementov,' *LitGaz*, 30 Sept. 1929. Two years later Leonov went out of his way to condemn Pil'nyak's *Mahogany* also (see his speech reported in 'Na diskussii v VSSP,' *NM*, 1931, no. 10, p. 124).
27 The first comes in a description of the anarchist forces in the Civil War: '... through the din and dust, roaring and screeching, hurtled these Hun-like chariots, and the spectre of another, yellow ancestor invisibly advanced above the heads of the human torrent' (4. 73–4). The second relates him to the threat of peasant protests against collectivization: 'The events on the Sot' prompted some minds to think that a peasant Attila was already sharpening his stave for more destruction' (4. 236).

28 This was pointed out by Kovalev, in *Romany Leonida Leonova*, pp. 171–2.
29 It is tempting to see a parallel between Leonov and Suzanna's experiences in the years 1918–20. In that case Suzanna's success in jettisoning her past is related with a certain envy:

> Everything melted away like a wretched dream [...] It is easy for a woman to avoid persecution: the scar on her temple she could explain plausibly enough as the result of a fall in childhood. Her masculine common sense appealed to a powerful figure who worked in the army for six months, and then she was sent to Moscow to complete her studies. Nowhere did anyone express any interest in her past. (4. 76)

30 It is perhaps significant that at the very end of the book two crows, symbols of memory and reason, fly over Uvad'ev's head, as he sits alone overlooking the river (4. 283).
31 N. Berdyaev, ' Predsmertnye mysli Fausta' in *Osval'd Shpengler i Zakat Evropy* (M., 1922). Quoted from K. Grasis, 'Vekhisty o Shpenglere,' *KN*, 1922, no. 2 [6], pp. 197–8. I am grateful to Dr Henry Elbaum for drawing my attention to this aspect of Vissarion. A.G. Lysov has pointed out that similar ideas had been expressed by Konstantin Leont'ev (see *Leonid Leonov: Tvorcheskaya individual'nost'...*, pp. 217–18.
32 Earlier in the nineteenth century liberal thinkers such as Gertsen (following John Stuart Mill in *On Liberty*) had argued that it was the rise of the bourgeoisie that threatened society with just such stagnation. Now their argument was stood on its head and turned against them.
33 Kovalev, *Tvorchestvo Leonida Leonova* (1962), p. 60.
34 It may be significant, however, that Belinsky's sobriquet *neistovyi* (fanatical) is the epithet that Leonov attaches to his master builder, Kalafat.
35 See Abdurakhman Avtorkhanov, *Stalin and the Soviet Communist Party: A Study in the Technology of Power* (Munich, 1959), p. 123.
36 See L. Bat', 'L. Leonov o literaturnom trude (Iz besed s pisatelem),' *VopLit*, 1960, no. 2, p. 188.
37 *NM*, 1930, no. 4, p. 31.
38 See for example, the authorial aside, recalling Pchkhov: 'everything in the world does not exist for man, but in its own right' (4. 146) with its rejection of the anthropocentrism of Marxism.
39 These ideas are sometimes parodied in the poetry of the period, for example: 'Nature doesn't understand anything, and you cannot trust her' (N. A.Zabolotsky, *Stikhotvoreniya i poemy*, M.-L., 1965, p.260); and 'Nature is an unreliable element – you can never get her to settle down' (Boris Pasternak, *Stikhotvoreniya i poemy*, M., 1965, p. 320.)
40 The 'hope come true' is later associated with Uvad'ev: 'He believed in the healing

properties of the forests, where he would have to fight every day just to survive [...] The Sot' had perhaps justified his hopes; wounds to the heart – assuming that personal circumstances could have so wounded him – healed quicker than a cut on the hand with him' (4. 91).

This explanation might be taken as an indication that the whole of the opening section is in fact seen through Uvad'ev's eyes, but nothing else supports such a reading. It is rather an example of Leonov's irony. Uvad'ev's attempt to escape from his personal problems may seem to have succeeded, but in the course of the novel it becomes plain that he continues to suffer from them.

41 In Dostoevsky's *Notes from the Underground* the anthill is an image of an inhuman, totally regulated existence. Leonov, however, loved ants, and regarded the destruction of their habitats as criminal vandalism. The wanton destruction of an anthill plays a part in Leonid Andreev's *Savva* (1906), a work which has already been mentioned in connection with Vissarion.

42 I suspect that in *The River Sot'* Leonov may often be alluding to Nikolay Klyuev's last major work, 'A Time of Fire' (*Pogorel'shchina*, 1928), an impassioned denunciation of the rape of northern Russia by the forces of industrialization: the fictional place name Lopsky pogost, and a scene in which the youths from the Komsomol mock the monks, are common to the two works. The word *pogorel'shchina* and its cognates occur several times in the novel. The poem could not be published at the time, but Klyuev is known to have given readings of it.

43 'This was a period when Stalin and Gor'ky were in love with one another. Later they both cooled off [...] I was afraid for my life. Writers were disappearing before my eyes, but what could one do? An Arctic chill had gripped the whole country [...] Stalin turned to me: "Tell me, has Vsevolod Ivanov written himself out?" I knew that the authorities were badly disposed towards him, and I tried to intercede on his behalf, but Gor'ky interrupted me and, I am sure, saved my life by his words: "Iosif Vissarionovich," these were his very words, "Leonov has the right to speak in the name of all Russian literature." Stalin turned his gaze on me, and for a full forty seconds looked straight into my eyes. I too looked into his eyes, absolutely certain that if I looked away I would be finished. Stalin turned to Gor'ky and said, "I believe you, Aleksey Maksimovich." If I had looked away, I repeat, I would have signed my own death-warrant.' Quoted from Sergey Vlasov, 'Leonid Leonov: Chudo otkryvaetsya tol'ko chistomu cheloveku,' *Kul'tura*, 10 Sept. 1994.

44 The resulting book was *Turkmenistan vesnoy* (M., 1932).

45 First complete publication in *Krasnaya nov'*, nos. 9–10, under the title 'Saranchuki.' A separate edition came out the following year. Even in 1930 Leonov was unsure how to entitle the work: it is called 'Sarancha' in the interview with Romov, *LitGaz*, 24 Sept. 1930, and for the 1945 reissue this name was finally

preferred. There are several differences between the earlier and later editions, most of them of a stylistic rather than ideological nature.
46 'Put' brigady,' *LitGaz*, 25 May 1930.
47 In Soviet literature such references often indicate time spent in the labour camps, and in later editions Leonov supports this possibility, when Maronov says of his time in the north: 'I came to understand why people are afraid of prison. The hardest thing to bear is your own company' (4. 291). But, as Leonov shows in other works, those returning from the labour camps were regarded with suspicion and would never have received the degree of trust and authority that is given to Maronov.
48 It is, however, a mark of respect when Leonov refers to his male heroes, Vekshin, Uvad'ev, Maronov, and their successors, by their surnames.
49 L. Leonov, 'Saranchuki,' *KN*, 1930, no. 9/10, pp. 41–2.
50 There is a story by Gleb Uspensky entitled 'Sarancha,' in which 'locusts' serve as an image of backwardness and barbarism.
51 S. Romov, 'Beseda s Leonidom Leonovym,' *LitGaz*, 24 Sept. 1930.
52 *Sobranie sochineniy*, 9 vols. (M., 1960–2), vol. 4, p. 335. In a later edition Leonov attributed the remark to someone else: 'One must hope, someone joked, that the spectacle of these fires would depress the mood of the insects' (4. 313).
53 See 'Na diskussii v VSSP,' *NM*, 1931, no. 10.
54 *Iz tvorcheskogo naslediya...*, p. 428.

CHAPTER 6   *Skutarevsky* 1932

1 Loren Graham, *The Soviet Academy of Sciences and the Communist Party* (Princeton, 1967), p. 88.
2 Quoted from the Gor'ky archives in L. Fink, *Dramaturgiya Leonida Leonova*, p. 145. See also Leonov's article 'Dvizhenie ne ostanovit'' in *LitGaz*, 4 Dec. 1930.
3 Mikhaylov, *Mirozdanie po Leonovu*, p. 100.
4 First published in *NM*, 1932, nos. 5–9. The novel came out in book form later the same year. There are several minor but significant differences between the journal text and the book versions. The more important of them will be discussed later in this chapter.
5 There is a reference to the the Sixteenth Party Congress of 1930 (5.122).
6 Thus he complains of his young Party assistant: 'He looks at science as though it was his Party obligation.' 'Is that a bad thing?' smiled the minister who was well aware of Skutarevsky's opinions. 'It's not enough' (5. 240).
7 The technical problems raised by the novel are discussed in V. L'vov, 'Komandarm elektronov. *Skutarevsky* kak nauchnyy roman,' *LitLen*, 15 Oct. 1933. The wireless transmission of electricity is technically feasible, but the vast

amounts of energy required would have made the project quite uneconomic in Russia in view of the immense distances involved. Interest in the idea has, however, recently been revived with the advances in the practical applications of lasers.

8 A partial success for Skutarevsky's experiment is hinted at by Leonov when a bird in the vicinity is electrocuted. The likelihood of any connection between them was hotly debated. Critics and some scientists among them asserted that it was impossible. Leonov declared that the incident was based on fact. On the other hand, one may also see in this scene a more ominous interpretation. The wireless transmission of electricity now becomes a sort of death-ray. This point is made by L. Fink (see *Uroki Leonida Leonova: tvorcheskaya evolyutsiya*, M., 1973, p. 85), but without comment. And like the innocent Polya in *The Sot'* a living creature in the here and now is killed in the name of future progress.

9 In the stage version, however, Skutarevsky's experiment is successful, and the play ends in a blaze of light and general triumph.

10 There is a hint that Skutarevsky's institute is more like the *sharashka* described by Solzhenitsyn in *The First Circle*. In these establishments prominent scholars were effectively imprisoned and forced to work virtually unpaid, though living conditions were much better than in other penal institutions, and compared favourably with the life of free Russian citizens. Thus the engineer Ramzin, the victim of the Prompartiya show trial, was said to have been shot in 1930, only to reappear at the end of the decade with a Stalin Prize. In this connection Leonov's remark: 'The work had been made top secret, and Skutarevsky with it; abroad they assumed that he had died' (5. 43), acquires a wealth of suggestion.

11 V. Katanyan, 'Skutarevsky,' *VechM*, 29 Dec. 1932.

12 For a similar situation see Volodya Safonov in Il'ya Erenburg's *The Second Day* (*Vtoroy den'*, 1932–3), another novel about the First Five-Year Plan.

13 Bukharin had called Stalin the 'Jenghis Khan of the Party,' as has already been noted.

14 Leonov concedes this point when he ironically translates Zhenya into the materialist jargon that is second nature to Skutarevsky: 'Perhaps she didn't exist at all; it was simply that Skutarevsky's lines of force and intellect intersected to form this lovely but unsatisfying phantom' (5. 251).

15 A version of the opening chapter appeared in *VechM*, 22, 23 Sept. 1931. The text is on the whole close to the final version of eight months later, but it is plain that at this stage Fedor Skutarevsky did not form part of Leonov's scheme: 'Five of them [Skutarevsky and his brothers] grew up on the streets and died in various ways, the surviving sixth [Sergey Skutarevsky]...' In the final version the 'five' was altered to 'four' to explain the survival of two of the brothers (5. 8). Leonov was himself the eldest of six children.

16 Compare 'A truly prominent scientist cannot be a reactionary by his very nature' (5.68) and 'A work that is artistically true will seldom be ideologically false' (*Vor*, 458).
17 F. Vlasov states that Fedor's aesthetic views echo those of Il'ya Ostroukhov, Leonov's mentor in the 1920s, but he offers no evidence in support of the idea (see F. Kh. Vlasov, *Epos muzhestva*, M., 1965, p. 289).
18 Vladimir Mayakovsky, *PSS*, vol. 7, p. 94.
19 *NM*, 1932, no. 8, p. 152. In the book version this was modified to '... replaced painting by topical subject matter' (5. 206).
20 V. E. Kaygorodova suggests that Nikolay Dormidontov's painting 'The Skier' may have served Leonov as a prototype for Fedor Skutarevsky's picture. See *Leonid Leonov: Tvorcheskaya individual'nost'*..., pp. 247–53.
21 *NM*, 1932, no. 9, p. 113.
22 The number may have other associations. Leonov was just 29 when he began work on *The Sot'*, and the year 1929 marks the beginning of the Communist Party's take over of the arts and sciences. One may also recall that the twenty-nine men who attended cadet school with Leonov in 1919 were all executed.
23 The red flags recall an image from *White Night*. There they had represented the cities under the Bolsheviks' control. It is then noticeable that the red flags in *Skutarevsky* are set to trap the red-haired fox and Skutarevsky. Leonov returns to an earlier image to suggest that the Revolution has begun to consume its own.
24 Kovalev, *Tvorchestvo Leonida Leonova...* (1962), pp. 236–7.
25 *NM*, 1932, no. 6, p. 46. In the book version this was modified to 'Unable as yet to dispense with the flashy, hackneyed phrase' (5. 68).
26 The italicized words *Soviet* and *open* were omitted from later versions of the novel.
27 Implicit in this image is Pushkin's tragedy *Mozart and Salieri*, which is alluded to twice in the novel (5. 82, 111), but it is nowhere explicitly related to the Prometheus theme. The conflict between the genius and the ambitious hack forms the basis of several of Leonov's plots.
28 E.g., 'Sergey Andreich realized that [the accountant] had come with a denunciation. He was unlucky, untalented and did what he could do to improve his prospects' (5. 293).
29 In *The Sot'* Uvad'ev is photographed in the doorway of his house just after he has expelled Zoya. There the episode is left undeveloped, but it presages the witch-hunts to come.
30 *NM*, 1932, no. 5, p. 59. Only the first sentence of this passage was retained in the book edition (cf. 5. 90). A Soviet reader could hardly avoid noticing that the age of the unfortunate meteorologist is the same number as the article in the Criminal Code governing counter-revolutionary activity, under which many intellectuals had recently been arrested. The number also happens to be twice 29.

31 See *NM*, 1932, no. 6, p. 87.
32 This pattern is repeated also in the scene of Arseniy's visit to Gerodov's wife in chapter 21.
33 The parallel between humans and cats mating in the moonlight recalls a similar scene in Leskov's 'Lady Macbeth of Mtsensk.'
34 Leonov originally intended to begin the novel in the spring. Thus one version of the opening chapter is explicitly set in April. (See *VechM*, 22 Sept. 1931, 'Nachalo romana'.)
35 'Shekspirovskaya ploshchadnost',' *SovIsk*, 26 Jan. 1933.
36 Cf. in *Locusts*: 'Maronov's eyes were catastrophically closing' (4. 329).
37 *Sobranie sochineniy*, 6 vols. (M., 1953–5), vol. 3, p. 99. This sentence has been rewritten in all later editions.
38 This paragraph is based on Kovalev's discussion in *Romany Leonida Leonova*, pp. 271–2.
39 It is noteworthy that it was the critics who complained of the complexities of the form of the novel; ordinary readers do not seem to have had any difficulties in following it. See S. Dzyubinsky and N. Izgoev, 'Massovyy chitatel' o khudozhestvennoy literature,' *NM*, 1934, no. 9, pp. 197–8.
40 An acquaintance of mine in Moscow told me that he liked to embarrass Leonov by asking him where the sentence '… хмель дружбы прошел, и осталась одна горькая похмельная фамильярность' ['the first intoxication of friendship had passed and there remained only the bitter hangover of familiarity'] came from. Any reader of Leonov would recognize it at once as a quotation from *Skutarevsky* (5. 32).
41 A.N. Bakh, 'Nashe slovo o literature,' *LitGaz*, 29 Oct. 1932. This attack was the more troubling since Bakh was regarded as a independent-minded intellectual, who was respected by the Communists. See Fleyshman, *Pasternak v 30-ye gody*, p. 354.
42 I. Anisimov, 'Novyy roman Leonova,' and G. Munblit, 'O pravde i pravdopodobii,' *LitGaz*, 17 Dec. 1932.
43 I. Nusinov, 'Ot Likhareva k Skutarevskomu,' *NM*, 1933, no. 6.
44 See 'Diskussiya o Skutarevskom,' *VechM*, 5, 6 Jan. 1933, and 'Spory vokrug Skutarevskogo,' *LitGaz*, 11 Jan. 1933. The latter account is more sympathetic to Leonov.
45 A. Selivanovsky, 'Ob odnoy diskussii,' *Lit Gaz*, 5 Feb. 1933.
46 'V sporakh o Skutarevskom,' *RabGaz*, 1 Feb. 1933.
47 The play was originally intended for the Moscow Arts Theatre, but because of the delay in producing it there Leonov offered it to the Malyy Theatre where it was first performed on 15 May 1934.

The play exists in several different versions. The earliest, in four acts and nine scenes, was published in book form in 1933. The following year another version,

in three acts and seven scenes, was published in *NM*, no. 6; the two scenes cut were Cherimov's visit to Butylkin and Arseniy's last monologue before committing suicide. The version acted by the Malyy Theatre consisted of three acts and eight scenes. It is clear from the cast list that it was the Butylkin scene that was omitted. Apart from these differences there were several variations in the text. The stage directions have been simplified, Arseniy's behaviour is made more reprehensible, and Petrygin's conspiracy is shown to be even more impotent in the later version. The text was revised again for the edition of Leonov's plays issued in 1935, and once more for the two-volume *Teatr* of 1960. The alterations here are of a mainly stylistic character; the structure itself is unaltered. In each case the play consists of three acts and seven scenes.
48 In fact, as was shown earlier the first version of the novel clearly did not include Fedor Skutarevsky: see note 15 above.
49 See M. Levidov, 'Zhertvy i zavoevaniya,' *LitGaz*, 20 May 1934, and Fink, *Dramaturgiya Leonida Leonova*, pp. 122–65.

CHAPTER 7 *The Road to Ocean* 1935

1 First published *NM*, 1935, nos 9–12. It appeared in book form early in the following year. There are several significant differences between the journal text and later editions of the novel.
2 For an excellent history of this idea see Rufus W. Mathewson, Jr., *The Positive Hero in Russian Literature* (New York, 1958).
3 So far as I know there is no Russian town called Revizan'. Much of the action takes place in a place called Cheremshansk, which is not to be found in atlases, but is presumably situated on the river Cheremshan in the Orenburg area. This would fit the other geographical indications in the novel. The area is associated with the Pugachev rebellion. *The Road to Ocean* also devotes some pages to a minor peasant rising.
4 These lines recall Mayakovsky's lines on the death of Lenin: 'I hate the way man is made and built, I hate his very appearance and dimensions. What are our hands meant to be?... Is this the way our respected machines operate?... [...] Enough? No more dawdling! Change the structure of the race of men!' (Mayakovsky, *PSS*, vol. 6, pp. 17–18.)
5 Eduard Bagritsky's poem *TVTs* (TB, 1929) is one of the few other Soviet works to raise the issue of death for a Communist.
6 *Zolotaya kareta. Materialy k postanovke p'esy L. Leonova* (M., 1946), pp. 4–5.
7 The source of this image goes back in Soviet literature to Gor'ky's eulogy for Lenin: 'the brow of a philosopher and the hands of a workman' (*SS*, vol. 17, p. 7). It later becomes something of a cliché, e. g., 'the Leninist skull of Socrates' in

Tikhonov's 'Story with a footnote' (*Rasskaz s primechaniem*, 1927), and in Valentin Kataev's 'Small Iron Door in the Wall,' ('Malen'kaya zheleznaya dver' v stene,' 1984). Behind all these stands Chernyshevsky's description of Rakhmetov in *What Is to Be Done?* The first use of the image, so far as I know, occurs in Turgenev's *Khor' i Kalinych*. But the image has also less positive associations: the Benefactor in Zamyatin's *We* is described in these terms (*My*, p. 166).

8 See too Gor'ky's words on Lenin's 'rare ability to look at the present from the future' (Vitaly Shentalinsky, *The KGB's Literary Archive*, trans. John Crowfoot, London, 1995, p. 259).

9 F.M. Dostoevsky, *PSS*, vol. 14, p. 290.

10 This idea goes back to Leonov's visit to Gor'ky in Sorrento in 1927. When sitting in a car he had become fascinated by the infinite number of concepts and interactions involved in the simple words 'We are travelling.' This incident had appeared in *Skutarevsky* only thinly disguised: 'Strange, the train is moving, various fabulous wayside stations are disappearing behind us and we know so little about the various parts of the engine that is drawing us' (5. 253).

11 Compare the photograph that Vekshin discovers in his sister's suitcase: 'He had smiled all these years [...] the Vekshin in the photograph [...] triumphing over death itself in this smile [...] And yet he, the real Veskhin, had lived all these years without a smile' (*Vor*, p. 59).

12 *Leonid Leonov v vospominaniyakh...*, p. 475.

13 The belief that history has no end, no final revolution, is one of several nods to Zamyatin's *We*. In another echo the giant hydroelectric stations of Ocean (a projection of one of the fetishes of the Five-Year Plans) are seen as 'the greatest triumph of reason and mankind' (6. 371). In *We* the engineer D. 503 is working on a spaceship, the Integral, that is designed to bring past civilizations into the Utopia of the Single State; the climax of the futurist chapters in *The Road to Ocean* is built round the return of the first stratonauts. This section is dominated by the pronoun 'we'; the 'I,' like D. 503 before him, is very much part of this collective, as he shows on the few occasions when he dares to express himself in the first person singular.

14 There is a reference to 'my hero' on the very first page of the novel, but this is likely to pass unnoticed by the reader.

15 In Ocean Kurilov and 'I' have their identities checked and are only admitted when the files turn up the names of Krylov and Leont'ev, which are reckoned to be close enough.

16 The sentence in italics is to be found only in the journal version of *The Road to Ocean*. It is somewhat prophetic as Leonov himself was within a few years to be accused of 'slandering Soviet reality.' The following paragraphs were also substantially rewritten. Originally Leonov had written:

'... a living man. *Well, do you deny that you are hanging on to the net, and that the children are trying to put out your pipe by spitting on it? Perhaps that is the most salutary thing that could have happened to us here.*'

'But they could have told us not to approach this infernal contraption.'

'*But who, my friend? They have no time to keep an eye on us. As human relationships become simpler, so an ever greater number of things will require constant supervision and maintenance.* And there was much else...' (*NM*, 1935, 9, 71)

17 Ironically, the Soviet authorities themselves confirmed the truth of Leonov's strictures. In the *NM* edition of the novel Peresypkin had believed that the 'Soviet state was strong enough to allow its historians to be objective and even dispassionate in their treatment of the vanquished enemy, whose ashes now awaited his verdict... but no, the virtues of old age were not for Peresypkin.' Any hint of criticism implied by the first of these two sentences might seem to have been neutralized by the second of them, but it still fell foul of the censorship. Later versions of this passage read: '... with the naiveté of youth [Peresypkin] believed that *he* was strong enough to be objective...' (6. 341). The idea of objectivity is thus assigned to Peresypkin, and is clearly not something that the Soviet state can be expected to approve.

18 Naturally, many Russians, even among those loyal to the Communist government, did not dare to answer all the questions truthfully, but they could not be sure that some other member of the family might not reveal a relationship that they had tried to conceal; another danger was that people could not be sure of remembering how they had answered a given question on a previous occasion. With the regular checking of *ankety* against one another there was thus a constant possibility of incrimination.

19 The families of the former aristocracy, the bourgeoisie, and the Church were specifically classified as 'exploiters,' and accordingly deprived of such rights of Soviet citizenship as the right to vote, to receive higher education, or to be employed in skilled work. They were known as *lishentsy* (deprived ones).

20 A similar plot line is found in Georgiy Nikiforov's novel *Under the Street-Lamp* (*U fonarya*, 1928–9) which Vyacheslav Zavalishin calls 'an attack on the Bolshevik practice of inventing class enemies where none existed' (*Early Soviet Writers*, New York, 1958, p. 325). There, however, the hero is eventually pardoned after a trial.

21 The motif of promoting unqualified workers played an important role in *Skutarevsky* also.

22 In March 1937 Stalin was to declare that this was one of the 'signs of a good wrecker.' See Robert Conquest, *The Great Terror* (London, 1968), p. 302.

23 For a detailed account of the traditional Soviet interpretation see Kovalev, *Romany Leonida Leonova*, pp. 361–3, 367.

24 See Mikhaylov, *Mirozdanie po Leonovu*, pp. 155–7.
25 The death of Kurilov inevitably recalls Pil'nyak's 1925 story, 'Tale of the Unextinguished Moon' (*Povest' nepogashennoy luny*), which was based on the death of Marshal Frunze after an unnecessary operation. Within a few months of the publication of *The Road to Ocean*, the death of Gor'ky was to lead to further accusations of medical assassination.
26 The type of doomed hero may be traced back to Pal'chikov in *White Night*, a story that reads rather differently in the light of *The Road to Ocean*.
27 In conversation in 1960. This remark is also made by Firsov in the revised version of *The Thief* (3. 673).
28 Leonov raises this possibility in Kurilov's reflections: 'But even so he could have spent the remainder of his life more sensibly. And he regretted that he had never had the chance to protect the life of the leader with his body or fall before a firing squad, so that someone might profit by his example' (6. 419).
29 In Ocean the narrator watches a moth 'hurling itself against a lamp and falling back, wings folded, sated, and dead. So that was how the problem of death was solved there' (6. 378).
30 Leonov expanded this section of the *NM* edition by some two pages, between 'Their craft still had not returned' (6. 372) and 'In the fourth point...' (6. 374). The episode is coloured by the death of the Soviet balloonists, Fedoseenko, Vasenko, and Usyskin, after attaining the record height of 22 kilometres above sea level. Stalin himself helped carry the men's coffins. In the reports of the time they were described as 'stratonauts'; Leonov uses the same word for his space travellers.
31 Suffering is still an essential element in the formation of character, but Leonov is now more cautious in expressing this idea. The actor Pakhomov pretentiously assures Liza that if she wishes to become a good actress she must be ready to 'buy herself unhappiness at any price. One great poet cut open his hero's breast and inserted a live coal instead of his heart.' Leonov ironically comments on this: 'however much life had knocked Pakhomov about he still had nothing to show for it' (6. 485, 486). Nonetheless the moral of *The Road to Ocean* is of the beneficent results of suffering: 'the disaster had imprinted the seal of serious concentration and independence upon [Sayfulla]; not a trace of yesterday's youth remained' (6. 438).
32 It may be noted that Leonov seems to make no distinction between the words *schast'e* (here translated 'happiness') and *radost'* (here translated 'joy').
33 The one literary figure who does appear, though not by name, is Maksimilian Voloshin (1875–1932). He is caricatured maliciously in the chapter 'Arkadiy Germogenovich and his contents.' This is all the more surprising since Voloshin had been married to Margarita Sabashnikova, the aunt of Leonov's wife. Athough

the marriage broke up in 1907 the Sabashnikovs remained on good terms with Voloshin. Leonov and his wife stayed with him at his house in the Crimea in May 1925. For more on this see '"Ochen' chasto vspominaem gostepriimstvo dobroe vashe..." Pis'ma Leonida Leonova Maksimilanu Voloshinu (1925 g.)' in *Iz tvorcheskogo naslediya...*, pp. 490–500. Many years later Leonov received a copy of Voloshin's watercolours with an inscription from the artist's widow.

34 The place name Borshchnya is very similar to Borshchen', the name of the Sabashnikovs' pre-revolutionary country estate.
35 I asked Leonov about these stories in 1960. He replied that they were purely ornamental.
36 The theme of the usurper is presented most boldly in two plays by Evgeniy Shvarts, *The Shadow* (*Ten'*, 1934) and *The Dragon* (*Drakon*, 1940).
37 *NM*, 1935, no. 12, p. 69. The italicized section was cut.
38 This may have been suspected by the critic who complained that the hero resembled Parsifal rather than a Communist. See A. Bolotnikov, 'Doroga na Okean,' *LitGaz*, 20 April 1936.
39 Gor'ky in fact advised Leonov to do just this. Stalin, as we shall see, felt the same way.
40 This is a Dostoevskian feature. Compare, for example, the dialogues of Porfiriy and Raskol'nikov in *Crime and Punishment* and Ivan and Smerdyakov in *The Brothers Karamazov*.
41 An account of this discussion can be found in Ya. E. 'Doroga na Okean,' *LitGaz*, 5 Nov. 1935.
42 I. Vinogradov, 'Za sovetskuyu klassiku,' *Literaturnyy sovremennik*, 1936, no. 5.
43 An exception to this generalization was A. Lezhnev who considered the book Leonov's best since *The Badgers*.
44 See 'Obsuzhdenie romana *Doroga na Okean* na Prezidiume SSP' in *LitGaz*, 10 May 1936.
45 Mathewson, *The Positive Hero...*, esp. pp. 301–10. Mathewson's enthusiasm for the novel, inspired a student at Columbia University, Olivia Ladd, to write one of the most interesting studies of the novel, its structure, and, in particular, its narrative strategies as her MA dissertation.
46 Notably David Burg, 'Popytka Leonida Leonova,' *Mosty*, 1961, no. 7, pp. 172–4, and Helen Muchnic, *From Gorky to Pasternak*, esp. pp. 294–5. Both these writers fail to discern Leonov's use of irony.
47 See Marc Slonim, *Modern Russian Literature* (New York, 1953), p. 328, and Zavalishin, *Early Soviet Writers*, p. 307.
48 For some examples of this hostility to Leonov see Mikhaylov, *Mirozdanie po Leonovu...*, p. 89–93.

CHAPTER 8 Three Plays 1936–1940

1 An earlier version of this chapter was published as 'The Lean Years of Leonid Leonov' in *Canadian-American Slavic Studies*, vol. 8, no. 4 (winter, 1974), pp. 513–24.
2 *The Thief* and *The Sot'* were translated into English in 1931, and *Skutarevsky* in 1936; *the Badgers*, *The Thief*, and *The Sot'* were all translated into German before the Nazi period; *The Badgers* and *The Sot'* were translated into Spanish in the pre-Franco years, *The Badgers*, *The Sot'*, and *The Road to Ocean* were all translated into French by 1936. Several of the early stories were also translated. This information is taken from Kovalev, *Leonid Leonov: Seminariy* (1964), pp. 228–9.
3 *LitGaz*, 17 Nov. 1933.
4 *LitGaz*, 23 Nov. 1933.
5 Fink, *Dramaturgiya Leonida Leonova*, pp. 126–7.
6 It was first published in Gor'ky, *SS*, vol. 30, pp. 399–402.
7 V.A. Kovalev, *Realizm Leonova* (M., 1969), p. 111.
8 Conversation with Leonov in 1960.
9 Apparently this was Vsevolod Ivanov. Leonov had told him about his interview with Stalin, where Ivanov's name had come up, adding: 'So long as Gor'ky is alive we are all like kids (*malen'kie*) around him.' Ivanov had in turn told Gor'ky, who took Leonov's words as a wish that he would soon make way for the younger generation (*Leonid Leonov v vospominaniyakh*..., pp. 335–6). Ivanov seems to have had no malicious intent, and he and Leonov remained on good terms afterwards.
10 Mikhaylov, *Mirozdanie po Leonovu*..., p. 100.
11 See E. Starikova, *Leonid Leonov* (M., 1972), p. 153.
12 Mikhaylov, *Mirozdanie po Leonovu*..., p. 102. It has been said that Gor'ky was upset by the suggestion that he had been the model for the dying Kurilov in *The Road to Ocean* (Mikhaylov, *Mirozdanie po Leonovu*..., pp. 102–3). Many Soviet critics have indeed seen elements of Gor'ky in this figure (see Kovalev, *Romany Leonida Leonova*, pp. 300–1, and Boguslavskaya, *Leonid Leonov*, p. 253). It may have been to reduce these similarities that Leonov replaced the 'Nietzschean moustache' (similar to Gor'ky's) of his hero in the journal edition (*NM*, 1935, no. 9, p. 6) by a 'Socratic brow.' For Leonov's own account of their relationship see *Leonid Leonov v vospominaniyakh*..., pp. 333–7.
13 This seems as plausible an explanation as any for the survival of Akhmatova and Pasternak, despite the victimization to which they were periodically subjected.
14 *The Orchards of Polovchansk* was commissioned in 1935 by the Moscow Arts theatre for the twentieth anniversary of the Bolshevik Revolution. It was completed in Jan. 1937 and an extract from it published in *SovIsk*, 11 Sept. 1937. The

Arts Theatre, however, insisted on several changes, and a new version was published in *NM*, 1938, no. 3, which remains virtually unaltered to the present day. The play was first performed at the Moscow Arts Theatre on 6 May 1939, but it was not a success; it ran for less than a year and only 36 performances were given. It was revived in the 1950s at the Moscow Mayakovsky Theatre under the title *The Gardener and the Ghost* (*Sadovnik i ten'*). This version is a free adaptation in three acts of Leonov's original four-act play, but the cuts and alterations were not approved by the author. Leonov also had hopes of turning the play into a film see 'Puteshestvie v neizvedannyy kray' (see *Kino* 29 Nov. 1938), but nothing seems to have come of this project.

15 First published in book form, M., 1938. First public performance in Tula in early April 1939. First Moscow performance at the Malyy Theatre 6 May 1939.
16 First published in book form, M., 1940. References to this edition will be indicated in the text by the initial *M*, followed by page number. First public performance in the Kazan' State Theatre on 17 April 1940. It was never publicly performed in Moscow. A revised version was published in *Zn.*, 1963, no. 2. It will be discussed with the other late revisions.
17 Leonov's first version in fact ended with the death of Makkaveev (see Fink, *Dramaturgiya...*, p. 235.)
18 The stigmatization of those who survived captivity anticipates the treatment of returned Russian prisoners after the Second World War.
19 *Istoriya sovetskogo dramaticheskogo teatra*, 6 vols. (M., 1967–71), vol. 4, p. 81. See also *Leonid Leonov v vospominaniyakh...*, p. 166–8.
20 See L. Leonov, 'Polovchanskie sady,' *SovIsk*, 5 March 1937.
21 Porfiriy's rank of *praporshchik* was the same as Leonov's when he entered cadet school in Archangel.
22 The plot of *The Snowstorm* had been anticipated in Mayakovsky's film scenario *Dekabryukhov and Oktyabryukhov* (*Dekabryukhov i Oktyabryukhov*, 1926). The film was released in 1928, but Mayakovsky's text was not published until 1936.
23 This symbol of manual labour to signify reintegration into Soviet society and spiritual regeneration recalls the destiny of Vekshin at the end of *The Thief*.
24 One may note here the reinterpretation of some of Leonov's earlier images. Luka Sandukov, the 'wolf,' does not possess any of the redeeming national qualities associated with the image in *The Breakthrough at Petushikha* and *The Badgers*. So too the concept of thieving is now rejected as utterly un-Russian: 'We live like thieves,' Elena complains to Roshchin (ostensibly about their clandestine love affair, but the words could also be interpreted in a more general sense).
25 Like other Communists in Leonov's work he is associated with the desire to level out all human individuality. He is the author of a paper on 'morality in a time of transition' in which he writes of the 'last revolt of the individual' (*M*, 31).

26 At the first performance of *The Orchards of Polovchansk* the scenery included a vast poster depicting an apple attacked by worms, as specified in the stage directions. It was forbidden by the censors because of its 'sinister implications' (see 'O povyshennykh esteticheskikh kriteriyakh i durnom vkuse,' *T.*, 1939, no. 5, pp. 3–11).
27 In the original version of the play the Pylyaev figure was called Usov. Leonov may have changed the name because Vladimir Lugovskoy had brought out a poem in 1937 called 'Commissar Usov,' or, alternatively, because the linguist D.P. Usov had been arrested at this time (see Nadezhda Mandel'shtam, *Vospominaniya*, p. 40). It was dangerous to use the names of un-persons even for villains.
28 'The theme of *The Orchards of Polovchansk* flows out of my last novel, *The Road to Ocean*. The play treats of the *podvig* of Soviet people.' ('Nad chem rabotayut pisateli,' *VechM*, 4 April 1938). The word *podvig* with its connotations of spiritual suffering and endurance has no exact English equivalent. Accordingly it will in future be used without translation or further comment.
29 By contrast with *The Orchards of Polovchansk* and *Wolf*, in *The Snowstorm* the younger generation plays no part in unmasking Stepan Syrovarov. This is left to the oldest characters, the aged aunts Marfa and Lizaveta, matriarchal equivalents of Makkaveev and Roshchin in the earlier plays. Marfa calls up Porfiriy to slap his face, but slaps Stepan instead.
30 See *SovIsk*, 11 Sept. 1937.
31 '*Volk* v Tule,' *LitGaz*, 5 April 1939.
32 This title was rejected by the censor Kerzhentsev. See 'O povyshennykh esteticheskikh kriteriyakh i durnom vkuse,' p. 8. It has been restored as the subtitle in all editions since 1955.
33 This too is paralleled in *The Orchards of Polovchansk* where it is said of Pylyaev: 'And you've become terribly nervy, you're always listening, running somewhere.' He replies: 'I've been on the run for six years now' (7. 194).
34 Gleb Protoklitov is twice called a 'wolf' (6. 171 and 500).
35 Like Gleb Luka also jumps off a train to begin a new life. The image goes back to Dmitriy Vekshin in *The Thief*.
36 Her name, Kseniya, recalls San'ka Velosiped's wife in *The Thief*, another *lishenka* (as the daughter of a Tsarist general), destroyed by the selfishness of a Communist.
37 This style of speech recalls the pomposities of Yakov Pustynnov in *A Provincial Story*.
38 The idea of Russia as a garden is of course found in many works, of which Chekhov's *The Cherry Orchard* and Mayakovsky's 'Sadu tsvest'' are only the best known, but there is a specific reference here. In early 1936 Stalin had said:

'cadres must be tended with as much love as a gardener tending his fruit-trees' (quoted from Fleyshman, *Boris Pasternak v tridtsatye gody*, p. 228). The gardener's story in *The Road to Ocean* acquires an additional sour note from this.
39 Although Vasiliy is included among the dramatis personae he never appears on stage.
40 Vasiliy drowns in the ocean that is celebrated in Leonov's preceding novel.
41 The closing lines of *The Gardens of Polovchansk*: 'I want us to be joyful today. It's my day, my day. Boys, where is your music?' spoken only a few hours after hearing of the death of Vasiliy, seem to echo Stalin's own: 'Life has become better, life has become merrier,' on the eve of unleashing the Great Purges.
42 When he revised the play Leonov made this line even more explicit: 'The well-being of a *country* is to be measured by the quantity of women's tears...' (7. 316).
43 Mikhaylov, *Mirozdanie po Leonovu...*, p. 193.
44 See Valentin Petrovich, 'Katastrofa v proezde Khudozhestvennogo teatra,' *Krokodil*, 1939, no. 14, p. 10. (Valentin Petrovich is the name and patronymic of V.P. Kataev, the originator of the first attacks on Leonov in 1933.) Leonov was in no doubt as to the author, 'An outrageous feuilleton by a certain well-known writer in *Krokodil*' (Mikhaylov, *Mirozdanie po Leonovu...*, p. 193). Kataev's hostility to Leonov would appear to be personal rather than political. He had displayed considerable courage in supporting Mandel'shtam during his years of exile in Voronezh and allowed him to stay at his Moscow apartment during his illegal visits to the capital. These visits were well known to the authorities. Stavsky, the General Secretary of the Union of Soviet Writers reported them directly to Ezhov (see Shentalinsky, *The KGB's Literary Archive*, pp. 186, 190).

Other articles in this vein include L. Nikulin, '*Polovchanskie sady*. Prem'era v Moskovskom khudozhestvennom akademicheskom teatre,' *MoskBol*, 14 May 1939; B. Rozentsveyg, 'O "rayskikh sadakh" Leonida Leonova' (*Polovchanskie sady* v MKhAT im. Gor'kogo), *KomPr*, 18 May 1939; D. Tal'nikov, '*Volk* v Gosudarstvennom Malom teatre,' *SovIsk*, 16 May 1939. Nikulin has been immortalized by the epigram 'Kain, gde Avel'; Nikulin, gde Babel'?' (Cain, where is Abel? Nikulin, where is Babel'?) He was one of the writers who was supposed to have accompanied Lidin and Leonov on their trip to Yaroslavl' in 1933.
45 See '*Polovchanskie sady*. Beseda s narodnym artistom RSFSR rezhisserom MKhATa V. G. Sakhnovskim,' *DMZ*, 1939, no. 14; I. Popov, I. Sudakov, A. Shumilin, 'O Leonove, o sovetskoy p'ese,' *SovIsk*, 27 May 1939.
46 A. Shin, 'Disput o p'esakh Leonida Leonova,' *VechM*, 27 May 1939.
47 E. Pel'son, 'Disput o p'esakh L. Leonova,' *LitGaz*, 30 May 1939.
48 'Itogi teatral'nogo sezona,' *SovIsk*, 2 June 1939.
49 E. Pel'son, 'Disput o p'esakh L. Leonova,' *LitGaz*, 30 May 1939.
50 'O povyshennykh esteticheskikh kriteriyakh...,' *T.*, 1939, no. 5.

51 See Mikhaylov, *Mirozdanie po Leonovu...*, p. 193. The article in *Izvestiya* would appear to be M. Serebryansky, 'Leonid Leonov,' *Izv*, 4 July 1939.
52 The censor's *imprimatur* is dated 17 April 1940.
53 See, for example, V. Zalessky, *'Metel'* L. Leonova v Kazani,' *SovIsk*, 18 May 1940, and A. Rappoport, *'Metel'* v dnepropetrovskom teatre im. Gor'kogo,' *Dnepropetrovskaya pravda*, 6 April 1940.
54 *'Metel'* Leonida Leonova,' *DMZ* (1939), no. 35.
55 'Klevetnicheskaya p'esa,' *SovIsk*, 22 Sept. 1940; V. Fomenko, 'Klevetnicheskaya p'esa,' *LitGaz*, 22 Sept. 1940.
56 The most significant of them is A. Gurvich, 'Pouchitel'nye neudachi,' *T*, 1940, no. 11. Its comparatively conciliatory title ('Instructive failures') reflects the fact that the journal had stood by Leonov at the beginning of these attacks, It may also have been trying to be even-handed, for the other 'failure' discussed in the article was Valentin Kataev's play *The Little House* (*Domik*).
57 Rostovtseva, 'Negativ, proyavlennyy vechnost'yu,' *LitGaz*, 1 June 1994.
58 Leonov claimed that in all six warrants for his arrest were presented to Stalin at one time or another, but that the dictator always declined to sign them (Maksim Shraer, 'Posledniy russkiy klassik na poroge stoletiya: predsmertnyy portret Leonida Leonova,' *LitOb*, 1998, no. 4, p. 41).
59 'Pered ukhodom v vechnost',' interview with Viktor Kozhemyako, *Pr*, 9 Aug. 1996. As early as 1962 Erenburg had also attributed the disgrace of *The Snowstorm* to Stalin's intervention (see his *Sobranie sochineniy*, 9 vols., M., 1962–7, vol. 9, p. 260). According to Mikhaylov Stalin had advised Leonov via Shcherbakov to transfer the material in the footnotes into the main text of *The Road to Ocean*. Leonov had refused and thus incurred the dictator's displeasure (*Mirozdanie po Leonovu...*, pp. 158–9). A photograph of Leonov in 1940 shows him in a deeply depressed mood, very different from the energetic and optimistic figure seen in other photographs (see *Tvorchestvo Leonida Leonova...*, 1969, p. 147).
60 Rostovtseva, 'Negativ, proyavlennyy vechnost'yu,' *LitGaz*, 1 June 1994.
61 For a detailed history of the reception of *The Snowstorm* in its two redactions see *Leonid Leonov v vospominaniyakh...*, pp. 177–94.

CHAPTER 9   The War Years 1941–1945

1 For an account of this period in Leonov's life see R. N. Porman, 'Chistopol'skiy period' in *Tvorchestvo Leonida Leonova...* (1969), pp. 459–63.
2 One sign of Leonov's rehabilitation was the invitation from Eisenstein to write the screenplay for *Ivan the Terrible*. This came to nothing, but Leonov was always interested in the cinema and composed several screenplays.

3 First published *NM*, 1942, no.8. It came out in book form later the same year. The first performance was intended for the Moscow Kamernyy Theatre, and rehearsals had actually begun when it was decided to abandon work on the play. *Invasion* was then offered to the Malyy Theatre. The first performance, however, was given in Chistopol' on the 25th anniversary of the Bolshevik Revolution, 7 Nov. 1942, and was produced by Leonov himself. The first Moscow performance was given by the Mossovet Theatre in March 1943. The Malyy Theatre premiere did not take place until 27 May 1943.
4 First published in *NM*, 1943, no. 5. It came out in book form later the same year. The play was apparently first intended for the Malyy theatre in Moscow. In January 1943 Leonov read the play to the company, but the theatre seems to have been uninterested. The first performance took place at the Griboedov theatre in Tbilisi on 25 Nov. 1943. It did not receive its Moscow premiere until 15 July 1946, when it was staged in the Moscow Theatre of Drama.
5 First published *NM*, 1944, no.6/7. It came out in book form later the same year.
6 This was first revealed in R. Porman, 'V surovoe vremya,' *LitTat*, 1957, no. 12, but the information was ignored for many years by other Soviet critics. In the 1980s Oleg Mikhaylov added some further details (see *Mirozdanie po Leonovu...*, p. 207).
7 Three years was the length of Luka Sandukov's 'absence' also.
8 A copy of the original text of the first act apparently still survives. See Porman, 'Chistopol'skiy period,' p. 438.
9 *Sobranie sochineniy*, 9 vols. (1961–3), vol. 7, p. 438. In the 1983 edition of Leonov's works, the material of the last act is substantially rearranged to provide a rather different ending. Ol'ga is weeping for her dead brother, Fedor, when her lover Kolesnikov appears:
 Kolesnikov. Why are you weeping, Ol'ga? this is a great victory for us.
 Ol'ga (as an echo). A great victory... (7. 528)
 This ending preserves the psychological implications of the original ending, while emphasizing the human cost of victory.
10 F. Peshchanskaya, 'Pisatel' i ego geroi,' *VechM*, 23 Nov. 1942.
11 In Leskov's story 'Peacock' (*Pavlin*, 1874), there is a character who is called a *grubyy biryuk* (a rough lone wolf) who proves to be an almost saintly character by the end.
12 See, for example, E. Surkov, 'O p'esakh Leonida Leonova *Nashestvie* i *Lenushka*' in *Teatr. Sbornik statey i materialov* (M., 1944).
13 At a writers' meeting in 1943 a letter from the officers and men of the tank corps appealing for a work devoted to their achievements was read out. Leonov was one of the writers who responded and he went to the Ukrainian front to gain impressions and material. Hence much of the story is based on fact: General

Litovchenko has been identified with General Kravchenko (*Sobranie sochineniy*, 9 vols., 1961–3, vol. 8, p. 553). Kovalev, however, states that Marshal Rybal'ko was the original for Leonov's hero (see 'Leonid Leonov,' *Don*, 1959, no. 5). On returning to Moscow Leonov undertook a detailed study of the mechanics of the tank and of the tactics and strategy of mechanized warfare. This experience explains the wealth of technical detail in the story. This has won the admiration of certain military figures, but at times tends to overwhelm the lay reader.

14 Leonov's horror at the use of poison gas had been voiced earlier by Agey in *The Thief* and Vissarion in *The Sot'*.
15 Leonid Leonov, 'Golos rodiny,' *Lit i Isk*, 5 June 1943.
16 See *NM*, 1944, 6–7, p. 21. The phrase was retained in all editions up to 1956.
17 It might be thought that the desperate military situation at the time might have made it difficult to think about putting on new plays, but in the circumstances anything that could be used as propaganda was welcomed.
18 See Porman, 'V surovoe vremya,' *LitTat*, 1957, no. 12.
19 Leonov told me that Stalin himself rang him up with the good news. Many years later Valentin Kataev circulated a rumour that Leonov had written a letter to Stalin, in which he had tried to recommend himself and his play by declaring that he was 'a pure-blooded Russian, and that there were too many cosmopolitans, Jews, and southerners.' See Chukovsky, *Dnevnik 1930–1969*, p. 306. I do not place much credence on this story. Kataev's vendetta against Leonov has been demonstrated in the previous chapter, and his reputation as a shameless liar is well attested from other sources.
20 S.K. Rudnitsky, 'Dramy Leonova,' *T*, 1958, no. 8.
21 Adapted for the screen by B. Chirskov. The film was released in 1944 by the Alma-Ata film studio.
22 Composer S. A. Dekhterev (sometimes spelled Degtyarev). Libretto in verse by Leonov and O. Leonidov. First published in *Sovetskaya muzyka*, 1952, nos. 6, 7. First performed in the Kirov theatre in Leningrad, 7 Nov. 1955.
23 See V. Gorodinsky, Ya. Varshavsky, 'Chernaya magiya. O p'ese Leonova *Lenushka*,' *KomPr*, 15 Oct. 1946.
24 See K. Simonov, 'O nekotorykh nedostoynykh metodakh kritiki,' *Pr*, 17 Oct. 1946.

CHAPTER 10 *An Ordinary Man* and *A Golden Coach* 1940–1946

1 First published in book form (M., 1942) in an edition of only 500 copies. The 1953 edition of Leonov's collected works gives the date of composition as 1940–3, though there are no textual differences between the first three editions (1942, 1944, and 1947). All three quote the same censor's *imprimatur* (27 Aug. 1942);

even the misprints of the first edition were corrected only in the fourth edition (1953), which also contains some minor revisions to the original text.

The confusion over the dating is probably due to the controversy over *The Snowstorm*. It has been suggested that Leonov had considerable trouble in persuading a theatre to take the play (see Yu. Yuzovsky, '*Obyknovennyy chelovek* v Moskovskom teatre dramy,' *SovIsk*, 3 Aug. 1945). In any case the outbreak of war would have lessened the chances of the play's being produced. In the latest edition of Leonov's works the date of composition is correctly given as 1940–1. The play was first performed on 22 May 1945 in the Moscow Theatre of Drama: producer F. Kaverin.

2 First published in a limited edition of 500 copies (M., 1946). The censor's imprimatur is dated 18 July 1946. The play was in rehearsal at the Malyy Theatre and receiving favourable publicity when the order to suppress it was given some time in Oct.–Nov. 1946 (see Kovalev, *Leonid Leonov: Seminariy*, 1964, p. 70). The original text has never been reissued. A substantially revised edition was brought out by Leonov in 1955, and this was further modified in 1957; a fourth version, which in some respects returns to the solutions of the 1946 edition, was released in 1964 in Leonid Leonov, *P'esy* (M., 1964). All references to the 1946 edition will be indicated by the initials ZK, followed by the page number.
3 For more details see *Leonid Leonov v vospominaniyakh...*, pp. 194–7.
4 Mikhaylov, *Mirozdanie po Leonovu...*, p. 188.
5 Some commentators spell his name Lodygin, so raising associations of 'laziness.'
6 His name Pavel relates him to the hard revolutionaries of Russian fiction, Pavel Vlasov, Pavel Rakhleev (or Comrade Anton), and Pavel Korchagin.
7 In this respect the play recalls *The Taming of Badadoshkin* and *Skutarevsky*.
8 Leonov suggested that he had in mind some place in the Pskov area. The remoteness of the town from all big cities, however, suggests somewhere much less accessible. In this and other respects it borrows from Chistopol', where Leonov's family had been evacuated during the war. Berezkin's home, 22 Karl Marx Street, was in fact their address in Chistopol'; Mar'ya Sergeevna was the name of the mayor of the city, who did much to help the Leonovs.
9 An earlier version of this section was published in 'Leonov's Play *Zolotaja kareta*,' in *SEEJ*, vol. 6, no. 3 (fall, 1972), pp. 438–48. I am grateful to the editor for permission to use the material here.
10 Mar'ya Sergeevna married Chirkhanov about two years after Karev's departure. She has been married for 25 years.
11 Kovalev, *Leonid Leonov: Seminariy* (1964), p. 69.
12 *Zolotaya kareta. Materialy k postanovke...*, pp. 17–18.
13 It is paralleled by the empty ikon frame which Leonov specifies in the stage directions.

14 Timosha's undemanding love for Mar'ka recalls that of Madali for Zoya in *The Snowstorm*. Madali comes from the Pamirs, and his last name, Niyazmetov ('Not I') points to his self-effacing character.
15 Berezkin and Timosha, respectively bereaved and blinded, are thrown back on their own inner resources, much like Kurilov in *The Road to Ocean*. It is significant then that Leonov took the opportunity to make this point about the novel in his notes on the play (see *Zolotaya kareta, Materialy k postanovke...*, pp. 4–5).
16 The idea is further discredited when Konstantsiya observes: 'Of course it's lovely to settle in an isolated cottage on the very edge of the sea' (7. 443).
17 In 1935 Leonov had written an article 'The Fall of Zaryad'e' (*Paden'e Zaryad'ya*), describing the squalor of pre-revolutionary Zaryad'e and the glories of the stadiums, airports, etc., soon to replace them. In revising the article for the 10-volume edition of his works in 1982, he added the following sentence at the very end: 'All the same, in spite of all the glaring horrors that I have enumerated I still feel sad today and regretful for something – for what?' (10. 420). I owe this idea to Groznova, *Tvorchestvo Leonida Leonova i traditsii...*, p. 63.
18 See Yu. Yuzovsky, '*Obyknovennyy chelovek* v Moskovskom teatre dramy,' *SovIsk*, 3 Aug. 1945, and L. Dmitriev, 'Dnevnik iskusstv,' *LitGaz*, 16 June 1945.
19 Scenario (unpublished) by Leonov and M. Romm; director: A. Stolbov, Mosfil'm, 1956.

CHAPTER 11   *The Russian Forest* 1953

1 Kovalev identifies the article in *Iz tvorcheskogo naslediya...*, p. 454. Shraer (see 'Posledniy russkiy klassik....,' p. 41) implausibly claims that it was 'Na bashne' (published in *Pr*, 9 May 1946). The former article has never been reprinted since the XX Party Congress, while the latter is concerned with Stalin only indirectly, and has been reissued several times.
2 'Slovo o pervom deputate,' *Pr*, 23 Jan. 1946.
3 *P'esy* (M., 1964), p. 114.
4 See Abalkin, *Sistema Stanislavskogo i sovetskiy teatr*, p. 238.
5 See his letter to Kovalev of 30 Dec. 1948 in *Iz tvorcheskogo naslediya...*, p. 429.
6 First published in *Zn*, 1953, nos. 10–12; in book form early in 1954. In the *Zn* edition the novel is dated Jan. 1950–Sept. 1953; in later reissues it is dated Jan. 1950–Dec. 1953. The discrepancy is probably due to the minor changes that Leonov made to the novel while the *Zn* edition was still being published. Alterations took the form mainly of adding adjectives and adjectival phrases to the text. In quoting from the novel I have indicated by italics passages that were added to the original edition. As will be seen, the vast majority have the function of underlining and intensifying (often unnecessarily) points that were made in the

original, rather than modifying or altering them. But some of them serve to sharpen the political point.

Max Hayward claimed that Leonov had told him that Stalin had personally censored the manuscript of the novel (see *The Soviet Censorship*, ed. Martin Dewhirst and Robert Farrell, Metuchen, 1973, p. 17). Since the dictator had died in March 1953 this seems unlikely; it is more likely that Leonov was referring to the first edition of *The Thief*, which Stalin had indeed read and annotated vigorously in the margins.

7 'Blagodarnost',' *Pr*, 18 Dec. 1949. The article has never been republished. In a letter to Kovalev of 8 Feb. 1965 Leonov wrote that such publications 'required an extensive commentary in justification' (see *Iz tvorcheskogo naslediya...*, p. 458).
8 Ibid., p. 459. And yet Leonov could also be taken in by official propaganda. Three months after the death of Stalin he and his wife were still unwilling to let their daughter be treated by the Kremlin doctors, a privilege granted only to artists enjoying official favour: 'What if all the medicines have been poisoned?' See Chukovsky, *Dnevnik 1930–1969*, p. 200.
9 For example, in the novel Leonov proudly quotes from one of his wartime articles: 'That famous aphorism that travelled through a hundred mouths to the columns of newspapers that "all the world's children cry in the same language"' (9. 602). The 'aphorism' originally appeared in 'Neizvestnomu amerikanskomu drugu. Pis'mo pervoe' (10. 109).
10 Aleksandr Blok, *Sobranie sochineniy*, 8 vols. (M., 1960–3), vol. 3, p. 362.
11 In all there are about fifteen explicit references to Stalin in the first editions of the novel. These were either cut or replaced by more general expressions after the XX Party Congress. The most substantial of these changes concern his famous appearance at the annual parade in November 1941 (cf. *Zn*, 1953, no. 11, pp. 120–1 and 9. 482–5). This does not seem to have been forced on Leonov. Sinyavsky describes visiting Leonov at this time and finding him cutting out every mention of Stalin's name in his works (Andrei Sinyavsky, *Soviet Civilization: A Cultural History*, trans. Joanne Turnbull, New York, 1996, p. 104).
12 Akhmatova was faced by an even sharper version of this dilemma over her cycle of poems 'Glory to Peace' (*Slava miru*, 1949–50), which she was forced to compose under threat of reprisals against her son, then in a labour camp. She protested strongly against Struve's including these poems in his 1965 edition of her works. He justified his decision on the grounds that the cycle was a 'document of the times' and exemplified the pressures under which she lived. For their part Soviet editors since 1962 have been reluctant to print these poems in their editions of Akhmatova's work.
13 Leonid Leonov, 'Pozabotimsya o zeleni,' *VechM*, 24 March 1945.
14 Leonid Leonov, 'V zashchitu druga,' *Izv*, 28 Dec. 1947.

15 In fact for some time Leonov was considering a novel about the oil industry of Baku. See *Leonid Leonov: Tvorcheskaya individual'nost'...*, p. 274.
16 For the prehistory of the composition of *The Russian Forest* see Kovalev, *Tvorchestvo Leonida Leonova* (1962), pp. 169–230, and E. N. Lopukhov, 'Za grazhdanstvo lesa,' in *Tvorchestvo Leonida Leonova...* (1969), pp. 472–81.
17 In *Skutarevsky* Petrygin suffers from diabetes; so too Gratsiansky's character is suggested by his anaemia, an ingenious image for the negativeness of his views and his own shadowy semi-existence.
18 As with *The Road to Ocean*, the theme of *The Russian Forest* might be summed up by a quotation from *The Brothers Karamazov*: 'If the forests are destroyed then the land of Russia too will perish' (Dostoevsky, *PSS*, vol. 14, p. 122).
19 V. O. Klyuchevsky, *Sochineniya*, 8 vols. (M., 1956), vol. 1, p.67. In his lecture Vikhrov echoes these feelings: 'a contradictory attitude to the forest – a mixture of an exaggerated affection (usually the consequence of a convivial get-together) and an indifference, not to say neglect, inherited from our remote ancestors, and at times open hostility' (9. 312).
20 See decree of Lenin and Sverdlov on controlled felling, 30 May 1918.
21 'The most valuable timber was sold at reduced prices. This involved a loss to the Soviet state of several million roubles in foreign currency.' See *Report of the Court Proceedings in the Case of the Anti-Soviet 'Bloc of Rights and Trotskyites,'* English ed. (M., 1938), p.123 (quoted from Robert Conquest, *The Great Terror*, London, 1968, pp. 375–6). The process began after the collapse of grain exports caused by the disastrous effects of collectivization in Ukraine, and is alluded to in *The Sot'*: 'In an attempt to patch the deficiency in wheat exports the country hurled vast quantities of forest abroad; in no time the Soviet Union became the third largest exporter of timber' (5. 320).
22 Several prominent names in Russian forestry appear in *The Russian Forest*, notably Tulyakov, who was arrested and executed in the later 1930s. Vikhrov himself is probably largely modelled on M. E. Tkachenko (1878–1950), who was a personal friend of Leonov's and was the source of much of his information. His name does not appear in the text. Many names could be adduced as models for Gratsiansky. One of them, N. Alekseychik, appears in Leonov's novel thinly disguised as the trinity of Andreychik, Eychik, and Chik.
23 Kovalev, *Tvorchestvo Leonida Leonova* (1962), p. 189.
24 *Zn*, 1953, no. 11, p. 44.
25 At the end of *The Thief* a spring is one of the two 'living creatures' that Vekshin meets in the forest, 'pulsing, like a never-freezing, thousand-year-old heart' (*Vor*, 539).
26 Conversely the expression *mertvaya voda* ('dead water' or 'the water of death') is associated with Gratsiansky.

27 The only other occasion in Leonov's work where the hero threatens to kill someone occurs in *The Badgers*, when Semen is appalled by Nastya's turning a machine-gun on the peasants. In both cases the hero is driven to these words by the urgent need to protect life; on neither occasion does he carry out his threat.
28 This aspect of Gratsiansky was apparently modelled on the musicologist S. Dianin, who was still alive in the 1950s (see Kovalev, *Tvorchestvo Leonida Leonova*, 1962, pp. 225–30). Leonov confirmed this in a letter to Kovalev (see *Iz tvorcheskogo naslediya*..., p. 442). The motif recalls the figure of Pustynnov in *A Provincial Story*, who had worked as an *agent provocateur* for the Tsarist Okhrana, and betrayed his friend Godlevsky to arrest and execution.
29 So too his ally Cheredilov has a 'skull that immediately adopts the curves and contours of his superior's hand' (9. 402).
30 The name indicates a Russian clerical family, and is reflected in Gratsiansky's studies in a theological college. The name had been used earlier in Russian literature for Tuberozov's successor in Leskov's *Cathedral folk* (*Soboryane*, 1872). In Leonov's novel, however, the righteous hero outlives his rival. The name may also suggest *grazhdansky* (civic), a word often misused by Soviet spokesmen.
31 Compare the attack on the scholar Boris Eykhenbaum in 1949 for 'aggressive idealism, eclectically combining in himself positivism, intuitivism, neokantianism, pluralism, "energeticism" as a variant of Machism. In practical terms this took the form of a hostile attitude to Marxism-Leninism. [...] A disregard for Russian culture and kowtowing to the West led him into cosmopolitanism.' (See B. Papkovsky, 'Formalizm i eklektika professora Eykhenbauma,' *Zv*, 1949, no. 9, p. 181). Probably many more examples of such jargon could be found.
32 This point is made by Ekaterina Starikova in her book *'Russkiy les' Leonida Leonova* (M., 1963), pp. 98–101, but she does not suggest any names.
33 Mikhaylov, *Mirozdanie po Leonovu*, 219. In fact Leonov anticipated these criticisms in the course of his novel. Morshchikhin asks Serezha: 'why Vikhrov, though conscious that he was absolutely in the right, should have kept his silence for twenty-five years?... or who gave Gratsiansky the right to make the most damaging political accusations, which can be raised only by the relevant articles of Soviet law... and then only after a thorough investigation?... or why Gratsiansky should have enlisted Vikhrov among his personal enemies, and what point there was in discrediting a colleague who was more knowledgeable in forestry matters?' He goes on to ask Serezha what he himself thinks about Gratsiansky. Serezha is "shaking all over" with embarrassment and tries to get away. But Morshchikhin refuses to let him go: "I am asking you as a member of the Komsomol why you are keeping silent." At this point Serezha reminds Morshchikhin that as the son of a *kulak* he is in no position to speak out. "Morshchikhin fell

silent: only now was he beginning to understand the full power of the poison, undetectable by any technical apparatus, that had been injected into this boy, who, it would seem, had no connection with the world of the past"' (9. 538–9).
34 On another occasion Vikhrov's wife mistakes him for the Communist Kraynov.
35 In *The Russian Forest* Leonov moves the critical events in the story back from 1918–20, typical of his earlier works, to 1910–12, and in particular the assassination of Stolypin on 1 Sept. 1911, when he himself was only a schoolboy. He underlines the importance of this period by referring to the fourth chapter (and in particular the 31st paragraph) of Stalin's *Short History of the Communist Party (bolsheviks)*, which is mainly concerned with the Stolypin period. The associations of a Tsarist police informer now working for the Communists with the Stolypin assassination reappear in *The Pyramid*. These allusions are clearly significant for Leonov, and perhaps contain coded references to Dianin. The '31st paragraph' is difficult to identify because of the sectional layout of the chapter.
36 See M. Shcheglov, '*Russkiy les* Leonida Leonova,' *NM*, 1954, no. 5. This aspect of the article later came under attack. See 'O kriticheskom otdele zhurnala *Novyy mir*,' *LitGaz*, 1 July 1954.
37 The first Soviet critic to examine this aspect of the novel was E.V. Starikova in her short but excellent study, cited above, '*Russkiy les' Leonida Leonova*. Published in the dying days of the Khrushchev 'Thaw,' the book is an intelligent and courageous elucidation of the implications of Leonov's novel.
38 See Edward Ellis Smith, *The Young Stalin: The Early Years of an Elusive Revolutionary* (New York, 1967) for an extended presentation of this case. At the time of the assassination of Stolypin Stalin paid a brief visit to St Petersburg, and was soon afterwards arrested but given a mild sentence, which has led Smith to suppose that Stalin was already working for the Okhrana (see *The Young Stalin*, pp. 244–5).
39 This sentence was added in the 1955 edition of the novel. This willingness to sacrifice individual lives for the sake of a dubious cause recalls the machinations of Petr Verkhovensky in *The Devils*. It is, of course, a recurrent theme of Leonov's.
40 Here Gratsiansky paraphrases some lines from Nekrasov's poem, 'The Poet and the Citizen' (*Poet i grazhdanin*, 1855–6): 'Enter the fire for the honour of the fatherland, for your convictions, for your love... Enter and perish without reproach. You shall not die in vain; the cause is assured when blood flows beneath it' (N. A. Nekrasov, *Polnoe sobranie stikhotvoreniy*, 3 vols., L., 1967, vol. 1, p. 234). In Nekrasov the self-sacrifice is voluntary; Gratsiansky thinks only of sacrificing others.
41 This sentence was added in the 1955 edition of the novel.

42 Another parallel can be found in Morshchikhin's conversation with Serezha: 'I recently came across one of [Gratsiansky's] articles. It is like a sniper's bullet from round the corner, with the advantage moreover that it leaves no hole in the victim. And just today I picked up a filthy pamphlet thrown out of an enemy plane, which invites traitors to put sugar in our fuel tanks. Take note: not poison, not acid, not explosives, but the most inoffensive *sweet* product' (9. 538).

43 R. A. Peace, letter to the editor, *TLS*, 1 Oct. 1976.

44 Alexander Gershchenkron, 'Reflections on Soviet Novels,' *World Politics*, Jan. 1960, p. 168. The comparison of the Western powers to vultures further allies them with Gratsiansky.

45 Leonov makes it clear that Lena is only an adopted child, but this is clearly an insurance device against the Gratsianskys still active in Soviet criticism. Lena's treatment would be no less unjust were she really a child of the landed gentry.

46 'The word "kinship" acquires the meaning of complicity' (9. 144).

47 Polya's interview with the NKVD is ominously reminiscent of an interrogation. (9. 549–56): 'Nobody saw her being led away to sleep in a half-buried hut on the edge of the village, from which she emerged several days later, without even being able to remember the name of the village' (9. 556).

48 The play on words occurs elsewhere in the book. For example, Kraynov asks Vikhrov if Gratsiansky is an 'honourable man.' 'I would say rather, an unhappy man' (9. 389).

49 'Purity' is of course also an important concept in Nazi ideology. For the purpose of *The Russian Forest* this connection is important, but the theme is also Leonov's own.

50 These thoughts are at first credited to Vikhrov. By the end of the paragraph, however, they have become Kraynov's. There is no apparent break in the train of thought or thinker.

51 The phrase 'the foothills of Communism' appears also on 9. 125.

52 In *The Snowstorm* Zoya Syrovarova's room too is 'memorable for its sterile purity' (*M*, 23), and the phrase was retained in the 1962 revision of the play. This passion for purity seems to be an expression of the child's sense of contamination by a rejected parent. In her case her shame at having a father in emigration is even stronger than her hatred of her stepfather's criminal activities. In this connection Leonov's words at the end of 'In Defence of our Friend' ring rather strangely: '... There are no lands on this earth, where man can breathe so freely. Then let us ensure that the material he breathes is sterilely pure in the literal sense of the word' (6. 409).

53 In a fragment of 1857 Marx asked why Greek art 'should still constitute with us a source of aesthetic enjoyment, and in certain respects prevail as the standard and model beyond attainment,' but without giving any clear answer (Karl Marx,

Friedrich Engels, *Literature and Art: Selections from Their writings*, New York, 1947, pp. 19–20).
54 In the journal version of the novel Leonov had written '... information about the composer and *the social underpinnings* of the work to be performed *and how the classics of Marxism had commented on music*, without which...' (*Zn.*, 1953, no. 11, p. 69). The italicized phrases were omitted or modified in editions published after 1956.
55 It may be noted that Serezha has the same name as the unattractive Komsomol leader in *The Snowstorm*.
56 In the *Zn* edition of the novel this quotation is given to Vikhrov. By transferring it to Serezha Leonov is making clear his dissociation from the idea.
57 The direct reference is to Gleb Uspensky's story 'She straightened me up' (*Vypryamila*, 1885), which contains the story of Heine sitting for hours before the statue. V. I. Khrulev has suggested that Leonov is hereby also recalling Heine's mixed feelings about Communism, for all its promises of social justice: 'I think with horror of the time when these sullen iconoclasts will come to power. With their rough hands they will mercilessly smash all the marble statues of beauty that are so dear to my heart; they will cut down the laurel groves and plant potatoes in their place.' (Quoted from V. I. Khrulev, *Mysl' i slovo Leonida Leonova* Saratov, 1989, p. 130). The passage from Heine is taken from his preface to the French edition of *Lutetia* (1855).
58 The 'monopolists' would be assumed by most Soviet readers to mean the capitalist West; but, as in *Skutarevsky*, Leonov is here implying that the monopolization of culture by the Russian Communist Party is just as culpable.
59 See Vlasov, *Poeziya zhizni*, p. 69.
60 The italicized words were added in 1955 to the original *Znamya* text. Gratsiansky is simply taking Bukharin's views on socialist culture to their logical conclusion. In fact only one section (§ 86) of the *ABC of Communism* is devoted to cultural issues and that takes up less than a page (see *Azbuka kommunizma*, pp. 162–3).
61 Before leaving for the front, Varya gives her copy of *The Voyage of the Beagle* to Polya (9. 318). Darwin's theory of natural selection is to play an important part in *The Pyramid*.
62 Starikova argues that Leonov envisages two kinds of purity: one is sterile, the other fertile. Thus she maintains that Polya comes to a more complex understanding of 'purity' when her rescuer from the Nazis turns out to be the former *kulak*, Demidka Zolotukhin, Serezha's father, now collaborating with the enemy ('*Russkiy les' Leonida Leonova*, p. 87): purity does not have to be absolute. It seems to me though that Leonov is indeed questioning the ideal of purity and has been throughout most of his creative life; it is impurity that is fertile.
63 The suggestion has been raised earlier. See R. Hingley, 'Leonid Leonov,' *Soviet Survey*, no. 25, 1958.

64 This is another reason why Leonov's forest is 'green' and not 'dark.'
65 Kovalev, *Etyudy o Leonide Leonove*, p. 190.
66 Another critic who attacked the novel at this meeting was called Dik. Leonov's comment was a witty misquotation of a famous line from Lermontov: 'Rvetsya Terek, Dik i Zlobin' ('The Terek rages, wild and angry [Dik and Zlobin]'). See Chukovsky, *Dnevnik 1930–1969*, p. 214. For more detail on this meeting see *Leonid Leonov v vospominaniyakh...*, pp. 198–204.
67 For a full account of Russian forestry policies and practices since the nineteenth century and the controversies surrounding Leonov's novel see Kovalev, 'Tema russkogo lesa,' in *Etyudy o Leonide Leonove*. Kovalev himself was to come under attack as late as 1957 for his defence of Leonov (see ibid., pp. 201–2 and *Iz tvorcheskogo naslediya...*, pp. 444–5, 447, 470, 485). In 1954 he was refused membership in the Union of Soviet Writers (see ibid., pp. 441–2) and again in 1975 (ibid., p. 477); he was finally accepted in January 1977 (ibid., 478–9). Leonov himself was proposed for membership for the Academy of Sciences, despite his attempts to withdraw his candidacy. His suspicions were well-founded, as he was blackballed. He was finally admitted in 1972 for his contributions to 'literary scholarship.' See ibid., pp. 464–5, 473.
68 This, however, does not mean that all these copies were sold or read. Tvardovsky recalled seeing unsold copies of *The Russian Forest* in every kiosk (see Chukovsky, *Dnevnik 1930–1969*, pp. 303–4). The size of an edition in Soviet times was more a signal of an author's standing in official favour than of popular demand for his books. The works of countless Soviet hacks met the same fate.
69 This point is made by M. Kuznetsov, 'Russkiy les,' *Pr*, 28 March 1954.

CHAPTER 12 The Late Revisions 1955–1962

1 First published in *Pr*, 1, 2, 4, 6, 8, 29 Jan., 3, 5 Feb. 1961. It was published in book form later the same year.
2 Fink, *Dramaturgiya Leonida Leonova*, p. 305.
3 Revised version first published in *Okt*, 1955, no. 4. It came out in book form in 1957 with a few minor changes. The revised version was first performed in Warsaw in February 1956. The first Russian performance was given in Karaganda in late 1956, and the first Moscow performance by the Arts Theatre on 6 Nov. 1957.
4 Revised edition first published in book form, *Vor* (M., 1959). Leonov continued to make changes up to the last years of his life.
5 Revised edition first published in *Sobranie sochineniy*, 9 vols. (M., 1960–2), vol. 1.
6 Revised edition first published in *Zn*, 1963, no. 2. Citations will be taken from the almost identical version printed in *P'esy* (1964) and indicated in the text.
7 First published in *Zn*, 1963, no. 11.

8 For a more detailed examination of the revisions to *Invasion*, see Fink, *Uroki Leonida Leonova*, pp. 357–9.
9 An earlier version of this section was published in 'Leonov's Play *Zolotaja kareta*,' in *SEEJ*, vol. 6, no. 3 (fall, 1972), pp. 438–48. I am grateful to the editor for permission to use the material here.
10 Leonov's words in conversation in 1960.
11 Similarly in *The Pyramid* one of the Gavrilovs raises his social standing by doubling a vowel, Gavriilov.
12 Leonid Leonov, *Sobranie sochineniy*, 9 vols. (M., 1960–2), vol. VII, p. 577. All references to this version of *A Golden Coach* will be taken from this edition and distinguished from the later 10-volume edition of 1981–4 by the use of a roman numeral for the volume. The play underwent further revisions after this date, and quotations from the later version will be taken from the 1981–4 edition, cited in the usual way.
13 1936 is associated in Leonov's mind with the beginning of the purges and his own fall from favour, as can be seen from *The Russian Forest*, completed only two years before the revised *Golden Coach*.
14 At the beginning of Act IV he says to her: 'We cannot get any answer out of you; (*harshly*) do you want to come to Pamir with us or not?' Mar'ka replies: 'You talk to me as though we were already at Pamir' (VII. 574).
15 When Timosha makes this plain the stage directions remark: 'Fortunately for him Timosha cannot see the changing emotions reflected openly in Mar'ya Sergeevna's face and bearing; relief, agonizing pity, renewed suspicions, and simply pangs of conscience. Mar'ya Sergeevna has to restrain herself twice from shaking Timosha's hand, which would betray her gratitude as a mother and her readiness to accept this sacrifice.' (VII. 540)
16 See, for example, A. A. Fadeev, *Za tridtsat' let* (M., 1957), pp. 768–9.
17 First published in Leonid Leonov, *P'esy* (M., 1964). For a fuller discussion of the changes see Starikova, *Leonid Leonov*, pp. 286–335, Fink, *Uroki Leonida Leonova*, pp. 352–3, and Mikhaylov, *Mirozdanie po Leonovu...*, pp. 222–9.
18 Mikhaylov, *Mirozdanie po Leonovu...*, p. 226.
19 Leonov's words, quoted in *Tvorchestvo Leonida Leonova...* (1969), pp. 201–2 and 249.
20 This version is published as vol. 3 of the 10-volume set that has been used here. There are also minor alterations from one edition to another.
21 Published as *Vor. Roman* (M., 'Profizdat,' 1991).
22 *Iz tvorcheskogo naslediya...*, p. 447.
23 Leonov quotes Firsov's novel: '[Vekshin] was merely a thief, that is the very lowest of the heroic generation, that had stormed the mighty citadel... but he was alive, and those who had not fallen in battle were now called upon to continue life

and to build a new world not only outside, but inside themselves, for otherwise all their endeavours and sacrifices would have been for nothing' (3. 426).

24 It may be noted that in 1927 the White officer's rank had been that of captain. In the new version he is an ensign (*poruchik*), one of the junior ranks held by such characters as Gleb Protoklitov who share certain features with Leonov himself.

25 The image of the eye as the repository of a secret knowledge that eludes the revolutionaries probably comes from Khlebnikov's long poem *Night Search* (*Nochnoy obysk*, 1921). In the 1927 *Thief* it appears only in connection with Agey, but there too it is linked to the theme of the place of evil in future history. Agey bayonets an Austrian soldier: 'Then I hit him with my rifle butt, and he looked at me, just like you're looking at me now, imploringly. I could see his eye was fading and blinking, looking for something. What was he looking for, Firsov (though it's true, when you're being beaten with a rifle butt, death is not in the butt, but in the eye itself!). The way he blinked, no way, I thought; do you want to climb into my eyes? So I wrinkled them up' (*Vor*, 128). Agey cannot bear the reminder that the eye contains, but Firsov, the novelist and chronicler has to endure it, unbearable though it may be. He is 'shaken by the blaze in Agey's eyes' (*Vor*, 125).

26 The following three paragraphs were inserted between the questions and their answers in the 1982 version:

Russians have always enjoyed their fruit before it ripens, and have then suffered throughout history from their teeth being set on edge.

Admittedly, the young everywhere are in a hurry to enter into their inheritance even during their parents' lifetimes, in the hope of achieving as much as possible before nightfall. And the secret of their work of obliteration lies in the fact that they know nothing, remember nothing, and never suspect that by the law of repetition and succession they too must meet the same fate. At first they are governed by a sort of aesthetic disgust at the sinful smell of corruption (in fact just an ageing body), which pervades the family home, but later purely practical considerations come into play. Unconstrained by any reverence for their patrimony they set to work, but then suddenly in the midst of their energetic activities in the acquisition of the property it transpires that the supreme treasure of the contemptible and vanquished old man consists not in hoards of diamonds, not even in the evidence of his material culture, not in underground vaults, but is to be found here, so close you could touch it, in the depth of his gaze, or rather in the elusive depths of the pupil, or better still, in that tiny and as it were slightly damp point of light in the weightless glint on its surface. No doubt this tiny particle of light is an older sister to the evening star, and that is why it can be seen from every corner of the universe. Without it the human race would instantly become a pack of wolves, trotting behind their leader over the sunset-coloured snow.

> And here a comic scene: the vanquished father with a gag in his mouth, leaning against the tree, while his impatient heir with his weapon bends over him, preoccupied with how to extract this priceless star from the loathsome and ironic eye. (3. 493–4)

27 Firsov specifically contradicts this imagery:
> ... the human soul is a rather strange kind of mechanism. Unlike a sewing-machine it cannot stand the intrusion of a screwdriver. It cannot tolerate any chemistry in the form of pills protecting it from evil, it wants its experience neat. In other words it wants to experience everything that makes up our reality, i. e., eternity, the struggle of light and dark, personally, with its eyes wide open [...] and not from the reports of the professional operatives of some literary guild. [...] In a word, I stand for an art that makes man better all round and not just in some particular administrative-organizational or domestic-hygienic field. (3. 461)

The image of the screwdriver occurs also in *The Pyramid*.

28 'Roundness' naturally recalls for Russian readers another near namesake of Chikilev's, Gogol''s Chichikov.

29 The 'cleared ground' (*ogolennoe mesto*) that Tolya speaks of recalls the 'naked man on a naked earth' that Vissarion had envisaged.

30 The phrase occurs several times in the book. Another example:
> Of course, the content of all the intemperate verbal effusions catalogued here should be left on the conscience of Firsov who communicated them. Though, out of the same old authorial cunning he related them not in his own person but ascribed them to his double of the same name. It would be fairer then to assume that this conversation never took place in reality. (3. 116).

31 The first paragraph of this passage has been almost totally rewritten since 1962. The idea of looking back at the cost of one's happiness is found in both *The Russian Forest* and *Evgenia Ivanovna*. In both cases the gesture is associated with fire, as in the story of Lot's wife. Elena Ivanovna, Vikhrov's wife, is about to surrender to her love for Mark Vetrov, when 'at the last moment she looks back at her daughter with regret and purely as a farewell gesture,' only to see the town on fire behind her and run back (9.371).

So too, as her car leaves the Alazan' valley Evgenia Ivanovna looks round for the last time:
> Through the cloudy oval of the back window she could see the bonfire blazing in the open field. The wind was combing handfuls of sparks from it that chased after her. Then the Buick turned round an olive grove, and the scratches of time on the windscreen were joined by scratches of rain... (8. 196)

32 *Sobranie sochineniy*, 9 vols. (1962), vol. 3, p. 147. This sentence was dropped from later editions.

33 The comparison of culture to original sin had been anticipated in the *Correspondence between Two Corners* of Ivanov and Gershenzon. See Vyacheslav Ivanov, *Sobranie sochineniy*, vol. 3, p. 391. Leonov's position is very close to Ivanov's in this debate, and there are several verbal parallels.
34 Rostovtseva, 'Negativ, proyavlennyy vechnost'yu,' *LitGaz*, 1 June 1994.
35 *Sobranie sochineniy*, 4 vols. (Khar'kov, 1929), vol. 1, p. 223.
36 *Iz tvorcheskogo naslediya...*, p. 454.
37 This rather undermines Stepan's rank as an important official – he has an 'impressive nomenclatured briefcase' (*P'esy*, 158).
38 This phrase was used by Serebrovsky of negative eugenics (see David Joravsky, *Soviet Marxism and Natural Science*, New York, 1961, p. 306).
39 In the 1940 version Porfiry had to earn his redemption by working on a collective farm. In 1963 he can spend only a few hours with his family, and he even refuses to see his daughter before setting off 'for the far North... where he intends to bury his head in the snow' (*P'esy*, 164). This last phrase is probably a euphemism for the treatment that awaited many returning Soviet émigrés in the immediate pre-war period. As Stepan says to Porfiriy: 'You'll find out soon enough what sort of coast and weather conditions you have been washed up on by the merciful waves. You fool: you've come back too soon. *It* hasn't finished yet. From now on you will spend sleepless nights listening to the footsteps on the staircase (as though they were carrying lead), and then the roar of a departing motor [...] And you too will be taken away, dumped in a large pit and covered with frozen earth. You will get the share of Russian snow that you once pined for' (*P'esy*, 139).
40 The play was not staged for some time; Polikarpov who had condemned the play in 1940 continued to obstruct it (see *Iz tvorcheskogo naslediya...*, p. 454).
41 Editor's note, 8. 311–2.
42 Kovalev has suggested that the name Pickering may allude to the colonel in Bernard Shaw's *Pygmalion* who falls in love with his protégée (see *Etyudy o Leonide Leonove*, p. 286).
43 Vikhrov also took his wife to Georgia in the vain hope of winning her love.
44 The areas of special interest to Pickering are the Egyptian pyramids, which provide the title for Leonov's last novel, *Assyria* (associated with megalomania in the recently revised *Snowstorm*), and, thirdly, Russia. Pickering's interest may be archaeological, but Leonov's choice of sites is based on other parallels.
45 Compare Vekshin's contempt for Firsov's writing in the revised *Thief*: 'You're a fine one; you swish around all that paper and flatter yourself that you're doing something of worldwide importance. But what does it all mean for us? Paper, and used paper at that, isn't going to clothe the working class or feed the world's hungry' (3. 126).
46 Leonov told Kovalev that this statement did indeed reflect his own beliefs (see *Iz*

tvorcheskogo naslediya..., p. 456). Compare in the revised version of *The Thief*: 'this insignificant something, this spark, hardly even a dot [...] is perhaps the most priceless treasure of existence, because it is the distillation of everything that is behind us, the entire experience of human history.'

CHAPTER 13 *The Pyramid* 1994

1. He was finally elected to the Academy in 1972 'for his services in the field of literary scholarship.'
2. Much of the material in this paragraph is taken from Leonov's correspondence with Valentin Kovalev, published in *Iz tvorcheskogo naslediya...*, particularly pp. 466–78.
3. Ibid., p. 487.
4. For more on Leonov's experiences in these years see *Leonid Leonov v vospominaniyakh...*, pp. 199–224.
5. Leonid Leonov *Piramida*, 2 vols. ('Golos,' M., 1994). The novel was issued simultaneously as a three-volume paperback by the 'Nash sovremennik' publishing house, with an almost identical introduction by the literary scholar Ol'ga Ovcharenko. References to the novel will be taken from the former edition and indicated in the text in parentheses by *P* with volume and page number.
6. Groznova, *Tvorchestvo Leonida Leonova...*, p. 44.
7. The chapter 'Mirozdanie po Dymkovu,' which was eventually published in 1974 is said be be almost identical with a chapter that Leonov had read to a friend in 1954 (*Leonid Leonov: Tvorcheskaya individual'nost'...*, p. 11).
8. The remark was retained in all later editions and revisions of the novel.
9. See the back cover of the journal *Zn*, 1963, no. 11.
10. Apparently a copy of this version survives, and one must hope that it will one day be released. Natal'ya Leonova told me that in many respects she preferred it to the published version.
11. The text we have is a composite of several different drafts dating from different periods, and is the product of much editorial work by Leonov's daughters and sympathetic scholars, in particular, Viktor Khrulev. For more on this see Ol'ga Ovcharenko's introduction to the novel (*P.* 1, 4) and *Leonid Leonov v vospominaniyakh*, pp. 388–95 and 577–607.
12. The name Matvey Petrovich Loskutov includes Leonov's mother's patronymic (Mariya Petrovna Petrova), a similar surname (Loskutov/Leonov), and a first name similar to Leonov's own patronymic (Matvey-Maksimovich). It may be noted in this connection that Vikhrov, who shares many features of Leonov's biography is also a Matveich.
13. The geographical indications suggest that Leonov is referring to the Church of the

Ikon of the Mother of God (1654), which was demolished in the 1950s to clear the ground for the Luzhniki sports stadium.
14 Dymkov is also left-handed (*P*. 2. 376). This allusion to the story of one of Leonov's favourite writers, Leskov, reinforces the theme of an innocent simpleton with a miraculous talent, who is destroyed by by the greed and indifference of the mighty of this world.
15 Leonov explicitly cites the Book of Enoch (see *P.* 1. 553 et passim).
16 Although Russian orthography once again permitted the spelling of God and the adjectives and pronouns relating to Him with a capital letter, Leonov frequently refrains from doing so. I have followed Leonov's practice in my translations.
17 Dymkov too is one of the 'children of fire,' and so his name, with its meaning of smoke, is a humorous allusion to his angelic origin: 'there is no smoke without fire.' He is fascinated by such toys as cigarette-lighters, and when Yuliya thinks of him, the words *zazhigalka* (lighter) and *dymok* appear in the text (*P*. 1. 677).
18 Vladimir Chivilikhin, 'Uroki Leonova,' in *Tvorchestvo Leonida Leonova* (1969), p. 484.
19 *NM*, 1932, no. 5, p. 7.
20 This episode is amplified in *The Pyramid* in part 3, chapter 7, a chapter that was published separately as 'Poslednyaya progulka: fragment iz romana' (see *Moskva*, 1979, no. 4, pp. 135–40). This can in turn be traced back to H. G. Wells's story, *The Time Machine*.
21 Compare Pchkhov's remark in the revised *Thief:* ' "... since every dream depends on one's existence what will happen to mankind when everything on this earth has been achieved? And when everything has become known, then won't mankind want to know a little bit less?" And [Pchkhov] continued with inscrutable logic: "... well perhaps the world is no longer for people and their offspring, but for birds and bugs that have not yet defiled themselves" ' (3. 490).
22 In some of the early drafts of the novel he is actually called Sataninsky (see 10. 564 *et passim*). He is also sometimes associated with Minos, the ruler of the underworld (*P*. 1. 589). The words 'Satanic,' 'devilish,' 'hellish,' and their derivatives recur throughout the book.
23 In this connection Leonov uses the word *nevozvrashchenets*, a word which might seem to mean no more than 'non-returnee' but has a specific meaning in Soviet conditions: 'a person who has not returned to his motherland from abroad and has treacherously gone over to the enemies of the USSR' (*Slovar' sovremennogo russkogo literaturnogo yazyka*, 17 vols., M.-L., 1950–65, vol. 7, p. 753). Its usage here is a fine example of Leonov's many-layered irony.
24 The expression parodies one of Stalin's many unofficial titles. It appears frequently in the text, and always sarcastically. Its first appearance is on *P*, 1, 19.
25 Shatanitsky's speech patterns and his slippery ironies often recall Gratsiansky.

When Leonov was asked about this he is said to have replied that Shatanitsky is not so much another version of Gratsiansky, as that Gratsiansky is one of the incarnations of Shatanitsky. It may be observed that the epithets 'Satanic' and 'devilish' are frequently used in connection with Gratsiansky and his allies.

26 The description of Shatanitsky's office evokes the Lubyanka, but it is also a hellish counterpart to the church pillar out of which Dymkov had appeared:

> [His] official building which descended like so many mine shafts into the depths of the earth and plunged high into the sky with its innumerable storeys, remained invisible to outsiders even on clear days. It could be discovered only by going right up to it, though at the risk of falling through a bottomless manhole on to the horns of the officer on duty. The security system operated more reliably than any office or pass system. All external doors were barricaded with boards because of ongoing year-round repairs, but apparently its own staff could pass directly through the walls. (*P.* 1. 124–5)

27 The phrase is taken from Gor'ky's play *The Lower Depths* (*Na dne*, 1902) in which Satin quotes the lines, 'All honour to the madman who inspires humanity with a golden dream,' itself a quotation from a poem by Pierre Béranger. In some ways the phrase would make a better title for the novel.

28 There are some striking parallels between Leonov's novel and L.P. Hartley's *Facial Justice* (1960). In the English novel the central themes are Envy and Equality; every kind of individuality, physical beauty, artistic talent, is discountenanced as antisocial, except for the 'Inspectors.' All this is done in the name of happiness, or the 'Fun Society.'

29 The words are taken from *The Thief*, where they form part of a cabaret ditty by Don'ka. I suspect that this was one of the passages marked by Stalin's red pencil.

30 'With us, as a result of Peter's heavy hand, the implanting of foreign exotica was always combined with the ruthless persecution of the social individual according to an imported and, frankly, abstract model, involving the ploughing under of the entire Russian way of life as mulch for a crop of as yet untested novelty' (*P.* II, 129).

31 The rejection of every form of 'elitism' in the name of democracy is not, however, confined to Soviet Russia. It has found its missionaries in the West too. See Robert A. Dahl, *On Democracy* (Yale University Press, 1999).

32 Leonov was also personally affected in this issue. Of the leading geneticists in the Soviet Union he knew Vavilov, while his wife was a student of Kol'tsov (until she was expelled from the university for her bourgeois origins). Both men were executed in the Purges.

33 In the revised *Thief* Chikilev had boasted of his 'screwdriver': 'I have a secret screwdriver [...] and what is this screwdriver? I can honestly tell you it is the aspiration to the highest well-being...' (3. 363).

34 Professor A. I. Pavlovsky of St Petersburg University contributed a paper, 'The Sign of Job,' to the 1998 conference devoted to *The Pyramid*. A summary of his paper can be found in *Russkaya literatura*, 1998, no. 4, pp. 239–40.
35 The life of hens in a coop was one of the images Dostoevsky used to discredit the Crystal Palace in *Notes from the Underground*. For Leonov even chickens can be the source of happiness.
36 Inna Rostovtseva, 'Negativ, proyavlennyy vechnost'yu,' *LitGaz*, 1 June 1994. Natal'ya Leonova told me that the other title her father considered was 'The Great Angel' (*Bol'shoy angel*), referring, I take it, not to Dymkov, who is hardly 'great,' but to Shatanitsky.
37 There are various plays on the word: it provides the name for a Tsarist police spy, Piramidov (*P*, I, 443, 463); elsewhere there is a reference to 'piramidon,' the Russian version of aspirin.
38 Leonov had not always shared this distrust of the pyramid. In Dec. 1927 he had written to Gor'ky apropos of the two versions of *A Provincial Story*: '... I am coming more and more (admittedly rather late in the day) to the idea that this is the time for work with a capital W. It's time to work, to make things, pyramids, bridges, anything that can absorb the accumulated energies of mankind. It's time that Russia stopped suffering and moaning, and time that she started living, breathing, and doing a decent job of work. And it's no accident that history has pushed on to the stage men who are tough, thick-skinned, men who have finally demolished our age-old stagnation...' (*Literaturnoe nasledstvo*, no. 70, p. 252).
39 The image is also found in Mandel'shtam; see, for example, his essay 'Humanism and Modernity' (*Gumanizm i sovremennost'*, published 1923) and the 1937 poem about Villon, 'Chtob priyatel' i vetra i kapel'...' In Evtushenko's long poem *The Bratsk Hydro-Electric Station* (*Bratskaya GES*, 1963–5) any resemblance between the Soviet and the Pharaonic systems had been angrily rejected, and it is possible that Leonov's novel was intended, among other things, as a rejoinder.
40 Miracles had appeared previously in Leonov's work, for example the rose that the blind Timosha manages to find for Mar'ka's name-day in *A Golden Coach*. The role of the fakir, Rakhuma, also seems to be intended as another pointer to the normalcy of miracles, though his receive a sort of explanation in the form of amazing coincidences. The word fakir and its cognates are often used in connection with Dymkov (e. g., *P*, I, 213).
41 The utilitarian enemies of art want to know 'how it is made' (*P*, II, 453). The reference is to such Formalist exercises as Eykhenbaum's 'How Gogol''s *Overcoat* Is Made' ('Kak sdelana *Shinel'* Gogolya',' 1918) and Mayakovsky's 'How to Make Poetry' ('Kak delat' stikhi?' 1926).
42 In earlier versions of the novel Shamin's name was given as Vtyurin.

43 Dostoevsky, *PSS*, vol. 14, p. 100.
44 My source for this is Natal'ya Leonova.

CHAPTER 14 The Art of Compromise

1 '... after the war one still believed in something and for twenty years I went to the voters, visited the offices of high officials, tried to protect the people in their misfortunes. But everything was out of joint, whatever one did, all the problems seemed artificially created and worse still there was no end to them' (*Leonid Leonov: V vospominaniyakh...*, p. 543).
2 Groznova, 'Leonid Leonov – grani leonovskoy metafiziki,' in *Nauchno delo akademika Milosava Babovicha*, pp. 22–3.
3 *Leonid Leonov v vospominaniyakh...*, p. 533.
4 I have not been able to trace the reference to Armillius. Perhaps Leonov is thinking here of Armilus, who, in Jewish legend, plays a role analogous to that of the AntiChrist. In the last days he will conquer Jerusalem and persecute the Jews before his final defeat.
5 Mayakovsky, *PSS*, vol. 2, pp. 16–17.
6 M. Gor'ky, *SS*, vol. 13, p. 185.
7 See in particular the two 'Letters to an American Friend' (1942, 1943) and the article 'Gnomes of Science' (1945).
8 Compare Leonov's comment on Vikhrov's first book: '... every outstanding piece of work, besides its main thematic purpose, is dictated by a parallel one, concealed from the reader in the creative biography of the author... '(9. 236).

Bibliography

There are several bibliographies of Leonov's publications. V.A. Kovalev produced an almost faultless bibliography of Leonov's work up to 1937, but this forms part of an unpublished dissertation, 'Romany Leonida Leonova' (L., 1951), and is not easily available. In 1958 V.M. Akimov published *Leonid Leonov: Ukazatel' literatury* (L., 1958), with a selection from the critical literature, but it was far from exhaustive, even within its own modest terms of reference, and was in fact severely criticized for its shortcomings (see *VopLit*, 1958, no. 8). A few years later my 'Bibliography of the Works of Leonid Leonov' (*Oxford Slavonic Papers*, vol. 11 (1964), pp. 137–50) attempted to bring these works up to date. Since then Akimov has returned to the field in the second volume (pp. 664–717) of the invaluable five-volume *Russkie sovetskie pisateli-prozaiki*, eds. V.M. Akimov and N. Ya. Morachevsky (L., 1959–72), but this work, the most complete to date, is not faultless: it contains several minor inaccuracies, but its two main weaknesses are, first, that it omits most of Leonov's contributions to the 'cult' of Stalin, and, second, that it records without comment many items that are abridged or amended or retitled versions of others included in the bibliography. I should also mention the two editions of V.A. Kovalev's *Leonid Leonov: Seminariy* (M.-L., 1964 and M., 1982). While inadequate as bibliographies they serve as invaluable sources of biographical information and guides to the critical literature.

The present bibliography aims to list the first publications of all Leonov's works, to correct errors where possible, and to add material from the last twenty-two years of his life. In the case of articles and speeches that were published in more than one location, even at the time of their first appearance, I have listed only the most accessible periodicals; items that have been abridged or revised or retitled have been noted accordingly. Several excerpts from Leonov's novels and plays were published as 'work-in-progress,' and since these often contain significant variants from the final versions I have included them. I realize, of course, that this compilation too will inevitably be found to contain its own omissions and errors.

The difficulties of producing an absolutely reliable bibliography are increased by the fact that both the surname Leonov and the initial L. are common; there is even a Leonid Leonov who has published in Belorussian journals. I have listed some of these items under Dubia.

The following bibliography consists of two sections: Primary Sources and Secondary Sources. The former is divided into four main parts: (1) the main collections of Leonov's work; (2) the artistic works of his maturity – prose, drama, verse, and translations; (3) his many articles, speeches, interviews, autobiographical essays, and his published correspondence; (4) his immature works, published in Archangel newspapers between 1915 and 1919, and his contributions to Red Army newspapers in 1921 and 1922; and, finally, the aforementioned 'Dubia.' The secondary literature is divided into three parts: (1) the many books that have been written about Leonov; (2) a selection from the thousands of articles that have been devoted to his life and work, with, I hope, a complete list of those in the English language; and (3) a list of books that I found helpful for the cultural and political background.

PRIMARY SOURCES

I. Collected Works

Leonov's works have been collected on five occasions. A four-volume edition was issued in Khar'kov and Moscow in 1928–30, and then extended with a fifth volume to include the recently published *Sot'*. A five-volume set was published in Moscow in 1953–5, later extended with a sixth volume to include his new novel, *Russkiy les*. A nine-volume set was issued in 1960–2, a ten-volume set in 1969–72, and another ten-volume edition in 1981–4, all published in Moscow. These contain most of Leonov's major works, but it should be noted that the original versions of *Metel'* and *Zolotaya kareta* have never been reissued, and exist in only single small editions (atrociously printed) of 500 copies each; the original version of *Vor* has also not been reissued in Russia since 1936, but a photo-reprint of the 1928 edition was published by Fink Verlag of Munich in 1975, with an introduction by Friedrich Scholz. All Leonov's major works have been subjected at one time or another to revision, and a full textual comparison of the various editions still remains to be done.

II. Artistic works

1. Prose

1A. Novels

Barsuki, *KN*, 1924, nos. 6, 7/8. The first *complete* edition was published as a separate book in 1925.

Vor, *KN*, 1927, nos. 1–7.
Sot', *NM*, 1930, nos. 1–5.
Skutarevsky, *NM*, 1932, nos. 5–9.
Doroga na Okean, *NM*, 1935, nos. 9–12.
Russkiy les, *Zn*, 1953, nos. 10–12.
Vor, revised version, *Vor*, M., 1959. Further significant changes were introduced in the third volume of the *Sobranie sochineniy* of 1981–4 and again in *Vor. Roman*, M., 1991.
Piramida, *Piramida*, M., 1994.

1B. Extracts from the Novels

'Shalman Artemiya Koritsyna' (*Vor*), *Narodnyy uchitel'*, 1927, no. 2, pp. 24–33.
'Konets tsirkachki' (*Vor*), *ZarV*, 30 April 1927.
'Tsirkachka' (*Vor*), *Krasnaya niva*, 1927, no. 6, pp. 2–7.
'Zaryad'e' (*Barsuki*), *Severnyy rabochiy*, 8 April 1928.
'Proekt' (*Sot'*), *30 dney*, 1929, no. 6, pp. 32–5.
'Pered proryvom' (*Sot'*), *LitGaz*, 9 Nov. 1929.
'Nachalo stroyki' (*Sot'*), *Krasnaya niva*, 1929, no. 47, pp. 2–4.
'Vozvrashchenie Suzanny' (*Sot'*), *30 dney*, 1929, no. 12, pp. 16–20.
'Vreditel'' (*Sot'*), *Izv*, 20 Dec. 1929.
'Otryvok' (*Sarancha*), *Turkmenskaya iskra*, 2 April 1930.
'Nachalo romana' (*Skutarevsky*), *VechM*, 22, 23 Sept. 1931.
'Banshchik i professor' (*Skutarevsky*), *VechM*, 24, 25 Sept. 1931.
'Vozvrashchenie domoy' (*Skutarevsky*), *LitGaz*, 23 May 1932.
'Glava iz *Skutarevskogo*,' *Izv*, 24 July 1932.
'Zhenya' (*Skutarevsky*), *KomPr*, 15 June 1933.
'Telo' (*Doroga na Okean*), *LitGaz*, 20 Oct. 1935.
'Ya razgovarivayu s A. M. Volchikhinym' (*Doroga na Okean*), *VechM*, 23 Oct. 1935.
'Otryvok iz *Dorogi na Okean*,' *Zvezda* (Dnepropetrovsk), 30 Oct. 1935.
'Zhizn' Kurilova' (*Doroga na Okean*), *Kommunar* (Tula), 30 Oct. 1935.
'Otryvok iz *Dorogi na Okean*,' *Moskovskaya kochegarka* (Bogoroditsk), 30 Oct. 1935.
'My berem s soboy Lizu' (*Doroga na Okean*), *VechM*, 7 Nov. 1935.
'Sadovnik' (*Doroga na Okean*), *LitLen*, 26 Nov. 1935.
'Otryvok iz *Dorogi na Okean*,' *Moskovskaya kochegarka* (Bogoroditsk), 11 Dec. 1935.
'Buran' (*Doroga na Okean*), *LenPr*, 12 Dec. 1935.
'Otryvok' (*Vzyatie Velikoshumska*), *Pr*, 9–17 July 1944.
'Kommunist Sapozhkov' (*Russkiy les*), *LitGaz*, 30 July 1953.
'Progulka' (*Vor*, revised version), *LitGaz*, 30 May 1959.
'Kudema' (*Vor*, revised version), *Lit i Zh*, 5 June 1959.

'V tsirke' (*Vor*, revised version), *Sovremennyy tsirk*, 1959, no. 7, p. 27.
'Somnenie' (*Vor*, revised version), *Sovremennyy tsirk*, 1959, no. 9, pp. 20–2.
'Mirozdanie po Dymkovu,' (*Piramida*), *Nauka i zhizn'*, 1974, no. 11, pp. 38–43. See also *Sobranie sochineniy* (M., 1981–4), vol. 10, pp. 561–82.
'Poslednyaya progulka' (iz romana), (*Piramida*), *Moskva*, 1979, no. 4, pp. 135–40. See also *Sobranie sochineniy* (M., 1981–4), vol. 10, pp. 583–92.
'Spiral',' (*Piramida*), *Pr*, 18 Feb. 1987.
'Otryvki iz novogo romana,' (*Piramida*), *SovR.*, 27 May 1989.

2. Shorter Prose Fiction

Buryga, *Shipovnik*, Al'manakh 1, M., 1922.
Gibel' Egorushki, *Al'manakh Krug*, 3, M., 1924.
Sluchay s Yakovom Pigunkom, *Literaturnaya mysl'*, Al'manakh 2, Petrograd, 1923.
Derevyannaya koroleva, Bubnovyy valet, Valina kukla, *Derevyannaya koroleva*, Petrograd, 1923.
Tuatamur, *Tuatamur*, M., 1924.
Ukhod Khama, *Rasskazy*, 1926.
Khalil', *Nashi dni*, Al'manakh 5, M., 1925.
Petushikhinskiy prolom, *Petushikhinskiy prolom*, M., 1923.
Konets melkogo cheloveka, *KN*, 1924, no. 3.
Zapisi nekotorykh epizodov, sdelannye v gorode Goguleve Andreem Petrovichem Kovyakinym, *Russkiy sovremennik*, 1924, nos. 1–2.
Provintsial'naya istoriya, *NM*, 1928, no. 1.
Temnaya voda, Vozvrashchenie Kopyleva, Priklyuchenie s Ivanom, *Zv*, 1928, no. 1.
Brodyaga, *KN*, 1928, no. 5.
Mest', *KN*, 1928, no. 6.
Belaya noch', *NM*, 1928, no. 12.
Saranchuki (later renamed Sarancha), *NM*, 1930, nos. 9–10.
Vzyatie Velikoshumska, *NM*, 1944, nos. 6–7.
Evgenia Ivanovna, *Zn*, 1963, no. 11.

3. Contribution to Bol'shie pozhary, Collective Novel of 25 authors

'Plokhie posledstviya,' *Og*, 1927, no. 5.

2. Dramatic works

1A. Plays

Starushki, *Al'manakh Krug*, no. 6, 1927.
Barsuki, *P'esy*, M., 1935.

Untilovsk, *NM*, 1928, no. 3.
Provintsial'naya istoriya, *P'esy*, M., 1935.
Usmirenie Badadoshkina, *KN*, 1929, no. 3.
Skutarevsky (4-act version), *Skutarevsky*, M., 1933.
– (3-act version), *NM*, 1934, no. 6.
Polovchanskie sady, *NM*, 1938, no. 3.
Volk, *Volk*, M., 1938.
Metel', *Metel'*, M., 1940.
Obyknovennyy chelovek, *Obyknovennyy chelovek*, M., 1942.
Nashestvie, *NM*, 1942, no. 8.
Lenushka, *NM*, 1943, no. 4.
Zolotaya kareta, *Zolotaya kareta*, M., 1946.
Zolotaya kareta, revised version, *Okt*, 1955, no. 4. Further significant changes were introduced in the 9 vol. *Sobranie sochineniy* of 1960–2.
Polya Vikhrova, a dramatized version of *Russkiy les*, written in collaboration with Yuriy Bondarenko, *Polya Vikhrova*, M., 1960.

1B. Extracts from the Plays

Act I of *Untilovsk*, *KN*, 1926, no. 8, pp. 57–73.
'Rasprodazha' (*Usmirenie Badadoshkina*), *VechM*, 4 Aug. 1928.
Act II, Scene 3 of *Skutarevsky*, *LitGaz*, 17 Dec. 1932.
'Otryvok' iz *Polovchanskikh sadov*, *SovIsk*, 11 Sept. 1937.
Act I of revised *Metel'*, *LitGaz*, 25 Oct. 1962.

2. Film Scenarios

'Liditse,' *Og*, 1942, nos. 38–40.
'Pir v Zhirmunke,' 1942, filmed but apparently not published.
'Nashestvie,' written in collaboration with B. Chirskov, filmed 1944, but apparently not published.
'Obyknovennyy chelovek,' written in collaboration with M. Romm, filmed 1956, but apparently not published.
'Begstvo mistera Mak-kinli,' *Pr*, 1, 2, 4, 6, 8, 29 Jan., 3, 5 Feb. 1961.

3. Opera librettos

'Sot',' for composer M. Starokadomsky, unpublished.
'Nashestvie' (written in collaboration with O. Leonidov), *Sovetskaya muzyka*, 1952, nos. 6–7, with music by V.A. Dekhterev. Produced at the Kirov theatre, Leningrad, in 1955 under the title 'Fedor Talanov.'

3. Verse

'Pyat' trioletov,' *Navstrechu*, M., 1923.
'Zapis' na bereste,' *30 dney*, 1926, no. 1.
'Sidim i grustim. Opyt tramvaynogo tvorchestva,' in *Literaturnye shushutki (Literaturnye sekrety)*, ed. A. Kruchenykh, M.-L., 1928.

4. Translations

'Dva lagerya' (from the Estonian of A. Jakobson), *Dva lagerya*, M., 1949.

III. Articles, Speeches, Interviews, Autobiographical Essays, Published Correspondence

1. Articles

Several of the items in this section consist of only a few lines, and were commissioned as representing the views or activities of Soviet intellectuals as a group. They were often published under general headings, not always appropriate to Leonov's own contribution. In such cases I have followed Akimov in providing titles that describe the contents more accurately and placing them in square brackets. Leonov claimed that in some cases his name had been attached without his knowledge.

1A. Signed by Leonov

'O politike partii v oblasti khudozhestvennoy literatury,' *Zhurnalist*, 1925, nos. 8–9, p. 31.
'Kasatel'no pisatel'skogo polozheniya,' *Zhurnalist*, 1925, no. 10, p. 37.
'Umer poet [Esenin],' *30 dney*, 1926, no. 2, pp. 17–19.
'Pisateli o sebe' (Otvet na anketu), *NLP*, 1926, no. 2, p. 57.
'Chto ya pishu...,' *VechM*, 12 Feb. 1927.
'O sochinitel'skom otdykhe,' *30 dney*, 1927, no. 4, pp. 14–15.
'Ot romana k p'ese,' *Sovremennyy teatr*, 1927, no. 5, p. 70.
'Nashi sovremennye pisateli o klassikakh' (Otvet na anketu), *NLP*, 1927, no. 5–6, p. 57.
'O predotvrashchenii voyny,' in *Protiv ugrozy voyny*, 20 June 1927.
'Foto-lyubov',' *30 dney*, 1927, no. 7, pp. 64–73.
'Poezdka v Sorrento,' *30 dney*, 1927, no. 11, pp. 63–4.
'Ya veryu,' *Kino*, 8 Nov. 1927.
'Oktyabr' i pisateli' (Otvet na anketu), *Oktyabr'skaya gazeta*, 8 Nov. 1927.
'O svoey rabote' (Otvet na anketu), *Chit i pis*, 11 Feb. 1928.

'O Gor'kom,' *Nizhegorodskaya kommuna*, 11 Oct. 1928, and *Zhurnalist*, 1928, no. 3, pp. 6–8.
[Privetstvie M. Gor'komu], *Izv*, 29 March 1928.
'Za vsechelovecheskoe,' *30 dney*, 1928, no. 4, pp. 8–9.
'Chemu my uchimsya u Tolstogo,' *Krasnaya panorama*, 1928, no. 36, p. 23.
'Moya pervaya veshch',' *VechM*, 29 Sept. 1928.
'O rabote izdatel'stv,' *NLP*, 1928, no. 18, p. 65.
[O svoey rabote letom 1928], *Chit i pis*, 6 Oct. 1928.
'O zayme industrializatsii,' *Chit i pis*, 6 Oct. 1928.
'Neobkhodimo obuzdat',' *Zhurnalist*, 1928, no. 10, p. 21.
'Sovetskie pisateli i Oktyabr'' (otvet na anketu), *Chit i pis*, 7 Nov., 1928.
[O roli pisatelya v period sotsialisticheskogo stroitel'stva] (otvet na anketu) *LitGaz*, 23 Dec. 1929.
[K 10–letiyu Gosizdata] in *Pisateli – Gosizdatu 1919–1929* (M.-L., 1929), p. 53.
'O sotsial'nom zakaze,' *Pechat' i revolyutsiya*, 1929, no. 1, pp. 68–70.
'O meshchanstve' (Otvet na anketu), *NLP*, 1929, no. 6, p. 27.
'V otvet na provokatsiyu kitayskoy voenshchiny usilim oboronosposobnost' nashey strany. Stroim tank "Sovetskaya literatura,"' *LitGaz*, 22 July 1929.
'Kak reorganizovat' Soyuz Pisateley,' *LitGaz*, 30 Sept. 1929.
'Dvenadtsataya godovshchina Oktyabrya,' *LitGaz*, 9 Nov. 1929.
'O deklaratsii VSSP,' *LitGaz*, 23 Dec. 1929.
'Poezdka v Margian,' *Izv*, 25 May 1930.
'Prodolzhat' rabotu pervoy chitatel'skoy brigady,' *LitGaz*, 25 July 1930.
'Privetstvie sovetu vseturkmenskogo ob"edineniya pisateley,' *Turkmenovedenie* (Ashkhabad), 1930, no. 8–9, p. 19.
'Pokhod v Baltiku,' *RabGaz, Krasnaya zvezda*, 17 Oct. 1930.
'Dvizhenie ne ostanovit',' *LitGaz*, 4 Dec. 1930.
'Ruki proch' ot Gor'kogo,' *LitGaz*, 14 Jan. 1931.
'Itogi pervogo goda,' *VechM*, 20 Jan. 1931.
'Gromkim golosom,' *LitGaz*, 26 Jan. 1931.
'Borot'sya za vysokoe kachestvo sovetskoy literatury,' *LitGaz*, 14 Feb. 1931.
[Nakanune Vsesoyuznogo stsenarnogo soveshchaniya] (Otvet na anketu), *Kino*, 18 March 1931.
'Chey eto golos?,' *LitGaz*, 25 Sept. 1931.
[O prizyve udarnikov v literaturu], *LitGaz*, 25 Sept. 1931.
'Tvorcheskaya diskussiya v VSSP,' *LitGaz*, 25 Sept. 1931.
'Kakoy nam nuzhen pisatel',' *NLP*, 1931, no. 10, p. 31.
'Esli vy molchite, to kto vy?,' *LitGaz*, 17 March 1932.
'Ko vsem rabotnikam literatury,' *LitGaz*, 5 May 1932.
'Sovetskie pisateli edinodushno privetstvuyut reshenie TsK,' *LitGaz*, 25 May 1932.

'O Gor'kom,' *Izv*, 25 Sept. 1932.
'Put' proletariata [Serafimovich],' *KrGaz (vech)*, 9 Oct. 1932.
'Boytsu za delo rabochego klassa,' *Pr*, 20 Jan. 1933.
'Shekspirovskaya ploshchadnost',' *SovIsk*, 26 Jan. 1933.
'Privetstvie zhurnalu *Yunyy proletariy* v svyazi s ego 15–letiem,' *Yunyy proletariy*, 1933, no. 1, p. 4.
'Kritiki poka net,' *Kniga i proletarskaya revolyutsiya*, 1933, no. 8, p. 48.
'My vse prochnee zanimaem nashe novoe mesto v mire,' *Izv*, 2 Oct. 1933.
'Bol'shoy chelovek [Lunacharsky],' *VechM*, 28 Dec. 1933.
'Bol'shevik-literator,' *LitGaz*, 29 Dec. 1933.
'Avtor o spektakle' in *Skutarevsky*, M., 1934.
'Syraya stenograficheskaya zapis',' *Sovetskoe foto*, 1934, no. 2, p. 25.
'Chestnost' v rabote,' *Teatr i dramaturgiya*, 1934, no. 3, p. 29.
'Stil' novogo cheloveka,' *Pr*, 13 April 1934.
'Prizyv k muzhestvu,' *LitGaz*, 16 April 1934.
'Tvortsam khudozhestvennogo masterstva,' *LenPr*, 8 Aug. 1934.
'Poezdka po Abkhazii gluboko pouchitel'na,' *Sovetskaya Abkhaziya*, 16 Oct. 1934.
[Privetstvie zhurnalu *Novyy mir* v svyazi s ego 10–letiem], *NM*, 1934, no. 12, p. 8.
'Paden'e Zaryad'ya,' *Moskva*, M., 1935, pp. 170–9.
[Privetstvie zhurnalu *Oktyabr'* v svyazi s ego 10–letiem], *Okt*, 1935, no. 1, p. 206.
'Egon-Ervinu-Kishu,' *LitGaz*, 30 April 1935.
'Sovetskie pisateli o rechi tov. Stalina,' *LitGaz*, 10 May 1935.
'Privet Romen Rollanu,' *VechM*, 23 June 1935.
'Poet i tribun,' *Pr*, 24 June 1935.
'Umer V. A. Gilyarovsky,' *Izv*, 3 Oct. 1935.
'Pamyatnye dni,' *LitGaz*, 1 Dec. 1935.
'Svetlyy obraz,' *LenPr*, 1 Dec. 1935.
[Tvorcheskie plany na 1936 g.] (Otvet na anketu), *Izv*, 1 Jan. 1936.
'Anketa *Izvestiy*,' *Izv*, 21 Jan. 1936.
'V odnikh ryadakh s nami,' *VechM*, 29 Jan. 1936.
'Plamennyy privet X s"ezdu VLKSM,' *VechM*, 10 April 1936.
'Novaya Konstitutsiya – sovershennoletie nashey strany i revolyutsii,' *LitGaz*, 15 June 1936.
'Chelovek bol'shoy zhizni,' *Izv*, 21 June 1936.
'Rukopozhatie naroda,' *KomPr*, 24 July 1936.
'O proekte Konstitutsii,' *NM*, 1936, no. 8, p. 195.
'Privetstvie geroyam,' *LitGaz*, 5 Aug. 1936.
'I pust' eto budet Ryazan',' *Izv*, 22 Nov. 1936.
'Golos istorii,' *Izv*, 20 Dec. 1936.
'Pamyati N. A. Ostrovskogo. Otlichnyy primer zhivym,' *RabM*, 26 Dec. 1936.

'Terrariy,' *LitGaz*, 26 Jan. 1937.
'Sergo,' *Izv*, 19 Feb. 1937.
'Polovchanskie sady,' *SovIsk*, 5 March 1937.
'Nikomu ne pokolebat' moshchi sovetskogo naroda,' *SovIsk*, 8 March 1937.
'Skutarevsky-Rybnikov,' *T*, 1937, no. 8, pp. 138–9.
'Velikiy i skromnyy chelovek [Suleyman Stal'sky],' *LitGaz*, 26 Nov. 1937.
'Narod golosuet,' *RabM*, and *ZarV*, 13 Dec. 1937.
'Nezabyvaemyy fil'm,' *LitGaz*, 20 Dec. 1937.
'Sovetskie pisateli na rodine velikogo Stalina – v Gori,' *ZarV*, 27 Dec. 1937.
'Podlinnyy Gogol',' *SovIsk*, 12 Feb. 1938.
'Artilleristy,' *Pr*, 23 Feb. 1938.
'Sozdat' teatr, dostoynyy velikoy epokhi,' *Malyy teatr*, 23 April 1938.
'Velikaya chest',' *LitGaz*, 20 June 1938.
'Nesokrushimyy blok,' *LitGaz*, 30 June 1938.
'Znamya russkogo teatra,' *SovIsk*, 8 Aug. 1938.
'Velichestvennaya zrelost',' *LitGaz*, 26 Oct. 1938.
'Vmeste so vsemi,' *Pr*, 27 Oct. 1938.
'Molodye artilleristy,' *Pr*, 10 Nov. 1938.
'Puteshestvie v neizvedannyy kray,' *Kino*, 29 Nov. 1938.
'Bol'shoe teatral'noe sobytie,' *Malyy teatr*, 2 Dec. 1938.
'Novogodnee rukopozhatie,' *Gor'kovets* (MKhAT), 1 Jan. 1939.
'Literatura – vsenarodnoe delo,' *LitGaz*, 5 Feb. 1939.
'Velichestvennyy podarok,' *SovIsk*, 1 May 1939.
'Davayte vmeste smotret' v budushchee,' *Internatsional'naya literatura*, 1939, no. 7/8, pp. 217–18.
'O p'ese *Volk*,' *DMZ*, 1939, no. 8, p. 6.
'Khoroshaya traditsiya,' *Izv*, 30 Oct. 1939.
'K chitatelyam *Dneprovskoy pravdy*,' *Dneprovskaya pravda*, 14 April 1940.
'Poryv vpered,' *LitGaz*, 30 June 1940.
'Putevye zametki,' *NM*, 1941, no. 3, pp. 147–57.
'Posleslovie Zaryad'yu,' *MosBol*, 1 May 1941.
'Smert' vragu!,' *MosBol*, 25 June 1941.
'Chto ty sdelal dlya pobedy,' *LitGaz*, 6 July 1941.
'Nasha bor'ba svyashchenna,' *LitGaz*, 20 July 1941.
'22 iyunya 1941,' *NM*, 1941, no. 7–8, p. 17.
'Vstavayte, narody,' *Trud*, 13 Aug. 1941.
'Nasha Moskva,' *Krasnyy flot*, 25 Nov. 1941.
'Negodyai zaplatyat vdesyatero,' in *Krov' za krov', smert' za smert'*, (M., 1942), p. 118.
'Neizvestnomu amerikanskomu drugu. Pis'mo pervoe' [2 Aug. 1942], in *Izbrannoe* (M., 1945).

'Tvoy brat Vladimir Kurilenko,' *Krasnoarmeets*, 1942, no. 19, later reissued as 'Geroy-partizan Volodya Kurilenko,' in *V tylu vraga* (M., 1943).
'Nashestvie,' *Og*, 1942, no. 36, p. 13.
'Leningradtsy' (later reissued as 'Dokumenty, sdelannye zhizn'yu'), *Lit i Isk*, 10 Oct. 1942.
'Dolg i chest' nashi,' *Lit i Isk*, 21 Nov. 1942.
'Vmeste s moim narodom,' *Lit i Isk*, 21 March 1943.
'Golos rodiny,' *Lit i Isk*, 5 June 1943.
'Slava Rossii,' *Izv*, 10 July 1943.
'Neizvestnomu amerikanskomu drugu. Pis'mo vtoroe' [15 July 1943], *Zn*, 1943, no. 9–10, pp. 274–8.
'Postup' gneva,' *Pr*, 24 Aug. 1943.
'Pervye vpechatleniya,' *Lit i Isk*, 7 Nov. 1943.
'Razmyshleniya u Kieva,' *Pr*, 8 Nov. 1943.
'Yarost',' *Izv*, 17 Dec. 1943.
'Primechaniya k paragrafu,' *Izv*, 18 Dec. 1943.
'Rasprava,' *Izv*, 19 Dec. 1943.
'Mshchenie i smert' nemetsko-fashistskim zlodeyam!,' *Bloknot agitatora Krasnoy Armii*, 1944, no. 29, pp. 28–9.
'Velichavaya slava,' *Pr*, 24 Feb. 1944.
'Otecheskaya zabota [Kalinin],' *Lit i Isk*, 1 April 1944.
'Nemtsy v Moskve,' *Pr*, 19 July 1944.
'Serdtse naroda,' *Pr*, 8 Nov. 1944.
'Fakel geniya [Griboedov],' *Pr*, 14 Jan. 1945.
'Vechno-molodoe,' *Izv*, 14 Jan. 1945.
'Pozabotimsya o zeleni,' *VechM*, 24 March 1945.
'Utro pobedy,' *Pr*, 30 April 1945.
'Vesna narodov,' *Pr*, 1 May 1945.
'Russkie v Berline,' *Pr*, 7 May 1945.
'Imya radosti,' *Pr*, 11 May 1945.
'Polden' pobedy,' *Pr*, 25 June 1945.
'Pobeda,' *NM*, 1945, nos. 5–6, pp. 5–9 (later reissued in abridged form as 'Siyanie pobedy,' *Krasnoflotets*, 1945, 10, pp. 1–2).
'Kogda zaplachet Irma,' *Pr*, 4 Oct. 1945.
'Poezdka v Drezden,' *Pr*, 24 Oct. 1945.
'Fashistskiy zmiy' (later reissued as 'Nyurnbergskiy zmiy'), *Pr*, 2 Dec. 1945.
'Lyudoed gotovit pishchu,' *Pr*, 10 Dec. 1945.
'Ten' Barbarossy,' *Pr*, 20 Dec. 1945.
'Gnomy nauki,' *Pr*, 22 Dec. 1945.
'Vospominaniya o B. V. Shchukine,' *Teatral'nyy al'manakh*, kn.1 (M., 1946), p. 236.

'Slovo o pervom deputate,' *Pr*, 23 Jan. 1946.
'Na bashne,' *Pr*, 9 May 1946.
'Tam, gde zhil velikiy pisatel',' *Pr*, 19 June 1946.
'Molodym druz'yam,' *KomPr*, 22 June 1946.
'Privetstvie v svyazi s uchrezhdeniem Dnya tankistov,' *Zhurnal bronetankovykh i mekhanizirovannykh voysk*, 1946, no. 8–9, pp.12–14.
'Preodolet' illyustrativnost' i poverkhnostnost',' *T*, 1947, no. 2, p. 6.
'Razgovor o spravedlivosti,' *Pr*, 31 March 1947.
'Nashe tridtsatiletie,' *Pogranichnik*, 1947, no. 20, pp. 41–2.
'Rassuzhdenie o velikanakh,' *LitGaz*, 27 Sept. 1947.
'Minuta molchaniya,' *LitGaz*, 5 Nov. 1947.
'V zashchitu druga,' *Izv*, 28 Dec. 1947.
'Beseda s demonom,' *LitGaz*, 31 Dec. 1947.
'Bessmertie,' *LitGaz*, 21 Feb. 1948.
'Nasha vstrecha,' *LitGaz*, 3 March 1948.
'Vengerskaya vesna,' *Pr*, 31 March 1948.
'Zolotoe zerno,' *LitGaz*, 5 May 1948.
'Soldat chelovechestva,' *LitGaz*, 19 May 1948.
'Pamyati aktera S.M. Mikhoel's,' *Og*, 1948, no. 7, p. 27.
'Neprimirimost',' *LitGaz*, 4 Sept. 1948.
'Ognevoy talant,' *LitGaz*, 20 Oct. 1948.
'Ptitsa, obletevshaya mir,' *LitGaz*, 23 Oct. 1948.
'Dostoyanie naroda,' *SovIsk*, 23 Oct. 1948.
'Zhaba,' *LitGaz*, 3 Nov. 1948.
'Otzyv o *Nashestvii* v Chistopole,' *Prikamskaya kommuna*, 3 Dec. 1948.
'Privet, druz'ya!,' *LitGaz*, 22 Dec. 1948.
'Ot perevodchika' in A. Yakobson, *Dva lagerya* (M.-L., 1949), p. 1.
'Pokhorony A.S. Serafimovicha,' *Pr*, 22 Jan. 1949.
'Soratniki po oruzhiyu,' *LitGaz*, 21 Sept. 1949.
'Malyy Teatr i russkaya kul'tura,' *Og*, 1949, no. 43, pp. 2–3; and *Sovremenniki o Malom teatre* (M., 1950), pp. 51–3.
'Ob unyloy i skuchnoy suete vozle nashego doma,' *Sovetskiy artist*, 7 Nov. 1949.
'Blagodarnost',' *Pr*, 18 Dec. 1949.
'Tvorcheskie plany sovetskikh pisateley,' *LitGaz*, 31 Dec. 1950.
'Schastlivogo puti, tovarishchi!,' *LitGaz*, 25 March 1951.
'Narody otstoyat velikoe delo mira,' *Pr* (as 'Za mir,' in *LitGaz*), both 6 Sept. 1951.
'Tvorcheskie plany sovetskikh pisateley,' *LitGaz*, 29 Dec. 1951.
'Narody otstoyat zhizn',' *Og*, 1952, no. 13, p. 8.
'Slovo proshchaniya,' *Pr*, 10 March 1953.
'Izoblachenie vraga. Slovo moskovskikh pisateley,' *LitGaz*, 22 Dec. 1953.

'V kanun vyborov,' *LitGaz*, 13 March 1954.
'V zashchitu lesa,' *LitGaz*, 30 March 1954.
'Opyt odnoy diskussii,' *LitGaz*, 22 May 1954.
'Torzhestvennoe zasedanie Mossoveta,' *LenPr*, 27 May 1954.
'Sestry. K 300–letiyu vossoedineniya Ukrainy s Rossiey,' *Izv*, 29 May 1954.
'O velikom druge [Chekhov],' *Sovkul't*, 15 July 1954.
'Volshebnyy gorod,' *Izv*, 1 Aug. 1954.
'Bol'shaya i svetlaya data,' *Kommunist Tadzhikistana*, 22 Oct. 1954.
'O novom ustave Soyuza pisateley,' *LitGaz*, 25 Dec. 1954.
'Vslukh o knige,' *Sovkul't*, 3 Feb. 1955.
'Slovo o luchshem druge,' *Pionerskaya pravda*, 29 March 1955.
'Prizyv k zdravomu smyslu,' *Izv*, 1 April 1955.
'Kruglyy stol pisateley mira,' *LitGaz*, 15 Dec. 1955.
Preface to D. Zuev, *Vremena goda* (M., 1956), pp. 3–4.
'V zashchitu zelenogo druga,' *Yunyy naturalist*, 1956, no. 1.
'Talant i trud,' *Okt*, 1956, no. 3, pp. 166–73.
'Priznanie druz'yam (later reissued as 'Khoroshaya pomoshchnitsa') in *Knizhnaya lavka pisateley* (M., 1957).
'Pisateli rasskazyvayut (Ob uchastii v podgotovke spektaklya *Zolotaya kareta* i o predpolagaemoy instsenirovke *Russkogo lesa* (Otvet na anketu),' *K i zh*, 1957, no. 1, p. 11.
'O *Doroge na Okean*,' *LitGaz*, 14 Feb. 1957.
'Sestra Pravdy,' *Izv*, 13 March 1957.
'Sozdadim obshchestvo druzey prirody' (later reissued as 'Ob"edinit' lyubiteley prirody'), *Pr*, 23 April 1957.
'Leninskaya premiya,' *VechM*, 26 April 1957.
'O nashem zelenom druge,' *LitGaz*, 7 May 1957.
'Edinstvo tseli,' *Iskusstvo*, 1957, no. 7, p. 38.
'Glavnoe v zhizni,' *SovR*, 28 July 1957.
'Zhivoy pamyatnik,' *MosKom*, 2 Aug. 1957.
'Stremitelen beg vremeni,' *LitGaz*, 5 Sept. 1957.
'U novogodney elki,' *Izv*, 1 Jan. 1958.
'Privetstvie Sovetskoy Armii v den' ee 40–letiya,' *Sovetskiy voin*, 1958, no. 3, p. 9.
'Pesni truda i mira,' *SovR*, 22 April 1958.
'Uspekha vam, druz'ya,' *VechM*, 10 May 1958.
'Yunosti nashey strany,' *LitGaz*, 28 June 1958.
'Pravo i pravda Kitaya,' *SovR*, 1 Oct. 1958.
'Govoryat chitateli,' *Inostrannaya literatura*, 1958, no. 12, pp. 270–1.
'Bratskiy privet,' *Kazakhstanskaya pravda*, 12 Dec. 1958.
'Krasota vospityvaet,' *Dekorativnoe iskusstvo*, 1959, no. 1, pp. 9–11.

'Srubil derevo – posadi dva,' *Master lesa*, 1959, no. 2.
'Bol'shoy drug lesa,' *Lesnoe khozyaystvo*, 1959, no. 5, p. 8.
Review of B. Shergin, *Okean – more russkoe*, *Izv*, 3 June 1959.
'Zhivaya svyaz' pokoleniy,' *Lit i Zh*, 29 July 1959.
'Molodezhi syavskogo lespromkhoza. V dobryy chas,' *Master lesa*, 1959, no. 8.
[Introduction to] N. Nogina and E. Lopukhov, *V zashchitu lesa*, *Tekhnika – molodezhi*, 1959, no. 8, p. 5.
'Velikaya missiya,' *Lit i Zh*, 11 Sept. 1959.
'Zamechatel'no – govoryat sovetskie lyudi,' *Lit i Zh*, 20 Sept. 1959.
'Krasota truda,' *Lit i Zh*, 13 Jan. 1960.
'Reki – krasa rodiny. Bud'te pervymi, vodniki,' *Vodnyy transport*, 21 Jan. 1960.
'Sputnik pokoleniy,' *T zh*, 1960, no. 2, p. 4.
'Vernyy, beskorystnyy i naibolee svedushchiy drug' (later reissued as 'Beskorystnyy i svedushchiy drug'), *Izv*, 5 Feb. 1960.
'Ne teryat' ni minuty zrya' (Otvet na anketu 'V chem ono chelovecheskoe schast'e?'), *UchGaz*, 17 March 1960.
'Ot vsey dushi,' *Soldatskaya pravda*, 24 April 1960.
'V zelenoe nastuplenie, tovarishchi!,' *UchGaz*, 9 June 1960.
'Slovo k s"ezdu,' *SovR*, 6 July 1960.
'O prirode nachistotu,' *LitGaz*, 22 Oct. 1960.
'Stroki priznaniya,' *LitGaz*, 3 Nov. 1960.
'Staroe bratstvo,' *VechM*, 11 Nov. 1960.
[O dekade ukrainskoy literatury i iskusstva v Moskve], *MosKom*, 19 Nov. 1960.
[O spektakle *Yunost' Poli Vikrovoy* v Kievskom teatre im. L. Ukrainy], *MosPr*, 23 Nov. 1960.
'Umnyy talant,' *LitGaz*, 17 Dec. 1960.
'Lyudi vysokoy kul'tury' in *Geroi nashikh dney* (M., 1961), pp. 143–4.
'O teatre budushchego,' *T zh*, 1961, no. 11.
Pryzhok v nebo,' *Pr*, 16 April 1961.
'Tost izdaleka,' *Vecherniy Tbilisi*, 12 May 1961.
'Esli vzyat'sya za delo s dushoy,' *Yunost'*, 1961, no. 6.
'Pisatel' s mirovym golosom,' *Pr*, 4 July 1961.
[Kakim dolzhen byt' kosmonavt], *MosKom*, 9 July 1961.
'Vladimir Soloukhin,' in Vladimir Soloukhin, *Liricheskie povesti* (M., 1962), pp. 3–4.
'Redaktsii *Sibirskikh ogney*,' *Sibirskie ogni*, 1962, no. 3, p. 5.
[Privetstvie k 40–letiyu *Sibirskikh ogney*], *Vecherniy Novosibirsk*, 2 April 1962.
'Poklon i slovo priveta,' *Pr*, 7 May 1962.
'Pokhvala zhanru: O nauchno-fantasticheskoy literature,' *LitGaz*, 4 Aug. 1962.
[Predislovie k glave iz knigi Mato-Nazhin, *Volnenie v rezervatsii*], *K i zh*, 1963, no. 5, p. 9.

'Zabota o blage narodov,' *Pr*, 1 Jan. 1963.
'Stanislavsky,' *T*, 1962, no 12, pp. 51–4 (later reissued in abridged form as 'O Stanislavskom' *T zh*, 1963, no. 1, p. 6).
'Snova o lese,' *LitGaz*, 22 Jan. 1963.
'Priroda i my,' *LitGaz*, 14 May 1963.
'Vmesto privetstviya,' *Pr*, 21 June 1963.
'Nakanune leningradskoy vstrechi,' *LitGaz*, 3 Aug. 1963.
'Forma i tsel',' *LitGaz*, 8 Aug. 1963.
'Roman, chelovek, obshchestvo,' *Inostrannaya literatura*, 1963, no. 11, pp. 141–7.
'Samoe glavnoe,' *Pr*, 6 Nov. 1963.
'Soyuz uma i serdtsa,' *Izv*, 31 Dec. 1963.
'Proshu slova,' *LitGaz*, 3 Oct. 1964.
'Brillianty dlya bednykh,' *Zhurnalist*, 1965, no. 10.
'Poka sud da delo,' *LitGaz*, 30 Oct. 1965.
'O bol'shoy shchepe: K voprosu ob okhrane lesa,' *LitGaz*, 30 Oct. 1965.
'Podvig lesnika nezameten,' *LesProm*, 1 Jan. 1966.
'Po koordinatam zhizni,' *VopLit*, 1966, no. 6, pp. 95–106.
'Lyul'ka, v kotoroy vzleleyan...,' *Nauka i zhizn*,' 1966, no. 10, pp. 44–9.
'Esli ne segodnya, to kogda zhe...,' *LitGaz*, 14 June 1967.
'Gorizonty zrelosti: K 65–letiyu so dnya rozhdeniya rumynskogo pisatelya Z. Stanku,' *LitGaz*, 11 Oct. 1967.
'Venok geroyu: O yunom partizane V. Kurilenko. pogibshem v 1942 g.,' *LesProm*, 27 Jan. 1968.
'Gor'ky segodnya,' *K i zh*, 1968, no. 2, pp. 14–16.
'Lyubite prirodu, no... bez ognestrel'nogo orudiya,' *LitGaz*, 7 Feb. 1968.
'Slovo o Gor'kom,' *LitGaz*, 3 April 1968.
'Glashatay novoy epokhi,' *VopLit*, 1968, no. 3, pp. 3–18.
'V zashchitu druga,' *Sem'ya i shkola*, 1968, no. 4, pp. 26–8.
'Moemu chitatelyu: Predisloviya k izdaniyu romana *Vor* na yaponskom yazyke i *Evgenia Ivanovna* na gruzinskom yazyke,' *LitGaz*, 4 Sept. 1968.
'Slovo o luchshem druge,' *Literatura v shkole*, 1969, no. 2, pp. 32–3.
'Rodnikovaya svezhest': O vystavke, posvyashchennoy 70–letiyu so dnya rozhdeniya peyzazhista i restavratora V.O. Kirikova,' *Pr*, 27 Feb. 1973.
'K sorokaletiyu pervogo s"ezda,' *VopLit*, 1974, no. 8, pp. 3–36.
'Istoriya vydvinula nas vpered...,' *LitGaz*, 14 Aug. 1974.
'Otechestvo,' *Knizhnoe obozrenie*, 22 Oct. 1976.
'Vysokiy dolg pisatelya,' *VopLit*, 1976, no. 12, p. 48.
'1957 – *Moskva* – 1977,' *Moskva*, 1977, no. 1, pp. 90–1.
'Ob A. S. Yakovleve,' *VopLit*, 1977, no. 8, pp. 216–223.
'Probivaytes' k glubinnym plastam,' *LitGaz*, 25 May 1977.

'Navstrechu tayne,' *KomPr*, 31 Dec. 1982.
'K slovu o Slove...' (1984), *Sobranie sochineniy*, 10 vols. (1981–4), vol. 10, pp. 555–6.
'Pis'mo k uchastnikam konferentsii' (1984), *Sobranie sochineniy*, 10 vols. (1981–4), vol. 10, pp. 557–8.
'"Mysli, kotorye neobkhodimo vyskazat'...": Razmyshleniya pisatelya,' *LitGaz*, 20 Oct. 1985.
'Pamyatnaya replika,' *LitGaz*, 18 June 1986.
'Razdum'ya u starogo kamnya: O neobkhodimosti sokhraneniya i vosstanovleniya istoricheskikh pamyatnikov,' *Sovkul't*, 23 Aug. 1986. Earlier publications (see *Tekhnika – molodezhi*, 1980, no. 9, and *Pamyatniki otechestva*, 1981, no. 2) were heavily censored.
'... Dlya razresheniya voprosov voyny i mira odnogo optimizma yavno nedostatochno...: Razdum'ya pisatelya,' *SovR*, 1 Jan. 1987.
'O Vladimire Chivilikhine,' *SovR*, 2 March 1988.
'Predvaritel'nye itogi: monolog serediny 70–ykh gg.,' *LitGaz*, 21 Sept. 1994.

1B. Joint Authorship

with V. Kirillov, 'Osnovy deklaratsii VSSP,' *LitGaz*, 23 Dec. 1929.
with V. Gol'tsev, 'Vserossiyskiy Soyuz Sovetskikh Pisateley za rabotoy,' *LitGaz*, 9 Jan. 1931.
with B. Yasensky 'Sovershennoletie naroda,' *Izv*, 8 July 1935.
'Umer V.A. Gilyarovsky,' *Izv*, 3 Oct. 1935 (one of 5 signatories).
with F. Gladkov and V. Stavsky, 'Imya Chkalova – simvol geroizma,' *Izv*, 16 Dec. 1938.
'Pamyati pisatelya,' *LitGaz*, 5 Aug. 1939 (one of 10 signatories).
'Bol'she sportivnykh matchey,' *VechM*, 9 Dec. 1944 (one of 4 signatories).
with O. Kurganov, 'Palachi bel'zenskogo kontslagerya,' *Pr*, 21Sept. 1945.
with Vl. Lidin and I. Erenburg, 'Stareyshiy pisatel'-skazochnik,' *Sovkul't*, 21 Oct. 1954.
with A. Volkov and M. Yakovlev, 'Shirit' dvizhenie "za zelenogo druga",' *Narodnoe obrazovanie*, 1957, no. 9; also published as 'Nad lesami Podmoskov'ya navisla opasnost',' *Izv*, 15 Sept. 1957.
with A. Yugov, 'Dumy o yazyke,' *Lit i Zh*, 8 May 1959.
with A. Tvardovsky, 'Nasha sovest' ne mozhet mirit'sya,' *Pr*, 16 Nov. 1961.
with A. Salynsky, 'O tvorchestve N. Tikhanova,' *Volzhskaya kommuna*, 11 Jan. 1962.
with S.T. Konenkov and P.D. Korin, 'Beregite svyatynyu nashu!,' *Molodaya gvardiya*, 1965, no. 5, pp. 216–19.

with Yu. Smirnov and I. Maksimov, 'Eshche raz ob okhote,' *LitGaz*, 12 June 1968.
with B. Ryabinin, 'Priroda prosit tishinu: O bor'be s brakonerstvom,' *Trud*, 24 Oct. 1968.
with E. Osetrov, 'Zolototsvet: S vystavki rabot khudozhnika A. Kulikova, Moskva,' *Pr*, 11 Jan. 1979.

2. Speeches

1A. Complete Speeches

'Donesti pravdu o stroitel'stve sotsializma do trudyashchikhsya kapitalisticheskikh stran,' *LitGaz*, 5 March 1932.
'Bol'shie mechty,' *LitGaz*, 17 Nov. 1933.
'Rech' po dokladu A.M. Gor'kogo na Pervom Pisatel'skom S"ezde Pisateley' [21 Aug. 1934], *LitGaz*, 22 Aug. 1934. Also published as 'Era, kotoraya ne povtoritsya nikogda,' *Pr*, 22 Aug. 1934, and as 'Vorota novoy ery otkryty,' in *Pisateli XVII parts"ezdu* (M., 1934), pp. 132–5.
'Rech' na obshchemoskovskom sobranii pisateley,' *Pr*, 17 April 1939.
'Rech' o Chekhove,' *Pr*, 16 July 1944.
'Sud'ba poeta [Griboedov],' *LitGaz*, 15 Jan. 1945.
'Gor'ky segodnya,' *LitGaz*, 14 July 1945.
'Rech'...,' *Izv*, 19 Jan. 1946.
'Rech' v Zagorske,' *Vpered* (Zagorsk), 3 Feb. 1946.
'Teatr nashego vremeni,' *T*, 1946, no. 10.
'Slovo k bumazhnikam,' *LitGaz*, 29 Jan. 1949.
Rech' na torzhestvennom zasedanii v Petrozavodske, posvyashchennom stoletiyu polnogo izdaniya karelo-finskogo eposa *Kalevala*, *Leninskoe znamya* (Petrozavodsk), 26 Feb. 1949.
'Mir miru. Rech',' *Pr*, 28 Aug. 1949.
'Rech' na otkrytii pamyatnika N.V. Gogolyu v Moskve [2 March 1952], *Pr*, 4 March 1952.
'Pamyati velikogo kazakhshogo poeta-prosvetitelya Abaya Kunanbaeva,' *KazPr*, 7 Sept. 1954.
Rech' pri zakladke pamyatnika Abayu, in *Russkie o kazakhskoy literature* (Alma-Ata, 1957), p. 88.
'Bol'shikh uspekhov v vashem vazhnom i trudnom dele,' *Lesnoe khozyaystvo*, 1958, no. 3, pp. 22–3.
Rech' na I sessii Verkhovnogo Soveta SSSR, [later reissued as 'Vslushaytes'' v golos blagorazumiya' and 'Golos blagorazumiya'], *Izv*, 1 April 1958.
'Slovo o Tolstom,' *Pr*, 20 Nov. 1960.

'Vsekh nas zhdut bol'shie dela' [Rech'], *Leninskaya pravda* (Belomorsk), 18 March 1962.
'Slava cheloveku!,' *LitGaz*, *Pr*, 8 Aug. 1963.
'Pisatel', tribun, gumanist [Gor'ky],' *LitGaz*, 3 April 1968. Earlier publications in *Pr*, 29 March 1968 and *Izv*, 30 March were heavily censored.
'"My perezhivaem rokovye minuty epokhi": Vystuplenie pisatelya po sluchayu vrucheniya emu premii im. L. Tolstogo 5 avgusta 1994,' *SovR*, 11 Aug., 1994.

2B. Extracts from Speeches

'Vystuplenie na VSSP' [14 Sept. 1931], *LitGaz*, 15 Sept. 1931. A different account of the same speech is given in *NM*, 1931, no. 10, pp. 123–5.
'V sporakh o Skutarevskom,' *RabM*, 1 Feb. 1933.
' V vagone i na palube,' *KomPr*, 24 Aug. 1933.
'Chestvovanie Romen Rollana v Parizhe,' *Pr*, 3 Feb. 1936.
'V Prezidiume pravleniya SSP. Obsuzhdenie romana L. Leonova *Doroga na Okean*, *LitGaz*, 10 May 1936.
'Iz rechi pered izbiratelyami,' *Izv*, 5 March 1950.
'Gor'kovskie chteniya,' *LitGaz*, 29 March 1951.
'Izmennikam Rodiny net poshchady,' *LitGaz*, 22 Dec. 1953.
'Po Sovetskoy strane,' *LenPr*, 27 May 1954.
'Priroda i my: Iz vstupitel'nogo slova za "kruglym stolom" redaktsii,' *LitGaz*, 14 May 1963.
'Uvidet' zavtrashniy den': Fragment vystupleniya na III Vsesoyuznom soveshchanii molodykh pisateley,' *UchGaz*, 31 May 1984.

3. Interviews

P. Kr – v, 'O Evrope,' *VechM*, 13 Oct. 1927.
Izgoy, 'Lidin i Leonov o Evrope,' *KrGaz (vech)*, 13 Oct. 1927.
'V gostyakh u Maksima Gor'kogo,' *Nizhegorodskaya kommuna*, 30 Oct. 1927.
N. Bakunin, 'Pisateli o Gor'kom,' *Nizhegorodskaya kommuna*, 11 March 1928.
'Untilovsk v MKhAT I,' *Novyy zritel'*, 1928, no. 4, p. 14.
'Soyuz Pisateley na novykh putyakh,' *VechM*, 26 Oct. 1929.
'Svoimi glazami,' *Turkmenistanskaya iskra*, 1 April 1930.
E. Korobkova and L. Polyak, 'Pisatel' o chitatele,' *NLP*, 1930, no. 5–6, p. 101.
'Put' brigady. Beseda,' *LitGaz*, 19 May 1930.
S. Romov, 'Vstrecha s Leonidom Leonovym,' *LitGaz*, 24 Sept. 1930.
'Na aktivakh VSSP: o perestroyke literaturno-khudozhestvennykh organizatsiy,' *LitGaz*, 5 May 1935.

'Leonid Leonov i Bruno Yasensky v gostyakh u chuvashskikh pisateley,' *Krasnaya Chuvashiya*, 10 July 1935.
D. K. '*Doroga na Okean*: Novyy roman Leonida Leonova,' *VechM*, 10 Oct. 1935.
[Tvorcheskie plany na 1936 g.], *Izv*, 1 Jan. 1936.
A. Rich, 'Vstrechi i vpechatleniya,' *VechM*, 20 Feb. 1936.
'Nad chem rabotayut pisateli?,' *VechM*, 4 April 1938.
'Novaya p'esa L. Leonova,' *LitGaz*, 10 Sept. 1938.
E. Pel'son, *Volk* v Tul'skom teatre,' *LitGaz*, 5 April 1939.
'Leonid Leonov o svoey p'ese,' *Malyy teatr*, 1 May 1939.
'Leonid Leonov o p'ese i spektakle *Volk*,' *Ural'skiy rabochiy*, 5 June 1939.
F. Peshchanskaya, '*Pisatel' i ego geroi*,' *VechM*, 23 Nov. 1942.
'Obrazy p'esy,' in *Materialy k p'ese Leonida Leonova* Nashestvie' (M., 1943), pp. 21–9.
'Neobyknovennoe v obydennom,' *Og*, 1945, no. 27, p. 10.
'O p'ese *Zolotaya kareta*. Beseda s L.M. Leonovym,' in 'Zolotaya kareta': *Materialy k postanovke p'esy L. Leonova* (M., 1946), pp. 3–25.
'Vruchenie Moskve ordena Lenina,' *Gorodskoe khozyaystvo Moskvy*, 1947, no. 9, p. 5.
[On the production of *Untilovsk* in the Moscow Arts Theatre] in Nikolay Abalkin, *Sistema Stanislavskogo* (M., 1954), pp. 238–40.
'Vasha novaya p'esa?,' *T*, 1955, no. 6, pp. 166–7.
'Beseda,' *VechM*, 26 April 1957.
'Milliony druzey. Beseda...,' *KomPr*, 11 June 1957.
'Budni pisatelya,' *LitGaz*, 4 March 1958.
Ya. Chernov, 'Talant na vsyu zhizn': v gostyakh u Leonida Leonova,' *VechM*, 4 Oct. 1958.
'Rezets khudozhnika,' *Lit i Zh*, 31 Oct. 1958.
'Kniga – drug,' *Molodoy kolkhoznik*, 1959, no. 1, p. 25.
N. Tikhanov, 'Interesnaya vstrecha,' *Volzhskaya kommuna*, 14 March 1959.
'V zashchitu zelenogo druga,' *Master lesa*, 1959, no. 2.
V. Tychinin, 'V gostyakh u Leonida Leonova. (Iz besed s pisatelem),' *Angara*, 1959, no. 3, pp. 149–51.
D. Starikov, 'U Leonida Leonova,' *LitGaz*, 7 May 1959.
E. Osetrov, 'Razdum'ya posle vstrechi,' *Lit i Zh*, 31 May 1959.
I. Osipov, 'Bol'shoy talant. V gostyakh u Leonida Leonova, *VechM*, 1 June 1959.
'Lyubit', berech', znat' prirodu. Beseda,' *Tsvetovodstvo*, 1959, no. 6, pp. 16–17.
'Beseda. Leonid Leonov,' *MosKom*, 6 June 1959.
I. Konichev, 'Sovety druzey,' *Lit i Zh*, 15 June 1959.
L. Bat', 'Leonid Leonov o literaturnom trude,' *VopLit*, 1960, no. 2, pp. 184–90.
'Trud i talant (Neproiznesennaya rech'),' *LitGaz*, 12 April 1960.

'Pritcha ob "ubiennom" geroe. Segodnya u nas v gostyakh krupneyshiy sovetskiy pisatel' Leonid Maksimovich Leonov,' *Leninskoe znamya*, 18 Sept. 1960.
E. Starikova, 'Leonid Leonov o pisatel'skom trude. (Iz besed s pisatelem),' *Zn*, 1961, no. 4, pp. 177–89.
I. Patrikeeva, 'V besedakh s L. M. Leonovym,' *T zh*, 1961, no. 16, pp. 2–4.
'O vospitanii u detey lyubvi k zhivotnym,' *Nauka i zhizn'*, 1961, no. 8.
I. Aleksandrov, 'U Leonida Leonova,' *Pogranichnik*, 1962, no. 3, pp. 55–6.
'Plamya tvorchestva,' *Lit i Zh*, 30 Sept. 1962.
A. Less, 'Rasskazy dlya nachinayushchikh. "Kak propal rubl'",' *VopLit*, 1962, no. 9, pp. 237–40.
'Vstrecha c Leonidom Leonovym,' *LitGaz*, 2 Oct. 1962.
E. Lidin and S. Razgonov, 'U Leonida Leonova,' *VechM*, 25 Feb. 1963.
P. Podleshchuk, 'Retsenziya, napisannaya prokurorom,' *Moskva*, 1963, no. 2, pp. 214–15.
V. Lyubavina and R. Rostislavov, 'Kak voznikayut syuzhety: V gostyakh u L. Leonova,' *SovR*, 25 Sept. 1964.
A. Pistunova, 'Iskusstvu opasna zazemlennost': Beseda s L. Leonovym o problemakh iskusstva i literatury,' *LitR*, 13 Nov. 1964.
E. Osetrov, 'Priglashenie k budushchemu: Vstrecha s L. Leonovym,' *Izv*, 4 Feb. 1965.
N. Sergovantsev, M. Aleksandrov, 'Razdum'ya o zelenom druge' (Beseda s Leonidom Leonovym), *Og*, 1966, no. 41, pp. 1–3.
G. Kapralov, 'Predvidet' khod istorii,' *Pr*, 26 Feb. 1967.
I. Rishina, 'Prazdnik sovetskoy literatury: K prisvoeniyu zvaniya Geroya Sotsialisticheskogo Truda gruppe sovetskikh pisateley: Besedy s L. Leonovym i drugimi,' *LitGaz*, 1 March 1967.
'Talantliv na vsyu zhizn'. Beseda s Leonidom Leonovym,' *T zh*, 1969, no. 3, p. 3.
E. Medvedeva, '"Gor'ky vo ves' golos: O podgotovke k pechati Polnogo akademicheskogo sobraniya sochineniy A. M. Gor'kogo." Beseda s glavnym redaktorom izdaniya L. Leonovym i zamestitelem glavnogo redaktora A. Ovcharenko,' *Izv*, 7 Jan. 1970.
R. Opits, 'Razum vsegda dostigaet to, chto uzhe znaet dusha,' *LitR*, 27 July 1973 (translation of interview, originally published in *Sinn und Form*, 1972).
'Khudozhnika sozdaet trud' (Beseda s pisatelem),' *KomPr*, 24 Aug. 1974.
'Iskat' cheloveka...,' *Literaturnaya ucheba*, 1978, no. 4, pp. 146–51.
'Beseda s bolgarami,' *Nash sovremennik*, 1979, no. 5, pp. 181–4.
V. Pomazneva, 'Razgovor o teme dnya: Otryvok iz besedy,' *LitGaz*, 21 Aug. 1980.
V. Dement'ev, '"Leonid Leonov: moya zhizn' v literature – syuzhetnaya novella...": Po materialam besedy s pisatelem,' *LitR*, 2 Jan. 1981.
'"Pompeyskie slepki": Leonid Leonov o problemakh kul'tury i kul'turnogo naslediya. Zapis' besedy i kommentariy k nei A. G. Lysova,' *Moskva*, 1983, no. 10, p. 183.

T. Men'shikova, 'Posleslovie k publikatsii "Razdum'ya u starogo kamnya": Beseda s pisatelem,' *Sovkul't*, 23 Aug. 1986.
O. Mikhaylov, 'Razgovor s Leonidom Leonovym: O besedakh s pisatelem,' *LitR*, 3 Jan. 1986.
T. Zemskova, 'Leonid Leonov: "Lotsiya po kotoroy idti": Beseda s pisatelem,' *LitR*, 5 June 1987.
Inna Rostovtseva, '"To, chto sozdavalos' podvigom, sokhranyaetsya lish' takim zhe podvigom": Formula cheloveka. Iz besed s Leonidom Leonovym,' *LitGaz*, 8 July 1987.
K. Smirnova, 'O prirode sovesti: Po materialam besedy s pisatelem L. Leonovym,' *Izv*, 16 Dec. 1987.
A. Lysov, 'Apokrif XX veka: Mif o "razmolvke nachal" v kontseptsii tvorchestva L. Leonova: iz besed s pisatelem,' *RusLit*, 1989, no. 4, pp. 53–68.
A. Anisenkov, 'Leonid Leonov: "Byt' blagodarnym prirode": Beseda s pisatelem,' *Sotsialisticheskaya industriya*, 31 May 1989.
V. Zhegis, 'V gostyakh u Leonida Leonova. Talant na vsyu zhizn',' *Trud*, 31 May 1989.
E. Shigaeva, 'Vslukh o predstoyashchem: Rasskaz pisatelya,' *LitGaz*, 31 May 1989.
V.Kalita, 'Leonid Leonov: "Kak greshno i strashno...": po materialam besedy s pisatelem L.M. Leonovym,' *LitR*, 29 May 1992.
V. Dement'ev, 'Leonid Leonov: "Razum otkryvaet to, chto dusha uzhe znaet": O pisatele L.M. Leonove,' *Pr*, 30 May 1992.
Inna Rostovtseva, 'Negativ, proyavlennyy vechnost'yu: iz razgovorov s Leonidom Leonovym,' *LitGaz*, 1 June 1994.
L. Vlasov, 'Chudo otkryvaetsya tol'ko chistomu cheloveku: O vstrechakh s L. M. Leonovym,' *Kul'tura*, 10 Sept. 1994.
Kim Smirnov, 'V zashchitu zdravogo smysla. Dialog s Leonidom Leonovym, ne opublikovannyy sem' let nazad,' *Izv*, 21 Sept. 1994.
Viktor Kozhemyako, 'Pered ukhodom v vechnost': chasy i minuty iz poslednikh sta zemnykh dney Leonida Leonova,' *Pr*, 9 Aug. 1995.
Maksim Shraer, 'Posledniy russkiy klassik na poroge stoletiya: predsmertnyy portret Leonida Leonova,' *LitOb*, 1998, no. 4, pp. 40–50.

4. Autobiographical Essays

In *Literaturnaya Rossiya. Sbornik* I (M., 1924), pp. 171–2.
'Vospominaniya o svoey rodoslovnoy,' in *Russkiy evgenicheskiy zhurnal*, vol. 4 (M., 1926), pp. 136–40.
In *Pisateli. Avtobiografii i portrety sovremennykh russkikh prozaikov*, ed. Vl. Lidin (M., 1926), pp. 159–61.

In *Pisateli-sovremenniki*, ed. V. Golubkov (M., 1928), p. 115.
In *Doroga na Okean* (M., 1954).
[Told to E.V. Starikova] in *Sovetskie pisateli*, vol. 1 (M., 1959).

5. Published Correspondence

5A. Private Letters

Correspondence with V.A. Kovalev (1948–93) in *Iz tvorcheskogo naslediya russkikh pisateley XX veka*, ed. N. A. Groznova (St Petersburg, 1995), pp. 426–89.
Two letters to Maksimilian Voloshin (1925), ibid., pp. 490–500.
Five letters to Maksim Gor'ky (1924–30) in *Literaturnoe nasledstvo*, vol. 70 (M.-L., 1963), pp. 248–59.
Two letters to V.I. Nemirovich-Danchenko (1937) in *Ezhegodnik Moskovskogo khudozhestvennogo teatra*, 1948, vol. 1 (M., 1950), pp. 426–7.
'Druzhba literatur,' letter to Tsa-Tszin-Khua (6 Dec. 1944), *LitGaz*, 12 Sept. 1959.
Letter to N. Pershin (undated), *T zh*, 1959, no. 6, p. 59.
Letter to E. D. Surkov, 7 June 1971, *Leonid Leonov v vospominaniyakh, interv'yu, dnevnikakh* (M., 1999), pp. 220–4.

5B. Open Letters

'Pis'mo v redaktsiyu,' *Izv*, 17 Feb. 1925.
'Pis'mo v redaktsiyu,' *VechM*, 10 March 1926.
'Pis'mo v redaktsiyu' *LitGaz*, 13 May 1929 (one of 15 signatories protesting at accusations of plagiarism made against Mandel'shtam by A. G. Gornfel'd and D. Zaslavsky).
'K pisatelyam zapada,' *LitGaz*, 9 Nov. 1929.
'Vashe slovo dolzhno zazvuchat',' *LitGaz*, 17 Feb. 1932 (one of 5 signatories).
'Ko vsem rabotnikam literatury i iskusstv,' *LitGaz*, 5 May 1932 (one of several signatories).
'Otkrytoe pis'mo Ivanu Nazhivinu v Bryussel',' *LitGaz*, 29 Sept. 1932.
'Otvet Valentinu Kataevu,' *LitGaz*, 23 Nov. 1932 (with Vl. Lidin).
'Skorb' i gnev' (open letter on murder of Kirov, signed also by Vl. Lidin, A. Novikov-Priboy, B. Pasternak, and I. Erenburg), *Izv*, 2 Dec. 1934.
'Steret' s litsa zemli' (joint letter on trial of Zinov'ev and Kamenev signed by 15 other writers, among them Fedin and Pasternak), *Pr*, 21 Aug. 1936.
'S kem vy, amerikanskie mastera kul'tury?' *LitGaz*, 20 Sept. 1947 (one of 13 signatories).
'Kniga nadolgo,' *LitGaz*, 7 Dec. 1957 (one of 11 signatories).

'K pisatelyam vsego mira,' *LitGaz*, 22 Aug. 1958 (one of 102 signatories).
'... Ego zhizn' dolzhna byt' spasena,' *Pr*, 8 July 1959 (one of 31 signatories).
'Pisateli Ameriki, my khotim slushat' vash golos,' *LitGaz*, 19 May 1960.
'My solidarny s vashey bor'boy: Otkrytoe pis'mo d-ru Spoku, Pisatelyu M.Gudmanu, direktoru Vashingtonskogo tsentra po izucheniyu vneshney politiki M.Raskinu, svyashchenniku U. Koffinu i aspirantu Garvardskogo universiteta M. Ferberu,' *LitGaz*, 7 Feb. 1968.
'Eshche raz o dome Dalya: O neobkhodimosti sokhraneniya arkhitekturnogo pamyatnika,' *LitGaz*, 19 May 1971.
'Ostanovit' bul'dozery: Problemy sochetaniya pamyatnikov arkhitektury s novoy stroykoy,' *LitGaz*, 26 May 1971.
'Bezzavetnost': Pis'mo uchastnikam vechera, posvyashchennogo marshalu bronetankovykh voysk P. S. Rybalko,' *LitGaz*, 19 May 1976.
'"My khotim, chtoby nas uslyshali..." Pis'mo deyateley nauki i kul'tury v zashchitu zhizni,' *Trud*, 10 Sept. 1992.

IV. Early Publications

1. Archangel Period

Pre-revolutionary Russia followed the Julian calendar, which by the twentieth century had fallen thirteen days behind the Gregorian calendar of western Europe. In February 1918 the government changed to the Gregorian system. Accordingly, in this section dates before 1918 are given in the Old Style; all subsequent dates correspond to the Western calendar.

Almost all Leonov's Archangel publications appeared in the newspaper founded and edited by his father, Maksim Leonov. Up until April 1918 the newspaper was titled *Severnoe utro*; after that date it was renamed *Severnyy den'*. There is therefore no need to specify the name of the publication in the following list before the end of 1918.

1. Early Verse

Leonov's early poems are for the most part signed 'Leonid Leonov' or 'L. Leonov.' Several, however, appeared over the initials 'L. L.' Some of these cases are simply reprints of poems that Leonov had published earlier over his full name, but there remains some doubt over some of the others, since there was at least one other poet with these initials, Leonid Lobachev, who contributed to the paper at this time. Leonov himself took no interest in his early publications and did not remember which he had written. I have included here only those poems which are signed 'Leonid Leonov,' or poems which scholars have attributed to him. In the case of these doubtful cases I have added the form in which the author is identified.

Severnoe utro
'Vecherom,' 4 July 1915.
'Rodine,' 5 July 1915.
'Drugu,' 26 July 1915.
'Pesnya,' 1 Aug. 1915.
'Son,' 14 Aug. 1915.
'Osen'' ('Rozy ottsvetayut...'), 15 Aug. 1915.
'Mysli,' 19 Aug. 1915.
'Uzheli,' 26 Aug. 1915.
'Osen'' ('Ya verit' ne khochu...'), 2 Sept. 1915.
'Noch',' 23 Sept. 1915.
'Im,' 24 Sept. 1915.
'Vavila,' 20 Dec. 1915.
'Rassvet,' 23 Dec. 1915.
'Rovno v polnoch'...,' 29 Dec. 1915.
'V bredu,' 6 Jan. 1916.
'Pesn' o royali,' 8 Jan. 1916.
'Kakaya tishina!...,' 9 Jan. 1916.
'Pri zvukakh strun zhivykh...,' 9 June 1916.
'V beluyu noch',' 23 June 1916.
'Arlekin,' 24 June 1916.
'Starye berezy grezyat...,' 25 June 1916.
'Osennie akkordy,' 28 Oct. 1916.
'Osen'' ('Na dorozhkakh...'), 2 Nov. 1916.
'Iz dnevnika' ('I uekhala vdrug...'), 10 Nov. 1916.
'Iz dnevnika' ('Pis'mo. Ee konvert...'), 11 Nov. 1916.
'Eto bylo,' 11 Jan. 1917.
'Karnaval,' 18 Jan. 1917.
'Net vremeni...,' 17 Feb. 1917.
'Vesna' ('Ya segodnya napilsya...'), 19 Feb. 1917.
'Sergey ubit...,' 22 Feb. 1917.
'K Dalekomu,' 24 Feb. 1917.
'V uzore skal...,' 25 Feb. 1917.
'V starinnoy komnate...,' 2 March 1917.
'Kuznetsy,' 14 March 1917.
'Veytes', veytes', krasnye flagi svobody...,' 15 March 1917.

Severnyy den'
'Peshchera zverya,' 3 April 1918.
'Khorugvi,' 12 April 1918.
'Tsinichnyy mistik,' 17 April 1918.

'Razdum'e,' 17 April 1918.
'N. Belinkomu' ('V pereput'yakh...') 20 April 1918.
'Ty kogda-to s litsom bogomateri...,' 20 April 1918.
'Dekabr'skaya mut',' 21 April 1918.
'Vesna' ('V lozhbinakh sneg...'), 21 April 1918.
'Orkhidey,' 23 April 1918.
'Zadremala polnoch'...,' 23 April 1918.
'Vesennyaya skazka,' 24 April 1918 (signed L.L.).
'Osen',' (variant of 'Osen',' 2 Nov. 1916), 24 April 1918 (signed L.L.).
'Skazanie o Krestitele,' 25 April 1918.
'Solntsu,' 26 April 1918 (signed L.L.).
'Starinnye zdaniya,' 26 April 1918 (signed L.L.).
'Tak mnogo raz sblizhalis' guby...,' 27 April 1918 (signed L.L.).
'Troe,' 27 April 1918.
'Segodnya,' 28 April 1918.
'Zavtra,' 28 April 1918 (signed L.L.).
'Lidii V-oy' ('Kogda nebesnyy luch...'), 30 April 1918 (signed L.L.).
'Zvony,' 30 April 1918 (signed L.L.).
'Sny,' 1 May 1918 (signed L.L.).
'Zhena Iyulya,' 3 May 1918 (signed L.L.).
Nocturno' (signed L. L.; variant of 'Iz dnevnika,' 10 Nov. 1916), 3 May 1918.
Noch',' 9 May 1918 (signed L.L.).
'Tak nado...,' 9 May 1918 (signed L.L.).
'Traditsionnaya elegiya,' 10 May 1918 (signed L.L.).
'My,' 10 May 1918 (signed L.L.).
'Poezdka v ray,' 11 May 1918 (signed L.L.).
'Zver'' (signed L. L.; variant of 'Peshchera zverya,' 3 April 1918), 11 May 1918.
'Vzryv,' 12 May 1918 (signed L.L.).
'Vtornik,' 12 May 1918 (signed L.L.).
'Korol',' 17 May 1918 (signed L.L.).
'Ya razrublyu veslom...,' 17 May 1918 (signed L.L.).
'Ispoved',' 18 May 1918.
'Goryashchaya gotika,' 18 May 1918.
'Mozhet byt',' 21 May 1918.
'Vecher,' 21 May 1918.
'Gorodskoy chort,' 22 May 1918.
'Monastyr',' 24 May 1918.
'Smert',' 25 May 1918 (signed L.L.).
'Osen'' ("U shirokikh alley..."), 25 May 1918 (signed L.L.).
'Nebyvalochka,' 26 May 1918.

'Tak mnogo raz...' (reprint of 27 Apr.), 18 June 1918.
'Troe' (reprint of 27 Apr.), 18 June 1918.

2. *Early Prose: Theatre Reviews*

The following items are signed 'L.L.,' Leon. L-ov,' or 'L.L-ov.' Specialists in Leonov's early work agree in attributing them to him, though other authors (e.g., Leonid Lobachev) published in the paper could also fit these initials.

['Zabastovki v Moskve'], extracts from letters of Leonov, *SevU*, 25, 26, and 28 Sept. 1913.

Reviews of
Fuente ovejuna (Lope de Vega), *SevU*, 5 June 1916.
Sharmanka Satany (N. A. Teffi), *SevU*, 7 June 1916.
Krov' (S. Shimansky), *SevU*, 7 June 1916.
Fuente ovejuna (Lope de Vega), *SevU*, 10 June 1916.
Na dne (M. Gor'ky), *SevU*, 11 June 1916.
Moryaki (S. Garin), *SevU*, 15 June 1916.
Baryshnya s fialkami (Shchepkina-Kupernik), *SevU*, 16 June 1916.
Varfolomeevskaya noch' (A. Linner), *SevU*, 17 June 1916.
Bluzhdayushchie ogni (A.N. Antropov), *SevU*, 23 June 1916.
Tsena zhizni (V. Nemirovich-Danchenko), *SevU*, 24 June 1916.
Izmail (Bukharin), *SevU*, 26 June 1916.
Boevye tovarishchi (Tarsky), *SevU*, 28 June 1916.
Deti Vanyushina (S.A. Naydenov), *SevU*, 29 June 1916.
Tsyganka Zanda (Tangofer and Brossener), *SevU*, 3 July 1916.
Dyadya Vanya (Chekhov), *SevU*, 5 July 1916.
Aktrisa Larina (Al. Voznesensky), *SevU*, 7 July 1916.
V starye gody (I. Shpazhinsky), *SevU*, 14 July 1916.
U belogo kamnya (L. Urvantsev), *SevU*, 6 June 1917.
Kasatka (A.N. Tolstoy), *SevU*, 17 June 1917.
Chernaya pantera (Vinnichenko), *SevU*, 21 June 1917.
Vtoraya molodost' (P. Nevezhin), *SevU*, 21 June 1917.
Charodeyka (I. Shpazhinsky), *SevU*, 25 June 1917.
Roman (E. Sheldon), *SevU*, 1 Aug. 1917.
Mysl' (L. Andreev), *SevU*, 3 Aug. 1917.
Magda (G. Zuderman) ('Gastroli E.T. Zhikharevoy'), *SevD*, 17 April 1918.
Chudesnye luchi (Fal'kovsky), *SevD*, 2 June 1918.

Pervaya lyubov' (Shakh) and *Gaudeamus* (L. Andreev) ('Teatr Gagarinskogo skvera'), *SevD* 4 June 1918.
Grekhi zhizni (L'vovsky) ('Otgoloski zhizni'), *SevD*, 9 June 1918.
Kovarstvo i lyubov' (Schiller), *SevD*, 12 June 1918.
Raspyataya (N. Lerner), *SevD*, 13 June 1918.
Flavia Tessini (T. Shchedrina-Kupernik), *SevD*, 21 June 1918.

Other Early Prose
'Pervaya lektsiya V.A. Posse,' *SevU*, 23 June 1916.
'Bibliografiya. *Yunost'. Ezhemesyachnik uchashchikhsya goroda Arkhangel'ska*,' *SevD*, 25 April 1918.
'Poet Severa (U khudozhnika S. G. Pisakhova),' *SevD*, 3 May 1918.
'G.V. Plekhanov. Nekrolog,' *SevD*, 7 June 1918.
'K predstoyashchey vystavke kartin khudozhnika Pisakhova,' *SevD*, 21 June 1918.

3. Other Works of the Archangel Period

'Puteshestvie iz Moskvy v Arkhangel'sk,' *SevD*, 14 Aug. 1918.
'Professor Ivan Platonych,' *SevD*, 4, 7, 8 Dec. 1918.
'Sonnaya yav',' *SevD*, 18, 19 Dec. 1918.
'Toska,' *SevD*, 20 Dec. 1918.
'Tsar' i Afonya,' *SevD*, 7 Jan. 1919.
'Malen'kie,' *SevD*, 12, 13 Jan. 1919.
'Telegrafist Opalimov,' *SevD*, 16, 18 Jan. 1919.
'Mal'chik Kolya,' *SevD*, 22 Jan. 1919.
'Epikha,' *SevD*, 27, 28 Jan. 1919.
'Prelude,' *Vozrozhdenie Severa*, 9 March 1919.
'O vystavke (Severnyy Parnas),' *Vozrozhdenie Severa*, 14 Sept. 1919.
'Pro soldata skazka,' *SevD*, 7 Oct. 1919.

Leonov also published two works, 'Korol'' and 'Tsar' i Afonya' in a school magazine, *Zhurnal '19,'* Izd. Kruzhka Samoobrazovaniya (M., 1918), pp. 34, 35–6, respectively. These works were later republished in *SevD*, 17 May 1918 and 7 Jan., 1919, respectively.

2. Contributions to Red Army Newspapers 1921–2

Publications before July 1921 appeared in *Krasnyy boets* (published at Kherson and Ekaterinoslav); after that date in *Krasnyy voin* (published in Moscow). Items marked with an asterisk are in verse. These items are signed with a variety of pseudonyms, 'Maksim Laptev,' 'M. L.,' 'Laptev,' 'L.,' 'Lapot',' 'La-ev,' 'La-v,' 'L-v.'

Krasnyy boets
*'Zapomni,' 21 March 1921.
'Poumneli,' 22 March 1921.
*'Vrangelevtsu,' 25 March 1921.
*'Aprel' (Dve mysli pro odno i to zhe),' 1 April 1921.
'O "neodushevlennykh" predmetakh. Opyt ironicheskoy matematiki. Krasnyy fel'eton,' 5 April 1921.
*'Pod dozhdem,' 6 April 1921.
*'Otpuskniku,' 19 April 1921.
'Tri milliona. Istoricheskoe,' 27 April 1921.
'Udary po sebe. (Bazarnye nabroski),' 29 April 1921.
*'V etot den',' 1 May 1921.
'Gibel' vtorogo [Internatsionala]. (Zheltoe v krasnom svete),' 1 May 1921.
*'Vokzal. (Otpusknikam),' 12 May 1921.
'Shchelchki v lob. (Mimokhodom),' 14 May 1921.
'S kamnem na shee. (Zaupokoynaya isklyuchennym [iz partii]),' 17 May 1921.

Krasnyy voin
'Na pomoshch'. (Ocherk),' 30 July 1921.
*'Zakat,' 2 Aug. 1921.
*'Krasnoy Armii,' 4 Aug. 1921.
'V. I. Lenin,' 6 Aug. 1921.
'Nasha torgovlya s Germaniey,' 9 Aug. 1921.
'Redkiy ekzemplyar,' 12 Aug. 1921.
'Na pomoshch' golodayushchim,' 17 Aug. 1921.
'Distsiplina i khozyaystvennoe stroitel'stvo,' 20 Aug. 1921.
'Kniga i krasnoarmeets,' 20 Aug. 1921.
'Boyarskaya armiya Rumynii,' 24 Aug. 1921.
*'Evrope,' 24 Aug. 1921.
*'Beregi do gryadushchego dnya,' 26 Aug. 1921.
'Chto delaetsya na golodnom fronte,' 27 Aug. 1921.
*'Tebe, voin,' 30 Aug. 1921.
'Beregi dobro,' 1 Sept. 1921.
'Mimokhodom. (Vpechatleniya),' 3 Sept. 1921.
'Glyadi v oba,' 3 Sept. 1921.
'Telefon so skrezhetom,' 8 Sept. 1921.
'Trubochki v vitrinakh,' 8 Sept. 1921.
'Na Shipke vse spokoyno,' 13 Sept. 1921.
'Pochtovyy yashchik,' 17 Sept. 1921.
*'Pust',' 20 Sept. 1921.
'V uchebno-inzhenernom batal'one. (Vpechatleniya),' 22 Sept. 1921.

*'Ul'timatum,' 27 Sept. 1921.
'Mel'kom,' 27 Sept. 1921.
*'Vse o tom zhe,' 1 Oct. 1921.
*'Kaul'bars za rabotoy,' 15 Oct. 1921.
'Osvetit' kazarmu,' 18 Oct. 1921.
*'Vokzal. Ukhodyashchim v bessrochnuyu' [variant of 'Vokzal,' 12 May], 20 Oct. 1921.
*'Antanta,' 20 Oct. 1921.
'Pochtovyy yashchik,' 20 Oct. 1921.
'Pochtovyy yashchik,' 25 Oct. 1921.
'V pokhodakh i v boyakh. Obrabotka Lapteva [i. e. Leonova],' 29 Oct. 1921.
*'K vam, za rubezh,' 7 Nov. 1921.
'Pochtovyy yashchik,' 10 Nov. 1921.
*'Tebe, nashemu. K 100–letiyu so dnya rozhdeniya Dostoevskogo,' 12 Nov. 1921.
'Otvet ot redaktsii,' 13 Nov. 1921.
*'V posledniy raz,' 16 Nov. 1921.
'Bibliografiya. "Zhurnal V. S. Sh.. Oktyabr'skiy (pyatyy) nomer",' 17 Nov. 1921.
'Pochtovyy yashchik,' 22 Nov. 1921.
'Pochtovyy yashchik,' 24 Nov. 1921.
'Pochtovyy yashchik,' 26 Nov. 1921.
'Vosh'. (Nedelya bor'by so vshivost'yu),' 1 Dec. 1921.
*'Vashington,' 6 Dec. 1921.
'Pochtovyy yashchik,' 10 Dec. 1921.
*'Moe slovo,' 24 Dec. 1921.
'Krasnoarmeyskaya zhizn'. V Spasskikh kazarmakh,' 27 Dec. 1921.
*'My – Devyatomu S''ezdu,' 27 Dec. 1921.
'Ne slovom, a delom,' 27 Dec. 1921.
*'Na Moskvu,' 29 Dec. 1921.
*'Na strazhe,' 1 Jan. 1922.
*'V etot den',' 1 Jan. 1922.
*'Na zov Chity,' 3 Jan. 1922.
*'Krasnoarmeyskie chastushki. (Naschet tekh, kotorye lezut),' 12 Jan. 1922.
*'Vozhdyu. (K godovshchine Krasnoy Armii),' 12 Jan. 1922.
*'Krasnoarmeets. (Vsem ne-krasnoarmeytsam),' 16 Feb. 1922.
*'Dvum v shubakh,' 17 Feb. 1922.
'O literaturnykh nasekomykh. (Vsem, pishushchim k nam),' 18 Feb. 1922.
*'Chetyre-pyat'. (Vsem vam, bezvestnym i velikim, nosyashchim krasnoarmeyskuyu shinel'), 23 Feb. 1922.
'Malen'kiy fel'eton. Kak my bumagu vozili,' 7 March 1922.
'Malen'kiy fel'eton. Kak odin zabolel i chto iz etogo vyshlo,' 16 March 1922.
'Malen'kiy fel'eton. 1,500,000,000. (Vrazumitel'no dlya vsekh),' 24 March 1922.

'Tresk Moskpechal'. Nepechal'no o pechal'nom),' 24 March 1922.
*'Genuezskoe. (Neokonchennaya poema),' 29 March 1922.
'Chelovek iz "Nospechati". (Sil'no tragicheskoe),' 30 March 1922.
'Zametki o tom i o sem. (Po okrugu),' 4 April 1922.
*'Pesenka gospodina Puankare,' 5 April 1922.
'Zametki o tom i o sem. Nechto vrode obzora,' 6 April 1922.
'Usilit' svoyu rabotu,' 6 April 1922.
'Kak oni prosilis',' 11 April 1922.
'Zametki o tom i o sem,' 12 April 1922.
'Pomni Perekop,' 3 Sept. 1922.

5. Dubia

The following items are signed by a 'Leonid Leonov' who appears to be unrelated to the subject of this study.

'Shchyry poklon,' *Belarus'*, 1949, no. 1, p. 20.
'Rusakova doroga: Byl',' *Sovetskaya Belorussiya*, 17 April 1963.
'Belorusskiy med,' *Pchelovodstvo*, 1968, no. 7, pp. 8–9.
'Sad ty nash batyushka,' *Neman*, 1969, no. 8, pp. 151–61.
'Vtoroy khleb,' *Neman*, 1970, no. 6, pp. 117–31.
'Grabezh i sud spravedlivyy,' *SovR*, 21 Jan. 1993.

SECONDARY SOURCES

1. Books Devoted to Leonov

Akimov, V.M., *Leonid Leonov. Ukazatel' literatury* (L., 1958).
Andruszko, Czeslaw, *Romany Leonida Leonova 20–kh godov* (Poznan', 1985).
Ben'kovich, M.A., *Filosofskiy roman Leonida Leonova* (Bel'tsy, 1970).
Boguslavskaya, Zoya, *Leonid Leonov* (M., 1960).
Bol'shoy mir: stat'i o tvorchestve Leonida Leonova (M., 1972).
Chivilikhin, V., ed., *O Leonove* (M., 1979).
Fink. L., *Dramaturgiya Leonida Leonova* (M., 1962).
– *Uroki Leonida Leonova: tvorcheskaya evolyutsiya* (M., 1973).
Groznova, Natal'ya, *Tvorchestvo Leonida Leonova i traditsii russkoy klassicheskoy literatury: ocherki* (L., 1982).
Harjan, George, *Leonid Leonov: A Critical Study* (Toronto, 1979).
Khimich, V.V., *Poetika romanov L. Leonova* (Sverdlovsk, 1989).
Khrulev, V.I., *Mysl' i slovo Leonida Leonova* (Saratov, 1989).
– *Simvolika v proze Leonida Leonova* (Ufa, 1992).
Kirpotin, V., *Romany Leonida Leonova* (M.-L., 1932).

Kondyurina, E.F., *Leonid Leonov i pisateli-sovremenniki* (Vil'nius, 1977).
- *Proza Leonida Leonova 20–30–ykh godov (Problema kul'tury)* (Vil'nius, 1982).

Kovalev, V.A., *Romany Leonida Leonova* (M.-L., 1954).
- *Tvorchestvo Leonida Leonova: k kharakteristike tvorcheskoy individual'nosti pisatelya* (M.-L., 1962).
- *Leonid Leonov: Seminariy* (M.-L., 1964).
- *Realizm Leonova* (M., 1969).
- *Etyudy o Leonide Leonove* (M., 1978).
- *Leonid Leonov: Seminariy* (M., 1982).

Kovalev, V.A., ed., *Tvorchestvo Leonida Leonova: Issledovaniya i soobshcheniya: Vstrechi s Leonovym: Bibliografiya* (L., 1969).

Kovalev, V.A., and Groznova, N.A., eds., *Leonid Leonov: tvorcheskaya individual'nost' i literaturnyy protsess* (L., 1987).

Kruk, I.T., *Leonid Leonov: Ocherk tvorchestva* (Kiev, 1985).

Krylov, V.P., *Filosofskaya proza Leonida Leonova; Voprosy poetiki* (L., 1977).
- *Osobennosti tipizatsii kharaktera v proze Leonida Leonova* (Petrozavodsk, 1979).
- *Kompozitsiya filosofskogo romana* (Petrozavodsk, 1981).
- *Psikhologicheskiy analiz* (Petrozavodsk, 1983).
- *Leonid Leonov – khudozhnik* (Petrozavodsk, 1984).

Leonid Leonov – master khudozhestvennogo slova (M., 1981).

Leonid Leonov i sovremennost' (Saratov, 1982).

Lepeshinskaya, E.L., *Nravstvennyy mir geroev Leonida Leonova* (Voronezh, 1977).

Lobanov, M., *Roman Leonida Leonova 'Russkiy les'* (M., 1958).

Materialy k p'ese Leonida Leonova 'Nashestvie' (M., 1943).

Mikhailov, O., *Mirozdanie po Leonidu Leonovu: Lichnost' i tvorchestvo: Ocherki* (M., 1987).

Mirovoe znachenie tvorchestva Leonida Leonova (M., 1981).

Nikitina, E.F., ed., *Leonid Leonov* (M., 1928).

Nusinov, I., *Leonid Leonov* (M., 1935).

Porman, R.N., *L. Leonov: Problemy metoda i masterstva* (Perm', 1976).

Shcheglova, G.N., *Zhanrevo-stilevoe svoeobrazie dramaturgii Leonida Leonova* (M., 1984).

Starikova, E.V., Russkiy les *Leonida Leonova* (M., 1963).
- *Tvorchestvo L. M. Leonova* (M., 1964).
- *Leonid Leonov* (M., 1972).

Vakhitova, T.M., *Leonid Leonov. Zhizn' i tvorchestvo* (M., 1984).

Vlasov, F., *Poeziya zhizni* (M., 1961).
- *Epos muzhestva* (M., 1965).

Zaytsev, N.V. *Teatr Leonida Leonova* (L., 1980).

Zolotaya kareta *Materialy k postanovke p'esy L. Leonova* (M., 1946).

2. Selected Articles on Leonov

Anisimov, I., 'Novyy roman Leonova,' *LitGaz*, 17 Dec. 1932.
'Anketa sredi deyateley teatra,' *NLP* (1928), no. 3, p. 38.
Bakh, A. N., 'Nashe slovo o literature,' *LitGaz*, 29 Oct. 1932.
Bolotnikov, A., 'Doroga na Okean,' *LitGaz*, 20 April 1936.
Burg, D., 'Popytka Leonida Leonova,' *Mosty* (1961), no. 7 pp. 159–79.
– 'Leonid Leonov's Search,' *Studies on the Soviet Union*, vol. 1, no. 3, pp. 120–36.
'Diskussiya o Skutarevskom,' *VechM*, 5, 6 Jan. 1933.
Dmitriev, L., 'Dnevnik iskusstv,' *LitGaz*, 16 June 1945.
Dzyubinsky S., and N. Izgoev, 'Massovyy chitatel' o khudozhestvennoy literature,' *NM*, (1934), no. 9, pp. 197–8.
E., Ya., 'Doroga na Okean,' *LitGaz*, 5 Nov. 1935.
Elbaum, Henry, 'Rhetoric and Fiction: Interaction of Verbal Genres in the Soviet Fiction of the Twenties and Thirties.' PhD dissertation, McGill University, Montreal, 1988.
Ermilov, V., 'Problema zhivogo cheloveka v sovremennoy literature: *Vor* Leonova,' *NLP* (1927), no. 5/6, pp. 65–81.
Fomenko, V. 'Klevetnicheskaya p'esa,' *LitGaz*, 22 Sept. 1940.
Futrell, M., 'A Central Soviet Novel: Leonov's *Sot'*,' *Renaissance and Modern Language Studies*, Nottingham (1959), no. 3, pp. 111–30.
Gerschenkron, Alex., 'Reflections on Soviet Novels,' *World Politics*, Jan. 1960.
Golubov, V., 'Barsuki,' *Zhizn' iskusstva* (1929), no. 13.
Gorodinsky, V., and Varshavsky, Ya., 'Chernaya magiya. O p'ese Leonova *Lenushka*,' *KomPr*, 15 Oct. 1946.
Grasis, K., ' Vekhisty o Shpenglere,' *KN* (1922), no. 2 [6].
Groznova, N.A., 'Leonid Leonov – grani leonovskoy metafiziki,' in *Nauchno delo akademika Milosava Babovicha* (Podgoritsa, 1996).
Gurvich, A., 'Pouchitel'nye neudachi,' *T* (1940), no. 11.
Hingley, R., 'Leonid Leonov,' *Soviet Survey*, (1958), no. 25, pp. 69–74.
Humesky, Anna, 'Leonid Leonov and Blok: Observations on *Dereviannaia Koroleva*,' *Russian Literature and American Critics*, ed. K. Brostrom (Ann Arbor, 1984), pp. 103–28.
'Itogi teatral'nogo sezona,' *SovIsk*, 2 June 1939.
Kain, Richard M., 'The Plight of the Intelligentsia in the Soviet Novel,' *Russian Review*, 2 (1942), pp. 70–9.
Kataev, Valentin. 'Otkrytoe pis'mo Vl. Lidinu i L. Leonovu,' *LitGaz*, 17 Nov. 1933.
Katanyan, V., 'Skutarevsky,' *VechM*, 29 Dec. 1932.
Kharitonov, A.A., Vtoroy seminar po romanu L. Leonova *Piramida* v Pushkinskom dome,' *RusLit* (1997), no. 3, pp. 223–7.

'Klevetnicheskaya p'esa,' *SovIsk*, 22 Sept. 1940.
Kogan, P.S., 'Pis'ma o literature. O leonovshchine, o *Barsukakh*, i o nezyblemykh ustoyakh,' *KrGaz (vech)*, 1 July 1925.
Kolesnikova, G., '*Barsuki*. Roman Leonida Leonova,' *Okt* (1925), no. 9–10, pp. 185–97.
Kovalev, V.A., 'Poet-surikovets M. L. Leonov,' *RusLit* (1957), no. 1, pp. 257–9.
– 'Gor'ky i Leonov (20–ye gody),' *Voprosy sovetskoy literatury*, vol. 1, ed. V.A. Desnitsky and A.S. Bushmin (M.-L., 1953), pp. 200–44.
– 'Leonid Leonov – sotrudnik krasnoarmeyskhikh gazet (1920–1922),' ibid., pp. 329–41.
– 'Zametki o yazyke i stile romanov L. Leonova 20–ykh godov,' *Voprosy sovetskoy literatury*, vol. 2, ed. A.S. Bushmin and K.D. Muratova (M.-L., 1953), pp. 180–217.
– 'Iz tvorcheskoy istorii romana *Russkiy les* Leonida Leonova,' *Voprosy sovetskoy literatury*, vol. 6, ed. V.A. Kovalev (M.-L., 1957), pp. 328–76.
– '*Vor* L. Leonova (Ot pervoy do vtoroy redaktsii romana),' *Voprosy sovetskoy literatury*, vol. 9, ed. S.V. Kastorsky and V.A. Kovalev (M.-L., 1961), pp. 136–91.
– 'Leonid Leonov: Bol'shoy pisatel': bol'shoy chelovek,' *Don* (1959), no. 5, pp. 172–7.
Kut, A., 'Doklad I. M. Nusinova,' *VechM*, 1 Feb. 1929.
Kuznetsov, M., 'Russkiy les,' *Pr*, 28 March 1954.
Lelevich, G., '*Barsuki*,' *SovIsk* (1925), no. 2.
'Leningradskie pisateli solidarizirovalis' s moskovskimi; soprotivlenie reaktsionnykh elementov,' *LitGaz*, 30 Sept. 1929.
Levidov, M., 'Zhertvy i zavoevaniya,' *LitGaz*, 20 May 1934.
Loks, K., 'Petushikhinskiy prolom,' *Pechat' i revolyutsiya* (1924), no. 2.
– 'Konets melkogo cheloveka,' *Pechat' i revolyutsiya* (1924), no. 6.
Lunacharsky, A., '*Barsuki*,' *KrGaz (vech)*, 14 Oct. 1927.
Lunin, V., '*Barsuki*,' *Knigonosha* (1925), no. 29.
L'vov, V., 'Komandarm elektronov. *Skutarevsky* kak nauchnyy roman,' *LitLen*, 15 Oct. 1933.
Lysov, A., 'K sporam o *Vore*,' *Nauchnye trudy vuzov Litovskoy SSR* (Vil'nius, 1974) 14, vyp. 2, pp. 25–42.
– 'O bibleyskoy kul'ture v tvorchestve L. Leonova,' *Nauchnye trudy vuzov Litovskoy SSR* (Vil'nius, (1980), vyp. 2, pp. 64–75.
– 'Chelovecheskoe, tol'ko chelovecheskoe...,' *VopLit* (1989), no. 1, pp. 3–25.
– 'Tri puti: zhivaya zhizn' kul'tury i tvorcheskikh iskaniy Leonida Leonova,' *Nauchnye trudy vuzov Litovskoy SSR* (Vil'nius, (1990), 32, vyp. 2, pp. 52–69.
Mel'nikov-Papoushek, N., 'Leonid Leonov,' *Volya Rossii* (1925), no. 1, pp. 241–5.
'*Metel'* Leonida Leonova,' *DMZ*, (1939), no. 35.

Muchnic, Helen, 'Leonid Leonov,' *The Russian Review* vol. 18, no. 1 (1959), pp. 35–52.
Munblit, G., 'O pravde i pravdopodobii,' *LitGaz*, 17 Dec. 1932.
'Na diskussii v VSSP,' *NM* (1931), no. 10.
Neznamov, P., 'Sovetskiy Churkin (*Vor.* Roman L. Leonova),' *Novyy Lef* (1928), no. 4, pp. 40–5.
Nikulin, L.,'*Polovchanskie sady*. Prem'era v Moskovskom khudozhestvennom akademicheskom teatre,' *MosBol*, 14 May 1939.
Nusinov, I., 'Ot Likhareva k Skutarevskomu,' *NM* (1933), no. 6.
'O kriticheskom otdele zhurnala *Novyy mir*,' *LitGaz*, 1 July 1954.
'O politike partii v oblasti khudozhestvennoy literatury,' *Pr*, 1 July 1925.
'O povyshennykh esteticheskikh kriteriyakh i durnom vkuse,' *T* (1939), no. 5.
'Obsuzhdenie romana *Doroga na Okean* na Prezidiume SSP,' *LitGaz*, 10 May 1936.
Papkovsky, B., 'Formalizm i eklektika professora Eykhenbauma,' *Zv* (1949), no. 9, p. 181.
Pavlovsky, A. I., 'Dva esse o romane L. Leonova *Piramida*,' *RusLit* (1998), no. 3, pp. 261–70.
Peace, R.A., Letter to the editor, *TLS*, 1 Oct. 1976.
Pel'son, E., 'Disput o p'esakh L. Leonova,' *LitGaz*, 30 May 1939.
Peshchanskaya, F., 'Pisatel' i ego geroi,' *VechM*, 23 Nov. 1942.
Petrovich, Valentin, 'Katastrofa v proezde Khudozhestvennogo teatra,' *Krokodil* (1939), no. 14, p. 10.
Plank, D. L., 'Unconscious Motifs in Leonid Leonov's *The Badgers*,' *SEEJ*, vol. 16, no. 1 (spring, 1972), pp. 19–35,
'Po literaturnym vecheram,' *NLP* (1929), no. 4/5, p. 126.
Polonsky, V., 'Oktyabr' i khudozhestvennaya literatura,' *NLP* (1926), no. 3, pp. 24–5.
'*Polovchanskie sady*. Beseda s narodnym artistom RSFSR rezhisserom MKhATa V.G. Sakhnovskim,' *DMZ* (1939), no. 14.
Polyakova, E., 'Dostoevsky v otrazhenii sovremennikov,' *Literatura i Marksizm* (1929), no. 6.
Popov, I., I. Sudakov, and A. Shumilin, 'O Leonove, o sovetskoy p'ese,' *SovIsk*, 27 May 1939.
Porman, R., 'V surovoe vremya (k istorii sozdaniya p'es L. M. Leonova *Nashestvie* i *Lenushka*,' *LitTat* (1957), no. 12, pp. 116–32.
– 'Obraz Fedora Talanova,' *Uchenye zapiski* (Kazanskiy pedagogicheskiy institut), vyp. 14 (1958), pp. 297–312.
Pridorogin, A., 'Leonid Leonov,' *Knigonosha* (1925), no. 31/32.
'Provintsial'naya idilliya,' *NLP* (1928), no. 6, p. 88.
Rappoport, A., '*Metel'* v dnepropetrovskom teatre im. Gor'kogo,' *Dnepropetrovskaya pravda*, 6 April 1940.

Romov, S., 'Vstrecha s Leonidom Leonovym,' *LitGaz*, 24 Sept. 1930.
Rosen, Nathan, 'The Fiction of Leonid Leonov.' PhD dissertation, Columbia, 1961.
Rozentsveyg, B., 'O "rayskikh sadakh" Leonida Leonova (*Polovchanskie sady* v MKhAT im. Gor'kogo),' *KomPr*, 18 May 1939.
Rudnitsky, S. K., 'Dramy Leonova,' *T* (1958), no. 8.
Sandomirsky, Vera, 'Leonid Leonov and the Party Line,' *The Russian Review* vol. 6, no. 2 (1947), pp. 67–76.
Sazonova-Slonimskaya, Yu., 'Kul'tura i zhizn': Leonid Leonov,' *Sovremennye zapiski*, (1929), no. 38, pp. 471–87.
Shcheglov, M., '*Russkiy les* Leonida Leonova,' *NM* (1954), no. 5, pp. 220–41.
Selivanovsky, A., 'Ob odnoy diskussii,' *LitGaz*, 5 Feb. 1933.
Serebryansky, M., 'Leonid Leonov,' *Izv*, 4 July 1939.
Shin, A., 'Disput o p'esakh Leonida Leonova,' *VechM*, 27 May 1939.
Simmons, E. J., 'Leonid Leonov and *The Road to Ocean*' in *For Roman Jakobson. Essays on the Occasion of His Sixtieth Birthday* (The Hague, 1956), pp. 467–74.
Simonov, K., 'O nekotorykh nedostoynykh metodakh kritiki,' *Pr*, 17 Oct. 1946.
Simonova, A.K., 'Pervaya drama L. Leonova, *Untilovsk*,' *Nauchnye trudy* (Erevanskiy gosudarstvennyy universitet), seriya filologicheskikh nauk, vol. 57, vyp. 4, ch. 2 (Erevan, 1956), pp. 3–24.
– 'P'esa L. Leonova, *Barsuki*,' *Nauchnye trudy* (Erevanskiy gosudarstvennyy universitet), seriya filologicheskikh nauk, vol. 66, vyp. 6, ch. 1 (Erevan, 1958), pp. 123–43.
– '*Provintsial'naya istoriya* L. Leonova (P'esa i povest'),' *Nauchnye trudy* (Erevanskiy gosudarstvennyy universitet), seriya filologicheskikh nauk, vol. 70, vyp. 7, ch. 1 (Erevan, 1960), pp. 183–204.
Smirnov, N., 'Leonid Leonov,' *Izv*, 18 Aug. 1924.
Spory vokrug *Skutarevskogo*,' *LitGaz*, 11 Jan. 1933.
Startseva, A.M., 'Osobennosti kompozitsii romanov L. Leonova,' *Voprosy sovetskoy literatury*, vol. 8, ed. P.S. Vykhodtsev and V.A. Kovalev (M.-L., 1959), pp. 367–401.
Surkov, E., 'O p'esakh Leonida Leonova *Nashestvie* i *Lenushka*' in *Teatr. Sbornik statey i materialov* (M., 1944).
Tal'nikov, D., '*Volk* v Gosudarstvennom Malom teatre,' *SovIsk*, 16 May 1939.
Tarasova, N., 'Ob istochnikakh zhivoy vody,' *Grani*, no. 23 (1954), pp. 113–30.
Terras, Victor, 'L. M. Leonov's *Russkii les*,' *SEEJ*, vol. 8, no. 1 (spring 1964).
Thomson, R. D. B., 'Leonov's Play *Zolotaja kareta*,' *SEEJ*, vol. 6, no. 3 (fall 1972), pp. 438–48.
– 'The Lean Years of Leonid Leonov,' *Canadian-American Slavic Studies*, vol. 8, no. 4 (winter, 1974), pp. 513–24.
Thomson, R.D.B., and Henry Elbaum, 'The "Naked Horseman in the Wilderness":

An Investigation into an Image in Leonov's Novel *Sot',*' *Canadian Slavonic Papers*, vol. 33, nos. 3–4 (Sept.–Dec. 1991), pp. 301–19.

Turkevich, Ludmila, 'Soviet Propaganda and the Rebellious Artist,' *The Russian Review*, vol. 15 (Jan. 1956), pp. 49–56.

'V sporakh o *Skutarevskom,*' *RabGaz*, 1 Feb. 1933.

Vinogradov, I., 'Za sovetskuyu klassiku!,' *Literaturnyy sovremennik*, (1936), no. 5.

'*Volk* v Tule,' *LitGaz*, 5 April 1939.

Voronsky, A. K., 'Literaturnye siluety,' *KN* (1924), no. 3.

– 'Literaturnye zametki,' *Prozhektor* (1925), no. 5.

Wilson, Edmund, 'The Sophistication of a Formula.' In *A Literary Chronicle 1920–1950* (New York, 1956).

Yakimova, L.P., 'Motiv sdelki cheloveka s d'yavolom v romane L. Leonova *Piramida*' in *Rol' traditsii v literaturnoy zhizni epokhi: Syuzhety i motivy* (Novosibirsk, 1995), pp. 146–59.

– 'Motiv bludnogo syna v romane L. Leonova *Piramida*' in *'Vechnye' syuzhety russkoy literatury: 'Bludnyy syn' i drugie* (Novosibirsk, 1996), p. 152–72.

– 'Motiv piramidy i kotlovana v romane L. Leonova *Piramida,*' *Gumanitarnye nauki v Sibiri*, Seriya filologicheskaya (1996), no. 4, pp. 3–12.

– 'Semantiko-esteticheskoe znachenie intertekstual'noy detali kak faktora preemstvennosti v razvitii literatury,' *Gumanitarnye nauki v Sibiri*, Seriya filologicheskaya (1997), no. 4, pp. 3–17.

Yuzovsky, Yu., '*Obyknovennyy chelovek* v Moskovskom teatre dramy,' *SovIsk*, 3 Aug. 1945.

Zalessky, V., '*Metel'* L. Leonova v Kazani,' *SovIsk*, 18 May 1940.

Zamyatin, Evgeniy, 'Novaya russkaya proza,' *Russkoe iskusstvo* (1923), no. 2/3.

– 'Pis'mo v redaktsiyu,' *LitGaz*, 7 Oct. 1929.

Zapevalov, V. N., 'Mezhdunarodnaya konferentsiya: "Roman L. Leonova *Piramida*. Problema miroopravdaniya",' *RusLit* (1998), no. 4, pp. 239–49.

3. Background Literature

Abalkin, N., *Sistema Stanislavskogo i sovetskiy teatr* (M., 1954).

Alexandrova, Vera, *A History of Soviet Literature*. Trans. Mirra Ginsburg (New York, 1963).

Averbakh, L., *Nashi literaturnye raznoglasiya* (L., 1927).

– *Na putyakh kul'turnoy revolyutsii* (M., 1929).

Averbakh, L., and V. Kirshon, *S kem i pochemu my boremsya* (L., 1930).

Avtorkhanov, Abdurakhman, *Stalin and the Soviet Communist Party: A Study in the Technology of Power* (Munich, 1959).

Bauer, R.A., *The New Man in Soviet Psychology* (Harvard, 1952).

Berkovsky, N., *Tekushchaya literatura* (M., 1930).
Blake, Patricia, and Max Hayward, eds., *Dissonant Voices in Soviet Literature* (New York: 1964).
Bogdanov, A.A., *Iskusstvo i rabochiy klass* (M., 1918).
- *O proletarskoy kul'ture* (M., 1924).
Boguslavskaya, A.O., and V.A. Diev, *Russkaya sovetskaya dramaturgiya 1917–1935* (M., 1953).
Borland, H. *Soviet Literary Theory and Practice during the First Five-Year Plan, 1928–1932* (New York, 1950).
Brodsky, N.L., et al., eds., *Literaturnye manifesty* (M., 1929).
Brostrom, Kenneth N., ed., *Russian Literature and American Critics*. Ann Arbor: 1984.
Brown, Edward J., *The Proletarian Episode in Russian Literature* (New York, 1953).
- *Russian Literature since the Revolution* (New York, 1963).
Brümmer, Christoph, *Beiträge zur Entwicklunggeschichte der frühen Romane L.M. Leonovs* (Munich, 1971).
Bukharin, N.I., *Revolyutsiya i kul'tura: Stat'i i vystupleniya 1923–36 godov* (M., 1993).
Bukharin, N.I., and E. Preobrazhensky, *Azbuka kommunizma* (n.p., 1921).
Bullard, Julian, and Margaret Bullard, eds. 'Inside Russia: The Diaries of Reader Bullard 1930–1934' (Charlbury, 2000).
Buznik, V.V., *Russkaya sovetskaya proza dvadtsatykh godov* (M., 1975).
Chamberlin, W.F., *The Russian Revolution 1917–1921* (New York, 1935).
Christman, Ruth, ed., *Soviet Science* (Washington, 1952).
Clark, Katerina, *The Soviet Novel: History as Ritual* (Chicago, 1981).
Chukovsky, K., *Dnevnik 1930–1969* (M., 1994).
Conquest, Robert, *The Great Terror* (London, 1968).
Dement'ev, A.G., ed., *Istoriya russkoy sovetskoy literatury*, 3 vols. (M., 1958–61).
Dewhirst, Martin, and Farrell, Robert, eds., *The Soviet Censorship* (Metuchen, 1973).
Drozda, Miroslav, *Babel, Leonov, Solženicyn* (Prague, 1961).
Eastman, Max, *Artists in Uniform: A Study of Literature and Bureaucratism* (New York, 1934).
Elagin, Yu., *Ukroshchenie iskusstv* (New York, 1952).
Eng-Liedmeier, A.M. van der, *Soviet Literary Characters: An Investigation into the Portrayal of Soviet Men in Russian Prose, 1917–1953*. Trans. B. Timmer ('S-Gravenhage, 1959).
Ermilov, V.V., *Za zhivogo cheloveka v literature* (M., 1928).
Ermolaev, Herman, *Soviet Literary Theories 1917–1934* (Berkeley, 1934).
- *Censorship in Soviet Literature, 1917–1991* (Lanham, 1997).
Ershov, L.F., *Russkiy sovetskiy roman. Natsional'nye traditsii i novatorstvo* (L., 1967).

Evgen'ev-Maksimov, V., *Ocherki istorii noveyshey russkoy literatury* (L., 1927).
Fadeev, A.A., *Za tridtsat' let* (M., 1957).
Fedin, K., *Gor'ky sredi nas* (M., 1944).
Fitzpatrick, Sheila, *The Commissariat of Enlightenment: Soviet Organization of Education and the Arts under Lunacharsky* (Cambridge, 1970).
Fleyshman, Lazar', *Pasternak v dvadtsatye gody* (Munich, 1981).
– *Pasternak v tridtsatye gody* (Jerusalem, 1984).
Friche, V.M., *Zametki o sovremennoy literature* (M., 1928).
Gasiorowska, Xenia, *Women in Soviet Fiction* (Madison, 1968).
Gibian, George, *Interval of Freedom: Soviet Literature during the Thaw* (Minneapolis, 1960).
Glinka, Gleb, *Pereval: The Withering of Literary Spontaneity in the U.S.S.R.* (New York, 1953).
Golubkov, V., *Pisateli–sovremenniki* (M., 1927).
Gorbachev, G., *Sovremennaya russkaya literatura* (M., 1928).
Gorbov, D., *Poiski Galatei: Stat'i o literature* (M., 1929).
Gorchakov, N.A., *Istoriya sovetskogo teatra* (New York, 1956).
Gor'ky i sovetskie pisateli, *Neizdannaya perepiska, Literaturnoe nasledstvo*, vol. 70 (M.-L., 1963).
Graham, Loren, *The Soviet Academy of Sciences and the Communist Party* (Princeton, 1967).
Groznova, N.A., *Rannyaya sovetskaya proza* (L., 1976).
Groznova, N.A., ed., *Iz tvorcheskogo naslediya russkikh pisateley XX veka: M. Sholokhov, A. Platonov, L. Leonov* (St Petersburg, 1995).
Gurshteyn, M., *Marksistskoe literaturovedenie* (M., 1931).
Hayward, Max, *Writers in Russia, 1917–1978* (London, 1983).
Hayward, Max, and L. Labedz, eds., *Literature and Revolution in Soviet Union 1917–1962* (London, 1963).
Hingley, Ronald, *Russian Writers and Soviet Society* (London, 1979).
Holthusen, Johannes, *Twentieth-Century Russian Literature: A Critical Study* (New York, 1972).
Istoriya russkoy sovetskoy literatury, 3 vols. (M., 1958–61).
Istoriya russkoy sovetskoy literatury, 1917–1965, 4 vols. (M., 1967–71).
Istoriya sovetskogo dramaticheskogo teatra, 6 vols. (M., 1966–71).
Istoriya vsesoyuznoy kommunisticheskoy partii (bol'shevikov): kratkiy kurs, ed. Komissiya TsK KPSS (M., 1950).
Ivanov, V.V., *Vstrechi s Gor'kim* (M., 1947).
Jackson, Robert Louis, *Dostoevsky's Underground Man in Russian Literature* ('S-Gravenhage, 1958).
Jensen, Peter Alberg, *Nature as Code: The Achievement of Boris Pil'njak, 1915–1924* (Copenhagen, 1979).

Joravsky, David, *Soviet Marxism and Natural Science* (New York, 1961).
Kasack, Wolfgang, *A Dictionary of Russian Literature since 1917*. Trans. Maria Carlson and Jane T. Hedges (New York, 1988).
Kedrina, Z., *Literaturno–kriticheskie stat'i* (M., 1956).
Kemp-Welch, A., *Stalin and the Literary Intelligentsia, 1928–39* (Basingstoke, 1991).
Kennan, George, *Russia and the West under Lenin and Stalin* (New York, 1961).
Khersonsky, Kh., *Boris Shchukin. Put' aktera* (M., 1954).
Kirpotin, V., *Proza, dramaturgiya i teatr* (M., 1935).
Klyuchevsky, V.O., *Sochineniya*, 8 vols. (M., 1956).
Knipovich, Ya., *V zashchitu zhizni. Literaturno-kriticheskie stat'i* (M., 1958).
Kogan, P.S., *Literatura etikh let 1917–1923* (Ivanovo-Voznesensk, 1924).
– *Proletarskaya literatura* (Ivanovo-Voznesensk, 1926).
– *Literatura velikogo desyatiletiya* (M.-L., 1927).
Koz'min, V. P., *Pisateli sovremennoy epokhi* (M., 1928).
Kratkaya literaturnaya entsiklopediya, ed. A.A. Surkov, 9 vols. (M., 1966–78).
Kruchenykh, A., *Zaumnyy yazyk* (M., 1927).
– *Novoe v pisatel'skoy tekhnike* (M., 1927).
Kruti, I., I.M. Moskvin. *Stat'i i materialy* (M., 1948).
Leyda, Jay, *Kino: A History of the Russian and Soviet Film* (London, 1960).
Lezhnev, A., *Voprosy literatury i kritiki* (M., 1926).
– *Sovremenniki: literaturno-kriticheskie ocherki* (M., 1927).
– *Literaturnye budni* (M., 1929).
– *Literatura revoliutsionnogo desiatiletiia*, 1917–1927 (Kharkov,1929).
– *Razgovor v serdtsakh* (M., 1930).
Literaturnaya entsiklopediya, 11 vols. (M., 1928–39).
Literaturnaya Rossiya: sbornik literaturno-kriticheskikh statey (M., 1962).
Lobanov, M., *Serdtse pisatelya* (M., 1963).
Losev, Lev, *On the Beneficence of Censorship: Aesopian Language in Modern Russian Literature*. Trans. Jane Bobko (Munich, 1984).
Lunacharsky, A., *Upadochnoe nastroenie sredi molodezhi. Eseninshchina* (M., 1927).
L'vov-Rogachevsky, V. *Revolyutsiya i russkaya literatura* (M., 1923).
– *Khudozhestvennaya literatura revolyutsionnogo desyatiletiya* (M., 1927).
Maguire, Robert A., *Red Virgin Soil: Soviet Literature in the 1920s* (Princeton, 1968).
Mandel'shtam, Nadezhda, *Vospominaniya* (New York, 1970).
– *Vtoraya kniga* (Paris, 1972).
Marx, Karl, and Friedrich Engels, *Literature and Art: Selections from Their writings* (New York, 1947).
Masing-Delic, I., *Abolishing Death: A Salvation Myth of Russian Twentieth-Century Literature* (Stanford, 1992).
Mathewson, Rufus W., Jr., *The Positive Hero in Russian Literature* (New York, 1958).

Medvedev, Zhores, *The Rise and Fall of T. D. Lysenko*. Trans. I.M. Lerner (New York, 1969).
Mel'gunov, S. P., *Krasnyy terror v Rossii 1918–1923* (Berlin, 1924).
Mikulašek, Miroslav, *Puti razvitiya sovetskoy komedii 1925–1934 godov* (Prague, 1962).
Mirsky, D.S., *Contemporary Russian Literature* (New York, 1927).
Muchnic, Helen, *From Gorky to Pasternak: Six Modern Russian Writers* (London, 1963).
Nikitina, E.F., *Russkaya literatura ot simvolizma do nashikh dney* (M., 1926).
– *V masterskoy sovremennoy khudozhestvennoy prozy*, 2 vols. (M., 1931).
Nikitina, E.F., and S.V. Shuvalov, *Belletristy-sovremenniki* (M., 1930).
Novitsky, P., *Boris Shchukin. Zhizn' i tvorchestvo* (M.-L., 1948).
Nusinov, I.M., *Burzhuaznye tendentsii v sovremennoy literature* (M., 1930).
Ol'khovy, B., *Na zlobu dnya* (M., 1930).
Oulanoff, Hongor, *The Prose Fiction of Veniamin A. Kaverin* (Cambridge, Mass., 1976).
Pakenkreyter, S., *Zakaz na vdokhnovenie* (M., 1934).
Paley, A., *Literaturnye portrety* (M., 1928).
Panina, A.L. and T.G. Pereslegina, eds., *Zapiski Mikhaila Sabashnikova* (M., 1995).
Pertsov, P., *Pisatel' na proizvodstve* (M., 1931).
Piksanov, N.K., *Khudozhestvennaya literatura v otsenke marksistskoy kritiki* (M., 1923).
Piper, D.G.B., *V.A. Kaverin: A Soviet Writer's Response to the Problem of Commitment* (Duquesne University, 1970).
Polonsky, Vyacheslav, *Ocherki literaturnogo dvizheniya revolyutsionnoy epokhi* (M., 1929).
Reavey, George, *Soviet Literature Today* (New Haven, 1947).
Rozanov, I., *Putevoditel' po sovremennoy russkoy literature* (M., 1929).
Rühle, Jürgen, *Literature and Revolution: A Critical Study of the Writer and Communism in the Twentieth Century*. Trans. Jean Steinberg (New York, 1969).
Salisbury, Harrison E., *The Soviet Union: The Fifty Years* (New York, 1967).
Sakhnovsky, V.G., *Rabota rezhissera* (M.-L., 1937).
Shcheglova, G.N., *Ocherki razvitiya geroiko-revolyutsionnogo zhanra v sovetskoy dramaturgii* (Tashkent, 1985).
Selivanovsky, A., *V literaturnykh boyakh 1927–1936* (M., 1959).
Shaginyan, M., *Literatura i plan* (M., 1934).
Shane, Alex M., *The Life and Works of Evgenij Zamjatin* (Berkeley, 1968).
Schcheglov, Mark, *Literaturno-kriticheskie stat'i*, ed. V. Lakshin (M., 1965).
Shentalinsky, Vitaly, *The KGB's Literary Archive*. Trans. John Crowfoot (London, 1995).

Shepherd, David, *Beyond Metafiction: Self-Consciousness in Soviet Literature* (Oxford, 1992).

Shklovsky, V., *Pyat' chelovek znakomykh* (Tiflis, 1927).

Sinyavsky, Andrey, *Soviet Civilization: A Cultural History*. Trans. Joanne Turnbull with the assistance of Nikolai Formozov (New York, 1996).

Sinyavsky A., and A. Menshutin, *Poeziya pervykh let revolyutsii* (M., 1964).

Slonim, Mark, *Portrety sovetskikh pisateley* (Paris, 1933).

– *Soviet Russian Literature: Writers and Problems, 1917–1967* (New York, 1967).

Slovar' sovremennogo russkogo literaturnogo yazyka, 17 vols., (M.-L., 1950–65).

Smith, Edward Ellis, *The Young Stalin: The Early Years of an Elusive Revolutionary* (New York, 1967).

Starikova, E.V., *Poeziya prozy* (M., 1962).

Stepun, F., *Vstrechi* (Munich, 1962).

Struve, Gleb, *Twenty-five Years of Soviet Russian Literature 1918–1943* (London, 1946).

– *Russian Literature under Lenin and Stalin 1917–1953* (Oklahoma, 1971).

I.Z. Surikov i poety-surikovtsy (M.-L., 1966).

Swayze, Harold, *Political Control of Literature in the USSR, 1946–1959* (Cambridge, Mass., 1962).

Teatr. Sbornik statey i materialov (M., 1944).

Treadgold, D.W., *Twentieth-Century Russia* (Chicago, 1959).

Trotsky, L., *Literatura i revolyutsiya* (M., 1923).

Velekhova, Nina., *Serebryanye truby* (M., 1983).

Vladimirov, S.V. and D.I. Zolotnitsky, *Ocherki istorii russkoy sovetskoy dramaturgii* (M., 1963).

Voronsky, A.K., *Iskusstvo i zhizn'* (M., 1924).

– *Literaturnye tipy* (L., 1925).

– *Literaturnye portrety*, 2 vols. (M., 1928).

– *Iskusstvo videt' mir* (M., 1928).

Yarmolinsky, A., *Literature under Communism* (Bloomington, 1960).

Zavalishin, Vyacheslav, *Early Soviet Writers* (New York, 1958).

Zamyatin, E., *Litsa* (New York, 1955).

Index

Academy of Sciences 125, 265, *351*, *356*
Akhmatova, A.A. x, 12, 104, 200, 215, 264, *336*, *345*
Alekseev, M.P. 62
Aleksey Mikhaylovich, Tsar 21, *308*
Alekseychik, N. *346*
Alexandrova, V. 76, *315*
All-Russian Union of Writers 13, 100, 103
Andersen H. 16
Andreev, L.N. 12, 111; *Savva 326*
Andruszko, Cz. *312*
Anuchin, N.P. 236

Babel', I.E. 53, *310*, *315*
Bach, J.S. 231, 235
Bagritsky, E.G. *331*
Bakh, A.N. 146, *330*
Bedny, D. 10
Belinsky, V.G. 113, *325*
Bely A. 4, 12, 16, 283; *Petersburg* 283
Béranger, P. *358*
Berdyaev, N.A. 112–13
Blok, A.A. 4, 12, 217, *315*
Bogdanov, A.A. *308*
Breughel, Pieter, the Elder 263

Brezhnev, L.I. 292
Bryusov, V.Ya. *306*
Bukharin, N.I. 69–70, 113–15, 162, 289, *308*, *328*, *350*; *ABC of Communism* 69–70, *350*
Bulgakov, M.A. 282, *322*; *The Master and Margarita* 236, 282
Bunin, I.A. 12

Chaadaev, P.Ya. *322*
Chavchavadze, I.G. 261
Chavchavadze, Nina 261
Chekhov, A.P. 191, 204, *338*; *The Grasshopper* 204
Chernyshevsky, N.G. 25, *332*
Chopin, F. 244
Christianity ix, 19, 53, 71–2, 119, 150, 163, 168–9, 209, 211, 220, 245, 253, 275–6, 282, 286, 293, *318*
Chukovsky, K.I. 104
Clausius, 112, 129
Conflictlessness 234

Darwin, C. 235, 274, *310*, *350*
Deborin, A.M. 126
Degtyarev, V.A. *See* Dekhterev, V.A.
Dekhterev, V.A. *342*

Dianin, S.A. *347*
Dobrokhotov A.P. *306*
Dormidontov, N.I. *329*
Dostoevsky, F.M. ix, 6, 10, 11, 12, 20, 24, 26, 33, 47, 56–7, 58, 66, 67, 68, 69, 84, 87, 130, 153, 156, 198, 213, 227, 230, 236, 246, 247, 266, 267, 272, 280–1, 283, 287, 289, 291–2, *312, 317, 319, 326, 335, 359*; *The Brothers Karamazov* 24, 57, 58, 69, 153, 253, 257, 272, 280–1, 283, 291, *309, 315, 335, 346*; *Crime and Punishment* 56–7, 130, 161, 247, *335*; *The Devils* 58, 69, 114, 235, 249, 277, 289, *317, 347*; *The Double* 24, 28, 67; *The Dream of a Ridiculous Man* 213, 230, 252, 281, 291; *The Idiot* 56, 267–8; *Notes from the Underground* 24–5, 69, 112, 255, *309, 326, 359*

Eisenstein, S.M. *340*
Elbaum, H. *318, 325*
Eltsin, B.N. 292
Engels, F. 101, 147
Erenburg, I.G. xi, 238, *328, 340*; *The Grabber* 100, *311*; *The Second Day* 328; *The Thaw* 238
Ermilov, V.V. 75, 76, 147, *319*
Esenin, S.A. 52, 281, *308, 312, 313*
Evtushenko, E.A. x, 238, *359*
Eykhenbaum, B.M. *347, 359*
Ezhov, N.I. *339*

Fadeev, A.A. 188, 200, *352*
Falileev, V.D. 11, 12, 62, *307*
Fascism 114
Favorsky, V.A. *307*
Fedin, K.A. *311, 322*
First Five-Year Plan 52, 98, 99, 101, 102, 105–6, 113, 120, 122, 127, 144, 177
Frunze, M.V. *334*
Furmanov, D.A. 115
Furtseva, E. 189

Genetics 235, 274–5, 279, 290–1, 294
Gershenzon, M.O. 11, 66, 110, 279, *310, 324, 355*; *Correspondence from Two Corners* 110, *324*
Gertsen, A.I. *325*
Gide, André *315*
Gladkov, F.V. 116
Goethe J. 161
Gogol', N.V. 24, 28, 140, 200, 205, 207, *322, 354*; *Dead Souls* 97, *354*; *The Nose* 28; *Story of How Ivan Ivanovich and Ivan Nikiforovich Quarrelled 322*; *Taras Bul'ba* 201
Goncharov, I.A. 150
Gorbachev, M.S. 238, 292
Gorbov, D.A. 75
Gor'ky, A.M. 12, 45, 50, 75, 76 78–9, 86, 87, 88, 103, 120, 123, 126, 175–6, 189, 233, 290, *308, 310, 313, 314, 321, 326, 331, 332, 334, 335, 336, 358, 359*; *Mother* 38, *343*; *Somov and Others* 126, 176
Griboedov, A.S. 261
Grossman, L.P. 104
Groznova, N.A. 20, *312, 313*

Hartley, L.P. *358*
Hayward, Max 226, *345*
Heine, H. 233, *350*
Hidas, A. 174
Hingley, R. *350*
Hitler, 191, 198, 216, 238
Hutchinson, A.E.W. *321*

Il'enko, V.P. 116

Ivan IV, the Terrible 256
Ivanov, Vyach. I. 12, 66, *324*, *355*
Ivanov, Vsev.V. 49, 120, 174, 175, *312*, *322*, *326*, *336*

Jenghis Khan 114, 131, 185, *328*
Job 152, 275

Kamernyy Theatre *341*
Kant, I. 104, 294
Kataev, V.P. 173–5, *331–2*, *339*, *340*, *342*
Kaverin, V.A. *319*
Khlebnikov, V.V. *316*, *353*
Khodasevich, V.F. 12, *306–7*
Khrushchev, N.S. 218
Kirov, S.M. 147
Kirpotin, V.Ya. 147, *318*
Klyuchevsky, V.O. 220
Klyuev, N.A. 4, 266, 281, *326*
Kol'tsov, N.K. *358*
Korean war 217, 223
Kovalev, V.A. 136, 255, *310*, *316*, *318*, *342*, *344*, *345*, *347*, *351*, *355–6*
Krasnaya nov' 13, 14, 76, 99
Kul'kov, N.P. *306*
Kuprin, A.I. 12
Kuzmin, M.A. *312–13*

LEF (Left Front of the Arts) 60
Lenin, V.I. 13, 70, 113, 128–9, 147, 191, 223, 233, *308*, *331–2*
Lenin Prize 237, 265
Leonidov, L.M. 81
Leonov, L.M., works:
  The Badgers x, 28, 31, 32–51, 52, 55, 56, 57, 67, 71, 72, 73, 75, 81, 82, 89, 95, 108, 113, 147, 166, 169, 173, 177, 187, 203, 209, 243, 264, 270, 285, 286–7, 288, *310–14*, *336*, *337*, *343*, *347*

  The Breakthrough at Petushikha 16, 17–22, 26, 27, 30, 31, 38, 39, 42, 44, 47, 55, 71, 74, 80, 82, 94, 119, 123, 149, 151, 172, 264, 266, 267, 286, 288, 292, *307*, *312*, *337*
  Buryga 12, 14, 15, 16, 17, 18, 26, 30, 47, 48, 80, 209, 219, 287, *307*
  Dark Water 89–91, 93
  The End of a Petty Man 14, 16, 18, 22–7, 28, 30, 31, 37–8, 47, 56, 67, 79, 82, 113, 128–9, 239, 240, 247, 254–5, 262, 287, *309*, *319*, *351*
  Evgenia Ivanovna 239, 257–64, 270, 277, 293, 294, *354*, *355–6*
  The Fall of Zaryad'e *344*
  The Flight of Mr. Mckinley 239
  A Golden Coach 200, 203, 206–14, 215, 224, 228, 237, 239, 240–4, 246, 286, 291, 293, 294, *343–4*, *351–2*, *359*
  'Gratitude' 216
  Ham's Departure 16, 28–30, 50, 66, 73, 84, 85, 120, 253, 285, 286, 288
  'In Defence of Our Friend' 218
  Invasion 191–9, 222, 228, 239, 240, 270, *352*
  Ivan's Misadventure 91, 98
  Khalil' 14, 15, *310*
  The Knave of Diamonds 16
  Lenushka 192, 193–5, 198–200, 202, 214, 215–16
  'Let's Think about Our Green Spaces' 218
  Locusts 105, 120–4, 129, 140, 144, 175
  A Note on Birchbark 6–10, 16, 17, 20, 28, 29, 42, 44, 48, 80, 94, 117, 293–4
  The Notes ... of Kovyakin 16, 18, 27–8, 31, 33, 67, 68, 79, 82, 85

The Orchards of Polovchansk 177, 178–87, 193, 195, 207, 216, *336–40*
An Ordinary Man, 200, 203–6, 209–14, 228, 237, *342–4*
A Provincial Story 79, 80, 81, 83–7, 88, 94, 96, 98, 106, *338, 347, 359*
The Pyramid x, xii, 20, 28, 73, 82, 94, 104, 115, 238, 239, 247, 255, 261, 265–84, 285, 286, 288, 291, *310, 352, 354, 356–60*
The Return of Kopylev 89, 91, 98
Revenge 92
The Road to Ocean 75, 78, 149–72, 173, 175, 176, 177, 179, 182, 184, 187, 197, 209, 210, 211, 216, 222, 231, 232, 235, 258, 264, 269, 286, 288, 294, *331–5, 336, 338, 339, 340, 344, 346*
The Ruin of Egorushka 14, 15, 16–7, 18, 30, 74, 94, *307*
The Russian Forest x, 25, 181, 188, 207, 215–38, 239, 244, 248, 249, 252, 255, 258, 265, 269–70, 271–2, 273, 274, 277, 278, 279, 280, 281, 286, 287, 288, 292, *305–6, 310, 344–51, 354, 357–8*
Skutarevsky 105, 109, 125–48, 149, 150, 151, 153, 155, 157, 159, 162, 167, 169, 170, 171, 173, 175, 176, 185, 207, 209, 216, 218, 222, 223, 224, 255, 288, *327–31, 332, 336, 343, 346, 350, 352*
The Snowstorm 177, 179–182, 185–90, 193, 194, 195, 200, 203, 207, 215, 222, 231, 239, 240, 242, 254, 255–7, 264, 267, 269, *337–40, 343, 344, 349, 350, 351, 355*
The Sot' 97, 99–120, 121, 122, 123–4, 128, 129, 132, 140, 141, 142, 144, 149, 150, 151, 155, 157, 162, 164, 173, 175, 185, 209, 219, 222, 233, 247, 255, 266, 273, 277, 281, 286, 288, 290–1, *322–6, 336, 342, 346, 354*
The Taking of Velikoshumsk 156, 192, 195–8, 200–2, 245, *306, 343*
The Taming of Badadoshkin 80–1, 87, 88, 96, 130
The Thief 47, 52–77, 78, 79, 80, 84, 87, 88, 91, 93, 94, 95, 97, 110, 114, 123, 133, 136, 142, 144, 153, 155–6, 157, 162, 166, 168, 171, 172, 173, 186, 189, 209, 210, 219, 222, 224, 226, 233, 234–6, 239, 240, 244–54, 256, 262, 263, 265, 266, 273, 274, 279, 281, 285, 286, 287–8, 290, 291, 294, *314–20, 332, 336, 337, 338, 342, 345, 346, 351–4, 355, 356, 357, 358*
The Tramp 72
Tuatamur 14, 15, 16, 30, 31, 123, *308*
Untilovsk 79, 80, 81–3, 87, 88, 95, 98, 184, 207
Unusual Stories about Peasants 89–93, 97, 103, 176
Valya's Doll 14, 16
White Night 6, 80, 93–7, 103, 121, 140, *323, 329, 334*
Wolf 177, 178–88, 195, 214, 216, 286, *337–40*
The Wooden Queen 16
'A Word on the First Deputy' 215
Yakov Pigunok's Little Adventure 16, 22

Leonov, M.L. 3–4, *305*
Leonova, E.L. 266, *306*
Leonova, N.L. 265, 266, *306, 356, 359, 360*

Leonova-Petrova, M.P. 4, *306*
Leonova-Sabashnikova, T.M. 12, 266, *310, 317*
Leont'ev, K.N. *325, 332*
Leskov, N.S. 14, *308–9, 330, 341, 347, 357*
Lezhnev, A.Z. 75, *319, 335*
Lidin, V.G. 173–5, *335*
Likhachev, D.S. 62
Lishentsy 168–9, 177, 181, 219, 221, 228, 256, 267, 268, *313, 338*
Lugovskoy, V.A. 120, *338*
Lunacharsky, A.V. 51, *308*
Lysenko, T.D. 225, 274
Lysov, A.G. *325*

Malyy Theatre 147, 187, 188, 189, 203, *330–1, 337, 341, 343*
Mandel'shtam, N.Ya. 79, 104, *319*
Mandel'shtam, O.E. *339, 359*
Mann, T. 283
Markov, P.M. 81
Marx, K. xii, 41, 147, 151, 231, 288, *349–50*
Marxism x, 21, 34, 37, 40, 49–50, 61–2, 100–2, 104, 115, 126, 128, 131, 134, 150–1, 216, 220, 223, 231, 232, 255, 272, 274, 278, 283–4, 286, 289, *313, 325, 347*
Mathewson, R. 171, *331, 335*
Mayakovsky, V.V. 10, 29, 79, 133, 162, 289, *314–15, 320, 322, 324, 331, 337, 338, 359*
Mel'gunov, S.P. *305*
Merezhkovsky, D.S. 12
Meshchanstvo 79–81, 87–8, 96, 103, 116, 130, 224, 248
Meyerkhol'd, V.E. 149, 173
Miller, E. General *307*
Molotov, V.M. 127, 217

Moscow Arts Theatre 81, 184, 187, 188, 203, 239, *323, 330, 336–7, 351*
Mossovet Theatre *341*
Muchnic, H. *314, 335*

Nekrasov, N.A. 4, 58, 347
NEP (New Economic Policy) 12, 52–3, 55, 59, 96, 98, 99, 100, 101, 123, 144, 249, 254
Nietzsche, F. *318, 319*
Nikiforov, G.K. *333*
Nikitin, N. *312*
Nikulin, L.V. 174, *339*
Novyy mir 14, 76, 170

Okhrana 83, 223, 226, *348*
Oktyabr' 13–14, 100
Okudzhava, B.Sh. x, 238
Olesha, Yu.K.: *Envy* 75, *318*
On Guard 13
Ostroukhov, I.S. 11, 62, 81, *307, 329*
Ostrovsky, A.N. 80
Ostrovsky, N.A.: *How the Steel Was Tempered* 38, 151–2, 170–1, 231, *309, 343*
Ovcharenko, O. 266

Pasternak, B.L. 12, 53, 75, *314, 325, 336*
Pavlenko, P.A. 120
Peter I, the Great 21, 63, 256, *312, 358*
Pil'nyak, B.A. 21, 49, 93, 99, 103, 126, *308, 309, 310, 311, 312, 313, 321–2, 322–3, 324, 334*; *Mahogany* 100, *323*; *Naked Year* 49, *312, 313*; *Tale of the Unextinguished Moon 334*
Platonov, A.P. 266, *317, 320*
Podvig 192, 193, 194, 195, 196, 197, 200, 209, 210, 219, 228–9, *338*

Polikarpov D.I. 215, *355*
Poputchiki 12–13, 14, 62, 75, 79, 99–100, 102, 103, 123, 127, 172, 294, *319*
Positive hero 150–2
Preobrazhensky, E. 69–70, 115, 289
Proletkul't 13, 62, *308*
Pugachev, E.I. 40, *318*, *331*
Pushkin, A.S. 289, 290, *334*; *The Bronze Horseman* 8, 26; *The Gypsies*, 7; *Mozart and Salieri* 178, *329*

Ramzin, L.K. *328*
RAPP (Russian Association of Proletarian Writers) 100–3, 106, 111, 127–8, 135, 146, *323*
Remizov, A.M. 12, 14, 16
Rosen, Nathan *309*
Rozanov, V.V. 12
Russian Association of Proletarian Writers, *See* RAPP
Rybal'ko, P.S. *342*

Sabashnikov, M.V. 12, 62, 117, *307*, *335*
Salisbury, Harrison E. *320*
Sannikov, G.A. 129
Sel'vinsky, I.L. 76, *313*, *315*, *317*
Serafimovich, A.S. *316*
Shaginyan, M.S. 116
Shakespeare, W.; *Hamlet* 52, 64
Shamil' 261
Shaw, G.B. *355*
Shcheglov, M.A. 225
Shcherbakov, A.S. *340*
Shklovsky, V.B. 147
Shkulev, F.S. 3
Shostakovich, D.D. 173

Shvarts, E.L. *335*
Simonov, K.M. 200
Simonova, A.K. *311*, *321*, *322*
Sinyavsky, A.D. 220, *345*
Skaz 14, 15, 16, 27, 45, 48, 75, 76, 90, 97, 102–3, 141
Socialist realism 149–151
Sologub, F.K. 12, 79
Solzhenitsyn, A.I. 104, 288, *328*
Stalin, I.V. xi, 75, 78, 99, 100, 102–3, 113–14, 120, 127, 160, 171, 185–6, 189, 191, 195, 199, 215, 218, 226, 238, 240, 249, 256, 260, 266, 268, 271, 272, 273, 274, 276–7, *326*, *328*, *333*, *335*, *336*, *338–9*, *340*, *342*, *344*, *345*, *348*, *357*, *358*
Stalin Prize 189, 191, 199, 222, 237, *328*
Stalinism 131, 139, 226, 227, 282
Stanislavsky, K.S. 81
Starikova, E.V. *305*, *311*, *347*, *348*, *350*
Starokadomsky, M.L. *323*
Stavsky, V.P. *323*, *339*
Stendhal 123, *315–6*
Stolypin, P.A. *348*
Struve G.P. *317*, *345*
Sukhovo-Kobylin, A.V. 80
Surikov, I.Z. 3

Tabidze, Nina, and Titsian Iu. 257, 260
Tairov, A.Ya. 199
Tal'nikov, D.L. *335*
Thaw, the x, 103, 218, 239
Tikhonov, N.S. 120, *320*, *331–2*
Tkachenko, M.E. *346*
Tolstoy, A.N. 12, *314*
Tolstoy, L.N. 88, 102, 293; *Anna Karenina* 276
Tovey, D.F. 244

Trotsky, L.D. 12, *308, 323*
Turgenev, I.S. *332*
Tvardovsky, A.T. *351*

Union of Soviet Writers 100, 103, 105, 123, 127, 171, 174, 187, 189, 236, 265, *351*
Uspensky, G.I. 223, *327, 350*

Vakhtangov Theatre 50–1, *311, 313*
Vanga 266
Vasil'ev, A. 11
Vasil'ev, P.V. 236
Vavilov, N.I. *358*
Vertov, D. *316*
Vishnevsky, V.V. 161
Voloshin, M.A. *334–5*
Voronsky, A.K. 13, 14, 76, 99, 103, *308*

Wagner, R. 145, 161, 291
War trials 215
Wells, H.G. 266, *357*

XX Party Congress 199, 217–8, 256, *344, 345*
XXII Party Congress 192

Zabolotsky, N.A. *325*
Zamyatin, E.I. 12, 14, 16, 23, 69, 79, 99, 103, 111, 123, 126, 260, 266, 274–5, 290, *310, 323*; *Attila* 111; *The Cave* 23; *We* 69, 93, 99–100, 236, 249, 253, 266, 274–5, 290, *309, 318, 332*
Zavalishin, V.K. *333*
Zhdanov, A.A. 200, 203, 215
Zlobin, S.P. 236, *351*
Zoshchenko, M.M. 200, 215